SEÁN Ó RÍORDÁIN LIFE AND WORK

SEÁN Ó RÍORDÁIN LIFE AND WORK

SEÁN Ó COILEÁIN

TRANSLATED BY
MÍCHEÁL Ó hAODHA

MERCIER PRESS

Seán Ó Ríordáin: Life and Work receives financial assistance from the Arts Council.

MERCIER PRESS
Cork
www.mercierpress.ie

Published in association with Cló Iar-Chonnacht, An Cheardlann, An Spidéal, Co. na Gaillimhe.

ISBN: 978 1 78117 610 8

10 9 8 7 6 5 4 3 2 1

A CIP record for this title is available from the British Library.

Printed and bound in the EU.

Contents

Acknowledgements

We are very grateful to An Clóchomhar and Cló Iar-Chonnacht, An Spidéal, who hold the original Irish-language rights for the monograph, Seán Ó Coileáin, *Seán Ó Ríordáin: Beatha agus Saothar* (An Clóchomhar, Dublin, 1982). We would also like to thank the Arts Council for providing us with a grant towards the publication of this translation.

Abbreviations

B	*Brosna*
D	Diary
ES	*Eireaball Spideoige*
IT	*The Irish Times*
LL	*Línte Liombó*
TÉB	*Tar Éis Mo Bháis*

Introduction

The Life and the Mind

The artistic oeuvre of the writer Seán Ó Ríordáin should never be considered solely in terms of the fact that he was an Irish-language writer. Fate decreed that he be a writer, and this is the first and the last of it. And yet Ireland has produced very few other writers of Irish whose intimate bond with this minority language seemed almost preordained from the beginning. Any discussion on Ó Ríordáin requires the act of writing itself as its starting point. What initially led him to the life of a writer and towards the act of writing? Ó Ríordáin was unusual in that he didn't have any real literary background at all. He certainly didn't become a writer because he knew other writers or their work, or because he had any literary example to follow; he didn't. What Ó Ríordáin set out to do was unique; the thoughts and feelings he sought to give voice to needed to be expressed for the very first time and he would be the pre-eminent writer of his generation and the first to express them. He would say what needed saying and then hold his peace. His story or personal narrative was the poem. Put simply, his life's work, the expression of his internal life, was an outward manifestation of the inner soul. He recorded this inner world in the form of poetry. He told his story to himself and if others expressed an interest in it afterwards, then it was probably because of the supreme openness and honesty with which he explored even the least attractive and most difficult aspects of his sensibility and being. This inner journey of his as expressed in the form of art was frequently a lonely and aimless one, but at least he undertook it. And there are very few people who undertook as harsh an artistic road as his, a journey that 'literature' had something to do with but which necessitated a great deal more of himself also. And, in truth, Ó Ríordáin's inner journey manifested itself in the form of literature only occasionally. The crucial aspect was the journey itself, the laying bare of that trajectory where human life and fate intersected and where his inner world and the reality of his daily existence overlapped. Ó Ríordáin was both author and subject of this unique narrative, and if literature was the ultimate expression of this strange fusion of humanity and fate, then so be it.

The narrative he recorded in the privacy of his diaries was more than himself – it was more than the chronicle of one individual's life at the mid-point of the twentieth century – it was also the story of life itself, or at least what he knew of it. His diaries delineated 'life' as he experienced it and for as long as he had the strength to go on. The 'word' was more than a simple medium of expression for him, however; it was the sole weapon he had at his disposal.

He would fight with this weapon to the very death and when the time came for him to succumb – as it eventually did – (in all truth, he was beaten from the very beginning, wasn't he?) no one could say that he hadn't fought hard. Acknowledgement would come in the shape of the writings he left behind and nothing else. He would have left his trace, the marks of the battle that were his life and death, and for once the ultimate victor would be lowly humanity itself. There was hope and courage in this alone – even if it often seemed a lonely and futile struggle at the time. Ó Ríordáin's body of work demonstrated that the narrative of the individual *is* important, the ordinary human being whose story so often remains unspoken or disregarded. Maybe this was the most important aspect of all; maybe it was the only story worth telling. Speaking of certain people who'd given him courage along the way, Ó Ríordáin once remarked:

> *We got to know people who are now in their graves. They live on in their words however. These people picked up words in the same way that another would pick a rock from the ground and they had thrown these rocks in the face of oncoming fate. The dead are more alive to me now through their words and writings than they are in any memories of their individual personalities. The men and the women and their fistfuls of words; it is all that remains in the memory now. After all, what is a man or a woman in their truest essence? They are the last stand, the final attempt to defeat fate. The braver this final struggle is the greater the standing of that last man or woman, the one who persists to the end.*[1]

1 'Caidreamh le Dia agus le Daoine' ('*The Relationship with God and with*

Making form of this earthly life and flinging it back in the face of life once more. Man and his destiny, and the relationship that defined each aspect; and then the creative act when the moment deemed it appropriate – then and only then.

There is no doubt that 1938 was the year when the creative bent first manifested itself in Ó Ríordáin and he felt the need to write; it's a sad irony, however, that death and its accoutrements were central to the writing process for this unique poet from the very beginning. And the same was true at his life's end, when death came as a form of release or redemption almost, from a life that was an unforgiving struggle as a consequence of lifelong illness. In fact, much of Ó Ríordáin's writing can be viewed as an ongoing dialogue between the poet and death, between the limbo of the half-living and the half-dead, a dialogue that became increasingly incomprehensible the more the two realms intersected. An often hostile and angry dialogue, it was one that encompassed the best part of forty years. Ó Ríordáin's writings are edgy and teem with life, and yet they also seek the peace that comes with silence or effacement. And paradoxically, it was in an effort to drown out this great silence that he first began writing the diaries that are the primary focus of this volume, diaries that sharpened his artistic sensibility at the same time as they functioned to protect him from the terrible, final last silence. The written word could not stave off death, however, unless the words had its exact measure. Their battle was a battle of equals and therefore a never-ending one:

> *This diary probably isn't writing at all but rather a fight against death. The battle is fought with sentences. Even if they're worthless sentences in themselves, it doesn't matter if they put off death. They prevent one from accepting death. I scrutinise and re-scrutinise every pain, every mistake, every insult, every enemy, every fault in myself and in others who hurt me, every heresy, until they are no more. If I didn't, they would all combine together and overwhelm me. I'd have been gone a long time ago if it wasn't for all the minute analysis that I do in this diary.*[2]

People'), *The Irish Times* (hereafter IT), 29 January 1969.

2 'An Taisceadán' ('*The Locker*'), *Comhar*, June 1963.

The diaries as we have them today begin on New Year's Day 1940, and he continued with them until the very end; in fact, Ó Ríordáin wrote the very last sentence in his diary while in his death-throes at 2 a.m. on 16 February 1977. The very first and last diary entries may differ greatly in terms of subject matter, and yet in terms of tone and sentiment they are redolent of the same mind and sensibility. As Ó Ríordáin's health declined during the last years of his life, his handwriting became weaker and more indistinct, even as he physically tried to trace the journey of his impending death on the page. By then, he'd spent his entire life trying to make sense of life via the exposition of words on an empty page. And even at the very end, in those very last written words of his, he recognised the shape of his old nemesis – death – the enemy he had come across years earlier. He'd been close many times himself, even as a very young man, and was familiar with death's presence and traces. Because illness and death were an integral part of Ó Ríordáin's life on the personal level for decades – from the very first day he was born. Death and all its aspects; it was what he traced in its dimensions, and through body and soul, in his four decades of writing.

Death or departure infused all of his work. After all, the three most definitive events in the poet's life were the leaving of Ballyvourney, his contracting tuberculosis (TB) and his mother's death. The worst tragedy by far was the way TB destroyed his life, but all three incidents were nonetheless intimately woven into the sensibility that was Ó Ríordáin the poet. Not alone was the disease a very frightening experience, but being struck down with TB meant that Ó Ríordáin found himself constantly returning to another, earlier era of his life in the solace of his imagination, to a time when he was healthier in mind and body. This hankering after an illness-free youth was also what bound the poet in a very close relationship with his mother.

By the time the diary entries explored here begin – the world of youth, health and sexual innocence as associated with Ballyvourney has already gone, even if the attempt to retrieve it or recreate it again on the imaginative level has only just begun. Worse still, Ó Ríordáin has to take this journey of memory completely alone because of the early death of his mother; she died just a few short years after the family's move to

Inniscarra, on the outskirts of Cork city. The seas he had to traverse at this point of his life were stormy enough, but they became more daunting still after he lost the constant support and help which his mother had always provided to him. There are regions of being and of the inner world that are so bleak and empty that words cannot give them meaning and where the only response is an uncomprehending scream of pain. And this is one poet who was very familiar with such regions. The early years of his diary serve as a preparation for this bleak reality; they are where Ó Ríordáin sharpens his tools for the brutal battle ahead, for the foe that is fate. It is not solely through poetry that the poet hones his survival skills either; in these earlier years, through the diary entries, we can trace Ó Ríordáin's daily struggle to hone his métier in prose and make it fit for his artistic purposes.

Ó Ríordáin may be known today primarily for poems as striking as 'Claustrophobia' and 'Fiabhras', but it was in the forge of prose and the diaries that the real preparation and polishing of his artistic sensibility took place. The poems that appeared in later years only came into being because of the extensive prose groundwork already laid. So we find him setting out his situation and goal from the beginning.

New Year's Day 1940 is the first recorded diary entry that we have, albeit that Ó Ríordáin indicates that he's written other fragments previously, fragments that must have disappeared over the course of time. Ironically, the poet's newly written diary entries are inscribed on old paper, the old jotters or account books once used in the family shop. The poet is just twenty-three years of age when he writes:

> *Monday. Tonight I started writing this in an old account book that my mother had when she was in the shop in Ballyvourney. The figures are still marked in the book. I will keep an account of what happens in my life in this book for the coming year. Only God knows who'll be alive by the end of the year. Last year, when I began recording some of my thoughts, I stated that I thought I was unlikely to survive or still be on this earth by year's end. (Perhaps it is worth stating here that the writer of this journal is not a healthy person – because I've had tuberculosis for the past two years now.) I had to get medical help to stay alive. And I'm still not better by any means. But no matter. I survived the year.*

> *This is something that people who were much healthier than me at the beginning of the year didn't manage. There were plenty of bold Russians who were in the full of their health last Christmas and who are corpses tonight, buried now in the frozen earth up north. Another crowd will join the legions of the dead this year. I wouldn't be surprised if the soul left this decrepit body of mine and I too was numbered amongst this same crowd by this time next year. But this much I promise – that I won't leave any gaps in this account for as long as I have the strength in my fingers to do so. I was often very sick last year, but no matter what, I made sure to write the daily account in my diary. Even when I was in the sanatorium, I noted what happened in my dairy daily, even if I thought initially that I might be too embarrassed to do so.*

The contours of what faces him are clear from the very beginning even if his writing changes and develops before long, the more he pares and strips back his subject matter and language over time. It isn't clear how long the poet had already spent practising and honing his writing skills in Irish prior to these first diary entries, but it seems likely – as partly based on the diary entry above – that he was already working on and perfecting his writing for at least two years prior to these initial diary entries. In a diary entry for 30 March 1958, Ó Ríordáin informs us that it is twenty years since he began composing poetry for the first time; tracing backwards, these initial compositions can be dated almost certainly to the first time that he set foot in a sanatorium. The confluence is significant. The poet comes of the sickbed that is his suffering reality and to the mystery of poetry at one and the same time, even if the form he uses to describe that reality on a daily basis in his earliest terrain of creative endeavour is actually prose. This is a private prose journal for the moment, even if the poet returns to prose writing again later in life (1960s) – this time in the public sphere – from a combination of financial necessity and failure (in creative or poetic terms). Be that as it may, the prose served as the basic building blocks for his poetic oeuvre, in the early years at least.

Ó Ríordáin's creative work in prose and poetry was very different in many ways, even if they share many similarities in style – so much so that the term 'Ríordánach' (Riordan-ish) was frequently used to describe his writing style by various scholars. Interestingly, it was this very term, i.e. 'Ríordánach', that literary critic Seán Ó Tuama used to distinguish Ó Ríordáin's poetry from that of his Irish-language contemporary, the noted Aran Islands poet, Máirtín Ó Direáin. Ó Tuama classified Ó Direáin as 'a community poet' whose poetry was primarily concerned with 'the island that was', whereas Ó Ríordáin was a poet of the private individual, a writer whose primary focus was on 'the Ó Ríordáin to be'.[3] Ó Tuama's assessment of Ó Direáin aside, it seems to me that Ó Ríordáin's poetry exhibits a far greater concern with 'the man that is', and that this is undoubtedly one of the central themes of his work as developed over time. At the very beginning, however, as we will explore here, it is a case of the poet mastering his craft word by word, hewing and shaping the Irish language as appropriate to his needs. This was a difficult process but it was only by learning the craft thus that he also came to discover himself and the nature of his own artistic sensibility. Not unnaturally, many of the early diary entries (as with many written at the end of his life) were concerned with the immediate exigencies of the moment and were frequently distressing – given how ill Ó Ríordáin was with tuberculosis.

Ó Ríordáin had this to say in *Scríobh 3* in response to a question from Seán Ó Mórdha regarding how he began writing in Irish:

> *I regularly wrote prose as well as poetry years ago; as far back as 1935, I was writing a diary. I burned some of these diaries by throwing them into the fire, thank God. And there's one diary for the year 1940, and whenever I get a really bad bout of illness, I'm scared that I won't make it home again, so as to make sure it gets thrown on the fire too.*[4]

There are many different varieties of prose, just as there is poetry, and it may well be the case, therefore that 1935 is the most accurate date for the beginning of Ó Ríordáin's life project. It is unclear, however, what is the basis of Diarmaid Ó Mathúna's assertion that 'the poet was just eighteen years of age when he wrote the poem "Ualach na Beatha"', unless

3 Ó Tuama, Seán, *Filí faoi Sceimhle: Seán Ó Ríordáin agus Aogán Ó Rathaille* (Oifig an tSoláthar, Dublin, 1978), p. 42.

4 *Scríobh 3*, p. 175.

Ó Ríordáin himself conveyed this to Ó Mathúna at some point.[5] Based on the poet's diary entries for 1940 (running from 1 January to 21 May of that year), where the poet outlines how seriously ill he feels and his anxiety that he might not make it home from the sanatorium in time to burn the writings that he doesn't want anyone else to see, one would assume that it is only fairly recently – i.e. within the last year or two (1938–40) – that Ó Ríordáin had begun writing poetry. He is familiarising himself with the terrain that is writing at this point and thinking how best to organise his métier, and so his biggest question at this juncture is that of his subject matter and his own role within the creative process. He records various occurrences in his life, big and small, local and international, whether reacting to the latest news from Inniscarra in Cork or a report on the war in Russia as seen in the morning's newspaper, *The Irish Press*. At this early stage, we witness the poet mentally scoping out a path for his writing and the subject matter that best suits him:

> *I kept a normal daily journal last year, a journal which had a particular slot for each day in it, but now, I think it's time to restrict my writing and to become more focused to a certain degree.*[6]

> *In a daily journal a person describes what they have done that day and what happened to them. Then he also describes other incidents that he has witnessed or which have happened to him, or that he deems worthy of noting. He follows local events as based on the information he finds in the newspapers if you like. I don't think that this is really the type of material that you usually include in a private account or record of your thoughts … Anyway, the truth is that if I didn't record what's happening in the wider world outside, I'd have very little to write about here, given that little enough happens in my own life. As I mentioned in this account last year, the only thing that happens in my life is this bit of writing that I do here.*[7]

---

5 Ó hAnluain, Eoghan (ed.), *An Duine is Dual* (An Clóchomhar, Dublin, 1980), p. 155.

6 Diary (hereafter D): 6 January 1940.

7 D: 10 January 1940.

Ó Ríordáin had a lifelong habit of occasionally looking back over what he had written to see whether it was of much value. He always had a fairly humble opinion of himself as a writer, however, and rarely considered his literary efforts to be particularly outstanding. This is what he thought of an excerpt of his written in 1939, even if it was then still a fairly recent piece of work: 'I wrote an account of the year '39, for example, and I can't look at it again now, it fills me with such disgust.'[8] It's unclear what happened to the diaries kept for this period and a number of other diaries that he refers to later; likely as not, they suffered the same fate as quite a number of the diaries that followed, i.e. he ended up burning them.

Ó Ríordáin clearly had his reasons for destroying some of his early diaries but surely he had even stronger reasons to preserve them? Surely, life itself, even as recalled by the poet in its most wretched or shameful or abject moments deserved to be documented?

> *I'm a hospital patient all the time and therefore I don't do anything. Consequently, all I have to recount to you now relates to what I didn't do today. I didn't drink whiskey. I didn't shave my beard. I didn't kiss a woman. I didn't make my Confession. I didn't sing a song. I didn't compose a poem. I didn't plant any oats. I didn't bury my mother-in-law. I didn't put a heel on a shoe. I didn't go swimming. I didn't make a speech. I didn't break any window. I didn't die.*[9]

Of note here already is Ó Ríordáin's usage of the negative 'Ní' to describe what he didn't do (as seen in the original Irish), a term that grew in significance and assumed a more singular role over the course of his artistic and working life. Over time, it is this discourse of negation or nothingness – nothing happening, nothing written, nothing done – upon which Ó Ríordáin the artist depends for his subject matter; ultimately, perhaps, it is his only subject matter worth exploring. Ironically, it is in the idle recesses and apparent futility of the mind that Ó Ríordáin finds sustenance the

8 *Ibid.*
9 D: 31 March 1942.

more he developed as a poet. There is no need to be concerned about what you have to say as 'To be conscious is not to be in time.'[10]

It has been ordained from the beginning that you attend the fair even if you've no produce to sell and no business being there in the first place. One can have too much business also, particularly when it concerns the argumentation and propaganda into which many of his public pronouncements later descended. But it was also in such newspaper articles that Ó Ríordáin fleshed out many of the thoughts and ideas that he initially confided to the diary – in articles, such as 'Éist le Fuaim na hAbhann' ('*Listen to the Sound of the River*'), 'An Taibhreamh Mór' ('*The Great Dream*') and 'Smaointe Fáin' ('*Random Thoughts*').[11] The poet was already reflecting on the meaning and function of writing as early as the year 1944:

> *Can anything meaningful be written without there being a worthwhile subject in the mind of the writer? I think so. I think that this is how writing should be done sometimes. It's difficult to do, however, because it's like jumping aboard a moving train. Look into the room of your mind unknown to anyone – when your thoughts aren't looking so to speak. That's when you'll find them behaving in a completely natural way. Then your words really have life.*[12]

We may compare this with a piece he wrote in 1973, almost thirty years later, a piece he'd originally confided to the diary and re-worked again later on for the (aforementioned) article entitled 'Éist le Fuaim na hAbhann'. As was frequently the case, however, Ó Ríordáin had another motive when he initially wrote the piece in the privacy of his diary, one that wasn't obvious to the people who read the newspaper article as provided for public consumption at a much later date. The beginning of the piece, as taken from the diary, reads:

> *Friday 29/3/73, 5.20 a.m. Awake. Why did I take up my pen? It wasn't because I'd anything to write – although I do find myself writing. It must be a protection*

10 From T. S. Eliot's 'The Four Quartets'.
11 IT, 7 April 1973; IT, 3 October 1974; IT, 30 November 1968.
12 D: 3 August 1944.

> *against fear – for me. But as for whatever it is I write, where do I get it from or what is it – when I have no inclination to say anything anyway?*

The excerpt that follows is taken from the published newspaper article and is simply a more polished version of the original diary entry:

> *Where does the thing that I write come from – when I don't have anything to say? How do I manage to write something when I've nothing to say? This is all based on the principle that our minds are constantly in motion ... What happens is that your pen sees your mind wandering by and it hops up on it and rides along with it. Your pen doesn't know where your mind is going. Even your mind doesn't know. It's a sort of mystery tour.*
>
> *But it's already clear that your pen has already interrupted your mind. While your mind was travelling, does it travel naked or does it have words cloaking it? That's an old question, one yet to be answered by the philosophers. There are two schools of thought in relation to this, as they say. But, one way or another, this interruption has happened, irrespective of what the answer to this (philosophical) question is. What does the interruption consist of? Your pen has realised that your mind is present and it's no longer the same any more. It's on alert now. It's aware of itself now. It's watching out. It's public. It's aware that it's being listened to and that it must, as it sees it, conduct itself carefully. Now we don't know what it would be up to if it hadn't been interrupted or disturbed. It has been awoken from its innocent form of reflection, from the great unconscious thought. It may be that it has been disturbed from consideration on the nature of Humanity and that now it finds itself meditating on the situation of just one individual, and even that in attenuated form. If one could hear the sound of this particular river, one would surely catch a trout.*

The proverb Ó Ríordáin cites has a contradiction at its heart, however, because listening and watching or being alert are not enough in themselves. The poetic craft also requires action, and this is where the poet often struggles or fails. He might hear the sound of the river of creativity as it rushes by, but it is others rather than him who are often out in the mid-stream of the world fishing or gathering poetry into their nets. As he says in his diary:

The immediate act is the one that matters. Awareness and knowledge are worthless without the act that must accompany them. There is nothing as powerful or as youthful as the immediate act. Life transforms itself anew when someone acts. To act is a heartfelt thing. In the absence of the act, there's no progress or life … Apparently, people are always letting life seep out of them – they let it go in the form of a new child or in words, or, alas, they just waste it completely, and let it escape in the wind – the wind of sin.[13]

This is a man whose life consists entirely of words – and the word itself was scarce and hard-come-by at times. The true reason he seeks sanctuary in writing is immediate and urgent and is clear to the young poet as early as the year 1942, when he says:

I am not calm. I have no peace. Although I'm writing this now, I'm really just waiting for something else to come along. This rubbish that I'm writing here now is just a means to avoid restlessness.[14]

As Ó Ríordáin frequently confesses, he often uses the diaries *to avoid* writing too. Early the following year, he notes the following, for example:

The morning is windy and wet. I've no interest in writing anything. I decided to do this so as to avoid the awful thoughts I have. These thoughts are all around me in the house today and my mind is trembling with fear. I'll make it lie down on this bed of papers here and see whether that will put it to sleep. There's my mind there now stretched out flat in front of me on the page.[15]

These excerpts reveal two aspects of Ó Ríordáin's sensibility: the first is that it is from the tangled confusion of his mind that the bulk of his writing emerges; secondly, his writings are evidence of this inner life, the mind of turmoil that he seeks to capture within the word and rhythm of his poetry, even if they reveal little enough about other aspects of his life at

13 D: 13 December 1953.
14 D: 27 June 1942.
15 D: 1 January 1943.

this juncture. As he says himself in relation to his diaries on 15 February 1956: 'I have left some account of my bedroom mind here but where is the account of my wandering or road-mind?'

As it happens, it is the inner world of his bedroom mind as documented in the diaries that most concerns us in this volume; this is the world of harsh imagery and loneliness: the winter, the storm, the night, the illness, the world of fear and despair – the man within. This is not so much the life *as is*, but rather the life as the artist imagines it and recreates it through the medium of the word.

And this created world encompasses more than a rural landscape. The back country of Ó Ríordáin's imagination has its own people, a people whose dreams and motivations he recreates through the window of his imagination, a seemingly far-away landscape that the poet rarely traverses in actuality or in the real world, given the limitations his illness imposes on him. The landscape of Ó Ríordáin's imagination assumes physical form solely in the poetry that he writes. Sometimes, we feel that we are familiar with this place or that we recognise someone or something in its fictional terrain and yet we realise as quickly again that it's just a shadow-world, a place where even the language that mirrors it is elusive or distorted. Even if Ó Ríordáin's writing is a form of mirroring, it's frequently a blurred or faded image that reveals itself.[16] Life mirrors art in the sense that this imaginary reflection of his terrain is all the poet possesses. It's as if the life and the word inhabit the same mirror but rarely venture beyond its confines. The word *is* the mirror and reflects Ó Ríordáin's life back to himself, a life of creative struggle, illness and frequent physical suffering. And our primary concern here is the way that the two minds collide – the private mind of his bedroom where he lives and writes, and the road-mind where he lets his imagination run untrammelled and free. These minds meet and intersect, and separate again. And yet, much of the time Ó Ríordáin appears a solitary figure in his diaries, alone by circumstance and as necessitated by the dictates of his art. In the diaries we only get brief glimpses of the youthful and healthy individual that he was as a

---

16 See *Eireaball Spideoige* (hereafter ES): pp. 46 and 84; *Línte Liombó* (hereafter LL): p. 9.

very young man. This nostalgic and almost-mythical figure seems to have disappeared at an early stage of his writing life, however, and we discover very little about this younger man or his sensibility as the years go by.

The diaries are primarily books of anxiety, fear and occasional neurosis that chronicle the life of the mind subsequent to Ó Ríordáin's youth and the world he left behind there. Whatever the 'younger Ó Ríordáin' *was* is but a distant memory by the time we meet him in the silence of his sickroom and he begins to record on the empty page the detritus of suffering and the titanic physical and mental struggle he endures in order to bring form to his art. His writing and poetry is to a large extent the material evidence of this harsh struggle. Some sample excerpts from the ten years between 1951 and 1961 tell us more about the battle:

> *Sunday 7.40 a.m. 22/9/51. A thundery morning and rain. I never write anything in this book except when I'm sick and when the weather is bad …*

> *15/9/51 … I haven't written in this book now for a long time because my life has been healthy and happy recently. The streptomycin has improved my health greatly …*

> *21/2/1956. Tuesday 8 p.m. A bout of depression! And so, I need to write something down – whether the words have any meaning or not. I was in Cork today …*

> *Sunday, 7/10/56 6 p.m. This life is a storm, it seems. Take a look at an old man's face. It's obvious that he's been through a lot – that he's been through a great storm and that he feels lucky to have survived it. I'm not an old man yet. So I'm right in the middle of the storm. I'm in danger of drowning. People use all sorts of things to try and drown out the noise of the storm – drink, women, football, religion, work, drugs, etc. This book is my escape, it seems. It's no wonder that there is so much childishness and messing in it. It is a drug. It is a shelter. It's a way of running away.*

> *27/11/56 Tuesday, 5.20 a.m. I woke up a while ago to find myself thrown on the bed here and my clothes still on. I started coughing. I put on the light. Then*

I became terrified. I was actually terrified for the first few minutes. Then, I remembered to say a few Ave Marias. This calmed me down for a while. Then, I took up this book and noted these words in it. Am I dying? … [A few pages later.] I won't write anything else now. The storm has abated.

30/1/57 Wednesday 9.35 p.m. … This book is coming to an end. I myself am coming to an end. What else is anyone doing except coming to an end. This book only lasted three months. It's a bad sign of my health that this book is filling up so quickly.

Tuesday 26/11/57 11.50 a.m. I'm going to go into Cork now straight away. A feeling of impatience came over me and I took up this book for fear of something worse coming in my direction. That's all. Thank you book.

8 p.m. I was in Cork since. That was a big relief.

4/11/58 Tuesday, 10.20 a.m. In bed again today. My idleness is worrying me today. I write in this book because I'm lazy and not because I like to be busy. I have the strength to write whenever I like in this book and to write whatever I like in it. This is the last page in this volume and it's lasted from the 16/2/58 until today. Usually, one of these books lasts for just a few months. They last longer in summer than they do in winter, however, as I'm struck down with illness more often in winter … Is there anything left in this book that is worthwhile reading? Hardly, I'd say.

27/1/61 4.40 a.m. What am I doing now? What am I doing here really as I write this? I'm dying. (I've spent more than twenty years dying.) I suffer pain and terror and the loneliness of death and I write it down on paper in the middle of the night. I've died thousands of times at this stage – cowards die many times before their death. I'm a cowardly person, without any doubt. A puff of wind would frighten me. I'm sat back in the bed now because I'm too afraid to lie back in it. And I'm not that short of breath at all really. If it was morning, I'd be able to relax and rest and I'd have no problem stretching back properly in the bed.

Friday 3.50 a.m. 21/4/61 … These notes aren't worth a damn; other than that they keep me going. Poetry is worth something if you put the work into it. But

> *this kind of writing isn't enough. It's a lazy business. You can write whatever you want and in whatever way you want. What's the point other than to conquer the anxieties of the night? So that nothing goes to waste. You'd never know what kind of trout you might catch in your net, even like this ...*

Even if the poetry was more insightful than the prose, it emerged from the same physical and mental storm as the diary, the sole difference being that it was in a far more polished form than the more mundane or rudimentary nature of the prose; the latter functions as an amanuensis in the face of fear.[17] Considerations such as these underscore the prose: when illness or pain besieges you in the middle of the night, where can you turn except to the blank page in front of you? The sky comes to weigh heavily on you and you need a release valve for the fear, the sorrow, the claustrophobia, the anxiety and the sense of impending death that engulfs you. There's just one way to escape the pain or release the tension and it is this. You take on the pain that flows through you and strip parts of it away somehow; you try and choke down the fear that floods through you and still your racing blood. If possible, you let the fear out in the form of words in the hope that it will somehow melt them on the page. If you don't release this fear and mollify it through the act of writing, you're doomed. Or, to use a marine metaphor, continue to manoeuvre against tide and current until the day brightens from the east and the storm eases. You constantly wait and watch by the light of a candle. And all the while, you carefully guard whatever light you have, for fear that it might go out – in case the darkness of night should invade those decaying lungs of yours and overwhelm you completely.

Write, control, pacify everything that comes within the range of your eyes and imagination. It was death to let down your guard or lie back on the bed. One must always be alert. Anything is preferable to that thing beyond which you cannot define but know for certain that nothing else really exists. Writing is the only act left to you now, the sole protection against the night. It may be a form of cowardice, but it is all you've left and

17 An amanuensis is a literary or artistic assistant, particularly one who takes dictation.

it's only with the arrival of the wan light of morning that you have peace, a peace that you've paid for dearly. The terrors and images that have haunted you melt away and disappear in the yard outside and your vision becomes open and expansive once more. The night world is the realm of poetry that is Ó Ríordáin's 'Claustrophobia', even if the daylight world that imbues 'Fiabhras' ('*Fever*') is not much better. Ultimately, the worlds of night and day are negotiated in similar fashion: through incessant writing, even if the writing sometimes amounts to no more than scarcely coherent scribbling.

Depending on the circumstances, there are times when he needs the healing balm that is the 'word' more urgently, needless to say. At times also, this healing effect manifests itself in a manner that is more cold and clinical. It depends on the nature of the pain, and whether it is psychological or physical. A couple of examples from the diaries here, separated by a gap of twenty years, show how the poet longs to expel his suffering and transpose it to the empty page; words and pills become interchangeable:

> *Sunday 17/8/47 … I say all these things to make sure that the texture of this day lasts, to secure it to the page.*

> *11.35 p.m. 19/5/67… I had a pain in my lower back today and I want to leave this pain behind me on the page now.*
>
> *I swallowed a sleeping pill because I want to get this oppressive night over with and, to leave it behind me, and never taste it again …*

The poet describes something similar in his essay 'An Taisceadán' ('*The Locker*'):

> *I watch this thing and then I note down the latest signs I've noticed relating to it. If this occurs as a dream, then I note down the dream. If it takes the form of an itch, then I write down a full description of the itch. If it's transformed into a form of thought, then I do the same thing … Watching and taking note is all there is.*

The entry can be as basic as a quick weather report or how the winter cold has entered his bones: 'I don't know anything more painful than the frost' (26 December 1964). He writes his diary at any time, day or night – while drunk, while falling asleep, or even while still half-asleep and ensnared in the dream – also when the medication is beginning to take effect, numbing the senses. One feels that Ó Ríordáin was frequently testing himself against reality, against the very truth itself. The likes of the following, as first written at 2 a.m. on 15 February 1969; you can actually see the poet's handwriting wandering on the page as he comes to the last few sentences:

> *The pill is working. Bit by bit, I feel my body going numb. My two hands are like pieces of paper. A force is going through me that feels like some type of energy. I can feel it in my lips and in my fingers. This force is getting control of me so that it feels as if the bodily part of me – that slow, dull part of me – is starting to melt. It's as if I and this force – this energy – have become one. It's as if I've become pure spirit. You'd think that I was out there somewhere – weightless. It's a lovely feeling. It's a kind of intoxication. Everything is light and free. Everything in the world, me included, feels light ...*
> ('Pill, a Pill, a Rún Ó' ('*Pill, Pill, my Darling*'))[18]

Firstly, he notes the date and then sometimes the day and the hour. It's important to record time's movements when you yourself are so intimate with them, when you're an essential aspect of the calendar, of the clock. These are days and nights and years that have little to divide them and which melt one into another. He wakes from sleep one winter's night and to reorient himself within the living world, he notes the requisite information: 'It's 3 or 4 a.m. I think, probably the 14th. I can't find my watch under the pillow.'[19] What function does such apparently mundane information have for anyone else, however? It is this: if the poet confirms that such-and-such a thing occurred at a certain time or on a particular

---

18 IT, 19 March 1969. A pun on the Irish song title 'Pill, pill a rún ó' where the word 'Pill' ('Fill') translates as '*Come back*' or '*Return*' (lit: '*Return, return my darling*').

19 D: 14 January 1959.

afternoon, who's to say what additional insight – as reflected in that piece of writing – this will provide one with in time? Also, one has 'captured' a particular moment in time in a certain sense, and what's to prevent one from returning and playing out that moment again in a different way?

> *3.45 p.m. A wave of despair just went through me just now. I felt as if I was trapped. If a wave of despair goes through me at a quarter to four in the afternoon, why do I feel it necessary to note it here? Who cares what I felt and when? But despair is something that you have no control over. It's a permanent thing. If a student reads these words in a thousand years from now, won't he have a clear understanding of this despair, if nothing else? If he reads them at a quarter-to-four in the afternoon, when he feels a sense of despair himself, won't he understand them better still?*[20]

> *A gloomy, grey afternoon. A stab of joy running somewhere through the gloom also, however. If someone was to read the above phrase 'gloomy grey afternoon' in ten year's time, I think they'd feel that there was some sliver of magic in this afternoon, or even if I read the phrase then that I will feel the same thing myself. There was an unbearable light in the evenings of ten years ago.*[21]

He would capture things as he captures time. To draw the world outside the mind in order that its very existence be confirmed. His pen circumvents the room and appraises the furniture; it gauges the dimensions of the chairs and considers their essence:

> *There's a chair here next to the bed. A wooden chair. There's a small hole in the seat of it. The timber in the chair was very weak and easy to damage. There's a small spur or splinter of wood jutting out next to this hole. There's a rosary hanging on the back of the chair also ... I have a fondness for dead things, things that you can put your hands on, tonight.*[22]

---

20 D: 6 December 1956.
21 D: 1 April 1964.
22 D: 5 October 1956.

The poet even describes how he writes what he writes; he might be lying back in the bed (as in the above excerpt noted on the 27/01/61) or stretched out on his left-hand side, as was his usual writing position.[23] His vision is not necessarily askew, but it may not be complete or whole either:

> *I'm writing this while stretched back on the bed. I'm lying on my left-hand side. It's easy to write like this. It's a struggle for me to sit up straight on a chair as I get a pain in my back and a shortness of breath. I could do a lot of writing like this, if I set my mind to it.*[24]

Each diary assumes its own importance as it fills with writing. This is where those aspects of the world that communicated with him most recently are stored away. He says his farewell to each book as he leaves it behind and it enters into another world, a world that can never belong to him – given that his is the life of the 'word' and the 'book' from this point onwards. It will now exist really as a book, while he must turn his attention to the present time and person. A completed book – a person over and done with. A new book begins. Book and writer take each other's measure. They observe each other with varying degrees of interest or disinterest:

> *I'm coming to the end of this book. I bought its successor today. This book has no further interest in what I'm writing any more. It knows that it's coming to an end, that there's just one more page left, and that it's not up to anything now, that the pair of us are just putting in time. It's difficult for me to write anything worthwhile in a book that has this mindset. The book understands that I've abandoned it really and that I'm already thinking of the new book.*[25]

You already know what is bound and shackled inside and that all is not well with it or with its author. It is sobering to think how much pain comes to be transferred from person to page in the course of a few months, overflowing the book. Unsurprisingly, it is the diaries that are

---

23 'A ghiolla tá cliathánach sínte' ('*O fellow stretched sideways*'), ES: p. 115.

24 D: 11 February 1956.

25 D: 25 May 1962.

the most detailed and richest in literary quality that last longest and are the most fascinating. Amongst them are the following in particular: the diary that covers the period 7 August 1947 to 24 April 1949 and from 4 December 1953 to 21 January 1956. The size and the thickness of the diary indicate a good deal. It might be a sign of poor health on his part, for example, if a certain winter diary is filled too quickly (e.g., the entry cited earlier for 30 January 1957 and referring to the diary from 20 October 1956 to 31 January 1957.) On the other hand, he notes on completion of another diary that lasted him almost seven months, from 27 April 1964 to 21 November 1964 that life had been relatively good to him during this period. The lifespan of the diaries, too, was dependent on the health of their author.

Ó Ríordáin usually welcomed each fresh book in similar fashion; maybe this new ledger is the one where he'll really find what it is he seeks: for example, 'Yes, a new book. I hope that it's better than the last one which did little to enhance the Irish or the poetry, or prose of its author, I'm afraid.'[26] Or maybe the new book will give him a new lease of life as regards his health and happiness, more so than its predecessor did (e.g., 27 April 1964).

This never happens, however, because before long we recognise the same outlook and sentiments manifest themselves as before: laziness, exhaustion, fear, cowardice, a lack of manliness, a feeling of madness or some other failing that the poet senses goes way back in his family, the 'Speckled Riordans'. The poet sees the same traits or faults resurface in the next generation of his tribe. Here he is again tormenting himself with questions that he already knows the answer to. And how disheartening it is – to be continually obsessed with issues and questions that you've already tortured yourself with endlessly already: that you are intimate with suffering and illness and ensnared by your difficult circumstances – seemingly forever. No writing or book can set you free from this predicament. In your heart of hearts, do you really want to be free, however, or are you happy to stay where you are? Haven't you set before you as your life's project to trace the contours of suffering in silence and won't you see

26 D: 28 November 1966.

this task out until the very end? Everything is in the past and the past is a long time ago now. It is gone, never to return. Back then, you were in a very different moment and time, so different that it might as well have been a hundred years ago. The people and the era you remember were so different and far away in time that it might as well have related to the era of the old sages and stories – the likes of Conán Maol Mac Mórna, even if you still give a lazy nod of acknowledgement to that time and place on occasion ...[27]

Ó Ríordáin describes each diary book almost as if it was independent of its content. The type of paper it contains, what it smells like, how it compares with the one that went before. The cover of the copybook is too light on one of them (14 May 1961) or the pages are too thin on another (16 May 1967). It's an important moment to him when he writes the first new words in each copybook (e.g., 25 May 1962). He places his hand on the pristine new page and it is so cold that it almost burns him (1 February 1956). It is similar with each new pen that he welcomes; supposing, for example, he'd disliked the one he'd worked with previously. Or maybe a new pen that cost too much and he was out of pocket because of it. Or, on occasion, the poet writes something as simple as 'a new nib on my pen here' as he does on 8 December 1961.

If there's no news, then you have to make up your own ... Even when there's very little to say, it is important to say something. You go out with your net and see what you can catch. Isn't this whole project a bit of a swizz anyway? It's as if your book has taken the place of your mother, the one you once ran to whenever you composed a new poem.

It is your neighbour in the absence of a neighbour, but that is all. And it is often a bad neighbour too, if the truth be told, especially when it serves to heighten your doubts and fears. Life has played a few nasty tricks on you in your time but maybe this is the biggest trick of all – because you are the one who has played it on himself. You claim to have a talent for poetry but maybe you're only fooling yourself? And how true is this project anyway when you have such difficulty facing the truth that is your own life? Where is the subconscious mind that you regularly refer to? Not

27 LL: p. 23.

here anyway. Could it be that this is all a form of posing and dishonesty at the end of the day? Have you actually the linguistic wherewithal to burden the Irish language with your poems and reflections, or what right do you have to write in Irish at all?

These and others are the questions that Ó Ríordáin anxiously spent his life asking himself in the privacy of his diaries. Not that his diary writing is always prone to self-doubt or self-effacement. Like all true artists, he kept knocking on the door until it opened for him. He bravely follows the trajectory of his sensibility, no matter where it takes him and there are times – and plenty of them – when his writing is smooth as silk and sparkles with energy and life.[28] The smallest things can spark the imagination. He's on the outskirts of the city one day when a thought suddenly occurs to him that sets his imagination aflame:

> *A thought came to me the other day and it set my mind afire. I was looking out at the houses and the trees. I was thinking of all those healthy leaves proudly growing on the trees outside. Then this thought came to me – like something long-forgotten that you suddenly remembered. The houses and everything around the place are full of thoughts in addition to the leaves that are still growing. Young thoughts and old thoughts, and you can't see them. A sort of a hidden life that surrounds us. A natural world of thoughts and ideas. Thoughts like people and weeds – growing on the houses. Noble thoughts with an aristocratic lineage that rule over the more commonplace ones. A host of thoughts that you could categorise as the working-class of thought. All these images mixed up together.*[29]

Interestingly, it's in a similar fashion that he speaks of the bird image that leaps out at him from the whispering of the saints and the trees in the poem 'Oileán agus Oileán Eile' ('*This Island and the Other Island*'), a poem he wrote the following summer. The frequency of such moments of inspiration varies over time and, in later years Ó Ríordáin was prone to reading back over the diaries again to reassess their value. In 1967, for instance, just ten short years before his death, we find him going back over

28 'Léaspairtí' ('*Witticisms*'), IT, 20 March 1971.
29 D: 7 September 1947.

his diaries again and judging them uneven. He begins his prose review with the year 1951:

> *It seems that I was much worse back then than I am now even, bad as I am. My health was bad and I hadn't a penny in my pocket. But it isn't all this bad luck that most interests me but rather my Irish. Again, bad as it is now, it was seven times worse then. It was poor and weak and in bad health. And there was nothing great in any of the thoughts that I tried to express in it either. (Only the very odd time would a spark of inspiration appear to me then.) And what I don't understand about it is this: if the critics are right, or at least those of them who like my writing, it was back then that I produced my best poetry. It's true that I was writing more poetry back then than I am now. And although I wasn't that confident about my poetry-writing back then, I'm still sure that it was way ahead of the rotten prose that I noted in the diary. Is there any explanation so for the way a person's writing changes when they switch from prose to poetry? It seems as if the ability for reflection becomes stronger as well. Maybe the only explanation for this is that the diary writing was just a trivial and incomplete type of work, a light form of work, whereas the poetry is something more whole that involves a lot of effort and time. I hope that there's inspiration evident in it also. Who'd put in that much effort if they weren't driven by some sort of inspiration? Indeed, I still remember the time when inspiration would come – that inspiration which no longer appears unfortunately, or, at least, not as often – and I get sad about it. When I looked at the diary for 1965 and the Irish I wrote and the style and the thoughts that I expressed that year, they didn't mortify me as much as the ones I wrote in 1951. But where are the poems for 1965? And if I composed one or two or three of them, were they as good as those old stagers of 1951? I'm afraid that they weren't. It's not easy to explain these things.*[30]

Whatever one's view of his work, Ó Ríordáin's prose writing didn't decline to the same extent as did his poetic output in later years – and this was particularly true from the 1950s onwards. And there's no doubt that Ó Ríordáin thought he'd left some material of value in his many diaries. For instance, when he went into hospital for what he knew was the last time, he

30 D: 18 January 1967.

instructed his nephew, Seán, to take good care of the diaries he'd left at home and which he'd spent years working on in case anything got mislaid: perhaps they'd prove of value someday. He also told him who could decide their value down the line if it came to it: Seán Ó Mórdha and Seán Ó Coileáin. Additionally, he handed the last diary he'd been working on to Ó Mórdha without stipulating anything relating to what he should do with it later. Any decision in relation to the diaries was now left in the hands of others.

With respect to how the diaries might be regarded after he was gone, Ó Ríordáin had already stated publicly long before this: 'His mind was an eternal dialogue. He expressed his thoughts and feelings in writings discovered posthumously' or 'this is how I perceived it in my diary and anyone can examine the diary after my death'.[31]

Ó Ríordáin didn't mean this in a self-deprecating way it should be said; he took his diary writing quite seriously. And, in this instance, the poet is addressing the individual who was happy to read the diaries from the very beginning. On 5 January 1940 this anonymous individual is the 'mocking reader'; on 6 April 1942 the reader is the friend he does not know. Thirty years later and the reader is still the same invisible friend, someone who isn't in a position to come to his aid at that particular moment in time: 'I've no one to make my complaints to, only this book, i.e. to you who will read it. But then, when will you read it, if ever? I'll be dead by then. That isn't much good.'[32] But it is not only his 'friend' who will read it when he's gone, the poet suggests at another juncture. Here's some advice for a certain person of his acquaintance who might read it after he has passed on. He begins by listing his attributes, and continues:

> *Maybe he'll read this when I'm dead. I hope that it'll benefit him in some way. The ugliest trait associated with him is his slyness. If he doesn't control this, it will be the ruin of him. Maybe it's a bit late for him now to be getting it under control.*[33]

---

31 'Céadna idir dhá comhairle' ('*Céadna undecided*'), IT, 12/13 April 1968; 'Bríonglóidí' ('*Dreams*'), IT, 25/26/27 December 1968.

32 D: 8 January 1972.

33 D: 26 October 1956.

What value do the diaries have in literary terms, is the most common question Ó Ríordáin asks himself. He's always awaiting the advent of the 'great' work; the following excerpts are typical in that the answers provoke even more questions:

> *They are probably nothing more than a writing exercise, so that my pen doesn't get rusty. Later on, when I begin writing publicly, people will be surprised at how fluent or easy my writing seems, or will they? But I'd be unhappy if these reports were nothing more than an exercise in writing. I never put any great effort into these books. To tell you the truth, all I ever did was dash off the words carelessly as a form of recreation or as some sort of remedy when I was so ill that I couldn't put up with the suffering any further.*[34]

> *3.45 a.m. Just awake. I'm improved from last night. The panic and the shortness of breath are gone – for the moment anyway. I think that the night has improved also. It isn't as bitter outside, or as damp. If I'd been lucky enough to have spent last night in a pub, in cheerful and happy company, I'd have managed to avoid the poison and the terror of last night. Is it necessary to say these things here? Will these diaries that I write survive after I'm gone? That depends less on the diaries themselves and more on my reputation. If my reputation as a writer lives on, then everything relating to me will be valuable. It was on the radio last night that a Petrarch manuscript, containing 70 pages of his poetry, was stolen from the Vatican Library. I think they said that this document was worth £170,000 pounds. How can they put a price on the likes of that? I'm getting on in years and I have yet to produce anything in these diaries to ensure their value after my death. Could it be that they will prove valuable for their own sake? Hardly. Much of this depends on the fate of the Irish language also.*[35]

> *This writing is nothing but a trick to put the terror and the panic on the long finger. God help any poor American creature who comes after me and tries to make any sense of them.*[36]

---

34 D: 10 February 1958.
35 D: 27 November 1965.
36 D: 31 December 1965.

Ó Ríordáin had a sense that a day would come when the diaries proved of interest to others, however. He imagined someone bent over the diaries, examining them. He'd have some work ahead of him! Good luck to him!

> *This paper is too thin. I probably should write on both sides of this sheet of paper as the writing is going through it. Isn't that the best way to have it? The more effort that the researchers (from the States, of course) have to put in later on, the better. They love difficulty and incomprehensibility and* variae lectiones.[37]

What follows is largely the result of such scrutiny: an exploration of the writings of a man who faced the blank page and honestly inscribed himself upon it. And this was how Ó Ríordáin wanted it to be: 'You're only one human being. Leave yourself behind as further testimony to the human condition as provided by one individual. The Human Being will see himself in you. He doesn't expect to find anyone else here, but you yourself.'[38] Others might have expected to find a different person – the poet as they had encountered him in life: the nice, tidy, neat and ordered individual with the ironic wit. This is not the person presented here but one behind whose smile lay a great sense of despair and suffering. And this is the theme or trope that defines his personal and artistic life. The stability, order, fulfilment and wholeness that he searched for in the symmetry of poetry engendered something very different. The constancy or faithfulness that he sought from art, the source of which he associated with the mind of God, frequently proved inaccessible except by walking the hellish path that was suffering and pain. One paid a very high price in the effort to source the well of poetry and Ó Ríordáin was the Irish poet who paid the highest price of all.

37 D: 16 May 1967.
38 'Teachtaireacht Amháin' ('*One Message*'), IT, 1 April 1970.

1

One Morning Long Ago

Seán Ó Ríordáin was born on 3 December 1916. Interestingly, Ó Ríordáin regularly gave 1917 as the year he was born in biographical notes appended to collections of his poetry, beginning with *Nuabhéarsaíocht* (Modern Verse), 1950. This wasn't a deliberate 'error' on his part as it was the birthday date that he always mentioned in his personal diaries also. It may have been a superstition that Ó Ríordáin had, however, i.e. that one didn't give the 'exact' date of one's birthday away, in the same way that one didn't give the correct date on a person's coffin, but either added or subtracted a year to the correct date; remember, that this was a man who was in continual fear of the thirteenth of the month. But the birth certificate leaves no room for doubt.

Slievereagh (An Sliabh Riabhach) is given as Ó Ríordáin's place of birth; his father was renting a house by the roadside to the east of the mills of Ballyvourney, one of four houses standing in a row. The poet was the eldest child of Seán Ó Ríordáin (John Riordan), cobbler, and his wife, Máiréad Ní Luineacháin (Margaret Lenihan). He was baptised by the local priest, a Fr Twomey, the day following his birth in Séipéal Ghobnatan (The Church of Saint Gobnait); people tended not to delay with the baptism of new children at this time. They didn't go too far away from home for his godparents either; they were his uncle, Conchubhar Ó Ríordáin, and his maternal grandmother, Elizabeth Looney – she was the widow of Timothy Looney. Seán was very fond of both his godparents; his grandmother was sixty-five years of age at the time of the poet's baptism and she lived on for another fifteen years, while his uncle was a much younger man and in full health at the time. Tragically, of the three members of the Ó Ríordáin family whom we know were present at the baptism ceremony – his uncle, his father (i.e. Seán the Cobbler) and the child also named Seán – they would all eventually succumb to the same killer disease – tuberculosis. The poet's father would die from TB just ten years later and his uncle died from it when he was in his early seventies – he died on 16 December 1957. Seán Ó Ríordáin (the poet) caught the disease quite young and suffered from it for the next forty years of his life. Tuberculosis was the scourge of rural Ireland at the time and Seán's mother's side of the family suffered their fair share of its ravages also. Seán's mother, Margaret, was the eldest of seven children, five of whom (all girls) were still living at this point; the two boys had both died of tuberculosis in their mid-teens. Their father, Timothy Looney, had predeceased them, dying on 26 October 1892 aged fifty-seven. He died suddenly one day while attending Coachford Fair and, needless to say, his death was a devastating blow to his young family. Margaret was the eldest of the daughters and she was just ten years of age at the time; their mother was pregnant when their father died so suddenly – another daughter was born subsequent to his death. The two boys in the family, Thomas and Timothy, didn't outlive their father by very long.

The Lenihans (Ó Luineacháins) had a little smallholding of about two acres, but this was supplemented by a shop, which meant that they weren't too badly off by the standards of the day. The two acres they owned was poor land and so the family survived primarily on the profits of the shop, where they sold flour and meal, in addition to the other usual provisions. Timothy Lenihan, the father, was referenced as a 'shopkeeper' (solely) on his death certificate. Their house in Coolalta which had previously been a Protestant church, was a mile west of Carrigadrohid on the road to Macroom. Seán's grandmother, Elizabeth, had a reputation for being devout, discreet, frugal and careful in terms of money – and God knows, she needed to be – given the time at which she lived.

An elderly neighbour of theirs told me that the parish priest in Macroom helped Elizabeth out financially from time to time until the girls were all raised and things got a bit better for the family. The five daughters were all very well-respected, honest and devout in equal measure: Margaret, Elizabeth (Lily), Mary (Mollie), Gobnait and Kathleen. Their reputation as good, honest, decent people was such that the others in the area referred to their house as the 'nunnery' (in the noblest sense of the word); it was even said that the mother wouldn't sell cigarettes in her shop in case this attracted local blackguards or the 'wrong crowd'. One of the sons, Timothy, had been thinking of going on for the priesthood apparently. Two of the girls, Lily and Mary, went on to become teachers, even if Mary never actually qualified as a teacher but worked as a Junior Assistant Mistress instead. Initially, Mary taught in the National School in An Com, in the townland of Aghinagh nearby. She lived in the family home for many years before moving to Walterstown in Cobh. Lily was teaching school in Dún Dá Radharc when she met and married Séamas Ó Críodáin. She died on the birth of her first child. (Interestingly, Julia, the mother of famous Irish composer Seán Ó Riada, was this Séamus Ó Críodáin's sister, with the consequence that Seán Ó Riada, composer, and Seán Ó Ríordáin, poet, were related by marriage.) Gobnait got into the business of butter-making; neither she nor Mary ever married. The youngest of the family remained at home and wed a man named Jack Reynolds, who married into the family business. Margaret, the poet's mother, had married the cobbler in Ballyvourney a good few years prior to this and had moved there to live with him. She never had any Irish and she wouldn't ever learn much of it while in Ballyvourney either. The man she'd married, the poet's father, on the other hand, was a native Irish speaker who belonged to Ó Ríordáins known as 'Na Ríordáinaigh Bhreaca' ('The Speckled O'Riordans'). The poet's grandfather had come from the neighbourhood of Kilgarvan in County Kerry originally, a man of whom his poet grandson would say one day – 'bhí duanaire bó bainne aige/Sa bhfeirm i gCiarraí' (*'he had an anthology of dairy cattle/On the farm in Kerry'*).

Whatever bit of land he'd come from in Kerry, he certainly hadn't moved on to any great wealth in Ballyvourney, now that he was living in that small, rundown house on the side of the road beside the mill. This Seán Breac (Speckled Seán) had married a woman named Bríd Ní Fhionnagáin (Finnegan) from Derrynasaggart. They had six children altogether, two sons and four daughters, barely surviving on whatever income the father made from breeding his boar with local pigs. They said of him that he wouldn't allow his boar to service any pigs except those of the Kerry breed! If this had really been true, needless to say, the family would have been on the breadline continuously! The local wits even assigned their house a new address: Seán Breac, Boar no. 4, Piggery 8th Street, The Mills – a clear sign that he'd been accepted by the local community. This man, the poet's grandfather, had two sons as mentioned earlier – i.e. Seán and Conchubhar; Seán went into the cobbling trade while Conchubhar stuck with farming. He bought a farm of his own in the townland of Gortnatubrid following his marriage to a woman by the surname of Ó Mainnín (Manning) from Clondrohid. Their father, the poet's grandfather, died before he ever got to know Seán the poet. He succumbed shortly after getting a bad wetting while doing the Pattern on Saint Gobnait's Day 1916 at the well in Ballyvourney, his death certificate citing 'Croupous pneumonia 8 days, cardiac failure' as his cause of death. A woman who remembered him recalled him as a very fine-looking man, over six feet tall and who held himself as straight as a die, even when elderly. But then as another person said of him: 'No wonder he was like this – a man who never did a day's work in his life.'

The poet's father was wild and cantankerous by all accounts, especially when he had 'a drop on board' prior to his marriage. As a younger man, it wasn't unusual to hear stories of him mad-drunk and fighting out on the street, three or four policemen hanging off him. They'd remove the shoes from him for fear that he'd hit out at them when they arrested him or marched him down to the local barracks; it wasn't far from the pub to the barracks. A cousin of his, Donncha Ó Fionnagáin (Denis Finnegan) told me how the poet's father was released once on condition that he kept the peace. His people brought him up to Gortnatubrid and locked him into a room at the top of the house so that he could cool off for a while. A short while later, they heard that he'd been spotted arguing and fighting down at the mill again; he'd managed to get out through an upstairs window and escape, unknown to anyone. It goes without saying that the police made sure that he didn't escape too easily the second time!

This Seán, the shoemaker, had relatives living east of Dripsey and he'd often pay them a visit on a Sunday afternoon. He'd call into the shop in Coolalta on the way, to pick up a treat and so that he didn't arrive empty-handed to his relative's house. It was in the shop there that he set eyes on Máiréad Ní Luineacháin (Margaret Lenihan) for the first time apparently. As it turns out, another relative of Seán senior was a neighbour of the Lenihans. This man was Tadhg Ó Ríordáin (Tim Riordan), a cousin of his (Seán senior's) father, and he arranged the match between them. A daughter of Tadhg's by the name of Malaí (Molly), the widow of Timothy Cahill, would recount this story to Seán the poet many years later (and she also confirmed how the match was arranged to this writer). This is how Ó Ríordáin, the poet, envisaged it:

> *Our native land is holy ground if you think about it properly. When I was back in Carrigadrohid, I never really thought much about the fact that my father and mother walked this same patch of ground and made love on bright moonlit nights or when it was pitch-black, long before they gave me as a gift to the world. Not only this, but if you think of all the people who tramped the holy ground of Carrigadrohid over the past two thousand years, you get some sense of what the words 'fód do dhúchais' (your native sod) or 'talamh do shinsear' (the land of your ancestors) really mean.*[1]

This description is in many ways the nostalgia of a man fondly recalling the past that is no more, a man who is getting old and weak and nearing the end of his life. As regards the men who arranged the marriage match itself, all Ó Ríordáin ruefully had to say was this: 'If only they'd minded their own business!' But there was no going back now that the 'damage is done'; such was life![2] On another occasion, this was how Ó Ríordáin envisioned what this marital union produced with respect to his own temperament and mixed inheritance:

> *Depending on what mood I'm in, sometimes I feel that I'm an Ó Ríordáin and other times, I feel that I'm more of a Lenihan. When I'm tormented, restless idle or angry, I'm a Ríordáin, but when I'm industrious and puritanical, I tend towards the Lenihans.*[3]

The father gave up the drink when he got married, and he didn't touch

---

1 D: 3 October 1969.

2 LL: p. 29.

3 D: 5 July 1971.

another drop of alcohol for the rest of his life by all accounts. The newly married couple rented a house from the Williams family and the father had a small shack at the back of the house where he did his cobbling work; prior to this, his workspace was a room upstairs in the old courthouse next to the mill. While the ruins of this former courthouse have long since disappeared, I was shown the bare shell of them and it was clear that a very fine building once stood there. The rent for their new house was somewhere between £7 10s. 0d. and £7 16s. 0d. a year according to Tadhg, the poet's brother. It had a quarter-acre of land going with it where they sowed a few potatoes, and they also kept two or three goats in another corner of the field. Other than the goats and the few vegetables they grew, they survived on whatever profit their mother made from the little shop she ran indoors (the Carrigadrohid woman had brought her shopkeeping skills with her on marriage). One of the surviving account books from this era lists the staples of country living back then – i.e. the produce that she sold in the shop: bread, sugar, tea, tobacco, butter, jam, paraffin, candles, etc. The one noteworthy item that stands out on this list is the entry relating to: 'Leather soles and studs 3s. 1d.' These were for the father's work in the shack outside, of course. Although they also sold other items in addition to these. They had to buy the milk, not having their own cow – the goats were mainly used for meat – and they'd knock the 'milk money' off the shop bill of anyone who supplied them with the same. One of the main people who supplied them with milk, according to the account book, was one 'Mrs. Sweeney the Mills'.

The cobbler and his wife had three children altogether: Seán was first; then Tadhg, the second son, was born the following year. Their last-born was Bríd, their only daughter. By the standards of the day, Seán's mother would not have been considered young when she got married; she was twenty-three years of age; her husband may have been a year younger than her. The children were sent about a mile and a half west of their home, to Slievereagh, to Saint Michael's National School. Interestingly, the school at Ballymakeera was a half a mile closer to them, and easier to reach by road, but Tadhg Ó Duinnín was teaching in Saint Michael's and he was related to the Ó Ríordáins, even if this relationship was fairly far-out; consequently, the future poet and his siblings were sent there.

(As it happens, Ballymakeera School was given the Ó Ríordáin children 'on loan' every now and then, whenever they needed to boost their numbers.) An additional reason, probably, that Seán's siblings were sent to the school back west was that Ó Duinnín was an excellent teacher, in addition to being a very friendly and decent individual – except when he was drinking or out 'on the lash'! This was a two-teacher school at the time and Iníon Uí Chríodáin (Miss Creedon) taught there with Ó Duinnín. Ó Ríordáin refers to Ó Duinnín in some of the biographical information he provided for the volume *Nuabhéarsaíocht* where he says that he learned 'Caoineadh Art Uí Laoghaire' ('*The Lament for Art O'Leary*'), the Catechism and 'Twinkle, Twinkle, Little Star' in his school in Slievereagh. Ó Ríordáin himself confirmed that he'd learned the famous Gaelic lament in this school as a young child all of thirty years later when he personally welcomed Seán Ó Tuama's version of the iconic poem in the metre of the original:

A Eibhlín Dubh Ní Chonaill,
Do léas do chaoineadh ar maidin;
Nuair a léas an dán san cheana
Do bhíos ar scoil im leanbh.
Cé shéid an óige tharam,
Níor chríon do cheol im anam.[4]

Oh Eibhlín Dubh Ní Chonaill;
I read your lament this morning
When I read that poem before
I was still a schoolchild
Although my youth has flown by me,
Your music did not wither in my soul.[5]

Ó Duinnín clearly taught the children a good range of subjects and gave them a rounded education, poetry included, as Ó Ríordáin noted in his diary entry for 6 February 1959, for example:

---

4 *Tar Éis Mo Bhais* (hereafter TÉB): p. 43.
5 Trans. M. Ó hAodha.

Ar maidin, a mhacaoimh óig,
iarr teagasg ar an dTríonóid …

(In the morning, young lad
Seek the instruction of the Trinity …)

It's a long time ago now that I learned this poem back on Sliabh Riabhach in Ballyvourney. It was the first poem in the old metre that I ever learned. Tadhg Ó Duinnín, one of the Dámhscoil (Gaelic Poetic School) poets, taught it to us.[6]

Even years later, Ó Ríordáin would call to mind various things that his old teacher had taught them, particularly phrases and sayings specific to the Irish-language dialect of that area: 'Sometimes my mind jumps back twenty years and I hear my schoolmaster Tadhg Ó Duinnín's (RIP) words again: "Druidíg anonn is anall go dtí imealla na mbinsí" (*"Shuffle over and back there towards the edge of the benches"*).[7] Or if one of the pupils asked Ó Duinnín could they leave the class for a moment, they'd be liable to hear the following rustic phrase in reply from him. 'Ar mharaíobhair seana-mhart le déanaí?' (*'Did you (lot) slaughter any old bullock recently?'*)[8]

He taught them mathematics through Irish and Seán still remembered some of these maths terms years later when he'd forgotten the intricacies of the mathematics itself; in fact, he'd use them in a completely different context a few decades on when he attacked those involved in the political agreement known as the Sunningdale Agreement as part of an article he wrote for the newspaper.[9] 'Who are they?' (i.e. the people involved in Sunningdale) he asks, and then goes on to say:

---

6 O'Rahilly, T. F. (ed.), *Measgra Dánta I: Miscellaneous Irish Poems* (Cork University Press, Cork, 1927), p. 17.

7 D: 10 April 1949; the same again on 9 January 1962 and 19 February 1972.

8 D: 6 February 1959; 9 January 1962.

9 The Sunningdale Agreement was an attempt in 1973 to establish a power-sharing Northern Ireland Executive, as well as a cross-border Council of Ireland.

> *I think that they are probably 'the highest common multiple' or 'the lowest common denominator', both of which are mathematical terms that I learned long ago, in Scoil an tSléibhe Riabhaigh (Slievereagh School) from one of the poets of the Dámhscoil there, Tadhg Ó Duinnín. I'm not sure what either of these terms means exactly but I reckon that they have some connection to Sunningdale.*[10]

Not everything that Ó Duinnín did was the best example ever to his pupils, however. Every now and then he'd break out and go on a bender. Initially his students would watch him make his way across the mountain from his home in the morning. They'd observe his demeanour carefully as he arrived into the classroom to see what kind of a mood he was in. He might light a cigarette or amble over to the window, his glance drifting out over the landscape towards Derrynasaggart. If he quenched his cigarette as quickly again, they knew that they were 'away on a hack' and they had the signal they were hoping for. He'd leave the room again and head for the mill and it would be a few days before they saw him at school again. Whenever he was absent, his classes were taken by Iníon Uí Chríodáin (Miss Creedon) and the pupils had it a lot easier. The schoolmaster would call into the Ó Ríordáins' house when he was on a drinking spree the odd time and, as a child, Seán remembered him once roaring and shouting around the house and looking for a few slices of bacon to eat from their mother, even though it was a Friday (Catholics usually abstained from meat on a Friday at the time); the children ran away in under the stairs in fear of him. Here are some of Seán's memories of him:

> *Many's the alcoholic drink that the same Tadhg knocked back over the years, God bless him. He died in 1935. [Christmas Day of 1934 is the correct date.] He fell off the back of a farmer's cart one day and he didn't live for very long afterwards. He was still a relatively young man at the time – between forty and fifty years, I suppose. Think of that puffed-up body of his, swollen by drink, being lowered into the grave. He was probably someone whom we'd too much respect for. He was a bad example to us, and yet he was one of a kind in other ways. We were afraid of him when we were going to school, needless to say.*[11]

10 D: 10 December 1973; 'Punningdale', IT, 15 December 1973.

11 D: 6 February 1959.

Tadhg Ó Duinnín, poet, schoolmaster, drunk, and whatever else. Related to my father. Ard-Ghaeilgeoir (Excellent Irish-speaker), as they say. His life went off-track. I wonder if he had any (literary) talent? He was a bad example to us. Whenever we saw Tadhg, we thought it was great to be drunk. He was a fine-looking man, tall and handsome. He won't be remembered as a poet. He left nothing of any substance behind. There is one poem [of his] in this volume – a literary type of poem … I don't think that I can remember his voice any more.[12]

He taught singing to any of us who were able to learn it. I wasn't in that class. I was a crow. But, I've all the songs and all the tunes and I hum them to myself sometimes when I'm in the toilet. The songs would have made a nice album. Where are Gaoth Linn?[13]

He mightn't have taken any of his poetic artistry from the schoolmaster but Ó Ríordáin often wondered whether he might have inherited his own fondness for the 'drop' from him; that said, the way that Ó Ríordáin's health declined so severely over the course of his life meant that he lost his fondness for alcohol to a large degree.

In addition to the classes during the day from Ó Duinnín, Ó Ríordáin occasionally went to a winter night class run by Dónall Ó Ceocháin (Keohane), (the editor of the book referenced above: *Saothar Dámh-Sgoile Mhúscraighe*). This is how Seán remembered him in his diary on the day that he heard he'd died back in Coolea:

I knew him well. I was in the school when he taught Irish classes at night in Slievereagh … He wasn't a native speaker of Irish, but he spent so much time in Coolea that he was close enough to it. He was a unique person …[14]

The only other formal education that Ó Ríordáin received while living in

12 Ó Ceocháin, Donall (ed.), *Saothar-Dámh Sgoile Mhúscraighe ar n-a sholáthar a croinicibh na dámh-sgoile* (Oifig Díolas Foillseacháin Rialtais, Dublin, 1933), pp. 56–7.

13 D: 9 January 1962. *Gaoth Linn* is a pun on *Gael-Linn*, an Irish-language and cultural organisation.

14 D: 11 November 1956.

Ballyvourney was the music classes run by the local nuns that he was sent to for a while. 'I was given this sentence to learn so as to remember the scales: "few can gain distinction and escape blame".'[15]

Ó Ríordáin obviously didn't set the world on fire on the musical front, however, as he didn't continue with the music afterwards. He later recalled this period of his life in a jokey way in a letter that he sent to Con Prior from the sanatorium on 12 August 1949: 'The Sisters of Mercy in Macroom had a f….ed-up piano on which I practised scales about twelve years after being procreated. Each key produced its particular note after being assaulted, and expired in a slow, nasal, choking yawn.' This was one of those vacuous or dark jokes that the poet made by 1949 – but then, he hadn't had a lot to laugh about when he was twelve years of age. His father was already dead by then, even if Ó Ríordáin himself had yet to become seriously ill at this point. Already, even before the young poet had reached his teenage years, the brightness and joy of youth was gradually being extinguished.

His father died in their house on 3 March 1926, aged just forty-four. He'd been ill for a year with TB, according to his death certificate, and Seán had seen him waste away over the course of the year until he was just skin and bone. A strong, handsome man, he'd aged almost overnight due to the ravages of the disease until he was a living corpse, a ghostly figure that stalked the house at night in the poet's nightmares years later:

Chonac seanduine uafásach thuas
Laistigh d'fhuinneoig i mbarr an tí,
Bhí féasóg fheargach ar a ghnúis
Is gráin ghráinneogach ina ghéarghuairí.

An ghráin a bheir easlán don slán,
An fuath a bheir an sean don óg,
Do chonac i súilibh an chorpáin
Do shiúil sa tigh mar shiúlfadh beo.[16]

15 D: 15 November 1957.
16 TÉB: p. 35.

I saw a terrible old man above
Behind a window at the top of the house,
On his face he wore an angry beard
And bristly hatred in his sharp whiskers

The aversion of the sick to the healthy
The enmity of the old towards the young,
I saw these in the eyes of the corpse
Who walked in the house as would a living person.[17]

Needless to say, these verses had an additional resonance by the time Ó Ríordáin came to write them; the glance from 'behind a window' would have a very different significance for him by then; to look outside his window was to gaze upon the world of the healthy and the strong and perhaps to view it with a jaundiced and almost hateful eye. But he could not have yet fully apprehended the disaster that lay in store the morning he woke to hear his mother tell him that his father had died during the night. And for a good many years afterwards, Ó Ríordáin gravitated between waking and dreaming with regard to this tragic and nightmarish event; every now and then, revealed by snippets from the diary, we're given brief insights into how this event affected him as a young boy: 'I was still a child when my father died and sometimes I managed to convince myself in bed at night afterwards that he was still alive. And there were times when I was awake in later years and I wasn't entirely certain that he might not still be alive.'[18]

His father's death was never discussed in front of the children, and especially not its cause. At this juncture, TB was a death sentence, but a death sentence that involved a simultaneous half-living, half-death. And it was a subject rarely openly broached for fear of who might be unfortunate enough to contract the disease next. And, unsurprisingly, Ó Ríordáin, as child and young man, would express confusion and doubt as to the exact nature of this disease that was all around them and yet which was so rarely referred to by anyone. What exactly was this awful thing

17 Trans. M. Ó hAodha.
18 D: 31 January 1951.

called TB and to which side of the void did it really belong? Unfortunately, the poet would later find out all about TB and the suffering that went with it in the most intimate and heart-rending way possible. It was mainly in the privacy of his diaries that he spoke of the dreaded disease and its effect on his young life: 'The heart was torn crossways inside me when the coffin arrived to take my father away to the grave.'[19] Sometimes, when he'd just about managed to negotiate another restless night, racked by illness, this terrible memory would come to mind again all of a sudden – the memory of that other horrible night over twenty-five years earlier – the night that someone so dear to him hadn't survived: 'I still remember the night that snatched my father away.'[20] And he'd relive this memory once more as he himself edged closer to the precipice of night – the suddenness with which death strikes, even when one's been expecting it for a long time, the frozen rigidity of the corpse in the bed, the old woman weeping for her son:

> *Earlier tonight I was thinking back to the night my father died. I only remember the year – 1926. We were told in the morning. He was stretched out on the bed, in his habit. He was like a bullet from a gun it was that sudden, and the way he lay there rod-straight in the bed. My mother explained to us what had happened. Our father had gone to heaven … My grandmother was there lamenting over the body and my aunt Han was there.*[21]

He'd remember too, needless to say, the coffin being lowered out through the west window of the house, the multitude following on, as his father's coffin was carried on people's shoulders along the narrow road and up the incline to Saint Gobnait's Cemetery. The rituals of death and of the tribe, that had more to do with the O'Riordans, the Finnegans and the other generations for whom Ballyvourney was their ancestral homeplace, than with the widow who had come from the more 'civilised' east. Then back into the Mills on their way back from the burial, the same place the dead

19 D: 19 February 1940.

20 D: 4 June 1961.

21 D: 10 May 1973.

man had frequented when he was young and in his prime, where there would be talk of drinking and throwing shapes at the police.

The widow returning afterwards to the house by the roadside that wasn't hers and the three young children that still needing raising, the eldest of them just nine years of age and her own relatives a fair distance away. (Not that her neighbours the Finnegans weren't good to her or always treated her well; but at the end of the day, they weren't her blood.) The small shop, the goats, the tiny patch of land: it was a subsistence lifestyle if ever there was one.

As the eldest son, all Seán was left with was his few small memories of his father, memories and images that he'd revert to from time to time in later years. Sometimes, even decades later, Ó Ríordáin would draw on such memories when he needed the past – home, childhood, a sense of permanence – as a form of support: 'I remember one afternoon when I went to Carraig an Adhmaid [Ballymakeera] with my father. He was looking to buy a yellow tie. I think we were probably talking to Johnny Manning's wife that afternoon …'[22] '"Donncha na gCipíní" ("*Matchstick Denis*") was what my father used to call me because I was always chewing matches.'[23] Occasionally, Seán would call to mind that he was a shoemaker's son himself and that this was 'the reason why I've such an affinity with *Séadna*.'[24] And he'd collect useful idioms and phrases from Fr Peadar's famous book, like someone 'recording the tapping of the cobbler's hammer or the pulling and tightening of the wax thread.' This with respect to his writing of prose; the relationship was closer again as regards poetry. Speaking of himself in the third person, Seán would say that he was a word-cobbler who'd 'made a lot of shoes. Used he not find himself stitched or written in his shoes? There was no question but that the shoes fairly reflected him …'[25] Poetry was his trade just as his father's was cobbling; and when he needed an image to approximate

22 D: 14 February 1955.

23 D: 8 October 1961.

24 D: 16 February 1956. *Séadna* is an old Irish folktale written by Fr Peadar Ó Laoghaire, which was published in 1904 and revolves around a cobbler named Séadna.

25 D: 18 June 1962.

the 'assuredness and dignity of the clergy' it was his father's trade that he drew upon in order to represent it.[26] The tip-tapping of the cobbler's hammer was audible once more in the metre of each sentence; the poetic class working again at this, the ancient craft of their ancestors; the son fulfilling his father's trade.

The young Ó Ríordáin would question elderly people he came across from time to time in a vain attempt to better acquaint himself with his father again. As one man told him – 'he [his father] was as straight as a schoolmaster' and the younger Ó Ríordáin no doubt enjoyed phrases of a similarly poetic tenor.[27] But then there was the other man in Macroom whom he left thinking that the dead were best left in peace rather than sullying one's own recollection with the mindless chatter of an old drunk.[28]

It was not only his father with whom Seán looked to 'reacquaint' himself when he was older, and he could appreciate fully the environment and cultural context in which he'd lived. His father's life was redolent of an older way of life that was disappearing quickly in Ireland and in other parts of Europe at this juncture, and Ó Ríordáin wanted to learn as much as he could about it, even if it was already too late in many ways. It was as if he wanted to immerse himself in that childhood life again, the old life, even if it was only in the imagination. In fact, Ó Ríordáin would spend the rest of his life interrogating the past, posing questions that had no real answers to them, a past that could never explain itself but from which the poet could never truly separate himself.

The house the Ó Ríordáins lived in was the second in the row; in number 1, on the western gable-end, lived the woman known locally as Nell Mhattie – Nell Ní Bhuachalla (Nell Buckley), who was married to Mattie Ó Tuama (Mattie Twomey). Because they were rented houses and people were moving in and out of them over many years, it is difficult to say exactly when she came to live there, but it was probably around 1929. As with his father, Nell was a figure whom Seán would return to aesthetically speaking and when citing his own qualifications in the

26 ES: p. 35.
27 D: 1 July 1967.
28 D: 27 October 1966.

native (Gaelic) language and tradition. We know very little now about the traditional stories and examples of Gaelic culture that the thirteen- or fourteen-year-old Seán wrote down from the oral tradition of Nell Ní Bhuachalla, one of the last surviving custodians of the oral storytelling tradition in the area. No doubt, the young Ó Ríordáin himself didn't fully understand the value of the tradition that Nell Mhattie had inherited and shared with him, or how they'd provide cultural sustenance for him years later on the artistic road ahead.

Over in house number 3 was Seán's aunt, Han. (Interestingly, just a few years before Seán and his family left Ballyvourney forever, Han married Tomás Ó Drisceoil, a stonemason from Clondrohid; this couple's son, Dónall Ó Drisceoil, is someone who'll play a part in this narrative later on, even if it will be far away from Ballyvourney.) Seán's grandmother, Bríd, stayed in Han's house frequently. She lived there most of the time after her husband died in 1916; both women would prove crucial to Seán in terms of his cultural and intellectual development. When asked about it in later years, Ó Ríordáin said that he'd been 'listening to the best of Irish from the day I was born … My aunt and my grandmother were right next door to me and they spoke Irish among themselves.'[29] A regular caller to the family also was Conchubhar Ó Ríordáin, from Gortnatubrid, who'd come down socialising with them as he'd relatives in both houses; the children were always up and down to him in turn, and helping out with bits and pieces of work on his farm. It was Conchubhar who used phrases such as 'ar buile nó ag bogadh chuige' ('*mad or not far off it*') to describe someone who was 'angry or about to boil over'.

Seán stored away such idioms and speech in his memory bank to be utilised later when the moment was appropriate.[30] Even when his uncle was fading away and dying, Seán was still learning Irish from him, as indicated in this description of a hospital visit he paid him: 'He felt very weak, he said, before he went into hospital. He'd felt weak too when he was piking hay and "making haycocks in summer" ("ag déanamh na

29 'Banfhilíocht agus Gaeilge' ('*Women's Poetry and Irish*'), IT, 27 November 1975.

30 For example, 'Daoine Buile' ('*Crazy People*'), IT, 19 December 1970.

gcreabhar sa tsamhradh"). That's a term you wouldn't hear too often these days: the word "creabhar" ["*haycock*"] used in that context.'[31]

Irrespective of who'd told Seán an old folktale or legend, or who'd taught him a new Irish-language term or phrase – regardless of whether the person in question was Nell Mhattie, Mícheál Ó Gaoithín, Conchubhar Ó Ríordáin or Pound – Ó Ríordáin never let a word or phrase astray. His only concern when he got older was who'd first used the phrase and whether he could find an opportunity to incorporate it into his writing.

The future poet was now collecting from all sides, unknown to him almost. It would be years yet before he really understood the value of what he'd gathered, that is if he ever properly understood it. While the language of the older culture was essential to Ó Ríordáin, it was the place itself and the emotional associations he had with the area that were most important to him, and this remained the case, even after everyone he knew belonging to the homeplace had passed on. That childhood life and the eternal quest for the associations and feelings that went with it might have faded into memory as the decades passed, but the poet's idealistic desire for the homeplace never waned. A few random examples of the cultural and nostalgic sustenance he sought there are:

> *Father Peadar refers to Carraig na Madraí ('The Rock of the Dogs'). No one understands the incredible magic that's in that place name for me – Carraig na Madraí. When we were children in Ballyvourney, we'd have* Mo Scéal Féin *read to us at home, and ever since then there's a magic attached to every place mentioned in that book for me.*[32]

> *There was an old woman named Beití Horgan near us on the road to Coolea, when we were children. She was well-known for the richness of her Irish and her lore. God knows why she came into my mind just now? She's probably dead and gone years ago by now. Who isn't?*[33]

31 D: 10 September 1956.

32 D: 17 October 1956.

33 D: 1.40 a.m., 23 November 1964.

Why did an image of the road and of the houses near Carraig an Adhmaid come into my head just now, an image of them as they were when I was a pupil in the school there?[34]

Reading James Joyce by Ellman tonight. One ought to be 'odd' and full of heart. Joyce was that way. (Why is it that a reek of turf that we had at home in Ballyvourney came to mind just now? I saw all the turf in my mind.) There's no doubt that Joyce was slightly mad ...[35]

He'd call to mind many others also from his childhood, the likes of Liam Ó Conaill, nicknamed Squint, a man who owned a gander with a reputation for randiness, a bird that had a song in English composed about it at one stage: 'When I was a boy in Ballyvourney this lad named Squint (Liam Ó Conaill) was the "Kruger" of that place. He was the main character in the area ...'[36] In fact, it was this man's son, Seán Ó Conaill, who gave the song 'Amhrán na Stagún' to Ó Ríordáin at one stage, or what he still had of it anyway.[37] This is a satirical song composed by Gael na nGael's father about Peigín Sheáin Aodha, the wife of Tadhg Breac Ó Ríordáin, who was actually Seán's great-grandfather.

Lá agus mé ag taisteal liom féinig
I mbarr Chúil Aodha agus mé ag rith,
Cá gcasfaí fé dheireadh lem cheird mé
Ach isteach go tigh Reardon Bhric ...

One day and I travelling alone
At the top of Coolea while running
Where'd I go when my trade was done
But into the Speckled Riordan's house ...[38]

---

34 D: 3 a.m., 10 January 1966.
35 D: 3 a.m., 23 November 1967.
36 D: 13 January 1976.
37 D: 9 January 1968.
38 Trans. M. Ó hAodha.

There were others in the house that day too who were also a bit wild by all accounts, and it wasn't long before a row broke out. The fight escalated and the house was in a right state by the end of it, the kitchen utensils upside-down and, however it happened, the cat gone completely crazy and even the woman of the house suffered a few scrapes, it would appear, because of the fracas:

Éistíg is neosad mo scéal díbh,
Agus geallaim nach aon scéal suilt,
Go bhfuil daoine ar an mbaile seo taobh linn
Atá le seachtain ó inné gan mhin.

Mo thrua-sa baitheas na béithe
Do ghearradh le faobhar an chait.

Níorbh é sin do mhairbh mé in ao' chor,
Ná a chiapaigh mo chroí-se istigh,
Ach an braon a bhí sniogtha chun té againn
Gur dhoirteadar é fén dtigh.

Listen and I will tell you my story
and it is not a happy tale
that there are people in this district near us
who have been a week since yesterday without meal

I pity the head of the maiden
which was scrawled by the (cat)-claw

It wasn't that which killed me at all
nor tormented my heart within
but the drop which had been milked dry for tea by us
being spilt around the house.[39]

39 Trans. M. Ó hAodha.

The reputed poetic prowess of this older generation was a form of pride rather than a source of embarrassment. It was with the simple songs and ditties of this older, earthier culture that Ó Ríordáin associated poetry as a child, and even years later he would have his doubts as to whether such rawer or more traditional compositions were actually healthier and more valuable than his own modernist poetry. And as Ó Ríordáin would note, there were no university professors present the night that this particular traditional poem was composed 'to find fault with its metre' – this with sarcastic reference to the criticism his own poetry had been subjected to in the interval. He sent the piece entitled 'An t-iolubh agus uibhe nach é' ('*the mother egg and associated eggs*') to *The Irish Times* for publication but immediately withdrew it again in a letter dated 13 August 1968. The battle and the defence was a constant one. Tradition, language and metre were what Ó Ríordáin sought in his own work later and if one had to return a few generations to find the roots of each, then so be it. The older saying or term would remain a slender thread in Ó Ríordáin's poetry as of yet, even if it became a more important one over time.

In the meantime, he would serve his apprenticeship. If he hadn't composed many poems as of yet, Ó Ríordáin was developing the sensibility necessary for the road ahead. And disease and illness would play a very significant role in his artistic development from this juncture onwards also. Seán was struck down with pneumonia that left him absent from school for the guts of a year, an important aspect of which was the move towards the solitary life – as mentioned by Ó Ríordáin himself in a literary journal subsequently: 'But I got pneumonia when I was thirteen years old in Ballyvourney – three times in succession … that was when the loner in me began maybe.' While the other two children were gone to school each morning, Seán had to stay behind with just his mother for company. She now came to act as intermediary with the world beyond as he began to cultivate his private thoughts and language. She would gain her own place in his poetry as she was the one who most nearly approached the loneliness from which it emerged. He would have good reason to recall these long periods of illness and the artistic world they instigated long after they were gone; the image of the hunched and sickly child and the mother tending to him was forever engrained in his imagination:

> *I thought back to our own mother, when we were children – and those long days of rain and the door closed and the house dark, and the racket, and the way that she'd have all of us playing on the floor there. Many's the long day that she spent minding us when we were in the cot and then disciplining us later as we got older. I can see all the passion of those years still …*[40]

The years slipped by and Ó Ríordáin's mother became restless in this new area she'd made her home. If she were honest about it, she'd never felt fully at home in Ballyvourney; she'd never grown to love the place. One story best illustrates Mrs Ó Ríordáin's uneasiness with the area she'd moved to after her marriage better than most. And all I can do now is repeat it verbatim, exactly as I heard it. Initially I had difficulty believing this story, given its bizarre nature, but I can vouch in the strongest terms for the credentials of the person who related it to me. Apparently, she was abducted from the house at one stage during the Troubles of 1920–21; she was taken away and brought back into the hills where she remained captive for several weeks until her captors chose to release her again. The IRA abducted her, apparently – perhaps because she was a stranger or a 'blow-in' to the area; and because the police barracks was nearby, it was felt that she couldn't be trusted. Her husband had nearly gone out of his mind with worry and had spent days going from one place to the next, looking for her; he didn't know whether she was alive or dead. The children were sent up to the uncle's place in Gortnatubrid when this happened. Needless to say, this frightening incident had coloured the outsider's view of Ballyvourney forever and it came as no surprise that she was keen to move back east and closer to 'civilisation' after what had happened. She hadn't had life easy anyway, but it became tougher still following the death of her husband. Given their straitened financial circumstances, she'd been forced to keep the driver and conductor for the Ballyvourney bus as overnight lodgers. A guinea a week was what she charged these two people for lodgings – not that there were major profits to be made there.

And yet, despite these hardships, the children – including the lad who suffered poor health, would later recall this period of their young lives

40 D: 9 February 1955.

as tinged with a somewhat romantic hue: the smell of roast bacon being prepared for the lodgers in the morning, the children competing with one another for cigarette stubs – for smoking or swapping – the lads riding the donkey around Peter's Field, the field where Coláiste Íosagáin was later sited, the walks over to the crossroads at Coolea for fresh water from the well, swimming and fishing with the changing of the seasons, the visits to the farms of various relatives, the spectacular summit of Mullach an Ois as their backdrop – it was at once a physical horizon and a horizon of the mind. The weekend jaunts into Macroom along with their mother when they called into Kelleher's house – that was a 'kind of paradise' to the children with the fine meal they'd have there before the long road home again through the winding hills.[41]

That road east was the same one that Seán Ó Ríordáin would follow now. The last entry in the shop's ledger was for the 12 June 1931 and then the place was closed down. It would be another seven years before the account books were opened again, back east in Inniscarra – a new account book and a new beginning. The other life had been left behind forever. And what was it they had left? For one lad, the young poet Seán, it was a life tinged with happiness and the memories that would sustain him when the storm-clouds drew in; it was the area that had formed him, the place of long summer days and relaxation, the innocent paradise of the imagination never buffeted by sin or worry, the blessed place of childhood memory. Memories such as these, that would come to him years later and in the darkest of nights:

> *I remember a river in Clondrohid – about a mile from my aunt Han's house … There was a tree growing on the opposite bank of the river. A beautiful summer's day. I was on holidays …*[42]

> *Very bad shortness of breath today and yesterday. Maybe death isn't too far away from me. It doesn't bother me. I remember a fine sunny day in Carrigadrohid long ago. We were living in Ballyvourney at the time. So I was younger than*

41 D: 14 June 1966.

42 D: 1.20 a.m., 30 June 1969.

> *fifteen at the time. I think that my aunt Kathleen (who's no longer alive) was there. I can't remember who else but there were a crowd of us there. I got a spin in a big car that had no roof. Life was very joyful then. It's just a memory. Everyone is dead.*[43]

The poet was about to enter a new phase of his life, one that was rootless and uncertain. From this moment onwards, he would no longer belong to any person or place; and for the rest of his days his imagination would drift between past and present, between what he had once been and what he was supposed to become.

43 D: 11.45 p.m., 21 March 1974.

2

From Ballyvourney to Inniscarra

The summer of 1932 saw the Ó Ríordáin family make the move from Ballyvourney to Inniscarra. It was Seán's aunts who made the big decision in the end, even if it was obvious what Seán's mother felt about it. They left behind a limbo-like area culturally-speaking, a place that wasn't fully Irish-speaking but which hadn't succumbed completely to the march of the English language either. They also left behind their memories – mixed as they were – happy times, hard work, the life and murmur of the shop and the dark spectre of TB that had imposed itself over time.

Inniscarra was on the western periphery of Cork city and more convenient for the children's secondary education, especially for Seán, who looked the most promising academically and whose fragile health decreed that he was unfit for manual labour. There was a tradition of education in the family; his mother's side had all trained to be teachers and who was to say that Seán might not go down that route too? And her sisters, the relatives to whom she was closest, were now her principal advisers in the crucial decision to uproot themselves and to move to the suburbs of the city. Whereas the 'Speckled Ó Ríordáins' were rural, mountain people who'd been reared on the border between two counties and two languages, his mother's people – the Lenihans – were shopkeepers and teachers alike. The younger generation would no longer be reliant on subsistence farming and cobbling to make their living. No one could have predicted then that someone who had experienced both worlds would eventually turn his back on the comfortable life of office work and the standing that went with it to return to the culture he had left behind. It was a journey from the hill to the plain, from wildness to refinement.

Seán wasn't to know then that one day he'd find himself retracing this same path in search of that elusive, eternal summer once more. And even if the poet eventually came to some form of accommodation with his past, it was always an uneasy one; uncertainty and doubt was always its principal characteristic. It was only when it became a necessity and when his writing demanded it that Seán retraced the steps of the pivotal journey his family made that day of their departure. In his imagination, the day of their leaving was always intimately bound up with the faded memories of his father, his lost childhood and his cultural inheritance from the Gaelic tradition. The day they left was more than just a journey from the country to the city in Ó Ríordáin's mind, however. It is more than one day of their lives; it is a day that will be reconstructed and reimagined in the years to come, a day the significance of which grows a great deal over time. The day of their departure proved more important in terms of what it meant to the family and how it would be recalled in years to come, than for anything else.

The family had been preparing for the move for some time. Gobnait, the mother's sister, had returned from Limerick where she'd spent a few years managing the butter production of a creamery there. She had made the initial move and Bríd, Seán's sister, was the first of the children to join her. A few weeks later, the rest followed them – Seán's mother and the two lads. They hired a lorry to transport whatever few possessions and furniture they had, including an old lean-to or shed that they reconstructed in the garden of their new home.

Conor Lucey drove the lorry as they moved off to this strange new place near Cork city where everyone spoke English. The road took them down by the Sulane River to their right-hand side until they reached Macroom, after which they turned left at the far side of the town and took the main road east for the rest of the way. The River Lee was on the right-hand side now for the rest of the journey. Ó Ríordáin would travel this same main road in his memory a thousand times in the years ahead. Sometimes, this road and this journey appear as the source of every difficulty to him; at other times, they serve as the bridge between one way of life or one way of 'seeing' and another. Maybe it could somehow merge the past with the present in the poet's imagination. And every rock and turn along the way had its own meaning and designation for Ó Ríordáin, particularly in his mother's homeplace of Coolalta. This was a place in which he had ever felt happy and fully at peace with himself, and to which he would return for holidays as he grew older. By a strange turn of fate, Seán's grandmother (his mother's mother) had passed away on 10 March 1932, just a few months before the family left for the city, and another link with his childhood was broken and gone. And yet, even if the importance of Ballyvourney to Ó Ríordáin grew rather than faded over time, he must have felt some of the same sense of loneliness that summer's day of their move in 1932 as he describes thirty years later in his diary:

> *I brought my aunt home to Carrigadrohid since … It was a beautiful, sunny evening … The sky this evening would have left anyone spellbound – with the sun going down, magnificent and menacing, all at the same time. The evening was full of dazzling colours and there was a feeling of the sea over the Lee. A stab of pain went through my heart, however, because this road has an extra magic associated with it as relating to my childhood, the road from Inniscarra to Carrigadrohid. This is my mother's country. The area around Ballyvourney is my father's country and my own country. But this here is my mother's homeplace and the place for holidays when I was a child. This area and the road there was like the Tír na nÓg of distant summers for us when we were young. One's childhood thoughts and memories have a power in them that can never be overcome and a loneliness beyond loneliness that can never be expressed. This is an English-language road. The Ballyvourney road was Irish-speaking when we were young. The English-language road was the posher road. This road between Inniscarra and Carrigadrohid relates to William O'Brien and the songs of Tom Moore and the Mardyke and 'The Banks of My Own Lovely Lee'. The other road west from Macroom to Ballyvourney relates to Father Peadar and* Séadna *and Daingean na Saileach, and May Day and the superstitious people, and Reilig Ghobnatan and Dámhscoil Mhúscraí, and Eibhlín Dubh Ní Chonaill and my own father. These roads pierce my heart and I feel them clashing in my mind. I know that sometimes I managed to merge both roads in my imagination so that they became as one – on that road from Slea Head and west from there again, to Dunquin.*[1]

1 D: 5 June 1962.

This latter road that he followed from the early 1950s onwards to Dunquin in County Kerry was in search of the cultural roots he had lost contact with in Ballyvourney as a child. And yet Ballyvourney was more than the road that went back into the past at this juncture. Ballyvourney was also an area of cultural intersection and struggle, a place where the English language was relentlessly imposing itself over time. And it must surely have occurred to Ó Ríordáin sometimes that it wasn't just a sense of completion or finding himself that drew him back there regularly, even after the family had moved to the city, but also perhaps there was a tinge of guilt too – at their betrayal or abandonment of the Irish language in this place, just when it was about to succumb anyway.

Even worse to Ó Ríordáin's mind would have been any suspicion of pretence that his entire project was a sham, a vain attempt or a cover, and that, therefore, he wasn't really qualified to call himself a poet of the Gaelic tradition. Such self-doubts would haunt Ó Ríordáin throughout his entire writing life. Imperfect Irish had been exchanged for imperfect English and he could count fully on neither. He'd draw on broken or half-formed traditions on both sides whether he liked it or not and on a people with an uneasy and complex relationship to language, whether English or Irish. (Interestingly, the English language in his new home was in a much poorer state with respect to the literary side of things at this point). For him, it could only be one of two extremes and the first was remote and unattainable: the English of the British upper-classes, as opposed to the Irish as spoken in the Gaeltacht.

And this was only one of the initial problems for a radically modern writer such as Ó Ríordáin. He'd have to put his own stamp on the tradition now, something far more unique and groundbreaking than any other writer. He'd have to mould the tradition to satisfy his artistic needs and ensure it expressed what he sought to say. The poet would have to carve out his own place within the racial memory and tradition of his people and then express himself through that tradition – and yet do this in a voice that was individual and his own. But it would have to be east or west from now on, or at least that would be his public stance. The east signified the city and the urbane, an education, a job and a respected role within the community, and this was both his focus and his destination – for the moment.

In Inniscarra, a new house and a nice tidy piece of land – six and a half acres – awaited the family. It was actually more than they needed, really; £650 pounds is what they had paid for the lot, a considerable sum that would have been far beyond the widowed mother's reach. Two of his mother's sisters, Mary and Gobnait, had purchased the land together as 'tenants in common'. As it happens, Mary never actually lived there much, even after it was theirs. She was teaching in Aghinagh at the time and living in the family home in Coolalta, so that she only visited Inniscarra occasionally; she often helped out her sister with the rearing of the children and helped out financially from time to time. These occasional 'hand-outs' never went down well with Seán the poet – especially when he got a bit older and his health failed; by then, he privately considered such occasional financial help an added insult to their penurious position and akin to an admission that they were mired in poverty forever. This was one thing that, somewhat perversely, he never really forgave his aunts for: the way that the family felt beholden to them, particularly when better health permitting, he would have been the one earning the money and supporting his mother and himself. Not that such concerns were particularly significant at this early stage, just following the family's move to the city. They must have been filled with new hope at this point; this was a new start and Seán was in reasonable health – they weren't doing too badly at all for themselves, it seemed.

Their house faced southwards and overlooked the road from a height and it had a magnificent view of the river stretching out before it in the distance. The field behind them had ten apple trees growing there and unsurprisingly, given the fine, expansive location of the place, wild strawberries were plentiful too. There were outhouses out back for cows and pigs, not that they had any. They reassembled the Ballyvourney shed at the side of the house to the west and Tadhg etched the year into the wet cement as they were setting it in place – 1932. Before long, Seán would find himself sitting out in this same shed each day, honing and perfecting his literary skills and attempting to write. The new family home was nothing special but it did the job for the mother and the three children. It was a one-storey house with two bedrooms, a living room, a kitchen and a back-kitchen or utility. In time, Gobnait added a small room to the side of the house facing eastwards where she started up a small shop, the same as her parents had had once in Coolalta and Seán's mother had kept back in Ballyvourney. Gobnait herself ran the shop, not that this took enormous energy or time on her part, given that provisions were still very limited in Ireland then, in the inter-war period; the demand wasn't great either given that people had such little money at the time. Still, the shop would prove a help that was badly needed until her sister's family grew older and could fend for itself. The five years or so after their arrival would be tough for them, now that the two eldest lads, Seán and Tadhg, were starting secondary school. It was hoped that they'd make the most of it. Unfortunately, as fate dictated, it was Seán, the most academically-gifted of the boys, who didn't get as much from his secondary school education as he should have, and this was purely because of absenteeism due to illness.

Mounting medical and other family bills would make it necessary for the family to sell off the small piece of land they owned bit by bit over the following years. In fact, all they had left in the end of the six-and-a-half acres they'd originally bought with the house was the small orchard at the back and a narrow stretch of rough and hilly land skirting the Bun an Chomair road, and the house itself – a plot of less than two acres in total.

Seán and Tadhg began secondary school together in the North Monastery CBS, Cork city, in the autumn of 1932. Based on the results of the entrance exam, it was decided to start Seán off in second year, this despite the fact that he already had large gaps in his schooling at primary level as a result of various chest problems. This decision may not have been based entirely on his perceived academic abilities, however, as Seán was nearing sixteen years of age at the time and he was probably a good bit older than most people starting secondary school at this juncture. His brother, Tadhg, went into first year but he never had the same interest in the academic side of things and left before completing his schooling in the North Mon. Interestingly, the school roll shows Seán skipping another year in the 1933–34 session when he moved on to fourth year without doing third year at all. Perhaps, we shouldn't read too much into this, however, as it was normal for pupils to skip at least one of the four years prior to sitting the Intermediate examination. In 1934, after just two years in school, Seán passed the Inter Cert, achieving the following results: Irish

520 (out of 600), English 307 (400), Latin 306 (400), History 171 (250), Geography 74 (150), Arithmetic 111 (200), Algebra 119 (200), Geometry 123 (200) and Science 137 (200). These were all common-level papers for which all students presented, except for Irish, English and Science. In the case of these three subjects, it was the Honours paper that Ó Ríordáin sat. The various Mathematics-related subjects (Arithmetic, Algebra, Geometry) were amalgamated as one when calculating the overall result and it was the same in the case of History and Geography. This meant that Ó Ríordáin got honours in every subject other than Mathematics and Science.

Ó Ríordáin completed his last two years in Secondary School between 1934 and 1936, at the end of which he did the Leaving Certificate exam. His results in the Leaving Certificate were as follows: Irish 485 (out of 600), English 278 (400), Latin 321 (400), History 118 (300), Geography 210 (300), Arithmetic 77 (100), Algebra 100 (250), Geometry 105 (250), Chemistry 145 (300). Other than Arithmetic, which was a common-level paper, in the absence of any another exam-level for that subject, these were all Honours papers. The various Mathematic-related subjects were still considered as a unit, although History and Geography were now separate and distinct subjects for exam purposes. Ó Ríordáin got honours in four subjects therefore: Gaeilge (Irish), English, Latin and Geography, while he got a pass grade in three other subjects (History, Maths, Chemistry). Taken as a whole, Ó Ríordáin's results weren't great; he had actually slipped backwards in most subjects from when he had done his Intermediate Certificate. He was certainly nowhere near one of the best pupils in the class results-wise – the likes of James Donoghue, Tadhg Carey and Leo Skentlebery, for example. Even in Irish, he only achieved third place. It was clear that whatever academic abilities Ó Ríordáin had lay in the linguistic sphere. You certainly wouldn't have marked him down as someone best suited to clerical work.

Looking to the West, Looking from the West

The four years Ó Ríordáin spent at secondary school were intended to achieve the necessary qualifications for a job; other than that, the period seems to have had very little influence on Seán. He refers to his secondary school days only very rarely in his diaries, and then only in the later years of his life. By then, the North Monastery School symbolises for him the people who have done well in life, unlike himself, former friends of his who were no longer friends – that is, if they ever were friends in the first place. As regards the teachers, whether Christian Brothers or lay people, it is clear that Tadhg Ó Duinnín made more of an impression on Ó Ríordáin than anyone in the North Monastery did. Only rarely does one come across the occasional reference such as the following in Ó Ríordáin's published writings: 'There was a Brother in the North Monastery long ago whose only knowledge of the Irish language was "aon, dó, trí, ceathair" ("*one, two, three, four*"). This is sufficient now apparently to indicate that you have enough Irish to be a candidate for the Presidency'.[2] Or memories that he had pushed to the back of his mind would come back to him whenever he came across an old classmate of his in later life. In the following instance, it's a lad named Eddie Golden: 'I remember him playing the part of Christ when Brother Byrne produced the Passion in the North Monastery years ago. Because girls weren't allowed to do so, the boys had to do both male and female parts.'[3]

These were all small matters assigned to his memory, images of the past that had never really made much impression on him, it seems. We might have expected a more detailed description of his schooldays in his earliest diaries given that it wasn't long since he had left school, but even in them he mentions only two teachers, a man they used to call Jer Bass (Dennehy being his proper name) and a Christian Brother named Brother Moynihan. Jer Bass was the English teacher Ó Ríordáin had for a while and a man whom the poet mentions as being particularly fond of Patrick Pearse's poem 'The Wayfarer', a poem which Ó Ríordáin wrote out fully in his diary entry for 25 March 1940. Elsewhere in his diaries, Ó Ríordáin quotes some advice which Jer Bass gave his pupils at one point where he said that people needed to find the direction or model that suited them best in terms of their creative endeavours in order to become fulfilled as human beings. 'The soul can only find peace within its own nature.' This

2 'Haveth Childers everywhere', IT, 26 May 1973.
3 'The People of Cork', IT, 6 November 1971.

idea fitted in well with the development of Seán's own thoughts on life and art, and it was one that resurfaced again repeatedly in his work under various guises:

> *I don't think I'll ever be at peace until every book I have, every letter, every piece of clothing, every minute, is in order – until I'm travelling within the legitimate limits of my own nature. Jer Bass once said that a friend of ours invented this proverb off his own bat 'The soul can only find peace within its own nature'.*[4]

The introduction to *Eireaball Spideoige* also sees the appearance of a similar idea, although it is unlikely that it was Jer Bass' thinking which influenced Ó Ríordáin in this instance. Suffice to say that the period the poet spent in secondary school seems to have had very little influence on him as a writer.

Brother Moynihan, his Latin teacher, was the other teacher that Ó Ríordáin refers to; he was from Ballyvourney originally and would've been known on a personal level to some of Seán's family. Interestingly, he is one of the few people who has left us with a report of Ó Ríordáin's progress at school, not an entirely positive one as it happens. It comes to us at second hand. As the story goes, Seán's mother had a sister named Kathleen who was married to a man named Reynolds and it was she who asked Brother Moynihan one day in 1940 how Seán had got on when he was at school a few years earlier. Brother Moynihan's response was to the effect that: 'He was good, but he was in no way persevering, and he was irregular.'[5] Seán, for his part, had a more positive take on Brother Moynihan as a teacher: 'He was a good scholar of Latin and the Irish language and who knows what other subjects' is how he described him in his diary. In a letter Seán wrote in Irish to this same Brother, published in *Agus*, April 1980, he comments: 'I see you as clearly before me now as when we were learning *De Senectute* from you.' This letter, written on 12 February 1952, is very interesting because of what Ó Ríordáin said in it about his own first book of poetry. (He wrote this letter in response to one he had received from

4 D: 2 July 1949.

5 D: 6 April 1940.

Brother Moynihan, congratulating him on the new book and the most important aspects of this letter will be outlined later in this volume.)

The schoolteachers clearly weren't expecting a whole lot from Ó Ríordáin in academic terms. Séamus Ó Coigligh includes the following anecdote in the essay he published in *An Duine is Dual* regarding a conversation he had with one of the Brothers about Ó Ríordáin:

> *While Brother Ó Broin was on a visit to the Museum here a few years ago I mentioned Seán and his poetry to him. 'Now that you mention it,' said the Brother to me, 'you most likely remember, the "véarsaíocht Ghaeilge" ("Irish verse") which we used as an extra subject for the Leaving Cert classes of the Thirties; strange to say, but there were at least two others in that class, in 1936, who were better than Seán at poetry, in my opinion.'*[6]

The truth is that we have very little information about Seán's life at this juncture. The sort of report that one might get from his friends would probably have gone something along these lines, however, as Tadhg Carey remembered him: the shy boy who anxiously chewed the top of his pencil – so much so that the other lads eventually bought him a cover for it. The lad who never wore a tie until he began his first job when he was obliged to do so; it was a brass button that secured his collar at the throat. He looked a bit out of place already, as if he didn't really belong there; he was the quiet fellow standing to the side – the observer. Looking back on his years at school, Ó Ríordáin says in his diary entry for 23 November 1962 that he never really felt part of the North Monastery school; nor did the school have much to do with him either.

Skentlebery was the one of his fellow pupils whom he seems to have taken stock of and not because he felt any great affinity with him – but rather how different he was to the other lads. He'd come across the Skentlebery type again later on in City Hall – the type of individual who was conscious of his station or place in the world. The names of Skentlebery and Turnbull, names that announce their difference in advance, crop up in the diary every now and then; these were people who knew their place in

6 Ó hAnluain (ed.), *An Duine is Dual*, p. 28.

the social scheme of things – and were proud of it to boot. It didn't matter what station somebody had in life as long as their demeanour and speech accorded with their behaviour and background. And even if Ó Ríordáin's background was very different from the other two lads, there was always a hint of jealousy evident in his references to them in the diary, because they fitted the model of how postcolonial Ireland ought to have been ordered according to his perspective – the Irishman acting in accordance with his nature and behaving as an Irishman and the Englishman acting exactly as it had been fated – as an Englishman. And to hell with the man from Bandon whose English was as intelligible as his Chinese; speaking Sino or Hiberno-English didn't suit him and he looked a right fool in the end.[7] And he who was ordained to be an Englishman should be just that – because this was how best he could express himself and be true to his identity; this was his rightful 'territory', his 'island'. Not only were people who acted thus being faithful to the persona or image that everyone else had of them but they were also being true to their own individual identity. And Skentlebery was the first example of such a person/'persona' that Ó Ríordáin had ever come across. In a sense, Seán viewed Skentlebery as the reverse archetype of the Gaeltacht-man and the same went for the persona whom Ó Ríordáin most closely associated with him, i.e. the English writer Chesterton. Indeed 'Chesterton' was the title and principal subject of an *Irish Times* article which Ó Ríordáin published in 1973, which makes honourable mention of Skentlebery by virtue of the fact that he was one of the few of this type that Ó Ríordáin had ever come across:

> *Hilaire Belloc and Chesterton were similar to one another in spirit. Someone who was a fan of both was referred to as Chesterbellocian. Chesterton was fat. There was a fat student in the North Monastery in Cork during my time there whose name was Skentlebery. He was in the same class as me. We all thought that he was the spit of Chesterton. He had the magic of Chesterton about him. He was funny but his humour was of the learned type even at that time, even if he was still just a secondary school student. He spoke an upper-class dialect of*

7 'Droichead na Bandanaise' ('*The Bridge of Bandon Language*'), IT, 11 May 1974.

> *English. That dialect came naturally to him. I think he must have been of English background. The essays he wrote in those days were a source of amazement and jealousy to the rest of us – essays that the teachers would read out to the rest of us as a mark of their admiration for him. He left the best writers of all in the halfpenny place in our opinion. None of us would ever have been able to write prose of the quality that he wrote. He was a Chesterbellocian, if my memory serves me correctly, and similar to many scholarly people who also happen to be fat, he was constantly laughing, not in a sarcastic manner but in an academic or Chestertonian way in relation to the absurdity of life. His sense of the academic and objective followed naturally from the learned good humour that had been bred in him. Although we all thought that he would pursue the literary route, he is now working as an ambassador in Argentina and the good humour and objectivity of the profession must surely serve him well in this role. I can never really think of Chesterton without Skentlebery also coming to mind.*[8]

'By the way, the man who's the current Irish Taoiseach was in the same class,' is the next sentence in that same essay. Jack Lynch was the person whom Ó Ríordáin had in mind and he was a long way from being a Chesterbellocian – in his estimation.

Ó Ríordáin held a deep dislike for Lynch throughout his life and took a swipe at him whenever he got the chance in his articles and essays; to Ó Ríordáin's mind, Lynch was the 'nobody', the person who was duller than ditch-water. He was the 'nobody' who – irony of ironies – would be appointed leader of the tribe. And when Lynch was appointed leader of Fianna Fáil and of the Irish government years later, Seán felt it necessary to compare how Lynch had got on in life with himself. It was a bizarre and tragic comparison. While one man had reached the top of his profession and the apex of society, the other (i.e. the poet) had seen very little in terms of achievement in his life at all – at least not on the surface of things. The latter spent his wintry nights alone fending off the terrors of sickness and the dark, a world and work of writing that appeared almost worthless in his own eyes much of the time. The thought of Lynch inspired that hidden fear that was always there at the back of Ó Ríordáin's mind, however:

8 IT, 3 February 1973.

could it be that Lynch had reached the right conclusion regarding the cultural and linguistic situation between Irish and English? Or how were success and failure to be measured? The answers are suggested by the following entries in his diary, even if we must try to situate them in their context as much as possible – just as Ó Ríordáin tried to do when he first wrote them:

9.20 p.m. 9 November 1966. I'm not too bad. If there was someone in the house here with me, it wouldn't be too bad – We'd chat and I'd have to engage with whoever was here. But as of now, the whole house – indeed, the whole world belongs to me and this cold. My whole focus is on this cold and on myself. The cold has assumed gigantic proportions now even if it isn't more than a source of discomfort really in the overall context of things. It has assumed death's proportions now and it is striding through the world like a Colossus. If we thought about it properly, everything in its proper context, our own deaths – every one of us – would be just another incident in our lives, the final incident, but just a minor incident perhaps.

Jack Lynch was elected leader of Fianna Fáil today: Lynch 52 votes; Colley 19 votes. I heard it on the radio tonight. He began his speech with a few words of bad Irish and continued on in smooth English. He was delighted to be elected leader of Fianna Fáil. But his 't' in 'toghadh' (elected) was slender and the 'F' in 'Fhianna' wasn't attenuated. It's obvious that his Irish is the same now as it was when he was in the North Monastery. His English has really improved, however. A nod is as good as wink …

1.30 a.m. 10 November 1966. Woken up. If I wasn't sick, I'd write very little, it seems. A bad cold that's stuck deep down in my chest. The drugs didn't make any difference despite how many of them I've taken, and how much I've spent on them. It wouldn't surprise me if I were throwing up blood in another day or two. I'm a hypochondriac all right but … I've got reason to be. Could this suffering have been avoided? Is suffering a positive thing? I always got plenty of it. If Jack Lynch was in my situation, would he be as scared as I am? He was a noted hurler and footballer. During the past few days there have been umpteen references on the radio to the medals that he won playing sport. I was no sportsman. Does being a sportsman mean someone is also a brave man and vice

> *versa? We were in the same class at school. He will be head of the Government tomorrow. I never received a promotion of any kind. Life is strange. When we were doing the Leaving Certificate, I couldn't remember the Latin word for 'bee'. Jack was just behind me. I passed him back a piece of blotting paper looking for the information and I got the word 'apis' back.*

Whether true or not, this anecdote about the bee was one Ó Ríordáin regularly told people down through the years, and it was probably the only word of praise he gave Jack Lynch – if praise it was. As it happens, Seán did better than Lynch in Latin and in every other examination. (The most interesting result perhaps, and the one which linked both men in a strange way again some decades later, was how they got on in History; Lynch failed the subject while Ó Ríordáin only managed a pass. It wouldn't be long after the exams that fate dictated both men pursue completely different paths in life and assigned them very different places in the world: one man to his lonely sickbed anxiously watching the night, and the other to the most important office in the land. But how is importance to be determined? It all depends on one's perspective and vantage point on the world.

The Young Dilettante

It was while Ó Ríordáin was in the North Monastery that he first became interested in drama. In fact, if it wasn't for Ó Ríordáin's interest in theatre, it is unlikely that there would ever have been a drama group at all in Inniscarra, given that it was he who set up and organised it initially and kept it going for a number of years until he became too ill to do so. They held their first drama practices out in the old shed that the Ó Ríordáin family had brought over with them from Ballyvourney. Most of the plays they put on were in Irish, although they also put on the odd one in English. It is difficult to understand how they managed to attract an audience for their shows in Irish given that English was the only language spoken in this part of Cork city, but they did. In fact, they proved quite successful in getting an audience. As regards the actors themselves, there are only two others, apart from Seán, that knew some Irish. Seán's brother, Tadhg, was one of them and the other was Dónall Ó hÉalaithe (Healy) whose family had also moved from Ballyvourney to the neighbourhood of the city. Other than these, it was the local lads that Ó Ríordáin relied on mainly to help with the shows. The names of a couple of these lads often appear in his early diaries: Eddie Hanlon (who was in charge of whatever English-language dramas they put on), Jeremiah Keohane and Jerry Goulding – the last in particular. While rehearsing, they would discuss the dramas in Irish among themselves in as far as possible given that some of the members were less than fluent in the language.

A new hall was built to serve the needs of the drama group, which was quite an achievement. Tommy Heelan provided the site free of charge about a half a mile to the west of Ó Ríordáin's house on the Macroom road. It didn't take long for the building to be constructed: the local people all helped out (particularly those who were involved in Fianna Fáil in the area, as Seán himself was at one point). They built it and paid for its construction themselves and worked on it in their own time. Not that it cost them a great deal of money, because it was very basic, particularly in the beginning. At first they had just a clay floor until they managed to raise enough money from the various dramas they held to install a proper cement one. The stage consisted of a series of barrels with timber planks stretched across them, and a curtain to the front dividing actors from the audience. A series of planks laid across concrete blocks served as rough-and-ready seats for the audience, not that everyone got a seat at the shows, such was the interest in them. Sometimes they organised a dance after the drama so that they would have both on the same night; it took only a few minutes to take apart the 'seating' and put it in against the wall, then put the blocks and the barrels outside the door so that you had a ready-made dance floor. It was mainly when there was a prohibition on dancing during Lent that the dramas did well; as a local wit put it:

> There are Judges that don't practise,
> There are Otters that don't swim,
> And they've built a hall at Heelan's Cross
> To keep the girls from sin.

The Judges and the Otters were two local families who had no involvement with the construction of the hall at all and this was how the local humorist preferred it too. We have the names of some of the dramas that were staged in the hall back then: e.g. *An Sprid* by Father Peadar Ó Laoghaire; *An Chúis Dlí*, Liam Ó Rinn's translation of *Der Prozess* by Benedix, and *Aiséirí Dhonncha*, Pádraig Ó Siochrú's translation of *The Resurrection of Dinny O'Dowd* as written by Seamas MacManus.

As regards the English-language plays, it was the works of Synge and Lady Gregory that proved most popular. Seán took part in the Irish-language plays only – as both actor and organiser – and he also painted the backdrop to the stage on a piece of cloth or timber when necessary. He even went so far as to write at least one short play of his own, although there is no trace of it today. A few lines from some drama or other that he worked on at this time appear occasionally in the diaries; the earliest of these small extracts is actually set in City Hall, Cork and appears to have been written sometime around Christmas 1942–43. Ó Ríordáin never managed to write an entire play that he was happy with, however, a piece that he'd have regarded as a serious work of art, although he frequently mentions that he would have liked to have done so.

This drama group of theirs travelled around County Cork sometimes with their plays also – out to Berrings, Tower, Killumney, Coachford – all English-speaking areas, needless to say. Seán mentions these travels of theirs in a diary entry for 5 June 1949, at least ten years after he'd given up his involvement with local dramatics. He says that it was on one of these outings in the Berrings area that he met the writer and scholar Daniel Corkery for the first time. Corkery was giving a lecture at the same venue that night as it turns out, and also provided a report of the event to the local newspaper afterwards. He gave high praise to the actors and particularly to the young director of the drama – i.e. Seán – in his report of that event. That was how Seán came to meet the most important person he would ever know. But he was also the person he would most have to contend with if he were to develop his own sensibility as a writer. Corkery was like a giant presence overshadowing Seán's writing for years, a shadow that he finally had to set to one side so that he could come into his own as a writer. This is an aspect of the poet's story that will be explored in greater detail later in this volume.

Another craft that Ó Ríordáin began at this juncture and to which reference was made earlier was that of painting and sketching. He often wondered in later years whether this was the art form that he should really have pursued in his early years and wondered whether he'd more talent in this area than he did in terms of writing.[9]

Unfortunately, it is impossible for us to know now whether Ó Ríordáin did have more ability as a painter than as a writer as almost none of his landscape paintings or portraits – paintings he regularly mentioned in his early diaries – have survived. In fact, just one (colour) painting of his mother and the many smaller sketches of people that he created from his imagination are all we have left of his artwork today. In addition to these are the thousands of versions of the facial features of de Valera, with whom he seems to have been endlessly fascinated.

To return to that period when the young Ó Ríordáin was involved in the local drama scene. At this juncture, we'd most likely have found him in the back of the hall, sketching quietly as the nervous actors waited for the curtain to go up. Seán was particularly interested in sketching the faces of striking-looking elderly people that he came across. When his illness ensured that he was separated from the rest of the community, he lost contact with the potential subjects of these sketches, however. In a diary entry for 20 March 1942 he speaks of 'drawing creatures that never really existed'. And earlier still, on 5 March 1940, he speaks of spending the entire day 'drawing pictures of men and women that were never in this world'; tragically, in one sense, these people were the family he never had. As it turns out Ó Ríordáin would also have a second brood in time – his 'family of verse', who would also bear his stamp.[10] Interestingly, it was in the sanatorium, where he found himself among people whom he was most comfortable with and most fond of, that he'd return once again to the subject matter of these early sketches.

Corkery urged Seán to enrol in the School of Art in Cork city but Ó Ríordáin never took him up on this advice. Despite this, he often called in to the school to see the latest exhibitions on his way home from work,

9 'Smaointe Fáin' ('*Random Thoughts*'), IT, 24 June 1969.

10 ES: p. 26.

even at times when he wasn't feeling very well at all. Ó Ríordáin described in his diary an exhibition of paintings that he saw there on 26 April 1944 as follows, for instance:

> *They made me happy but they also made me jealous. Still, they gave me joy overall. It is difficult for an untrained person like me to describe them.*
>
> *All I can say is that I could look at them forever and I'd never get tired of them.*

Ó Ríordáin never did get any formal training in art and even had he done so he would have had little enough to bring to his creations by way of nourishment, such was the straitened nature of his life and experience. In the end, the art form that he chose to express himself through had the singular advantage to it that it could retreat into itself, thereby becoming a true and unchanging mirror-image of the self over time. The downside of the dramatics and the painting for Ó Ríordáin lay in the fact that they were art forms that required a certain amount of travel and a good deal of interaction with other people, neither of which he would have been able to do, given the way his personal circumstances developed over the following years. And even then he would often express the fear that his compositions were insufficiently grounded in everyday life.

At this early juncture, however, before the TB forced him to retreat into himself, Ó Ríordáin could still draw upon a fairly wide range of people and a reasonably active social life. This was the most sociable or public stage of his life, the period where his health had yet to fail, a life that made sense through the then-common simple English-language ditties and witticisms that Seán and the others invented for the fun of it. These expressions and rhymes as relating to local events and people were still remembered and repeated by his surviving companions. The poet's friends and neighbours would recall bits and pieces of these ditties and rhymes even in later years; they were verses that cemented their identity and created a sense of solidarity among their community even long after Seán had retreated into his sickroom at the back of the house and retreated into himself. And 'Jackie Riordan', as he was commonly known in the locality, would always be associated with this community and belong to them, long after the people who knew him through his poetry or the more official Irish-language groups and organisations called him 'Seán Ó Ríordáin'. In their everyday eyes, the 'Seán Ó Ríordáin' who became something of a public figure decades later had little affinity with them really – he belonged to a different world. He was always 'Jackie Riordan' to them and that was the end of it. Indeed it might be said that 'Jackie Riordan', man of the local community, belonged to that community more than Seán Ó Ríordáin, for whom writing was always a singularly lonely craft, would ever belong to the literary set.

At that moment in time, however, Jackie was woven into the fabric of the neighbourhood as much as the next man – whether it was sharing witticisms or jokes, playing pitch-and-toss, or road-bowling along the road that stretched up towards Bun an Chomair (Seán bowled left-handed and, even if he wasn't the strongest in the world by any means, he was still a nice handy player by all accounts). In addition, there might be the odd trip away for the day to Bantry or Youghal or down into An Rinn (Ring), the Irish-speaking area of County Waterford, on a bus as hired for the day by the women of the locality. For now, Ó Ríordáin – even if he was always fairly shy and tending towards the edge of the crowd – has the verve and energy of youth and the hope that accompanies the possibility of new opportunities in life about him.

When we return to him in the next chapter, however, his circumstances have altered greatly. The dark cloud of illness has drawn in and we find him ensconced most days in the claustrophobic sickroom separating him forever from the life he had previously known and shared; the world outside coming to him now in the sounds and voices of his former companions that reach him from the crossroads below. Serious illness will lay him low but then raise him up again so that the window of his world has a new and unique perspective, one that requires a very different form of expression.

3

The Public Self

The final segregation had not yet occurred, however (and indeed, there would always be a tenuous, grudging accommodation forced on him by circumstance), when Ó Ríordáin successfully applied for a job with Cork City Corporation shortly after publication of the Leaving Certificate results. Three other lads from his class also applied to the Corporation and got onto the same panel. They were then called for jobs one by one, as based on their Leaving Cert results. Seán was the first of them to be called as he had got the best exam results and the other three lads followed him into the Corporation in due course – Con Twomey, Con Prior and John O'Donovan. Seán was interviewed on 7 November 1936. His interview lasted nearly an hour, which was a lot longer than normal. A man who met Seán on the morning of the interview told me that Seán had drunk a half-glass of whiskey beforehand to calm his nerves and maybe this contributed to the interview panel dragging on a bit! Interestingly, when Con Twomey was called himself a few days later, his interview lasted just a few minutes.

Anyone applying for a clerical job position in the Corporation at this juncture was obliged to provide a certain amount of information about themselves. To that end, a question-and-answer form had to be completed. The archives of City Hall still hold a copy of Ó Ríordáin's application form, albeit the official typewritten version rather than that in his own handwriting. Seán didn't have access to a typewriter in those days. The questions were all in English even if Ó Ríordáin responded to them in Irish, a sign of things to come. (Of necessity, both question and answer appear in English below.)

Give particulars of appointments held and of employment during the past ten years ... I had no job at all prior to this; I was attending school.

Whether engaged in the sale of spirituous liquor of any kind, tobacco, groceries, or provisions ... I am not involved in any business such as this but I am living in my mother's sister's house and she sells tobacco in her shop. Her name is A[bina, i.e. Gobnait] Linehan [*sic*].

Whether person to be appointed has been hitherto, and is now, a person of sobriety, peaceable demeanour, and moral conduct ... Brother Ó Broin, President of the North Monastery will provide a character reference on my behalf.

Give full particulars of educational attainments (including knowledge of Irish) and of any examinations passed ... I got Honours in my Intermediate Certificate and in my Leaving Certificate. I was born and reared in the Gaeltacht.

Give particulars of knowledge of bookkeeping and accounting ... I have no knowledge of either of these skills.

The interview was held on a Saturday. Seán was appointed to the job and as per the instructions of the City Manager, Philip Monahan, he was due to commence work the following Monday, 9 November, dressed in a shirt and tie. What appears in the archive next, however, is a second instruction from the City Manager dated 12 November, indicating that Con Twomey be appointed in place of Ó Ríordáin and that he begin work on the thirteenth of the month. This was a peculiar if not unique arrangement – i.e. that the person originally appointed to the job didn't commence work on the appointed day but was given flexibility in the matter instead. On enquiry, Ó Ríordáin's contemporaries from that era had no explanation for this; they were surprised that he'd managed to come to this agreement with the manager. Nor does Seán refer to it anywhere either. None of his diaries survive for this time (and may never have existed) so there is no contemporary account of the precise circumstances from his point of view. Whatever the case, Seán spoke solely in very positive terms about Philip Monahan (his manager) in the early days of his working in the Corporation. This tune wouldn't be too long in changing, however, as we'll see in due course.

It was customary at this time for new employees in the Corporation to be appointed but then to await official approval from the Department of Local Government. Accordingly, although he was approved for official duties commencing on 7 November, official departmental approval in this regard wasn't received until 15 December. Below is the letter sent to the manager that day. Judging by its tone, the civil service official in question wasn't overly impressed with Ó Ríordáin's appointment and made a point of reminding the Corporation that their new employee had best be able to fulfil his new clerical duties to the required standard. Two pounds a week was Seán's pay for the first year, and this would increase by ten pounds per annum based on satisfactory performance of his duties:

> *A Chara,*
>
> *I am directed by the Minister for Local Government and Public Health to refer to your letter of the 9th instant enclosing query form in connection with the appointment of Seán Ó Ríoghbhardáin as Junior Clerk in the Offices of the Cork Corporation, and to state that the appointment is sanctioned at the scale of salary proposed, viz. £100 by annual increments of £10 to £200 per annum, subject to the passing of an efficiency test when on the salary of £150 per annum. It is noted that the appointee has no knowledge of bookkeeping or accountancy and as it is considered necessary [sic] that some knowledge of these subjects is necessary to efficient performance of the duties which he may be called upon to perform, you should ensure that a working knowledge of the subjects is acquired as soon as possible.*
>
> *Mise le meas,*
> [illegible signature]
> *a/s Rúnaí.*

There was no mention of Seán's absence in the interim, nor, it would appear, were the officials in the department aware of this. Seán didn't commence work in the Corporation until 25 January 1937 when he took up his duties for the first time. He was assigned to work in the motor tax office and when the time came for him to be made permanent in his job after six months, there was no question about it; Ó Ríordáin hadn't been in the office much anyway since he'd officially commenced work and when he had been, no one could find any fault with his work. Séamus Ó Coigligh's account of this period, as published in the influential essay in *An Duine is Dual*, isn't entirely accurate in every regard with respect to these details. It is precisely because of the importance and general reliability of this essay that reference is made to such minor slips. (One small but critical inaccuracy, for example, is the date Ó Coigligh gave for when Ó Ríordáin finally resigned from his job in the Corporation; he cites 1960 as the year he resigned, 1965 being the correct date.)[1] Here is Ó Coigligh's recollection of the events outlined earlier:

> *Seán was appointed as a clerical officer in Cork Corporation on 10 January 1937 [sic] … According to the rules of the Department of Local Government, anyone appointed at this juncture was on six months' probation prior to being made permanent, six months where they checked that your health, competence and conduct were up to scratch. Seán was unable to commence work on 25 January and not for a long time afterwards. He was ill and confined to bed – 'the captain of all these men of death that came against him to take him away was the Consumption.' But the City Manager, Philip Monahan didn't enforce the rules in this case; Seán wasn't disqualified from the job.*[2]

The first inaccuracy here is that the date 10 January was never in the equation and wasn't cited in the typewritten copy of the essay that I was given to read, but rather 25 January in both instances; the other date must somehow have occurred in the editing process. And even if Seán was delayed in starting in the job, as discussed earlier, he actually commenced work on Monday 25 January 1937. More crucial still is the approximate date given for Seán's diagnosis with tuberculosis as indicated in this same essay; it is more than a year out in my opinion. Based on the evidence of his work file and Seán's own later diary references, it was in early 1938 that he first contracted tuberculosis. Or at least, this was the first time that he *knew* he had contracted this life-changing disease. Therefore, whatever kept Seán from work in November and December of 1936, it is unlikely

1 Ó hAnluain (ed.), *An Duine is Dual*, p. 51.
2 *Ibid.*, p. 29.

to have been TB. Ever since he'd got pneumonia a few years earlier, Seán had been very susceptible to chest problems and he'd often been absent from school as a consequence; Brother Moynihan hadn't lied when he said he was 'irregular'.

It was in City Hall that Séamus Ó Coigligh – as formerly appointed on 12 November 1934 – worked. The motor tax office was in Parnell Place when Seán began work there, while City Hall was the location of the Corporation's other offices and where his old pals from the North Monastery were based. Perhaps, this explains Ó Coigligh's confusion regarding the date that Seán began work. Another thing is that Séamus didn't know Seán very well at the time, as it was his brother Pádraig who had been in Ó Ríordáin's class when he was in his last year in the North Mon. (Their friendship wouldn't be long postponed, however.)

From the day he began in the Corporation, Seán went more than a full year without missing work: from 25 January 1937 until 7 March 1938 when he first fell seriously ill with TB. Once he was infected he had to leave work immediately, needless to say. We have a detailed account of this first bout of sickness and all the smaller ones that followed it in Seán's diaries for most of the next six and a half years.

In a letter dated 18 September 1944, we find an enquiry from the Corporation wondering what salary Seán was entitled to, given his protracted absence from work. The arrangement was that one was kept on a full salary for the first six months of absence, and then on a half salary for the following six months, after which payment ceased. The question of most concern to the enquirer on this occasion was what salary scale Seán should be on if he returned and what level of increase he was entitled to – or whether he was allowed back to work at all. Edward J. Twomey, the City Accountant, addressed his query to the City Manager as follows:

Dear Mr. Monahan,

I wish to report that Mr. Seán Riordan [sic] resumed duty in the Motor Taxation Office on Monday, 11th instant. He has been absent since the 9th September 1941 and I shall be obliged for a direction as to the salary payable to him on resumption.

Since his appointment on 25th January 1937, his position has been as follows:

Absent from	*8/3/38 to 8/9/38*	*Full pay*	
	8/9/38 to 8/3/39	*Half pay*	*@ £110 p.a.*
	8/3/39 to 31/5/40	*No pay*	
	Resumed on 1st June 1940 at £120 p.a.		

Absent from *14/10/40 to 16/10/40; 21/1/41 to 1/2/41;*
26/4/41 to 28/4/41; 1/5/41 to 3/5/41;
21/6/41 to 22/6/41; 24/6/41 to 30/6/41
at Full Pay.

Absent from	*9/9/41 to 9/3/42*	*Full Pay*	
	9/3/42 to 9/9/42	*Half Pay*	*@ £130 p.a.*
	9/9/42 to 10/9/44	*No Pay*	
	Resumed on the 11th September 1944.		

I presume sanction will have to be obtained to his re-employment in this Department,

Yours faithfully
Edward J. Twomey
Local Taxation Officer

As it happens, Ó Ríordáin was returned onto the previous salary scale, a move which didn't please him one bit. He'd lost out on a year's salary increase or more and he duly complained about this to the manager. It would be another two years, however, before he plucked up the courage to write this letter of complaint on 17 July 1946. When in Rome, one should do as the Romans do, and so the letter was written in the style and jargon of bureau and officialdom:

Dear Sir,
My salary for the year commencing June 1941 was £130. I went off duty in September 1941 and was paid for one year (during which period I was on sick leave) at the £130 per annum rate. When I resumed duty in September 1944 I was placed on the £130 per annum scale again. It would appear that my salary at that stage should commence at £140 per annum and not £130.

He didn't get much in the way of satisfaction from the manager, however, because his response simply confirmed the previous decision. The reply came the following day, dated 18 July 1946:

> *Increments in salary are payable only on certification by the City Manager that the person claiming increment has satisfactorily performed his or her duties during the previous twelve months. In the case of a member of the staff who is absent or on sick leave for a period of twelve months, it would be impossible for the City Manager so to certify as to the performance of duty …*

This might have been the first 'falling-out' they had, but it was far from the last. And behind these barbed official missives there was a great deal more going on. For Ó Ríordáin's part, he was very bothered at all the days he was missing from work due to his chronic illness, and the fact that he'd no choice but to engage in this official to-and-fro as regards sick leave, holidays and the conditions of the job only added to his predicament. As well as the constant bickering, there was his very real fear of losing the position on which he and his mother were utterly dependent, there being no other available to him in his condition.

The official-speak of the letters between Ó Ríordáin and the Corporation aside, it is to the diaries that we must turn to find the real human suffering and feelings that underscored these years. The following, as relating to a prolonged bout of illness in the two-year period that was 1938–40, for example. The poet has been absent from work now for a full two years and he is still very unsure and worried as to whether he'll be able to return to his job by the specified date. In this instance, Ó Ríordáin's suspicions regarding 'plotting' against him on officialdom's part are completely unfounded; he would have more reason to worry about such a possibility at a later date:

> *I went up the hill at half-past eleven. I lay down on the heather. I didn't feel the joy today that I felt yesterday. Maybe my mind was a small bit troubled. I received a letter from the City Manager this morning and there was a sting in it, I can tell you:*

Dear Mr. Riordan,

I would be glad to have a line from you indicating when you are likely to resume duty here.

Yours faithfully,
P. Monahan
City Manager

If I'm not able to return to work this time, there's a danger that they'll take the job from me ... I have no other way of making a living and even if my health is bad, I must go to work ... We've no money coming in to us and I have to go out and earn some.[3]

On 1 April 1940 Ó Ríordáin sent a letter to the manager promising that he'd be back at work by the end of the month. Needless to say, the promise was not fulfilled. On 26 April Seán visited the City Manager in person to try to agree a solution to the situation. Their discussion was amicable and Ó Ríordáin was quite pleased on his return home again that evening. His job would be left open for him until he was well enough to return to work again:

If there is any good Christian left in the world, Philip Monahan, the City Manager is that Christian. I asked him for another month. 'For God's sake,' he said, 'take May and June if you want it.' I said I was sorry for causing him so much trouble. 'You have more trouble than us,' he said.[4]

None of their correspondence for the period of 1938–40 is now available in the files of City Hall, but the files do contain many of the letters they exchanged for the period 1941–44. Even if some of the correspondence for this later period is lacking, enough has survived to understand the general tenor of their interactions. Ó Ríordáin was normally excusing himself for his absence from work due to illness and Monahan's replies were short notes acknowledging same and wishing him a speedy recovery:

3 D: 28 March 1940.
4 D: 26 April 1940.

'I hope your health continues to improve,' as noted by Monahan in August 1943 is typical of these exchanges. Their correspondence was always in English, even right down to the spelling of Seán's name as the self-styled 'Seán Ó Ríoghbhardáin' becomes the 'Mr Riordan' of the prompt reply.

21/8/'43

Philip Monahan Esq.
City Manager and Town Clerk
City Hall
Cork

Dear Sir,

I regret that I am still unable to resume duty.
I should be very grateful to get an extension of leave for another month.
Yours faithfully
Seán Ó Ríoghbhardáin

23 August 1943

Dear Mr. Riordan,

I am obliged for your letter of the 21st.
I am sorry that you are not able to resume work at present.
Sincerely yours
Philip Monahan
City Manager and Town Clerk

On 16 June 1944 Seán was still sick but hoping he might be well enough to return by early August: 'I regret I am still unable to resume duty. I should be very glad to get extension of leave until the end of July. I expect to be fit to resume duty by then.' As usual, however, he wasn't well enough to return by the promised date or for another month or more; by this point he'd been absent from work for a full three years and had been alternating between home and periods spent in the sanatorium. He finally managed to resume work by Monday 11 September 1944, and this is his diary entry for Thursday 7 September, just four days prior to his return:

> *I'm going to work in the office on Monday. There'll be no welcome for me. No matter. My mind is getting older and sleepier. I hope that this change in my life will awaken it. I am worried all the same, however. My body is damaged. If only I could buy a new body. The tea is ready.*

That is the last word in the form of prose from him for two years. The life of the office takes over and blots out his inner reflections for a substantial period of time, it appears. Even his mother's death on 21 January 1945 isn't enough to prompt him to resume the diary again. And interestingly, when he eventually did explore this other enormous tragedy of his life, it was in the form of poetry that his first thoughts emerged – in the seminal poem 'Adhlacadh mo Mháthar' (*'My Mother's Burial'*). His life was either too empty or too full – depending on what perspective you took on it – to say what he had to say solely in prose. The daily rhythm that could be followed and traced in the diary was now at an end. We can rule out the possibility that some diaries for the period have been lost or destroyed, because when we next meet him a few years on, he gives a brief update on what's happened in the intervening years.

The odd random mention of Ó Ríordáin and the office as contained in the files of City Hall is all we have to go on for this interval, not that they provide us with very much in the way of information. Ironically, to be at work in the office for an uninterrupted period is akin to the poet neglecting his most essential duties, tracing the inner world of the soul in the diary accounts. And this wasn't the first such derogation of duty either. The first continuous run of the diaries pertained to the period 1 January 1940 to 21 May 1940 when he was ill. Then his return to work on the first of June and the pattern is repeated. He abandons his diary entries just a few days before his return to work and we don't hear from him again until he falls ill again; and, even then, he's sick for a while before he speaks to us. The next time he makes an entry in his diary is Saturday 10 January 1942, when he mentions the time that has gone by and the world that has gone unrecorded: 'I am at home without work since September. I was sick and exhausted, and supposed to be sick …' It's as if he has already jettisoned City Hall again in his mind and is ready to put out to sea once more; his illness has that one small silver lining to it that it gives him time to recover himself in seclusion and draw on his inner resources again. Ironically too, the sanatorium and City Hall bear many similarities in terms of their influence (or the lack of it) on his writing, as will become evident shortly. It's not that he doesn't mention either place occasionally but rather that they are an inhibiting influence more than anything and have very little role in his poetry. Both environments are important only in the sense that they help us come to a better understanding of Ó Ríordáin the human being. It is only by tracking his journey between these environments and home that we can come to some realisation of the truly solitary human being, the solitary artist, as Ó Ríordáin came to create such an individual in his life and work.

City Hall and Ó Ríordáin's work environment in the Corporation highlight the dualities that characterise the young poet's life at this juncture. His work is a relief because it gets him out of the lonely house for the day, and the office represents activity, masculinity, the company of others. A series of opposites define his bouts of prolonged illness at home: they encompass idleness, eternity, ennui, self-contempt. Because you've been infected with this disease for which there is no real cure, he seems to say, you are the same miserable, filthy person that is always oppressively present, the same foul smell of sickness clinging to everything in the house and to yourself. The early years saw Ó Ríordáin oscillate between both of these environments and world views but he knew deep down from the beginning which side of his existence would prove more significant in the long-run, particularly in terms of his artistic development.

The time spent with other people would be lost to him. Engagement with them he would come to see as part of a common conspiracy to set aside the individual, at least for the time being. So the person who is revealed to us in the diaries is very different from that which we might construct from the anecdotes of his acquaintances; the merry witticisms they recall are nowhere recorded in his private writings, although they would re-emerge in the later public prose. But, while we must search indoors for what truly endures, the *dramatis persona* which he presented to his fellows in City Hall and elsewhere cannot altogether be ignored.

Interestingly, Séamus Ó Coigligh says in his essay in *An Duine is Dual* that City Hall wasn't as Anglicised or as unsympathetic an environment for the Irish language as people might assume during Ó Ríordáin's first years there – even if some people may have given the opposite impression at times. Ó Coigligh was undoubtedly correct about this, as evidenced from a quick list of the people working there who spoke Irish on a daily basis during the 1940s and 1950s. In addition to Ó Coigligh and Ó Ríordáin, there were people such as Clára Ní Annracháin (who was high up in the Cork branch of the Gaelic League at the time), Diarmaid Ó Murchú, Seán (Fear) Ó Tuama (appointed president of the Oireachtas in 1956), Bríd Nic Ghiobúin, Seán Standún and Val Deasy, all of whom spoke Irish whenever they had the opportunity to do so. Not that Seán ever had much to do with the various Irish-language revival organisations or with the work promoting the language that some of his colleagues were involved in – the advertising campaign they had in Irish, the names of their soccer teams as provided in Irish, and the like. As Séamus himself put it: 'It goes without saying that Seán had no part in these initiatives. The Motor Tax department had no involvement really with the everyday work of other sections of the Corporation.'[5] There is one brief diary entry of Seán's coming towards the end of 1946 (he refers to the fact that his thirtieth birthday is approaching) where Ó Ríordáin describes a half-jokey exchange regarding language activism and Irish generally between himself and Clára Ní Annracháin. Seán is dropping subtle hints about the major work of literature in Irish he is supposedly working on and how much of a boost this will give the Irish-language movement when published, only to receive her slightly sardonic reply: 'If you would only like to set up a new Branch.'[6]

Unfortunately for that point of view, Ó Ríordáin was never one for establishing branches or language activism in that sense. And anyway, he was very private about the Irish-language side of his writing and rarely mentioned it; if his literary work got a hearing in the end, so be it, but it was primarily for his own audience. While Seán shared a few of his poems with Séamus Ó Coigligh at this point and valued his opinion of them, this was in the knowledge that Ó Coigligh would give

5 Ó hAnluain (ed.), *An Duine is Dual*, p. 30.

6 *Branch* – i.e. set up a new branch of the Gaelic League.

them a sensitive and sympathetic hearing. Or the verdict might come uninvited as happened in the case of 'Oilithreacht Fám Anam' ('*My Soul's Pilgrimage*') published in the journal *Comhar* in September 1947. According to the poet himself, it was Clára Ní Annracháin who told him that certain references in the poem disgusted her. This is almost certainly a reference to the poet's own shock and coming to terms with an understanding of sexuality and the mechanics of it, the realisation of which had disgusted him too, initially. All the more so because it had meant the sudden and brutal sundering of the poet's world of 'ungendered' innocence and sacred beauty, his youthful idyll desecrated in one swift moment:

from **Oilithreacht Fám Anam**

Ach thuirling eolas buile
A scoilt an mhaidin álainn
'Na fireann is 'na baineann,
Is chuir ruaig ar chlúracána

Mar ghadhar ag déanamh caca
Ar fuaid an tí istoíche,
Nó mar sheilmide ag taisteal
Do bhréan an fios mo smaointe.[7]

from **My Soul's Pilgrimage**

But an insane knowledge descended
to divide the beautiful morning,
into male and female,
and chased the cluricaunes away.

Like a dog taking a shit
all over the house in the night,

7 ES: p. 71.

or like a snail trailing along,
knowledge fouled my thoughts.[8]

Ó Ríordáin responded to Clára Ní hAnnracháin on that occasion, however; his poetic response is included below. In truth, it wasn't what he'd said in the poem that Seán felt ashamed of, but rather that which he couldn't say at all and the way that his mind seemed in perpetual flight from reality, the same reality that should have been the basis of all that he wrote or was yet to write:

> *You'd immediately recognise a piece of prose by Shaw or by Father Peadar or Chesterton or some poetry by Yeats or Máirtín Ó Direáin. They have their own special personality about them. This gave me a shock. 'Oilithreacht Fám Anam' (that I wrote) was published in Combar this month. Something in it disgusted Miss Hanrahan. There are elements of my personality that disgust myself – those elements that are remote and cute. One should be scouring the inner world constantly. I try and hide the ugly parts of me but I'd be better off just getting rid of them. There are those who argue that the best poetry ever written was the poetry of San Juan de la Cruz. Because he is a saint? But then Yeats was no saint. He was honest, however. He never hid anything. There is no sin but duplicity. I have to expel the ugly things from my mind before I can expel them from my poetry.*[9]

Ó Ríordáin's resolution to this human dilemma goes as follows: given that it is impossible to accept or separate the aspects of his human nature that he finds repulsive from the rest, it is simpler to incorporate them into the whole and learn to live with it – no matter how much he hates to do so. Similar to the whore who is almost saint-like in her pure devotion to her nature or trade, all sins are forgiven if they are done openly and with real integrity.[10] The mind must be 'stripped' of all accoutrements so that

---

8 Sewell, Frank (ed.), *Selected Poems: Seán Ó Ríordáin, 1916–1977* (Yale University Press, New Haven, 2014), p. 79. Trans. Denise Blake.

9 D: 2 October 1947.

10 TÉB: p. 30.

only that which is raw and pure remains. Dishonesty is the one sin that cannot be forgiven: it is the sin that damns you. There is only one way to repel the demon and that is to expose it for what it really is. The worst sin of all, the one that is beyond forgiveness is prevarication or evasion: 'you aren't permitted evasion' in such matters, as Ó Ríordáin explained in more detail years later as part of his essay 'Aistriú ó theanga go teanga' ('*Changing from one language to another*').[11] The examination of conscience and confession, this is the ultimate cleansing of the soul. There is no place for alternative understandings of the literary and artistic act. The artistic act is the ultimate act of exposition.

The 'outside man' or the observant self could stay where he was; he had no time for him because the inner world and the 'inner man' was Ó Ríordáin's concern now and forever. And to reach that inner voice or 'inner man' or recognise him, Ó Ríordáin had no choice but to separate himself from others and follow the lonelier path of isolation and the solitary night-writing of the diaries. Bizarrely, in much the same way that the TB sufferer was shunted away to a separate realm that the uninfected avoided at all costs, so too did Seán's writing function as a sanctuary, the threshold of which few people ever crossed. In the discussion that follows, partly with the aid of the diaries, we trace Ó Ríordáin's construction of this wall around his private suffering, particularly from the 1940s onwards, a wall that hid his striving at poetry too. From that point onwards, and as TB became a greater obstacle in his life, we meet Ó Ríordáin more frequently in the poetic realm – but for as long as he worked in the Corporation there was almost no one who knew the creative or writing side of him at all. He had the public face and the private face, each befitting the separate aspects of his day. Less than a handful of people knew Seán Ó Ríordáin as poet and for the vast majority of people who came into contact with him, it was as Ó Ríordáin the clerk that they knew him. It was only when he returned to the silent sanctuary of the house each evening that he let his guard down as, alone, he faced the fearful silence of his room. The pretence was over for another day and he faced his true self in the form of the empty page. It was then that he came to understand better than most

11 IT, 7 July 1975.

the meaning of community but also the meaning of loneliness. It was in one of these solitary moments that he noted down the following extract, by which time it is clear that he has tasted loneliness in all its fullness and when the public life of work and office is no more than a salve to the gaping wound. Ó Ríordáin notes this at 7.30 on the morning of 12 April 1962, the long day still stretched before him in the office. While this diary entry comes near the end of his working life, it is a succinct summation of the sentiments that he's been expressing already for two decades previous to this, as ensconced within the solitary, protective world of thought and writing. In this instance, the world of people and the 'outer man' is more suffocating and claustrophobic to him now than is the solitary life of the loner:

> *A long day in the office ahead of me. Sold out to the enemy. Life is an enemy. Everyone's an enemy. We have to hide our true mentality here and adopt a disguise. If you meet me in the office today, you won't actually meet me but rather the person that I am presenting to the world. This is someone who doesn't actually exist at all, but it is the person that people are expecting, I think, and so that's what I give them. You wouldn't mind so much except that the real person has to die during the day. Not only that, but there is the risk that the real person becomes smothered completely, in the absence of air. I hope he hasn't been wiped out already. If so, I will inhabit nothing but a false personality, day and night. I'll just be a full-time actor …* [12]

Ó Ríordáin had only a few short years left to go in City Hall when he wrote this, if only he'd known it at the time. And when the time comes, he'll describe in some detail the ritual that went with his leaving the office behind forever, as if to say that he understood very well the significance of what that change in his life entailed. This day is further down the road as of yet, however. For now, it's sufficient for Ó Ríordáin to indicate the to and fro of his existence and the way that he misses work when he's absent for a long time and wearies of his own thoughts and company. And this should come as no surprise, really. After all, the poet – to Ó Ríordáin's

12 D: 12 April 1962; cf. *Comhar*, June 1963, pp. 27–8.

eyes – was in essence someone who'd lost the music and rhythm of life, someone who'd awoken from the dream of this life and had been unable to return to it again.[13] No wonder he yearned for the music and rhythm of dreams from time to time! And almost inevitably, it is when he felt most abandoned and alone that Ó Ríordáin needed to fill the silence and emptiness with words, with poetry – with anything. 'It is difficult to be all alone, to be all alone/the calling is too lofty, and too narrow.'[14] If one was fated to be alone – even while amongst the crowd, so to speak – it was important to acknowledge this and make one's own of this allotted station. And this is exactly what Ó Ríordáin did to a degree that was unusual amongst Irish people of his generation and even amongst the literary class. Not that he didn't look back sometimes longingly on the times when he'd had a more active social life. In this brief diary entry for 25 June 1949, for example, he mentions some of his occasional callers, the likes of Fr Valkenburg, Fr Tadhg Ó Murchú and Seán Ó Tuama: 'I always get a break from the animal of myself whenever they call, i.e. the learned priests, etc.' Still and all, it was the animal in him that most interested him in literary terms, and not these occasional visitors. And he knew too, deep down, that no matter how wretched a figure he cut – both in body and soul – that he had one quality that set him apart from the others. This was his ability 'to be present', a state that he would explore in greater detail in his writing – not that Ó Ríordáin was always entirely clear about what he meant by this quality of 'presence'. Was it a reference to himself being present – being fully present – when poetry emerged, or was it a reference to being present in order to attest to the humanity of others around him? Or was it necessary to make a distinction between either of these possibilities at all? The following is what Ó Ríordáin says when he is filled with the joy that is composing a new poem and proudly understands his place within the creative process. Surely there is nowhere else one would rather be?

> *What is a poet? This answer came to me tonight. [A poet is] a person who is present when a poem is born and, similar to a nurse, cares for the new child. I*

13 D: 15 February 1951.
14 LL: p. 17.

> *was present myself when a poem (by Seán Ó Ríordáin so-called) came into the world. 'Stand back woman, stand back!' I know that Father Tadhg and Riobard Mac Góráin and Seán Ó Tuama are all a level or two above me in life. I feel a snobbery there. They're university people. As for me, I'm just a pleb. But I AM PRESENT and that's something that they'll never be, never – not till kingdom come.*[15]

No one knows which poem emerged on the occasion alluded to here – unless perhaps it was the one simply titled 'Dán' ('*Poem*'), a poem which expresses a similar understanding of poetry – the idea that a poem is something that emerges organically and independent of other aspects, forms itself and matures in the mind, given appropriate sustenance.[16] Here's an excerpt from 'Dán':

Mar thoircheas i mbroinn.
Bíodh an véarsa so a chím,
Ní iarraim ach í a iompar
idir an dá linn …

Let this verse that I see be
in the womb like a pregnancy;
all I ask is to carry it
in the interim.[17]

Ó Ríordáin was committed to his poetic endeavours from an early stage and wasn't one to waste his time or limited energies on surface friendships or sparring with others for the sake of it. There were plenty of people out there who would waste your time and who were the enemy to your endeavours. At worst, they were privately hostile to you, and at best, they delayed you or were a hindrance. You had to be alert and wary of the motives of others. Weren't many apparent friendships false in the sense

15 D: 8 April 1949.
16 ES: p. 113.
17 Sewell, *Selected Poems*, p. 117. Trans. Colm Breathnach.

that they were based on one person's need of another? Sometimes, the other person wanted something from you, something that wasn't even yours to give in the first place. And in a sense it was this enemy, the hidden or covert one, who was the worst of all. Once they got what they wanted from you, they abandoned you as quickly again and you were left all the poorer for it. Ó Ríordáin remained guarded in whom he let into his trust.

> *There is no light in the afternoon. I'm in bed all day. People playing ball, a dog howling. No one has friends. Where are my friends now? If you have friends, they are always sucking something out of you. They like your company. They like to listen to you giving descriptions of the city. They can tell you their troubles. You know about some subject that they like. They receive a physical or lustful pleasure from you. You can be sure that they are getting some sort of advantage from their dealings with you – always. As for yourself, as regards you as an individual, you don't really have any friends at all (outside of your mother) nor has anyone else. There is nothing as lonely as the human being in the end. People constantly disguise this reality from themselves – they talk of friendship and love, and let on that these are things which we (human beings) all get for free. If you don't have something to buy them with, however, you will no more get these things than the penniless man who tries to buy tobacco. A human being isn't fully human until he loses his health, his youth, his kindness, his wealth, i.e. until the beard is shaved off and you can see the white face as clear as day. Who will give the barefaced person friendship or love? There is no one, no friend nor anyone else, in this room tonight.*[18]

Maybe he was as well off. Friendship was not his vocation; devotion to your trade, your craft, the same as your father before you – this was your real business, your reason for being. The short poem 'Profanum Odi Vulgus', 'that I wrote in memory of my father because he was a shoemaker,' as Seán put it, elucidates this perspective better than most.[19] Every craft is a combination of friendship and hostility, solidarity and competition – it makes no difference whether it is cobbling or poetry:

---

18 D: 22 April 1949.

19 ES: p. 35.

Ní fada bhíonn duine ag cleachtadh gréasaíochta
Nuair thagann claochló ar a iompar,
Is labhrann sé feasta mar labhair leis na blianta
Gach bráthair a dhealbhaigh buatais.

Ní fada bhíonn duine ag cumadh filíochta
Go scarann le daoscar na céille,
Is gabhann sé go huaigneach mar gabhadh leis na cianta
Le tuairim is dínit na cléire.

A man is not long at the cobbling trade
When his bearing is transformed,
Henceforth he speaks as every brother
Who's shaped a boot has always spoken.

One's not long composing poetry
When he parts from the rabble of little sense,
And he takes the lonely path of the ages
With the mind and dignity of the clergy.[20]

And Ó Ríordáin is an accomplished craftsman by the time he notes the following in his diary at midnight on 21/22 July 1957:

> *I fell out with all of my friends and relatives. I never had any friend that I didn't have something against him. I'm too restricted and confrontational as a person. In order to tell the truth, I am the enemy. This is my calling: to be the enemy. I can't maintain a friendship or believe in one either. I have to always be picking and provoking until friendship changes and becomes hostility.*

Hostility and resentment were the reality of things. The other thing was just a syrupy pretence. Or at least this is what you told yourself later when you'd destroyed the friendship and you finally admitted the harsh truth to yourself. Yours had never been a friendship really; it was actually the

20 Trans. M. Ó hAodha.

opposite of friendship even if you'd tried to convince yourself otherwise all along. Here's an excerpt from the diary where he recounts how the scholar Seán Ó Tuama and he fell out after being friends for many years:

> *I met a man recently. He greeted me. He has no time for me whatsoever anymore. We're enemies now. I'm just something to be avoided in his eyes – someone whom one can talk to occasionally, but only in a very evasive way and only when it can't be avoided. We both understood this when we ran into one another and this was how we spoke to each other. It's not a bad basis for a conversation really. It must have been fated since the beginning of time that we'd be enemies. We started out as friends years ago. But the enmity soon revealed itself and, slowly but surely, it picked away at the friendship until there was nothing left but the bare bones of it. The friendship between us was always an unhealthy, uncharitable and tormented thing. Again and again it just made us angry with one another. It was a release for both of us when we admitted that we were no longer friends but enemies. That put an end to the tension. Our hostile relationship was easier and healthier. Our friendship was false and unhealthy, and vulnerable and uneasy, it was always very anxious and edgy.*[21]

It isn't so much who he's fallen out with or the circumstances around it so much as the understanding that this was an alien aspect that had impinged upon his mind and that needed to be driven away or expunged in order to be at peace with oneself once more. Not that Ó Ríordáin always felt relieved when such 'distractions' had been eliminated. Sometimes it was only a temporary respite as indicated in the two following snippets from the diary. They might be short paragraphs but they reveal more about the poet's mindset than one might assume on a cursory glance:

> *9 p.m. Concert in the Hall tonight. They're all gone to it. This is always the way, I've noticed. The Kellys all left with their husbands. Neilo [Donovan] went to it. Kitty Mahony went. Therefore, I become a writer. With God's will, I will become one.*[22]

21 'An fhírinne' ('*The truth*'): IT, 26 March 1969; D: 20 March 1969.
22 D: Sunday, 11 March 1951.

It might be a different Hall from City Hall in this instance but it is part of a continuous motif that runs through his work – with respect to those people who are 'outside' his realm – when he is trying to write. Just six months before he died, he wrote the following from his hospital bed:

> *My brother and a good many of his family are going on holidays next week, as they rarely go. A son and a daughter of his are already on holidays. My friend, Brother Brendan is going to be gone on a retreat. Seán Ó Coileáin and his family are going to Tralee for the week. Seán Ó Mórdha is already on holidays in Dunquin. My doctor, Hickey, is in France. It is then that you write poetry. There is nothing else left.*[23]

In a sense Ó Ríordáin viewed chat, friendships (outside of immediate family) and socialising as a waste of time and he became more entrenched in this view as soon as he realised that he was a person with a unique and unusual artistic talent. He'd always been keen to cut to the marrow of the truth and to expose it in as pure a form as possible, the marrow of his private and inner self. Even if the following example doesn't relate exactly to what we are discussing here, it is nevertheless revealing of his mindset, as early as 1942. 'I agree with the *Imitatio Christi* – talk is but the passing of time' (21 January 1942). And this was the approach Seán followed for the next twenty-five years. This was the mindset he had heading out to the office each morning in order to spend the day in small talk and dull bureaucratic exchanges. It wasn't easy but it was the sacrifice that had to be made. Only at night, when he came to write his diaries, did he weigh up the worth of his work as against the price he paid for it in terms of time and energy expended. A few random examples from the years 1956–8 are below, but one can find diary entries of a similar sentiment for many other phases of his working life:

> *I know one place in the world where the mind neither grows nor expands and that's in Cork City Hall. (6.40 p.m., 28 January 1956)*

23 Ó Mórdha (ed.), *Scríobh 3*, p. 31.

I wish to leave this (diary) account after me. An enemy of mine is [X] in City Hall. He has made every effort to harm me in any way he can. When he isn't playing games and trying to damage me behind the scenes, he is openly insulting me. But worse than all of this is the image of friendship that he cultivates towards me. He's an enemy that's very difficult to crush, because he is strong and sinister as well as malicious and unscrupulous. And he's completely blind to his own rottenness. It is difficult, but with the help of God I will get the better of him in the long term hopefully. (5.30 p.m., 30 January 1956)

I haven't written much since I started working in the office again. I'm exhausted. But I'm happier in my own mind. What's to be done? If I could spend all day in the office writing, would this solve the problem? Devil knows what the best option is. (9 p.m., 30 October 1956)

(He'd been absent for five weeks preceding the diary entry above. It's clear that he enjoys the routine of the office, even if he has no particular fondness for the type of work it entails.)

As regards the writing, it is clear to me by now that I need to devote myself to this craft properly or give it up altogether. I've no other choice. Goodbye to English. Goodbye to Local Government. I'm not young. The hill I'm facing is a high one. What was I delaying for? (11.20 p.m., 5 November 1956)

I'll be going to work in the office in a while. I'm going to get up now. A day for scallops [i.e. windy]. The room is full of dictionaries and books. Our Father who art in Heaven … (8.10 a.m., 7 November 1956)

I have spent the day in the office. I'm exhausted. I must lie down now to recover. City life is coming between me and the lines of Irish poetry that are inscribed on my memory. (6.45 p.m., 7 November 1956)

Another morning as given to us by God. Who knows whether it came from God? I'm going to work in the office today after being out sick for three days. This work will affect my thinking – the reflections that were developing while I was here alone. Still, it's necessary to go and mix with other people – for the moment. (8.10 a.m., 16 November 1956)

I'll tell you – if you have any interest in it – how I spent the day. I got up at eight. I washed my face and ate my breakfast. I went to Cork. I reached the city at nine. I was just in time for mass in St Augustine's Church … I drank a cup of coffee in Wren's pub after mass and reached City Hall at half-past-nine. (Can I not write 9.30 instead?) I spent the morning speaking in that dog-like way with members of the motoring public, I went to the courthouse then (11 a.m.) as I was called as a witness on behalf of the office. Many very minor cases were tried. Most of the people being tried in court were from poor backgrounds – people from Knockpogue Avenue and similar places … I left the court at 12.30 p.m. and returned to the office. I went for dinner with Riobard Mac Góráin in the Imperial at 1.10 p.m. Back to the office at 2.30 … I won't bother recalling how I spent the rest of the day. I am very tired and it's not worth it. (7.15 p.m., 21 August 1957)

The lungs weren't good this morning and I stayed away from the office. I've changed already. I've been a ghost since morning. I'm nearly a writer. I've spent the time since this morning quite peacefully. I'm a different man today from the man who spent the day amongst his papers in the office. There is no limit to the human mind when it is given time, when it is given some freedom. The mind is limited and impeded when it spends the day surrounded by papers in the office. The mind is hindered when it's confined to an office all day. In fact, the office serves as a protective device for the human being because, if it wasn't for the office, the mind might prove so strong that it would actually kill the person in question. It's not easy to put up with your own mind. My mind proved to be great company today, however. And I was excellent company for her. But before long, she'll torment me and disturb me again and I'll be looking for barriers to protect myself against her. (1.30 p.m., 5 September 1957)

I won't return to the office for another week. It's difficult for someone to live alone. It's difficult to be amongst people. Whatever way you look it, it is something that one suffers. When I'm at home like this, I'm completely alone. I often do nothing. I don't write and I don't read. I have no protection against my own mind therefore. This is why offices, meetings, motion pictures, political parties,

> *churches, etc., are there – to come between us and the bluntness and severity of our own minds. Think of that poor person who leaves all forms of protection aside and addresses his own mind head-on! God help him! It isn't long before this loneliness without any form of security breaks him down and slashes away whatever drive or pride he has. It doesn't take long for the person who is reliant solely on his own company to be brought low. 'I'm the king of loneliness,' says Mícheál Ó Gaoithín, poet. I'm afraid that loneliness is king over me. (3.35 p.m., 22 September 1958)*

Three days later, on 25 September, he writes:

> *Here are two lines that came to me a while ago but their comrades have yet to appear:*
>
> *Is deacair bheith id aonar id aonar*
> *Tá an ghairm ró-ard, róchúng …*
>
> It is difficult to be all alone, all alone
> the calling is too lofty, and too narrow …[24]

In fact, it would be a decade later before those accompanying or 'comrade' lines arrived and the completed poem was published as 'Tionlacan na nÓinseach' ('*The Fool's Accompaniment*') in *Comhar*, December 1968. But the die was cast already it seems, and the poet increasingly withdrew into himself. And yet, despite what Ó Ríordáin said about his own company, friendship and City Hall, it was at work that Ó Ríordáin got to know two of the people he'd remain most fond of for the rest of his life: Séamus Ó Coigligh and Cáit Ní Fhoghlú. Needless to say, in the case of Miss Ní Fhoghlú (Kay Foley), it went deeper than just friendship. Indeed, such was his affection for her that she was the 'C' he dedicated his haunting collection *Eireaball Spideoige* to when it was first published in 1952.

The significance of this dedication should not be underestimated, bearing in mind how few people ever penetrated the poet's 'exterior' self or

---

24 Trans. M. Ó hAodha.

played any significant role in his private life. Not unless they came looking for sanctuary, barefoot and broken by life, as many of his fellow sufferers in the sanatorium did. And it was during those extended periods when he was confined to the sanatorium that the poet really came to understand the meaning of friendship and how lucky he was to have met those few good friends he had through work. Whether someone visited in person or sent a short letter, it always proved memorable for him. The following relates to a visit by Kay Foley to him in Heatherside and is extracted from a letter he wrote to Séamus Ó Coigligh dated 13–14 September 1949. The traces of his old and established pattern reveal themselves here – the poet's desire for a quick bout of sociability but then the equally swift retreat into the isolation of himself afterwards – but there is no denying his fondness for the colleagues in City Hall and the friends he mentions in this letter. In this instance, Ó Ríordáin temporarily flees from his own shadowy half-light, and basks in the refracted light that the person he loves most in the world emits:

> *When I returned to the room, who was there before me in the flesh but K[ay] F[oley]? I got a real fright. The atmosphere of the room fell asunder and I suddenly felt the freedom and initiative of City Hall around me. I'm not joking. The Body (which is really an absence of faith in the form of a physical body – with respect to the mind) dissipated there and then. I hate the bareness of the body. … But the Spirit still burns bravely in City Hall. What I mean by C.H. is K.F, you, Con Prior, Bill Daly and Miss Hanrahan. As regards K.F., as you know she walks like a form of poetry. I don't think she has ever taken a prose step in her life. As for you, when I think of you, and you travelling between the languages and the way that you never get mentally tired, I think that I'd actually die if it wasn't you who was there. As if at a football match, that thought of Con Prior's. When Bill Daly says 'yes' or 'no' you feel as if he has already amassed the knowledge of the entire world and curiosity has ended forever. There is a rural friendship to be found there also. As for Miss H., she sees things beyond herself. Her mind is full of bridges and oats and small country churches and Conradh na Gaeilge people and they all safely saved away within Grianán-like phraseology [An Grianán was the headquarters of Conradh na Gaeilge (the Gaelic League) in Cork at this time] – it's like she has a small, powerful motor inside her, God bless her.*

City Hall was more than one place, depending on what vantage point you viewed it from and whether yours was a despondent or a joyful perspective. Certainly, as viewed from the literary perspective, and through Ó Ríordáin's eyes, one would be forgiven for considering it a dour and sterile place. But then, as evidenced in some of the diary entries, there were other more positive aspects to the poet's workplace as well. Undoubtedly, however – setting certain individuals and Ó Ríordáin's friendship with them aside – he found the actual work in the tax office humdrum and tedious at the best of times. Seán was subservient to the system or 'sold to the foreign tyrant' as he put it himself, even if he had a small circle of friends there, and even if some of them were Irish-speakers to boot. At heart, the bureaucratic mindset that he implemented every day at work was an alien or Anglophone one, as Ó Ríordáin saw it, one that had been introduced under the previous colonial era, a mindset that he felt it necessary to subvert in his own writing in order to try and draw upon the half-buried Gaelic tradition that was his. And, needless to say, there were others working there whom he didn't trust, people who may even have pretended to be his friends from time to time. The likes of X, as mentioned in his diary on 30 January 1956. One of the main reasons why Seán couldn't stand this person, even if this isn't mentioned in the diary excerpt is that he was very hostile to anything that related to the Irish language and was quite open as regards his denigration of those who spoke the language. Additionally, he was someone who liked to exercise power over others, according to Seán; at one stage Ó Ríordáin even went so far as to defend the institution that was City Hall itself against X in his diary, which is no small irony, given what the poet himself said about the place on occasion:

> *He's not your average person [X]. He's a dour and destructive type. Forever bullying other people. As far as he's concerned, the City Manager is a tyrant who thinks of nothing else but power. The officers in the Hall all lack manliness and intelligence. They're all just nothing types with this false air of dignity about them, this air that he refers to as the 'build-up'. X himself is an awful and ignorant tyrant if he could get away with it. He's just a nothing who's full of 'build-up' himself. I never met anyone in my life as lacking in generosity as*

> *him. And as for subterfuge and political games behind the scenes, he's an absolute master of that ...*[25]

Ironically, Ó Ríordáin himself was far from generous about the denizens of City Hall in the brief biographical note he provided for Seán Ó Tuama's seminal collection of modern Irish-language poetry, *Nuabhéarsaíocht,* when it appeared in 1950. There is little difference between T. S. Eliot's 'the hollow men, the stuffed men' and the 'build-up' of X in the Corporation; the same empty posturing underscore both. No doubt, Ó Ríordáin also had another analogy in mind with the term 'hollow men', given that there was little difference between the sound of the words 'Hall men' and 'hollow men' in the English of that part of Cork city, a form of English that Ó Ríordáin hated with a passion. The poet himself applied the apostrophes in the excerpt below by all accounts:

> *After school in North Monastery in Cork, he got a job in the City Hall where you find all 'the "hollow men, the stuffed men" going around, papers in their hands.'*

It is the daily 'small death' that was the routine of the office all over again – and you wouldn't have minded only that Seán was in the same boat as all the 'hollow men' himself. The daily turn of the bureaucratic machine. The circulars, all of which sounded equally listless and dull – the likes of 'Circular No. MT 329' – that arrived to City Hall from the Department of Local Government when Seán was considering a return to work after being out (according to his own calculations anyway) for three years. This particular circular required urgent information as relating to American cars (imports) that came under the aegis of the Corporation, a circular dated 24 August 1944. It isn't the date of the circular that is significant but rather the bureaucratic mindset that underlies it, the same mindset that underscores the entire system.

> *A Chara,*
>
> *I am directed by the Minister for Local Government and Public Health to*

25 D: 7 January 1948.

request you to be good enough to furnish on the enclosed forms a return of the numbers of mechanically propelled vehicles of American make (a) registered with your authority and (b) under current licence with your authority.

Particulars are required of the number of vehicles of the various American makes in the Private, Commercial, and Agricultural categories and lists of the American makes are set out on the 'Private' and 'Commercial' return forms enclosed. (If there are any vehicles of American makes not enumerated on the enclosed forms the names of the makes and the number of vehicles should be added to those shown.)

A spare set of forms is enclosed to enable you to retain a copy of the return for your information.

This information is required urgently, and I am to request you to complete the enclosed forms and return them to this Department as soon as possible.

The necessary information was duly furnished as soon as the sick man returned to work. One almost senses a sigh of relief in the City Manager's response to this request; perhaps he was struggling to find a project that would keep Seán busy on this, his latest return to work. One way or another, this is the task that Ó Ríordáin, budding poet, was engaged in for one week of his life.

15th September, 1944

A Chara,

I beg to acknowledge receipt of your letter of the 24th ultimo, asking for a return of the numbers of mechanically propelled vehicles of American make registered at the Cork County Borough Motor Taxation Office.

In reply, I desire to say that Mr. Sean Riordan will be employed in the Motor Taxation Office, preparing this return, for one week. Mr. Riordan has now resumed duty in the Motor Taxation Office to which he was attached when he became ill.

On completion of the return, an effort will be made to find other employment for Mr. Riordan.

Mise le meas,

Bainisteoir agus Cléireach na Cathrach

It is unsurprising that Ó Ríordáin stopped keeping a diary at this point, and for quite a while afterwards, in view of the regulatory mindset that he was now dealing with, day in and day out. Neither should we be too surprised by the somewhat cynical way he spoke in the biographical note he wrote relating to his education and early working life. From now on, he was a cog in the wheels of the system and had to abide by its rules and regulations and the system of pretence or hypocrisy that he personally hated. Not unnaturally, this led to a tension within himself as manifested in his everyday dealings before God and his fellow man. The regulatory culture there meant that it was necessary for him to give evidence every now and then in the local circuit court, where prosecutions were taken against people who hadn't abided by the motor-tax laws. In the same way, he was obliged to help the Guards when they came around making their enquiries beforehand. Ó Ríordáin also spent his days checking and recording the weight of the transport lorries while sitting or standing next to the counter and making sure that the relevant forms were filled out correctly and that the people filling out the forms were honest and fit to work as drivers. Entrenched within this local bureaucracy was how he passed his days now, even if, deep down, he knew that he wasn't really suited to this type of work and had very little in common with this, the bureaucratic class, the purveyors of paperwork and officialdom.

This was a type of work that had an eternal or unending nature about it, a bureaucratic haze that was only made worse for the person who didn't really believe in it. And, needless to say, it was rare for this form of timelessness to crystallize itself in the form of a poem, unlike the eternity of loneliness of his sickroom at home. Interestingly, it is in the occasional early English-language poem of his that we see Ó Ríordáin most at ease with his workplace and coming to an acceptance of the rhythms of his working life and the institutional life of the office. Amongst the first of these poems (overleaf) is one where the sense of civilization and order that the institutional life brings with it finds celebration.

Bill Daly and Jim Turnbull are people who know their place in the institutional scheme of things and understand the mindset that accompanies the system. They are at one with themselves. Turnbull had a careful and measured manner and the most frequent phrase that Ó Ríordáin associated with him was 'it's not done old chap'. Turnbull was a natural speaker of received English, a person who spoke with the authority of someone who'd been formed in the long-established British tradition and was comfortable in his own skin. In a sense, the contrast couldn't have been greater between the likes of Turnbull and Ó Ríordáin – the latter was a man who found himself between cultures and social strata and not entirely sure whether he belonged to one tradition or another. Privately, Ó Ríordáin acknowledged the assurance and confidence that one associated with the likes of Turnbull, even if he did so half-mockingly. In the final analysis, Turnbull and his like were of a type whose world view and manner complemented one another and fitted neatly within the parameters of the language that defined them.

It is restful to sit in an orderly room
Where the tongs seem to follow the thought of the mat,
And an ink bottle strictly adheres to the rule
That the curve of a yawn be described round the room,
And the feeling of ease that Bill Daly can find
On the first of December fits over your mind,
Like a pure plucky seam on a plump nyloned leg,
Like a thought in a feathery verse put to bed,
Like a Turnbull answer that leaves you no doubt
That old Turnbull sorts all his dapper thoughts out.
It is restful to sit in an orderly room,
And to think 'twas a nun that said that to her class,
Without knowing what an orderly thing she was doing,
What an anapaest nun to be teaching a class!

The poem begins with the reptilian gestures of the nun. 'Then I remember the nun who said, "It is restful to sit in an orderly room", and this line as I composed myself, "What an anapaest nun to be teaching a class."'[26] Everything in the room begins to move in accordance with the rhythm: the arrangement of the room, the regular instructions of the nun, the

26 D: 10 April 1949.

strict mathematical patterns that reveal themselves in the black bottle or in the yawn, and the stitching of the stockings, the thought that is at peace with itself within the form of the poem, the same peace of mind and assuredness one associates with Bill Daly and the English-language tradition of Turnbull – everything is arranged correctly and is in its correct order. When would the poet's life ever approach a similar sense of order or what could Ó Ríordáin, the poet, build upon within the broken Gaelic tradition that would approximate to that which the likes of Turnbull had inherited? Was what remained of Gaelic tradition adequately developed already or could the remnants of the Irish-language be stretched and expanded further or in a new way?

In the excerpt below, Ó Ríordáin was exploring the difference between the two traditions and world views that he saw around him in the Ireland of the 1940s and the enormous differences that delineated them. The British or Anglo-Irish tradition as exemplified within Turnbull's ordered and measured speech and use of language is a cultural attribute that Ó Ríordáin always felt was lacking in his own mindset or perspective on the world:

> *A country is left bereft once she loses all her institutions – the misery of development, the misery of belief, the misery of unbelief. I never noticed this miserable mindset in Turnbull at all. 'I sort out my mind biannually old man.' It had a tradition behind it. Professor Corkery is right ... This sense of the bereft is the biggest flaw in modern Irish-language literature. Despite how good Máirtín Ó Cadhain is I couldn't help thinking of him in relation to this. This sense of richness, this formulism, this civilization, the nobility was all in Ireland once when the language was healthy, it seems.*[27]

The system that was gone had encompassed formulism and order and wasn't dependent on the artist's ability to harness it and shape their own emotions to it as based solely on instinct. And, from an artistic viewpoint, it was easier and better if the cultural mindset of the majority of the people corresponded to the aesthetic reach and creativity of the artist. It

27 D: 11 April 1949.

was healthier this way. Otherwise, one stood out or was deemed odd as the aesthetic order was ruptured: 'It's not done old chap.' And, on those few occasions when the ordered pattern was breached, as when Turnbull himself was inserted into the poem 'Malairt' ('*Switch*'), for example, it was necessary that Ó Ríordáin justify this exception to the normal scheme of things; an exception similar to this was the only way to circumvent the rule and the ordered pattern of tradition. Because it was the poem, rather than the subject, that made both world views and traditions correspond with one another and made them whole – even if only for a while. And the poet didn't mind going partway along this road of exception or mixed tradition on occasion if it ensured some company or human interaction. Rarely did each of these traditions or mindsets work in tandem as well as they did in this poem and in the one that follows. 'On seeing Artie Mannix's knees wobble mechanically in the presence of Mr. O'Brien' is the title of this second piece. In the same way that Bill Daly and Turnbull belonged to City Hall, so too did Niall O'Brien or 'Mr O'Brien' as he was referred to at work. He filled in for Seán sometimes when the poet wasn't well and was one of Seán's best friends. Artie Mannix worked with the Eagle Printing Company and called into City Hall regularly to pick up new orders. Mannix functions as the 'exception' or the 'odd one out' in the following poem while the observer (or poet) is apparently a regular or established part of the bureaucracy or system.

And slowly through the crowded street
Of faces looked at and forgot,
With thoughtful compromising feet
We both unscrewed ourselves and caught

A glimpse of Arty Mannix's frame,
As with pants-wrinkling trembles slow
A human egg-beater he came,
Knee-wobbling past the G.P.O.

And then we laughed at fervent length,
De-selved ourselves in rural roar,

Packed into it each ounce of strength
In vast abandon like a whore.

We yelled our love incontinent
For all things strange, fantastic, odd,
The crooked things of accident,
The fumbles of our funny God.

Here it is the city that is in the ascendant and the poet is a willing participant in the urban environment. In this instance, the poet is engaged in the act of 'de-selving'. The term 'de-selving' is one that reappears in the introduction to his seminal collection *Eireaball Spideoige*. Ó Ríordáin borrowed the term from the Welsh poet Hopkins and subsequently applied it to one of the major difficulties that confronted him in all of his poetic endeavours. Ó Ríordáin's act of 'de-selving' might be different in this English-language effort as compared to his Irish-language poetry, but it is no less significant for this. In the poem, the poet links his will with that of the crowd and has fun at the expense of the peculiar individual who has found himself ensnared within the tangle of regulated behaviour or decorum. Before long, however, Ó Ríordáin himself found it necessary to do the opposite of this and abandon the will of the crowd so as to align himself with the marginal man, the peripheral man who was made fun of – in essence, the man who is the same as him. Ironically, you couldn't have got a more fitting example of the 'awkward' individual who embodies the memorable phrase 'the fumbles of our funny God' than Ó Ríordáin himself. The significance of Hopkins' observation on human nature is very clear to him in this instance: the necessity to maintain the search for self-expression and the elucidation of the inner man when the temptation is to remain peripheral by hiding oneself away amongst one's neighbours and friends – such as is described in the following from Hopkins in 'As Kingfishers' Catch Fire':

Each mortal thing does one thing and the same:
Deals out that being indoors each one dwells
Selves – goes itself; *myself* it speaks and spells
Crying *What I do is me: for that I came.*

The cruel irony is that when a similar narrative became part of Ó Ríordáin's life – as it inevitably did – there would be nothing joyful or humorous about it. That said, there were other days again when the realm of humour was the sole avenue to which Ó Ríordáin could assign such sentiments. It often seemed easier and more appropriate to cleave to the general consensus of 'otherness' or singularity and go with the flow, a fact that the poet recognised increasingly over time and particularly towards the end of his life when it was too late to do anything about it. Life itself dictated that Ó Ríordáin pursue the indistinct and arduous path, the one that was apparently without definite destination, the one that necessitated him turning his back on whatever happiness life promised him in anticipation of something else, something that he could never fully understand. Worse still, he could never be fully sure that he'd made the right decision in adopting the solitary existence. In a diary entry for 1973 we find him thinking back to a day nearly thirty years earlier when they had buried Niall O'Brien, a friend of Seán's who'd died young, of heart disease, in 1947. Remembering those days long gone, Ó Ríordáin is haunted by all the people who have already walked the eternal path, and the years that have passed and are gone forever. The poet is haunted by who and what has gone before – he is haunted by himself:

> *Niall Ó Briain came into my mind just now. He died in 1947. He would be sixty years old by now … I remember the day that I was told he was dead. I wept … I remember the afternoon of the funeral and the brightness of the sky. This part of my life is long dead. There's more of me dead than there is alive. The self of that time is as dead and gone as Niall is … Is that world, those events, are they all lost completely? Something sickens me in relation to it. Is it that I didn't experience my youth properly – that I went through life without experiencing it at all? I was waiting for the right thing to happen, the big thing, waiting for it as it was already happening.*[28]

The phrase 'Heavier the interval than the consummation', from Eliot's 'Murder in the Cathedral', was one that disturbed Ó Ríordáin the first

28 D: 3 a.m., 11 March 1973.

time he came across it, on 22 February 1951. Every day that passed in which he didn't make poetry, or even one small or simple aspect of it, was a failure in the poet's eyes. Or, at least, these are the sort of days that he left us descriptions of in his diaries at any rate. If it wasn't for his diary writing, time was eternal and interminable to him. One aspect or turn of the day, just one thing, and the diary entry noting the date and the time was as a protective barrier between you and the moment that follows it. What lies on the other side of that invisible divide doesn't bear thinking about. There are few other resources within your gift to challenge the void when one is writing in the dead of night; you know only too well what is waiting and watching you from the other side of this particular darkness. And one inevitable consequence of this solitary struggle, even if it wasn't the most pleasant, was that one turned in more upon oneself and the 'interior' life became more expansive.

Even if Ó Ríordáin is in the process of leaving the youthful and unruly life of the city streets behind at this juncture, there is still some small part of him left on those streets – not that he always finds it easy to admit this to himself. And, not unnaturally, the poet sometimes cut loose and made for the city for a drinking session, a bit of craic, and the company of others, even if TB was already ravaging his body. And whatever place we assign to those few (aforementioned) English-language poems of his in Ó Ríordáin's overall oeuvre, it is difficult not to forgive him the fleeting moments of happiness that they evidently brought him. It wouldn't be long before he'd abandon this, the English-language side of his creative sensibility completely, never to return. These poems are just a temporary stopover in his development as a writer, therefore, a fleeting visit to another place, a place often deemed more sophisticated or urbane in the Ireland that formed him as a writer.

This is not to say that the urban world of the city doesn't have its place in his Irish-language poems also; they are just one element of the author's sensibility, however, and by no means the most central. In 'Teitheadh' ('*Flight*') for example, the streets function to reflect the turmoil or disorder of the poet's mind as the outer and inner worlds mirror one another – the 'cith ar leacaibh' ('*rain that showers the pavement*') and the 'smaointe ag cith ar m'anam' ('*the images that shower my soul*').[29] It is the inner world of the mind that is paramount and the external environment is just its reflection or outward manifestation. The same holds for the poem 'Malairt' ('*Switch*'), a poem which has City Hall as its setting and its place of composition.[30] The image of the person and the horse exchanging natures is the main motif here; the poem's setting is of little real consequence in this instance. In fact, if it hadn't been for the fact that Ó Ríordáin supplemented the poem with an unpublished essay as part-preparation for a radio talk, the poem's setting wouldn't concern us at all really: '… a poem I wrote quickly in the office in Cork when Turnbull showed me a horse and he spoke exactly as cited in the poem "Malairt".' This is the same Turnbull 'persona' as before and yet it isn't. In this instance, Turnbull abandons his normally staid position and status and is transformed; he becomes an element in the 'sensibility' of the horse; he becomes the horse and merges apparently seamlessly into the mysterious world of poetry unknown to himself; his transformation is analogous to that of the child described in the introduction to *Eireaball Spideoige* – even if such moments of transformation were a very rare occurrence in City Hall!

Ó Ríordáin was retreating into himself at this juncture, partly as necessitated by the nature of his illness and the societal strictures of the time with respect to TB. Back to that small room that faced out onto the road from a height and was set at an incline above the river; this was the sum of his world from now on, the river and the road, and they filled his poetry with their voices, each voice with its own special weight and significance. The constant echo of footsteps echoing over and back along the road, carrying with them the vertigo and the dizziness of the poet's mind, disoriented and wandering across the night; the road that endlessly attracted him and rejected him in equal measure.[31] All the evenings when the shouts and messing of the lads down below him on the road came between him and the page. The poet struggling with the mood and the moment that was a new poem so that, in the end, the struggle and the

29 ES: pp. 106–7.

30 ES: p. 63.

31 ES: pp. 97 and 46.

success or the failure generated something new; the absence of the poem was the poem itself.[32]

If the road below his house signifies the dazed struggle and confusion of the creative act, the river is symbolic of something else. Ironically, the image of the river has more of a sense of permanency and rootedness about it than does the road in Ó Ríordáin's poetry. The poet listens to her growl on stormy nights as she tumbles noisily over the weir below; either that or he follows her on her prayerful path and when she sings her 'water-bareness' and celebrates her watery nature, a nature that is unchanging and true to itself – unlike the uncomfortable and tormented soul that writes of her, a person who is never fully at one with himself or the world around him. [33] On another occasion, he'll describe the river as sauntering by, refined and pompous almost, when his mood is most in tune with hers, her river-nature linking the unbroken nature of the poet's youth with the life he has now, the disembodied existence of the city where he is far away from his people, from his roots – from himself. [34] Because Ó Ríordáin was born close to a river, as he mentioned a number of times in his diaries over the years (e.g., 27 July 1958), for the poet it's the river that still holds all of his childhood memories and the beauty of the world that once was – a world the voices of which survive solely in his memory. It is amongst these voices that fate dictated he, the poet, carry his burden in this life and it is amongst them too that he reveals himself and what is left of them all in the communal memory. There was a tactile shape and reality to these memories in the shape of the road, the river and the long-lost speech carried in the voices of the past. It was real, even if the poetry, like all writing, had an element of performance or re-imagining about it. And Ó Ríordáin was always tormented by doubt about the poetry. How much of it was a pretence and an attempt to recreate something that had never really existed in the first place, and how much of it was a reflection of the real – of the truth? The poet or artist was by nature searching and full of doubt, and none more so than Ó Ríordáin. And the probing and

32 ES: p. 41.
33 ES: p. 68; ES: pp. 38 and 47.
34 ES, p. 70.

criticisms of his poetry by certain other writers and critics added to his self-doubt even if it also affirmed him and made him more dogged about his writing and more determined to persevere. Certainly, the hostility or negativity that he met with from certain critics would shake Ó Ríordáin badly in the coming years, but he'd gone through too much already in the isolation of his solitary calling to be deflected from his chosen path. Whatever flaws were in his work would actually prove his strength in the long-run because they'd drive him on to demonstrate that he was a writer – to prove his status as a true artist. He'd suffered too much in his quest for the truth of his art. He wouldn't be silenced. He would give voice to the voiceless. He would pay an enormous price for his art but he would write what needed to be written and say what needed to be said.

4

In the Valley of Shadows

Like all poets, Ó Ríordáin drew on the subject matter of the life he saw around him and made art of it, when he could. Unsurprisingly, much of his work explored illness in all its manifestations and effects. He went into a sanatorium for the first time ever on 1 April 1938. There was no small irony in the date itself, April Fool's Day, and Ó Ríordáin wasn't beneath marking this day in the diaries. He'd made a fool of himself in more ways than one and would remain the 'outsider' or fool to a large degree for the rest of his life. Heatherside (or Leitir Fraoigh as he referred to it, when using the Irish name) was the small hospital near Doneraile to which he was sent. Back then, even relatives of the sick person wouldn't dare to put the word 'sanatorium' in the address on a letter to one of the patients there. Tuberculosis was a taboo disease, one that had strict and unspoken laws associated with it. And because he'd contracted the disease as a young man, Seán was assigned to the status of leper and understood this clearly from the first day, the same as his fellow patients in the sanatorium. He now belonged to a hidden group that had a stricter set of unspoken rules than any religious order. We have the poet's own word for one of these *rites de passage* in an article entitled 'Aicme Íseal' (lit: '*Low Class*'): 'I remember the first morning I woke in the Sanatorium. Another patient walked into the room and greeted us as follows: "Good morning, my tubercular friends."'[1] Ó Ríordáin had been duly stamped with the mark that he would faithfully carry for the rest of his life, whether he liked it or not. It wasn't always the physical suffering that defined the disease in question that was the worst aspect either, as Ó Ríordáin explained in the same essay:

1 IT, 13 February 1971.

> *To be a TB patient at that time was to be a leper. Visitors refused to take a cigarette from you. You weren't put into an institution to be cured but rather to protect the public from you.*
>
> *There was no mention of streptomycin that time. It was all* Kyrie Eleison.[2] *You'd see a healthy, young girl, a fine-looking bed-mate one day and three weeks later, she'd be nothing but the bare bones – eaten away by the* bacilli. *She'd be as thin as a wisp of straw …*
>
> *The life of the healthy person was completely different – i.e. robust, alien, with a sense of permanence. His personality remained calm, robust, while we others faded away. Years after this, when I'd see healthy people, I'd think back to all those boys and girls who had TB, and the way they just wasted away before your eyes. Not only did we not have a penny to our name – most of us – our health gone and no chance of ever recovering, without any hope left for this world … but we were also ashamed of our lives that we'd got such a disease. You hid yourself away as did your family, in case they'd (i.e. the family) be driven out of the locality or in case no one would marry your sisters.*

There might have been an element of exaggeration in this, but only just. Fate had dealt Ó Ríordáin his hand and one needed to know the contours of one's appointed place so as to be disabused of any notions from the beginning. Whatever about the suffering of the body, Ó Ríordáin would find plenty of support and advice on the spiritual front while in the sanatorium. When streptomycin was unavailable to him, he'd have to rely solely on the *Kyrie Eleison* instead: his condition as the will of God, in accordance with the common understanding of this at the time as explained by His representatives on earth. Ó Ríordáin must have accepted such understandings and explanations generally at the time, even if the cynicism and resentment of the older man comes through clearly in that later, influential essay of his: 'Aicme Íseal' ('*Low Class*'). By the time he came to write that essay, the hesitancy and trepidation of the younger man of thirty years earlier had long since disappeared. The poor boy from the

2 Streptomycin is an antibiotic used to treat a number of bacterial infections, including TB. *Kyrie Eleison*, on the other hand, is the name of an important prayer. The term translates as 'Lord, have mercy'.

rural background who had recently contracted the dreaded TB and who still accepted without question the meaning of existence and suffering as correctly elucidated by the clergy, if theirs was indeed the correct explanation, or if Ó Ríordáin had read correctly what they were saying – that innocent young man was long gone by the time he came to write the following diary excerpt, recalling an incident from the summer of 1938. Ó Ríordáin states that he was just twenty years old then, but he was a year out; he was actually twenty-one. But there is more than one person and one year in question really. In the following extract, the youthful hopes and dreams of a generation are trampled on shamefully, and in a way that the poet never forgot:

> *One fine summer's day we were all told to go down to the church straight away. This was the only church I was ever in, that I didn't hear people coughing in it [sic]. A priest was going to speak to us. A big jovial-looking Franciscan, who was tending towards fat, although he was still only a young man, appeared before us. He was already raising his belt because of the weight … He patted his big blessed stomach, may he be glorified further in heaven if he is now dead and gone. Then he spoke. 'People of God,' he said, 'yours is a fine community of young people that I see before me today.' (It was mainly young people who got TB that time. Former soldiers in the British Army were the older people who caught it and they'd have to steal the spits of the younger patients so as to keep getting their pensions from the army.) 'The rude glow of health is reflected in your faces; unfortunately, however, this is not really the glow of health but the glow of disease instead, the glow of death. Because you have an incurable disease amongst you and there are very few of you here today who won't be buried beneath the graveyard clay within the next two years …' That was a nice sermon to be giving on a fine summer's day when you were just twenty years of age. But the human spirit is difficult to vanquish. That same church was actually a meeting place for young people who were courting – until two people were found together loving one another or sinning in the confession box. They got the road and were sent home. There was a ban on mixed visits to the church after that.*

It is hardly necessary to say that Ó Ríordáin wasn't one of the two. And he'd learned his lesson only too well. The many efforts he made in his poetry to rid himself of lustful thoughts or the problem of 'sin' is evidence enough.

That young Franciscan's sermon in the church that summer's evening was poor enough fare from a spiritual perspective, especially for a young man to whom life had already dealt a harsh hand, and who was just setting out on his career as a writer to boot. Where else could he turn his face to try and find refuge but in the solitude of the blank page? He'd no control over this horrible disease, but maybe he could regulate and shape the word instead. And inevitably, the bleak loneliness of his station would leave its imprint on his work. It was as if he'd been assigned an existence that was bereft of the love of God or of human love. Was there a companionship that didn't frustrate the search for the spiritual way? Where could he source the joy and tranquillity that one associated with being fully human? How could he flourish in the artistic sense at all in a world so hopeless or filled with despair? Experience was all; everything else was false and a lie, even if he had only his own limited experience of the world upon which to base his art. And what had he really anyway in terms of subject matter or life experience, penned in now as he was in the sanatorium, surrounded by corpses in regular prayer and the fear and hostility of the public to the TB sufferer beyond the institution's walls? A young man ever-present to the reality of his own disease – his pollution. The greatest surprise of all is that Ó Ríordáin didn't lose hope completely and give up. Years later, when recalling her criticism of the flaws she'd found in some of the poems from the collection *Eireaball Spideoige*, Máire Mhac an tSaoi observed that the misgivings or qualms expressed by Ó Ríordáin in some of his more personal poems were no more than 'the regular scruples of conscience of the normal young Catholic' of his generation.[3] What surprised Mhac an tSaoi more than anything was 'that a poetry so promising could emerge from a terrain that was so bleak'.[4] However bleak the terrain of Ó Ríordáin's artistic endeavours, however ostensibly foolish the task – writing in a language that he had only half brought with him and that he was attempting to

3 *Feasta,* March 1953.

4 *Scríobh 1*, p. 112.

reclaim – he had undertaken it to the best of his ability. The fool might speak but at least he would speak in his own voice. If the entire project was an exercise in foolishness, at least he would be professional about it.

An important step towards such professionalism, ironically enough, was Ó Ríordáin's first stint in the sanatorium. 'I think the degree of TB was more useful to me than the BA degree', he said himself towards the end of his life.[5] Not that such a thought would have been much comfort to him in 1938, if it had occurred to him then at all. However long Ó Ríordáin spent recuperating on this occasion, we know that he was discharged from the sanatorium sometime in 1938, because we find him berating himself for going a bit crazy, particularly on the money side of things after he'd come out. He was the main provider financially for his mother at the time, as you'd expect, given that he was the eldest of three children, but he'd let her down now instead of supporting her and the others. Ó Ríordáin of the scruples blamed himself entirely for the situation:

> *I didn't look after my health in time. I left the sanatorium in 1938, before I should have left, by rights. Then I didn't look after myself properly after I returned home. The drinking killed me and I used up whatever little money I had. We're dependent now.*[6]

By the time he wrote this, the Corporation had cut back completely on his sick pay given that he'd been absent for work for over a year, and he hadn't a penny coming in. It looks as if he went back west to Ballingeary drinking at one point and blew whatever small bit of money he had left, as the diary entry for 11 March 1973 says that he spent his holidays back there with the Ó Mainnín's that year. (This family's son would later be appointed Cardinal of Los Angeles in 1973, an appointment that decades later brought back many half-forgotten memories of that summer.)

He was back in the sanatorium again the following year, 1939. Nothing of his diary for this year survives, although Ó Ríordáin later mentions

5 *Scríobh 3*, p. 169.
6 D: 17 January 1940.

that he was keeping a daily account at that time. In his diary entry for 3 September 1963, the poet refers to the fact that he was in the sanatorium when the Second World War broke out twenty-five years earlier.

From New Year's Day 1940, when we find him home again in Inniscarra, the TB already taking its toll on him both physically and mentally, his diaries revert to a regular or daily description of his life. The significant psychological transformation, a response to the deadly disease that he describes in his essay 'Teangacha Príobháideacha' (*'Private Languages'*), has already occurred and the institutionalised life of the sanatorium and the hospital has become one of the most significant aspects of his sensibility and indeed his life now, even if we know little or nothing of his literary endeavours at this juncture.

Ó Ríordáin suffered three major or prolonged bouts of illness in the years leading up to the publication of *Eireaball Spideoige*: 8 March 1938 to 31 May 1940, 9 September 1941 to 10 September 1944, and 5 May 1949 to 8 October 1951. In a sense, there is little to distinguish these three periods from one another because, as with many TB patients of the time, the months and years of serious illness all seemed to melt into one another so that they became lost years. We know, for example, that Ó Ríordáin was out of work continuously for a full three years in the period 9 September 1941 to 11 September 1944 as outlined previously, and for the next five years he was affected by the illness and absent from his clerical job at regular intervals – up until the end of May 1949. After this, we have quite an accurate account from the poet himself of how his illness impinged on his life and got steadily worse. He complained to the local government regarding the injustice he felt the Corporation had done to him. In a letter dated 18 May 1954, Ó Ríordáin wrote as follows:

> *I was granted sick leave from 5/5/49 to 1/10/50 and because I was being treated for pulmonary tuberculosis I was paid as follows:*
>
> *5/5/49 to 4/11/49, full pay*
>
> *5/11/49 to 4/5/50, three-quarters pay*
>
> *5/5/50 to 1/10/50, half pay*
>
> *I resumed duty on 2/10/50 but was taken ill again with pneumonia and pleurisy on 14/10/50. I received half pay until 28/10/50 but was on sick leave* without

> *pay from 28/10/50 to 8/10/51 (a period of 341 days). During that time I had no pay, no T.B. allowances, and no source of income whatever. Nevertheless, I survived and returned to work on 9/10/51 and I have continued to work in the Motor Taxation Department since then ...*

His diary-keeping was irregular, needless to say, and none of his letters from the sanatorium to people outside prior to the year 1949 have survived, letters that would have provided us with a better picture of his 'institutional' life then. The first references to him entering the sanatorium in his diary relates to the week beginning 5 July 1942:

> *I went to the doctor last Monday. I lost 5 pounds in weight during the past fortnight and he's sending me into the sanatorium. My weight now is nine stone two pounds, unless I've gained or lost some weight since. Since I got this disease, I was never as light – as far as I know, anyway.*[7]

> *This is the last Sunday that the Inniscarra people and I will be in one another's company for a long time. I don't think that the Inniscarra side is too worried about it and I don't feel too down in myself either. A windy showery day. There's a 'sports' taking place in Leemount and all the rabble are gone. That's an advantage. But I haven't any of my company around. That's another advantage, I suppose.*[8]

The account from which this excerpt is taken comes to a halt on 9 July 1942 and we don't hear from him again for a long time afterwards. When we do he is writing from Heatherside and it is in the form of a dozen lines or so of a letter as written on a torn piece of paper. Christmas is drawing near and he is a long way from either company or rabble – perhaps the two were one and the same thing in Ó Ríordáin's mind by then anyway. The poet addresses himself in the letter – given that he's the only person he can share this secret horror with:

---

7 D: 25 June 1942.

8 D: 5 July 1942.

15/12/42

> *Dear mind*
>
> *It is to you that I write the most indiscreet letter I've ever written in my life – myself writing to my mind. I wonder did anyone else ever think of this trick? I'm here in the '13-bedded ward' in Heatherside and the fading winter sun gently stroking my hair like an elderly grey-haired gentleman, an old man saying: 'I've seen the world young lad – be brave.'*

He was let home at Christmas, a few days after this, and we have another excerpt from him as written on New Year's Day. This short paragraph is one of two that he wrote during his life where he appears to discuss the nature of homosexual feelings. (The second is from 27 February 1976 where he denies that he ever had any such feelings himself, in as far as he can tell; the explanation that he gives for his musing on this subject is that he finds himself drawn to a religious brother.) This excerpt comes just after a piece where he described a bout of despair that he had eventually managed to get under control; the following appears all as one paragraph:

> *How come I felt like crying, and am just keeping it under control? Loneliness. And why the loneliness? I came home from Heatherside on the 18/12/42, having spent six months there. Plays and short stories and romance novels and poems have all been written on the subject of love – the love that happens between a man and a woman. But very little is written about the love that happens, that grows, that matures, between one man and another. Augustine understood this love, as did Francis Xavier; and they both understood the pain that is suffered when male lovers separate. And I understand it.*[9]

The diary account is incomplete from this point until September of the following year. On 15 September 1943 we find him still at home and complaining about his health problems. He was not long home, however, before he had to go back in again. Silence and a lack of commentary in the diary are indicative of periods when Ó Ríordáin was away in the

---

9 D: 31 December 1942.

sanatorium, as the poet himself explains the next time we meet him – on 11 July 1944. It's unlikely that he was in Heatherside for the entire time between September/October 1943 and when we next meet him in the diary. Six months or less at a time was the usual period spent in the sanatorium by TB patients at this juncture:

> *My first day at home. I came home yesterday ... My first full day. I couldn't write anything worthwhile while I was in Heatherside. Lack of privacy, lack of books, lack of freedom, lack of time. I am home again now and I have all of these at my disposal but my mind is still raw. I'm confident in myself, however.*[10]

Even if none of Ó Ríordáin's letters to his relatives or friends outside the sanatorium survives today, there is one that he received in Heatherside which is of much interest and is particularly poignant. This is a letter that was found amongst the poet's effects after his death, tucked inside an envelope marked 'litir mo mháthar' ('*my mother's letter*') in Seán's handwriting. The letter is dated 4 March 1944 and there's no doubt that this is the 'dirty, stained old letter' the poet refers to in his seminal poem 'Adhlacadh mo Mháthar' ('*My Mother's Burial*'). (Ó Ríordáin's mother died on 21 January 1945 and it was in June of that same year that he wrote this poem, by all accounts.) The contents of the letter are difficult to decipher in places today, but we can get the gist of it nonetheless, even if we can never really comprehend the extent to which it affected Seán, particularly as he grew older. A wing of the sanatorium in Heatherside had gone on fire shortly before this, an accident that the poet's mother had seen reported in the newspaper:

> *My dear Jackie,*
>
> *I am very disappointed and very troubled indeed at not hearing from you since the Fire there, I am thinking all sorts – I one time think you are ill or suffering from shock. I sent Pullover etc., tob[acco] and cig[arette]s last week and* [Irish] Presses *did you get them? I hope you are all right if you are not able to write would you get some one to write to me to ease my mind as you know this*

10 D: 11 July 1944.

> *old world is not a bed of roses, and not knowing how you are drives me nearly crazy. You know the house is so lonely now that sometimes I get so down and out. But things could be worse. I hope and trust you are all right … I am sending you pyjamas, a pants of one and jacket of another, they will fill a gap for you and I'll try to repair another pair of old ones. I am also sending you two [?] hankies you ought to have three or four in the suit case, also the* 'Comar' *which came to-day and as you don't trust me about the coupons I am also sending you those to send away. When writing next tell me do you get enough 'Butter, Tea and Sugar' if it would be any good to you I could send you some of each at any time. I wrote to you the day I saw the Fire on [sic] the* Exam[iner] *and you never answered – I hope you are all right. Everything here is just as usual …*

Small wonder that the thought of his mother and the heartrending tone of this letter brought tears to the poet's eyes on reading it again the same summer she died. The memories of those nights came flooding back to him, the pair of them in the room together, his mother trying her best to fend off the dark, the pair of them struggling against this awful sickness and the night terrors drawing in – battling death. *'I hope you are all right …'*

But we're not home from the sanatorium with Ó Ríordáin yet – there's still a way to go.

The other notable event relating to this bout of recuperation in Heatherside was that Ó Ríordáin saw his first ever poem published. (As it turns out, this poem, 'An Dall sa Studio' (*'The Blind Man in the Studio'*), wasn't actually the first of Ó Ríordáin's poems to see print but that's a discussion for the next chapter.) 'An Dall sa Studio' was published in the March 1944 edition of *Comhar*. 'This is a little poem that I composed about a patient who was in the same hospital ward as me – the bedroom as our only studio' was how the poet introduced the poem in *Comhar*, in an essay where he also discussed the genesis of the poem 'Malairt' (*'Switch'*). Ironically, Ó Ríordáin and this fellow TB patient were a long way from any artistic 'studio' when this poem first saw the light of day.

The most common sketches that Ó Ríordáin did during this time were 'head-shots' or profiles of people's faces, both real and imaginary, but this time the sketch is of a blind person whose fingers are caressing the air, his fingers stroking the dark as he tries to locate a chair to sit down on. Initially, this image puts Ó Ríordáin in mind of fingers stroking water or a musician caressing the strings of a musical instrument. But as suddenly again, the spell is broken and the only thing sitting opposite him is a sickly, broken-down and pathetic old man, who is suffering from blindness. A simple sketch wouldn't do justice to the figure sitting before him now. It is the fleeting image of the individual whose fingers sift the air, searching for that which it cannot see, that Ó Ríordáin seeks to recreate in this instance:

An Dall sa Studio

'Suigh síos agus déanfaidh mé pictiúir díot,'
Adúrtsa leis an dall,
'Tá cathaoir id aice ansin sa chúinne,'
D'iompaigh sé a cheann,
Is do shín amach an lámh sin oilte ar chuardach,
Gach méar ag snámh go mall
Mar mhéaranna ceoltóra ar a uirlis,
Is bhí an uirlis ann:
Do sheinn sé ar an aer táin nótaí ciúnais,
Goltraí bog na ndall,
Na snámhaithe critheaglacha gur thuirling
Ar bhruach na habhann –
An suíochán sin a luas-sa leis, sa chúinne,
Is do shuigh sé ann.
Siúd láithreach é ag cíoradh a chuid gruaige,
Mo réice dall![11]

The Blind Man in the Studio

'Sit down and I'll paint your portrait,'
I said to the blind man.
'There's a chair beside you in the corner.'

11 ES: p. 28.

He turned his head
and stretched out his hand long used to searching,
every finger swimming slowly
like the fingers of a musician on his instrument,
and the instrument was there:
he played a fistful of quiet notes on the air,
a slow air of the blind,
until the fearful swimmers
landed on the bank of the chair
where he sat down
and straight away began combing his hair,
my blind rake![12]

Quite a few examples of Ó Ríordáin's sketching survive, as do the many references in his diaries and letters to his perceived ability or lack of same. We know that sketching was a popular pastime of his while in the sanatorium. He mainly sketched imaginary faces and figures rather than real people, but at least he had plenty of subject material while in the sanatorium. Sometimes he'd compare these real-life sketches with those he sought from the other Creator. (Such comparisons weren't an entirely pointless exercise in Ó Ríordáin's eyes because he associated them with a fundamental problem as relating to his primary métier, poetry: how to evaluate the piece that was imbued with a sense of humanity with that which wasn't; the work that necessitated the living breeze of creation blew through it and assumed form – as against the forms of anti-creation that lurked menacingly in the wings awaiting their opportunity.) Sometimes, of course, the two forms of creativity came together and melded into one another. Such was the case with regard to the many sketches of de Valera that Ó Ríordáin did over the years. The image of de Valera's face had captured the poet's imagination ever since the first time he had seen him in the flesh, on the Grand Parade in Cork in 1933, and interestingly, we see de Valera's face ageing throughout the course of the diary, mirroring

12 Sewell, *Selected Poems*, p. 5. Trans. Peter Sirr.

the ageing of the man himself.[13] The artistic image that is humble and reflective of its master. It's a similar story with regard to an image he describes sketching in the sanatorium, except that the stress is more on the sketch than on the individual that is its subject in this instance:

> *Years ago I had worked out one particular face – straight out of my imagination – without any outside help. I was in a sanatorium at the time. One morning I was brought down from the top of the house, where I'd been imprisoned for a good while prior to that, and what did I see sitting right there in the chair in the Day Room but that very own sketch of mine in human form. I nearly died. I was livid with anger. The Other Man had infringed on my copyright and it was difficult to forgive Him. It was I who first made up that shadow-person in the chair.*[14]

The poet describes the same occasion or one similar to it, in a letter he wrote in English to Con Prior from Heatherside on 14 January 1950:

> *I saw a little gnome of a patient here the other day. He is about fifty and a lovely specimen. But there was a flaw somewhere. After a while I realised that he was a sketch that I drew years ago. The* Ens Entium *stole the sketch in defiance of the laws of copyright and the sketch was made flesh and dwelt amongst us.*[15] *The divine slipped up a bit and got the forehead wrong. That was the flaw.*

'I will remember him for his wonderful skill in pencil sketching, and how sorry I was years later to have lost or mislaid a sketch he made of me,' one of Ó Ríordáin's fellow patients in the sanatorium would write to me years later. (Jimmy Ronan was the man in question, a man whose name will crop up again shortly.)

Measuring time, sharing time, counting it down – this was a central aspect of Ó Ríordáin's life. In the sanatorium, the days and years melted into one another the same as the people in his sketches. The same dull lethargy that characterises the slow passage of time. The routine life of the

13 'De Valera', IT, 18 September 1975.

14 'Sceitseanna agus uachtaráin' (*'Sketches and Presidents'*), IT, 12 May 1973.

15 *Ens Entium* translates from the Latin as 'the being of beings', i.e. God.

non-patient appears very far away from these unfortunate TB sufferers, who have disappeared from the physical space that is 'normal life' so that it is as if they inhabit a separate realm of the imagination, one that appears almost non-human or far away.

The people Ó Ríordáin sketches now are his own people, the forgotten ones, the people whom the outside world has jettisoned or assigned to the dung heap of society and history. They are a community deemed weak or marginal; their illness has rendered them a stigmatised group in the eyes of others, a group whom the rest of society should avoid at all costs, in case they too become impure or damned, or disregarded and banished to the limbo world. As we see later, Ó Ríordáin would fight back against this ostracisation of the weak by the strong, the law of might and right, through the medium of his poetry. He would not forget what had happened and he would even the score with the establishment or the 'consensus' people when the time came – the nobodies, the big-shot sportspeople, the rich man, whoever was powerful and prepared to walk on others to maintain their status. His time would come – just not yet.

No doubt, the medical routine was becoming familiar to Ó Ríordáin at this stage. The initial indications and the warning from the doctor that he needed to go for treatment, the quick preparations at home, the bus into the city and then the train northwards as far as Buttevant, where the ambulance was waiting and ready to bring him the rest of the way. This was the normal pattern. If he was very sick and weak, as happened in 1939, he made the entire journey by car, even if it was a struggle to pay for it. The sudden flood of silence as one entered the hospital and the slog of that first day as he settled in and was introduced to his fellow patients and friends, both old and new. The latest news about the TB patients he'd met previously there – one old pal who had died and was being prepared for burial – others who were still alive but only just. Then, after this initial flurry, the world of monotonous and dreary routine would take over. How could one recuperate in a place where no one could really be cured, a place where the only constant was the murmur of prayers or the flurry that accompanied the rounds of the nurse each afternoon? Anything at all to puncture the tedium that was the endless passage of time, the eternity of the clock.

It is autumn 1949 and he has been in again for a month already, since 6 August. 'Death is the frost that obscures our lives':

> *How can one write anything in this grave? There's a radio on next to me here. Harry Smith is reading a book. Bernie Lucey and Denis O'Leary are playing draughts. Willie O'Sullivan is scratching himself. There's no life or movement here. There's neither the sovereignty of the mind nor God's sovereignty here. There are just people praying here. There is no joy anywhere. Sanatorium. People praying grimly together. The people here are broken, just as the monks in Mount Melleray were. Sometimes a fit of despair goes through me and I am terrified.*[16]

> *There's a man's next to me – Smith – and he's smoking a damned pipe. He's killing me. I'd love to grab a hold of that pipe of his and fling it out the window. My soul and my mind and my lungs are tormented by the stink of that pipe. Please appear among us Christ and spread your light. This morning, I understood that I have no connection with the people around me. I imagined that I wasn't present. I felt as if they were all about to surround me here as I lay stretched out dead in front of them.*[17]

One of the things that bothered Ó Ríordáin most in the sanatorium was the lack of privacy, which meant that he couldn't do any real writing there.[18] The individual and his primary concern as a writer was denied him by the culture of control and regulation that worked against him. Whenever he heard about others in later years who railed against this institutional culture – those independent individuals who'd been sent away and 'who never wanted to be part of the community; the person who was his own man' and who resisted being institutionalised – Ó Ríordáin always took their side. The injustice of it was always paramount in the poet's mind, this and the way the system insured that your bodily integrity, your privacy and indeed your very freedom were put into the hands of others:

---

16 D: 4 September 1949.
17 D: 9 September 1949.
18 D: 11 July 1944.

> *We are under the control of diseases and of death – they invade the sanctuary of our privacy and make us human the same as everyone else. No one has any privacy or independence. As I said, he was struck down on Friday morning and his privacy was immediately gone. He had to be brought in amongst strangers in the hospital. He's now paralysed. One of his arms is dead. His face is completely distorted. His privacy is in ashes. It is obvious that neither his face nor his body belong to him any more. The public laws of nature or of the body entered his house and told him that he didn't belong to himself any more and they reduced his privacy to smithereens.*[19]

Based on his own experiences, it was no surprise to find Ó Ríordáin expressing sentiments such as the following:

> *I want to escape into my own soul now and again. I'd like to be somewhere for a while where no one would see my face or these bright teeth of mine. Somewhere private. The only place you can get any privacy here is in the lavatory. When I remember sometimes how I'm an inmate who's imprisoned here I feel short of breath. And to top it all off, nothing ever happens here. The patient across from me was being given streptomycin until recently. Every evening at seven the nurse came into the room, needle in hand, and jammed the streptomycin into his arse. Jerry is the name of this patient. Another patient who's next to me said to me just now: 'Do you know what I'm missing now? The nurse's afternoon visit to jab Jerry in the arse.' It's true for him. It's the little things like that make the time go by for us here.*[20]

The world described here is the mundane world of the poem 'Siollabadh' ('*Syllabication*') except that in 'Siollabadh' the world has been startled or awed into life.[21] In the poem, too, it is the nurse's arrival that jump-starts the rhythms of life again amidst the grey tedium of the day. Her entrance into their world sees their room come to life once more, so that everything moves with the same rhythm. We feel the steady throb of all the pulses 'ag

19 D: 8 October 1968.

20 D: 19 September 1949.

21 ES: p. 111.

preabarnaigh go tomhaiste' (*beating rhythmically*) as the nurse places her fingers on them and as the murmuring of the Angelus spreads throughout the room; the nurse is about her business and it is as if 'the act of nursing prays through her' as Ó Ríordáin described it elsewhere with reference to the sound of her regular footsteps leaving the room.[22] All of these separate rhythms are borne along by the overarching rhythm that is the poem where they find peace. The world is accentuated until it forms the physical rhythm of sound and metre, all beating in unison, as if in celebration. In the end, it fades away and becomes one with the evening prayer as intoned by the patients. The world becomes rhythm, the world becomes a prayer, the world becomes one.

Siollabadh

Bhí banaltra in otharlann
I ngile an tráthnóna,
Is cuisleanna i leapachaibh
Ag preabarnaigh go tomhaiste,
Do sheas sí os gach leaba
Agus d'fhan sí seal ag comhaireamh
Is do bhreac sí síos an mheadaracht
Bhí ag siollabadh ina meoraibh,
Is do shiollaib sí go rithimeach
Fé dheireadh as an seomra,
Is d'fhág 'na diaidh mar chlaisceadal
Na cuisleanna ag comhaireamh;
Ansin do leath an tAngelus
Im-shiollabchrith ar bheolaibh,
Ach do tháinig éag ar Amenibh
Mar chogarnach sa tseomra:
Do leanadh leis an gcantaireacht
I mainistir na feola,

22 ES: p. 16.

Na cuisleanna mar mhanachaibh
Ag siollabadh na nónta.[23]

Syllabication

A nurse in a hospital
on a sunlit afternoon,
and pulses in sick-beds
beating to her measure,
she stood above each patient
in studied concentration,
jotting down the rhythm
that beat between her fingers,
then left the pulses beating,
and beat it from the room,
leaving behind a chorus
of pulses beating on:
then the Angelus sounded
on syllable-shaken lips
till round the room it faded
to a dying Amen;
but the chanting continued
in the abbey of the flesh,
the pulses like monks
reciting the syllables
of afternoon prayer.[24]

I have to admit that I can't hear the 'sound of the church bell' (*fuaim chloig an teampaill*) in this poem as literary critics such as O'Brien felt they heard it at the time, nor that this sound signals the end of the 'chorus of veins'

23 ES: p. 111.
24 Sewell, *Selected Poems*, p. 115. Trans. Seán Ó Coileáin, Seán Ó Mórdha, Frank Sewell and Robert Welch.

that is indicative of the 'brevity of life that is their fate' (i.e. the patients).[25] Instead, I hear it as this hospital room and its occupants being temporarily transformed and made distinctive, and it is this rare transformation that is celebrated in the moment. And if it wasn't for such rare moments, death would have already taken hold in that place, the same as the tyranny of the clock, the eternity of time. The parameters are simple – life/death or death/eternity – and yet occasionally they momentarily melt into one another so that it is difficult to distinguish them. The sanatorium is only one such place wherein Ó Ríordáin could have composed the poems that make up the collection *Línte Liombó*. There were others too, even if he may have felt the oppressive time weigh more heavily on him in the sanatorium than anywhere else.

There were the occasional other small bits of news that broke the tedium of the poet's days in the sanatorium, needless to say. It might be the arrival of a letter from Séamus Ó Coigligh, Clára Ní Annracháin or Con Prior, or the occasional visit from one of them. Even Corkery himself might pay him a visit every now and then. And they'd all have brought a bit of news for Ó Ríordáin. Other times, it might be a book of poetry that someone had sent in to him, or even a humorous anecdote or witty comment as made by one of the other patients that would lighten the mood and keep the poet going. Because Ó Ríordáin had two sides to his writing really, the blunt, sardonic (country) humour of the diaries and then the other – the poetic speech that was written for a different audience and was of a different type.

The two visits alluded to below may not correspond exactly chronologically speaking, but they give an indication of the differences in attitude and tone between them. In one, Corkery and some of his followers came to visit Ó Ríordáin:

> *Professor Ó Corcora, Miss Hanrahan, Eibhlín Ní Choitir and Mícheál Ó Cuill came to see me here on Saturday. I hadn't a word to say to them. Look, God, just finish me off.*

---

25 O'Brien, Frank, *Filiocht Ghaeilge na linne seo* (An Clóchomhar, Dublin, 1968), p. 306. The title translates as *Contemporary Irish Poetry.*

Me: *Will you go to the Oireachtas this year?*
Miss H.: *I don't know yet.*
The Professor: *Were you there last year?*
Me: *I was. I saw* The Last of Friday's King's Men *while I was there.*[26]
The Professor: *What did you think of it?*
Me: *There wasn't a lot in it.*
The Professor: *Rubbish. Molloy sent a copy of it to me. I told him that I'd never heard the word 'shillelah' in the mouth of any Irish person ever.*
Michael Coll: *Stage Irishman.*
The Professor: *In the years 1907, 1908, 1912, they wouldn't have been allowed to produce it.*[27]

The following extract is from a letter Ó Ríordáin sent to Con Prior in English, beginning 'Hades, Nov. 1949':

> *It is necessary to piss beautifully in these days of the B.B.C. I heard Terry de Valera broadcasting a talk on Chopin some time ago. I thought that he fashioned his sounds with care, and the whole thing gave me pleasure. Next day Dan Corkery and others were here. One of the others said that Terry Dev spoke with an Oxford accent, and that he was not a bit like the old dad. I said that I caught echoes of the dad. Dan said that the accent [was] not quite Oxford, that it was merely Holy Ghost Father. I felt some resentment when I thought of the slovenliness of current speech. Of course Dan is a dote and speaks like an angel and should be bathed morningly [sic] by perfumed virgins on their way to Solomon to be raped.*

The way of thinking revealed in the Irish-language letters he sent to Séamus Ó Coigligh is probably closer to the mindset of Ó Ríordáin's diaries and resonates more with the poet's inner thoughts and artistic development. Ó Coigligh was unusual in that he was on the 'inside' in terms of what Ó Ríordáin was trying to achieve poetically. He understood him better than almost anyone else, so the poet was only ever open and brutally honest with him. This letter was dated 13 September 1949:

---

26 The correct title of this play by M. J. Molloy is *The King of Friday's Men.*
27 D: 16 August 1949.

> *I'm not producing anything (poetry) at all these days. There are six of us in this room. One of them has a radio and the Light Programme is on from morning until night – 'The Wedding of Lily Marlene' and 'Clancy Lower the Boom'. Whenever the people in the room aren't talking they are praying. I despair completely sometimes and life is nothing but claustrophobia and the Bishop of Galway. There's one fellow here and he says the Holy Rosary eight times a day, the religious poems of Tadhg Gh. Uí Shúilleabháin written across his pus. A little light appears occasionally. Letters from yourselves. The book on Houseman's poetry that I got from you. That was the first book that I managed to read since I came here. There was a letter in* The Irish Times *recently describing the Galway debate about schools. The Bishop's speech was referred to as the 'Galway bay'. This was another light. How to read or write something? A number of patients were chatting in this room the other day. I suddenly realised that I wasn't alive at all, that I had no connection with them, but that I was looking at them from somewhere completely beyond this world. I was listening to someone talking about medical matters there about three weeks ago and I felt so tired that I fainted and fell on the floor … This place is much further away than the desolation of death. Here is where the bird fell that didn't believe in wings.*

Then there was Christmas, when the odd bout of drunkenness, humanity and pagan antics won out over the strictures of the Church, the Bishop of Galway and the oppressive atmosphere of the sanatorium, for one day at least. Here is an excerpt from another letter to Séamus Ó Coigligh, written on 29 December 1949:

> *I never had such a Christmas before. I gave a sermon against drink to the other patients here before Christmas and then when the afternoon of Christmas Day came, I was mad drunk. We all got out of bed that day. The younger nurses came into the room and they were as twisted as we were by the time they left. We were too drunk to have had anything to do with them. I never saw the likes of it ever before – women and men falling down drunk everywhere. Some of the lads here went over to where the women were on the other side of the River Boyne and there's no knowing what they got up to. As for myself, I was so drunk that I couldn't move and I was put back into bed. The tradition was fulfilled in all its fullness and Christ did not err when He came into this world. If you want*

> *to pass Christmas in a really traditional and full-blooded way, then go into a sanatorium. And while all this chaos was going on, the priest was anointing some poor person below us here.*

This was just one day of escape, needless to say, and it wasn't long before Ó Ríordáin was back in the grip of that society where the Church outside the walls was all-powerful and had a firm grip on his conscience within. If Ó Ríordáin could only have achieved some sort of equilibrium with himself and his inner 'self', then he would have been at peace with himself, one imagines. What follows is an excerpt from a letter he sent to Séamus on 9 February 1950, addressed from Heatherside as before:

> *As for the Bishop, I am watching what he is doing. A sanatorium was opened recently. The Bishop spoke. There is a great danger, he says, that the patients would be too comfortably off, more comfortable than the workers outside. Watch, watch, Séadna! I don't care about being comfortable but how despairing for someone seeking the Church to hear of a bishop being up to the likes of this? How is it that the Church didn't shine its wealth of intellectual richness into Browne's mind? ... Maybe this fool isn't a Catholic at all.*

Occasionally too, in letters sent to Con Prior, one can penetrate beneath the surface to where Ó Ríordáin reveals the true horror of what he felt, passing his days and years in the sanatorium. At one moment he rebels against the strictures of the church more generally, while the next it is the strictures he imposes on himself personally that he rails against; it is a struggle that can never be resolved because there is no release in this eunuch-like world where any chance of fulfilling one's desires or sexual awakening has been taken away. The TB sufferer is rendered more impotent in the sexual sphere than anyone else. In the privacy of his diaries, we get intimations of Ó Ríordáin's awful struggle in this regard, the forcing under of his natural sexual desires when his body cries out for release. The ceaseless pendulum of longing and refusal, and the private torture that accompanies it. The women who are his fellow patients, their bodies thin and weak, withering away physically as the terrible disease decays them. Life and death and the chilling *danse macabre* they perform together. And no escape from the smell of sickness, the constant presence that is one's own decaying body in the bed, that peculiar putrefaction that renders one inert and helpless in body and soul. The increasingly shapeless body that is under the dominion of disease, infection, nurses, doctors and proposed medical treatments. One's individuality, one's body, is a contrivance upon which others exert control. One can almost envision the observers of the disease as grey harbingers of death standing about and waiting.

Strangely, this process is not so dissimilar to that which happens when the poem is written and the artistic work revealed. The observers gather around, the critics huddle in and give their judgement; they map out the contours of the poem and sketch its weaknesses, metaphysical and otherwise, wherever they find them: 'Tá an dán fite fuaite den tinneas/ Is muintir an eolais á mheas …' ('*The poem intertwined with sickness/the qualified ones examining it* …')[28]

The examination and the prognosis in both cases are very similar and are delivered clinically, mercilessly and without emotion by this all-knowing authority that appears indifferent or impersonal. The invisible trace that is surveillance culture and external authority. Sometimes, it is the weak attempt at humour – for example, the ironic letters that Ó Ríordáin wrote in English occasionally at this time – that serves as a protection against the true horror of his situation, the sole bulwark against despair. Irony or sardonic humour as a defence mechanism against the reality that cannot be faced full-on, that is always best postponed. This is a writing that disguises more than it reveals. It is the discourse of 'putting off' for another day, another time. *Aliud facere.* Anything rather than the true horror of the moment.

We see the same tactic in the diaries, of course, even if in this case Ó Ríordáin is really talking to himself – to the body that is already 'dead' – more than anyone else. The refusal to face the reality of TB, because it is a disease that no one can truly face. Who else would listen anyway? Who else could hear him? Who else would understand except he who is a fellow sufferer? If he could only jettison this diseased body of his for a while, that which has subverted the laws of nature and which hems

---

28 ES: p. 104.

him in. Death is the only release and even then his body seems intent on accompanying him every step of the way. The following extracts are testament to the enduring inner struggle that was Ó Ríordáin. In the first extract, the poet speaks as if to his recently deceased self, the one who still remembers the life that has just passed – life as it was before:

12 August 1949

Your letter seems to come from a pre-grave world. I entombed feel your unburied contempt. I have come to a contempt, no a horror, of flesh. I feel utterly hostile to the palms of my hands. My arse fills me with an undying hatred. When in black moments I remember that I am enclosed in the filthy stuff I would fain bray with disgust. There is something beautifully turn-your-back-on-everything about the braying of an ass. When in the universal presence of a good bray I feel independent of Picasso and the Pope and people I like too much. That seems to be my reason for straining deathwards – I can't bray. I must shake off things and people that are essential to me. Your sense of humour and huge brushing aside of things, your burly ridicule, are of no avail. I abjure wit, reason, humour, hope, soup, Shakespeare and my own Gaelic O. I want death and nothing else. You can bray. I'll say that for you. No poem, no Turnbull, no whore can move me now. I got the faint whiff of the old breeze from fleshdom yesterday – a female radiologist with diseased, dilated eyes and a good figure. It vanished as quickly as Quigley (no pun intended) learning a language.

Forgive this poppycock. It shut out consciousness for a while, acting as locum tenens *for death. It is a dreadful thing to be caught in the trap of life when one is dead.*

11 October 1945

I always feel that there is a kind of civilised and spacious Christian blasphemy blowing over Europe at all times. I should like to spend a month in Italy where one could create things uncringingly. I should like to taste the Vatican and V.D. in juxtaposition. Pope Alexander VI was the greatest man (Quigley excepted and Jesus Christ) that ever lived, because, whoremonger that he was, he was not too uppish to take the job of Pope. Here in Ireland rosaries are said listlessly and lustlessly. When I hear them pray around me I feel that I have eaten wet towels. The few European words I know seem to go trippingly on the tongue when the words of these island languages stagger along like aged plough-horses. (Of course I'm too lazy to learn a European language.) Fellows here read The News of the World *between rosaries and X-rays. The words 'intimacy took place' are repeated about fifty times. This is totally disgusting. Latin Europe would never do that, I think. They understand ritualistic sin in Europe as Byron did. The ritual is half the secret. The other half is that a man should be in love with a woman, no matter how transiently, before he makes a human lodgment. Otherwise his progeny is bound to be uninspired. Such offspring approach religion without sexual excitement and approach sin without religious feeling or ritual.*

September 1949

I am surrounded by females here. They are fascinated of my bald head. When they wish to be seduced they retire in ones to the Linen Room. Now that Lenin is dead it should be called the Stalin Room? To date I have not pleasured a single damsel here. I am conscious these days of the existence of a higher intelligence in Ireland. Her name is Frances Cox and she is accused of murder.[29] *Her mind is free and full of light and she doesn't care a hen's shit about the lawyers.*

14 January 1950

I visited Mallow Chest Hospital a week before the Nativity to get a bronchoscopy. I was fitted with a cap and gown and white Cistercian socks and wheeled to the op. theatre where I was received by a squadron of the Ku Klux Klan. They promptly pushed a pipe down my throat on the principle that there are more ways of killing a cat than choking him with butter. I did not choke because I am accustomed to getting things shoved down my throat, e.g., the Ecclesia Catholica, *the King's English, the art of motor taxation, Murphy's Stout and Christian Brothers' education. The surgeon-in-chief proclaimed his belief that I was a bit of a poet.*

---

29 Frances Cox was a Protestant from County Laois, who fell in love with a local Catholic man. As her brother did not approve of the match, Cox decided to poison him, so as to speed up the wedding process. She was found guilty of murder after a six-day trial in December 1949.

Needless to say there were other people in the sanatorium with Seán who were far worse off than he was – people who hadn't the strength to battle fate and the consequences of this awful disease, nor the resources to deal with this ordeal on an everyday level, never mind make sense of it. Sad as it may be, the majority of these people, many of whom died young, dealt with TB by referring to themselves and their condition as if from the perspective of healthy people or likely survivors. The fact that this form of denial was the strongest protection that they could muster against the grim reality of their situation is all the more pitiful and disturbing. And in a sense, Ó Ríordáin became the spokesperson for this community who were unable or unwilling or too afraid to speak. He'd be the one who'd speak on their behalf. He'd be the poet of those whose ability to express themselves had been nullified, those who'd sometimes yet to realise the true horror of their predicament. These were Ó Ríordáin's people, the people he evoked in his memorable essay 'Aicme Íseal' ('*Low Class*'):

> *There was a great demand for cigarettes and they were scarce sometimes. There was a Limerick man who had an unbelievable craving for them. One day, he failed to get even one smoke from anyone. 'It doesn't matter,' he said, 'as long as we all have our health.' The poor man wasn't joking, may the Lord have mercy on him. He was just leaning his weight on the cliché. You wouldn't have minded if he was joking. I often saw people passing the day comfortably, leaning on one phrase and then the next, their only crutches or oars being the clichés.*

On the face of it, such 'jollity' seems out of place in a sanatorium but the joke had its own power and it certainly wasn't meant in sarcastic terms in this instance. Essentially, he was remembering all his friends from the sanatorium years, the people he'd become closer to probably than any other group of people in his life, the friends whom he'd grown to love in that special way that is the solidarity of sickness and pain. Interestingly, one of these fellow patients and friends of Ó Ríordáin's from those days, Jimmy Ronan, wrote to me spontaneously years later and shared a very touching memory of Seán and the sanatorium. He wrote down this recollection of his for no reason other than that, as he put it, 'I consider myself very honoured to have known Seán Ó Ríordáin and to be have been his friend in distress for so many years and fellow sufferer.' Ronan was admitted to Heatherside a year earlier than Seán and they ran into each other at regular intervals in the sanatorium afterwards.

> *I was first sent to Doneraile Sanatorium in 1937. It was better known as Heatherside. The word 'sanatorium' was never used when people at home were addressing letters. That time Dr. Ahern was the Dr. in charge. The stethoscope was the only instrument used for examination of the patient as no X-ray had been installed there until 1938 or '39. Cod liver oil and malt extract were used in the treatment. Raw eggs were also given out at 11 o'clock and many a battering match took place when the nurse left with the empty dish. [He returned home in September 1937.] Twenty months later I was back again in Heatherside and there I met Seán Ó Ríordáin and he learned me how to play draughts. A very quiet shy man … I was discharged home in December 1939. I didn't meet Seán for ten years. When I got off the train in Buttevant Seán got off a few doors down further so we were coming back together to the San. It was August 1949.*

The pattern appears fixed at this stage and whether it's the sanatorium or at home, or talking to some of the local corner-boys or eccentrics on the street outside, Ó Ríordáin has by this juncture chosen the person on the margins, the outsider, or the one who is down on his luck as his preferred companion. They take their place in his private pantheon alongside the saint, the prophet, the madman and the child – essentially anyone who still has some form of unsullied innocence about them. As for the overly logical man, the dull man of reason or the person who signified status, power or the authority and the establishment in those days – they could forget about it. They'd never be accepted within his world because he'd had enough of them to last a lifetime. 'He used to always enjoy listening to an argument and he would always back out anyone giving stick to the Government or the establishment anywhere,' as Jimmy Ronan put it in his letter. Those who protected the establishment and authority needed to be questioned and confronted, even if they were the poet's own friends:

Dom Chairde

Cuireann sibh olc orm agus ní gan fáth;
Seasaíonn bhur gcainteanna lánmhara,
bhur dtuairimí údarásacha,
bhur dtacaíocht d'bhur n-aicme bheag,
don éagóir atá ag an láidir á imirt ar an lag
sa domhan so inniu, agus leis na mílte bliain,
ar scáth an teagasc éithigh,
tá sibhse fós a chraoladh,
thar ceann na fírinne dá gcreidfí sibh,
in ainm Chríost tá coillte agaibh:
troidfead sibh go bás,
cé sibhse mo chairde,
mar cloisim macalla ard
bhúr gcainte, fán pasáistí
ar fuaid na staire,
ag déanamh eirligh,
ag satailt.[30]

To My Friends

You make me sick, and not without reason:
your smug speeches, your high opinions,
the way you protect your own little coterie,
they represent the unfair play
the powerful pit against the weak
in the world today, and for thousands of years,
under the cover of false intelligence
you still broadcast in the name of truth
or the Christ whom you have castrated.
I will fight you to the death,
even though you are my friends,

30 LL: p. 41.

because I can hear echoing loudly
throughout the passages of history
your rhetoric shocking and awing.[31]

Whether this poem successfully expresses Ó Ríordáin's fury towards the establishment is debatable, but he makes his statement very clearly. Because not every biographical poem has, of necessity, to be a good poem, the poetic impulse is brought to the same mill for grinding irrespective of tenor or approach, and there are occasions where the poem as statement serves best. The same is true as regards the poem 'Ní Ceadmhach Neamhshuim' (*'Indifference is not Permitted'*), another poem from *Línte Liombó* and a work where Ó Ríordáin reveals his understanding of the societal nexus that is the weak and the strong. The poet leaves us in no doubt which side he is on in this particular struggle – it is that of anyone who has been hurt or marginalised in life as he has, essentially; it is their needs he considers paramount.

Ní Ceadmhach Neamhshuim

Níl cuil, níl leamhan, níl beach,
Dár chruthaigh Dia, níl fear,
Nach dualgas dúinn a leas,
Níl bean; ní ceadmhach neamhshuim
A dhéanamh dá n-imní;
Níl gealt i ngleann na ngealt,
Nár chuí dhúinn suí lena ais,
Á thionlacan an fhaid
A iompraíonn thar ár gceann,
Ár dtinneas-ne ‹na mheabhair . . .[32]

31 Sewell, *Selected Poems*, p. 183. Trans. Frank Sewell.
32 LL: p. 40.

Indifference is not Permitted

There's not a fly nor a moth nor a bee
that God created, not a man
nor a woman made we're not
obliged to aid, whose anxiety
we're allowed to disregard;
no man buried in his asylum
we shouldn't sit beside,
keeping him company as long
as he carries on our behalf
our own sickness in his mind.[33]

These poems were written later in Ó Ríordáin's career and yet they express a truth and an understanding that was his from the very earliest days. Ó Ríordáin always felt a strong sense of injustice at the way he and his kind were treated, particularly with respect to the medical treatment then offered to TB patients and the shunting away to the institution that society deemed the norm in those days. Unsurprisingly, given the degree to which he was reliant on his own resources to fight the disease and his tense interactions with City Hall as regards his long periods of absenteeism from work, his sense of combatting perceived injustice only increased over the years. So much so, that when it came to the attacks on his work by later critics he became instantly suspicious that people had set themselves against him and were whispering behind his back or conniving against him in some way. His sensitivity regarding criticism of his work verged on paranoia at times, but then that is hardly surprising when one sees how harsh some of the attacks on his poetry proved to be.

Exacerbating this feeling of injustice was the poet's conviction that the authorities in the sanatorium had treated him badly when they'd refused to prescribe him streptomycin as a treatment for his TB between the years 1949 and 1950, even though streptomycin had been available since 1944. Apparently, the explanation given to Ó Ríordáin for this was that it would

33 Sewell, *Selected Poems*, p. 181. Trans. Peter Sirr.

have made no difference in his case, given that he'd already had TB for a good number of years at this stage and that the drug was more effective in treating more recent TB patients. This was an explanation that the poet never accepted and he was convinced that a particular doctor had something against him for some reason. Ó Ríordáin would often find himself in dispute with this same doctor about a range of issues relating to the treatment. For example, Seán was convinced as early as the year 1940 that he was better off staying in bed for his recovery when the medical advice was that he should get out of bed regularly and walk around.[34] Once Ó Ríordáin dug his heels in, however, the doctors were wasting their time advising him otherwise, as is clear from a letter the poet sent to Con Prior in October 1949:

> *I am resting in bed against the advice of all doctors. Three doctors endeavoured to get me up but Bernard Shaw would have none of it. He says that God puts all men of genius to bed for six months at certain stages of their careers … The patients here are majorityists and therefore stagnationists. They dislike my attitude. They say I must know more than the doctors. And I say I must.*

When the doctor in question wanted to find out whether Ó Ríordáin would transfer to Skibbereen for a while, because there was nothing else that they could do for him in Heatherside – not that they could do anything much in Skibbereen for him either – Seán asked a woman named McCarthy who he was friendly with to act as mediator. This mediation was to no avail, however, as she got the same response as the doctor would have gotten. Ó Ríordáin was staying where he was and that was the end of it. Such interactions only exacerbated his hostility and distrust of the 'system'. Ridiculous as it seems, the poet's suspicions regarding not being prescribed streptomycin weren't entirely without foundation: there were other patients there who'd had the disease longer than Seán had had it, Jimmy Ronan amongst them, who'd been prescribed the drug sooner than he had.

Whatever basis Ó Ríordáin had for his suspicions in this regard –

34 D: 8 February 1940.

and it's probable that there was very little basis to them at all – he went home again from Heatherside on 13 March 1950 in pretty much the same state as he'd gone in – with the TB still making inroads inside his body. It was ten years since he'd first contracted the disease and if there were patients who were more hopeful then because of ongoing medical developments in relation to TB, the poet certainly wasn't amongst them – not yet, anyway. As it turns out, it was July 1951 when Ó Ríordáin was injected with streptomycin for the first time and he continued taking it for years afterwards. He had to pay for the drug by then, however, whereas if he'd received it earlier, he would have been prescribed it free of charge – something which Seán made a point of noting in his diary (6 December 1956). Another thing that has to be said with regard to the question of Ó Ríordáin's treatment is that his own local doctor told him that he wasn't convinced that the streptomycin would make any major difference to his life, even if it wouldn't do him any harm to try it. Not that this lessened the poet's dislike and mistrust of the other doctor he'd had dealings with in the sanatorium to any extent.

Years later all his suspicions came to the fore in an embarrassing moment of rage when the poet took his opportunity to vent his anger on this man. This incident took place in a clothes shop in Cork city in April 1976, just after it had been announced that the National University of Ireland were to award Seán an honorary D.Litt., *honoris causa*. The medic recognised Ó Ríordáin in the shop and felt it an opportune moment to congratulate his former patient. Seán hadn't forgotten his old grievance with the doctor, however, and he let him have it with both barrels, unconcerned that he was in a public place and that other people would see them. 'F… off, you f…er,' he roared at the top of his voice as he saw him approach and the doctor left the shop in a hurry. A quarter-century of grievances and suffering exploded from Ó Ríordáin's mouth in that one moment of pent-up rage, emotions so powerful that a D.Litt. degree was as nothing compared to them.

1949–50 was his last stint in Heatherside, a place where he'd only ever managed to write the odd poem and a small few pages of the diary. These and the handful of letters sent to his friends outside, letters where he gave hints of what he was going through or how he felt and, very occasionally, what he might be trying to write. To what extent were these few brief writings from the sanatorium a 'construction' or a false history and to what extent were they true? To what degree were they pretence or a smokescreen for the reality of his days there, the truth that didn't bear elucidation? And what difference was there anyway between such discourses, whether true or false – because wasn't the act of writing itself a form of pretence, even if writing to oneself privately or in the form of poetry? Silence or the absence of speech was probably the proper and most appropriate response in the heel of the hunt. *Ex nihilo nihil.* Life in the void, and the abyss of speech or writing as its true expression.

And where else could Ó Ríordáin seek perfect sanctuary? It wasn't in the representatives of the institutional side of the Catholic Church anyway, even if there was the odd person in its fold who was very close to him. The likes of Fr Tadhg Ó Murchú, for example, a man he met in Heatherside for the first time around 1944, engaged in his charitable work and nationalistic activities as was his wont. 'I was a patient in a sanatorium when he came in one day. He spoke Irish to everyone. He went around and handed cigarettes out to any of the patients who wanted one. He was very "down-to-earth".'[35] Although they became good friends, they spent as much time arguing as anything else, and I'm convinced that the poem 'Dom Chairde' ('*To My Friends*') is addressed to Fr Tadhg above all others. Fr Tadhg was one of Seán's closest friends in the world, but Ó Ríordáin viewed him as having more than one aspect to him, and that included the institutional side of him, a side which Ó Ríordáin always struggled with. Not that Ó Ríordáin ever abandoned this aspect of his own life or cut his ties with Catholicism. Even if there were negative aspects of the Church that he was critical of, he remained a Catholic his entire life. His pattern of rejecting and seeking again within the philosophical structures of Catholicism remained constant. Who had the answers to the fundamental questions – now or at the hour of our death? It is on the edifice of his uncertainty and doubt – his own personal doubt – that we find Ó Ríordáin exploring most often. The search was the source and wasn't it almost better to search without finding much of the time, particularly

35 'An tAthair Tadhg' ('*Father Tadhg*'), IT, 18 December 1971.

once one realised that there was no explicit resolution or answer to be found? In essence, the search is but a reference point that can never be realised, a confirmation that you have failed. Still and all, Ó Ríordáin had to continue with the search. The search for your original heritage, and the language that articulated it; shaping the forms and contours of this life and the words that would express this for you; the search for that unsullied beauty of youth that wilts and fades just when you think it is within your grasp again; the search for all that is the glimpse of heaven; the attempt to trace the secret contours of God's mind and fashion it in the form of poetry. And when you failed, as you surely would, all that was required was to acknowledge your imperfection, make your confession, compose the poem and stand naked before the world as the living manifestation of failure. In essence, that was your responsibility, your vocation: to be as a witness to the individual, the life, the god that had failed.

And the irony of ironies underlying it was this: it would be difficult to imagine anyone more suitable for the task than Ó Ríordáin, an individual who appeared a failure, both internally and externally, a man to whom the gift of a normal life had been denied, a writer who was writing in a language that was only half his (irrespective of which language he expressed himself in, perhaps), a poet who was not a poet or writer most of the time, but a clerk instead. And hadn't he failed even in his role as a clerk too – initially because he hadn't fulfilled all the duties of the office and then because his body had let him down and his health had failed? Ó Ríordáin was now increasingly absent for six months at a stretch and his salary had been halved as a consequence. Another full six months out and he'd have no salary at all, so he'd be entirely reliant on others whose resources were as meagre as his. His situation saw a slight improvement when the Coalition of 1948 came to power and Dr Noel Browne ruled that an extra period of six months at three-quarters of their regular salary be permitted to workers such as Ó Ríordáin who were receiving treatment for an infectious disease like tuberculosis and who had been out of work for successive six-month periods.

Money was not the most crucial issue in March 1950, however, when Ó Ríordáin returned home to an empty hearth and a house where no one had ever been born and or would ever be born either. It was a life-and-death tussle for the poet from now on and a struggle that would take a huge toll on him, both physically and psychologically. Because, not only was there the physical isolation the disease necessitated, but there was also the knowledge that this one was taboo and that there was a shame that accompanied it. One had to be kept away from others and remain hidden from the neighbours. And now that he was home from the sanatorium once more, Ó Ríordáin had to begin his writing and his attempts at poetry all over again, as if from the very beginning. He'd have to muster his resources and try again, as the smith beating out the frail slivers of his anguish on the cold iron of dead tradition hoping to leave his mark. On the face of it, this wasn't a project that any sensible person would have taken on. On 15 May 1974 Ó Ríordáin wrote to Con Prior as follows:

I left City Hall eight years ago. T. P. O'Connor [doctor] told me the other day that he thought at the time I would not live a year. In 1949 Maurice Hickey [surgeon] said that I could scarcely live six months. The strange thing is that they were not wrong. I hung on to life when I should have died. I am paying for it.

In essence, this was a form of living death, the contours of which were delineated and suffered far away from the sanatorium or City Hall. On 25 April 1950 Ó Ríordáin sent this letter to Philip Monahan, City Manager:

Dear Sir,

Dr. Hickey has advised me not to return to work before June lest it should be still necessary to undergo surgical treatment.

The City Manager replied the following day:

Dear Mr. O'Riordan,

Thanks for your letter of the 25th inst.

I hope you continue to do well and that we will see you here at the beginning of June.

Monahan didn't see him back at work in early June but in early October instead, when Ó Ríordáin worked for two weeks but fell ill again. It was another year again – 9 October 1951, to be exact – before he was able to return to work. In retrospect, the Manager should probably have required that the poet undertake a medical examination before he was permitted to return to work in October 1950, something that he didn't insist on. He probably regretted this later, however, because when he wanted to cut back on Ó Ríordáin's salary at a later date on the basis of all the time the poet had been absent, the Department of Local Government informed him – on foot of an official request from Seán – that the regulations didn't permit this.

However, we'll leave City Hall and the sanatorium behind for the moment and return to Inniscarra with the aspiring poet.

5

None Were Ever Equal

Ó Ríordáin returned home from his first-ever stint in the sanatorium in 1938. The diaries and letters are silent for this period but we know some of the circumstances of his life at this juncture. Officially the poet went home to his own house and family, but the strictures and laws of the time as associated with TB were less straightforward. The TB patient was required to remain separate from others and this was a regulation that was strictly adhered to in Ó Ríordáin's case, as with others. A new room was built, an extension measuring 11.25ft x 8ft, that began at the shop to the rear of the house and this was where Seán lived from then on. The poet would become intimate with the shape and contours of this room because it was here that he lived and worked for years to come, separate and cut off from his family, even if he was at home. To be a TB sufferer in those days was to suffer the frightening, taboo status assigned to the leper of an earlier era.

The disease meant that Ó Ríordáin had reduced contact with his next-of-kin but initiated even less contact with the public. It is as if he has finally discovered his allotted place in the social order is to be separate and cut off from others, from that very social order. The terms of reference for his new life are clear. He is to stay at the 'back of the house' ('ag cúl an tí') where no one can see him – even if this 'cúl an tí' is very far from the idyllic, imaginary existence and the magical world of the celebrated poem. The sole inhabitants of this new world are 'the four-legged crowd who come walking by', the dog and the cat, along with the hens and ducks. As for human contact, the only visitors to this remote world are the occasional passing beggar or the ghost and it's not all of the latter that receive welcome either, as is clear from the diaries. These are his new neighbours and, like the wanderer who scouts his terrain, Ó Ríordáin soon becomes intimate with every shade and nuance of the place, both physically and psychically. If there are wonders to be seen on the rubbish heap in the corner of the yard there, it isn't the neighbour passing outside who'll notice them but rather the poet or the children whom he sometimes addressed in his poems – those who can still appreciate wonder and transcendence.

New Year's Day 1940 is the first day we find ourselves in the room with the poet. He is only getting used to the new room yet, settling in. Before long, the door will close and the walls will seem to move in on him, extinguishing him almost within the confined world, the sole redemption for which he'll express through writing – the slow grind of the diaries or the sudden explosion of the poem. Essentially, Ó Ríordáin has begun his retreat from other people and the outside world, the slow withdrawal into himself that is the domain of 'Claustrophobia'.

His retreat is lazy and hesitant in the beginning. A neighbouring lad has called in on a quick visit and has just gone home again one day when the poet is left alone. He looks around and takes in his surroundings properly for the first time. He notes what he sees. Before long the vista of his inner world narrows:

> *When he left, I came out to the room here. I sat down at this table and this book and the vessel that I have to spit into in front of me here.*[1]

Another day learning the shape and form of disease and the contours that might serve to express it:

> *I stayed in bed for most of the day. The small room that I sleep in is at the back of the house. (To describe it as a 'bedroom' is to do it a disservice, as this room is also an office, a library, a dining room, and also still a sanatorium.) … There are probably fewer than three people in this parish who haven't passed by on the tiny path that's right outside my window, not to mention all the wanderers from outside the parish who also pass by. I always have the windows open and consequently, as is clear to you, my dear friend, I can't do anything in here without it being in the full view of the public.*[2]

1 D: 8 January 1940.

2 D: 23 January 1940.

Wanderers and local people approached the family shop and the house from the western side, even if, by rights, they should have been taking the path that led down from the road. Even when it was probably common knowledge that Ó Ríordáin was suffering from TB, the informal 'rules' of society could not be transgressed. One couldn't admit openly to having the disease and so the words 'asthma' or 'bronchitis' were always used in relation to Seán, even if most people knew otherwise. This was the 'code' Irish society followed at the time, their understanding of how one dealt with such a taboo subject. Only within the community that was the sanatorium could the illness be called by its real name: 'Good morning, my tubercular friends.'

News reaches Seán one day that the dance master who used to visit the area giving classes has recently been admitted to Mount Desert (convalescent home). Anyone sent there was 'finished' because the common view was that you were only sent there if you were close to death. As it happens, Mount Desert wasn't far from Seán's house at all; it was less than three-and-a-half miles away. On hearing such grim news, Ó Ríordáin imagines where he may end up himself if or when his health worsens. A local lad named Dan Healy delivered the shocking news to Ó Ríordáin:

> *That's a hospital for people with tuberculosis. I wouldn't be surprised at all if it was in there that I died myself. "Asthma and bronchitis is what he has," he says. Isn't it terrible that no one will admit to TB now? And Dónall [Dan] knows well what's going on above with the dancing master. And, furthermore, he knows well what's wrong with that man up there, although he never says it openly.*[3]

Tuberculosis was such a taboo at this time that, in theory, you couldn't have it because it didn't officially exist. Beyond the disease itself, the two worst things about TB were the hiding that went on with it and the shame associated with it. While out walking with a number of other local young people Ó Ríordáin's face gets all flushed and he makes up an

3 D: 29 January 1940.

excuse on the spot, quickly turns on his heel and returns home.[4] Another time, he's at a wake in a funeral home when he feels himself get flushed and he slips outside quickly, hoping that his face hasn't betrayed him or divulged his guilty secret.[5] Had he left on time or had anyone noticed? Not that he'd ever know – if someone had noticed, they wouldn't tell him, anyway. The strictures of the taboo are adhered to fully. You never heard what you heard and you never saw what you saw. The signs that there's something wrong are never recognised because they don't really exist. The diseased person keeps their side of the bargain and so does everyone else, and the unspoken regime is never disrupted. And Ó Ríordáin, the poet, follows these unspoken laws to the letter, even in his dreams. Years later, he describes an awful dream he had, a nightmare he found himself trapped in: people on every side of him and he hasn't the strength to escape them. 'I wanted to go somewhere private because I needed to cough ... Then I had a feeling that I've often had during the course of my life – I was afraid that someone would hear me coughing. The fear of this woke me.'[6]

But there is probably more to all of this than one might imagine. I am strongly of the opinion that the part of his family history as relating to TB was never fully explained to Seán himself. Otherwise, how can one explain the fact that he never explicitly says anywhere what caused his father's death at such a relatively young age. The fact that he never alludes to his father's death is all the more curious, given that he so frequently commented on the family traits and apparent defects he'd inherited from the 'Speckled Riordan' side of the family, and the fact that he was stuck with them whether he liked it or not. As far as I'm aware, however, Seán never once referred in conversation or in writing to the fact that he himself was suffering from the same disease that his father had also suffered from. If Ó Ríordáin really did know the full truth, then his decision never to mention it at any point of his life is all the more tragic, given that this was the same taboo or 'marginalising' mentality that he'd elected to fight

4 D: 26 January 1940.
5 D: 18 February 1940.
6 D: 11 November 1957.

against every day of his life, and especially when he became a regular patient of the sanatorium and had nothing else left in his life but this.

It's still a mystery how much Seán knew about the history of TB within his immediate family and how his understanding of the disease may have impacted on his own treatment and as relating to his health. After all, when he first contracted the disease, public opinion was still strongly of the view that healthy people had to steer clear of people who were infected in case they contracted the disease themselves; and tragic as it may seem from the vantage point of today, this was also Seán's strongly held view as a young man. It should not come as a surprise to find out that, towards the end of his life, the poet seriously considered burning these very diaries that we are exploring now, in which he'd tracked the onset of the disease and its physical and psychological effects on him; we hope that Seán will forgive this intrusion on his diaries and see it as a brief but important window on that other far more serious incursion – the disease that destroyed his childhood and his entire life.

Another anecdote pertaining to this same question centres on Christopher Reynolds, a cousin of his who comes to their house on a visit one day but with whom Seán is very fearful of spending too much time: 'I don't like it when he comes close to me and I carefully move back out of the way as best I can, because, God with us forever, but I'm not a clean person.'[7] The same went for any of the neighbours who happened to call in. Even worse, Seán was afraid that it might be possible for the dog to catch TB and sometimes he kept his distance from it also:

> *Two of the Murphys are in here every night … [One of them] is often coughing. I am very afraid that he'll catch TB from me … The likes of me are always watching out closely and petrified that every cold is a sign of TB. I remember that our little dog was sick-looking last year and, would you believe it, I thought that he had tuberculosis and I myself was to blame for it. Maurice O'Reilly told me that he thought the same about his own dog at one stage.*[8]

---

7 D: 4 January 1940.

8 D: 12 February 1940.

Everyday life goes on as before, except that Ó Ríordáin becomes increasingly marginal to it. This marginality becomes his poem, and it is frequently Seán's chosen status also. He supports the unofficial societal rules in solidarity with the community to which he belongs, until he becomes peripheral to that same community. The collective view of him changes then – at least in the poet's eyes – he goes too far with his rejection of the unwritten rules that are the collective and from then on *he* becomes the transgressor or the one who has sinned against the norm. The sole satisfaction the poet receives from this altered relationship is the fact that the poet can now view the community as if in a mirror and ignore them when it suits:

> *There was a time when the community respected me, or maybe it would be more accurate to say that the neighbours respected me and had empathy with me. But apparently they have turned against me now. When I first got sick, they used to ask how I was. I used to go out amongst them then, and I'd be in their company. I'd go to Mass on a Sunday and I'd drink a pint. After I came home from the sanatorium in 1938, I did all the things that a Christian should do if he wants to continue living amongst his fellow Christians. Now, I am cut off from them. I am alone and I am lonely. I don't go to the church or to the pub. I don't go out and meet up with the lads on a Sunday. I rarely appear outside at all. I am sick but I don't think I'm so bad that it's necessary for me to hide away completely. I'm not one of them any more. There is a growing hostility and distrust between me and the local community. I'm not one of them any more. They talk to me in a grim tone and watch what they say to me. I speak to them in a dour way also and I'm in a hurry to get home again. The long and lonely period that I was separated from them is now a barrier between us. I've breached the laws of common humanity and I've got to pay now accordingly. It's as if I insulted the public by the way that I stopped interacting with them. I gave them the impression that I could continue with my life without them and they hate me as a consequence. That's the situation I'm in, dear reader, here at the beginning of my life (and I suppose it is probably the end of my life also – and may the release not be too far away). I have little self-respect and I hate myself.*[9]

9 D: 2 February 1940.

Another definitive break with the younger people in the local community occurs for Seán when he no longer has any involvement with the local dramas and plays. Ironically, it was he who had initiated the drama group in the area; he had directed many of their plays and often painted the backdrop for the stage when needed. By now others were doing this work, and the Irish-language side of them – the main reason why Ó Ríordáin had set up the drama group the first day ever – was in rapid decline. His own work with the group is in the past now and forgotten – and it's probably better that this is so. The new drama producer is Éamonn Ó hAnluain (O'Hanlon), a man whose name comes up in the diary extracts below:

> *Éamonn O'Hanlon was with me on the bus [into Cork]. He was telling me about the drama group that I set up last year and he told me that they're not doing well in promoting the plays. His conversation made me lonely when I thought back on times past, and it made me depressed as regards what the future may hold, and the condition that the Irish language may be in, the language of my heart in those days.*[10]

> *We produced* An Sprid, *the drama by Father Peadar Ó Laoghaire back in the Hall approximately three years ago. It is necessary to display a graveyard in one scene of this play. We got some plywood in Cork and I painted a picture of a graveyard on it. I found it a great effort. I drew the ruins of a church and white headstones and trees in the graveyard and the moon above it. I remember that myself and Kevin [Murphy] (who lives next door to us here) spent an afternoon over in the graveyard next to the river, the bitter cold going through us, and I doing my best to draw a picture of the place. Well, our Taidhgín here and Éamonn O'Hanlon, they brought that scene back to the hall with them this afternoon. They're going to make a new tableau for the play they're putting on in a fortnight's time or so and they need to cut a bit off the tableau because they have to have a door in that scene. I understand of course that they are only doing the right thing with this. And yet, a sense of loneliness came over me when I saw that the lovely graveyard of mine that I put so much effort into is about to disappear. And I got a little bit angry I'm afraid, although I hid my*

10 D: 22 January 1940.

thoughts from everyone. Out of pride, I could only praise what they were doing. I'm finished with plays and tableaus from now on as my world has gone dark.[11]

As I said before, there is a polite hostility between me and the local people whom I used to socialise with once. I used to be in charge of the plays one time and it was I who started them off here originally. But now I'm like the person who's been thrown out onto the road, looking in at the stranger who's taken over my house. It's the same in Cork where my job is being done by someone else. I'm alive after my death and I feel the eyes of the community as if they are saying: 'Get yourself out of the way now, let you. Why don't you just stay in the grave, the same as all the rest of the dead do?'[12]

The drama group went to Crookstown with the plays. There was a big crowd in the lorry. All the losers in the parish went with them except for me. I felt a sort of loneliness after they were gone. I was left behind. I was like Oisín after the Fianna were gone.[13]

The more Ó Ríordáin retreated into his inner world, the more he retreated physically from social contact with the outside world also. The more he develops his poetic aesthetic and the words required to express it, the less dealings he has with those on the 'outside' – the likes of the thin women on the fence, figures who are already present in his imagination, even if they have yet to assume a specific human form.[14] He still makes the odd effort to socialise with others, not that he's always very successful:

I spent the day in bed until evening. Night had fallen when I heard a group of lads below at the gate. I went down to them. I spent a while down there with them. Eventually, they left and disappeared back up the road and the TB man was left alone with himself.[15]

11 D: 7 February 1940.
12 D: 25 February 1940.
13 D: 3 March 1940.
14 LL: p. 23.
15 D: 7 March 1940.

And he'd be on his own a good deal from then on. There is little to distinguish the solitude or loneliness of day from night for him now. And it is no help whenever he comes across former fellow pupils from his secondary school days either. They just remind him of the life that has disappeared from him now: health, a particular status within society, the chance of university even. They have a stability and a standing to their lives that means his interactions with them are strained. How else could it be now really? They go through the ritual out of politeness, but they know the score. It would be easier for all concerned if they'd never run into each other at all. In the following excerpt, it's as if the bus takes him from one person to the next and from one life to the next:

No sooner had the bus pulled in but I noticed an old friend inside – Joseph Murphy from Macroom. He was a student with me in the North Monastery … He's a student now in the University, a place I'd also like to be, if my family were able to afford it … Joe gave a happy rundown to me of all our mutual friends who are now at University – Skentlebery, Paddy Hooper, Tadhg Carey, Jim Donoghue, etc., etc. According to Joseph, all of them are voraciously assimilating knowledge and falling in love. They are the future leaders of Ireland, I suppose. I felt a mixture of joy and sadness on meeting Joseph today. Anyone would normally be filled with joy on meeting one of their friends, but it reminded me of the time when great ideas and plans were burgeoning in my mind and my 'joy was overcome by a great melancholy' when I thought of how these plans came to nothing. I said goodbye to Joseph Murphy (perhaps for the last time) and made for the library.[16]

Seán Ó Riain from Cork came out this way. We had a chat. We'd prefer not to meet each other at all. It's strange that. But of course, it isn't strange or unusual really. This is what happens: two friends; they separate; one of them succeeds in life; the other fails; they meet one another years later; they have spotted one another before either of them has the opportunity to go in a different direction; the poor man is ashamed that the more successful man sees him in this state; the

16 D: 8 April 1940.

> *rich man despises the poor man, and, anyway, he has better things to be doing than talking. Do you get it? Yes.*[17]

He moves away and leaves the road to those who are still capable of experiencing all the joyful madness of youth, but not before looking on enviously at them. Meanwhile, he drifts over in the direction of those 'others' whose status is marginal at the best of times – the elderly sailor, he or she who has been martyred already and for whom death is a constant presence. They're not all necessarily TB sufferers in the same boat as himself but that's not to say he forgets them either. They are figures and types who reappear constantly in his work and he shares with them what he can of his artistry, even if it's frequently the artistry of despair:

> *The women are having some kind of a party in the Hall tonight. I was invited to go to it but I didn't. They are all gone back to it now except for myself and my mother. There's an old sailor who lives not far from us here. He lives alone … While I was a talking to him, some of the boys and girls from this house left for the Hall. When they were gone he looked at me, a lonely look in his eyes and said, 'Isn't it terrible thing to be a loner? No one gives a damn whether I go over to that crack or not' … I was in the same boat myself as I watched the young people leaving, like a Caitlín na Clúide, but do you think the sailor thought of this at all?*[18]

This sailor lived to a very good age as it happens and when he died in April 1967 Seán celebrated his individuality and integrity in a diary entry, later published as part of a newspaper piece entitled 'Beirt Fhear Mhacánta' ('*Two Honest Men*').[19] In fact, Ó Ríordáin also wrote a short piece in English as based on this sailor's experiences towards the end of his diary for the period 10 January 1942 to 26 April 1942. The journey that is the night bus from Cork city to Inniscarra has become the retired sailor's ship. He and Seán often get off the bus together at the same stop: 'I often

17 D: 14 May 1940.
18 D: 11 January 1940.
19 IT, 25 November 1968.

thought that it must be sad for him to go to his smoky fireside, leaving his ship and visions behind. On the bus he was on his ship, and the rest of the world was outer darkness and he was alone with his visions …' Both the poet and the sailor share the same role now in many respects given that their ability to function 'normally' in society has been denied them and they've been thrown back on the power of the imagination forever more.

Another day and a neighbouring man is dying of cancer, and his wife is looking after him at home. The poet senses the similarities between this sick man and his own situation – the pair of them (his mother and himself) left alone together in the house when everyone else is gone about the 'everyday' business of living:

> *Me and my mother were left here by ourselves and a strange thought came to me. There were two people left behind in the house next door also. A broken individual and his wife in there, and a broken individual and his mother in here.*[20]

Another time again and summer has arrived, and the young women have come out from the city on their bicycles and are cycling around Inniscarra as they have always done. Himself and Denny O'Hanlon (Éamonn's brother), the latter another local young lad whose health was poor, are the only two people who are left on their own because their illness prevents them from joining in with the fun of the other young people. In Ó Ríordáin's imagination, the crossroads they are left standing at becomes the image of Christ's Suffering Cross:

> *You'd imagine that the city had just given them all up and they'd emerged out into the heat from their caves. And oh Mary, their lovely legs – legs and knees that would even make a priest lustful. The young people here were given free rein for the day and boy did they take full advantage of it. But the two who were wasting away here were left imprisoned by their disease and nailed to their own cross. What bad odds we got! A living spirit trapped within a decayed body!*[21]

---

20 D: 11 January 1940.
21 D: 12 May 1940.

It was the same thing again the following Sunday:

> *Another sunny day. We're at the cross again. Poor Denny Hanlon [sic] and I, the two of us just about alive still and we watching the people going here and there, experiencing all life's joys. And us two – hungry and weak, thirsty, lonely. I'd prefer to be out fighting in the war. I'd prefer to be dead and gone, buried beneath the clay.*[22]

Other than the friends he made while in the sanatorium, people such as these are Ó Ríordáin's secret 'tribe': the man whose unexpected death he saw reported in the newspaper one day, or the unnamed girl he passed while walking along a city street whose natural beauty withered under the onslaught of TB. They all fade away or disappear, the world apparently deaf to their sufferings. Ó Ríordáin wasn't averse to citing Hitler or the IRA in the early diaries, anyone or any group that would 'sweep' away the terrible occlusion and silence regarding the 'taboo', and the double-standards and hypocrisy that characterised the country at the time – both Church and State – and the societal establishment's treatment of those deemed 'marginal' or 'untouchable'. It was the same burning righteous indignation that suffused some of Ó Ríordáin's first newspaper articles as published in *The Irish Times* decades later. He was still only sharpening his quill at this point, however:

> *My still-beating soul was torn right out of me just now when I saw Seosamh de Barra's death announced in the* Evening Echo. *He was with me on the train when we went to the sanatorium last year. I'm just a year older than him and I thought he was as strong as you'd expect for the like of us … God bless your soul Seosamh. You have no tuberculosis or any other disease tonight, neither do you have the hungry look of the man spotting the legs of the young women passing by – as you had that afternoon on the train.*[23]

> *I saw a girl on the South Mall. I removed my hat politely, immediately. We*

22 D: 19 May 1940.
23 D: 20 January 1940.

stopped. Maria O'Mahony. A pretty young girl with a fine set of legs on her. But she has TB. I met her in Heatherside before. I didn't know her well. I don't think I've ever had a proper conversation with her. She was the nicest and the prettiest girl in the place and she didn't look unhealthy at all. Lots of fellows were after her of course. I think that one of the doctors there had the eye on her ... She gave me a shock, all the same. 'This Maria Mahony isn't the same Maria Mahony as before however.' Quantum mutata ab illa! She's lost a lot of weight. She's a big woman no more. 'Consumption hath no pity for blue eyes or golden hair.' She had a small touch of redness in her cheeks. That redness is a deadly sign. Some of my other comrades are in Saint Patrick's Ward. She had news about most of them. We said goodbye to one another. It's a terrible thing, really awful. A beautiful-looking girl in the bloom of her youth a while ago and she's now she's fading away to nothing. The disease is really powerful. Nothing stands in its way. Poverty is the root cause of a lot of this disease. And people are afraid that Hitler will destroy this civilisation of ours. If he did it wouldn't be before time. Christianity without depth or healing![24]

His initial reaction here is to flee the body in all its aspects and so he develops a hatred for everything associated with the human body and denies the 'lust', the 'filth' and the 'sin'. He rejects that which he cannot have anyway. If he falls prey to the powerful temptations of the flesh from time to time as sure as not he'll have to pay for it later. The significance of his relationship with a local girl that he went out with for a while becomes manifest solely in a negative and destructive fashion – the sin, the poem and the pain:

I went to confession on Saturday and I received Holy Communion yesterday. Herself back on the hill is more enticing than ever. A poem in English came to me, and what came out of it then was just confession and heartache ... Each act has its own brood ... The accursed brood of this act surrounded me and gave me an awful battering, a battering that I won't forget in a long time.[25]

24 D: 26 April 1940.
25 D: 28 June 1943.

It's likely that the poem 'A Wet June Day 1943' is the one being referred to here. It's the only English-language poem of Ó Ríordáin's that can hold its own with anything that he wrote in Irish. In the poem, Ó Ríordáin describes how the frenzy of lust is gone and life hasn't the same lustre or fullness to it as it had the previous day. The detritus of drunken lust is on his tongue and it has a bitter taste. The sweat and the heat-lust on his body chills and evaporates in the form of cold rain. The death of the soul and the death of the body close on its heels – one reflecting the other. The pleasure and the disgust that is the sexual, merging as one:

Rain fell all day, all day grey rain,
Hen-plumes clung bald, tin sheds shone wet,
Eyes quenched, you felt June-sunned joy wane;
Sky-lines last night so thin and set
Now mist in melting shivers like
A drunken guess of fainting eyes.
I felt this June-December strike
My sun-puffed soul and now she lies
In wrinkles like a burst balloon,
The vein-blue wine of slow June streams,
That filled her and the whiskey noon,
The fat trees plumping shades, the dreams
That trickled down like hay-field sweat,
Extinguished by the clammy breath,
The brooding spirit of the wet,
Blew from his rainy lair of death.

Whether consciously or not, in my opinion Ó Ríordáin was imitating Daniel Corkery with that phrase 'tin sheds shone wet'; he'd noted a sentence similar to this in his diary three years earlier, having read Corkery's short story collection *Earth out of Earth*, 'to show you the type of images he likes to record – "We could see the surfaces of the canvas shining with wet, they were blowing about".'[26] The remainder of the poem

26 D: 23 February 1940.

is Ó Ríordáin's idiom and no one else's. A thousand artists had asked this question of life and death before him but Ó Ríordáin needed to resolve it for himself – all the more urgently in his case given that he'd regularly skirt both states of being with the TB. In fact, the poet's exploration of the boundary that is life and death had begun in one of the earliest poems he ever wrote – 'An Cheist' ('*The Question*'), which was originally published in *Combar* in April 1944; we first come across this poem in his diary entry for 15 September 1943. Actually, it may be that he first wrote this poem even earlier than this, early that same summer perhaps. We see death accompanying the poet here every step of the way. It is the most powerful obstacle he has to overcome if he wishes to truly develop himself as an artist and create an art that makes him whole within the realm that is eternity. In the end, the resolution to the artistic question and the question of belief are one and the same:

Tá bás sa tsamhradh chugham gan mhoill:
An stathfad blátha roimh a thíocht,
Nó an sáithfead crúb go ciúin im mhian
Le súil go stathfad sa tsíoraíocht?[27]

The death of summer with us soon
Will the flowers wilt by then
Or my longings quietly stolen
In the hope they too will wilt forever?[28]

Another time, and it's a feeling of desire or lust in him that makes him retrace his steps in disgust – as a pilgrim in search of the sinless purity of youth. He employs the same metaphor again. It is necessary to waylay sin before it overcomes you and corrupts what it is you seek:

Do chuala an deamhan trím chodladh
Ag satailt ar mo smaointe,

27 'An Cheist' ('*The Question*'), ES: p. 31.
28 Trans. M. Ó hAodha.

Is do sháigh isteach a chosa
Im fhéitheacha mar bhríste.[29]

I heard the demon in my sleep
trampling through my thoughts,
thrusting both his feet
into my veins like trousers.[30]

'Fóir ar m'Easpa Creidimh' (*'Aid My Lack of Faith'*) is the title he gave to the poem 'An Cheist' in the diary, the first verse of which demonstrates how his unfulfilled desires were distressing him:

Tá uamhan uafásach ar mo chroí,
Is radharc an áthais 'om róchloí,
Tá amhras ársa im dhá shúil,
Is saint gan sásamh 'om thruailliú.

A terrible dread fills my heart,
And the glimpse of joy tears me apart,
My eyes wide with ancient disbelief,
An insatiable hunger corrupts my soul.[31]

He brings his sins with him to the holy place, therefore, to the church and to the poem, and makes reparation for them by confessing to them. Or he goes back in time in his mind, back to the healthy period of his youth when he felt a wholeness or balance to this life, a time so innocent that one couldn't have associated any hint of the sexual with it – a time as pure and unsullied as a mother's words or a small child's fingers.[32] Each image and reality fades and dies one after another, however – health, childhood, his mother, his health, and before long he finds himself in a place very

29 'Oilithreacht Fám Anam' (*'My Soul's Pilgrimage'*), ES: p. 71.
30 Sewell, *Selected Poems*, p. 79. Trans. Denise Blake.
31 Trans. M. Ó hAodha.
32 ES: p. 72.

far away from the dewy plains of youth. He realises that his is a purely romantic view of the world, one that no matter how beautiful it may seem in the imagination bears no significance now. The 'nostalgia-tinged' life that once was has been completely blown apart, 'the beautiful morning' split wide open, never to return. And how it has been sullied beyond all recognition now! In the poet's mind, they all run together, the filth, the poverty, the disease and the pollution that is sin. They go together in his mind, as does the shame that accompanies poverty. One day he spies his mother's leg as sullied and dirty and:

> *I got angry there with the rich and with the whole world, and with fate, and my mother being reduced to such insignificance. But she's only been elevated in my mind. My love for her increased and I felt sorry for her and understood better how I've let her down myself. The dirt on my mother's foot put me in mind of my own conscience.*[33]

She is cleansed in the fresh snow, in the Host (the Eucharist) and in the poem 'Adhlacadh mo Mháthar' ('*My Mother's Burial*'):

> *Gile gearrachaile lá a céad chomaoine,*
> *Gile abhlainne Dé Domhnaigh ar altóir*
> *Gile bainne ag sreangtheitheadh as na cíochaibh,*
> *Nuair a chuireadar mo mháthair, gile an fhóid.*[34]

> The brightness of a young girl at her First Communion,
> The brightness of a host on the altar of God,
> The brightness of milk spurting from a woman's breast,
> The brightness, when they buried my mother, of the very sod.[35]

He'll wash the filth or lust that's in his heart clean away again in similar fashion when he buries her in fresh soil following her death. But her

33 D: 3 January 1940.

34 ES: p. 56.

35 Sewell, *Selected Poems*, p. 47. Trans. Paul Muldoon.

memory fades too over time, the same as the world when it was young. Short-lived as they may have been, Ó Ríordáin's memories of his mother and his youth provided him with a form of redemption at a particular juncture of his life.

6

The Inner Self

There were two worlds in Ó Ríordáin's life – the world of Seán's room and the world beyond – and his mother was always the only person who had true access between them on the physical level. Sadly, she was more than familiar with this division, given that two of her own two brothers had suffered from TB. Her husband had died of the disease also and now her eldest son was seriously ill with it. It was difficult to believe that all that worry and uncertainty had entered into her life one more. They had to keep Seán's illness to themselves, and whether she and the aunts discussed the disease or not, its existence certainly couldn't be acknowledged anywhere beyond the walls of their house. This was just another aspect of the seclusion or monk-like nature of their existence – the sense of enclosure or claustrophobia. Seán's mother had to go outside and leave her house to reach his room every time she went to see him and mind him, and this wasn't easy at the best of times. It was particularly difficult at night and in winter when the weather was wild and stormy and she was in and out regularly to check on Seán and to make sure he wasn't too anxious or afraid. The poem 'An Stoirm' refers to one such night.[1] This poem was written sometime in early 1943 as Ó Ríordáin informs us almost a year and a half later – on 16 August 1944 – when he also mentions that he won an Oireachtas prize for it. (This was the second prize that he'd won for his poetry; he'd won a prize the previous year for 'An Leigheas'.)[2] The roof of Seán's room was galvanised and it made a hell of a racket whenever it was lashing rain. 'An tseanbhean' ('the old lady') of this storm is his mother – even if she wasn't actually an old woman, really, seeing as she was barely sixty at the time; she is the one who protects him from the madwoman

---

1 ES: p. 43.
2 ES: p. 29.

that is the storm, the woman who screeches and roars wildly about the house and who rattles the galvanised roof in her rage. The room is filled with chaos and the violence of the storm, so that the metaphorical rain that inks his page is black and anarchic, the unruly night taking form, the rain easing off as the storm leaves, dripping onto the page. Then, as the noise outside fades, the darkness presses in once more. We're getting closer here to the world that imbues 'Claustrophobia' when the 'government of the night' takes over completely and the darkness of the night outside enters the poet's room and presses in on him.[3] The dark shadows enter his rotted lungs and everything is shrouded in black. At least Ó Ríordáin has his mother beside him now to light the candle and fight off the encroaching darkness. His mother might be his physical sanctuary in the poem here but Ó Ríordáin can't find any true spiritual shelter at this juncture. The old woman's prayers are as weak and feeble as the apparently powerless 'statue of my Lord' in 'Claustrophobia'. The only response their prayer receives is the hellish racket of the winter's storm and the howling night that silences them. Just two years on from this poem, Ó Ríordáin's mother has passed on and he's on his own against the night. There will be no one to support him and it will be him against the dark and the terms of reference for his struggle are clearer and more fundamental than ever before – presence and absence, light and dark, life and death. He has some form of shelter for the moment but the strange void of human emptiness is just two years away when he writes:

An Stoirm

Tá an doras á chraitheadh is gan Críostaí ann
Ach gaoth dhall stuacach ag réabadh
Go liobarnach siar is aniar san oíche.
Tá a gúna á stracadh anonn is anall
Is á pholladh ag snáthaidí géara
Na fearthainne, atá ag titim 'na mílte.
Tá an tseanbhean fá chritheagla ag féachaint suas

3 *Brosna* (hereafter referred to as B): p. 13.

Trí dhíon an tí, ag lorg Dé,
Is port gainmheach na fearthainne go diablaí thuas
Ag báitheadh an fhocail ar a béal.
Siúd léi go himníoch is coinneal 'na glaic
Ag daingniú na fuinneoige;
Nuair thit an solas coinnle ar an ngloine, las
Na ceathanna bolgóidí.
Do ghortaigh dealg fhuar fearthainne mo lámh,
D'fhéachas de gheit;
Braon duibh as an bpeann reatha dhein an smál,
Bheadh braon fearthainne glan.[4]

The Storm

The door is rattled and no Christian there
but a blind belligerent wind tearing
clumsily westward and back in the night.
Her dress dragged this way and that,
performed by sharp needles
of rain falling in their thousands.
Trembling with fear, the old woman looks up
through the roof of the house, for God,
while the rain's grating tune, like a devil above,
smothers the words on her lips.
There she goes, warily, clutching a candle,
securing the windows.
When the candlelight fell on the pane,
showers of bubbles lit up,
a freezing dart of rain stung my hand,
startled, I looked down:
a dark drop from the moving pen made the mark,
a drop of rain would be clear.[5]

---

4 ES: p. 43.
5 Sewell, *Selected Poems*, p. 23. Trans Frank Sewell.

Many's the night that Seán and his mother passed in one another's company like this, as is indicated in the various diaries. Passing the time when they were too anxious to sleep; the pair of them recounting the old days in Ballyvourney, Seán remembering the summer days when he had gone swimming in the Sullane river with all the other lads, and his mother telling him what life was like back there when she first married into the village. Anything rather than another anxious night invading their company, invading the room:

> *It's raining heavily tonight. Chatting with my mother, I was recalling my schooldays and the days when we used to go swimming. I get really down now when I remember back on those wonderful times compared to the state I'm in now.*[6]

> *I didn't sleep a wink yet and I don't feel a bit sleepy. Since I got that last turn, my mother is in the room with me. She's snoring away at this very moment … I'm very anxious tonight – that's if you can refer to what is really morning as night. Earlier tonight I was asking my mother about the different people who were in Ballyvourney when she first moved there. I was just trying to get through the night with talk, afraid that at any moment I'd be coughing and spitting up blood.*[7]

This is just one of many short fragments written in the dead of night. The following was written in daytime rather than at night:

> *I hunted my mother out of this room last night. It's better for her to be inside. Another fine day. Normally, I don't notice time passing …*[8]

When Seán's mother died, aged just sixty-two, it is hard to know whether the poet held himself partly responsible for her death. He left us no account of how he felt at the time, or how this huge tragedy impacted

6 D: 21 January 1940.
7 D: 4 a.m., 14 March 1942.
8 D: 20 March 1942.

on him. There is one short piece of writing, from 'Prima Donna eile' that seems to indicate that Seán felt at least partly to blame for her early death.[9] In this excerpt, the poet alludes to the kind of people 'who can accept everything that happens to them in this life as if it's part of some preordained plan as laid out from the beginning of time.' Needless to say, Ó Ríordáin wasn't enumerating himself as one of these types; he was one of the other crowd instead:

> *The first crowd remembers particular dates as if they were set down and assigned from the beginning of world [sic]. So-and-so died on the 21 January 1945. This is a date that's unchangeable, in their view. But the second crowd considers this date a mistake and that it was never set in time – that the person who died that day could have lived a lot longer if he'd been cared for better.*

Interestingly, Seán's mother, too, died of lung problems; she passed away on 21 January 1945. Perhaps it was just a random coincidence, but her death certificate ascribed her death to 'Lobar pneumonia, two days. Myocardial degeneration.' She'd certainly been suffering breathing problems for quite a while prior to her death, and when she felt weak her sister Gobnait would bring her over to sit near an open window so that she could breathe more easily. The constant to-ing and fro-ing between the main house and Seán's room at the back in all weathers and at all hours of the day and night couldn't have done much for her health. It was snowing the night that she died, just as it was the day of her funeral and burial, and the weather was some of the hardest weather within living memory. The roads were so slippery and dangerous that she couldn't be brought back to Ballyvourney for burial there, the weather so severe that it was even a struggle to reach the graveyard in Inniscarra. The roads were so dangerous that quite a number of Ó Ríordáin's family were unable to make it in from Ballyvourney for the funeral. She was buried in Inniscarra, in the 'white graveyard near the river' – and it was certainly blanketed in white that day.[10] In a strange way, maybe this was how she'd have preferred it – given

9 IT, 2 June 1973.
10 ES: p. 56.

that she'd never really felt she belonged back in Ballyvourney. And wasn't this place also closer to her mother's people and the English-speaking area of Cork, after all? Ó Ríordáin's mother was a woman who had never had much of an understanding of the Irish language or the culture that went with it. We don't know what she thought of Seán's literary pursuits other than what we can infer from something she said one day regarding his diary writing: 'Yourself and that fairy book of yours should be burned.'[11] And yet it was she who regularly threw the newspaper (*Scéala Éireann – The Irish Press*) in through the open window to him in the morning and brought him home the most recent edition of *Comhar* or *Dublin Opinion* or *John O'London's Weekly* from the city. She also regularly got him the books of Chesterton, Belloc, Yeats, Shaw, Ibsen or Hardy on loan from the library. On top of that, she had a nice dinner ready for him each day and she was his closest and most supportive companion in the whole world, especially when times were difficult. Her death in winter left the poet alone at the worst time of the year and he missed her greatly. And it's those wild and stormy nights when she sat with him, her hand stroking his forehead, that he associated forever with the night she died and that he immortalised in the poem 'Adhlacadh mo Mháthar' ('*My Mother's Burial*'):

Lámh a thál riamh cneastacht seana-Bhíobla
Lámh a bhí mar bhalsam is tú tinn.[12]

A hand as distinctive as any face.
A hand that had a Biblical charitableness.[13]

Another time and it's the winter cold and the cold that is death that are as one – in the poem 'Reo' ('*Stiff*').[14] He can tell that there's some buried memory associated with the frosted handkerchief but he needs to 're-search/seek out' the image in his mind so that it comes to him again – the

11 D: 28 January 1940.
12 ES: p. 56.
13 Sewell, *Selected Poems*, p. 47. Trans. Paul Muldoon.
14 B: p. 17.

image of her frozen mouth – the mouth that he hasn't kissed in so long. Once he stumbles on the correct image, he is at peace and the anxiety that gripped him when he initially glimpsed that frozen handkerchief is dissipated.

Reo

Ní héadach beo a léim óm ghlaic
Ach rud fuair bás aréir ar sceach:
Is siúd ag taighde mé fé m'intinn
Go bhfuaireas macasamhail an ní seo
  Lá dár phógas bean dem mhuintir
  Is í ina cónra reoite, sínte.[15]

Stiff

One frosty morning as I ventured out
a handkerchief on a bush seemed to carry such clout
I seized on it and tried to pay
it into my pocket but, being frozen, it slipped away.
This was no living remnant torn
from my grasp but something that expired last night on a thorn.
I cast about for a likeness till something fetched
up from deep within
my memory – that day I kissed one of my own kith and kin
who was stiff as a board in her coffin, stiff and stretched.[16]

In 'Éadóchas' (*'Despair'*), a much earlier poem of his than 'Reo', his loss is much more evident.[17] 'Éadóchas' was published in the March 1951 edition of *Comhar* under the title 'Tuambaí' ('*Tombs*'), but we find a draft of it in his diary for the period 3 April 1950 to 3 February 1951, indicating that

15 *Ibid.*
16 Sewell, *Selected Poems*, p. 137. Trans. Paul Muldoon.
17 ES: pp. 103–4.

he originally wrote the poem earlier than its publication. The completed poem appears in a letter of his to Séamus Ó Coigligh on 22 December 1950, where it is clear that Seán has penned the poem recently. 'I don't have time right now to write a proper letter but here's that poem,' he says at the beginning of the letter, which he signs off with the comment 'it's weak'.

This is a poem of blackest winter. 'And this, I think, is the loneliest poem I ever wrote. I think that I was of similar mind to the people in deepest hell when I wrote this' was the poet's description of the poem in some notes he prepared for a radio talk at one point. His description is very apt. There is no escaping the stultifying 'encroachment' of night here; the poet has no sanctuary and is forced into 'tasting the black chalice night' all alone. He is completely exposed and no one is there to offer him support – there is no longer any 'wall' that he can lean against when his cross becomes too heavy, and he can only wait for daylight to banish the dark. 'My mother is dead and I see her fleeing from me in the darkness' he wrote on the 28 October 1948. All traces of her have disappeared by now:

Éadóchas

Níl éinne sa tuama ag freastal
Ar chúngracht oíche ná lae,
Ná múscail aon tuama le machnamh
Ach umhlaigh do cheann nocht don chré.

Ná glaoigh ar an rud atá imithe,
Ná hiarr ar an bhfírinne sos,
Ná hiarr ar an Slánaitheoir aisling,
Ní déirc ins na Flaitheasaibh duit

Is lámh chaoin i dtuama á lobhadh,
Is aisling i dtuama fé leith,
An aisling dob annsa a lobhadh,
I dtuama san intinn istigh;

Is cailís dhubh na hoíche á blaiseadh,
Is Peardshuan thall is abhus,
Nuair a thairg Veronica an falla,
Nuair a lomadh san oíche an chruit.[18]

Despair

No one in the tomb is serving
The encroachment of night or day,
Do not awake any tomb to reflection
But bow your bare head to the earth.

Do not call back that which is gone,
Nor seek respite from the truth,
Do not ask the Saviour for the dream,
Nor for your charity in the Heavens

A gentle hand decays in one tomb,
And a dream in another tomb yet,
The dearest dream it decays,
In the inner tomb of the mind;

Tasting the black chalice of night,
The odd delusion here and there,
As when Veronica proffered the wall,
And the harp it was night-bared.[19]

The memories would fade over time, even if they are still alive in the piece cited below. The nights his mother spent chatting with him flood into Seán's mind again on his return to the room after a while spent in the main house with the others. His mother was dead at least six years by this point:

---

18 ES: pp. 103–4.
19 Trans. M. Ó hAodha.

> *I'm back in my own room again – the small, little room. Thank God. I'm home again. Isn't it lovely to be back in my own room again. My mother used to be here with me, God bless her soul. She'd sit on the chair opposite me here in the corner, her apron on her. Whenever I was sick, she'd tell me stories about when she was young.*[20]

Ó Ríordáin was very fond of Ibsen's writings and read them often in the early 1940s, particularly *Peer Gynt.* In this diary entry, some years on, by which time he's not as taken with Ibsen any more, he describes how reading the Norwegian playwright as a younger man influenced him:

> *I'm reading Ibsen and Chekhov again recently. I read them first in 1940. The first time I read Ibsen, I imagined that the Creator had been reborn and that he'd created everything anew again just for me. I got a new Bible. Ibsen Christ; Tolstoi, Chekhov, Strindberg, Turgenev, the four evangelists. But now, I'm not sure. I'm getting older. I don't have the same enthusiasm any more. A light hat is better than any other. That's why I bought a 'Christy Rollaway' [sic] the last time.*[21]

By the time he wrote this, the hat was nearly more important to the poet than Ibsen had once been. It had been very different story on 17 April 1942, however, when he imagined himself as Peer, a man whose sole form of heroism consisted of brave words and a gallant imagination. On 9 August 1944 he says: 'I read the death of Aase in *Peer Gynt* when I came home today and I shed tears.' And he writes this in the piece 'Ciotrúntacht' ('*Awkwardness*'): 'I knew a man once who'd weep after reading the account of Aase's death and before his own mother's death. After she died, however, he could read that account without it having the slightest effect on him.'[22]

That the man the poet refers to here is actually himself is clear from the diary entries – and given to be understood in at least one other piece

20 D: 4 June 1951.
21 D: 23 April 1949.
22 IT, 3 July 1975.

written by Ó Ríordáin.[23] Ó Ríordáin imagined the same mother–son relationship might have existed between Mícheál Ó Gaoithín, the Poet (An File) of Dunquin, and his mother Peig Sayers.[24]

On reading the account of Aase's death in the play *Peer Gynt* it's easy to see why it would have affected Ó Ríordáin so deeply: the long and rough nights of illness and the stories he and his mother told one another and embellished in order just to get through till morning. Similar to Seán in the piece from 4 June 1951 quoted above, Peer is back home now and remembering the stories his mother told him long ago. Aase is drifting closer to death and learning its contours. The following passage is from Rolf Fjelde's translation:

PEER GYNT

No, let's talk now, you and I –
But only of this and that.
Things that are twisted and wry,
That hurt – we can forget.
You're thirsty? Do you want a drink?
Have you room? That bed's like a toy.
Let me see – but, yes, I think
It's the one I had as a boy!
Remember the evenings you sat
By my bedside when I was young
And tucked me under the coverlet
And sang me ballad and song?

AASE

Of course! And when your father
Was out, then we played sleighs.
The spread was a lap robe of fur,
And the floor was a sheet of ice.

23 'Brendan Behan', IT, 13 August 1970.
24 'Aindreas Ó Gallchóir', IT, 13 May 1972.

PEER GYNT

Yes, but all else above –
You remember, Mother, too –
The dashing horses we drove –

AASE

Yes, don't you think I know – ?
Our cat, and that other one –
Kari's, we had her on loan.

PEER GYNT

To the Castle East of the Sun
And the Castle West of the Moon,
To Soria-Moria Castle
The high and the low roads wound.
You had a whip with a tassel –
It was just a stick we'd found …[25]

It would be no surprise if 'the Castle West of the Moon' was the inspiration for the 'gealt-teach iargúlta tá laistiar den ré' ('*from the desolate madhouse behind the moon*') in 'Oíche Nollaig na mBan' ('*Women's Christmas*'), the magic of Ibsen's old castle swelling up in the stormy world that is the abandoned poet's. (This poem was composed in 1947 in my opinion – see below.)

Peer Gynt's influence on Ó Ríordáin waned over time, in much the same way as the poet's memories of his mother also became fainter. (I have attempted to demonstrate elsewhere how influential this play probably was in the philosophical system that Ó Ríordáin was devising for himself in the 1940s.)[26] Then, when 21 January comes around again, it reminds him of his mother's death. Seán has long abandoned the room outside by the time he notes the following:

25 Ibsen, Henrik, *Peer Gynt* (Signet Classics, New York, 1964), pp. 115–16.
26 Ó hAnluain (ed.), *An Duine is Dual*, pp. 85–8.

> *My mother died in this same bed that I'm in now, eighteen years ago today, God blessing [sic] on her. I don't miss her any more, I'm afraid. She's been completely dead to my mind for a long time. It's a long time since I thought of her at all. I don't get upset any more when I think of her. When she was alive I couldn't read the death of Aase in* Peer Gynt *without a tear coming to my eyes. I could read that piece now without any emotion at all, I think.*[27]

His thoughts are similar when he recalls her anniversary six years later:

> *Twenty-four years ago today, my mother, Máiréad (Aggie) Ní Luineacháin (RIP), may God give her grace, died in this room. I don't miss her one way or the other now. Oh! A flea. It's a long time since I saw one of them …*[28]

If 'An Stoirm' was written in early 1943, then 'An Doircheacht' ('*The Dark*') came before that again.[29] Both were entered for Oireachtas competitions in 1944, as was a third poem 'Bacaigh' ('*Beggars*').[30] ('An Stoirm' was the only poem that won a prize as it happens; this prize was worth three pounds which was a good deal more than he'd have got in a week working in City Hall.) If the fragment below was written around the same time as 'An Doircheacht' and both are similar in terms of rationale, then this means that 'An Doircheacht' is the very earliest of Ó Ríordáin's poems that we now have. (But, as we shall see later, it was only two months ahead of 'An Leigheas' ('*The Cure*'), a work that secured another three-pound prize in the Oireachtas festival of 1943, the first ever money prize Ó Ríordáin received for his poetry.)[31] Ó Ríordáin noted in his diary for 30 January 1957 that he enjoyed storms as a child and this particular storm recounted in the poem reprises his earliest memories now, even if the storm also usurps his childhood. The past and the present are very different places and yet it is the contrast between these two worlds that ensures their power for him. The wind that blows here is softer than that

27 D: 21 January 1963.
28 D: 4.40 a.m., 21 January 1969.
29 ES: p. 42.
30 ES: p. 37.
31 ES: p. 29.

which rages in 'An Stoirm' and it is easier to deal with as a consequence. Here is the diary excerpt:

> *A howling windy day, the wind strong on the window; it's the kind of wind that reminds me of the weather when I was an innocent child and the sins that have tainted my soul since. A wintry wind such as this fills my heart with loneliness and regret – always and without fail. She quenched the candle on me just now as I was noting this. It's the same way that a person's hope is extinguished with the advent of a sudden idea. When this bitter wet wind blows, I think back with regret on the young ego of times past, that young, ignorant, fearless ego that disappeared years ago, and which – like the years that can never return – make an old man of me. And I'm only twenty-five years of age. But when a fit of regret [such as this] comes over you, my unknown friend, just remember Hardy's thrush:*
>
> *An aged thrush, frail, gaunt, and small*
> *In blast-beruffled plume,*
> *[Hath chosen thus to fling his soul*
> *Upon the growing gloom.]*
>
> *and the fog disperses, the despair disappears and your courage returns, if you still have courage left in you. But maybe such unreasonable fits of despair only afflict fools and people who are sick, or people who have both these faults, like me.*[32]

Let's leave the 'young, ignorant, fearless ego' and the sins that hinder his attempts to source the innocent youthful days behind for the moment; this is a struggle that comes to the fore again in Ó Ríordáin's later poetry, needless to say.

It is the smothering of the candle of hope that he addresses in the diary entry that corresponds with the poem below:

---

32 D: 6 April 1942. The extract is from Thomas Hardy's poem, 'The Darkling Thrush'.

An Doircheacht

Ag luí dhom im leaba anocht
Is daille na hoíche ar mo shúilibh
Smaoinim gan feirg gan tocht,
Gan oiread is deoir ar mo ghruannaibh,
Ar na soilse do múchadh im shaol:
Gach solas dár las ann do múchadh
Le tubaist dochreidte do shéid
Mar an ghaoth seo ag béicigh im chluasaibh.
Is ait liom gur mise an té
A chaill gach aon dóchas a fuair sé,
Is ait liom go rabhas-sa inné
Go dóchasach ainnis im bhuachaill,
Ach tá an doircheacht codlatach séimh,
Níl cúram ar bith ar mo shúilibh,
Is ní saoire ina buile an ghaoth
Ná an té tá gan solas le múchadh.[33]

The Dark

Lying in my bed tonight,
the blackness of night on my eyes,
I think without anger or emotion
or a single tear on my cheeks
of the lights that went out in my life:
every light that was lit was quenched
by unbelievable disaster that blew
like this wind screeching in my ears.
I find it strange that I lost
every hope that came my way,
I find it strange that only yesterday
I was the awkward hopeful boy;

33 ES: p. 42.

but the dark of sleep is gentle,
my eyes are free from care,
and the wind is no freer in its frenzy
than the man with no light to quench.[34]

The metaphor of the candle has appeared by this point, a metaphor that features ever more strongly in his poetry as time goes on. In fact, this metaphor had appeared in the diaries long before we came across it in the poetry or in 'An Doircheacht'. The following passage is from his diary for 10 January 1940. The death of the candle and the death of life are used as a metaphor for one another:

> *It is night and I am sitting here in my own little room in my writing, a lighted candle next to me. The candle is fading and coming to an end. The night is fading. I myself am fading and coming to an end.*

Needless to say, this was a metaphor that Ó Ríordáin didn't ever need to source in literature given that it was always there beside him, right between the four walls of his room. It was a metaphor that he could scarcely avoid, given his long-term illness. The image of fragile life extending its finger towards death, lighting up the dark momentarily before it is swallowed up, the threatening rustle of the wind around the house at night, the sudden asthma attack and the night-terrors and the helpless anger that follows swiftly on its heels. 'An Doircheacht' is simply the next stage on the journey; he has moved to somewhere that is beyond the brutal extinguishment of the candle in the dark; the choice has been made, and the darkness of night comes as a form of release, a release that needs to be experienced for itself. In truth, he couldn't really have been expecting any other form of release from the beginning, could he? *Una salus victis: nullam sperare salutem* is Virgil's Latin phrase that consoles him in the diary.[35] It's the poet's embrace of death – the death of health and youth.

34 Sewell, *Selected Poems*, p. 21. Trans. Peter Sirr.

35 27 January 1940. Virgil's phrase roughly translates as 'The only hope for the doomed is no hope at all.'

His reasons for hope were all a misunderstanding, a mistake he'd made when he was weak and sick. Someone else could take the blows from now on because he is finished with all of that, he decrees.

In reality, this was very far from the end of it for Ó Ríordáin, however. In many ways, his story had only begun. There would be plenty of other nights where he would take a hiding – physically and metaphorically from the darkness, plenty of nights where he would be joined by the slew of night-creatures that share his room, the moths and the insects of all kinds that batter themselves against the walls and get burned in the flame. On one such night, the poet crushes one of these creatures and leaves it dead on the open page as evidence of his 'human' treachery. The relatives of the dead creature gather round then, ready to take their revenge, their shadows magnified and enormous in the dark in an attempt to intimidate the poet further. He quenches the candle and listens to the flutter of wings as they go quiet where he cannot see them on the wall. He lights the candle once more and the moths and other insects gather around him once more. One of them gets caught in the flame and incinerates itself and the distress that accompanies this is blown into the half-finished page in front of Ó Ríordáin so that the writing of the poem is moved along:

????[36]

Smaoineamh beag mailíseach

A thosnaigh thíos in ifreann
In inchinn an diabhail féin,
Is a eitil tríd an oíche,

Mar leamhan ag lorg solais
Go ráinig lampa an Tiarna
Is gur chrom ar Dhia do chiapadh …[37]

36 This poem is untitled in the conventional literary sense. The four question marks are its title.

37 ES: p. 98.

????

A small malicious thought

Which originated below in hell
In the mind of the devil himself,
And which flew through the night,

Like a moth seeking light
And reached the lamp of the Lord
And began to torment God …[38]

Another time and he's reading late into the night and a moth gets caught in the flame again and singes itself; it falls to the ground, its wings burned. The poet looks on from his bed – from the region of forgetfulness, sleep and dreaming – then remembers back to that other night when he was the one who crushed those same small wings and stopped them beating. The scorched moth enters into his dream and the dream-moth emerges into the room and changes the atmosphere there. In this case, the dream-moth highlights the inability of the person in the bed to protect another fragile life, the way a 'real man' would. This is a poetry sometimes found in the diaries in which it becomes difficult to distinguish between dreams and reality; we are in a between-space, a place we drift in and out of.

Ó Ríordáin wrote a number of other poems at this juncture that have a strong dream-like quality to them. They are poems imbued with the strange atmosphere that is halfway between waking and sleeping – that anxious and 'unsettled' mood that permeates poems such as 'Fiabhras' ('*Fever*'), 'Tromluí' ('*Nightmare*'), and 'Roithleán' ('*Whirl*').[39] 'Tromluí' is the first of them to appear in his rough notes: an early draft of it appears towards the end of a copybook where Ó Ríordáin noted some of his thoughts and activities for July and August 1944; one assumes that it was some time around then that he began this poem. He writes out the poem – or as

38 Trans. M. Ó hAodha.

39 B: p. 26; TÉB: pp. 35–6; ES: p. 53.

much of it as he has completed – in his diary for 13 April 1949, where he also says that it's 'five or six or seven years' since he first began working on it. The mysterious world of sleep and dreaming permeates 'Roithleán' also; it may be frightening sometimes, but it isn't the worst thing in the world to see the truth in the clarity and bright light of morning. When exactly the poet wrote 'Roithleán' isn't entirely clear, but it was first published in the journal *An Síol* in 1948 – making it relatively contemporaneous with the following diary excerpt:

> *I often half-woke in the morning, my night of sleep done, or almost done, and I'd weave an element of dream onto the last little stretch of sleep that remained as best I could. But I couldn't progress at all; I'd just be going around, around, around in the same place until I became tired and frightened. In the end it was a great relief to give up altogether.*[40]

'Awake! Frightened!' Two of the most frequently cited words in Ó Ríordáin's diary, perhaps, and two of the states he was most familiar with. The 'music of the night' – that which carries over into the 'sigh of morning'. Or perhaps the poet has a good part of the night to run yet and the sleeping pill is already long-taken and beyond having an effect. And, worse still, the fear of taking a second pill – because you can't remember any more whether you took the first one or not. And still the remainder of the night – as bled into words in the diary and the poem – where he can't hide beneath the blanket that is dreaming any more. Was a poem such as 'Roithleán' composed in such circumstances or was it taken straight from the diary as formed in cold blood, as Ó Ríordáin had no compunction doing later in his writing life? Let's assume that it is a poem that was spontaneously created in the moment:

Roithleán

Bhí ceol na hoíche seinnte
Is cnead na maidne im chluais

40 D: 2 October 1947.

Nuair do rugas-sa mo ghreim docht
Ar urla bheag den suan,
A chlúdaigh m'anam thuas
I gceantar na míorúilt
San oíche mhór ealaíonta
'Na rinceann treabh na dtaibhreamh
Le ceolta míréasúin
Anonn is anall gan chúis.

Do choinníos uirthi greim docht,
An urla bheag dem shuan,
Lena sníomh i bhfoirm taibhrimh
Ach bhí an mhaidinchnead im chluais,
Is bhí an urla bheag róchúng,
Is níor shníomhas ach an tús,
Nuair do chas an tús sin timpeall
Gan trócaire ina roithleán:
    Do bheinn im ghealt go buan
    Ach gur scaoileas uaim an suan.[41]

Whirl

Night-music had drawn to a close
and morning whispered in my ear
when I laid firm hold on
a little wisp of sleep
that clothed my soul up there
in the miracle zone
of the great firmament
reeling to the dream-plough
illogically lilting
back and forth for no cause.

41 ES: p. 53.

I held it firm as firm could be,
my little wisp of sleep,
that I might spin a dream thereof,
but morning whispered in my ear,
and the wisp was next to nothing.
All I had spun was the beginning
whereupon it turned about me
mercilessly whirling:
    had I not let slip that little sleep
    I would be forever moonstruck.[42]

In 'Feithideacht' ('*Insecthood*') we meet another dizzy insect of the night, one that nature has allowed to go clean out of all control.[43] As the poet has already foreseen the 'apocalypse of dreaming', he imagines that he has traduced 'the law of tiny things' so that the insect had become 'misshapen' and assumed gigantic proportions in his imagination. We are in strange and unfamiliar territory here once more, in a place that is neither day nor night, waking nor sleeping, big nor small, and we must accompany the poet on his journey through it. If this isn't the place the insane inhabit, we are certainly somewhere in its vicinity, and we may well have traversed its invisible border unknown to ourselves. This is the journey Ó Ríordáin undertakes at night when a combination of illness, fear and various medicines including sleeping pills frequently forms a mist and obscures his normal route or way. The world is alive and shapeless with motion and the only stability here is the anchor of his pen and the trace of his inked words on the page. It's not as if literature is even the poet's primary objective here, even if this is the outcome of his struggle when morning eventually comes around and the world is at rest again; it is the strict necessity of the moment that propels him to write. And there are plenty of nights when Ó Ríordáin is so terrified of the dark and, more particularly, the choking feeling and breathing difficulties induced by TB, that (understandably) he can't bring himself to extinguish the candle that's propped next to his bed. All he can

42 Sewell, *Selected Poems*, p. 41. Trans. Ciaran Carson.
43 ES: p. 89.

do is transfer his frightened bedroom thoughts onto paper and bring them under the jurisdiction of the 'word' whenever possible; in this way, maybe fear will loosen its grip somewhat. The important thing is to try to manage the fear, wrap it up in words before it gets entirely out of control. The point of reference the poet observes until morning is the small light of the flickering candle; otherwise, the darkness will overwhelm both the light and the poet. This is the terrain that is 'Claustrophobia' all over again. And, unsurprisingly, Ó Ríordáin recognises a fellow traveller on this rocky and obscure road, when he comes across the writings of Spanish mystic Saint John of the Cross. The simple truth as a companion on the arduous road:

> *It is unlikely that John of the Cross had any book in his possession when he was in prison. He had only the most important library there is. He (himself) as* en una noche oscura. *But it was during this period that he wrote everything worthwhile.*[44]

Ó Ríordáin understood quite well what St John of the Cross meant when he spoke of searching for the truth.

> *a oscuras y en celada,*
> *estando ya mi casa sosegada*

> In shadow and stealth
> From my silent house[45]

Even if one believes that it isn't just the bleak voice of the individual that is the medium for the most powerful poetry, as he seeks to imply in the essay from which the excerpt (cited above) is taken, one must nonetheless acknowledge the person who speaks faithfully in accordance with that voice. In a sense, the ability to speak faithfully is more important than what is actually said. Ó Ríordáin's inner voice might have spoken differently if he'd had another life experience beyond that of the 'una

44 'Teachtaireacht Amháin' (*'One Message'*), IT, 1 April 1970.
45 Trans. M. Ó hAodha.

noche oscura', but that was not his fate. He tried to reconcile what he'd personally experienced and reflect it in his art. Here was his experience – here was his poem.

But let us return to the storm-filled nights of the 1940s, those Ó Ríordáin had fashioned poetry from. Composed slightly later than 'An Doircheacht' was 'Oíche Nollaig na mBan' ('*Women's Christmas*'). It seems to have been written in or around 6 January 1947 and is associated with that feast day. This poem and 'Oilithreacht Fám Anam' ('*My Soul's Pilgrimage*') both secured prizes in the Oireachtas competitions of 1947; Ó Ríordáin's initial drafts for 'Oíche Nollaig na mBan', 'Oilithreacht Fám Anam' and 'Sos' ('*Relief*') all appear in the same copybook that he was using as a diary at the time and, in an entry for 23 January 1948, he notes that he'd published 'Oíche Nollaig na mBan' almost exactly as it came to him on the night in question and with very little change, and that it was 'at least a year' since he composed it. In 'Oíche Nollaig na mBan', similar to 'An Doircheacht', the storm is blowing and the light is being extinguished and the silence of death is palpable towards the end of the poem. One also senses a hidden joy or thrill in the observer, the poet who is safely tucked up in bed and listening to the wind gusting outside – as he once did as a child – the squalls of the wind and the neighbour's gates 'squawking' on their hinges like the 'cackling of a goose'.

'I think that there's a magic in gates. Wherever there are gates, there is poetry,' he says in the diary entry for 21 January 1957. It's the 'loneliness' of the gate outside in the night that engenders feeling. In a similar vein, Ó Ríordáin's diary for 12 December 1967, a full decade later, notes the poetry he always senses 'in gates and in goats'. In 'Oíche Nollaig na mBan' the night is filled with wind and the sounds of gates and birds and other animals. The gust of wind that extinguishes the candle is like a sudden slap across the face. Where there was some relief in the quenching of the light in 'An Doircheacht', the poet doesn't mind the wind and storms that accompany him into the eternity of 'Oíche Nollaig na mBan' to the same extent. In the end, any noise is better than eternal and deathly silence – because silence is another form of suffering.[46] The window of the poet's

46 ES: p. 40.

room won't be shut this time and the people returning from the dance won't realise it but they're lucky that they cannot hear what the poet hears, that they don't have to listen … And he hears their exuberant shouts as they return back along the road from the dance now and their shouts are as one with the crazy roar of the storm. The poet hears it all – he listens and waits, and the shouts of the young people, like the storm, fade back into night and the world goes silent once more:

Oíche Nollaig na mBan

Bhí fuinneamh sa stoirm a éalaigh aréir,
Aréir oíche Nollaig na mBan,
As gealt-teach iargúlta tá laistiar den ré
Is do scréach tríd an spéir chughainn 'na gealt,
Gur ghíosc geataí comharsan mar ghogallach gé,
Gur bhúir abhainn shlaghdánach mar tharbh,
Gur múchadh mo choinneal mar bhuille ar mo bhéal
A las 'na splanc obann an fhearg.

Ba mhaith liom go dtiocfadh an stoirm sin féin
An oíche go mbeadsa go lag
Ag filleadh abhaile ó rince an tsaoil
Is solas an pheaca ag dul as,
Go líonfaí gach neomat le liúrigh ón spéir,
Go ndéanfaí den domhan scuaine scread,
Is ná cloisfinn an ciúnas ag gluaiseacht fám dhéin,
Ná inneall an ghluaisteáin ag stad.[47]

Women's Christmas

There was power in the storm that escaped last night,
last night on Women's Christmas,
from the desolate madhouse behind the moon

47 ES: p. 68.

and screamed through the sky at us, lunatic,
making neighbours' gates screech like geese
and the hoarse river roar like a bull,
quenching my candle like a blow to the mouth
that sparks a quick flash of rage.

I'd like if that storm would come again,
a night I'd be feeling weak
coming home from the dance of life
and the light of sin dwindling,
that every moment be full of the screaming sky,
that the world be a storm of screams,
and I wouldn't hear the silence coming over me,
the car's engine come to a stop.[48]

The critic Seán Ó Tuama posited that this is a poem 'where God is being rejected completely and formally'.[49] But perhaps he was reading too much into the metaphors Ó Ríordáin employed here ('the light of sin', 'the car's engine'), which don't comprise a philosophical argument in themselves but are instead the recourse of one individual struggling alone against his fate and expressing this in the form of poetry. If there is a rejection here, it is certainly not a complete or formal one, but rather a kicking-back, as demanded by the necessities of the moment. And that this rejection is but a temporary one has been ably demonstrated by Seán Ó Tuama in other works of his.

The Oireachtas adjudicator focused more on Ó Ríordáin's use of language in 'Oíche Nollaig na mBan' and the fact that some of his terminology was new and modern as compared with that traditionally used in Irish-language poetry – the likes of 'the car's engine come to a stop'. The adjudicator liked the poem, however. Here is part of his feedback on it:

48 Sewell, *Selected Poems*, p. 73. Trans. Theo Dorgan.
49 Ó Tuama, *Filí faoi Sceimhle*, p. 47.

> *The influence of the evil spirits is evident in this draft as is the seal of the true poet. It would be easy to list its special attributes – the imagination, the freshness, the power of description that it has. There is strong and precise imagery here and thoughts that startle the mind. I know it's stupid to award marks to a draft such as this … I didn't give this draft full marks because I wasn't entirely happy with the final line – maybe I'm a bit old-fashioned when it comes to poetry.*

Whatever mark the poem received, Ó Ríordáin secured first prize on this occasion again. With respect to the literary critics, one could hardly argue as Seán Ó Tuama did that 'Sos' was 'one of his very earliest poems', particularly if one accepts, as Ó Tuama does elsewhere, that the poem 'Adhlacadh mo Mháthar', as written in 1945, constituted a definite change of direction in terms of Ó Ríordáin's work.[50] 'Sos' had been entered in the Oireachtas competition of 1948, but wasn't published until December of the same year, in the journal *Feasta.* But even if 'Sos' came later than the other aforementioned poems, it corresponds very well to the mindset evinced in some of the poet's earliest diary writings. Such diary entries often recount how he'd go back to the local hall with the intention of trying to flirt with (or ask out) some local girl (her name isn't mentioned), but his courage would fail him and he'd return home as quickly again, back to the cold walls of the room where he might write down what had just happened; then, as if to compound his isolation, the sound of the revellers returning from the dance later that night just adds to the resentment towards the world 'outside' that's been building in the poet's heart. But it's not all timidity in this poem either, because psychologically, the poet has already separated himself from the 'raucous crowd' – much the same as they've put a distance between them and this 'damaged' person who inhabits the fringes. The excerpts below can be compared with the poem itself:

> *He opened the hall and we went in. There was a lot of noise going on and there were a lot of boys and girls there. There was a pretty young girl there that I loved once from afar, except that I didn't have the guts to approach her. I was there*

50 Ó Tuama, *Filí faoi Sceimhle*, p. 74.

> *barely five minutes when a feeling of shyness came over me and I slipped off home, feeling alone. As I said before the connection that was there once between me and the local community no longer exists any more.*[51]

Another occasion – the saddest and most pitiable of all perhaps – is when the drama group from Ballyvourney visits Inniscarra. Seán Ó Cronin is the director of a play he's written himself. He drops over to the house to enquire about Seán, but Ó Ríordáin is too ashamed to meet this man he once knew in Ballyvourney and hides himself away until the man is gone again. Over the course of the afternoon, others from the group call over and it is Seán's mother who gives the poet the latest news on everyone who comes in – after they've all left, needless to say. The girl who has grown up and who is a real beauty now, the man who has put on a lot of weight, the person who has got very old-looking – and yet, the worst of them all is still in a much better way than poor Seán. They perform the play and hold a dance immediately afterwards, as they always do:

> *The drama crowd came over from Ballyvourney. They stopped at the hall. Before long, they were coming over in groups to the shop here. I didn't see any of them. I hid from them. And, oh Mary, I would've loved to have seen them really! Eight years ago! Yes, it's eight years ago now since they knew me. I had my health at that time. Now that I'm no longer healthy, I'd sooner the frost than meet any of them. That's why I hid myself away from them … I couldn't stay in the room any longer. I went up the hill. I fled from my own people as they're thriving and getting stronger while I'm fading and going into decline. Soon, I was up on the top of the hill, looking grimly downwards. I heard the joyful laughter coming over to me and the powerful and lively sounds of the dancers, and every spirited clout their shoes struck the ground with was a blow of sorrow to the heart of this young old person here. And there was pride in each wallop they gave the floor. And my poor health cowered before them and I was glad of the darkness that concealed me from them and hid my decline and my weakness from them; I imagined that those sturdy legs of the dancers actually despised my thin and emaciated self. I imagined myself as a wounded animal*

---

51 D: 7 February 1940.

> *that is thrown into the ditch and the healthier animals gone off triumphantly in search of food.*[52]

The 'echoing sound' of the dancer's feet can still be heard in 'Sos' but the nostalgic loneliness of it has dissipated in the intervening seven years. Ó Ríordáin knows his place in the community now better than anyone. The wind can blow where she likes, the dancers can dance their own dance. His life is set on a different course now and has a different destination. And the inner world speaks a very different language to the outer world and neither can understand one another because he writes in Irish, a hidden idiom that is almost a secret language. And yet this isn't the principal difference between the inner world and the world outside as the poet sees it now in 'Sos':

Sos

Mar sceach fé thathaint na gaoithe
Tá m'anam á lúbadh anocht,
Thiar ná thoir níl dídean
Mar is poll im cheann gach smaoineamh
Trína liúnn an ghaoth gan sos.

Raghad go halla an rince
Mar a múineann fuaimint cos
Is béarlagar na mianta
Bodhaire seal don intinn,
Is gheobhad ansan mo shos.

Ach do labhair gach aghaidh go líofa,
Ach m'aghaidhse bhí i dtost,
I dteanga nár airíos-sa
Á labhairt amuigh san iasacht
'Na mbím go haonarach.

---

52 D: 10 March 1940.

Cumfad féin de bhriathra
Scáthán véarsaí anocht,
As a labharfaidh aghaidh scoraíochtach
A mhalartóidh liom faoistin,
Is gheobhad ansan mo shos.[53]

Relief

Like a thorn-bush battered by the wind,
my soul is twisted and turned tonight;
west or east, there's no shelter,
every thought a hole in the head
the wind howls through without relief.

I will go along to the dance hall
where the sound of stamping feet
and the codewords of desire
will numb the mind a while,
and then I'll find some relief.

But every face, except mine
which was silent, spoke fluently
in a tongue I'd never heard
out in the wilderness
where I exist alone.

Tonight, I will craft from words
a looking-glass of verse
where a neighbourly face will speak
and exchange confession with me,
then I'll find some relief.[54]

53 ES: p. 46.
54 Sewell, *Selected Poems*, p. 29. Trans. Robert Welch and Frank Sewell.

The word 'scoraíochtach' (*house-calling in the evening*) is one that Ó Ríordáin took straight out of his past life in Ballyvourney, when people would call in to one another and have a chat and a laugh and exchange gossip or tell a few stories next to the fire. As the simpleton or 'fool/jester' who speaks on the poet's behalf in another of Ó Ríordáin's poems 'Na hÓinmhidí' ('*The Jesters*'), he'd test the shape and texture of the Irish word before he elected to use it during those nights of socialising, repartee and witty talk at different hearths – *'oícheanta ag scoraíocht/Cois tine gach aon fhocail'* ('nights spent house-calling/next to the fire, every word').[55] Here, we can almost see the words gathering momentum as he goes back to the old days and the old firesides that he can still remember and resurrects the half-forgotten memories and languages. Either that or travelling back west in his imagination and sifting amongst the 'dead' of Gaelic literature until he discovers again that 'house-calling mindset' – as a still-living tradition back in Dunquin, County Kerry. 'I feel guilty whenever I go socialising anywhere now except in the Gaeltacht,' he notes in the diary for 18 October 1956. Not that such socialising is a form of confession in itself, either; rather, it better equips him to hone the confessional or inner self of his writings and to do so more eloquently.

Other early poems which demonstrate the tension Ó Ríordáin sees between himself and those 'others' who inhabit the world outside are 'An Leigheas' ('*The Cure*') and 'An Peaca' ('*The Sin*').[56]

Initially, of course, it was obligatory that Ó Ríordáin avoid the company of other people for health reasons, and especially for the health of others. Before long, however, it is they that are deemed unclean in his work, and he's the one who feels that he's better off keeping his distance from them. He explains the rationale behind 'An Leigheas' in this excerpt from a radio script: 'Here's a short poem that emerged from the nostalgia, and the sentimentality of youth. "Peataíol" [petting/spoiling little children] is what my grandmother used to call it.' It's clear that there's more to this poem than this, however, as evident from the diary entry that relates to it. Also, it is the diary entry that allows us to date the poem (which was

55 ES: pp. 85–8.
56 ES: pp. 29 and 41.

first published in *Comhar* in April 1944) more accurately. It seems to be the second-earliest of his poems, the composition of which can be dated with reasonable accuracy. The background to the poem is the most crucial aspect of all, however:

> *I spent yesterday evening chatting with the louts outside until darkness fell. My mind was in torment. I knew that the best cure for my troubles was to go and read or write something rather than feeding on the louts and the scum. But I'm weak and I need to mix with my fellow animals. There isn't the least shred of dignity or manners [or] brains about any of them. All they like is filth and dirt of all kinds and they're never mean or miserly with one another or with me. The truth, in another guise, is to be found amongst the likes of them. This is better than a lie, disguised in the habit of a nun. I was right there amongst them as a demon mixed in with the most rancid shit in hell and them around me gorging all the filth they possibly could with their eyes and their ears, and shouting and roaring with infernal pleasure. There wasn't a girl who went back the road that they didn't ingest every morsel of her in their minds. I swear that there wasn't even the slightest smidgeon of soft calf or the brief, tasty sight of knee belonging to any girl who cycled past that was wasted on any of them, or on me either. If it wasn't that the truth, incredible as it is, didn't manifest itself – the incredible truth that manifests itself amongst a shower of whores, whores that are whores in public – then Dante's hell would burn up all around us.*
>
> *The sky to the east was so red in colour that you'd have imagined the sun was going under over there. But it wasn't the sky that was red really but the large clouds stretched across the sky that was as a new country anchored in a bay of blue. But those clouds reminded me of Russia, they were that red – covered with blood. And I thought that I'd found the Crimea and Sebastapol. The red was duly absorbed into the clouds and we were left with the lonely, dirty detritus of clay.*
>
> *I came home and wrote a few verses.*[57]

There's no doubt that the 'some verses' he mentioned that evening are the ones found in the poem confided to his diaries – 'An Leigheas' ('*The Cure*'):

57 D: 13 June 1942.

An Leigheas

Do chaitheas tráthnóna le caidreamh,
Is scamaill go fuilteach sa spéir,
Gur súdh an fhuil as na scamaill,
Is fágadh ann salachar mar chré,
Im thimpeall bhí daoscar cuideachtach
Ag magadh is ag eascainí baoth;
Níor fhéadas suí socair sa bhaile
Ag suirí le leabhraibh an léinn
Is pianta go fuilteach ar m'anam,
Mar bhí fear ar an gcnoc thiar le bé.
Do thomas an fhuil ins an salachar,
Sin priomhleigheas an daoscair ar phéin.[58]

The Cure

I spent an afternoon chatting
With clouds blood-red in the sky,
And the blood was sucked out of the clouds,
And there was left there dirt like earth
Around me there was a sociable crowd
Joking and cursing foolishly;
I could not sit quietly at home
Flirting with learned books
And there were cruel pains on my soul,
Since there was a man on the hill behind in the company of a woman.
I plunged the blood into the dirt,
That is the rabble's principal cure for pain.[59]

The clash between the blood and the clouds in the sky above reflects the battle that's going on in the poet's mind. The cold, frigid 'courtship' of his

58 ES: p. 29.
59 Trans. M. Ó hAodha.

books is useless when he's plagued by his own sexual desires and thinks of your man 'on the hill behind' keeping company with a woman. One way or the other, it's the 'pollution' or 'filth'; initially, he drains the pain away through the blood that he gives up, the blood he spits up with the TB and the suffering – and attempts to heal himself. But he has already abandoned his observation post; it's too late – he's gone down and rolled himself in the dirt and it has left a bad taste in his mouth. This is the pollution that he can't forgive himself for; this was his blood and he shouldn't have fouled it and corrupted it like this. In the end, his blood is all he has; what else has he got that makes him distinctive from the rest? But it's the same spilling of blood that the demons recommend for him in 'Oilithreacht Fám Anam' when he has already become familiar with sin and it's clear what 'sin' he means here:

Bhí ceol na ndeamhan á sheinm
I solas chíoch na mban.[60]

The music of demons was playing
In the light of the woman's breasts.[61]

He struggles with the same inner battle in 'Ualach na Beatha' ('*The Burden of Life*') as well as in 'Na hÓinmhidí' ('*The Jesters*'), a struggle and a tension that's heavily influenced by the puritanical outlook, or 'Victorianism' that Seán Ó Tuama cited.[62] Interestingly, when Ó Ríordáin received his copy of Ó Tuama's essay as published in *Studia Hibernica*, this word 'Victorianism' was the one word that he marked with his pen. Put another way, these were 'the normal scruples of conscience of any young Catholic' of this era, except that they were exacerbated in Ó Ríordáin's case by the disgust he felt at the disease that was martyring his own body. The likes of this in 'Ualach na Beatha' ('*The Burden of Life*') is a case in point:

60 ES: p. 72.
61 Trans. M. Ó hAodha.
62 Ó Tuama, *Filí faoi Sceimhle*, p. 75.

Iar mbíogadh as aisling na feola
Tháinig fuaire agus baine ar mo ghné
Do scrúdaíos an dara ródchomhartha,
Cé go mb'fhionn liom éalú gan é léamh,

Ardchnoc is sneachta ar a bharr
Agus umhalmhachnamh uaigneach sa spéir
Gaoth bhorb gan fothain mhná,
Staonadh agus cúngfhocal Dé.[63]

After rousing from a dream of flesh,
a coolness and a pallor came over me;
I studied the sign for the second path
though I wanted to flee without reading it:

a mountain peak with snow on the summit
and the humble reflection of loneliness in the sky;
such a bitter wind without the shelter of a woman,
abstinence and the narrow word of God.[64]

The problem is identified even if its resolution in this instance is far too neat to be deemed of any great literary merit; it's a problem that must be taken into consideration nonetheless when discussing Ó Ríordáin as a human being and as a poet. This issue of natural sexual desires and feelings was one that bothered him a lot, to the point that he often marked in his diary the days that he went to confession and mentally kept tab of his 'chaste periods' as he himself referred to them. Returning to the poem 'An Leigheas', however, it has to be said that Ó Ríordáin's explication of the poem (as provided in the diaries) proved far simpler and more satisfying than Frank O'Brien's complex and somewhat mysterious reading of same:

63 ES: pp. 33–4.

64 Sewell, *Selected Poems*, p. 9. Trans. Denise Blake.

> *In this poem, there is a concern with the merging and re-merging of unrelated aspects together. During the course of the poem, the natural world and human nature cleave apart from one another and then become as one again through a sequence of elements that, at a first glance, don't appear to have any connection between them. In the first line of the poem, we are reminded that the persona is among friends, but, in reality, such feelings are being routed in his mind. This human company (or the ideas that have been given a humanity) are very similar to the blood-coloured clouds that have gathered and blended together in the sky …*
>
> *The same as those dead clouds, when the blood has been drained from them, the persona loses whatever interest he had in his own problems: 'I couldn't sit still at home.' As some of this company breaks up, the company that created the persona, the cloud-blood mingles with the colour that is the poet's living pain. As this mingling or mixing of the clouds takes place, a part of himself fades and dies and another comes to life …*[65]

The poet, in contrast, noted how he came to compose 'An Leigheas', the 'cure' that isn't a cure really, in his diary: 'The evening is cold and my comrades, the proletariat, are gone off for a walk to warm themselves. I'll make myself warm with a spot of writing.' As Ó Ríordáin frequently acknowledged, his attempts at warming himself with words and writing proved fruitless as often as they culminated in anything worthwhile. In fact, one senses from some of his diary musings that he would actually love to join the 'proletariat' outside more often than he would admit to, with a view to further subject matter or life experiences; that he would like to go around begging almost amongst the community, like the last of the Gaelic poets, if only the subject matter he sought was available there. He is too nervous to take a chance on it, however, and afraid that he won't find anything worthwhile, so he simply avoids it. And wouldn't it have been worse still in a sense if you actually had found what you sought there? In such circumstances it wouldn't have been out of place to include Ó Ríordáin amongst those:

65 O'Brien, *Filíocht Ghaeilge*, pp. 322–3.

Na droinge sin bacaíochta
A shíneann lámh don deirc
Is ná labhrann focal choíche.[66]

of that crew of beggars
who stretch out their hands
and never say a word.[67]

This is a reference to the wanderers and tramps who hang around the back of the house sometimes and whom the poet had a lot of time for. He might go 'around the houses' in his imagination but he always ends up back in the same place and with the same 'marginal' people in the end. In a way, the journey and the poem 'The Cure' prove one and the same.

Similarly, the subjects of many of Ó Ríordáin's poems are as often as not the poems that were not written. This is understandable given all the weeks and months and (indeed) years that he was rendered immobile with illness, meaning that it was all he could do to compose a poem or even write new sentences in his diary. Unsurprisingly, even on those rare occasions when literature is not the main subject of his discussion, he finds himself drawing on terms that come from the world of writing or publishing for his discussions and comparisons. The organised rhythmic life of a monk in Melleray puts him in mind of the 'metricality, purity, assonance of the poem'.[68] The complex male sensibility he envisages with Blessed Finbarr and Gandhi only reveals itself to him as he struggles to put an order on the lines and express this sensibility in the physicality and form that are words on a page; once again, it is art that actually serves to explicate and define the world 'outside' and the life that he has distanced himself from: 'Mar scríbhinn breacaithe ar phár/Is scríbhinn eile trasna air/Chonaic geanc is glúin is spág.' ('*I saw, like writing on a piece of parchment/with more writing across and over it/a snub nose, a knee, a hump, a clumsy foot.*')[69]

66 'Bacaigh' ('*Beggars*'), ES: p. 37.
67 Sewell, *Selected Poems*, p. 13. Trans. Peter Sirr.
68 ES: p. 66.
69 'Oileán agus Oileán Eile' ('*This Island and the Other Island*'). Sewell, *Selected Poems*, p. 95. Trans. Denise Blake.

Ó Ríordáin imagines the duck as a bird that craves the dignity and prestige of the older and more esteemed 'dán díreach' form of Gaelic poetry, even if, in reality, she struggles even to create 'vers libre'.[70] Some of his dead aunt's things, as scattered on the table, become a collection of poems in Ó Ríordáin's mind, a collection that have the authoritative seal of print on them, and the 'cold formality of the editor about them'.[71]

And, the verse Ó Ríordáin writes is a creative reflection of his own self as much as anything else. The poetry forms a mirror in which he sees the imprint of himself; that or a series of imprints and reflections, both pleasant or unpleasant, as dependent on what aspect of his sensibility reveals itself while writing. The poet speaks of 'a mirror of verses', of 'the word regime that reflects me in the glass' and of 'which self or anti-self/ will reveal itself in the mirror'.[72] It is in the permanent and enduring nature of the written word and of print that the power lies – they are the traces that Ó Ríordáin returns to when he needs to and when he wants to see himself again as he really is:

> *While I was reading some of my poems tonight, it occurred to me that it is time for me to return to this type of poetry. I'm not saying this because the thing that I read was either good or bad, but because that's me – the poetry. When I'm not doing this work I'm not there at all – I'm absent.*[73]

As an immediate follow-up to this, he asks the blunt question: 'Have the years that weren't formed in poetry been lost forever?' If so, then the story of why they've been lost needs explication. The two best examples of poems that he really struggled to shape in the form of words from *Eireaball Spideoige* are undoubtedly 'An Peaca' ('*The Sin*') and 'Ifreann' ('*Hell*'). Much the same understanding underscores both poems and, in fact, the title of the first poem seems more appropriate to the second in many ways. Interestingly, the poem entitled 'An Peaca' also bears certain

70 B: p. 30.

71 LL: p. 20.

72 ES: p. 46; ES: p. 84; LL: p. 9.

73 'Sliocht Sleachta' ('*Extract of Extracts*'), IT, 24 July 1975; D: 11.20 p.m., 4 June 1964.

similarities with 'An Leigheas' ('*The Cure*'). The same conflict or tension between Ó Ríordáin and the 'rabble' marks both poems, except that the threat that he thinks they pose seems farther away this time.

In the first two verses of 'An Peaca', the silence and beauty of the night echoes the poet's mood well; the night and the poet's words work in tandem together to 'write' one another; the night gently imbues itself into his words and takes them back. The world appears ordered and in harmony with itself – and once again it is the terminology and jargon of the craft of writing that forms one of the poem's central metaphors – 'assonance like music drifting through the poem' – until someone out on the road lets a shout out of them and the spell is broken. In 'An Peaca' the rabble-shout reaches the poet through the window of his room and shatters the 'glass of night'. The atmosphere of eternal beauty has now been shattered irrevocably and they're being forced down into the muck by the hooves of the animals in their imagination. The night is no longer in a pure state of grace any more; sin permeates the air as the precursor to 'prose' rather than poetry. It is the same failure here as in 'An Leigheas', except that the poet isn't the guilty party on this occasion; it's the others who have sinned this time:

Ach teilgeadh daoscarscread míchumtha ard
'Na urchar trí ghloine na hoíche
Is cheapas go bhfaca na blúiríní fáin
Fé chrúbaibh an mhasla san aoileach.

D'fhéachas arís ar lámhscríbhinn an dáin,
Ach prós bhí in áit na filíochta –
An ré is na scamaill is an spéir mar ba ghnáth –
Mar bhí peaca ar anam na hoíche.[74]

But a loud, shapeless rabble-scream was hurled,
smashing the glass of night,
and I thought I saw scattered shards
under trotters of insult on a dunghill.

74 ES: p. 41.

I looked again at the manuscript of the poem
but it was prose instead of poetry –
the moon and the clouds and the sky as usual –
because there was sin on the soul of the night.[75]

Ó Ríordáin had begun incorporating the terminology of the scruple in his writing and art, the same as in his own personal life. This is a discourse that never fades fully in his poetry over time either. He gradually develops a terminology and system around this aesthetic and aligns it with the religious tradition in which he has been raised. If a major element of this discourse is the avoidance of 'sin', then the corollary of this is that he needs to source the 'prayer' that is outside of himself somewhere and unite it with his own private prayer within the poem.

Another or third hope manifests itself then in the form of the poem itself, until it becomes natural to this aesthetic that each aspect sustains the other and forms a unity of sorts.[76] Each of these disparate 'prayer-forms' can only become the poem and assume a new life together if they are 'sparked' in unison and if the conditions for their creation are perfect and pure.[77] If one prayer-form fails, the entire poem fails or never assumes form. In 'An Peaca' ('*The Sin*'), for instance, the night prayer dies before it has even been crystallised – simply because its development has been interrupted in mid-flow. In the case of 'Ifreann' ('*Hell*') the poet's own private prayer fails and falls apart even before it has begun, so that he produces a different poem completely:

Ifreann

Cé go bhfacasa adharca
Chomh cumtha le teampall,
Is óigbhean ag iompar
Banúlachta seanda,

75 Sewell, *Selected Poems*, p. 19. Trans. Noel Monahan.

76 ES: p. 11.

77 ES: pp. 15 and 24.

Is suaimhneas na gaibhneachta
Ar mhiotala sleamhaine,
Tá mo smaointe chomh coillte
Le déad fiacal mantach.

Tá fairsingeacht smaointe
San abairt is lú,
Tá síneadh don intinn
I mbeag is i mór,
Tá iascaireacht machnaimh
Sa tsolas máguaird,
Ach tá m'anamsa i gcarcair,
I bpeaca beag duairc.[78]

Hell

Although I have seen horns
as shapely as a temple,
and a young woman bearing
ancient womanliness,
and the serenity of smithy work
on smooth metals,
my thoughts are as ruined
as the ivory of a chipped tooth.

There's breadth of thought
in the smallest sentence,
and stretching of mind
in what's great or small,
there's fishing for thought
in the light all around
but my soul's imprisoned
in the gloom of venial sin.[79]

---

78 ES: p. 105.
79 Sewell, *Selected Poems*, p. 113. Trans. Theo Dorgan.

Ó Ríordáin recognises the flawless structure of the truth in the long-established forms and objects about him but he cannot source this truth within himself as of yet. He comes across a set of ram's horns, so perfectly formed that they are as a chapel/church of themselves (the same 'temple' that is the introduction to *Eireaball Spideoige* also perhaps, a chapel that represents the abstract architecture as unique to each chapel), and the ancient form of femininity that passes between one person and the next. He listens to the smooth and regular rhythm of the blacksmith's hammer in the forge and hears the sounds of that ancient trade as practised since the beginning of time. The past can be heard here again in 'the ancient harp of the everyday' upon which he seeks to sing his poetry and trigger the echoes of the time that has passed.[80] The poet goes in search of this eternal racial memory and Gaelic inheritance, even if his attempt to source it frequently ends in failure.

He can't source these older forms because he's proved inadequate in the area that he considered himself to have some control over (i.e. his own personal system and balancing aesthetic of purity and sin); while the older forms continue to function in accordance with their natural function, this isn't true for the poet. Sin has hindered his odyssey and hobbled him from the beginning of his quest. The expansiveness of thought and imagery that he seeks is denied him and he's tied up in 'claustrophobic' knots, all as a consequence of his own perceived inadequacy and failings. 'Expansiveness of thought', 'the extending of the imagination', 'thought-fishing' – the poet is refused all of them and has to make do with what he sees as the restricted and sterile circuit of his own imagination – when what he really sought to tap were the pure and clear waters of tradition. What the poet really sought was the 'child-mind' that is the exact opposite of his own convoluted aesthetic; the child's sensibility as set free rather than oppressed or restrained. The childish imagination runs wild with the horse – it is with the horse and on the horse and in the horse. It becomes part of its very nature, an element of a poem itself:

80 ES: pp. 48–9.

> *And there doesn't [have] to be a reference to the horse in the poem that I'm talking about, nor does the horse have to have anything said about it. Maybe a horse wouldn't be mentioned at all except that you'd sense the presence of the horse in it, in the same way as you'd detect a child's spirit or the spirit of poetry there, because to say a poem is simply a form of being.*[81]

The initial draft of this section – the introduction where Ó Ríordáin considers the power of the 'child-mind' and the immediacy of the childish imagination – appears in the diary entry for 3 April 1949. Not that these were new ideas on his part. He'd already been thinking along these lines for most of the previous two years, as evidenced here:

> *A 'Narrative Poem' is not poetry. My guardian angel told me this tonight. Poetry is not storytelling or any form of narrative. Poetry happens on the inside, not on the outside. We recognise the two voices. The first voice is as a photograph – it is an impersonal thing, and the newspapers are replete with this. It is something without value. This voice – the exterior voice – speaks like this: 'The grass is growing'. But the inner voice, this voice eats the grass first and the grass becomes the voice. Then the voice speaks but it doesn't mention anything about the grass. But everyone knows that it's the grass speaking. That's poetry. Or let's put it like this. A poet wishes to write a poem about grass. He absorbs its soul from the grass, as everything has a soul (i.e. the idea of it) and he transfers that soul into the poem (i.e. into words) and that poem has life if the idea behind it is the soul that is the grass.*[82]

We find him exploring these conceptions further and bolstering them on 3 April 1949, when he moves closer to crystallising his ideas as they finally appeared in the introduction to *Eireaball Spideoige.* His interaction with the 'world outside' and the things of that world, and the relationship or potential balance or harmony between the 'self' and the elements of that other world are the subject of his enquiries, as evidenced in the following, written just nine days later:

---

81 ES: p. 11.
82 D: 28 October 1947.

*I look at the bottle and I become bottle-ised. I think of a woman and I am womanised. That is to say that the bottle and the woman raise me out of myself. They assume the burden of the 'self' that I normally shoulder. I become a bottle, I become a woman, on thinking about them. A thought is like a magic wand. This escape is necessary. You'd go mad if you were always your-*self *– if you were always the 'self'. You (yourself) and life are different and interchangeable. We ought to become bottles and horses and prayers, so that we don't go crazy. A madman is someone who tripped and fell into him-*self *and couldn't escape out of it again … And a madman is someone who tripped and fell into a bottle and couldn't get out of it. That's what it is. 'No loitering'. A person ought to be travelling between one self and another.*

Note: A travelling 'Self' is what every reasonable person is.[83]

It is in this potential balance or contrast between elements, and the relationship that defines them, where poetry reveals itself. If you fail to maintain the direct association that is the 'self' and other (i.e. the object outside, in this case, the bottle) you'll go off the rails and drift into the realm of madness instead. It's necessary to go out there and source the structures that shape the aesthetic you wish to express – and this is something Ó Ríordáin fails to do in 'Ifreann' ('*Hell*') or when he goes 'down amongst the people', as he tries to do in 'Saoirse' ('*Liberty*').[84] This latter poem is his attempt to escape the first form of insanity as circumscribed by 'the person who tripped and fell into himself' – he/she who nonetheless continued the process of creation, irrespective of the world outside. As the last verse of 'Saoirse' goes:

Is atuirseach an intínn
A thit in iomar doimhin na saoirse,
Ní mhaireann cnoc dar chruthaigh Dia ann,
Ach cnoic theibí, sainchnoic shamhlaíochta,
Is bíonn gach cnoc díobh lán de mhianta

83 D: 12 April 1949.
84 ES: pp. 100–2.

Ag dreapadóireacht gan chomhlíonadh,
Níl teora leis an saoirse
Ná le cnoca na samhlaíochta,
Ná níl teora leis na mianta,
Ná faoiseamh
Le fáil.

Weary is the mind
that has fallen in the deep trough of liberty,
no hill erected by God exists there,
only abstract hills, the particular hills of the imagination,
and each hill is full of desires
climbing, unfulfilled,
liberty is without limit,
so are the hills of the imagination
the desires are unlimited,
and there exists
no release.[85]

One could give too much credence to the 'other' that is the world outside, however, and place too much emphasis on the views and opinions of others around you, needless to say. The following diary excerpt depicts Ó Ríordáin's existential struggle better than most. He wants to be accepted and yet he doesn't; he wants to be in tune with the 'common view' of the community and surrender to it and yet he doesn't hear it or understand it correctly, even when he tries. He can't find sanctuary and rest because his mind has turned in upon itself to such a degree:

I went back the road to the graveyard. The day was fine. Everywhere calm and healthy. God's will radiating across the countryside. The holy patience of the cow. I looked at the cows and I tried to suck some of that bovine calm of theirs up into my lungs. The children industrious and solemn, playing games. The peace of the cows be upon them also. Two men working patiently in a field. There was no

85 Sewell, *Selected Poems*, p. 111. Trans. Seán Ó Ríordáin.

> *hurry on anyone – not on the cows, not on the children, not on the men. All of them working calmly in accordance with the Will of God. Everything happy in God's Will. All of them acting in accordance with God's Will, except for me – a person without peace. I went into the graveyard. I said a prayer at my mother's grave, but it was an anxious form of rosary. I read a few poems from* Measgra Dánta *but my mind was not broadened in line with God's will. I came home and even the road itself extended outwards, in the direction of God's Will. I walked through the place as if as a living sin. Is there anyone else out there as despicable as me?*[86]

He'd written 'Saoirse' just four months earlier, a poem in which he'd tried to elucidate his true heart's desire:

from **'Saoirse'**

Don bhfeirmeoir ag tomhas na gaoithe
Sa bhfómhar is é ag cuimhneamh
Ar pháirc eornan:
Don chomhthuiscint, don chomh-sheanchuimhne,
Do chomhiompar comhdhaoine,
Don chomh-mhacrud.[87]

from **'Liberty'**

To the farmer measuring the wind
in the autumn as he thinks
of a field of barley:
To co-understanding, to co-tradition
to co-behaviour of co-people,
to the co-copied thing.[88]

---

86 D: 22 January 1951.
87 ES: pp. 100–2.
88 Sewell, *Selected Poems*, p. 111. Trans. Seán Ó Ríordáin.

He hadn't succeeded very well in this endeavour by all accounts, even if we can date exactly when he wrote the poem:

> *Wet day. Rain. Thoughts. A poem came to me yesterday afternoon: 'Raghaidh mé síos i measc na ndaoine'. Poetry – true poetry – only comes in the autumn.*[89] *It was in the autumn that I wrote 'Ní Raibh Sí Dílis' and there was poetry in it.*[90] *How is it that the power in me doesn't always work, as it did yesterday afternoon? Because I don't stay on the island, is it?*[91]

Because he'd spent too long alone on that 'island' is a more likely answer to this question perhaps – or at least this is what the poem seems to indicate. It's worth noting, perhaps, that Ó Ríordáin invented the word 'macrud' – as based on the word 'maicleabhar' – from King Diarmaid's official judgement in the *Foras Feasa*: 'the judgement that Diarmaid gave was as follows: to every cow her calf, and to every book his book-son.'[92] Frank O'Brien posits that Ó Ríordáin borrowed the image of the hounds closing in on their prey from Patrick Pearse's work. In fact, it may well be that the original model for 'Saoirse' was the poem 'Cad Chuige Dom Chiapadh' ('The term "conairt-smaointe" [*sic*] ("*pack-thoughts*") would put you in mind of the poem "Cad Chuige Dom Chiapadh" ("*Why Do I Torment Myself*") and maybe it was this that inspired the poem "Saoirse"').[93] The sentence 'Fiadh fadtuirseach 's an chonairt ina dhiaidh' ('*The deer long-tired and the pack in pursuit*') is the line from Pearse that may well link both poems.

As if continuing the 'hound' trope in relation to his work, Ó Ríordáin's diary entry for 24 December 1950 says: 'And I can't lie down and relax as the ideas begin barking immediately'. Another potential literary source for 'Saoirse' might well have been Gerard Manley Hopkins, a poet whom

89 'Raghaidh mé síos i measc na ndaoine' ('*I shall go down amongst the people*').

90 'Ní Raibh Sí Dílis' ('*She Was Not Faithful*').

91 D: 8 September 1950.

92 *An Foras Feasa Ar Éirinn* ('Foundation of Knowledge on Ireland') is a narrative history of Ireland written by Geoffrey Keating in the seventeenth century.

93 O'Brien, *Filíocht Ghaeilge*, p. 316.

he'd read and re-read: 'O the mind, mind rested mountains; cliffs of fall/ Frightful, sheer, no-man-fathomed. Hold them cheap/May who ne'er hung there.'[94] Or we could also bring Wordsworth's contention regarding 'the weight of too much liberty' into the discussion, given Ó Ríordáin's noting of same in his diary for 4 October 1965. Not that we don't have plenty of evidence from the poet's everyday life and the regular bouts of suffering and hospitalisation – as sources for the complexities and difficulties he was trying to work out while developing his writing aesthetic.

Seán Ó Tuama identifies the fundamental difficulty Ó Ríordáin attempted to resolve at this juncture (one engendered primarily perhaps by the fact that he was standing splay-footed on the periphery of two very different literary traditions (i.e. the Gaelic (Irish) and the British (English) traditions) and seeking to give due regard to both. To neglect either of these traditions completely would have seen Ó Ríordáin doing himself down and belittling the dual nature of his own cultural inheritance. The same goes in relation to the 'extended series of concepts/dualities' that one finds in Ó Ríordáin's work, concepts which are 'in complete contrast to one another' – freedom and slavery, sin and prayer/confession, death and life, darkness and light, the individual and the rabble, the inner self and the outer self, the English language and Irish.[95] We frequently see the poet avoiding one aspect while seeking to maintain or bolster the other. To side with one of these dualities is the path to the salvation of his soul and to profligacy in terms of his poetry. The other side means eternal damnation and spiritual death as an individual and as a writer. Of course, it is often the case that more than one of these dualities coalesces and is found on both sides of the struggle. The rabble and the night for example – aspects that function in tandem to threaten the individual and his night-candle, and set him astray somehow. Such dualities engender the vast majority of the poems that Ó Ríordáin wrote; the contradictions and dualities merge and then separate again, often in new forms and configurations. Ó Ríordáin's 'self' or identity is always restless and where

94 From the Hopkins poem, 'No worst, there is none. Pitched past pitch of grief.'

95 Ó Tuama, *Filí faoi Sceimhle*, p. 74.

the 'ego' is dominant at one moment, in the next it's the rabble that is in the ascendant. Repression transforms itself and manifests as freedom, and liberty replaces oppression; the rabble outside his window become a community of their own because, unlike the isolated, tormented individual who writes poetry inside, they are healthy and comfortable in themselves and know their assigned places within the greater scheme of things. Themes sunder and form sub-themes and each individual aspect assumes its appropriate position within the discourse of binaries, for example, the writer's position in terms of tradition, or the voice and personal language of the individual with respect to the language of the community.

The message of 'Ifreann' ('*Hell*'), albeit that the message of itself isn't its primary function, is that the poet can only avoid spiritual aridity and remain 'in step' with the world and with the Creator if he steers clear of sin in all its aspects.[96] If he should become estranged from the fundamental truths and the nature of creation through sin, however, his poetry is a failure. Or, worse still, his poetry is a form of 'anti-creation' that ultimately serves to damn the person completely since they had the temerity to beget a false or misshapen form of creation.

> *And he who is damned, what happened to him? I think that he denied the truth: that he refused to acknowledge the forms of the truth and endlessly continued on creating his own false forms of the truth, as an anti-creator would do, so that he stagnated within himself like a badger. This sentence is to be found in the sermon titled* 'On Mortal Sin: The Maynooth Sermons': *'They (the sinners) normally desire that which will never happen, and they don't desire that which has always existed.' This (latter) person never went down courting near the church buildings … Eventually, he created his own version of himself, his own body, rather than in the likeness that God created for him.*[97]

Based on this explanation, it is clear that Ó Ríordáin wasn't simply 'making a statement' or exaggerating when he titled his poem 'Ifreann' ('*Hell*') in

96 B: p. 23.
97 ES: pp. 18–19.

this instance. The horns referenced in 'Ifreann' belong to a ram that strayed between the islands that were 'Oileán agus Oileán Eile' ('*This Island and the Other Island*'), and here's his explanation of the image from the radio script mentioned earlier; he composed the poem out in Gougane Barra:

> *I went out on the Island to meditate on Blessed Finbarr. I came across a horned ram. I couldn't manage to achieve the serenity or the truthfulness of that ram. And I couldn't compose a poem either, a poem as truthful, or perfectly shaped or as authoritative or as replete with ancestral memories as those horns. Although I didn't have the ram in this poem, I composed the poem under its influence. I put the ram into another poem later on.*

'Ifreann' is this other poem. But there is no question that the principal inspiration for 'Oileán agus Oileán Eile' is the image of the horned ram and what it represents – the truth as naturally ordered and fated for every living thing. This is the essence of his poem as uncompromisingly stated in the fourth section of the poem:

I bhfírinne na haigne
Tá oileán séin ...[98]

There's an island of serenity
In the mind's truth[99]

Interestingly, Ó Ríordáin initially struggled to incorporate the ram image in his earliest drafts of the poem, as indicated in his notes:

Chonac reithe ar oileán,
Tráthnóna sa tsamhradh;
Bhí adharca an reithe
Chomh cumtha le teampall.

---

98 ES: p. 80.
99 Sewell, *Selected Poems*, p. 93. Trans. Denise Blake.

I saw a ram on an island
One afternoon in summer
The ram's horns were well-formed
Chapel-perfect[100]

When I saw the ram, it was as if I'd suddenly walked back into the old days … Ancient, ancient, ancient. You'd have imagined that Finbarr had left the island just a short while before this in search of the ram …

He might have failed on this occasion but he managed to accommodate the ram image within the poem later. He wrote 'Oileán agus Oileán Eile' in the summer of 1948 (it was six months before it saw publication in *Comhar* in January 1949). In the case of 'Ifreann' ('*Hell*') he probably wrote this sometime during spring 1951, given that the poem's first line appears in one of his diaries for the end of the period 3 February 1951 to 18 April 1951.

The same sense of encroachment or repression that imbues 'Ifreann' is also very evident in 'Domhnach Cásca' ('*Easter Sunday*'), a poem, the beginning of which:

Domhnach Cásca, mór an náire,
Baineadh tuisle díomsa,
Thiteas faon isteach sa chorp …[101]

On Easter Sunday, what a great shame,
I tripped,
And fell limp into the body …[102]

is based on the second part of the traditional Gaelic saying that Ó Ríordáin had heard in his childhood and which he cites more than once in his diary: 'It's a real curse to drink milk on Good Friday; it's a great shame not to have meat on Easter Sunday.'

---

100 Trans. M. Ó hAodha.
101 ES: pp. 74–5.
102 Trans. M. Ó hAodha.

Not that a lack of meat or flesh was Ó Ríordáin's main concern at this juncture; it was his excessive love of the sins of the flesh. ('Sin' has the same meaning in his diary almost all of the time.) The room that was built as a physical sanctuary for the person whose body is fouled by TB has also become the place where the soul is now at risk of corruption. The symptoms are clear and familiar: the 'black-night', the quenched light, the ceiling of his room seemingly hemming him in. The creatures that inhabit this bizarre dream-world are strange and don't bear much resemblance to reality: thoughts and images endlessly circling his mind in the form of bizarre-looking midgets or monkey-peoples, creatures that resemble human beings but aren't actually human at all. The dirty and defiled rabble of the road has temporarily transformed into something else, even if, in the diary entries, the monkey-people are actually academics – with their formal and ever-polite behaviour at all times. Ó Ríordáin notes them as a 'new class of people coming to the fore in Ireland – a new type of aristocracy':

> *They're not fully there yet. They've yet to hatch. But I can see that they are developing various traits naturally, traits that are common amongst similar classes to theirs in other countries. University types, I mean, the kind who are Irish-speakers. These types [or the ones that I know for a long time] look down on those classes of people that are beneath them. They never like to exhibit anger. 'Not done old man.' But I can see – and I think it's a good thing – that they are inventing a new etiquette, a new model of living …*
>
> *I saw three monkeys picking lice from a comrade of theirs and they exhibited such formality and nobility and university-like gentility! Accuracy, greatness, good conduct, discipline. And picking out lice and eating them is what they were at!*[103]

In the indeterminate state that is sickness, sleeping pills and various heavy drugs for the control of the TB, scholars, dwarf-like creatures, the rabble and the monkeys all appear much the same in the poet's eyes. In truth, he too is a member of their broken tribe, both body and soul. From 'Domhnach Cásca' ('*Easter Sunday*'):

103 D: 11 April 1949.

Do múchadh na soilse
Thíos anseo,
Tá an lá ina dhubhoíche
De shíor sa chorp.

Is abhac gach smaoineamh
Thíos anseo,
Tá díon an tí íseal
Istigh sa chorp.

Ta moncaithe im thimpeall
Go tionscalach
Ag piocadh na míola
Dá chéile anseo:

Nuair bheirid ar mhílín
Ardaíd crobh,
Is slogaid gan mhoill é
Siar mar dheoch.[104]

The lights were extinguished
Down here,
Day is as pitch-black night
In the body, always.

Every thought is a dwarf
Down here,
The roof of the house is low
Inside in the body.

There are monkeys around me
Busily

104 ES: p. 74.

Picking the lice
From each other here:

When they catch a little louse
They raise a paw,
And they swallow it back without delay
Like a drink.[105]

To follow The Trace of the Christ/as a flow through the Bible is a form of redemption or escape and is the essence of the poem. (This, and the release that is the act of writing the poem itself, no doubt.) The poet negotiates an analogous form of escape in 'Teitheadh' ('*Flight*') – in this case an escape from the torment of ideas and images in his mind. 'I remember the afternoon that relates to this poem well. The rain fell, the wind blew, trees fell down on the road home' is the prelude Ó Ríordáin gave to this poem in another talk of his. We can't know for certain what evening this was, but it seems to have been on 7 April 1951 that he wrote the poem, or at least began writing it anyway. The following excerpt from his diary encompasses his initial thoughts on it. (Another part of this poem is found at the end of the same diary/copybook for the period 3 February 1951 to 18 April 1951.)

> *When it becomes clear to us that the woman that we gave our love to isn't as angelic or as innocent as we first thought, then we get angry; it is when we have to face up to these insufferable things that we discover what is really pure; it is then that we really need to show her how much we love her, if possible. This love will be permanent as it is based on the truth. And when all our confusion regarding God and the Church has been taken away, and when we see God and the Church through the prism of imperfection – only then are we truly able to honour and love God and the Church fully.*
>
> *I walked all day once in the city.*

The poet is struggling with these thoughts and intentions. On the same

105 Trans. M. Ó hAodha.

page as the comments above, he drew a sketch of one man and the lower torsos of two others across the page; and across one of the men he wrote the initial lines of poetry of 'Teitheadh'. This poem links the storm that is his mind and the physical storm that is the sky outside; they merge together in the poem so that one imagines the city and the countryside have entered his room, the same as the slates that are smashing and the trees falling onto the cows outside. And the storm has indeed entered the room now because it is his soul that is at risk in this instance, and it is spiritual danger that has him retreating into himself. Just as the psychic battle coalesces in the imagery of the storm, Ó Ríordáin visualises his sins arranging themselves in a book of poetry so that the world can witness for itself how flawed an individual he is. The storm that tears through the poem highlights one of the most long-established themes in Ó Ríordáin's poetry: the relationship between poetry and confession, and the sense of release that ensues following both – but only if the contrition is real and true; it's a theme that appears in the diary as early as the year 1942:

> *It's difficult to put the tussles of the mind into words, in the form of a play or a poem or a novel, or a confession ... Literature is a sort of confession. A full and satisfactory confession is an act that is without limits; it's difficult to know whether such a complete confession has ever been done ... I wonder whether his own confessions (the ones he wrote) were the best confessions that St Augustine ever made? Ibsen couldn't reproach in any way the person who made a satisfactory confession.*[106]

(Ibsen was one of Ó Ríordáin's favourite authors at this juncture, needless to say.) The concept of tearing things apart in storm-like fashion in order to expose what lies beneath appears again on 12 December 1947. 'I'm reluctant to begin writing in the same way as someone would be reluctant to make their confession. Both are linked in a sense.' And again in the following excerpt – from an essay, written in 1969:

> *Has anyone ever made a proper confession? Has anyone ever composed a poem*

106 D: 4 July 1942.

that was entirely to his satisfaction or entirely without fault? Probably not. We are all incomplete. Failure is everything we do.[107]

Failure is the end result in this instance also, however:

Do rugas liom don eaglais
Mo chnuasach nuapheacaí
Do chuireas iad in eagar
Don fhoilsitheoir a bhíonn
Ag clódhearmhad peacaí.

Ach do lean an cith im chathair,
Is do lean an cith féin thuaith,
Do scoilteadh slinn ar leacaibh,
Is do leagadh crainn ar bhuaibh,
Is do chúb mo chroí ón ruaig.[108]

I took with me to the church
My collection of recent sins
I put them in order
For the publisher
Who deletes sins.

But the shower continued to fall in my city,
And also in my countryside,
Slates were smashed on flagstones,
And trees fell on cows,
My heart shrunk back from the attack.[109]

Is this the form of failure Ó Ríordáin meant when he commented in one of the diary entries on the importance of maintaining one's love for God

107 'Ár n-easpa foirfeachta' (*'Our lack of perfection'*), IT, 21 January 1969.
108 'Teitheadh', ES: pp. 106–7.
109 Trans. M. Ó hAodha.

and the Church even when one no longer has any illusions about the nature of the human condition or the fallen nature of the institution? Is the final verse here his full acquiescence to both, and his attempt to share his own suffering and his fallen nature through the words of the poem – on the understanding that both he and the world have failed? This is the sole path available to him aesthetically speaking, he says:

Ní raibh aon áit le dul aige
Ach suas i measc na ndeor,
Suas dréimire na hatuirse
Go Vatican an bhróin,
Is do thit an cith sa Róimh.[110]

It had nowhere to go
Except up among the tears,
Up the ladder of dejection
To the Vatican of sorrow,
And the shower fell in Rome.[111]

The sanctuary that is religious belief may be part of the poet's solution, but it is also part of the problem for him. His relationship with religious belief is tense. His spiritual journey is complex and over time, it's a road that proves far more challenging and wearisome even than the 'ladder of dejection' or another perusal of the Bible. And perhaps it's the journey that is most crucial to the poet at this juncture anyway, rather than any definitive response or resolution to his question – (in this poem, his response or resolution is slightly at odds with the main thrust of the poem, and perhaps overly facile or conventional). He says as much to us in 'Guí' ('*A Prayer*'), as seen below:

Is bás, dar liom fós, freagairt,
Is beatha fiafraí

110 'Teitheadh', ES: p. 107.
111 Trans. M. Ó hAodha.

Ragham amú tamall eile,
Is chífeam an tír.[112]

To answer is death, to my mind,
to be alive is to inquire;
let us go astray yet a while
and take in the countryside.[113]

It might be the same country but he is still lost in it and we readers are equally confused too and struggling to find our way through this terrain. The second verse of 'Guí' provides us with our most coherent clue as to the direction he is taking; the poet links perfection in poetry with purity of heart and a joyful spiritual state or soul:

Iarraim filíocht bheag a cheapadh
Anois is arís,
Ní iarraim go ndéanfainn peaca,
Ba bhaoth mo ghuí,
Ná go gcuirfeadh neach eile a anam
I mbaol an dlí:
Dá mbeimis ó bhaol an pheaca
Dob fhearr filíocht.

I ask that I should compose
some little poems now and again;
I don't ask that I should sin
that prayer would be in vain –
nor that another would put his soul
in danger of conviction:
if we were free of sin's peril
poetry would be better then.[114]

112 B: p. 16.
113 Sewell, *Selected Poems*, p. 135. Trans. Colm Breathnach.
114 *Ibid.*

The biggest shift in thinking here is that Ó Ríordáin no longer sees it as a necessity to constrain his questions solely within the philosophical context. Even if the fundamental question still intrigues him, its resolution doesn't worry him in the way that it did previously.

The poem 'Oileán agus Oileán Eile' ('*This Island and the Other Island*') was one of Ó Ríordáin's most definitive responses to the intersection that was the metaphysical and the religious in his poetry. He spoke of the way 'his thoughts danced' on his mind like a shower in 'Teitheadh' ('*Flight*'). And, interestingly, the poem 'Oileán agus Oileán Eile' emerged from his reading and preparation for a much longer poem, later titled 'Rince ar mo Smaointe' ('*Thought Dancing*').

Similar to Ballyvourney, Gougane Barra was one of those blessed or sacred places in Ó Ríordáin's imagination as associated with his childhood. There was nowhere more appropriate for him to go in search of his spiritual essence than the Gougane (unless he was to go to the 'source' that was Ballyvourney itself, as he did in a different way in 'Oilithreacht Fám Anam'). According to his diary, the poem's genesis went something like this (below) – these diary excerpts appear one after another, as a continuous stream of thought: the poet's mind is animated and awash with thoughts and images that seek expression within the shape that is the poem. He feels so alive and inspired during this journey on the island that his thoughts dance and leap impatiently onto the page:

> *16 May 1947 [1948]. Sunday: Long poem 'Rince ar mo Smaointe'. The thoughts swimming in lake Gandhi. Immersing themselves in the waters of Jesus Christ and the odour of Christ from them. They go to Heaven at night – dreams. Come to life again in the morning. Don't stray too far away from humanity.*
>
> *23 May 1948. Sunday: There was a terrible heat all week but the weather broke last night and it's bitterly cold today. I went to confession yesterday – Fr Mel. My mind was at ease yesterday afternoon. It is women who destroy and sully the world. Freedom. To deny the ego.*
>
> *2 June 1948. I'm on holidays since yesterday. The Gougane, the Island, until*

next Friday – the pasture where they used to have prayers – thoughts – Holy Finbarr grazing.

I would like to be able to see into you Finbarr but it is painful just to see into myself. Am I everyone? Freedom and a joyous mind produce poetry. Fear, fear, fear. Oh, I'm afraid of composing a poem. Freedom from desire, freedom from fear, freedom from the ego, freedom from belief, from tradition, from ignorance, from blame. I'd like to speak to Jesus Christ here. Blessed Finbarr and Turnbull, the pasture and the quay – the same person, the same Christ, the same Wilde, but a different project. The same author but a different play.

10 June 1948: Thursday: I'm in the Guagán. I'm here since last Friday. I'm worn out now, worn out by the loneliness and by my own company.

Seven years later, when the well of his inspiration has dried up – according to Ó Ríordáin himself – the poet thinks back fondly to those days among the trees where his poetic impulse was alive and animated:

But remember 1948 in Gougane Barra when I wrote 'Oileán agus Oileán Eile'. I'd spend the whole day amongst the trees on the Island thinking. After every meal in the hotel, I'd head out in search of those thoughts as a man seeking out his lover.[115]

The poem 'Oileán agus Oileán Eile' begins with him preparing himself to receive the sacrament. Ó Ríordáin had a habit of translating Latin hymns into Irish, and in this instance, the main stimulus for the poem is Psalm 25, a psalm he would have known quite well from the Catholic Mass. The poet's translations of *O Salutaris, Tantum Ergo* and *Adoro Te Devote* always remained a separate entity from his poetic work but, in this instance the poet managed to incorporate the message of the psalm into his work in a way that makes the poem more multifaceted and expansive:

Lavabo inter innocentes manus meas: et
circumdabo altare tuum, Domine.

---

115 D: 13 October 1955.

Ut audiam vocem laudis: et ennarem universa
mirabilia tua.
Domine dilexi decorem domus tuae: et locum
habitationis gloriae tuae.
Ne perdas cum impiis, Deus, animam meam: et
cum viris sanguinum vitam meam.
In quorum manibus iniquitates sunt …

Here, we find him washing his hands before he listens for the 'essence of the saints' thoughts' (through which he tries to express himself subsequently); he praises the house and his surroundings and attempts to eradicate the image of the rabble that he has mentally brought with him, despite himself, to this special place:

from **'Oileán agus Oileán Eile'**

Tá Sasanach ag iascaireacht sa loch,
Tá an fhírinne rólom ar an oileán,
Ach raghad i measc na gcuimhne agus na gcloch,
Is nífead le mórurraim mo dhá láimh.

Raghad anonn is éistfead san oileán,
Éistfead seal le smaointe smeara naomh
A thiomnaigh Barra Naofa don oileán,
Éistfead leo in inchinn an aeir.

A Bharra, is aoibhinn liom aoibhneas do thí
Agus caraimse áitreabh do smaointe,
Ach ní feas dom an uaitse na smaointe airím
Mar tá daoscar ar iostas im intinn.

from **'This Island and the Other Island'**

An Englishman is fishing in the lake,
over on the island the stark truth rests.

I will go among the rocks and memories
 and bathe my hands with reverence.

I will go across and listen to the island,
 listen to the essence of saints' thoughts
bequeathed by St Finbarr to the island,
 listen to them in the mind of the air.

Finbarr, your joyous home delights,
 this genial place of reflection,
but are these thoughts sourced from
 the rabble dwelling in my mind?[116]

He doubts, however, whether the aforementioned rabble always have the upper hand in this place and not Finbarr. The poet is a man who neither listened nor spoke for many years as he should have and the grey plumage or stubble of time has occluded his thoughts and obscured them; and ironically, the only thing that has mined beneath such thoughts or pared them away in all the years is the 'pollution' of the mind, of his aesthetic; because he failed to unsheathe his thoughts and set them free, they have stultified and become polluted and stagnant. He must become like a saint or a child again, therefore, in order to see the world anew once more. Now that he is on the island, however, the humidity and aridity of summer stretches out and weighs heavily on his soul, thereby threatening to obscure the true spirit of this holy place for the poet. The next moment, he feels the motion of a breeze amongst the trees and thinks that perhaps this is the stirring or impetus he requires. How can he know that this journey of his to the island is not in vain or that he's not just fooling himself, however? But then, to be stirred or roused poetically in any way at all is better than to remain stultified and dead to the muse, as he had been before his arrival to the island; even the 'blindness or the devil' stirring his poetic impulse is better than nothing at all or this endless weariness of body and soul. Ó Ríordáin waits for a sign that will express the meaning of this place to him

116 Sewell, *Selected Poems*, p. 89. Trans. Denise Blake.

fully – his image of the ram as an exemplar of clarity and purity has failed – just as he waited the day of his mother's burial long ago. And as happened on that day too, the poet seizes on the symbol of the bird as the vehicle for that which he seeks to express in 'Oileán agus Oileán Eile':

Do chuala tarcaisne don saol
I nguth an éin bhí 'clagar ceoil

An ceol a raid sé leis an mbith
Dob shin oileán an éin,
Níl éinne beo nach bhfuair oileán,
Is trua a chás má thréig.

I heard contempt for our chosen world
in the sound of a bird's clacking chorus.

The song he shared with the universe
was the bird's own island.
No one is born without an island—
a pity for anyone who deserts.[117]

The symbol of the bird proves burdensome before long and he abandons it again. (It would probably have been to Ó Ríordáin's advantage if he had realised that the image of the robin wasn't powerful enough to ensure the redemptive emotion or release he sought in 'Adhlacadh mo Mháthar' either, but that's a subject for another time.)

Then, suddenly, the poet stumbles on the thing he wanted to say and, better still, expressed in simplicity and poise and rhythm and sweet language. If there's a philosophy here, it is the one as elucidated in poetry's shadow; the coercing of words and images and the literary appropriation of ideas is at an end. In one brief instant he has recognised the forms of the truth. Ó Ríordáin noted this crucial shift in approach on 9 April 1949 when he wrote:

---

117 Sewell, *Selected Poems*, p. 93. Trans. Denise Blake.

From time to time, when someone is composing poetry the best thing to do is to surrender. i.e. not to make any effort to compose something. A sort of a listening. Let the lines mold you. The poem forming itself masterfully … The language and the past and the dead blow themselves through you. I felt it when I started the lines that began with 'I bhfírinne na haigne', or when they composed themselves, I mean. Our race plays its music through us.

He moves in tandem with the music, even if he doesn't know where it will take him:

I bhfírinne na haigne
Tá oileán séin,
Is tusa tá ar marthain ann
Is triall fád dhéin,
Ná bíodh ort aon chritheagla
Id láthair féin,
Cé go loiscfidh sé id bheatha tú,
Do thusa féin,
Mar níl ionat ach eascaine
A dúirt an saol,
Níl ionat ach cabaireacht
Ó bhéal go béal:
Gé gur cumadh tú id phaidir gheal
Ar bhéal Mhic Dé
Do scoiltis-se do thusa ceart
Le dúil sa tsaol,
Ach is paidir fós an tusa sin
Ar oileán séin,
A fhan go ciúin ag cogarnach
Ar bheolaibh Dé
Nuair do rincis-se go macnasach
Ar ghob an tsaoil.

There's an island of serenity
in the mind's truth.

It is you who resides there,
so go to meet your self.
Don't tremble with fear
in your own presence,
although your self
will burn you alive,
as you're just a curse
uttered by the world,
just some loose talk
from mouth to mouth:
though formed as a prayer
on the mouth of our Lord,
you cleaved from the right you
to craven life,
but the right you
is still a prayer
on an island of serenity,
and stayed whispering softly
on the lips of God
while you went romping
on the gob of the world.[118]

In Section V of the poem 'Oileán agus Oileán Eile' we find him reverting to the 'old' way of composition and mechanically sourcing the image, if possible. The tree limbs and branches as waving in the sky overhead must serve to inscribe meaning now. They are as a corpse 'being burned alive', a corpse burned away by the searing essence of the humanity it once contained – they are as a sketch of Gandhi and of the 'duel' that Finbarr fought between the 'God that is you and the God that is the world'. Gandhi and Finbarr are identified as one in the 'name-place' that is 'geanclann', a place they both inhabited at one time. As based on his various diary entries, one would assume that this poet's entire meditation here began with Gandhi rather than with Finbarr, but that Ó Ríordáin

118 Sewell, *Selected Poems*, pp. 94–5. Trans. Denise Blake.

had to come to Gougane Barra to ensure one of the sages was made manifest in the other. (Ó Ríordáin was very taken with the life and death of Gandhi; earlier that year, on 2 February 1948, for instance, he noted: 'And they killed Gandhi, the deed of deeds in this world.')

In a sense, the actual historical personage, whether it be Finbarr or Gandhi or someone else again, is not the most crucial issue here. The poet isn't interested in these figures for themselves but rather because they have remained loyal to the 'island' – because it is this island that is their most authentic and enduring aspect in the end. The poet leaves their two islands quickly again later, having passed a brief period in the presence of the 'truth' after he returns back to 'the chatter of life' again. Not that it's ever entirely clear what the poet's truth actually entails – despite how beautifully he speaks of it and proclaims its existence in the poem. Is it solely the experience that is the poem or does it extend beyond this again? What is 'his own telling of God's Realm', as revealed to him here in this place that he's now about to abandon? If it is anywhere in the poem it is surely somewhere in the following verses:

Nuair ghlanann ceo na feola léi
Tig áilleacht ait i rocaibh,
Is féidir cló a mheas ann féin
Sa tsolas cnámhach folamh.

Tá sult na saoirse i gcló na gcrann
Is grá don tsúil a fiaradh,
Tá dúil sa rud tá casta cam
Is gráin don bhog is don díreach.

Is fireann scríbhinn seo na gcrann,
Níl cíoch ná cuar in aon bhall,
Tá manach scríte abhus is thall,
Sé Barra lúb na ngéag seo.

When the fog of the flesh disappears
it leaves the strange beauty of scars,

true forms will be judged for themselves
in the empty skeletal light.

Freedom joys in the script of the trees
and here love warps the eye,
there's passion for things jagged and crooked,
abhorrence for the smooth and untried.

This tree-script is masculine,
there's not a breast or curve in sight.
Monk is written everywhere,
and this tangle of limbs is Finbarr.[119]

He is best staying on this hard and masculine island where one can appraise the human being in the fullness of truth and without the hindrances and fog that is the call of the flesh – the form that has the clarity of bare and corrugated human limbs. It seems that there is a place for the 'distorted eye' and the 'crooked twisted thing' and the individual that is different, after all; and also for 'the joy of freedom' whatever this may be – the 'freedom from desire, from fear, from ego, from faith, tradition, from ignorance, from blame' which Ó Ríordáin had sought from the beginning. And perhaps this is what the poet really found there ultimately, even if only for the shortest time.

The poet meets the Englishman again just as he's about to leave the island. Initially, he senses that this other visitor to this place has little enough regard for it, but he quickly reconsiders and posits that 'fishing on a lake' better 'explains' the Englishman's *raison d'être* on the 'island'. Ó Ríordáin says this somewhat derisively, even if it's consistent with the motif of the Englishman as 'other' in much of his work. Here again is the Turnbull and Wilde of the diaries, people who are as different from Blessed Finbarr as it's possible to be but who are nonetheless willing to display the truth of themselves openly and without fear. 'The same writer but a different play,' was the way Ó Ríordáin put it in his diary. The poet

119 Sewell, *Selected Poems*, pp. 95–7. Trans. Denise Blake.

too is author of another play, one that he has to rewrite again and again – a play without an ending.

And this play was the one that he also brought to the stage in the poem 'Cnoc Mellerí' ('*Mount Melleray*').[120] Here he brings his collection of sins to the Church once more in the hope of finding sanctuary from the demons that torment him. It's a landscape that we are more familiar with now than the storm and the night that is 'snoring' in and around the monastery – his illness which prevents him sleeping and weighs heavily on his soul, the ticks of lust that plague him when he's in the bed where he dressed himself within the 'plumage-joy of life'. It's as if he has moved his room from Inniscarra to this place in his imagination and endeavours to transform it into a spiritual site of sorts, as befits a site of pilgrimage; here the physical suffering that he normally undergoes at home is re-embodied as a spiritual illness that seeks to eat away at his soul:

from **'Cnoc Mellerí'**

Sranntarnach na stoirme i Mellerí aréir
Is laethanta an pheaca bhoig mar bhreoiteacht ar mo chuimhne,
Laethanta ba leapacha de shonaschlúmh an tsaoil
Is dreancaidí na drúise iontu ag preabarnaigh ina mílte.

from **'Mount Melleray'**

The snore-snortle of a storm in Mount Melleray last night
brought back days of concupiscence hanging over me like a disease,
days that were featherbeds in which I would luxuriate
and lusts would hop around like so many fleas.[121]

That strange amalgam of images and symbols once more – the 'God me' that is the figure of the young boy who'll 'never taste the ecstasy of women'

120 Mount Melleray Abbey is a monastic community of Cistercian monks found in the Knockmealdown Mountains in County Waterford.

121 Sewell, *Selected Poems*, p. 71. Trans. Paul Muldoon.

any more than Finbarr did on the solitary male island that had no 'breast nor curve anywhere' there. And contrasting with this is the worldly sinner – the 'me' who hasn't the humility to accept the instruction of the abbot, the clock or the rule:

'Ní bhlaisfidh sé choíche tréanmheisce mná
A chorraíonn mar chreideamh na sléibhte,
Thug léargas do Dante ar Fhlaitheas Dé tráth,
Nuair a thuirling na haingil i riocht véarsaí.'

Sin é dúirt an ego bhí uaibhreach easumhal,
Is é dallta le feirg an tsaoil,
Ach do smaoiníos ar ball, is an ceol os ár gcionn,
Gur mó ná an duine an tréad.

D'fhéachas laistiar díom ar fhásach mo shaoil

D'fhéachas ar bheatha na manach anonn

Do bhlaiseas mórfhuascailt na faoistine ar maidin …

Ach do bhlaiseas uair eile iontaoibh asam féin

'The power of a woman who can move
mountains as surely as faith is one in which he'll never be immersed.
It was such a woman who afforded Dante a vision of Paradise
in which even the angels were strictly versed.'

That's how the ego weighed in, so full of itself,
so blinded by life that's out of control,
though it struck me later, while the music hung over us,
how the flock triumphs over a single soul.

I looked back at the waste of my life …

I looked at the life of that monk over there …

> I'd tasted the great lightening of confession that morning …
>
> At another time I tasted something like self-reliance …[122]

A worthless trip, one might say, if it wasn't for the few monks 'made of sun' that he incorporated into the poem along the way. When exactly Ó Ríordáin visited Mount Melleray Abbey or composed this poem is unclear. As mentioned earlier, his diary contains significant gaps during the mid-1940s. We have only one small entry between 7 September 1944 and 7 August 1947 and even in this case, the exact date of the entry isn't provided. All we know is that 'Cnoc Mellerí' was written sometime during this period when there were many gaps. In the Oireachtas poetry competitions of 1946, Ó Ríordáin claimed four of the five-pound cash prizes for his poetry, and 'Cnoc Mellerí' appeared in print for the first time in the December 1946 issue of *Comhar*. The diary entry where he references the trip he made to Melleray for the first time appears a few years after this again. The poet is discussing a priest named Fr Valkenburg in very positive terms, even if the poem itself betrays a certain small degree of tension between Ó Ríordáin and the apparently 'perfect' people he describes.

> *It is clear that he rides on the back of his learning and culture and yet the animal never really takes a bite out of him. All of this intellectual purity mortifies me as regards my own life just as Mount Melleray and Fr Tadhg also made me ashamed. God preserve me. My friends have all surrounded me.*[123]

The poet never managed another visit to Melleray, even if he often mentioned it afterwards. For instance, in 29 April 1950 he says that he's been to confession but that he hasn't felt the normal sense of peace afterwards that he normally does. The diary entry asks:

> *Have I no faith left at all? I should go to Confession at Mount Melleray and confess my entire life there. I also have to turn my back on the music of sin. This*

122 Sewell, *Selected Poems*, pp. 66–9. Trans. Paul Muldoon.
123 D: 22 June 1949.

> *music is still in my ears – sweet music. I'm reluctant to deny this music. No wonder I have no peace.*

Although he didn't visit Melleray again, he did visit Glenstal Abbey in March 1951 and this is how he felt on his return home:

> *I went in search of God, as far as Glenstal. I watched over the Blessed Sacrament for half an hour in the church and promised God that I would never sin again. Look at me now, my face to the wall ...*[124]

In a letter Ó Ríordáin sent to Fr Valkenburg, he mentioned this visit to Glenstal and in a reply dated 7 April, the priest advised him to avoid sin and clerics in equal measure: *Fuge prelatum sicut peccatum.* Wise words indeed, if one could only follow them.

Ó Ríordáin wrote 'Oilithreacht Fám Anam' ('*My Soul's Pilgrimage*') a year before 'Oileán agus Oileán Eile' and the former saw publication in September 1947; both poems bear many similarities. Not only is the way that the poet set about writing both poems quite similar, but so too how he sought inspiration in both instances. There is the atmosphere associated with the sacred place of refuge, a feeling that manifests itself physically in the form of certain animals he comes across there. Just as the poet fails to be 'as accurately formed, as authoritative as the ancient ancestors' as signified by the ram's horns on the island – in much the same way, he fails in his attempt to prove as 'respectful' as the Pilgrimage's *Ortsgeist.* Unlike the ram, the image of the small respectful donkey is inserted into the poem in this instance, albeit proving a much less effective image, poetically-speaking. It seems likely that the old woman the donkey puts the poet in mind of is an old woman from Ballyvourney and his childhood long ago; after all, it was back to the 'source' there that the poet usually went whenever he wished to draw on deeper religious feelings and the atmosphere of a holy place as he sought to imbue his verse in this instance. 'I felt a sudden urge there a while ago to do the Stations of the Cross in a church in Ballyvourney' the poet writes in the diary for 9 April 1963 when

124 D: 2 April 1951.

the draw of the older or half-lost tradition came to him unexpectedly again. Not that there was anything very spontaneous or unexpected about the composition of the poem itself – as Ó Ríordáin himself explained during one of his radio presentations:

> *This is a poem I wrote because I set out to write a poem. I got a bicycle and visited a certain area and then stayed around there idling, supposedly thinking – until these words eventually came to me. I spotted a donkey and came across a few thoughts. I think that it probably had a lesson for me but I failed to be as humble as the donkey.*

Where was this place that Ó Ríordáin spoke of returning to in search of his 'fairy youth', as he referred to it in another poem, and where he sought a similar sense of home or harmony?[125] I think that it was probably the graveyard in Inniscarra where he buried his mother just a few years earlier. The place that was 'the white cemetery by the river' on that fateful day, but where the river now flows 'pompously' next to her, similar to the blend of joy, peace and sanctity that forms the atmosphere of his poem's initial verses.[126] His mother rises from the grave and the pair of them head back together to Ballyvourney again in their imagination, the same as they would have done during the long winter nights they spent telling each other stories years earlier:

from **Oilithreacht Fám Anam**

Do labhair an tír mar theampall,
Bhí siúl na habhann boimpéiseach,
Do chrom go glúin na gleannta,
Bhí fíor na croise ar ghéaga.

Mar sheanabhean dheabhóideach
Ag déanamh Turas na Croise

125 ES: p. 48.
126 ES: p. 56.

Sheas asailín ómósach
Gan aird aige ar dhuine.

Le soiscéal gaoithe d'éisteas,
Bhí naofacht ar an dtalamh,
Anseo do mhair mo chéadshearc,
Níor ghabhas an treo le fada.

D'aiséirigh 'na taisléine,
Is solas ar a leacain,
Is do thionlaic mé go gléineach
Ar oilithreacht fám anam …

from **My Soul's Pilgrimage**

The country spoke like a temple,
a river shuffled on past,
valleys were bent to their knees,
the sign of the cross upon the branches.

Like a pious old woman
making the Stations of the Cross
a reverent little donkey stood
paying heed to no one.

The gospel was carried on the wind,
and there was holiness on the earth.
This was where my first love lived.
I hadn't passed this way in a while.

A vision arose wrapped in a shroud
with a brightness from her cheeks,
and she escorted me vividly
on the pilgrimage of my soul …[127]

---

127 Sewell, *Selected Poems*, p. 77. Trans. Denise Blake.

Another element of the older tradition the poet had experienced as a child, which he recalled again now, was the storytelling in the evenings at different houses: listening to his grandmother (his father's mother) or Nell Mhattie, the withered hag in the corner, and their renditions of the old stories. He recreates these forgotten people and the nights they told their stories again in his copybook in preparation for the poem:

> *A morning of my life. My grandmother. 'Light my pipe.' 'The man who went to the Orient.' 'The man who cut his daughter's limbs off.'*

Raghad siar ar bhus na cuimhne
A dá ordóig ag casadh timpeall mar roth
Ar oilithreacht ar fuaid m'aigne – áiteanna naofa.

I'll return on the bus of memory
Her two thumbs spinning wheel-like
On a pilgrimage through my mind – the holy places.[128]

The wonder of the story and the wonder of youth; there was a time when they fused together, when he was an element of both. They were one and the same, and the world formed anew:

from **'Oilithreacht Fám Anam'**

Chonac saol mar scéal fiannaíochta
Fadó, fadó, ar maidin,
A mhúnlaigh an tslat draíochta
A bhíonn 'na láimh ag leanbh.

Bhí cailleach chríon sa chúinne,
A dhá hordóig ag casadh
Go tionscalach mar thuirne,
Ag piseogaíocht go gasta

128 Trans. M. Ó hAodha.

Iar n-éisteacht lena glórtha
Ba chomharsa an clúracán dom,
Ba chlúracán gach comharsa
Is drúcht na hóige ar bhánta ...

from 'My Soul's Pilgrimage'

I saw life like a tale from the Fianna,
long long ago in the morning,
the way a magic sword takes shape
in the hand of a young boy.

There was an old shrivelled shrew
turning both her thumbs
tirelessly like a spinning wheel
while she quickly recited spells.

After listening to her piseogs,
those cluricaunes became my neighbours
until every neighbour was a cluricaune
and the mist of youth on the meadows ...[129]

Whether he likes it or not, however, the poet has no choice in the end other than to leave the graveyard and Ballyvourney behind and face the real world again – the same as he had to say farewell to the 'essence of the saints' thoughts' of Gougane Barra rather than bring them home with him. And it's the same familiar canvas that awaits him on his return, one that, as Seán Ó Tuama says, is dominated by images of 'demons, frogs, winds, storms, derision and female breasts'.[130] One could say that this atmosphere and these images were always with him at the back of his mind, even when he sought to flee them or follow an alternate imaginative trajectory through the occasional trip to places like Glenstal or Melleray. The order

129 Sewell, *Selected Poems*, pp. 78–9. Trans. Denise Blake.
130 Ó Tuama, *Filí faoi Sceimhle*, p. 43.

of things is disturbed in this poem, however; time and the world are not as before, and when he begins again he is as the sinner who felt it necessary to set out on pilgrimage the first day ever. They are the first cornerstones for his new plan of life, his new aesthetic:

> *Image one – the individual scrutinising themselves. Lustful thoughts. I had a revelation – Hell. I was looking at myself. I escaped from myself into the city. The symphony of the city – pictures of it. The drama of the city taking place. The city shattered the depth of my thoughts. It was only just drowning out the river of sound that is the ego, the same as a withered old virgin who remembers only occasionally when she was corrupted, but who always carries the bitter memory with her nonetheless. Redemption – the tradition of our ancestors maybe or Faith. A morning of my life. Begin. Write it in the morning. I am happy when I remember my soul …*

'Redemption – the tradition of our ancestors maybe or Faith.' It might well be, but the poet's concept of redemption now incorporates very different understandings from those that were his as a youth. The demons have been released within his mind and he cannot defeat them, whatever about conveying their nature. The female 'ghost's' advice proves inadequate; her message remains solely on the level of fable, a fable which is never acted upon. It was a 'Gospel wind' in every way. But if he belongs to the denizens of hell, then hell is his proper subject and not simply the soothing memories of years that are long gone. Memories won't suffice in themselves, and neither will they banish the filth of the sweet lust that takes possession of his thoughts. In literature, hell always seemed more real a place than paradise ever did, and it was this hell too that the adjudicator took most note of when adjudicating on the poetry competition in the Oireachtas competition of 1947:

> *There is more of the magic and mystery of poetry in this piece than in any of the other entries in the competition. It is clear from the thoughts expressed in this piece that an imagination that is unusual and strong and independent is at work here. For example it would be difficult to better verse IX and verse XI as a reflection of filth that is sin and the effect it has on the human mind …*

The section of 'My Soul's Pilgrimage' that begins with the line 'Mar ghadhar ag déanamh caca' (*'like a dog taking a shit'*) is the one he meant here. And, curiously, it is when the poet abandons what he truly feels to engage with the cold instruction his mother's mouth emits that this poem goes off-kilter. One would be forgiven for thinking that the objective of this poem was clear and set from the beginning and that it would wrap itself up in neat and tidy fashion no matter what: this only barely happens in this instance, however.

In his introduction to the anthology *Nuabhéarsaíocht*, published in 1950, Seán Ó Tuama wrote about Seán Ó Ríordáin that 'there most likely wasn't a poet as important as him writing in Irish for hundreds of years'.[131] That was some statement to make, when you consider that Ó Ríordáin was only twenty-three years of age and hadn't even one book of poetry published by then. And Ó Tuama particularly had in mind the longer poems, as it is in them that he says 'we get the greatest sense of the poet's exceptional promise, above all in the four poems "Cnoc Mellerí", "Adhlacadh mo Mháthar", "Oilithreacht Fám Anam" and "Oileán agus Oileán Eile".'[132]

Not that the poet himself felt this way, as evidenced by the radio script he prepared contemporaneous with the publication of *Eireaball Spideoige*. In his diary entries for the time, he was critical of all of his poetry barring one long poem entitled 'Saoirse'; the latter wasn't available by 1950 when *Nuabhéarsaíocht* came out. He praised this poem in the aforementioned radio script, the same as in the diary interestingly, and it was one of the few poems that Ó Ríordáin was consistently very proud of – even in later years. For example, in his article in *An Síol* he referred to 'Saoirse' as follows:

> *... my favourite poem in the family. A little poem that I wrote that I didn't come to hate sooner or later. I think that this poem is female, that it came to me in the autumn and that it stood next to me as a woman. I'm afraid that I was a bit*

131 Ó Tuama, Seán, *Nuabhéarsaíocht, 1939–1949* (Sáirséal agus Dill, Dublin, 1950), p. 11.

132 *Ibid.*, p. 12.

> *strong-handed with the truth and with life in the other poems, as a man can be – but that this poem accepted the truth and life as a woman does. This poem wasn't composed; it was such that it came of itself.*[133]

He had said the same thing in the diary for 9 April 1949 with reference to section IV of 'Oileán agus Oileán Eile' where he felt the poetry had composed itself, even if the poem as a whole – and indeed, the rest of his longer poems – were ones that:

> *... were plucked from the tree but didn't fall. Maybe I wasn't ready for them. Maybe I went in pursuit of them. Their scope was broader than the needs of the moment. I'm afraid that I was strong-handed with them. I'm really afraid that the composition that went into them is very obvious, and that's a term that is used with sarcasm in Dunquin.*

It's unlikely that he changed his views on his poetry later either as, when interviewed in *Scríobh 3*, published in 1978, he stated 'now things such as "Adhlacadh mo Mháthar" – I don't think that's a good poem. I don't think that it's a healthy thing.'[134] Interestingly, such poems didn't leave any progeny after them either in any of his later collections, not unless you count those poems where he sought to delineate the human being's different forms and manifestations while simultaneously engaging with various philosophical questions. It was the shorter poems that the poet was always happiest with, as he'd made clear in that same radio script: 'they were ripe so that the wind blew them off the tree ... I'd arrived at them. And each of them fulfilled a certain need, whether big or small at that particular moment in time, and no other.' Shorter poems like these formed the bulk of the collection *Brosna* and were cited by Seán Ó Tuama as his favourite poems also. Another longer poem that wasn't published in time for the *Nuabhéarsaíocht* anthology was 'Na hÓinmhidí' ('*The Jesters*') as written in the summer of 1949. Ó Ríordáin submitted it for the Oireachtas competition, number 11, later that year, but it wasn't

133 *An Síol*, 1969, p. 15.
134 *Scríobh 3*, p. 174.

published until July 1951, when it appeared in the journal *Feasta.* There are significant differences between the version of the poem submitted for the Oireachtas competition and the one published in *Feasta*, however, and the poem was revised again before it saw publication in *Eireaball Spideoige.* The biggest difference between the two published versions of the poem was that one of the verses that appeared in the (earlier) *Feasta* version of the poem was omitted from the 'final version' in *Eireaball Spideoige.* This was the verse that began section III of the poem (An Óigbhean ag Labhairt/*The Young Woman Speaking*):

> *Ná héist leo, na hóinmhidí,*
> *Iompaigh-sé chugham,*
> *Féach mise beo led thaoibh,*
> *Bean lán de stuaim,*
> *Shiúil mise bóthar leat,*
> *Bean na dTrí mBó is mé,*
> *Bean Dubh an Ghleanna mé,*
> *Is Eibhlín a rún.*[135]

> Don't listen to them, the jesters,
> He turned to me
> See me here right next to you
> The wise woman
> I've walked the road with you
> I'm the Woman with Three Cows
> I'm the Black Woman of the Glen
> And beloved Eileen.[136]

We'll refer to the different versions here as appropriate.

The poet's diary entries prove useful in our attempts to understand this poem and this is important because even if many of the same questions are explored here as his other poems, there's no question that this is one

135 ES: pp. 85–8.
136 Trans. M. Ó hAodha.

of the darkest and most enigmatic of all the metaphysical poems that Ó Ríordáin ever wrote. As with other compositions, he returns – as on a pilgrimage almost – to his early childhood days in Ballyvourney, back to the wellspring, and the earliest version of the poem (the Oireachtas version) highlights this best. The hill known as Mullach an Ois, which overlooked the town to the rear of the poet's house, becomes the jester of his imagination. The verse is as yet only half-formed but it is still clear in the following:

Do chonac i gcéin Mullach an Ois
Is mé i dtús na hóige,
'Sin é an solas leanfadsa
An solas ar Mhullach an Ois,'
Do sheas an cnoc mar óinmhid
Ar tháirsigh an tráthnóna.

As a child once more,
I saw Mullach an Ois far away
'This is the light that I will follow
The light on Mullach an Ois,'
The hill stood as a jester
On the threshold of evening.[137]

The jester, who takes shape in the form of the hill as the second verse proceeds, emerges neither from his childhood nor from the contours of the poet's everyday life, however, but from the pages of a book entitled *Guaire an Oinigh* by Cormac Ó Cadlaigh, a book that Ó Ríordáin had been reading from January 1942 onwards.[138] It was one of the few books he'd bought at this juncture as his illness meant he had to be frugal in his spending. Seán's copy of it still survives, as do the two poems by Hopkins ('Spring' and 'As Kingfishers Catch Fire') that he'd scribbled on the blank pages at the start of the book. Indeed, the words of the first jester, and

137 Trans. M. Ó hAodha.
138 D: 11 January 1942.

his allusion to having been there at the time of 'Guaire an Oinigh', are an acknowledgement of the literary source for the poem. And Seán added this note to one version of the poem while he was still working on it: 'Their iniquity led them astray, the buffoons. They noticed the colour of existence but never bothered with its interpretation. The joint poem of Mac Dá Chearda and Conall Clogach, the two jesters.'

Why had Ó Ríordáin plumped on the notion of the jester as an image of the state of mind that one associates solely with pure poetry? His notes provide us with further information on the genesis of this idea. His thoughts here are rooted in his reading of the story 'Guaire agus an dá Óinmhid' and the idea that the jesters were a race who 'noticed the colour of existence', yet he fails to interpret the meaning of this to any great degree.[139] The jesters had communicated with the language of colour rather than with the language of the expert or theoretician – i.e. that language as spoken by the scientist or the man of grammar, or the legalist who has been blinded by knowledge; this latter language is what the poet is left with when 'the intoxication passes'.[140] In the poem 'In Absentia' it is the lunatic and the saint only who remain housebound and responsible for the 'fireside of the abandoned God' when 'the people of the world are outside'.[141] (Another lunatic or 'crazy fool' whom Ó Ríordáin sourced in the literature was the Suibhne Gelt (Mad Sweeney) of 'In Absentia', needless to say.) And in the essay 'Teangacha Príobháideacha' ('*Private Languages*'), the poet extends the wellspring of inspiration so that it encompasses the madman or crazy fool, the saint and the poet in unison:

> *They are a different people altogether, the people who compose the most elevated of the private languages – they are people who were completely transformed, like Saint Paul, John of the Cross, the great poets, great writers of prose and crazy people. These are people whose homeplace left a particular mark on their speech as happened to everyone who grew into holiness or poetry or madness – so that*

139 Ó Cadlaigh, Cormac, *Guaire an Oinigh* (Oifig an tSoláthair, Dublin, 1939), pp. 118–56.

140 ES: p. 44.

141 B: p. 20.

their native language was transformed or whatever language it is that they use when in this transformed state … There is no one with a purer ability to create a private language than the madman. The madman goes into the realm of insanity and for as long as he's there, he speaks the dialect of that region faithfully. The realm of madness is another region of the mind, the same as every other form of inspiration.[142]

This madman/saint/poet is the jester(s) of this poem. The misery of the first jester is one that is more worldly or earthbound and there's no doubt that he speaks for the poet as he once was (the poet who has (newly) sinned against buffoonery) when he states:

Do bhíos-sa anseo fadó, fadó,
In aimsir Ghuaire an Oinigh,
Do chleachtas óinmhideacht lem ló
Is níor pheacaíos riamh 'na coinne,
Do leathadh doirse focal romham,
Is do fáiltíodh romham cois tine.

Do chaitheas oícheanta ag scoraíocht
Cois tine gach aon fhocail,
Is do chuardaíos féin le solas croí
Tinteánachas gach focail,
Sara bhfágas riamh aon ghin dem bhaois
Fé chúram lucht an fhocail.[143]

I was here long ago,
In Guaire an Oinigh's time,
I practised holy wisdom by day
And never sinned against its tenets
The doors of perception opened for me,
And I was welcomed in.

142 *Scríobh 4*, p. 15.
143 'Na hÓinmhidí' ('*The Jesters*'), ES: p. 85.

I spent nights house-calling
By the fireside, every word,
And I sought with an enlightened heart
The language of home,
This was long before that foolish progeny of mine
The verses I left in the hands of the wordsmiths.[144]

The poet had written this in his diary earlier that same summer:

> *When I'm looking for a particular word while writing a poem I try a few different words like this: I go down the stairs of words and find the fire and I sit next to it warming myself and before long I know in my heart whether this is a house that I could leave my child in.*[145]

The child cited in this piece represents that which begat foolishness in 'Na hÓinmhidí'. It is necessary to taste or sift the physical texture of the word initially in order to test its suitability for the emotions he seeks to embody it with. The poet goes from one person to the next in the company of words in a sort of a 'house-calling' (or 'scoraíocht') of the imagination and, similar to the poem 'Sos', the mere texture of the word is enough to recall the older rural world of his youth again and imbue it with the necessary power.[146] Another variation on the same metaphor occurred with his sourcing from memory of the phrase – 'ag siúl na sráide' ('*walking the street*') in the poem 'A Sheanfhilí, Múinídh Dom Ghlao' ('*O Ancient Poets, Teach Me the Trade*'), even if he doesn't recognise them any more because it's so long since he had any link with them.[147] But the door is still wide open and he's welcome next to the fire. He'll knock on the same door in 'Fill Arís' ('*Return Again*'), the door of the older Gaelic world view and tradition, the door to the world of the forgotten generation that he seeks to recreate in his work. In the case of 'Fill Arís', it isn't the former

144 Trans. M. Ó hAodha.
145 D: 26 May 1949.
146 ES: p. 46.
147 ES: p. 36.

neighbours who are waiting for Ó Ríordáin inside the door but actually his own 'self' – as it ought to be. Take the following from 'Fill Arís':

Sin é do dhoras,
Dún Chaoin fé sholas an tráthnóna,
Buail is osclófar
D'intinn féin is do chló ceart.[148]

that is your door,
Dún Chaoin in the evening light,
knock and there will be opened
your own mind and your right shape.[149]

And not only does Ó Ríordáin see himself as a crazy fool or buffoon as understood within the older tradition and culture, and as encompassed by Mac Dá Chearda, Conall Clogach and Suibhne Geilt, but he is a buffoon in worldly terms as well. One state accompanies the other. After all, it's with the human versions of such 'fools' and 'jesters' that the poet had always registered his affinity – particularly from that crucial day he'd first found himself in their midst – April Fool's Day 1938. Wasn't it the evening of that very day that he'd properly assumed his trade of poet for the first time ever, as the poem itself explains?

from 'Na hÓinmhidí'

An cuimhin leat tráthnóna
Gur thuirling an solas
Ar ainnise óinmhid'
Is sinne ad lorg?
B'shin é an tráthnóna
Gur baisteadh do chloigeann
Le solas na n-óinmhid
I gcreideamh an Fhocail.

---

148 B: p. 41.
149 Sewell, *Selected Poems*, p. 163. Trans. Barry McCrea.

B'shin é an tráthnóna
Gur dhúisigh an Focal
As toirchim eolais
I suainliosaibh leabhar,
As míogarnach cainte
Ar bheolaibh an phobail,
Is gur thosnaigh na meamraim
Sna sléibhtibh ag cogar.[150]

from **'The Jesters'**

Do you remember that evening
When the light fell
On the jester's desolation
While we searched for you
That was the evening
When your head was baptised
In the light of the jesters
In the faith of the Word

That was the evening
When the Word awakened
Fecund with knowledge
From the ancient slumber of the fairy-book,
From the murmur of speech
On people's lips,
When writing began once more
Off in the whispering hills.[151]

Wasn't it this too that had happened to Chomhdhán Mac Dá Chearda when he'd been made a jester for life?

---

150 ES: p. 87.
151 Trans. M. Ó hAodha.

The wizard came to him and struck the illusive magic ...

One way or another it's the same 'bald-headed jester' here at the beginning of the poem, except that he's assumed the shape of a hill, a hill that enjoys the 'play of light on his bald head'.[152] And what are those notes that he senses stirring again in the mountains? What else but the Irish-language tradition that's been there since the beginning of time and that's being shaped again in order to better attune it to the twentieth century? The language is rousing itself slowly now, waking from the long, deep slumber of the old books where it's been mumbling sleepily to itself for far too long, just waiting to be fired up and imbued with thought and feeling again. Has the poet already cut himself off from inspiration and from the poetic craft and from the community of the jesters because of his dalliances with the 'young woman' back on the hill, however? This is the poem's central question, an inevitable question, really, given the poet's understandings with respect to the pollution of the soul and the enjoyment of sensual pleasures. In the Irish-language versions of the international ballad 'I am Stretched on your Grave', it is the clergy who are at loggerheads with the man whose love for the dead girl is deemed immoderate:

Tá na sagairt is na bráithre
Gach lá liom i bhfearg
De chionn bheith i ngrá leat
A óigbhean is tú marbh ...

The priests and the friars
Approach me in dread
Because I still love you
My love and you're dead ...[153]

The jesters are the 'priests and friars' of our poem here and the ones who

152 A phrase taken from 'Na hÓinmhidí' as translated by M. Ó hAodha.

153 'I Am Stretched On Your Grave', lyrics, Sinéad O'Connor – www.azlyrics.com/lyrics/sineadoconnor/iamstretchedonyourgrave.html.

remind the *persona* that he's drifted away from the gospel they had once practised together in order to sing his thoughts in the church of the flesh instead. The fact that the girl is alive again now in the imaginary is the source of sin:

Tá óinmhidí Éireann
Go mór liom i bhfeirg
De chionn bheith i ngrá leat
A óigbhean is tú id bheathaidh,
Is do chiúinigh an Bíobla
Im chluasaibh go hobann
Nuair a chanas mo smaointe
I meadaracht do cholla.

The jesters of Ireland
Are very angry with me
Because I love you
A young woman like you … alive,
And the Bible suddenly fell silent
In my ears
As I sang my song of desire
To your body's tune.[154]

The way the poet sees it in 'Na hÓinmhidí', he is only wasting his time trying to write poetry if his will is not attuned with that of the Creator. The 'Cat-Priest' is the name given to the animal jester who attempts to bring the two aspects together – the metaphysical impulse and the worldly call of the flesh. This call is no common *das Ewig-Weibliche* (the eternal feminine) and the woman in question was no passing attraction for the poet. This wasn't a theoretical problem that Ó Ríordáin had to solve because for the first time in his life he was really in love. He was in love with Kay Foley. She encompasses the woman full of wisdom, the woman with three cows and the dark-haired woman of the valley as referred to in

154 Trans. M. Ó hAodha.

the version of the poem Ó Ríordáin published in *Feasta*; and she is every seductress there ever was in the Irish-language literary tradition. It is near midnight on 2 July 1949 when he notes:

> *Woman, woman, woman. The woman who was waiting for her chance and who took my shirt with her and the woman who's full of wisdom and the woman of the three cows and the black woman of the glen, there is no power like yours! The Church is it? The woman is stronger. Literature? Pride? Philosophy? Manliness? Will? She's stronger than all of these put together. Is the Virgin Mary listening to me? Can it be that she is listening to every useless person like me? If you have a private hearing oh Virgin, or if you have oh God, or if you have Augustine, then help me one of you. How come no one else can cure me except she who took my shirt with her? Was anyone else in as desperate a situation as I am? There are other women out there – there aren't. There is no one in this world but her. No one else has my shirt …*

In Ó Ríordáin's first real description of her, as noted in the diary for 9 December 1948, he says: 'She's infinite goodness even if I know that her goodness may not be at all an uncommon one. My portion of beauty, my portion of God's Reign is gathered within her, it is stored up in her.' On 20 December, in the middle of his account of his day at work, he mentions 'K.F. on the stairs.' This sighting had been in City Hall, and it was an image that would stay with him and the memory of which he would embellish in the years ahead, such as in 'Na hÓinmhidí':

> *Bhí bean ar an staighre*
> *Chomh faiteach le smaoineamh*
> *Bhí solas 'na súilibh*
> *Nuair a iompaigh sí aniar chugham.*

> A woman on the stairs
> Anxious as thought
> A light in her eyes
> As she turned back towards me[155]

155 Trans. M. Ó hAodha.

By May and June 1949 he is skirting closer to the subject that really concerns him. He's about to return to the sanatorium again for another bout of treatment. He takes sick leave from work on 5 May and, as usual, he begins to feel more manly or whole. We'll let the diary account speak for itself, as appropriate:

> *17/5/49. I gave up work in the office a fortnight ago. My soul returned to me tonight. It had been drowned beneath the opinions of others for a while and also with love for a woman. Seán Ó Ríordáin has returned to life again and if this world was good to him, he would take care of himself.*
>
> *26/5/49. Tuesday night, I went to the Opera House – Ballet – Joan Denise Moriarty. Peer Gynt. Ballet and speech mixed together. Pure ballet without speech, everything other than Peer Gynt. As for the music, and it's said that it was good, I don't understand music and it was lost on me. [It is after this that the extract relating to "the stairs of words" as cited earlier appears.]*
>
> *11/6/49. I went to confession in the Church of Peter and Paul.*
>
> *19/6/49. You are sorry, Seán. You are lonely. I'm afraid that you abandoned your light. You composed poems but you don't know whether they are poems. Life is too hard for you. You gave your love to a woman and you don't know what you got in return. How could a woman love the likes of you? Look at how your health is. Aren't you dying? The world is written on your face. The woman is that world. They are one and the same. They are both hard, fixed. But when you fail and when the light of this life and this woman disappears you'll still have this small room and this notebook and words will come to you as if back from your ancestors. These same words visited many rooms over time and they took something with them from every room. We're all words on God's lips and we live for as long as he speaks. When God's Mind abandons us we are nothing but a dead shell until God's Mind returns to us again. Call them back out of the dictionary and give them life in the same way as God put life into us.*
>
> *Cáit Ní Fhoghlú (Kay Foley) and Eibhlín Ní Cheallacháin (Eileen O'Callaghan) visited me from Cork last night. We went back over to the graveyard. A beautiful evening. Me saying stupid things and both of them slagging*

me, nice and relaxed. Me acting the fool. They took off their shoes. I prefer C. Ní Fh. when she's by herself. Something ruined the evening. Sin was thundering in the air. You can't have a proper conversation when there are more than two people present. It's a struggle when there are three. Oh, the pain of it!

I was drawing pictures of children this afternoon. I saw something beautiful, something pitiable, and with a small bit of cowardliness running through it. A pretty little girl aged about seven and boy of roughly the same age but not as handsome. He's squint-eyed and I like him. It's obvious that he's in love with the girl. He was talking to her and caressing her. She paid no attention to him. He was fighting with her because he was fond of her. She was fighting back with him coldly. Where's the coward? In heaven? Maybe that small boy has a room of his own there ...

How could love survive or prosper in such a cold atmosphere, one asks? The sanatorium threatens the poet on one side and the 'thunder of sin' on the other. And whatever glimmer of light he sees at the end of the tunnel will be ruthlessly snuffed out as before – so that he retreats again to his only sanctuary, the room and the books. The hearth of the 'word' is the only hearth he'll find a welcome at, ultimately. And for all he knows, and there's always that sneaking doubt at the back of his mind, perhaps this sanctuary is no refuge either; that the shelter that is the 'word' has abandoned him too and there's nothing left there for him there either – not the company of women nor the company of the other jesters/holy fools.

In the following verse of 'Na hÓinmhidí' he's neither one thing nor the other, neither fool nor man of substance, nor man of deed:

Tá an seomra folamh anocht
Gan solas gan áilleacht gan bhaois,
Má tá focail ag feitheamh amuigh
Is ag cnagadh ar dhoras mo thí
A deirim leo 'Deoch níl istigh',
Ta na hóinmhidí imithe le gaoith,
Is an óigbhean dar thugas síorghean
Níl baint aici siúd le filíocht.

The room is empty tonight
Without light or beauty or folly,
If words are waiting outside
Or tapping on the door of my house
I tell them 'No drink here',
The jesters have gone with the wind,
And the young woman I always loved
Is unknown to poetry.[156]

Because he believed this, consequently this is how it was. He returns to Heatherside in August and is at the lowest ebb of despair.

> *16/8/49. Tuesday. I'm here [in Heatherside]. Six of us in the room. The radio is on. 'The Light Show', curse it. The sun shining but there is no God at all. I came here on the 6/8/49. The night before that, the Friday night, God abandoned me completely. I've been suffering because of that night since. I've hardly got the courage to mention her. I should maybe mention what happened that night here but I can't – not yet anyway. It's a terrible thing to love a woman. It's even worse to kill off that love while it's still alive, alive. For a week, since I came here, I wanted nothing but to die. But the love is still alive. I suppose I deserved it. The last night. The person I loved more than anyone else in the world beside me. Then the ugly thing that happened. The night fell apart. There were two of us in it. There used to be a magic between us. But we failed to protect the magic from that night. We had to watch the magic dying. Oh Jesus Christ! I can't suffer it. Oh! Oh! Oh! Pain, pain, pain. Pain forever. It was my fault – a failing that can never be healed.*

It would heal, or at least for a while, anyway. Kay Foley's visits to him in the sanatorium and the letters she sent him there – every visit and every letter was a ray of hope lighting up the dark. It doesn't take long for memories to lose their sheen, however, and before long, he's back again in the dark prison of night. He receives a letter from Kay on 7 September 1949:

---

156 Trans. M. Ó hAodha.

> *That letter and that contact with her made me happy for the day … She asked me to write a play for the Abbey Theatre. She has full confidence in me, she says. I'm incarcerated here. There's no way out. I'm trapped finally. A claustrophobia engulfs my life. Oh Jesus Christ. I will go completely mad. I'll scream. Is there any help anywhere? I collapsed one day because I heard a story that upset me so much. This life and suffering is too much for me at the moment. Will it be long before I collapse completely and die. If I could do something for her and write a play. Am I a 'great man'? There isn't a cat in this world that isn't wiser or more sensible than I am …*

In contrast, the summer of 1950 was the happiest period of Ó Ríordáin's life since childhood. He had been home from the sanatorium since March and his life seemed to have a new scope and breadth to it again. There was a fragrance of honey on the air for the first time in years. He makes his first trip to Dunquin during this period in an effort to return to the well of tradition, and all goes well. The poet feels at ease with himself once more. He's in love with Kay and Kay with him. There's the prospect of a normal and happy life on the horizon – marriage, an improvement in his health. Five days after the doctor tells him that there's no problem with him marrying Kay, if he so wishes, he writes the poem that goes 'I will go down among the people' – 'Saoirse' ('*Liberty*') – in the space of one evening. Finally, he feels whole – he's the same as everyone else after all. His anxieties and self-doubts are always there at the edge of his mind, however; he can never be shot of them, no matter how hard he tries. They're not long returning either and by the year's end he has regressed to where he was for many years. He doesn't go to a sanatorium in Switzerland, after all, but takes refuge in his room and closes the door behind him instead. But before retreating into himself again he observes the world one last time from this newer and more positive perspective, the perspective of someone who has attempted to immerse himself within it and engage with it. Cited here are some of the main steps on the journey:

> *Wednesday 5/7/50. I went to play Blarney today with C. Ní Fh. Saturday. Happiness. A rainy afternoon but it doesn't matter. We went to the Hydro for some tea but we were refused. It doesn't matter. Her shoes got wet. It doesn't*

matter. There was magic everywhere. She is an able and intelligent person. I am certain that I am in love with her. She can be bitter sometimes. It doesn't matter. There's no one in the world as good as her or as beautiful as her. Seán Ó Tuama would say that I need an objective correlative in this moment.

If God's there I ask him to provide what I'm lacking, to direct my step, and to save my body and my soul. Give me a different form of music other than this pain and eternal suffering.

Saturday. 8/7/50. We went to Ballycotton. We had a great day.

Saturday, 15/7/50. I'm in Dunquin. I came up as far as Dingle on Wednesday. I spent the night in Benner's Hotel. I arrived here by car on Thursday. 25/-. Kruger is a big personality. He is multitalented. 'I failed in one trade,' he said, 'making small things …'

Sunday 20/8/50. The two of us went to the Guagane last Sunday. We'd a lovely day. We went to Blarney on Friday night. We were down in ourselves coming home. It's easy for the worries to creep up.

Sunday. 3/9/50. We went to Kinsale yesterday – C. [sic] and I. Dr O'Brien told me on Friday that there's no reason why I can't get married! I'm surprised. C. said to me that she was happy to go with me to Switzerland and to marry me. This is the reason that I asked the doctor the question. She said to me last night again that she was happy to marry me. What'll I do in God's name? There is a disease in me still. Would it be fair?

I'm afraid. A fear that freezes me and stops me in my tracks. It's easy to do something if you just go and do it. But it is difficult to pass over that border. The world expands beyond all measure when fear disappears. Because the only difficulty in this life is the fear of difficulty …

Tuesday. 12/9/50. Woe to he who puts his faith in women. Saturday was a disaster. Drinking. I was blind drunk. I nearly killed myself. God abandoned me. I haven't seen sight nor sound of Him since. I ask the Virgin Mary to come to my aid.

> *23/1/51. I received a letter from herself this morning and love is finished completely. Goodbye to love! And now, God – but, of course, you are not there. There is no God. Life is empty …*

> *24/1/51 … 'We were lucky,' she said, 'that we didn't fall into a Strindbergian Stew …'*

> *25/1/51. 11.12 p.m. 'Married Alive' by Strindberg on the BBC tonight. Strindberg faced life head-on, i.e. the women. It's a big relief. It's almost like a confession …*

It's difficult to know what Ó Ríordáin understood by this expression that he'd come across – 'Strindbergian Stew'. Could it be that he shared a similar view of women as Strindberg did – that they were at the root of everything that went wrong? Or was it a vague reference to the life that was his, as he described it just over a month later? 'There was a character in a Strindberg play that had no life of his own and so he spent his time leeching off other people's lives. That's me.'[157] Or did the poet better elucidate what he meant in that letter that no one ever saw?

Whomever he had in mind, the poet isn't long integrating her within another drama – this time it's the one they'd seen together on 26 May 1949, the one in which he'd also assigned a role to his mother long before this – *Peer Gynt*. Literature is always a safer bet than messy reality. If his mother was always Aase, then Kay is Solveig.[158] He himself is Peer, as usual, the one whom 'A Great Calamity constantly awaits him like Boyg', a calamity that one must go through in order to be free of it.[159] Ó Ríordáin makes a few half-hearted efforts to make the play a reality in his actual life but his heart isn't in it any more and he closes the door again on another opportunity in his life. There will be no Solveig waiting for him to fall asleep in her arms when the curtain comes down on this particular play:

157 D: 1 March 1951.
158 D: 16 April 1951.
159 D: 25 April 1951.

> *15/9/51. Terrible rain last night. I was in Cork with K. She told me that she's in love with a man whose name she wouldn't mention. Is my heart broken now? Is there a sweetness in people whose search for love remains unanswered? I know people like that. They are smooth and perfumed. Tonight was a beautiful moonlit night but when I went out walking I was on my own. She wasn't with me. The terrible beauty of the night but a searing pain – her absence. When I was returning down the steps to the house I sensed the perfume of flowers. God is above, praise be to Him forever …*
>
> *I haven't written anything in this book for a long time because I am living a pleasant and healthy life. The streptomycin improved me a great deal. I still get down about that woman every now and then. It would be better if I could wipe her from my mind completely. She often made me happy but also caused me anxiety and despair more often still.*

This diary excerpt is the last one we have from him until 6 February 1953 when another calamity occurs in his life, one that shakes him to the absolute core, on both the private and public levels.

7

I Spent Nights House-Calling

'No one fails us but it's rather the false and inhuman rules that are in our minds that let us down … It was from Miss Foley that I learned the philosophy of false constructions,' Ó Ríordáin wrote in a letter to Séamus Ó Coigligh on 14 November 1950. This wasn't entirely true, however, as this 'philosophy' predated their relationship by a long way. In one sense, it might have seemed a relief to him and most appropriate from a literary point of view, that he'd banished Kay Foley to an 'island' other than his. And this construction that was the 'island' could be shifted between one sphere and another, even if its significance always remained the same: the idea that one should always remain faithful to one's primary essence or vocation. There was Blessed Finbarr's Island on the Gougane that the visitor could deem their 'oileán séin' ('*island of serenity, in the mind's truth*'), needless to say. And there was also the Great Blasket Island, a place that he needed to source also if he was to survive the 'cultural dilution' and inadequate linguistic sustenance that had been the reality of life for him since his family left Ballyvourney years earlier.

The poet also saw this return to his cultural source as redemptive not just on the literary level but also on the spiritual level; the only way he could become complete and be true to himself on the spiritual level was through the perfection of his art and to reject this was to accept a false understanding of his own nature and to be insincere in aesthetic terms – i.e. to have one's syntax tied up in knots as alluded to in the poem Fill Arís ('*Return Again*') – 'do theanga a chuaigh ceangailte i gcomhréiribh/'Bhí bunoscionn le d'éirim' ('*your tongue which got tied up in syntax/at odds with your intellect*').[1] And

1 B: p. 41; Sewell, *Selected Poems*, p. 163. Trans. Barry McCrea.

such a sham would be exposed sooner or later. One can almost substitute paragraph IV from 'Oileán agus Oileán Eile' (*'This Island and the Other Island'*) (*'There's an island of serenity/in the mind's truth'*) in terms of theme and conception with the following from 'Na Blascaodaí' (*'The Blasket Islands'*). The 'seanaigne' (*'ancient mindset'*) of the Blasket community corresponds with the mind of God in terms of the truth it holds – the truth that he (the poet) had let go of long ago:

Ach do thugabhair libh an aigne
Chomh húr le leanbhán
A thréigeamar i leabharaibh
Is pairilis ina cnámha,
Is a fhanann linn sa duanaire
Mar a fhanabhair ar oileán
Go dtí go dtagann fonn orainn
Suirí le seanadhán.[2]

but bring with you
the mind as fresh
as a new-born babe,
which we left paralysed
in pent-up tomes,
but which waits for us
in our book of songs
like you did on an island
till the notion took us
to indulge in old poems.[3]

You would imagine sometimes that Ó Ríordáin thought that all he (and the Irish people generally) had to do was call on the Irish language and our ancestral entitlement again and that she would come streaming back to us from under the surface of the national subconscious, uninterrupted

2 ES: p. 94.
3 Sewell, *Selected Poems*, p. 101. Trans. Frank Sewell.

and unaffected by the fog of forgetting and abandonment that she had been subjected to for hundreds of years – that she could mould our modern sensibility once more as if the long interval in between had never happened. If such were possible, then the modern mind and the mind of tradition could merge again as one with all the authority and peace and order that this would engender. Such a possibility would give true meaning to what he'd previously set out to do in 'Saoirse' (*'Liberty'*): to enjoin with that 'Don chomhthuiscint, don chomh-sheanchuimhne/Do chomhiompar comhdhaoine' (*'the co-understanding, the co-tradition/the co-behaviour of co-people'*).[4]

Unsurprisingly, the poet himself would visit the Gaeltacht (the Irish-speaking area) closest to him to attempt this project or to see if the dream could be realised. It was from Peig Sayers that Ó Ríordáin had learned where this ancestral subconscious mind could be sourced, the cultural 'wash' that was hidden from him in his everyday life:

Tá tigín fo-intinneach bán
Ag machnamh ar imeall Dhún Chaoin
Inar chuala caint chianda mná
Is í dall ins an leaba le haois,
Is do chonac an fho-intinn ar barr,
Is an bharrintinn deascaithe thíos.

Bhí aigne Pheig mar naomhóig
Ár n-iompar ar dhromchla na dtonn,
Chuaigh ár gcúrintinn éadrom go tóin
Nocht ár bhfo-intinn folaigh mar chúr,
Ghaibh imigéiniúlacht ár nglór,
Bhí mianach macalla sa bhfuaim …[5]

Deep in thought at the edge of Dún Chaoin
is a white house in the subconscious

4 *Ibid.*, p. 111. Trans. Seán Ó Ríordáin.
5 ES: p. 96.

where I listened to the ancient speech
of a bed-ridden woman, blind with age,
and saw on the surface the deeper mind,
shallow reason dumped to the bottom.

Peig Sayers' brain was like a currach
that carried us across the waves,
sinking the froth of our foam-thoughts,
and raising the deep mind from the foam
until a strangeness came over our speech,
and an echo rang in the sound.[6]

Ó Ríordáin saw this return to tradition as the same journey that composer Seán Ó Riada had pursued. Whether his 'take' on Ó Riada in the excerpt below is accurate or not, there's little doubt that it accurately reflects Ó Ríordáin's own view at this juncture in time:

> *He recognised his most appropriate ego in the perfection of the language … He wanted to reach his self in all its completeness … The aesthetic of the language and of music was born much earlier than was his own mind … Until he gained full control of this aesthetic, his work would only be a pastiche, a series of random works as separate from one another.*[7]

It is unlikely that such a theory would have much backing in linguistic circles today given that it was premised on a number of concepts, including the idea of 'linguistic relativity', none of which are taken seriously in scholarly circles nowadays. This theory fitted the dualities and contradictions that fascinated Ó Ríordáin with respect to language – freedom and tyranny, the individual and the community – albeit that they only satisfied him temporarily: 'Is níl laistigh d'aon daoirse/Ach saoirse ón daoirse sin' (*Daoirse*). ('*And all that's in any limitation/is freedom from its limits*'.)[8]

6 Sewell, *Selected Poems*, p. 105. Trans. Frank Sewell.
7 'An Riadach' ('*Ó Riada*'), IT, 7 October 1972.
8 B: p. 27; Sewell, *Selected Poems*, p. 149. Trans. Celia de Fréine.

If you were enslaved, at least it was best to be enslaved in accordance with the dictates of your own tyranny rather than someone else's. For as long as you remained cloaked within the language that was your ancestral birthright, you were free from outside interference and rules. But go across to the other language and you were immediately subservient to its grammar and structures, the structures that you are obliged to adhere to in order that you may come to understand it and 'home' yourself within it – becoming almost unknown to yourself after a while. This is almost a 'foreign' language; it is so seductive and exotic, its exoticism a very function of its unfamiliar rhythm and nature. It was this very exoticism – the strangeness of the new – that inspired Ó Ríordáin to write the poem 'An Feairín' ('*The Maneen*'), a poem where he's surprised in a joyous way by the accuracy and absolute appropriateness of the woman who refers to Pound as a 'feairín'. Here's the unpublished account of the moment when this poem 'happened', one evening while he was visiting someone's house in Dunquin (in the Kerry Gaeltacht):

> *It was one night when we were socialising in Seán Ó Conchubhair's house. They were arguing about the people moving over from the Island. The woman of the house, referencing Pound, said that this poor little man ('fearín') would need a house and a field the same as any island-man. I took note of the way she pronounced the word 'fearín' (the maneen/little man) and I put this together:*
>
> *'Theastódh tigh is gort ón bhfeairín bocht,'*
> *A dúirt an bhean 'dtaobh Pound,*
> *Is bhailigh Pound isteach sa bhfocal di*
> *Is chónaigh ann …*
>
> *… Tá beirthe ar Phound sa bhfocal sin aici,*
> *Mar feairín is ea Pound,*
> *Do réitigh gach a bhfuil dá chabhail sa bheatha léi,*
> *O bharr a chinn go bonn.*
>
> 'He'd need a house and land, the maneen,'
> said the woman about Pound,

and Pound crept into the word
and settled there …

… Pound has been reborn in that word of hers
because Pound is a maneen;
from the top of his head right to the ground,
the whole of his body agrees with her.[9]

Who else would be interested in a 'nonsense-word' like this, other than the likes of Ó Ríordáin, who was visiting the area and wished to sample the cultural inheritance or richness of the place in all its facets? The suggestion here is that this was the first time Ó Ríordáin had ever really 'seen' or understood this local character Pound properly and that it was this one word/term that permitted this 'insight', given its complete summation of Pound. He has Pound's 'measure' now; he understands him wholly and completely because, thanks to one of the locals, a native speaker has encapsulated the man perfectly and all within the dimensions of a single word.

Mentally, Ó Ríordáin adopts this house and landscape as his permanent cultural home or inheritance; a single word has opened his door of perception to the reality that he always sought and the place where he can be at peace. Incredible as it seems, he has captured this crucial moment in his project of cultural reclamation and the figure of Pound under the auspices of just one single word – a word that incorporates realisation and precision, a word that is perfection or wholeness. The poet considered such precision to be a long way from the feeble and impoverished version of the English language that was the *lingua franca* of most Irish people in his generation. The English Ó Ríordáin heard around him almost every day of his life was a low and inadequate form of communication and expression, as he saw it; it was neither English nor Irish, really; neither one thing nor the other, but a collective imagining that had fallen between two stools and belonged to neither. This was the tragedy of Irish history as Seán saw it; the loss of language had ensured the vast majority of Irish were a betwixt-and-between people, a bewildered or pathetic race whose

9 B: 15; Sewell, *Selected Poems*, p. 133. Trans. Peter Sirr.

poor patois had rendered them mute and symbolised all that had gone awry for them culturally. Not only had the Irish people been rendered mute, but the watered-down or clumsy dialect through which they expressed themselves symbolised their lowly and miserable condition. This muddled speech was Ó Ríordáin's daily diet, except for those occasional visits he made to the Gaeltacht, and on the morning of 11 May 1951, for instance, he notes the following brief encounter as overheard one muggy morning, back home in Inniscarra:

> *'Did you see the fog?' 'What?' 'Did you see the fog?' 'I did. 'Twill be mad warm. Will I bring in the wather now, I'm going to town?'*

In conversation, Ó Ríordáin often joked about 'awkward speech' the likes of this, such as the mangled English the women mumbled when they were giving out the decades of the Rosary in the funeral home, for instance.[10] Or the English he heard that was the priest's, a language 'so parochial and backward and as far from proper English of the colleges as is possible, so incredible, so true to its own heresies of pronunciation and syntax, so funny, so democratic, so lacking in grandeur, so ugly, so common, as mangled as that of the radio storyteller himself. *"He marrid Cissy and they're doing fierce bishness ... He got fierce excited after the match."*'[11]

Here's how Ó Ríordáin described the different mentalities he envisaged as associated with the landscapes he journeyed through on his way westwards to the Gaeltacht and from Tralee to Dunquin. (*From an unpublished lecture.*)

> *There is a big hiatus between Tralee and Dingle i.e. Gleann na nGealt*[12] *– it is a bare and hungry glen, a big empty glen. I've never seen this glen that I didn't feel fear and despair coming over me. I knew that it had nothing to do with space or with time. Mentally, I associate the region around about with this glen; it has the mindset of those parts of Ireland where the Irish language*

10 'Sos', IT, 25 November 1967.

11 'Caint shagartúil' ('*Priestly talk*'), IT, 28 August 1968.

12 Gleann na nGealt – lit: 'the glen of the mad/crazy [people]'.

> *has disappeared. There is neither life nor death there. There's just a stasis. The Irish language is gone and the only thing spoken there now is broken English. A subdued class of people makes their home there now. The mentality of the people and the place is broken. The mentality is still there but it has come to a standstill. When Dante saw the Devil himself he was so terrified that he said: 'I had neither death nor moral life. Imagine yourself, if you have any bit of intelligence in you, how I feel.'*
>
> *But go West from Dingle. Travel west along the Slea Head road to Dunquin. There is nothing empty about this place. You will see the Great Blasket and Inis Mhicileán, an Tiaracht and Inis Tuaisceart, Sliabh an Iolair and Na Trí Deirféaracha. You'll feel enlivened by the vitality and the energy of the sculpted landscape. Days that passed us by, days when we wrote nothing and read nothing, days when we never said a prayer nor opened our minds, this is what Gleann na nGealt puts us in mind of. This other landscape reminds us of those miraculous days when God was with us, however. And the mentality of the people here is far from bare or empty …*

But even if Ireland's true imagination or sensibility inhabited Dunquin (as he stated in his diary entry of 26 June 1955) and still had the wherewithal to express itself there, the place was not without major flaws either, as the poet admitted during the course of that same lecture:

> *All the same, the Gaeltacht is at a standstill. It is frozen in time. The Boyg, i.e. Gleann na nGealt, stands between it and the wider world. This leaves it hemmed in and without the possibility of development or of tapping into the energy of the larger world outside. Not only are the people hemmed in but the language is too. If one hears an adjective as accompanying a particular name in the Gaeltacht, be certain that this adjective has been ascribed to this name for at least 100 years. There is no interaction between her and languages and thoughts from outside; all that she can feed on is herself.*

And again, in a letter he sent to Donncha Ó Laoghaire, secretary of Comhdháil Náisiúnta na Gaeilge (under whose auspices he'd spent time in the Kerry Gaeltacht), where he gave his impressions of St Patrick's Day 1953 in Dunquin:

> *Unfortunately, however, some of the language itself is dead, even in the Gaeltacht. I'm not saying that life in the Gaeltacht is more limited or narrow compared to life in Dublin or in Cork. It's the opposite I'd say: the intellectual life of Dublin wouldn't hold a candle to the intellectual life of Dunquin, as I understand it, particularly. There are aspects of life that the people of the Gaeltacht never mention, however. And there's a finesse and a mental energy and a privacy of thought that they do not practise.*

Visiting the Gaeltacht every now and then wasn't sufficient to bolster the poet's linguistic needs anyway, needless to say. It wasn't as if the everyday life or language there tallied with what he was writing about, and the idiom of the rural world was often of little value to a poet writing poetry that expressed metaphysical concepts or emotions.

Ó Ríordáin sought to carve a new way through the Irish language and develop an idiom that was more expressive of the twentieth century individual than it was of community. He needed to return to the source but only so that he could shape the language for his own purposes and make it his own. He wanted to bring the Irish language along a new path and mould it in a way that incorporated new concepts and thinking, adapt it to a new tradition, bring it on a fresh and original journey, if it proved willing. This wasn't an issue of terminology or technique at all, but rather that the Irish of the Gaeltacht 'has been excluded for so long from the form of writing that engenders continuous thought or philosophy … There are hollows and caves that the Irish language has never entered as yet,' he wrote, in his seminal essay 'Teangacha Príobháideacha' ('*Private Languages*'), when he explored the vocation of writing in terms of the individual and as relating to the proverbial power of language in some detail.[13] Because Ó Ríordáin's ultimate destination in terms of his artistic journey was the individual and his sensibility in the twentieth century, and because he was one poet who wouldn't compromise for any language, dialect or tradition, he began to suffer a great deal of criticism from others before long. In the final analysis, it was tradition that would have to come looking for him rather than the other way around, the reified linguistic

---

13 *Scríobh 4*, p. 16.

forms and sayings and the wisdom pearls of the older tradition renewing and reshaping themselves again for a modern sensibility.

Down the years, both in Dunquin and in his memory of Ballyvourney, he had gathered his share of these 'older linguistic pearls', calcified and half-forgotten, and he would give them sparkle again in his poetry of the individual; for their part, this wealth of the older tradition would prove his deliverance when he went through the most difficult period of sickness and despair, when the world was falling apart around him and when he needed to extricate himself quickly from the 'back of night', lest it engulfed him.[14] Those periods of illness were extremely testing for him both physically and mentally and it was then more than at any other time that he was assailed by doubt as to the objective he'd set for himself. Which tradition or place did he really belong to? Was he Ballyvourney or was he Inniscarra, or Dunquin? Or was he none of these and stuck somewhere between the two languages – Irish and English? Which of these traditions was his really by rights? Or did he belong to either of them? He would follow the shades of the past that flickered across the wall of his sickroom and hope that they would lead him back to where he wanted to begin again. And if he had faith enough maybe they would lead him back to Aogán Ó Rathaille and Céitinn (Keating) and the Four Masters and Dámhscoil Mhúscraí (Muskerry Poetic School), and the Gaelic tradition would be one again and he would bring it together in his work. Because this was what tradition meant essentially: the individual who goes back and stirs the embers of the older generations, their humanity and their culture, and nurtures it once more lest it expire completely. And when Ó Ríordáin spoke from now on in his poetry, he would speak with the echo of tradition in his work; in a sense, the older generations would prove his audience. They would be the community he would write for in the absence of a community who could read or understand Irish. In one of those strange ironies of literature, it was just when it seemed that the Gaelic tradition was at an end that he had found himself back and breathing life into it once more. The idea of the individual as artist and the process of eternal questioning consumed Ó Ríordáin – the interrogation of yesterday and

14 ES: p. 116.

tomorrow. It's during the course of this constant questioning, he realised, that the tradition re-forms itself and goes on. The present is all. It's the only time that ever existed.

Here's Seán Ó Ríordáin, that poor miserable person out on the ocean of the night in a bad boat and every indication is that it will sink into the depths. He was awoken abruptly just now. He lit his candle. He's just burned five matches in addition to putting a razor blade into the candleholder and three stubs of wax. There is a small bottle on the table between the candle and the wall. The shadow of the bottle is on the wall. This shadow is ten times the size of the bottle. The shadow of my hand and the pain is on the wall next to me. You'd imagine from the size of the shadow that there was a great importance or mystery attached to whatever writing was emerging from that hand. I suppose that there was a similar shadow on the wall when they were writing Annála Ríochta Éireann. *I suppose that the hand of Aogán Ó Rathaille and the hand of Séathrún Céitinn must have been reflected in great shadows on the wall back then too.*

Last night, I was reading Dámhscoil Mhúscraí. *It's a long time since I read this book and there are many people who have very little respect for these poets. But I don't remember reading anything as good in terms of ability or artistry than this poetry for many a long day, nor for many a long night …*[15]

I'm in bed. The neighbours are asleep – or at least I imagine they are. I think it's time to bring my Irish on another step. Maybe the day will come when I'll reach as high a level of ability and power in Irish as the language itself ever reached. Amn't I getting cocky! Is anyone else as particular about their Irish as I am? And yet I still don't feel that I'm making progress in her [i.e. the language]. I'm too lazy. But it's not right to rush the man who has diarrhoea too much. Is this a load of shit? Is there any connection at all between this hand and this here pen, and the pens that wrote Lebor Gabála Érenn *or* Annála Ríochta Éireann *or* Foras Feasa ar Éirinn*? But will people remember me after I am gone? There are far more memories behind the words that I'm writing that haven't gone into these words themselves at all …*[16]

15 D: 5.50 a.m., 6 March 1956.
16 D: 1.45 a.m., 22 December 1969.

One couldn't but recognise the voice. It was the same voice from the beginning, except that it had become more strident over time. He has a poem in *Eireaball Spideoige*, 'Fan' ('*Wait*') where he discusses what his writing might possibly be a reflection of: that 'little mirror on the wall'; this mirror isn't a reflection of his 'proper self', however.[17] Similarly, he'll wait 'until a more pleasant reflection/Appears in my glass' before replicating his 'self' in the 'word-regime' of the poem.[18]

The poem 'Ná Fan' ('*Don't Wait*') also explores this concept: no matter how good or bad the perspective of representation may be, one must grab a hold of it when writing the poem as best one can. One may end up with a form of 'inexpressible disorder' when one attempts to express what is vague, but so be it. Or, at times, the poem may run away with itself and become so abstract that it becomes almost incomprehensible. The polar concepts that are good and evil or right and wrong no longer have the same relevance as before provided you communicate the poem's subject as fully and as sincerely as possible. The medium is still the message, as the examples that follow make apparent:

Ní lot go tost.
Ná caill ar d'aigne,
Fág í neadaithe
I mbréithre in aice leat,
Dá fheabhas, dá ainnise,
Cuir ainm ar
Gach ar ghaibh trí d'shúil, trí d'chluais anocht,
    trí d'aigne,
Cum tranglam
Má chaitheann tú,
Dolabhartha,
Ach cuir snaidhm ar shnáth sin d'aigne.[19]

---

17 ES: p. 84.
18 *Ibid.* Trans. M. Ó hAodha.
19 LL: p. 43.

Silence is the greatest hurt.
Do not fail your mind,
Leave it nestled
In words near you,
However excellent, however poor,
Put a name on
Everything which went through your eye, through your ear tonight,
    through your mind,
Compose something confused
If you must,
Something difficult to express,
But tie a knot on that thread of your mind.[20]

In his prose pieces at this juncture, we frequently find the poet regretting he hadn't accepted life as it was, rather than hoping for some kind of a great leap forward in literary terms, a leap that never seemed to happen. Take the following from 'Teachtaireacht Amháin' ('*One Message*'):

> *Sometimes I feel that we read too much – that we never stop. I don't say, for example, 'sid é Mise agus scríobhfad Mise' (This is Me and I will write Myself) and yet I hope that a more perfect Me, a more learned Me, a Me with better Irish will manifest itself in a while. This is a mistake. It might be that I'll smother this Me completely beneath a great weight. This Me (self) is always there and I should give it immediate room to speak, despite how paltry its utterances are. It isn't the learning or the richness that this voice has that's the most important thing – but rather itself. If there's any importance attached to it, it's the importance of itself, the way it emerged the first day ever, and how it's been ever since – and not its weight.*[21]

The time for 'listening' is over; it is time now to express oneself – and as never before. And no matter how many times he reminds himself of

20 Trans. M. Ó hAodha.

21 IT, 1 April 1970; 'Saol, samhradh, stair' ('*Life, summer, history*'), IT, 25 August 1973.

this necessity, it is always a struggle, both on the personal or inner level, and also with regard to those who pronounced on his poetry publicly and who placed such great store on the role of tradition with respect to the Irish language. The latter always had 'the tradition' as their buffer and sanctuary, and were very reluctant to step outside that discourse now and engage with material as radical and new as Ó Ríordáin's poetry. There were times when the poet even envied those literary 'purists', who basked in the constancy of tradition, and yet he had understood from the very beginning that their literary concerns were not his. As Thomas MacDonagh had put it so succinctly, tradition was both a source of joy and a scourge:

> *We have not reverence for the same things. We cannot pray to the old gods. We are of a different day; a different light shines upon us. History is between us and our heroes.*[22]

It would prove necessary for Ó Ríordáin to reiterate MacDonagh's sentiments once again, however.

Brosna, published in 1964, was the first book of poetry where Ó Ríordáin really broached the subject of Ireland's dual-language inheritance and the complexities and problems this engendered. This theme was played out most fully in poems such as 'A Ghaeilge im Pheannsa', 'A Theanga Seo Leath-Liom', 'Éisteacht Chúng' and 'Fill Arís'. Whenever the subject of the Irish language itself had been broached in *Eireaball Spideoige*, on the other hand, it was as a form of completeness or fulfilment; a release or pathway into his true self – the subconscious that contained the racial memory, which gave him the authority of expression he required. Dunquin was where he renewed himself and became whole as a person again. 'Dán Áthais' ('*Poem of Joy*') might have seemed a strange title for any poem of his, but this was the original title Ó Ríordáin gave to the poem 'Múscail do Mhisneach' ('*Awaken Your Courage*').[23] The mind of God and

22 MacDonagh, Thomas, *Literature in Ireland: Studies Irish and Anglo-Irish* (The Talbot Press, Dublin, 1916), p. 112.

23 B: p. 19.

the outlook that circumscribes this earthly life flowing in harmony as one. This new-found release and sense of freedom puts Ó Ríordáin in mind of the passage in the Acts of the Apostles where the angel sets St Peter free from prison, and he notes it alongside the poem in his notebook: *Oratio autem fiebat sine intermissione ab Ecclesia ad Deum pro eo.*[24] And we meet this sentiment again within the poem itself: 'As the Church will pray for you.'[25] Even if the poet confuses the words *fiebat* with *fiet*, the essence of his thinking is clear.[26] He has emerged from a very dark place into the light and can expand his vision accordingly. It's as if he has tapped into his creative essence or life-spring and is in harmony with the world again. The imagery of ebb and tide has almost sexual overtones here, something that was very rare in Ó Ríordáin's work. From: 'Múscail do Mhisneach' ('*Awaken Your Courage*'):

Boladh na feamnaí is sobal-ghol
Éireoidh sobal as an bhfarraige,
Sobal glégeal is éanlaithe …

The smell of seaweed and foaming tears
Froth will rise out of the sea,
Pure-white spray and flocks of birds …[27]

For once, his physical illness and the despair that accompanies it doesn't hold him back; it isn't the same as the spiritual illness or artistic barrier that he associated with being in a sinful state or cut off from God's light. Indeed, his physical suffering with TB almost serves to heighten his art at this point rather than drag it back – it's as if the closer one is to the precipice that is death, the richer the experience of life and the expression of the light.

It is spiritual and artistic completeness that he seeks very overtly

---

24 Acts 12:5. 'But prayer was made without ceasing by the church unto God for him.'

25 B: p. 19.

26 Fiebat – 'used to become, used to be made'; fiet – 'will become, will be made'.

27 Trans. M. Ó hAodha.

here, that energy and life that manifests itself when everything that hitherto clouded his artistic vision is stripped away. This search for artistic wholeness or vision is a tricky one, as he alternates between being outside and inside the tradition, as well as being sometimes at odds with his racial inheritance as delineated by the Gaeltacht and all it stands for. Ó Ríordáin seeks to elucidate a new vision and a new way of speaking but it's a difficult balancing act, this push-and-pull between the Irish-language tradition and the language as spoken traditionally there (and Seán's everyday reality, as lived in an English-speaking part of Ireland). The entire endeavour (cultural reclamation or rejection) is a complex balancing act and a two-edged sword:

> *The speech of the neighbours is both a form of sustenance and a form of poison. If you believe it or if you imbibe it, you're finished. If you don't hear it, you're finished also. Beware that you don't become dizzy with too much information or too much loquaciousness.*[28]

And in 'Múscail do Mhisneach' it's significant that it isn't the 'idiom of the neighbours' or 'easy talk' or the 'nice turns of phrase' that the poet seeks to emulate, but rather the essence of what is hidden behind the language. The word is as a submerged rock, similar to the elderly man in the poem. More surprising still is the way he speaks of the elderly man as an island like Beiginis, when it isn't anything of the kind:

> *Imeoidh deisireacht cainte anseo,*
> *Is nochtfaidh focail as do smaointese*
> *Mar a nochtann fochais as an bhfarraige*
> *Oileáin mhara tabhair id dhá shúil leat,*
> *Cuir chugat Beiginis is an Seanduine.*[29]

---

28 'Aistriú ó theanga go teanga' ('*Moving between one language and another*'), IT, 17 August 1975.

29 B: p. 19. Beiginis is one of the Blasket Islands off the coast of County Kerry. An Seanduine is a dangerous rock near Dunmore Head.

The nice turn of speech will depart here,
And words will appear out of your own thoughts
As a submerged rock appears out of the sea
Bring islands of the sea with you in your two eyes,
Take to yourself Beiginis and An Seanduine.[30]

But woe to the person who assumes that this 'nice turn of speech' consists of the poet's own regular idiom and thoughts, let alone his subconscious mind. The poem itself confirms otherwise. If it was necessary to set aside such 'easy talk', then the use of a term such as 'deisireacht cainte' (*'neat/tidy speech'*) in the poem itself was an example of the terminology he claimed to be wary of. In fact, Ó Ríordáin had heard this phrase from the local Dunquin poet Pound as it happens, as he explained in one of his notes:

Pound doesn't like people who try to speak in a very posh fashion. 'Don't bother at all,' he says, 'to posh up your speech.' Irish is a thing that can't be poshed up at all. If I have to posh up my speech I'd rather not talk at all. When the river is dammed, she gets dirty. Let her speak as she wishes to. Let her free and she'll remain pure. That's just the fanciness of Siobhán Stac.'

And yet, wasn't including such a phrase in the poem itself a form of 'poshing up'? Similar to this was his use of the term 'éasc' (*'fault'*) in the line 'Mar caithfir géilleadh don éasc ionat' (*'Because you have to accept the fault within you'*), another term that came clean out of one of his copybooks where he noted down rich words and sentences that he heard spoken by the locals in the Kerry Gaeltacht. Dunquin 24/9/52 to 23/11/52 and 16/5/53 to 14/7/53 is the lifetime of this particular diary.

On another occasion, Donncha Ó Conchubhair, the man who owned the house in Kerry that Ó Ríordáin always lodged in, is leaning a ladder against the side of the house one day when:

Me: *That's a good ladder.*

30 Trans. M. Ó hAodha.

> The Man of the House: *'It is long and it isn't heavy. I need to take the window out – there is some kind of flaw ('éasc' – pron. iasc) in her.'*

Shortly after this in his diary, we come across Ó Ríordáin's use of the term 'comhartha cille' (*a mole or birthmark*), and his reference to Pound's use of the term 'deisireacht cainte' again.

And there are many other similar examples in the poet's writing, including well-known storyteller Peig Sayers' turn of phrase 'cuma na hainglíochta' ('*look of an angel*') that really caught his imagination one evening. Ó Ríordáin explains the context in which the phrase was first used – it's one where An File and Pound are almost competing to find the 'tidiest' or richest turn of phrase – a very old tradition in the Gaeltacht and one that was not entirely dissimilar to the wordplay and 'rap battles' of poets and singers in the African-American community today:

> *An File (The Poet) has the Irish of the Islands, and I think that this language has a greater flourish to it than it does in Dunquin. An File has the word 'gliondar' [joy] for example, and this word is in Peig's book also. Pound had never heard that word before. 'It's going through me since I heard it,' said Pound. 'It's a good word,' I said. 'Indeed and it isn't,' said Pound, 'it's just a fat word.' We got thirsty sometimes needless to say and we had to go into Dingle to pay a visit to Peig in the hospital. That phrase 'cuma na hainglíochta' [angelic appearance] is hers and it's an example, I think, of the creativeness that we're looking for here in writing matters at the moment but which is to be found only rarely in the Gaeltacht. It's lovely to be listening to Peig. She's easy-going and she speaks clearly …*

Ó Ríordáin had Peig Sayers at the back of his mind again when he recalled an incident relating to someone mislaying their key in 'An Eochair' ('*The Key*'):

> *Ach fan!*
> *Cad é seo ar an bhfaiche*
> *Is gaethe na gréine á soilsiú?*
> *Is í eochair an dorais í a cailleadh,*

Is gan fiú an fhocail aisti –
an cladhaire.[31]

But wait!
What is this on the green
With the sun's rays illuminating it?
It is the door key which was lost,
And not even a sound out of it –
The rogue.[32]

This was another of Peig Sayers' turns of phrase that Ó Ríordáin had come across: 'Féach ansan é, an cladhaire, agus gan focal as.' ('*Look at him there, the coward, and not a gig [a word] out of him.*') It was the Kerry scholar Seosamh Ó Dálaigh who gave Seán this phrase and it was one that had proven particularly appropriate to them one day when they actually really did lose their house key for a while. (In the case of storyteller Peig, it was probably her clay pipe that she mislaid most often.) It goes without saying that a poem such as 'An Eochair' ought to be understood on the level of light humour and fun rather than anything else. This is the same joy in the humorous that can be read in every line of Seosamh Ó Dálaigh's very fine essay in the volume *An Duine is Dual.* And what more appropriate and necessary an occasion for Seosamh to recall such joyful moments than when he visited a dying Seán in his hospital room in December 1976 when Dunquin was just a distant memory and they both knew it. Significantly, Seán actually wrote his name at the bottom of this poem as follows: 'Seán Ó Ríordáin 12/11/76', as if signing off on the closure of his life's work in poetry and the fact that he was satisfied with what he'd achieved. He'd only sign his name like this one last time, and that was on finishing the poem 'Clóanna über Alles'.[33]

While it's true that Ó Ríordáin had deliberately set out to try and find his real artistic voice and his true 'self' in Dunquin twenty-five years earlier,

31 TÉB: p. 49.
32 Trans. M. Ó hAodha.
33 TÉB: p. 29.

this isn't to say that he was completely in awe of everything and everyone (even the so-called 'biggest personalities') relating to the Irish-language culture there and that he couldn't bring them down to the same level as everyone else in his mind. An File was perhaps the most important or influential of the personalities he came across during his visits to the Gaeltacht and yet he could still speak of him as in the excerpt below where, on the short journey by road between Dunquin and Baile na nGall, he abruptly cuts through all the idealisation or hero-worship. Both men observe one another closely and see through one another quite easily; neither of their perspectives is the 'inward eye' of Wordsworth, that's for certain. (Ó Ríordáin wrote the following in a letter to Neans Eichthigheirn, a person who worked with him in City Hall for a while, one stormy day in the early summer of 1953.)

> *I went to Baile na nGall about ten miles away with 'An File' today. The road was often invisible. Sometimes I felt the wheel being torn out of my hands. The File said that every day has its own delights. We stopped at various pubs. One of the File's eyes looks out at the Atlantic while the other looks inward at Tralee and hops. I never saw his inward eye hop so much as it hopped today. And the more we drank the more An File's eye hopped, and the more precise and evocative and unearthly his Gaelic became. Whenever I try to communicate something of the Gaelic world to the English-speaking world I am dumb. There seems to be no common ground. They are utterly at variance. Neither world wants to hear of the other and I seem to feel a painful obligation to tell them of one another. The strangest thing of all is that this world here – the Gaelic one – seems to me the more sophisticated of the two. They seem to be beyond the stage where you take things seriously here. It makes me feel dull and stodgy. They secretly despise you if you are slow enough to take anything seriously.*
>
> *Nobody here marrying. There are still twenty people on the Blaskets. Houses are being built in Dunquin for them. The whole transaction has been transferred into some weird cynical part of their minds. It would take a magician to unravel their comments.*

The English-speaker he was writing to would have found it next to impossible to unravel what the locals were really saying, but Ó Ríordáin wasn't too far behind sometimes, either. He was as blind as most when it came to the subtleties of what might be said and functioned as an interlocutor more often than anything else. Ultimately, he was searching for a sense of peace within himself. Over the years, he'd get closer to whatever it was he sought to find in the Gaeltacht, sometimes too close for his own good. In a sense, it was always the easier option to remain on the 'outside' and to romanticise the Gaeltacht people on the abstract level and highlight their positive Gaelic qualities than it was to do anything else. Whatever special knowledge he sought in his trips to the Gaeltacht – whatever exotic patterns of thought or insights he had as a poet – they really would have only pointed to his lack of insight, Ó Ríordáin would most likely have argued. One of the greatest paradoxes of his work – if one were to be honest about it – was that his distance from the reality of his subject (i.e. Irish-language culture and tradition) for most of the year allowed him to imbue it with a magic or a wonder that was nothing more than a form of misunderstanding or insecurity. In the excerpt below, we see the poet attempting to get to the basis of this very magic and misapprehension. He's the man who is inside here, even if he'd much rather be on the outside in this particular instance:

> *Anything that you get to learn too much about, you lose it – in so far as you don't recognise it any more. I met Seán Ó Súilleabháin (ex Raidió Éireann) in Dunquin. He doesn't have much Irish either. You couldn't say that he has a Dunquin accent one way or the other. He noticed the music in the Irish of Dunquin, however. I understood what he meant immediately and from then on I heard that 'music' all over the place, although I hadn't heard it at all until he mentioned it. It's someone like him who'd hear it, a man who came in from the outside and was getting to know Dunquin for the first time. I suppose that I'm used to the dialect in Dunquin by now, and that this is why I found it difficult to recognise at first.*
>
> *I'm listening to some German choirs now on the radio. I remember hearing a German choir in the City Hall in Cork years ago. I suddenly realised that I'd got an insight not only into German music but also into the German people themselves, the German nation. I knew that I could sense their masculinity in the same way as a woman would.*[34]

34 D: 30 June 1964; 'Babhta suibiachtúil', IT, 23 January 1971.

And yet, even after all this, he needs to eradicate each and every persona from his imagination, one after another, lest he be caught 'inside' and permanently trapped there. Eventually, he says goodbye to Dunquin and the Dingle peninsula again, because his quest is not for them after all – but rather for the essence that is his 'self'. The Sunday morning sun shines brightly as he makes his way home again through Churchtown, where he stops to attend Mass.[35] As he passes the stream near Ballynahow, the morning is still fresh and bright in the poet's imagination – its voice is a young girl giggling with laughter and 'hiding in behind the ditch'. But his mood is already changing on the drive home; he becomes more than one person. An hour later and he's changed from youthful joy to the one who has left 'a trail of his foot in the mud'. [36] He's not the same person at all. And as for all the nice turns of phrase that he made his own during his sojourn in the Gaeltacht, the sheen has already worn off them and the bulk of them are being committed to his notebooks for posterity rather than for use in any future poetic work – phrases the likes of: 'Ní raibh peidhleacán thiar ar an gCill inniu' ('*There was no butterfly behind in the Church today*'). We don't know where the poet picked up this particular saying, but we see him ask St Columcille for his intercession in incorporating it into some future poem of his. Rather than Ó Ríordáin, however, it is the native speaker and the story of the saint that manifests itself in the quatrain he eventually composes:

Ní raibh peidhleacán thiar ar an gCill inniu,
Ná níor thaistil cuil an Laidin;
Níor chuir aigne duine aon adharc amach
Ach oiread le slua na marbh.

There was no butterfly behind in the Church today,
Nor did a fly travel the Latin;
No human mind put out a horn
No more than the host of the dead.[37]

35 B: pp. 11–12.
36 *Ibid.*
37 Trans. M. Ó hAodha.

It was sometime between the years 1956 and 1957 that Ó Ríordáin tried to write this poem and he left it to others after him to give it an appropriate title. It was one day in 1954 that he overheard Máirín Feiritéar ridicule the priest in a jokey way with the phrase: 'Bainfeadsa an scrogall bán díot.' (*'I'll pull that long streaky white neck of yours clean off.'*) The priest appears in another of Ó Ríordáin's Gaeltacht-inspired poems, one that also features An File, Pound and Bríd, and Kruger and Kate, and the others who were in the company also:

Tá sagart na Gráige, is scrogall glan bán air,
Ag éisteacht le faoistin an Phobail ...[38]

The priest in An Graig, has a clean white neck,
And he listening to the community's confession ...[39]

And it was the same community that the poet referenced once again in the paragraph that follows, as relating to a summer trip he made to the Gaeltacht in 1961. Himself and An File together again:

I discussed death with An File today. I said to him that this is our only release. He agreed with me and said that death was the only wealth that we have. 'But still,' I said, 'we're afraid of death.' 'The fear is there,' he said. 'Life is sweet and the body finds it strange to die – to separate from life.'

4.15 a.m. We (An File and myself) discussed the poems that he composed recently. We both praised them. We mentioned the lament that he composed for Monsignor de Brún. The lament was a little bit better than the Monsignor. It was Father Tadhg who asked him to compose the lament. Máire Mhac an tSaoi was mentioned. 'She isn't a poet,' said An File. 'She is a poet,' I said. 'No, she isn't,' he said, 'because a woman was never a poet and never could be. A poet is there to praise the flower that God created. The flower is the woman. The beauty of a woman is the poet's subject. How can a woman praise another woman? Ireland used to visit the poets in the form of a woman. Máire Bhuí composed one of those

38 *Comhar*, May 1977.
39 Trans. M. Ó hAodha.

> *aislingí (vision poems) but it was unnatural because she was a woman …' If you were to meet An File tomorrow, he'd have the opposite take on this.*[40]

Seán spoke of death in much the same way, however, it has to be said. It's the same 'richness of death' that his poem 'Mo Bhás Féin' ('*My Own Death*') celebrates. He's still exploring the idea here, just as he was in the prose piece from which he took the concept initially, even if he is yet to fully mature it to his satisfaction.

Fear saibhir is ea mise
Ar chuma an uile dhuine
Mar sé an bás mo chiste …[41]

I am a rich man
Just like every other person
Because death is my treasure …[42]

The theory An File put forward regarding the female role in the composition of poetry underpins Ó Ríordáin's 'Banfhile'. And there's no question but it's the same woman whom the poet had in mind when he wrote the following:

Is ait liom bean a bheith ina file;
Tuigtear dom gur gairm staile,
Cúram fireann, dúthracht raide,
Is ea filíocht a bhaint as teanga

Ag luí léi féin a bhíonn banfhile,
Trom léi a bhíonn banfhile,
Ní file ach filíocht an bhean.[43]

---

40 D: 14 June 1961.
41 TÉB: p. 44; initial prose piece in *Comhar,* May 1967.
42 Trans. M. Ó hAodha.
43 TÉB: p. 45.

I find women poets strange.
It's stud-hard work, I think,
a man's duty, a devotion granted,
to draw poetry from language.

With male force, fury, violence,
the impulse to art is birthed safely,
so a female poet is unnatural, for me.[44]

Even if neither of these verses officially saw print, it was no accident that he recited the second of them at the literary school, Dámhscoil Mhúscraí, in 1971. Ó Ríordáin could have quite comfortably taken up permanent residence within this Gaeltacht tradition or aesthetic but that wasn't his path. The way he saw it, he would have been doing an injustice on both fronts: to the man (i.e. himself, as poet) who would have set his stall and gone home forever within the comfortable confines of the 'native' and the 'traditional', and those (i.e. the Gaeltacht people he was learning new aspects of the tradition from) whom he'd have had as his collaborators in this strange enterprise. His visits to the Gaeltacht were just that – temporary visits or a few weeks of the summer holidays. And his poems were never summer poems or created on the back of a sensibility that had the temporal at its heart. Ó Ríordáin rarely yielded to the 'tradition' camp – as characteristic of many of his critics and fellow writers within the Irish-language establishment – and when he did occasionally lapse into their way of thinking, he always regretted it fairly soon afterwards.

In the following except, written on 8 August 1967, we see him ruefully recalling how this erroneous aesthetic had damaged the quality of some of his poems, as he saw it. But then, who can say for certain where the truth lay and whose literary approach was superior in the long-run?

This afternoon I was reading some verses that I composed years ago – 1960? 1958? – for the opening of Raidió Éireann in Cork. I never published them

44 Sewell, *Selected Poems*, p. 201. Trans. Mary O'Donoghue.

because I didn't think they were worth publishing and even if they were, I don't have full texts of them. Here's an example:

B'í a ngairm dul thar triúch' anonn
Ag sealgaireacht prátaí na Mumhan —
Tá a dteist go fial ar fuaid Chorcaí
Is soir go Déisibh Mumhan.[45]

They aren't worth much. Light verse is all they are. But they are based on Irish-language poetry. They are more traditional and healthier maybe than my normal poetry. The words suit the metre better. You feel more comfortable here. Maybe I was always trying to marry the tradition with what is foreign to it and I never succeeded. Is this a sign? Is it easier to stay within the framework of tradition including metre and all? It is easier for sure. Would I compose more if I stayed sheltered? Would I write better poetry?

Ó Ríordáin almost certainly didn't believe that he'd have written superior poetry if he'd stayed entirely within the bosom of tradition, however. But then, what business had he going back to the 'source' in the Gaeltacht then, one asks? This was the paradox of his writing life at this juncture and he was caught between two stools. Why was he visiting the Gaeltacht at all if he didn't intend incorporating the richness of poetic phrase and tradition that he found there into his writing and attempting to enrich his own poetry in the process? Was it because whatever he found in the Gaeltacht was under the 'chaptaentaíocht na bun-teangan' ('*stewardship of the root-language*') so that he found it both natural and cohesive and beautiful in equal measure?[46] Did the remnants of the tradition he found in the Gaeltacht engender a wholeness within himself and an enhanced sense of form in his writing? Wasn't this what he'd always been sourcing, really – the natural flow of language, poetry running unhindered from the underground stream of

45 From over the hills, that was their trade
Harvesting Munster's potatoes
And well-known for it throughout Cork
And eastwards to the Decies. (trans. M. Ó hAodha)

46 'Teangacha Príobháideacha', *Scríobh 4*, p. 21.

tradition, his ancestral inheritance coursing as natural as day through his own rhythm and blood – as in the poem titled 'Dán' ('*Poem*')?

Ná ní mian liom a cheistiú
Mura seoltar chugham a bhrí,
Mar ní liomsa féin a bhrú,
Ná ní liomsa féin a bhrí.

Bhí lámh ag mo sheanathair ann,
Gé nár chleacht sé riamh filíocht,
Ach bhí duanaire bó bainne aige
Sa bhfeirm i gCiarraí.

Is do thuig sé cad ba chrú,
Is do thuig sé cad be chíoch,
Is do bheirimse mo bhuíochas dó
Gur chuimil sé siní.[47]

Nor do I wish to interrogate it
if its meaning isn't delivered to me
because it's not my womb gestates it;
I am not the one who gives it vigour.

My grandfather had a hand in it,
though he never practised poetry,
he had a milch-cow anthology
on his farm in Kerry.

And he knew about milking,
and he understood the pap,
and I give him thanks
that he stroked the teats.[48]

---

47 ES: p. 113.

48 Sewell, *Selected Poems*, p. 117. Trans. Colm Breathnach.

Wasn't this what he'd always sought through writing – to coalesce the many personas he'd made his over time, that diversity of tradition and modernity that he'd tapped into down through the years on the road of his imagination, the road he'd always journeyed between Inniscarra and Dunquin? Even if he was tormented by doubt, couldn't he prove to be the artist that might bring it all together in his work? Aogán Ó Rathaille and Peig Sayers, *Parliament na mBan* and the Kerry 'community poet' Pound – meshing the Gaelic oral tradition with the literary tradition and even breaching the gaps where Ireland's tragic history and linguistic change had rendered the Irish language silenced or invisible?

Ó Ríordáin seemed to be moving towards this way of thinking in a letter he sent to Donncha Ó Laoghaire on Saint Patrick's Day 1953. Commenting on Maghnas Ó Domhnaill's book *Betha Colaim Chille* (*The Life of Columcille*), he says:

> *Maghnas Ó Domhnaill wrote this book in the year 1532. It is in the language of this era and the decades prior to it that one sees the real breadth and scope of the Irish language; and it is in the Irish of this era that one can infuse that older richness with a naturalness and a life that complements the breadth of the older language. I took everything by Aogán Ó Rathaille with me to read also – the* Dánta Grádha, Measgra Dánta, Peig *in addition to a couple of other books. I forgot about writing and focused on learning. I didn't write more than four poems while I was there. I gathered some dirt, some vulgarity while I was there also that lifted my heart. A frequent phrase in Pound's mouth when describing women was the following: 'Is áil liom agus ní háil liom.' ('I care for her and I don't care for her.') I noticed that this phrase also appears on page 107 of* Parliament na mBan *– as follows: 'As áil leis agus ní háil leis deaghobair… do dhéanamh.'*[49] Parliament na mBan *is more alive and real to me now that I have heard Pound speaking and Pound's speech has more authority to it now that I have* Parliament na mBan *also. Céitinn has the focal 'buannacht' ('billeting') in his work and the word 'buannaíocht' ('imposition'/'presumption') is in*

49 *Parliament na mBan* is a late seventeenth-century didactic work by Domhnall Ó Colmáin, based in part on the 'Senatulus', one of the *Colloquia familiaria of Erasmus.*

> *Dunquin. Mícheál Ó Gaoithín describes the thoughts that are 'ar chúlaibh' (at the backs of/behind) speech and this same sentence is to be found in* Parliament na mBan, *page 27…*

The term 'buannaíocht' (*'presumption'/'imposition'*) was another that Ó Ríordáin had stored in his memory and for which he was waiting for the correct poem to find a place – it eventually appeared in the poem 'An Feairín' (*'The Maneen'*). The poet understood this term, 'buannaíocht', in the sense of it being a complete sense of 'unity' or 'integration', a sense of completion, a perfect wholeness. The mind of God and mind of man unified and whole, in so far as they could ever be with respect to the artistic act, i.e. poetry. The subject and the message perfectly unified in the form of art. Each aspect reflecting the other – as absolute and perfect. The poetry that is no longer of this world of man but which speaks entirely for itself as if in celebration of creativity. (I'm strongly of the opinion that the essay excerpt below was prepared by Ó Ríordáin as part of a speech he gave to the Ciorcal Staidéir (Study Circle) in Cork on 5 March 1954.)

> *On a winter's night last year An File stood in his own kitchen in Vicarstown and read out a poem that he'd written that morning. He himself wrote it, he said. And it was him too. In another way, it wasn't him however. I imagined that his ancestors in the graveyards were writing that day also, that they were walking all over An File and that he was so choked by them that there was barely any of the poet left in him – that the forms of Irish poetic tradition were too strong for An File and that these forms needed to be broken. An File is a master of language when he's speaking to you. I've never met anyone who'd best him in this regard. But he was imprisoned within the poetry …*[50] *I remember going home that night and composing this quatrain:*
>
> **Conas?**
>
> *Conas go ndeirimid an rud ná rabhamar chun a rá?*
> *Conas go leanaimid an múnla ceanann céanna cnámh?*

50 'Cnuasach filíochta ón Oileán Tiar', IT, 15 August 1968.

Conas nach féidir linn a mhalairt d'abairt riamh a rá,
Fé mar ba chreatlach an teanga agus sinne smior na gcnámh?[51]

How?

How is it that we say that which we were not going to say?
How do we follow the exact same pattern of bones?
How is it that we can never say a different sentence,
As if the language were a skeleton and we were the marrow of the bones?[52]

The neat expression of metaphor occurs to him again on seeing the lads from Farranferris training on the beach, running and playing football in the light of the setting sun, young lads jumping out of their skins and yet trapped within the unique essence of themselves, the sinew that traces bone. He observed, and confided his thoughts to the diary:

Swimmers on Clogher Beach – the boys mentioned in Father Tadhg. They were running and playing ball in the sunlight. Whatever moves they made they couldn't escape their human form and condition. They were going wild and yet they were still under the control of their form/skeleton.

How can we say that which we'd never say? An elbow here and a knee there decided to try and break free but it didn't matter what a particular knee or elbow did, the law of human form always prevailed. They could just fulfil it and nothing else. It's the same with a person's thoughts. No matter how crazy the idea, one cannot go beyond the pattern that is fate.

That said, at least the poet could engage with the language and the world view he found here on his sojourn in the Gaeltacht, something which he could never do back in Inniscarra. Indeed, when we call to mind Ó Ríordáin's belief in the link between the writing of poetry (the artistic process) and man's effort to reflect the will of God, one sees how absolutely essential those periods he spent in the natural Irish-language environment

51 B: p. 40.
52 Trans. M. Ó hAodha.

of the Gaeltacht were to his development as a writer. The other question remains nonetheless, however. What benefit was there to the constant solitariness, this eternal sameness, the eternal void that he frequented for the rest of the year? Wasn't it necessary for one to renew oneself in someone else, in an act, in a word or in somewhere that was outside of you? When one lost one's grip on the person beyond, one lost one's own identity as well. It was this contact with the outside that explained who you were and that enabled you to retain your own humanity. Everything falls away or fades in its absence, in the absence of this necessary steer or structure from the outside.

> *I am not* divina institutione formatus. *Ah, that word* formatus. *That is the word that frightens me. I know that I'll have to face it sooner or later but I don't dare do so.*[53]

As far as form and structure went, the basis of it had to be Dunquin and the grace of God working in harmony together. Why the increased doubts in Ó Ríordáin's mind then about his Irish-language poetry, as characterised by his writing in *Brosna*? Hadn't he already decided that Irish was his chosen form as a writer, once the language had been shaped and adjusted to express his experience? Was it that he'd failed to attune the language adequately with his subject matter or vice versa? This was what others said about his poetry, and such criticisms of his work had certainly left their mark on him. It's not unlikely that it was the critics who had sown the seeds of doubt in the poet's mind as to whether his knowledge of the Irish language was up to scratch. If what they said was true (and we'll return to the character of these criticisms shortly), then Ó Ríordáin's entire poetic oeuvre had been undermined, as had the entire philosophy he'd built around it. Not that the poet would capitulate to them, not publicly anyway. The report letter he writes to the secretary of Comhdháil Náisiúnta na Gaeilge on St Patrick's Day 1953 is a case in point. The poet reviews his qualifications to be an Irish-language writer and defends them; he might not be the best qualified in the world for

---

53 D: 26 November 1950.

this role but one had to start somewhere. And what else could he have done except what he did? And isn't it his right anyway? What other way or approach could he have taken? Initially, he describes what his life was like in the years 1932–50 in Inniscarra, before he'd become familiar with Dunquin and the Kerry Gaeltacht and this 'Irish-language voice in my mind as the face of a friend that I hadn't seen for years and that I'd difficulty calling to mind'. It is the same face ultimately whether east or west, the friendly house-calling face of older Gaelic tradition. It was literature and the books he'd read that had fostered the flame of Gaelic culture in him for the guts of the eighteen years prior to the publication of *Eireaball Spideoige*. His childhood had been his sole sustenance prior to this accessing of the literary tradition, he says. Such was the choice he had to make, if a choice really needed to be made at all:

> *Maybe it would be no harm if I made reference to my childhood in Ballyvourney since there is so much talk about my lack of Irish. My father was a native speaker. My grandmother and my aunt were next door to us and we children were in and out to them during the day. Both of them were native speakers and the old woman had just a few words of English. My uncle (another native speaker of Irish) had a farm a small distance from us and he'd visit us – socialising every night. There was an old woman named Nell Mhattie next door to us also and I used to write down stories from her (e.g. 'Dearg mac Deirg agus an Claíomh Solais'; 'Cac Money a Chapaillín Bháin', etc.), stories that Maidhc Gaoithín (i.e. the son of Peig Sayers) had never heard, and Maidhc is a superb storyteller. Here's an example of the English that Nell Mhattie had. When Mattie, her husband, would come home she'd say 'Mattie is came'. The teachers we had in school were native speakers. There was one big thing lacking in me, however, with regard to Thersites. My mother was like Seán McEntee, she had no Irish … Was I entitled to write in Irish the first day ever? I didn't care about language or about country or about religion itself when I began writing. I'd give a damn about what happened to Ireland. I was without English or Irish. 'Mattie is came' and Book English would have been my background if I'd written in English. I felt that the Irish I had was more suitable for my writing, whatever type of Irish she is. Máire Mhac an tSaoi said that I put an Irish cloak over ideas that were in English initially and that there was a falseness to what I wrote. She isn't right*

about this. That's something that I never did. From the beginning of this journey until its very end, I always thought in Irish. Another thing: it wasn't just the subject matter that moved me to write poetry. The language itself moved me also. A good many of my poems, whether good or bad, emerged from the current, from excitement, from the flow of the very language itself (e.g. 'Scagadh'). Most often, it was the language that worked me more than anything else. If that woman understood the smallest thing in relation to poetry she'd know that lines of poetry happen and form themselves more often they are invented. Take this line, for example:

Tá an fhírinne ró-lom ar an Oileán.

That line happened. If things came to me in English then I would write in English. But the poem 'Oileán agus Oileán Eile' seems lifeless to me and I was never fully satisfied with any poem that I ever wrote. I'm not defending myself here. But believe me – and I've spent a long time thinking about this – it's my right to write in Irish.

Ó Ríordáin bolstered his defence further in his essay 'Banfhilíocht agus Gaeilge', when he'd just begun publicly responding to the critics (and to Máire Mhac an tSaoi in particular) and their attacks after twenty-five years of silence. The fact that he'd delayed his response for so long meant that he was able to make the case for his defence in a more measured way than would have otherwise been the case. He went to the heart of the question immediately when he declared, contrary to what was being said about him:

… that it's the same Irish that I am always writing, a sort of personal language, as skimmed from the speech of the people – a type of Irish that's within me – a small voice or a small logic that I associate with my own ego. This voice would have been drowned out long ago if it wasn't for my trips to Dingle …

If I understand myself correctly I turned my back on anything to do with the mindset of the community and the tradition of the community in order to reveal whatever insight or sensibility I felt I had. This leaves its own mark on my Irish. I've intended for a long time to write a different type of Irish but I don't think

> *that I will. You are circumscribed forever by your own internal style and your personality. Maybe also, they are really both one and the same.*[54]

There is far more to this than a simple imitation of Buffon's speech in *Le style est l'homme même.* There's a huge portion of Ó Ríordáin's life in this one short paragraph: the Irish language that he had in him and the outlook, personality and style that he wished to bring to this tradition and the language as he'd found it. This is the same thing, albeit in another form, that he outlined in his essay 'Má Nuad' ('*Maynooth*') – another essay where he was on the defensive. This time it's the voice and legacy of Daniel Corkery that he still feels 'listening without pause/as a re-conscience', this despite the fact that Corkery had been dead for eight years by then.[55] It was Corkery's opinion of him that bothered Ó Ríordáin more than anything else; needless to say, out of respect for the dead, the poet's comments were more restrained here than they'd normally have been in the diary:

> *Corkery said to me once not to write any line that wasn't based on a line from the older poetic tradition. But what does one do when elements from outside that tradition enter your sensibility – when the person becomes more wide-ranging than the tradition. (Undoubtedly, one can be narrower than the tradition also.) It's fine to remain within the understandings of the Irish language but it is a different thing to leave one part of yourself out of the reckoning. It's necessary then to build upon and expand upon the tradition, dangerous as this is.*[56]

We can but observe Ó Ríordáin as he attempts to resolve the struggle that was going on in his mind with regard to tradition and the influence of Corkery and others. This was a struggle that had been there since the very beginning, or at least until Ó Ríordáin found his own personal voice. And it was one that always brought Corkery to mind for him, as evidenced in the passage below:

---

54 IT, 27 November 1975.

55 ES: p. 52.

56 'Má Nuad', IT, 12 August 1972.

> *I remember certain thoughts that would come to me at night long ago when I was in bed ... They were important and basic thoughts, I felt. Or maybe it would be better to say that they were understandings that I had or a certain mind/way of thinking. I don't remember when this mind first appeared. Maybe I had her when I was fifteen years of age. I was definitely no more than twenty years old when she came to me. This is what those thoughts consisted of – her mindset or thoughts: a certain understanding or mind/mindset exists – the understanding of the writer, the artist, the loner; this mind is honest and independent: she's independent of belief (religion), of politics and of teachings; it belongs to you; she's an independent witness; she belongs to the inner world and not to the outer. I understood without question that I'd this mind and I was proud of her. It wouldn't have been right to have let the church or political opinions overrule this mind. The virginity of this mind has to be protected forever. I remember asking myself the question one night – what would happen if this mind contradicted the faith that I had in Christianity at the time? The only answer that I had to that was that belief would have to give away. This choice wouldn't be much of an issue today but at that time it was a very serious question, I felt. Myself and this independent mind were one and the same, it seems.*[57]

The basis for this thinking can be found in the diary entry for the previous week, the entry for New Year's Day 1972, when he mentions that he'd already decided to pursue the solitary impetus in his work at a very early stage indeed, even before he'd left Ballyvourney. And that he hadn't separated himself from the remnants of the Gaelic tradition there too readily either. He'd had to pay his dues to this tradition and it would had to have its cut of him also. Ó Ríordáin had to work out his own relationship with tradition, independent of the advice of others who would seek to advise him, or who assumed they knew better; this is the primary issue here. The segment below, as included in a paragraph on the writing of poetry on the sleeve-note of a Gael-Linn album, is based on the diary entry for 1 September 1967 and was published in final form in *Scríobh 2* (1975):

57 'Trotsky agus Ó Corcora' ('*Trotsky and Corkery*'), IT, 8 January 1972.

> *I surrendered to the Irish-language tradition. I humbled myself before it. I'd nothing within me and nothing could ever be within me. I was in my teens then and in my early twenties when I was like that. The beautiful poetry that was written in Irish frightened me. The only thing that I really understood and related to at that time was the poetry of Dámhscoil Mhúscraí. I'd nothing inside me except the tradition. It was in the tradition that everything lay. I was smothered by it. Then, suddenly, I threw it the hell away from me and I found something that I wasn't expecting. I was given the right to speak. It wasn't long again before I felt that I wanted to escape from this right to speak and escape from myself and return again to the tradition. That's how the person is; over and back following his own personality sometimes and other times following the tradition. Whichever one he follows the other always accompanies him. It's the accompaniment of the fool.*[58]

Even still, the old tradition was no real burden for him, really, in his early years as a poet – it was the opposite, in fact. It was rather that the poet was inevitably dazzled by its power and capacity, and the assurance and fluency as associated with the Dámhscoil, and it had left him floundering slightly as a younger writer. This had led Ó Ríordáin to take a different approach from the beginning. His call to arms was always far more understated and had none of the bombast associated with the older tradition. In fact, the poem 'A Ghaeilge im Pheannsa' ('*To the Irish in My Pen*') is more of a question than it is an answer:

A Ghaeilge im Pheannsa

A Ghaeilge im pheannsa,
Do shinsear ar chaillis?
An teanga bhocht thabhartha
Gan sloinne tú a theanga?

Bhfuil aoinne inár dteannta
Ag triall ar an dtobar?

---

58 *Scríobh 2*, 1975, pp. 72–3.

Bhfuil aon fhocal seanda
Ag cur lenár gcogar?[59]

To the Irish in My Pen

O Irish in my pen
have you lost your ancestors?
Are you a poor fosterling
without any surname?

Is there anyone amongst us
drawing from the well?
Is there any old wise saying
to give volume to our whispering?[60]

This is another entreaty to the Irish-language tradition to accompany him for some of the journey, even if his allegiance to it might appear foolish, given how quickly it was fading or dying. In ways, Ó Ríordáin's dubious relationship with the English language had the same hesitance about it as his allegiance to Irish. English was the 'alluring whore' who was always there in the background, the temptress who never hesitated to accompany him, even when he journeyed back to the source or the 'well' of (Gaelic) tradition:

Do d'iompar atáimse,
Do mhalairt im chluasaibh,
Ag súrac atáirse
Ón striapach allúrach
Is sínim chughat smaointe
A ghoideas-sa uaithi
Do dhealramhsa a chímse,
Is do mhalairt im shúilibh.[61]

59 B: p. 9
60 Sewell, *Selected Poems*, p. 125. Trans. Noel Monahan.
61 From the poem 'A Ghaeilge im Pheannsa' ('*To the Irish in My Pen*'), B: p. 10.

I am carrying you,
your opposite in my ears,
sucking as you are
on that foreign trollop
while I slip you thoughts
that I've stolen from her.
I see your true image,
and your opposite in my eyes.[62]

If English was always generous with her charms, the Irish language certainly wasn't and the metaphors of the languages as whorish and frigid even made their way into his work in poems such as 'A Theanga Seo Leath-Liom' ('*Language Half-Mine*').[63] The poet's comment regarding the apparent futility of this 'half-mind/mentality' is based on a similar idea: the precariousness of being caught between two completely different linguistic and cultural traditions and being master of neither. Indeed, Ó Ríordáin based that very term – 'leath-aigne' ('*half-mind*') on the older Irish maxim 'Ní mheileann leathbhró' (lit: '*Halfway (i.e. a half-job) is a waste of time/useless*'), a phrase which he'd used in his diary as far back as 20 April 1940. In Irish, this term was frequently used in the metaphorical sense to refer to the futility of doing something involving a woman if that woman's heart wasn't in it. To put it another way, it takes the coalescence of two mentalities or two wills. And if Ó Ríordáin was to knock a child out of the Irish language, he'd have to court her with true devotion, no matter how reluctant she might be for congress with him, as suggested in 'A Theanga Seo Leath-Liom':

Ní mheileann riamh leath-aigne,
Caithfeam dul ionat;
Cé nach bog féd chuid a bhraithim tú,
A theanga seo leath-liom.

62 Sewell, *Selected Poems*, p. 125. Trans. Noel Monahan.
63 B: p. 25.

Half a mind to do won't do,
I have to fully enter in,
Though you're a hard one to get round,
language half-mine.[64]

And even if he denied it in his public writings, it's difficult to escape the impression that the poet's attempts at congress with the Irish language were an awkward fumble or a grope in the dark more than anything else sometimes.[65] We'll follow the poet some way along the road nonetheless and observe his tortured relationship with Ireland's two main languages, Irish and English, whether in the solitariness of his bedroom at home, or in the bustle of the hospital ward – when he listened to the brief and almost alien voice of the announcer speaking a few words of Irish on the radio ('The crowd here deaf to the Irish/I hear spoken on the radio tonight/I'm trapped within a narrow realm/Within the inner deafness of English')[66] – or in a café in Cork city when he sits at a table with a small group of Irish-language enthusiast friends and it's as if all of them are party to the same make-believe world, each of them unsure as to whether they were completely mad to speak Irish together like this.

But if these were some of Ó Ríordáin's thoughts as he came closer to the end of his artistic journey, he had a different view entirely when he set out on the road the first day ever.

64 Sewell, *Selected Poems*, p. 145. Trans. Mary O'Malley and Frank Sewell.
65 e.g. 'In vacuo', IT, 6 May 1972.
66 B: p. 38.

8

The Choice and the Road Followed

In the important interview that Ó Ríordáin did with Seán Ó Mórdha, the poet spoke of the short poems and sayings that were essential sauce to the everyday conversation of his childhood in Ballyvourney. Even if the Irish language was already in decline in that part of Cork then, the local speech was still replete with many of these linguistic pearls, incorporating philosophical insights and poetic gems; if nothing else, they were a reminder of how rich the Irish spoken there had been at one time. The fireside game called 'Deirín Dé', for example, where the child would spin a glowing twig around and around, causing sparks to twirl in the air. 'And that element of the child is deep within the human spirit – the Last sparks of God's light, the Last sparks of God's light – the greatest poetry in the world is in this.'[1]

Such statements often appear in the diaries, each of which provides a unique glimpse of this other life that had formed him as a child: the abstinence and renewal of Lent and of Easter, socialising on bright moonlit nights, the poverty and the misery. 'An old verse that I learned in Ballyvourney long ago: "Good Friday is a day of great torment"' etc., from a diary entry from 22 March 1940; 'The first two lines of poetry I ever learned: "The night is bright and the road is fine/Yet wait still until day"': 14 February 1956. Another verse couplet that he didn't mind citing with reference to his own situation: 'Always hungry and a lack of shoes/ That's what made a decrepit old man of a young boy': 3 November 1958. At one point Ó Ríordáin can't remember the words of whatever saying or rhyme it is correctly and we're left with only a snippet of writing referring to 'an old rhyme that my father used to have long ago' : 6 February 1940.

1 *Scríobh 3*, p. 170.

Another time, he has the quatrain exactly right and on the tip of his tongue, just as he learned it the first day ever; this was one that 'Nell Mhattie gave me long ago back west in Ballyvourney and it's unlikely that this poem was ever published':

Is mairg a bheith fé tharcaisne ag mnaoi,
Is ná fuil aon earra ar an dtalamh is measa ná í;
In aghaidh na géige ar an gcrann tá cor claon 'na croí,
Is í a dhein an peaca do chuir fearg ar Chríost.

Woe to the one who is held in contempt by a woman,
Since there is nothing on earth that is worse than her;
Her heart is twisted like the branch on the tree,
She is the one who committed the sin which angered Christ.[2]

'Yes now there you go, as she used to say herself' (3 February 1940). These fragments of verse were a far cry from the rich poetry produced by the Dámhscoil (Poetic School) that had been located in that area many years earlier, and yet they are hints of the type of material that still lay in Ó Ríordáin's memory and which he tried to draw on from time to time. Indeed, he was reliant on these random poetic pieces for a small yet significant aspect of his poetic development. Not that such fragments of memory were ever enough in themselves to bolster his evolution as a leading Irish-language poet. And this much was clear to Ó Ríordáin himself from a very early stage. This was like learning another life or an older and different language and, ironically, it obligated him to seek out the company of the dead and the recovery of half-buried memories when there was no companionship available to him closer to home. This was the first step he had to take. Never mind those who were outside for the moment, or that part of you that sought to extract its tribute from you on a regular basis. When we met Ó Ríordáin for the very first time, in the diary entry for New Year's Day 1940, he had yet to make up his mind whether to recognise the tempting call of 'the foreign prostitute' (i.e. the English

2 Trans. M. Ó hAodha.

language) or not. Not that he was blind to how she tried to entice him over to herself. He had already journeyed way back in his mind, however, back to an earlier and different time:

> *I need to improve my Irish. I prefer Father Peadar's style to that of any other writer in Irish that I have come across, as of yet. I better read one or two books of his again, if I want to put a shape on any of this nonsense of mine. I read An tOileánach as well. I liked Ó Criomhthain's pure Irish. There is a big difference between his Irish and that of Céitinn but I'm fond of them both. The echoes of these three writers will make my pen dance from page to page. The historical music of the English language is always strong in my ears however, I'm afraid.*[3]

In so far as something strays from this theory and its implementation, then it's a defective piece of work in his view. Ó Ríordáin's interpretation of the past and its role in his poetic development changed over time and became more nuanced as evidenced in his piece 'Teangacha Príobháideacha' ('*Private Languages*'). His thinking here is that the 'old saying or turn of phrase' is still crucial and can be juxtaposed alongside the 'private account', although he holds neither idiom in quite the same high regard at this particular point in time; not as compared with later at any rate. The date is 14 January 1940:

> *It was extremely cold, a cold that went right to the pith and the marrow of me ('go smior agus go smúsach'). That's an old turn of phrase in the Irish language – go smior agus go smúsach. I wonder if it's better to stick with existing idioms or words rather than hitch words and terms together that were never married to one another before? If the idea you have in mind can be constructed with older words and long-established idioms, then it's better to use them. I don't think anyone has yet proved (maybe they did, but that I didn't hear of it) that there's any idea that cannot be expressed using existing or older Irish-language idioms. Father Peadar Ó Laoghaire wrote the Irish that he inherited from his ancestors and I don't think that he ever joined two words together in a phrase for the first time that hadn't been joined together previously. He warned Irish-language writers*

3 D: 1 January 1940.

against inventing a new form of Irish off their own bat. He felt that the Irish language was good enough as it was and that they'd only damage it if they were spreading a form of Irish that they'd made up themselves. He was right then and he'd still be right, perhaps, if he said the same today. A living language grows and develops but she needs to develop at her own pace. Irish-language writers need to immerse themselves in the language before they've the right to construct the idiom in a way that differs from the older forms. Unfortunately, the sin that I'm critical of is on my own conscience. My only defence is that this is a private account.

The writers were there in the tradition already and there was no shame in following the approaches that they'd adopted in earlier decades. Years later, Ó Ríordáin would reassess the long-established referents as followed by various Irish-language writers and opine as follows:

As for the File Mór (Great Poet), I think that he's still a kind of a pioneer, irrespective of whether he appears during the era of a worn-out tradition or a tradition that's fully flourishing. He is the type who always tries to initiate a new tradition. The pioneer is never the slightest bit afraid. He abandoned the way. He did two things that were forbidden – he created a new way at the same time as he destroyed an old one. He was the catalyst for a new linguistic energy and inventiveness even if he wasn't inventive himself. Poets will come after him who'll tease out this new inventiveness. He's out of tune, emotional, foreign. It's clear that simplicity is not his forte. He's an amateur when the minor poet is deemed a professional. Maybe he isn't a poet at all but the plunderer of graves. How can he be recognised? By his lack of richness? What keeps him in the ascendant? That his energy is clear? That he is none other but himself? That he's easily recognisable? And what makes the minor poets what they are? That they make use of that which has already been smoothed out and crafted within the language before them? Inventing is what they do, inventing something that was there before them. Creating is what this other man does, however. From what? From nothing. It isn't a form of creation unless it is from nothing.[4]

4 'Mionfhilí agus neamh-fhilí móra' ('*Minor poets and non-poets with big reputations*'), IT, 29 July 1968.

In retrospect, we can see now that it was easy to talk like this when the battle was as good as over. Ó Ríordáin had already been recognised in the pantheon of new and unique Irish-language poets when he wrote these words towards the end of his life. Writing three decades earlier, at the end of the year 1940, it was much more difficult not to surrender to the pessimism that enveloped the death-throes of the older Gaelic culture and the inevitability with which many people spoke about the disappearance of Irish and the attendant decline of its poetic tradition. It was even more difficult still for Ó Ríordáin personally, given that he claimed a relationship with the very area that this tradition had survived in so strongly for centuries.

The poet sent a letter to the organisers of the Oireachtas in mid-February 1940 enquiring about the competitions, and enclosed in their reply to him was the poem entitled 'Duan Aithbheochaint an Oireachtais 1939' ('*Poem on the Revival of the Oireachtas Festival 1939*'). It was 'Tórna' (the pseudonym of Tadhg Ó Donnchadha, 1874–1949) who composed the poem and yet, in another way, it wasn't him (entirely) either, or at least that's what Seán thought. 'I know highly literate Tórna where you got that last verse – or what verse was in your mind when you composed the last part of that poem.'[5]

The Duaisliric an Oireachtas (Winning Lyric) of 1939 was published in the newspaper *Scéala Éireann* on 7 March 1940 and Seán noted the full poem down in his diary. Pádraig Mac Suibhne ('An Suibhneach Meann') from Coolea was the author of this piece, which celebrated his native area. 'An Peidhleacán' ('*The Butterfly*') was the title of the poem and there was a richness, a simplicity and a facility for writing evident in each and every line of it. His métier was a literary one, even if it was beginning to lose its sharpness. Go over to the other side, however, and what did you have to draw on except 'Book English' or worse again, the likes of 'Mattie is came' – the type of speech that Ó Ríordáin really hated. While there was no chance that the poet would embrace the latter form of speech, there was no doubt a certain attraction for the poet in the 'Book English'. There was a sense of community amongst writers in English that was often lacking

5 D: 16 February 1940.

amongst Irish-language writers, and this undoubtedly made the English-language literary tradition attractive to the poet. Perhaps the best option, however, was the one that the poet chose in the end – i.e. that he helped make both literary traditions (English and Irish) more familiar with one another. While the poet was very familiar with the tradition of rhyme from an early age, it was Yeats who gave him an understanding for the meaning of poetry for the first time. As Ó Ríordáin put it in 1940:

> *Yesterday or the day before, I can't remember which, I was reading a poem by Yeats and it suddenly struck me that I was reading poetry and that it's good for someone to read poetry and that I understood what poetry is, and how to enjoy it. When I write, there are four ideas in it but when it came to me like that, it came in one sudden and joyous thought ... 'An Irish Airman Foresees His Death' was the poem that I was reading.*[6]

Ó Ríordáin liked some of Yeats' poems better than others. For instance, 'Ego Dominus Tuus' was one poem that he really related to, even if just for emotional reasons: the image of the boy in the street outside looking in through the shop window at all the treats inside. It wasn't just the imagery of this poem that he appreciated, but the fact that the poet Keats, who is referenced in the poem, had also died young, his body racked with the same disease that would shorten Seán's life too:

> *His art is happy, but who knows his mind?*
> *I see a schoolboy when I think of him,*
> *With face and nose pressed to a sweet-shop window,*
> *For certainly he sank into his grave*
> *His senses and his heart unsatisfied,*
> *And made - being poor, ailing and ignorant,*
> *Shut out from all the luxury of the world,*
> *The coarse-bred behalf of a livery-stable keeper –*
> *Luxuriant song.*[7]

---

6 D: 9 January 1940.
7 Yeats, 'Ego Dominus Tuus'.

This was a poetic voice that was worth imitating even if the substance of what Yeats said was as a form of exclusion to Ó Ríordáin's class of people. What was it that Yeats also said in relation to the same people, a people who might recite the poem 'A Coat'? 'Song, let them take it,/For there's more enterprise/In walking naked.'[8] This was actually the essence of it: to 'stand naked' and listen to 'the advice of our fearful heart', without simultaneously coveting the wealth that wasn't yours.[9] Who knows but maybe Ó Ríordáin could add some small bit to that same tradition he'd found before him, no matter how poor the contribution. Maybe he could add the tenets that had shaped him into the mix, couldn't he? His misfortune – his obscured or contorted vision. And surely, over time, his input to the tradition would be understood and would be forgiven? He'd be accepted eventually and then, as soon as not, he'd be forgotten and his work rendered insignificant again. In the meantime, there was nothing left to him but to observe and to keep his distance from all things – because to unify one's vision with the 'consensus' or the establishment was as good as a form of death:

> *When the author sees anything – a custom or someone's reputation or a political movement or a certain act – this is something that no one else sees. Another image entirely than that which the public sees is what the author stores in his memory. According to the author, the public's image is a false one – an image based on a lack of comprehension, a simplistic image. He gets angry when he sees anyone disagreeing with him and he knows that he is right. He has a poisonous disregard for the public, as did Ibsen and Yeats. Of course, the public believes that he's angry. When everybody is against you don't care any more about what the public thinks. You write the truth for yourself without any delay so as to explain yourself to people who don't have the same insight as you so to speak. It is from this that the ambivalence which is said to characterise the writers of today emerges, I think. I also think that all the great writers appeared unclear or slightly incomprehensible in the eyes of their contemporaries. It was only in the twentieth century that the writers of the nineteenth century came to be*

8 From W. B. Yeats' poem 'A Coat', published in 1916.

9 LL: p. 39; ES: p. 26.

> *understood. That is to say that I wasn't right when I said that the author writes for himself and ignores the public completely. He writes for the generation that comes after him. There are people and it is in their nature to be looking inside themselves and weighing themselves up. This isn't a pastime but rather a form of torture and there is no cure for it because there's no escaping human nature. They don't see anything healthy within and they are usually disconsolate as a result. Their only company is themselves.*[10]

> *It's clear to me that some form of transformation occurs in those people who are always exploring their inner world, something that means one could refer to such people as unique or different from others. They are all unlucky. They don't belong to the world. The other people don't need to look into themselves because the world is as a mirror to them. The world belongs to them. They are the world and they have great fun. They aren't lonely. But the ones who explore the inner world are always lonely. The world is a strange and wonderful place in their eyes. Also, they initially think that there's something wrong with themselves, so that they cannot relate to the world ... They become curious. They avoid the company of the living and seek out the company of the dead.*[11]

Eoghan Rua Ó Súilleabháin wasn't a poet in the realist sense because there was one great flaw in his work according to Ó Ríordáin:

> *It is understandable. There is nothing obscure in his work. The absence of obscurity in poetry is like the parting of the soul from the body ... Now for the lesson: 'Don't read Eoghan Rua Ó Súilleabháin, read James Joyce' – even if Shaw threw it into the fire.*[12]

Life must permeate the language and be felt through it. It was better to imitate speech rather than subject matter, even if they usually reflected one another in a form of unity. What is Ó Ríordáin's solution to the conundrum – a solution he moves towards gradually nearing the late 1940s?

10 D: 13 June 1942.
11 D: 25 June 1942.
12 D: 31 March 1942.

> *Immerse ourselves in the old literature? But Mac an Bháird has a grey down on him. Well, let's dry ourselves beneath the sun of life after we've first immersed ourselves. I think that 'the disciples of the tradition' don't understand why such an immersion is necessary. To build up courage, I think. A person needs to dry themselves off immediately, however, in case they catch cold. The rhythmic and eternal flu of Eoghan Rua Ó Súilleabháin seems to afflict the poets of Coolea, I think. They're always dripping wet and have a grey down growing on them.*[13]

It wouldn't be with old words covered with grey that one could 'loosen the damp moss/from the features of Christ/or from thoughts'.[14]

Language had to be viewed in a new way; there had to be a new way of seeing – in the same manner as a saint would see the world anew, or a child, or a Beckett. To fail in this new and fresh perception of the world wasn't an option, even if this new vision of his revealed only a world of horror – the same horror that had to be broached, day after day, night after night. In the end, there is nothing left but God and the elemental scream, one tearing itself against the other in unnatural fashion – but then, was there ever a scream that was normal or natural?[15]

> *Suffering enters a person's life and it increases slowly but surely. The person himself is looking on at this and trying to make little of it – half-thinking that the bad luck is just toying with him and that it will leave him be after a while. This helps him be more patient – the expectation that he'll be free from this later on. A moment comes, however – the moment when the suffering goes too far – a terrible moment. The spirit rises suddenly and she screams out. This is a scream against God. Patience is at an end; wisdom has come to an end. Hope no longer matters. It's almost as if hope no longer exists. Say that it is illness that is tormenting the spirit. While the illness may not wane at all, the scream ruptures the torment of the soul. This is a moment of madness. A challenging of God. And there's a sweetness in the air after the battle is over. A good way to face*

---

13 D: 7 August 1947.

14 ES: 79; from 'Oileán agus Oileán Eile' (*'This Island and the Other Island'*), Sewell, *Selected Poems*, p. 95. Trans. Denise Blake.

15 ES: p. 60.

death. It's a terrible sight to see a whole person fade away. His body, his mind, his hope dissipated each day. There's some kind of horrible slyness in such a thing. And the ugliest sight of all, the sight of him praying humbly. Oh God, sustain a sense of stoicism and a lack of humility in us, so that we may be strong enough to kick against you if necessary. My own spirit screamed this afternoon. Isn't the personal note an ugly thing, Professor Corkery?[16]

By the beginning of that same year, 1948, Seán has come to a clearer understanding of poetry and his vocation as a poet and yet he still feels it necessary to submit his thoughts to the Professor – at least in his own mind, anyway. It's clear that he misses the institutional 'imprimatur' that goes with University, even as he sends his first collection of poetry out into the world.[17] On one side of the equation are metrics and form, tradition, control – and on the other are unlimited imagination, the ego, that restless and unpredictable individual who can't find a secure place in the scheme of things and who doesn't believe in anything, really – even in disbelief itself. This is a poetry of the disconsolate as shaped by the language and culture of an abandoned and downcast race. Doesn't one always follow the other in the end? And even if his poetry might scream of an unheralded purity and sweetness occasionally, more often than not it's the hollow and mute voice of the river that he reflects. The sense of listlessness and disgust that gradually takes hold of his mind and of the room he lays sick in for months on end; the individual sensibility that goes astray in the absence of any structure that can keep him on track or in harmony when he needs it most of all. Such an absence of structure or form was a long way away from the likes of Fr Tadhg or Corkery or Turnbull, the regular and upstanding people in society. The various musings on this are provided here in the order in which they made their appearance:

Professor Corkery would like to control poetry. Control the spontaneous imagination. Control the ego. Control the form. I look for our gospel to contradict

16 D: 19 March 1948.

17 ES: p. 26.

him: e.g., I say to myself 'This is a cunning thought: "the impersonal literature of the Professor is just folklore".' Little by little however, I am divesting myself of the Professor's philosophy. Bad cess to him, he has me tormented.[18]

When I was finished my work today in Cork I was between two minds as to whether I should stay in the city or go home. I had no business to attend to at home and neither did I have anything to do in the city. There would be no one waiting for me at home and there would be no one looking for me in the city. Truth be told, I have neither home nor city at all. I have no family. I am neither a Christian nor a Gael nor an Irish person, nor an English person. I don't go to Mass or to the theatre. That is my life. I suppose that Professor Corkery is right. The lack of tradition. Too much of the ego. A lack of metre – i.e. a lack of control.[19]

I can't help but notice that the things I write are very thin. This is a consequence of the lack of tradition as Professor Corkery says. There's no doubt that there is a richness in the tradition. It is like the earth. Right now, I have a terrible lack of respect for what I have written. And, wonders never cease, there are some poor creatures out there who think that there's good in some of it.[20]

I wasn't well today. A fine day. I was reading The Hidden Ireland *by Corkery, for the third time, I think. I remember a day that I met him on the South Mall about a year ago and I said to him that the Irish-language tradition is a poor one. What sort of a blindness or stupidity came over me? The good man nearly fainted on the spot. The chances are that he is entirely correct with respect to the metre and the tradition, and maybe the ego.*[21]

This was what he'd recommended himself in a poem entitled 'Do Dhomhnall Ó Corcora' ('*To Daniel Corkery*') written at about this same time. (It was published in an edition of *An Síol* that appeared later in the year.) Eoghan Rua and Corkery setting out in tandem on 'roads full of

18 D: 13 January 1948.
19 *Ibid.*
20 D: 19 January 1948.
21 D: 13 March 1948.

Munster-people', one of them on foot and the other following along close behind in the imagination: 'One thinks of him as setting out with high heart and quick nostril: the roads were crowded with life; and taverns were frequent, the coaches swinging noisily up to them in noise and dust and bustle; and in every tavern there would be new stories of highwaymen, of duelling, of kidnappings, of elopements and forced marriages ...'[22] The narrative had musical accompaniment and people had entered into the words. Even when referring to Corkery's words in the diary, however, Ó Ríordáin makes use of the old distinction between music and the meaning of the words. And, once again, it isn't to Eoghan Rua that the tendency towards purity of idiom is ascribed but rather to Joyce, of whom Corkery once said – while Seán was present apparently – that his work was just 'the biggest literary trick ever played on the world'.[23] In the following piece, it isn't a 'shower of music' that he wishes to fall down upon the 'foreign floor of this day', nor a 'shower of poets' either, but rather the diverse meanings that the words might set free if Irish-language writers approached them correctly and sought admittance – i.e. managed to get inside the hardened shells of the language:

> *I'm reading* Ulysses *by Joyce. Corkery said that the parts of the eighteenth century brought a music from the language that never resounded from it before. Tricks were played with the music of the language and music fell upon them as in a shower. There is no harm in us playing with the meaning of words and a shower of meaning falling upon us. Let us play with the meaning of words. Wordplay. Joyce.*
>
> *Ní fear gníomha sinn*
> *Gé taoi tinn dár ngrádh*
>
> *A word man – words, words, words, words, words and words.*[24]

22 *An Síol*, 1948, p. 199.
23 'Dónall Ó Corcora' ('*Daniel Corkery*'), IT, 11 November 1967.
24 D: 24 April 1948.

The Professor's words weren't similarly amended in the praise-poem – but then Ó Ríordáin could hardly do so given that it was a poem of praise composed specifically for the occasion in question: a special issue of the university's Irish-language journal that was being produced in honour of Corkery's retirement from University College Cork after spending fifteen years of his life working as Professor of English and as a primary literary personality there. It wasn't as if you'd expect the entire truth, warts and all, in such a poem. While there might have been traces of 'pomposity' perhaps about lines such as 'The doe of our poetry awoke/ in the woods one year' in this poem, perhaps they are even more apparent at the beginning of the only other official praise-poem he wrote – 'Colm' – on the birthday of his old friend's child (Colm, the son of sculptor, Séamus Murphy), a child whom he stood as godfather for on 2 February 1959:

Buanghol, a Choilm, do cheol,
Ach oireann an deor do d'aois,
Taoi bliain ar an saol anocht
Is do thugais le gol trí mhí.[25]

Eternal crying is your music, Colm,
but at your age tears are no surprise.
You're a year in the world tonight
and you've wept at least three months of that.[26]

Without doubt, these lines were partly based on that famous poem which begins as follows; needless to say, it's a different 'colam' that Ó Ríordáin has in mind in this case:

Tuar guil, a cholaim, do cheól!
mo chroidhe ní beó dá bhíth;

25 B: p. 31.
26 Sewell, *Selected Poems*, p. 159. Trans. Peter Sirr.

> *do bhréagais mo dheór óm rosg;*
> *is truagh nách id thost do bhís.*[27]

Further confirmation of this is the fact that the first line of this quatrain appears in his diary for 28 February 1951 – as included in amongst some other 'lines that come to me from time to time'. But then, wasn't it only natural that the echo of tradition should underscore praise-poems as written for various public figures – the likes of 'Do Dhomhnall Ó Corcora' – given that they were such a public figures? This isn't to say that he publicly endorsed Corkery to such a huge degree in that particular poem, though this is a subject for another day, perhaps. Ó Ríordáin would continue to pick at Corkery privately, as if by disparaging him like this, he might bring him down to a level that he could really understand him and even wound him. But what weaknesses or defects could he identify in him, really? Wasn't Corkery much the same in terms of strengths and weaknesses as anybody else who'd ever been involved in the world of the arts?

The next excerpt in the diary following on from 24 April 1948 is provided below. Another of the old comrades is gone; those who are left now are just the damaged or crippled few who somehow continue to seek out the truth that is the fool's – and put another winter of this life behind them. Let us each recognise the poverty of our own truth and yet keep our distance from one another while keeping mercy close at hand at all times. Rather than bring him low, it was more that Ó Ríordáin wished to accept Corkery as a member of his same tribe; in a way, to leave him secure on his pedestal of pontification was akin to a lack of real solidarity with him:

> *Patrick Cronin was buried today. The man from Galway. T.B. I have a cold, yesterday and today. Imagine a room in Patrick Street on Tuesday night in winter. (A savage deity and no two ways about it.) 'The Study Circle.' Professor Corkery – old and lame– he can't get a woman. X – young, ugly – she can't get a man. Y – she is choked with asthma – a wren. We have neither man nor woman*

27 O'Rahilly, T. F. (ed.), *Measgra Dánta II: Miscellaneous Irish Poems* (Cork University Press, Cork, 1972), p. 155.

> *– we'll have a lecture. Is this how it always is? Is it always the same story in relation to every form of intellectual endeavour? Shaw? Ibsen? da Vinci? 'Take your pick.' 'You can't be whistling and eating oats.' Is it true that there'd be no whistling in the world if it wasn't for the lack of oats?*[28]

It makes no difference, really, given that they are both amongst the whistling brigade, even if the tune they whistle is not the same, unless it's for public show.

Ó Ríordáin headed for Gougane Barra the following month, in search of relief on both the personal and public levels, a simultaneous relief from personality and ego and tradition. He needed to get away badly, even for a few days; he needed a rest from the literature and its theorists, even if he was far from finished with Corkery in his mind as of yet. In fact, the very first article of his that he published in *The Irish Times* was about Corkery: 'Just as the people of Dunquin live under the shadow of Sliabh an Fhiolair (Mount Eagle), we lived in the shadow of Daniel Corkery. You'd write something and you'd be satisfied with yourself until you remembered him. And then you'd get worried ...'[29] Indeed, Ó Ríordáin was so influenced by him that he filled pages of his diary with different things that Corkery said over the years, some of which also made it into print in the same newspaper later on, as part of an essay.[30] Ó Ríordáin always assigned Corkery to the highest pantheon of *literati,* even when he might be in dispute with him about something or other. Even Joyce was sent to the margins in English literature by the poet when it came to defending Corkery's theories and teachings; they were almost an article of faith.

'The two emotions' is how Ó Ríordáin referred to him on one occasion when he needed Corkery as a stick with which to beat Thomas Kinsella.[31] It was Corkery, in his important pamphlet *The Philosophy of the Gaelic League*, who provided cover for the counter-argument that Ó Ríordáin expressed in this essay that 'no literature that had a genius of

28 D: 8 May 1948.

29 'Dónall Ó Corcora', IT, 11 November 1967.

30 'Comhrá Dhónall Ó Corcora', IT, 2 March 1968.

31 IT, 26 February 1969.

its own could have emerged from English language as spoken in Ireland. "It lacks character; it has never developed from within. It is thereby unfit to represent that reality that is [the] Irish mind."'[32] As Ó Ríordáin continues:

> *All right, I feel a lack in the English language as regards us. It encompassed the feelings of other people for too long – people who were completely different from ourselves. This alien feeling can be felt all over the English language. Undoubtedly, this same feeling shaped and coloured the English language and must have inculcated itself in the younger English people at an early stage of their lives. The Irish language contained a different range of feelings and shaped our people here in Ireland. The Irish language shaped the people in addition to the English language and therefore this Gaelic sensibility has had an indelible influence on us as a people.*

This isn't such a bad summation of the argument Corkery put forward that it is nearly impossible to produce an Anglo-Irish literature of substance because it would never access the innermost heart of the Irish race:

> *Our national consciousness may be described, in a native phrase, as a quaking sod. It gives no footing. It is not English, nor Irish, nor Anglo-Irish; as will be understood if one thinks a while on the thwarting it undergoes in each individual child of the race as he grows into manhood. Though not quite true, let us take it that the Irish-born child is as Irish in his instincts, in his emotions, as the English child is English: the period of education comes on: all that the English child learns buttresses, while it refines, his emotional nature. Practically all the literature he reads focuses for him the mind of his own people; so also does the instruction he hears. At a later stage if he comes to read a foreign language he seizes what he reads in it with an English mind. He has something of his own by which to estimate its value for him.*
>
> *How different with the Irish child! No sooner does he begin to use his intellect than what he learns begins to undermine, to weaken, and to harass his emotional nature. For practically all that he reads is English – what he reads in Irish is not*

32 'The two emotions', IT, 26 February 1969.

> *yet worth taking account of... In his riper years he may come to see the crassness of his own upbringing, as, doubtless, T. C. Murray and Padraic Colum see it; but of course the damage is done: his mind is cast in an unnatural because unnative mold. So does it happen that the Irishman who would write of his own people has to begin by trying to forget what he has learned.*
>
> *If it be so, and it cannot be otherwise, with T. C. Murray and Padraic Colum, men sprung from the people, sharing their national memory in all its ramifications, what chance of expressing the people of Ireland have those writers who, sprung from the Ascendancy, have never shared the Irish national memory, and are therefore just as un-Irish as is possible for them to be?*[33]

The 'reality that is [the] Irish mind', 'national consciousness', 'emotional nature', 'unnatural because unnative mold', 'national memory': it would be difficult to argue that such notions began solely with Corkery; it was more that he rooted them firmly within Ó Ríordáin's world view. It's a 'gospel' that manifests itself in the final verse of the poem 'Do Dhomhnall Ó Corcora':

Tráthnóna na teangan in Éirinn,
Is an oíche ag bogthitim mar scéal,
D'éist sé le creagar i véarsa,
Is do chuala croí cine soiléir.

The evening of the language in Ireland,
And the night falling softly like a story,
He listened to a cricket in a verse,
And he heard clearly the heartbeat of a race.[34]

One couldn't source a better example of the two traditions coalescing than in the above excerpt from Corkery. A sensitive and moving critique of English books as incorporating some of the older concepts associated

33 Corkery, Daniel, *Synge and Anglo-Irish Literature: A Study* (Cork University Press, Cork, 1931), pp. 14–15.

34 Trans. M. Ó hAodha.

with the Gaelic world: a nice long story of the tribe as related at the hearth in the old days, with due accompaniment from the evening music the grasshoppers made in the meadow outside. In this instance, one happens upon the beating heart of the older tradition within the English language – even if such a thing runs contrary to Corkery's normal theories. The flow of the older tradition as encompassed in Corkery's melodious English catching one unawares, this was what Ó Ríordáin sought to identify here. Such moments were very much the exception, however, and Ó Ríordáin generally proved more successful in his poetry when he set Corkery's theorisations aside and focused on the subject matter before him.

After all, a significant aspect of his modus operandi, as we have already seen, was the selection of the best model or vehicle for what it was he wished to express: the shaping of language and tradition, the shaping of the spiritual and the human, and the amalgamation of these diverse aspects within the one form. Art and spiritual development were intimately linked in Ó Ríordáin's conception of creativity; each aspect was entirely dependent on the other. It is immaterial to a certain extent which author or discourse moulded Ó Ríordáin's sensibility – whether Corkery, Hopkins, Ibsen or even Saint Augustine or the sermons that made up *Seanmóirí Muighe Nuadhat* (The Maynooth Sermons) – they wouldn't have inculcated themselves into his world view unless the poet welcomed the insights of these various writers himself. In fact, such insights were an absolute necessity for Ó Ríordáin; they helped him to get through the days when the poetry wouldn't come or when he was too weak or sick to do anything. Sometimes, it might be argued that Ó Ríordáin goes overboard with his attempts to amalgamate the theorists within his work (e.g., 'Saoirse'), but more often than not his poetry is played out on a more impersonal or clinical canvas without the specifics of particular characters or individuals – e.g., 'Daoirse'.[35] The necessity of his art follows much the same pattern at all times: the impetus to gather all the aspects and the people he feels slipping away or eluding him and finding a way to unify them in his work. Until then, i.e. until his death, the dualities repeat themselves and there is only hunger and nausea, humanity and the rabble,

35 B: p. 27.

the ego and the tradition, each duality interrogating the other. And this isn't true solely of his poetry either. The same deficiency characterises his sketching: lines that seek out their subject from him, a subject he fails to provide. There was a time when this wasn't the case – those summer afternoons long ago when he was backstage setting up the scenes and props for the play. But when was the last time that there was any drama in his life? He looks at some of his abstract sketches now and thinks:

> *When I look at those 'pictures' now, I don't have any affection for them any more and I never will – even if it was the morning of Candlemas (Lá le Muire na gCoinneal) in the chapel. They make me tired. I said to myself: 'Release the constraints in yourself – be free.' There is an awful restrictiveness in them. I tried my best to throw aside all types of knowledge I might have so as to set my mind free. I would create a new form! I tried my best and this is the result. How come there isn't any life in them? How is it that there is no joy in any line or corner of them? Wasn't I free? Didn't I have freedom? There is a terrible control over these lines that excludes them from the fields of joy. Even if no two of them are the same, the same lack is in all of them. The absence of life is that lack. Death is the most terrible control of all. I oppressed the forms that I knew best. That is to say that oppressed the thing that was alive. I placed an Iron Curtain around my mind. What was left? Nothing. There's not a pick left in me. I imagined that I'd be able to create amazing forms that would surpass nature and the tradition. But I failed because I expelled the living thing (that which the forms create) and the tradition (the forms made by others from that which is living) from my mind. The mind is dried-out and if the river of life doesn't come flowing through and the ancestral memory flooding along with it, then there's no point in going fishing.*[36]

> *I'm alone from 6 p.m. until 8.30 a.m. each day. I'm alone every Sunday. My mind is like the pictures over there – shapeless and unformed; i.e. the lines of my mind do not form pictures, nor do they create any music from the sounds of my mind.*[37]

---

36 D: 29 March 1949.

37 D: 30 March 1949.

He frequently describes his sketches in those terms: that the people he drew in them were never 'human' enough, or the places he sketched not familiar or local-enough looking. The poet speaks of the sketches as being controlled or restrained in some way, something that 'precludes them from the fields of joy', when what he really has in mind is the control or enslavement that is really complete freedom. In the poem '????' the word is the line, and the idea or thought is the picture that he wishes to sketch. He goes even further with respect to the composition of the poem, however. He himself is the word or the body; but is he a suitable enough carrier for the thought, the captive or the soul? This is the question. Is there another idiom or another poet who'd be more suited to the task? If he was to release the captive within him, would his thinking become more expansive perhaps, and inhabit another or different poem, one that would release its meaning out over 'the fields of joy' rather than remaining that cramped and stilted or unnatural idiom that is trapped within him? The poet can only express what is within him, however, and if his speech is cramped or stilted, then so too is the purveyor of the message:

An focal mé gan fuinneamh,
A mhoilligh smaoineamh diaga,
A dhorchaigh an smaoineamh?

An bhfuilimse ad choscadh,
A chime úd, am bhíogadh,
Ar pháirceanna an aoibhnis ?

Dá dtabharfainn cead do chos duit
An bhfaighfeá corp le bíogadh
Do fhairsinge comhlíonadh?

Ach cá bhfios dom nach focal mé
A bhrostaigh smaoineamh diaga . . .[38]

38 ES: pp. 98–9.

Am I a lifeless word
That delayed the spiritual thought
And clouded the mind?

Am I a hindrance to you
Oh prisoner-thought
That rouses one to joy's fields

If I set you free,
Would you find a form of inspiration,
Or fulfil your lavish bounty?

For all I know, I am the word
That spurred the spiritual thought …[39]

In 'Saoirse', however, we saw Ó Ríordáin leaving his lofty perch and heading down amongst the regular people in search of more humanity, much as a pilgrim might do. Given that it was in the Gaeltacht that Ó Ríordáin would find the common values that he wished to source, it is no surprise that he headed there from time to time. He needed more than the idiom and subject matter of the Gaeltacht to fulfil his needs, however, and there were other forays and trips that he probably should have undertaken also, ones that would have allowed him to expand his range of vision even wider, rather than going over the same roads, literary-speaking, repeatedly. He could have written a play, for example. Ó Ríordáin did publish a short story entitled 'Morrissey' in the journal *Feasta* in February 1952, a story in which he himself assumed the character of Morrissey much as he took on the role of Céadna in *The Irish Times* later. 'I call him Morrissey because the word Morrissey resembles the word "Pharisee." The name "Céadna" was formed from a similar amalgam – in this case a fusion of the word "Séadna" and "céanna" [the latter word meaning "same" in Irish]. The persona "Céadna" was therefore a man who saw every person and every

39 Trans. M. Ó hAodha.

day and every fate as exactly the same.'[40] Ó Ríordáin had planned for this persona Morrissey that he would send him on a journey on his behalf and that when he returned to him again, they'd both be able to get on with living and have normal lives and adequate health for life's journey. It seemed a strange message, really, particularly given that the man who had created this new persona had never known what such a journey consisted of and had no knowledge of the way either. Unsurprisingly, neither poet nor persona ever actually moved beyond the theoretical stage and followed up on the idea in the end. The persona remained entrapped within the writer's mind, the pair of them left with no subject matter but themselves and whatever other abstract concepts may have come their way, concepts which neither the poet nor the persona can ultimately provide sustenance for or find peace in. Morrissey sits down at the same table as the two other creative poles of the poet whose imagination has invented him, the two poles whom his life, pendulum-like, has alternated between – Christ and the prostitute. (If one of them would only just get up and leave! Moreover, the poet had never experienced a sense of wholeness or totality within either one of these poles or aspects, but rather its opposite: an abstract or tortured corporeality as juxtaposed with an agonised and corporal spirituality – neither aspect of which he'd ever managed to attain in any integrative sense.) Ó Ríordáin had identified the problem in an unpublished essay entitled 'Le súilibh gan solas' ('*Eyes that cannot see*'):

> *Rather than bringing Morrissey into the world, I went into his mind in search of him and I presented more of his thoughts and life of the mind than I did any of his life amongst the people. I'd prefer if Morrissey went down amongst the people so that he'd be constrained while I healed the claustrophobia within myself. My idea was to accompany Morrissey through every sin and every disease and every heresy and then to accompany him up onto the stage of truth and health once he had searched through all the nooks and crannies of humanity.*

Morrissey was left where he was, however, and neither was the play ever written, albeit that the poet has certain poems which explore the concept

40 IT, 26 March 1968.

of 'exchanging one's skin (form) for another' – that which Ó Ríordáin imagined as the essential function of drama.[41] The poems where such an exchange of personas or sensibilities occurs are nearly all amongst Ó Ríordáin's later work, with 'Malairt' being the most well-known of all.[42] Such poems exhibit diverse and hybrid shapes and forms melting into another – a man entering the mind of a horse ('Aistriú') or a human being becoming a cat ('An Cat'); or, alternatively, a cat transforming itself so that it becomes human ('Eireablú'), the head of one man stolen by another ('An Cloigeann Mícheart'). These are all poems that will be discussed in greater detail later in this volume. Ó Ríordáin also has another series of poems which involve shape-changing aspects and contrasts, including the swapping of part-personas solely amongst human beings: the female eyes that become male in ('Súile Donna') ('*Brown Eyes*') are more of a confirmation of the eternal than its opposite (by this stage eternity encompasses earthly eternity only).[43] Then there is that unfortunate person who is the poet – he or she whose personality or fate was always there amongst his or her ancestors and who must endure the regular evidence of such same inherited traits, even after their antecedents have passed on ('Toil');[44] Ó Ríordáin's sketch of the hound, the one that is, in reality, a really poor sketch of himself, and the face of the person found in the bog after two thousand years. And irrespective of how broken or contaminated these various things are, they nonetheless memorialise or make steadfast all the hounds and dogs there ever were.[45] The world is falling and being renewed again within these poems and sketches; it is a play of movement as appropriate to its ever-changing and ever-uniform nature and bears many similarities with the changing scenes of a drama in this sense.

In essence, and despite such shifting personas, images and forms, Ó Ríordáin remains essentially trapped, however. He hasn't achieved what he set out to do: to go out under the auspices of his other persona in search of people and human beings while simultaneously remaining inside with

41 LL: p. 28.
42 ES: p. 63.
43 LL: pp. 10–13.
44 LL: pp. 27–9.
45 'Clóanna über Alles', TÉB: p. 29.

the persona that is himself. His fate seems to be an endless circularity whereby he goes back in upon himself so that his only experiencing is himself, a *self* that's eventually worn out and exhausted. The constriction of his world and actual life experience ensures a weaker and more barren poetic voice over time – this despite the fact that Ó Ríordáin knows it is happening and tries again and again to explain it in his non-poetic writings. Ironically, it is in the introduction to *Eireaball Spideoige*, his most celebrated collection, that Ó Ríordáin provides one of the best explanations for the gradual failure of his poetic voice:

> *Because no one can savour their own self. And no one can inspire themselves or set off poetry within themselves. It is rather that they set off something else (often an abstract thing such as shoe-making or architecture or nursing). They act on one another. Not alone does he awake himself to prayer, but the prayer that is in the other thing comes alive also ...*[46]

He might have identified the problem, but it becomes worse over time nonetheless. 1969 goes by and there's no play written or characters written for it either. Neither had he managed to go down amongst the people and gather their idiom in Molière-like fashion. In truth, the poet has been telling the same story for the guts of thirty years by then – there is no other – and he is already tiring of it himself. His words and life experience narrowing at the same time as his poetic vision:

> *Every new writer likes to explore a new terrain of thought and break open a new quarry of words. I don't say that you can't do this by giving expression to your own thoughts. But maybe it is easier to express this by speaking on behalf of others. He collects other people and puts them talking just as a dramatist or a storyteller would. He speaks through the crowd. Or the crowd speaks through him. Everyone he sets to speech, expands his range of thought and his language, apparently. I don't know if it's really that simple, however.*[47]

46 ES: p. 15.
47 'Personae dramatis', IT, 28 May 1969.

It is others who'll put on the play and who'll inhabit the personas that will serve to free them from themselves: Niall Tóibín taking on the part of Brendan Behan, for instance; Seán Mac Réamoinn assuming the role of every cardinal Ó Ríordáin has ever met, or spreading his persona throughout Cork city via telephone.[48] These are the ones who have the run of things with them as they go around tóibín-ising and mac réamoinn-ising everything. But what has Seán Ó Ríordáin to 'ó ríordáin-ise' with or inhabit a new persona with – other than that old persona, which he's already done to death? And regardless of whether it's poetry, sketching, sculpture or drama that's in question, one needs more than an author, or a sketch without a subject, or personas that have no life left in them and nothing left to give. Or what use is the sculptor that carves an individual's head if he has never really known that individual or understood their persona or nature? An excerpt from the diary that later appeared in the essay 'Seal im aonar' elucidates this further:

> *I saw a small sketch of a person's head a while ago. It was very similar to a goat's skull. It had the look of a goat's skull as well as that of a human skull. It was a treacherous form and yet it had something special about it as well, like a word-play or a pun, and a real sketch looked boring compared to it. You'd need to be on your guard looking at him – that's to say alive. How about writing a play with people or contemporary* personae *in it, albeit that you'd see other historical people through them? Or what about a play where the characters exchanged characters with one another for a while and yet the character initially assigned to them could still be read on their faces all the time? Say that there were two in the play, Peter and Paul. After a while Paul would become Peter-ified, and Peter would become Paul-ified because of the interaction they had with one another. That's not to say that Peter would turn into Paul completely or that Paul would turn into Peter completely, because Paul would still be Paul except that he would be a Peter-ified Paul and Peter would Paul-ified in much the same way. I don't think that this thought is as mad or as crazy as it might seem. I visited an exhibition of heads recently as created by a certain sculptor. There was a great gathering of*

48 'Niall Tóibín', IT, 24 July 1971; 'Mac Réamoinn i gCorcaigh', IT, 30 January 1971.

heads in attendance there. Amongst those present, as the newspapers say, were Seán T. O'Kelly, Éamon de Valera, the Archbishop of Dublin, Frank O'Connor, Maurice Walsh, Orla, the sculptor's daughter and many others. Each of them was recognisable by his own head but the sculptor was most recognisable of all, for it was he who was in the know. If I am right, this means that each personality transmitted the sculptor into their heads and that he couldn't escape again. To tell you the truth, none of the heads would have amounted to much if it hadn't been for the sculptor marking them with his own essence.[49]

Séamus Murphy was the sculptor in question here, a man who had inherited the craft and tradition of 'stonies'. But what else was tradition but the attempt by the artists of each generation to explain or represent the life around them as best as they could through the medium at their disposal – in this case, the medium of clay? In another instance, it is the appropriate ordering of the words within the sentence, the action within a play, or the lines that circumscribe a drawing and give it meaning. While nothing can ever be expressed fully in the artistic sense, the artist will nonetheless come to the fore if the subject matter wills it, irrespective of medium. We witness Séamus Murphy again, Murphy and Galway writer Máirtín Ó Cadhain, dancing together and exchanging form:

It's a strange one then to see Séamus struggling with Máirtín and trying to bring shape to him anew in clay and tussling with the clay to make Máirtín of it and Máirtín in the clay of the graveyard all the while. Máirtín spent a large part of his life writing, solving problems with writing, trying to express himself. Now that he is dead, and Séamus is trying to express him in another way … Máirtín has changed form. Now, he's a subject rather than being an author. (He was his own subject at one time, also, just as Séamus is his own subject while he is engaged in expressing Máirtín.)

I see both of them toiling with the same problem – that is Máirtín Ó Cadhain. They both arrived at this problem and they both did their best to resolve it.[50]

---

49 *Comhar*, March 1960.

50 'Dhá thriúr', IT, 25 March 1972.

It is at this point, perhaps, that the question of public and private languages comes into play and its inadequacy in carrying both functions with it. The most important thing about the medium is that it functions to express what it seeks to express. One recalls the following words of Ó Ríordáin's: 'Not only does the individual speaker have one eye on his locality and his family but he also has an eye on his own mind and he transforms and adapts his local and family discourse accordingly.'[51] The question Ó Ríordáin often asked himself was whether he'd done enough to integrate his sensibility and world view with that of his homeplace/locality and family, or whether he had any real homeplace or family to write for, in actuality?

Had the medium of his work taken a place that was better assigned to its subject matter? Had he a subject other than the 'self'? Was he exploring that which lay beyond the inner world adequately? Wasn't the battle fought 'between you God and you the world' a reflection of poetry itself?[52] The battle would go on, the poetry, until one side or the other gave in, or until the response was issued. Maybe it wasn't the worst thing in the world to go with the flow of the world outside, rather than spending too long lingering by 'God's abandoned hearth'.[53] Outside was the community and the brotherhood of man and it was as well knowing that it was there. Rejection was hopeless if there was nothing appealing to reject; they both should go together:

Ach iarraim go mbraithfinn tarrac
An tsaoil im chroí,
Iarraim go bhfeicfinn trí Phól is a theagasc
An Pól atá thíos
Ag gliúcaíocht aníos tríd an Laidin
Is cealg ina chroí:
　　Ós amhlaidh atá, ós amhlaidh ár ngairm,
　　Is amhlaidh mo ghuí.[54]

---

51 *Scríobh 4*, p. 14.
52 ES: p. 82.
53 B: p. 20.
54 'Guí' ('*A Prayer*'), B: p. 16.

But I ask that I'd feel the appeal
of the world in my heart,
and that I'd see through Paul and his teaching
to the Paul under it, standing apart
peering slyly from beneath the Latin
with guile in his heart:
    as things are thus, as our calling is such,
    that is what I ask.[55]

Has the poet's prayer got a hearing, however? It hadn't in the case of *Eireaball Spideoige* – according to some of Ó Ríordáin's critics, anyway. Ironically, Ó Ríordáin had included another prayer in his notes as part of his entreaty – i.e. that his 'family of verses' would avoid the worst fate that he thought could befall them:

Má castar libh fear léinn sa tslí
Bhur rún ná ligidh leis, bhur sians …

Should you meet a scholar on the way
Don't reveal your secret to him, your sense …[56]

In fact, Ó Ríordáin would soon meet both in reality, and they'd include scholars both male and female.

55 Sewell, *Selected Poems*, p. 135. Trans. Colm Breathnach.
56 Trans. M Ó hAodha.

9

The Battle Commences

As with many other writers of his ilk, Ó Ríordáin had always been beset with doubts about his project, as relating to producing art in the marginalised and minority language that was Irish. There was always that sneaking combination of anxiety and fear at the back of his mind. Was he on a fool's errand, trying to carve out a place as a leading Irish-language poet? Would the authors or critics make a mockery of his work or would his life's work prove in vain? One of the first critics and writers of Irish to exacerbate such doubts in Ó Ríordáin's mind was Flann Mac an tSaoir (the pen name of Tomás Ó Floinn), who posed the question in an article of his published in the literary journal *Comhar* (May 1953) as to whether the system of emphasis the Cork poet employed in his poetry was indigenous to the Irish-language tradition. His comments (below) regarding the accent (emphasis) being placed equally 'on the syllables in each word' in Irish-language poetry from the 'beginning of time, and until it began to decline', and this still being the case 'in two of the three main dialects now left in Irish' (the exception being Munster Irish, where the emphasis is 'thrown forward onto the final syllable') is difficult to take seriously from the vantage point of today. For one thing, given the paucity of sources, it is next to impossible to make comparisons between the various historical periods of Irish, whether on the oral or written levels and with respect to any of the various dialects. And anyway, even if this was the 'native' pattern of emphasis that was common to the other dialects outside of Munster (or the 'indigenous' form, as Ó Floinn understood it) – why he should seek to find it in Ó Ríordáin's writing, given that the latter was a Munster writer, is baffling, to say the least:

> *In Irish poetry since the beginning of time, and until it began to decline, it was the norm, the model, the standard, to lay equal stress on the syllables in each word, as is*

still the case today in two of the three main dialects now left in Irish, in Connacht and Ulster. In the Munster dialect, however, it became the norm to stress the final syllable of the word. But even in Munster, this wasn't ever the normal practice for as long as poetry was being composed. Now the stress patterns of Munster Irish are being brought into poetry – for the first time ever – by Seán Ó Ríordáin. I find it surprising that no one has noticed this, as it is a minor revolution in itself.[1]

It is correct to say that Ó Floinn gives Ó Ríordáin a pass as regards the pattern of emphasis the poet utilises in his poetry – as following the system of stress in spoken Munster Irish. Again, however, what other pattern would he expect Ó Ríordáin to use? Leaving aside the doubts raised by Ó Floinn, on the dialectical and literary levels (other than to say that Ó Floinn's analysis of the question in another article published in *Comhar* the following month – June 1953 – was more measured and accurate in tone), let us examine the evidence for another, more serious 'accusation' directed at Ó Ríordáin's poetry at this juncture – i.e. the inference that his poetry was strongly affected by the English metrical system rather than the Irish-language one. Ó Floinn posits:

Now, look at the following quatrain by Seán Ó Ríordáin (An Cheist, 1.31):

Tá bás sa tsamhradh chugham gan mhoill
An stathfadh blátha roimh a thíocht.
Nó an sáithfeadh crúb go ciúin im mhian
Le súil go stathfad sa tsíoraíocht.

The fourth line here is correct as regards the form of the iamb. The poet stresses the vowel in the second syllable of the word 'tsíoraíocht.' It doesn't matter about this. But, in doing so, he is forced to stress the vowel in the word "sa". But this does matter. Because the likes of this goes contrary to the normal rhythm of the language – in speech or in poetry. You can find another hundred samples of this in Seán Ó Ríordáin's poetry.[2]

1 *Comhar*, May 1953.
2 *Comhar*, June 1953.

Is it true to say that the emphasis is on the word *sa* here or, if so, is it the poet or the critic who has highlighted this apparent emphasis? Is it actually the iamb running inside his own mind – or as felt beating beneath the line itself, even if it isn't always evident – that leads the critic to claim that Ó Ríordáin usurps the 'normal rhythm of the language'? Couldn't it also be argued that it's the reader who usurps the 'normal rhythm' in this case, by placing undue emphasis on a pattern that it isn't actually necessary to complete in its entirety anyway? In reality, every single example of the type that the critic has highlighted would have to be assessed on its own merits before one could come to any definitive conclusions in this regard; (interestingly, only one other example of this apparently English-inspired metrical rhythm is provided in the above-cited review and this is itself untrustworthy, given that the print in the text is faded and unclear).

The truth is that the question of metrics and perceived metrical systems is a sensitive one and one cannot assign an exact system or pattern to any piece of writing, independent of the context in which it is has been written. Frank O'Brien was much more sympathetic than others to Ó Ríordáin when these criticisms were first directed at his poetry. This is part of his response to those who claimed 'that his [Ó Ríordáin's] rhythms were imitative of the rhythms of the English language':

> *Firstly, no English-language rhythm exists per se. It is usual for every type of poetry to have its own rhythm and this rhythm can be identified, even if not very accurately, according to the stress structure associated with English-language poetry …*
>
> *There are many ways of identifying the rhythmic structure of a poem; these patterns are intertwined with one another; they aren't always applied with the same effect, sometimes; other times, the application (or not) of the structures depends on the thematic interpretation that people take from a particular poem. Put simply, the stress-pattern of a poem can change depending on the interpretation of that poem and from reader to reader. One might assume that this is only speculation on my part or that this is overly complex. But after all, no rhythmic structure can exist independent of anything else: the rhythm is always dependent on the subject under consideration, on the person one is conversing with, on our impression of that person, on our own health, on what time of*

the day it is – and on many other circumstances that create the character of the conversation. It is the same in the case of poetry. Poetry is equally as dependent on such similar aspects and circumstances.[3]

It may be helpful to add Ó Ríordáin's reading of this controversy at this juncture. For instance, as an addendum to his own private notes regarding O'Brien's book, the poet referenced the two primary objectives he had with his poetry: '(1) To observe humanity (2) To create a new sound pattern. Such an approach should take a prayer or an inscape or an *haecceitas* to itself – not that which it represents but rather that which it infuses itself with.' A metre is nothing more than the rhythm of the prayer that it initiates; it is from the inside out that one identifies the emergence of both.

The issue of metre in Ó Ríordáin's work was also bothering Máire Mhac an tSaoi in her review of *Eireaball Spideoige* in *Feasta*, March 1953, even if this wasn't the worst aspect of his poetry in her view. She advises Ó Ríordáin to take note of the ditty that goes: 'and the word went out in loud lamentation', similar to Seán Ó Duinnshléibhe in 'Beauty Deas an Oileáin':

A quatrain of his comes to mind:

Ní ar log na ngéan a dineadh sinne a thraenáil
Ná ar na hoileánaibh rua atá thuaidh fé bhun Imileá
Ach ar fharraigí féine go dtéann dosna lachain a snámh,
Is nár mhagúil é a dtuairim go mbuafaidís orainn an rás.

We were not trained in the place of the geese
Nor on the russet islands which are up north under Imileá
But on wild seas where the ducks are not able to swim,
What a joke that they thought they would best us in the race.[4]

(Note: A few minor errors have been corrected here; 'dineadh' rather than 'déineadh' (*loco*) is more correct in the first line.)

---

3 O'Brien, *Filíocht Ghaeilge*, pp. 330–2.
4 Trans. M. Ó hAodha.

The biggest lesson Ó Ríordáin would learn from the likes of this, in Mhac an tSaoi's opinion, is that:

> *It is the counter-rhythm here that emphasises the interaction of the conversational aspect and the metrical rhythm. This is a valuable protection against the accompanying rattle-beat assonance here, and it would do well for our poet to learn the likes of this. The first requirement for this is to be familiar with the stress-rhythms of the spoken speech, and it is very clear that he is not familiar with these …*

It is clear that it's the 'rattle-beat assonance' that's bothering her here, much as it did Tomás Ó Floinn at this juncture and even well before this; i.e. that the poems are based on the regular metrical patterns of English and that the Irish-language cadences were usurped and out of sync as a consequence.[5] That said, if one examined the quatrain Mhac an tSaoi provided as an example of the native grace that Irish-language poetry ought to reflect, it is clear that there is nothing even mildly 'radical' about Ó Ríordáin's placing the emphasis on the second syllable of the word. If the likes of 'thrae*náil*' is appropriate usage, for example, then the usage of a word such as 'tsíor*aíocht*' is no less appropriate or groundbreaking either.

In *Comhar*, May 1953, Máire Mhac an tSaoi bolsters her advice to Ó Ríordáin as follows:

> *He understands the importance of poetic form. We have his own word for this in his introduction. The person who believes in this has no right to feel complacent, standing behind the fence-wire of cheap street poetry. One can only write ballads under the auspices of the ballad rhythm. The most profound poem here has been destroyed by the petty loitering of such lines. The poem I intend discussing now in this regard is 'Oileán agus Oileán Eile'. Look at how good this verse is:*
>
> *Tá Sasanach ag iascaireacht sa loch,*
> *Tá an fhírinne ró-lom ar an oileán,*

5 *Comhar*, December 1951 and February 1952.

Ach raghad i measc na gcuimhne agus na gcloch,
Is nífead le mór-urraim mo dhá láimh.

It's no harm to compare this with the first lines of the poem 'Athalie' by Racine, Oui je viens dans son temple adorer l'Eternel. *See this now, part of the same piece:*

A Bharra, is aoibhinn liom aoibhneas do thí,
Agus caraimse áitreabh do smaointe,
Ach ní feas dom an uaitse na smaointe airím
Mar tá daoscar ar iostas im intinn.

Does anyone else see an echo of the following here: 'You are old, Father William'?[6]

Seán Ó Tuama's response to Mhac an tSaoi, and it was an immediate one (and one of a number of responses she received with respect to her initial critique in March), was simply that there was 'superb craftsmanship evident in that verse'; he also posed the question 'Does anyone recognise the echo from *"Domine dilexi decorum [sic] …"* and "Cnocáinín Aerach Chill Mhuire" in these lines?'[7]

Even if Mhac an tSaoi was correct with regard to her doubts concerning Ó Ríordáin's use of gurgle-sound/assonance (and Ó Tuama thought that she was, apparently), he didn't need to apologise for such use of internal rhyme, irrespective of whether it was in English, Irish or in Latin (or all three languages) that he wrote his line. I don't believe that Ó Ríordáin would have put it like this, as Ó Tuama did, however:

There is gurgle-sound assonance evident in that verse, it's true, when read immediately after the measured quatrain that precedes it. Didn't Máire Mhac an tSaoi understand that this was entirely deliberate on the poet's part? *Is it that she didn't read the second section of this poem, the entire theme of which is that same gurgling rhythm which infused the poet's mind? Is it that she didn't understand the meaning of the line that followed the above quatrain?:*

6 Taken from 'You are Old, Father William' (1865) by Lewis Carroll.
7 *Comhar,* April 1953.

Le bréithre gan bhrí,
Le bodhaire na mblian
Thuirling clúmh liath
Ar mo smaointe.

From words without fervour
and the deafness of my years,
there is a mossy mould
growing over my thoughts.[8]

The 'controversy' went quiet for a while then, until Frank O'Brien returned to the fray once more. He sought neither to attack nor defend Ó Ríordáin, and neither did he use the terms 'gurgle' or 'assonance' but rather the 'ordering' of the lines. It's the same verse ('A Bharra, is aoibhinn liom', etc.) that's under consideration again here:

> *There is as much order in these lines written to Saint Finbarr as there is in the iambs we mentioned earlier. But, within the orderliness, a graceful movement underscores the lines that makes this a major poem. The stress on every alternate syllable is four/three [four stressed syllables in lines 1 and 3, and three stressed syllables in lines 2 and 4 is the pattern apparent here] and your word 'bá' aside, iambic pentameter is the most common movement in the lines here. Elsewhere in the poem, the tempo is often changed but each change entails an internal cohesion that demonstrates Ó Ríordáin is a master of a rhythm when he wants to be.*[9]

Clearly, opinions differed on the question of Ó Ríordáin's use of metre and rhythm in *Eireaball Spideoige* and given the sensitivity and complexity of the issue at hand, the old Irish phrase 'mór saítho, becc torbai' ('*to commit no evil, to act bravely*') doesn't seem out of place here.

The next aspect of the Ó Ríordáin's reviews was one that took up a good deal of the critic's time and had more significance in ways – this was the issue of whether Ó Ríordáin's use of the Irish language was proper or

8 Sewell, *Selected Poems*, p. 89. Trans. Denise Blake.
9 O'Brien, *Filiocht Ghaeilge*, p. 334.

correct. This issue proved most divisive amongst the Irish-language critics, and discussions regarding his alleged 'lack of mastery of the language' hurt Ó Ríordáin most of all. Whatever criticisms he might possibly have envisaged with respect to his extending of tradition and the use of new forms and rhythms, he could never have imagined that his Irish-language inheritance on the familial level would be questioned or denied him – as Ó Ríordáin saw it. While it is a continuous undercurrent in her various reviews, it was in the essay below that Máire Mhac an tSaoi most seriously attacked Ó Ríordáin's (in her view) inaccurate Irish:

> *The most heartfelt aspect of this book is what he says on its cover where he demonstrates his desire to express himself comfortably in a language that isn't too far away from the Irish Gaeltacht. If he's serious when he states this, then he ought to have good sense enough to fill his head with this type of Irish for as long as he has opportunity to do so. He focuses his efforts for a while on reading rather than writing, on listening rather than talking; and let him hope that this isn't too late for him, and that he is still capable of learning, and that there are still masters out there that can teach him.*
>
> *Because one of the difficulties associated with Irish is that it is a living language. One can't experiment too much with her without doing her mischief. One especially can't make a new designation that a particular type of Irish is really Irish if it is actually a specific type of English, or do this solely in order to facilitate one particular writer. The result of such a discourse is that it says nothing at all and consists of a series of signs that can't be read without a key. If we were dealing with a dead language, there would be no loss in this, even if it wouldn't be of any benefit to it either. It is another thing altogether when one is usurping a language that has a long-established history of catering to all human needs. This would be a crime against culture that would only result in a bizarre form of language as made available to a small group of individuals. This is the violent death that threatens the Irish language. Those who use it as a medium who will succeed in squeezing every bit of substance and nature that is left in it, and kill it off altogether during the experiment. It would be a tragedy if it were someone such as Ó Ríordáin, someone who is talented and coming into his own, who was to partake in such treachery and all because he received indiscrete praise for the faults in his use of Irish.*

> *There is no doubt that this poet has a natural talent for composing in Irish. Undoubtedly, this type of creativity is to the benefit of the language. It needs to be restrained, however, and in particular, the living language should not be unjustly and unnaturally bent out of shape. One terrible effort that fails is far more damaging than the value of all the successful efforts combined. Ó Ríordáin is right to remind us that there is no aspect of the modern mind today that can't be expressed through Irish. It would be dangerous for him to think that he has demonstrated such a thought, when what he has written isn't Irish at all.*

It takes her a while but eventually she gets around to identifying particular examples, which she considers demonstrate a 'misunderstanding of the meaning of words or, to put it bluntly, ordinary bad Irish' in Ó Ríordáin's writing. At first glance, and even assuming for a moment that she was correct about the points she highlighted, it is difficult to see how the following meagre examples support the 'build-up' or the seriousness of the claims Mhac an tSaoi has just made:

> *Experience and study will teach the poet that it is* ligeann liú *or* tá ag liúraigh *that is required where he currently has* tá ag liú *[ES: 100]; that the Paidrín Páirteach is a prayer and not a rosary [ES: 65]; and that the world will be filled* de náire *and not* le náire *[ES: 66] if such were to happen at all. These are minor points, but a poet's conscience ought not to countenance them. A more dangerous misuse again is this one:* 'Tá drúis sa chime-scaoileadh' *[ES: 98]. This is a sentence that would remind you of the pattern* 'Pity is a vice' *in English, but it's difficult to figure out what in the world the Irish used here means.*

Three writers responded to Mhac an tSaoi on these specific points and on other issues: Seán Ó Tuama, Máirín Ní Mhuiríosa (*Feasta*, April) and Máirtín Ó Direáin (*Feasta*, May). Máirtín Ó Direáin was the most senior of these writers and the one with the best credentials to comment; interestingly, he'd been one of the first highly regarded poets in Ireland to identify Ó Ríordáin's poetic talent at an early stage, when he'd been amongst a select group of judges for the 1943 Oireachtas prize, awarded to Ó Ríordáin's poem 'An Leigheas'. 'We knew immediately that we'd caught a lobster' was his comment on that occasion.[10] Both other writers had written important reviews of Ó Ríordáin's work even before *Eireaball Spideoige* was published for the first time: Máirín Ní Mhuiríosa in *Feasta,* September 1950, and Seán Ó Tuama in *An Síol* 1949–50 and again in the introduction to *Nuabhéarsaíocht.* As part of her response to the controversy, Máirín Ní Mhuiríosa wrote:

> *[Máire Mhac an tSaoi] bluntly criticises the Irish of the poet but she supports her criticism with just a few minor points ... She reminds us that Irish is a living language and that one can't stretch it too far without causing damage to it. This is true, but isn't a poet allowed to shape his language to a certain degree if this helps him to express his thoughts in a clearer and more innovative way? If it could be proved that Seán Ó Ríordáin did so much damage to the Irish language that he actually tore it from its natural roots, he'd deserve criticism. But can this be proved?*

Seán Ó Tuama opined that this hadn't been proven and neither had it occurred. He made no attempt to defend Ó Ríordáin's use of the phrase 'phaidrín páirteach' but defended him with respect to his Irish in the poems as a whole:

> *The phrase 'tá ag liú' is just as correct as 'tá ag liúraigh' ('ligeann liú'). Ó Ríordáin has both (cf. Dinneen; Father Peadar). The phrase 'líon le náire' is as correct as 'líon de náire' (cf. McKenna 'full'; Dinneen 'líonta', 'tuillte'). The words 'Tá drúis sa chime-scaoileadh' are as correct as 'Tá dainséar sa chime-scaoileadh.'*

Máirtín Ó Direáin's response was similar and equally accurate:

> *The world can be filled* with *shame,* with *grief,* with *joy (i.e.* le *náire,* le *brón,* le *háthas) as much as it can be* de *all of these things. I myself have never heard the word* de *used in such cases, until I read this. I don't feel that it's bad Irish to say 'Tá drúis sa chime-scaoileadh'; and I still don't understand how this could be bad Irish, I have to admit. She is correct in relation to the Rosary ... The Rosary is a prayer or a series of prayers of course, and it couldn't be sweating ... A rosary*

10 *Combar,* May 1977.

> *beads is the apparatus ... or the stones/beads with which each prayer is recited but the word 'páirtín' wouldn't be used just after it.*

This was Ó Direáin's reading of the situation:

> *I'm not saying that Máire Mhac an tSaoi's review is knowingly unjust, but when a poet is accused of bad Irish and when this claim, or parts of it, is subsequently proven to be false, then all that needs to be done is that a humble apology be given to the poet.*

No apology was forthcoming, however. The most powerful response in such circumstances is no response at all – or so they say. And although Máire Mhac an tSaoi took no part in the debate that followed on that very critical review of hers, it can be argued that some sections of an article by her entitled 'Scríbhneoireacht sa Ghaeilge Inniu' ('*Writing in Irish Today*') and published in *Studies,* Spring 1955, were actually a follow-on or continuation of the controversy. Moreover, rather than toning down her previous criticisms, she intensified them instead. Ó Ríordáin's writing was now a form of Esperanto in her view: 'For as long as his Irish remains an (artificial) imitation of English, he only has a sort of Esperanto.' Aside from that one individual example that she offered in her *Feasta* review – the far-fetched comparison between 'Tá drúis sa chimescaoileadh' as imitative of the English-language pattern 'Pity is a vice' – Mhac an tSaoi provided no evidence to back up her assertion in this instance. The same was true with regard to her comment regarding 'signs that cannot be read without a key' that she repeated in this latest essay. No examples or evidence to bolster this assertion were provided. The sole instance where she could find fault with his Irish was with regard to the following (the meaning that's ascribed to the 'Family Rosary'), an example which escaped the notice of those who rose to Ó Ríordáin's defence (other than Máirín Ní Mhuiríosa, who questioned this particular usage) and even if we accept the few minor errors that are evident in Ó Ríordáin's poems, they are hardly enough that his writing constitutes a 'sort of Esperanto'.

The greatest irony in all of this was the fact that Ó Ríordáin himself would never have claimed that his Irish was entirely faultless. In fact, even when the battle of the critics was being waged at its most intense around him, he wrote a report-type letter to Donncha Ó Laoghaire saying: 'I'm the first to admit that my Irish is weak compared to the likes of Peig Sayers. Why wouldn't it be? It's both a source of despair and joy to me when I hear the people in Dunquin speaking Irish.' It would come as some considerable relief to Ó Ríordáin when scholar Séamas Caomhánach, a man whose Irish-language credentials were impeccable, said years later that no one had ever really had Irish.[11]

Not that this meant the critics wouldn't write what was on their minds and what they wished to say. And, while he didn't respond publicly to Máire Mhac an tSaoi's criticisms when, by rights, he should have, he always had it in for her after this and when he eventually saw an opportunity to get her back, he did. And even if he didn't mention her name publicly as of yet, there was no doubt whom his sarcastic comment regarding the 'aphorists that are around today' and their meaningless words was directed at in his essay 'Teangacha Príobháideacha' ('*Private Languages*'). He'd go closer to the bone again with reference to Mhac an tSaoi in some of his *Irish Times* articles at a later date.

The piece below is taken from the essay 'Teangacha Príobháideacha' and even if it's not so much an attack as a form of ridicule, a bitter laughter underscores it nonetheless. It is attack as a form of defence – whereby Ó Ríordáin subtly defends his work and the thought processes that have underpinned it for years, and even if he includes himself amongst the 'aphorists' here, it's despite his best efforts that he's amongst them – if he is indeed to be included in their company at all, that is. It's the opposite of such linguistic swagger or showing-off that best defines the writers, Ó Ríordáin says, and the same is true for the work of art itself, the language, the tradition:

> *There are Irish writers, however, and they spend their time creating sentences, each of which is more rustic and ragged and overstated than the next, and dragging them into their writing so that everyone will know how great their Irish is. This is a disgusting sight, however; watching them preening themselves,*

11 'Banfhilíocht agus Teanga', IT, 27 November 1975.

> *like cats, with their amazing Irish. It is a sin against the light, this false Irish. One clearly comprehensible phrase by itself would be enough, without overdoing it completely. Writing is a form of sifting and filtering, not a process where you lay it on thick; it's an awakening of language, not a drowning of it. This fancying up and luxuriating in language is a form of suffocation. Father Peadar Ó Laoghaire started the spread of this disease the first day ever but, if so, it was as a teacher that he did it, and he was able to incorporate this aspect into his own writing without doing it too much harm. It was his example that ruined us and most of us are brazen idiom-makers ever since. Father Peadar was a native speaker of Irish and even if the number of sayings and idioms he used were excessive, they were part of a greater whole, i.e. organic. He had the basic shoe even if it was too decorated or full of trimmings. But the idiom-makers who are around these days, especially those who don't have the language from its source, they are just all decoration and no shoe, or, to put it in a more disgusting or more accurate way still, they are all just puffed-up poseurs without substance. There is a fundamental dishonesty at the core of this constant use of idioms and sayings.*[12]

As Ó Ríordáin saw it, it was dishonest to deny the two aspects that underlay every form of artistic expression – i.e. the private convictions and the private language that had to become public in the form of poetic expression; one ought to acknowledge the fact that the most private and truthful thoughts and emotions only became art if they were faithfully expressed through the medium of public idiom. The thinking upon which Ó Ríordáin based 'Teangacha Príobháideacha' appears in increasingly edited form in his diary entries for the years 1956–7. (While the final essay 'Teangacha Príobháideacha' didn't appear in print until 1963, he did use some of it as part of a talk he gave on Raidió Éireann in 1958.) Most of his talk was based on his own hard-earned experience as a poet, but he likely received confirmation for some of his ideas about writing and literature from books that he may have been reading at the time. On 26 August 1958 Ó Ríordáin mentions two books that he'd been given to read by Séamus Ó Coigligh 'recently when I was giving talks on private languages on Raidio Éireann'. The books in question were *Essays*

12 *Scríobh 4*, p. 21.

on Language and Literature (ed. J. L. Hevesi) and *Concerning Marxism in Linguistics* (by J. R. Stalin). The first book was the most important of the two for Ó Ríordáin and it's not difficult to understand why; the essay by Paul Valéry entitled 'Poetry and Abstract Thought', for example, is a piece which ends as follows:

> *Think of all that goes on inside a man before he can give voice to a single intelligible phrase, and then calculate all that must occur in order that a poem by Keats or Baudelaire may take form upon the blank sheet of paper lying under the poet's eye.*
>
> *Think, too, that of all the arts, ours is perhaps the one that has to co-ordinate the largest number of independent parts or factors: sound, sense, reality, imagination, syntax and the double invention of substance and form … and all this through that most severely practical of all media, the perpetually changing, muddied, maid-of-all-work, our common language, from which we must evoke a pure and ideal Voice capable of communicating, without weakness, without apparent effort, without offending the ear and without breaking that sphere of the poetic universe which has been created in a moment of time – an idea which shall express a* self *that is miraculously superior to* Me.

I don't know whether Ó Ríordáin had ever read John Press' book *The Chequer'd Shade*, a book that follows a similar line of reasoning as Ó Ríordáin's: in fact, the extract Ó Ríordáin included from Ezra Pound concerning the place of literature in the *res publica* also appears in this book. Given that Press didn't publish his book until 1958, however, and the fact that Ó Ríordáin never mentions it at any stage – and it would've been strange for him not to, I think – then it's likely that both writers came to the same philosophical conclusions regarding poetry independently of one another.

The 'war of words' between Ó Ríordáin and his critics, and the arguments regarding the use of language, would rumble on for another while yet, with further comments concerning the use of syntax and the copula in Irish poetry. Ó Ríordáin entered the fray himself on occasion, for example: 'Tradition has it by now that nearly every review of an Irish-language work has to find some faults in the language used, even when there is no defect to be found in the text. Máire Mhac an tSaoi isn't without skill in this area. Let's return to our explorations …'[13] This is a subject for discussion later in this volume, however.

Unsurprisingly, Ó Ríordáin gave considerable time to any changes or 'minor edits' he wished to include for the second edition of *Eireaball Spideoige*, some of which had no connection with his use of language, for example, 'Sin capall Mháire ag dul thar bráid' instead of 'Sin capall X uasail ag dul ar an aonach', or omitting the sentence 'Ní féidir liom anam éinne a shamhlú le rud ar bith eile'.[14] There were a few other minor edits that did relate to the fine-tuning and improvement of language usage, however. These included changing the famous line 'Allas ar phaidrín páirteach' to 'Allas ar phaidrín brúite im láimh'.[15] He didn't pay any heed to any other potential changes as identified in earlier reviews, however. Any other additional changes or improvements he made off his own bat, including 'A sheanfhilí múinídh dom glao' and 'Inis Tuaisceart' instead of 'A sheanfhilí múin dom an glao' and 'Inis Tuaiscirt'.[16] Not that Ó Ríordáin was too easy to deal with on these various changes, however, as evidenced from the letters he sent to Seán Ó hÉigeartaigh's wife, Bríghid, at the time – the various edits to the text were made towards the end of 1969 and the beginning of 1970. The following, for example, as written on 16 December 1969:

> *As for the cover: There's no need for anything on the cover. It's not as if you'd think I'd include something about myself on that. Máire Mhac an Daoi [sic] would do that for you … In the first edition of* Eir. Spid. *there were three mistakes: that I left Ballyvourney when I was five instead of fifteen … McEnteeeee and her gang got great mileage out of that … I asked Seán [Ó hÉigeartaigh], may God have mercy on him, when they were bringing out* Brosna *to say that this mistake had been made in* Eir. Spid. *He said that it was all right just to have the correct information on the new book. Anyway, the less that's said, the better.*

13 'Banfhilíocht agus Teanga', IT, 27 November 1975.

14 ES: p. 9.

15 *Ibid.*, p. 65.

16 *Ibid.*, pp. 36 and 95.

Or the following, which came afterwards again as relating to the same issue in another letter from him, dated 22 January 1970:

> *What you have to put on the cover of* Eir. Spid. *is concise and to the point. I'm always finding fault with my own Irish and rightly so. I wonder should I be writing in Irish at all when you live somewhere where your Irish isn't getting any daily sustenance. Signs on it, I write very little. But Máire Vac an Daoi [sic]. I know that I hate everyone of that breed ... But what I'm getting to is this: I don't know whether I like this on the cover 'Le ceartúcháin an fhile'. [The poet's corrections included.] This is correct. If it wasn't for the aforementioned woman I'd let it go. Instead of 'correction' would you be happy with this: 'with some changes made by the author himself'. I wonder whether you should refer to me as a poet. I'm agreeing with Mary McEntee now. She said previously that I'd made mistakes that weren't mistakes at all e.g. 'líonaim* le *náire.' As you probably remember, I made this correction to the text: 'A sheanfhilí múinídh dom glao' instead of 'A sheanfhilí múin dom glao' which is clearly incorrect. That said, I often heard Eoghan Ó Súilleabháin finishing one of his radio programmes with 'seachain sibh féin' rather than 'seachnaídh sibh féin.' Máirtín Ó Murchú said that to me that this is an error that's common everywhere in the Gaeltacht, even in Scotland.*

It would be a brave person at the best of times who would claim to know what was right or wrong in terms of language usage or what was deemed beyond the bounds of legitimacy. The main theme of the essay 'Teangacha Príobháideacha' is that the poet ought to inhabit the border region that is insight and language. If the poet should happen to traverse that boundary and wander over into the region of madness, obscurity or confusion, then he is essentially sacrificing himself or selling out his craft.

In such circumstances it is the role of the critic, who is the arbiter of the public voice or language, to guide the poet back on track – in Ó Ríordáin's case, this was the road west to Dunquin. It should be said, however, that this was a road that Ó Ríordáin had journeyed often – and well before Máire Mhac an tSaoi recommended it to him. As we shall see, there would be some confusion as to what Mhac an tSaoi actually meant by this recommendation of hers, confusion that lingered on well after the event.

If one assumes for a moment that Mhac an tSaoi's review published in *Feasta* was an in-depth analysis of Ó Ríordáin's poetry (and it clearly wasn't in some parts, given various unsubstantiated criticisms that she made), the controversy regarding *Eireaball Spideoige* that ensued in the pages of *The Irish Times* in January and February 1953 was of a different hue. The columnist known as 'Thersites' (Thomas Woods) initiated the discussion on 10 January with his article 'Private Views'. He began his essay by praising Ó Ríordáin's poetry, particularly given the historical, literary and linguistic environment in which he was working. 'Thersites' then focused on the main issue he saw with regard to his poetry – i.e. the context in which he was writing Irish and the communicative aspects of same:

> *[Ó Ríordáin] has an interesting and sensitive mind, and possesses remarkable skill in rendering his poetic thought into a language of which he is not a native speaker. This should be enough to guarantee that his first book is valuable, though difficult, reading. Yet, I confess to a little doubt in my mind. There can be no doubt of Mr. Ó Ríordáin's quality as a poet in the abstract. But has he chosen the best channel for communicating? It must be extraordinarily difficult to write poetry in a language that is not native to one (in fact, I suspect that it has never been done). But the problem seems to me almost insoluble, if to this you add the difficulty of your audience. For to whom are Mr. Ó Ríordáin's poems addressed? Hardly to native speakers, who would find difficulty in appreciating fully their import – not only from differences of environment (Mr. Ó Ríordáin is a city dweller), but also because, no matter how excellent Mr. Ó Ríordáin's command of the language is, it can never comprehend that instinctive feel for the connotations of words and phrases that only a native speaker can have. It is possible for classical dons to write Latin and Greek verse, grammatically and metrically beyond reproach and of considerable charm for modern readers; but these verses would indubitably have seemed rather meaningless and possibly absurd to an ancient Roman or Greek. Mr. Ó Ríordáin's audience is rather like that of the classical dons: it is people, like myself, who have acquired Irish in school and at college, and the communication involved must necessarily be somewhat artificial. In other words, it is difficult to avoid the impression that what is going on is a highly ingenious but academic exercise, which, whatever its charm, has really very little to do with poetry.*

These were all pertinent questions as relating to poetry and to Irish-language writing generally, and Ó Ríordáin responded to them as best he could in an article which was published in the same newspaper, *The Irish Times*, entitled: 'In vacuo'.[17] Unfortunately perhaps, 'Thersites' didn't apply his thoughts with reference to any specific poems of Ó Ríordáin's but spoke in a more general way about poetry in Irish, a point made by publisher Seán Ó hÉigeartaigh in a letter published in *The Irish Times* on 15 January:

> *Although 'Thersites' has made Ó Ríordáin's poems the occasion of his disquisition of the importance of writing in one's native language, he has not rested his theories on any criticism of the content of the poems.*

This letter didn't seem to faze 'Thersites' unduly and he reiterated his doubts concerning Ó Ríordáin's poems in a piece published in *The Irish Times* on 24 January (1973):

> *I still think that a man who is not a native speaker of Irish and has lived most of his life in an English-speaking environment, and whose work can be directed only to an artificial, non-native-speaking audience, cannot write poetry in Irish in the accepted meaning of the word, and I am convinced neither by Mr. O'Riordan's [sic] work nor by Mr. Ó hÉigeartaigh's special pleading … While there is a real Irish there is no room for pseudo-Irish and least of all, for pseudo-Irish poetry.*

Needless to say, Thersites' sole authority for assigning Ó Ríordáin's work to the category of 'pseudo-Irish poetry' was the theory he himself had postulated. This time it was Máirtín Ó Direáin who responded to what the columnist had said. 'Thersites', he argued, was incorrect in his assumptions on the theoretical and practical levels. As Ó Direáin opined:

> *In any case 'Thersites' has made no real attempt to show how the work of Seán Ó Ríordáin falls short of the standard he, 'Thersites', would expect from a native*

17 IT, 6 May 1972.

> *speaker. One wonders why? Surely this would be the only honest method of criticism in a case like this.*[18]

Meanwhile, Seán Ó hÉigeartaigh and 'Thersites' had begun to bandy about the names of some of the writers who'd successfully written poetry in a idiom that was not their native language. (Ó hÉigeartaigh had admitted in his first letter that Ó Ríordáin wasn't an Irish speaker.) Some of the best-known writers were mentioned and the list of names extended far beyond Ireland also. In the end, Brendan Behan couldn't stomach such literary musings any longer and intervened in the debate with a typically down-to-earth contribution:

> *In Saturday's paper [24 January] 'Thersites' had a 'sudden sinking feeling that somebody was going to miss his point and bring up the glib text-book stuff about Merrill, Moréas and Apollinaire.' In between times he must have remembered something; for on the opposite page he tells us that he will shortly get round to making up his mind and describing the disturbances within caused him by the works of Samuel Beckett.*
>
> *The French have made up some time ago their minds about the works of Mr. Beckett ... 'Thersites' informs us that there are parts of Ireland where Irish is the living language. He may be right. I was never far enough out of Dublin to find out what goes on in the bog. I see them all running out of it ... I don't see, however, that Seán Ó Ríordáin, born in Baile Mhuirne, is not as well entitled to write in Irish as Samuel Beckett, born in Dublin, is to write in French. Both are friends of mine, and bedamned if I'll make fish of one and flesh of the other.*
>
> *Though, when all is said and done, I do not think Ó Ríordáin will be much the worse of 'Thersites', nor Samuel Beckett anything the better of a pull on the peak of the caubeen from him.*[19]

Patrick Kavanagh then entered the fray with two letters: on 24 January and 2 February. 'Thersites' might have been lacking in any textual examples

18 IT, 29 January 1973.

19 IT, 28 January 1973.

to back up his theory on Irish-language poetry but Kavanagh required no evidence at all apparently to assert that the subject under consideration – i.e. poetry written in Irish – was nothing but 'the doodling and phrase-making of mediocrities'. It was irrelevant if one didn't understand Irish or poetry written in Irish – as in Kavanagh's own case, for example – that shouldn't hinder someone from judging it, he claimed; if Seán Ó Ríordáin was a true poet, then this should be obvious just by seeing him walking along the street. Seán Ó hÉigeartaigh might have spotted Ó Ríordáin walking along the street a number of times, but this didn't preclude Kavanagh from saying that Ó Ríordáin definitely wasn't a real poet. Or as Kavanagh put it in his first letter:

> *If Seán Ó Ríordáin is a poet, one might well say that it would be a good thing to read him before judging him. But this, for the reasons given, is not always necessary. As Gertrude Stein would say: A poet is a poet even in his walking down a street. And judging by what Whitehead calls 'the act of negative prehension', I would be inclined to think that anyone Mr Ó hÉigeartaigh thought a poet would surely be the opposite.*

Kavanagh got 'caught' nicely on this one, however, because Seán Ó Ríordáin was just one of many poets whom Seán Ó hÉigeartaigh had regularly spotted passing him on the street and as Ó hÉigeartaigh responded:

> *This is extremely embarrassing for both of us, because I have always thought Mr. Kavanagh a poet – and not merely from having seen him walk down a street.*[20]

The to-and-fro in *The Irish Times* had barely come to an end when the 'controversy' was begun again anew in *Inniu*. The writer C.Ó.N. (Ciarán Ó Nualláin) had his own particular 'understanding' of the history of Irish and of Christianity and he added his tuppence-worth on 30 January 1953. One ought not to take the representation of animals in Irish-language literature – to take but one example – too seriously, he advised, because

20 IT, 27 January 1973.

to do so would have run counter to the world view of our ancestors who'd placed great emphasis on 'the truth':

> *It's an ancient, sensible and Christian habit in Irish literature not to take animals too seriously. This view has a 'Pangur Bán' in the story of Mochua's three jewels and in 'Druimín'... Laughter is more important than fondness and grief in these stories. Ó Ríordáin abandons this tradition, as based on the truth, on the proposition, on the 'conceit', that is without truth:*
>
> *Do deineadh díom leathchat*
> *Ba dhuine an cat dá réir*
>
> *A poem must always contain the truth.*

One wouldn't have minded these criticisms so much if he'd left it at that – as some of the other letters to *The Irish Times* had – but he didn't. Ó Nualláin went much further on the same theme, delivering his judgement in the same solemn style. He had problems with other aspects of Ó Ríordáin's collection, and said that some of the subjects he'd explored should never have been examined in poetry given how odd they were: 'The strange concepts explored in poems such as "Roithleán", "Na Fathaigh", "Ceol", "Fan!", "Feithideacht", "Cláirseach Sean na nGnáthrud" should never be the subject of poetry.' Ó Nualláin regarded the introduction to the collection as odd and ridiculous in equal measure. He denigrated Ó Ríordáin's use of the word 'paidir' (prayer) in *Eireaball Spideoige* and then dismissed the collection as a whole in the following terms:

> *It's best for me not to say anything about the ridiculous ideas here concerning the soul, concerning eternity, concerning Christ's Body, etc., that float to us through metaphorical speech, like clouds emerging through the fog, as based on some amazing meaning that Seán reads into the words 'geit' and 'cimilt' and the aforementioned 'paidir'.*
>
> *It was really stupid to publish this introduction.*

Ó Nualláin didn't neglect to fulfil another aspect of the Irish-language review tradition by finding fault with the line 'Thit réal na gealaí i scamall-sparán'.[21] He commented that 'This sentence is a complete and utter Anglicism, in terms of both thought and language.' Máirtín Ó Direáin saw the sentence and its import completely differently. The only fault he could find with it was that he hadn't thought of it himself! 'I have to say that I saw nothing wrong with this sentence when I first read it, only that it was terrible that it wasn't me who'd thought of it.'[22]

Given that they were mainly philosophical issues that Ó Nualláin highlighted in his critique rather than grammatical questions, these formed the bulk of ensuing correspondence in the journal's pages. The main bone of contention was the 'lay baptism' or looser interpretation that Ó Ríordáin had applied to various theological terms and the critics weren't long citing various leading theological writers and experts to support their arguments and interpretations of Ó Ríordáin's poetry. The critic Máire Bhreathnach based her reading of Ó Ríordáin's theological musings on the Bible (13 February), although she also referenced '*A Companion to the Summa,* Vol. 1, p. 332'. For his part, Sean Ó Tuama mentioned Saint Thomas' '*De Veritate,* C2, A2' and Saint Paul's 'Romans VIII, 19–22' (20 February). Máirtín Ó Direáin was left in the 'haepenny place', given his sole reliance on the *Catechism,* not that it didn't bolster his argument. Peadar Bairéad, on the other hand, couldn't see fault in Ó Ríordáin's 'Introduction' other than to say that perhaps 'Seán Ó Ríordáin forgot about God' (27 February). Ciarán Ó Nualláin circled the wagons and returned to the scrap again, lashing out all over the place (6 March). He even engaged an anonymous theologian to better explain the issues more clearly given that 'There's probably none of us involved in this controversy who's a philosophical expert' and published his view on Ó Ríordáin's use of theological terms in his poetry (March 13). The same theologian doesn't really come down on Ó Ríordáin's side with respect to the poet's theological explorations or expertise:

21 ES: p. 41.

22 *Inniu,* 20 February.

> *... and this is the biggest weakness in the Introduction: a lack of precision in the use of terms that have had a precise meaning for hundreds of years. It is clear, of course, that Ó Ríordáin writes not as a theologian but as a poet. All the same, anyone who interprets terms such as 'soul' and 'prayer' too loosely will find nothing but a twisted form of the truth in the end.*

Seán Ó Tuama admitted that he was neither a philosopher nor a theologian himself, but that this didn't mean he couldn't source the information he required – Dr James O'Mahony, Professor of Philosophy in Cork, was placed at his disposal for this – albeit that Ó Tuama contradicted him point-by-point a short while later (20 March). C.Ó.N. didn't forget to add a revised appendix (incorporating theological terms etc.) to his subsequent refutation of Ó Tuama when it appeared in print. The last word went to Peadar Bairéad (20 March), who had changed his mind because he now understood that C. Ó. N. was 'dead-serious' in his argumentation and 'also a philosopher' to boot. His argument went the full circle and concluded with: 'From the philosophical perspective, I'm of the same mind as C.Ó.N. as I amn't happy with the philosophical aspects of the Introduction.' That was the end of the 'kerfuffle' and not before time, either.

In essence, Ó Ríordáin's 'Introduction' was a poem that went astray in the form of prose (in similar fashion – the poem titled 'Paidreoireacht' ('*Prayer*'), is prose gone astray.)[23] As Ó Ríordáin wrote to an Bráthair Ó Muimhneacháin on 12 February 1952, when the controversy regarding his 'Introduction' was at its height:

> *As for that introduction, it was going to be a poem initially. I had some notes written for it. Then, before I had a chance to write the poem, I was asked to a lecture and I used these notes for it. Then, lacking enough time again, I used the lecture as the introduction to the book. Out of cheekiness and a lack of humility again, because, as you know, I have no knowledge of philosophy.*[24]

23 ES: pp. 108–9.

24 *Agus*, April 1980.

He provided the same interpretation, and made the same distinction between poetry and philosophy, when he said in an article for the editor of *An Stól* a long time afterwards:

> *... this Introduction consisted of notes made for a poem that I intended writing. I knew that I'd got a small spark in relation to the word 'prayer', and I had a particular meaning with the word 'prayer' in this instance. I was then asked to give a lecture in Cork, and instead of composing a poem as based on the notes, I put them together for the lecture and then as an introduction to that book. Well, the spark that would be suitable for a poem wouldn't work for a logical statement ...*[25]

It is clear that the first section of the 'Introduction', where he describes the child and the horse praying in one another's chapels, was based on his diary entries. It's the opposite to 'Malairt' ('*Switch*'):[26]

> *But the child – it hears the sound of the horse. It tastes the sound of the horses for the sake of the sound itself. And it listens to the sound of fading and falling back into the silence. And it is amazed at this sound and amazed at the silence. And it considers the hind legs of the horse and is surprised at their authority and their ancient nature. And the world is filled with horse-wonder and trot-magic. That is to be ... to be enthralled by another dimension. And I think that this is poetry.*

And it is really Ó Ríordáin himself, as we saw earlier, who has assumed the role of the child-poet in his room, listening to the voices of the night and trying to preserve the authority and 'antiquity' of the forms beyond.

The mistake that Ó Ríordáin made in his 'Introduction', if mistake it was, was to go beyond the scope of his experience as relating to philosophical issues which he'd thought out and felt but didn't have the appropriate terminology to express fully. He'd had the temerity to wander beyond his 'patch' and he was quickly told this and sent off home again.

25 *An Stól*, 1969.
26 ES: p. 63.

Because the publication of *Eireaball Spideoige* was itself a journey, a journey the directions of which he was only learning along the way. More importantly, the book was a journey out amongst the people, including various intellectuals, and as Ó Ríordáin always knew deep inside, not every friend remains entirely loyal. There were those who defended him and the 'Introduction', but there weren't enough of them. Ó Ríordáin even suspected that one of his closest friends of all, Fr Valkenburg, was actually the 'anonymous' theologian cited in *Inniu*: 'Got a very friendly letter this morning from Fr Valkenburg but I know (although he doesn't know that I know) that he wrote an essay in *Inniu*, criticising my Introduction in *Eireaball Spideoige*,' is how the poet put it in the diary.[27] That wasn't the worst of it either (because, at least, Ó Ríordáin could say that his 'Introduction' was more of an adopted child to his poetic work, as compared with his family of poems, anyway); most embarrassing of all was that the poet had revealed so much about his most intimate thoughts and philosophical outlook in the poems and now they'd received a resounding rejection from the world at large. After all, these poems of his hadn't been composed as a bit of fun or as a hobby but had emerged from a great deal of torment and suffering. And this was the treatment he was getting!

He understands now whom the unforgiving rabble of the night are. They have bayed loud and clear from the darkness outside and revealed themselves. They are his neighbour, his friend, his enemy and the critic – those who were born to the task of crushing the individual and his sensibility. Not that you should ever really have expected anything different from them. Go out your door in the early morning or later that evening and they will be waiting for you there, all friendly and welcoming – and wearing that half-smirk that is really a jeer of mockery on their faces. Stay indoors and they will come to you via the radio or just via your thoughts. You don't need any more proof – they are there all right, all the time, even if you can't see them. And sure enough, they will gather around you in the darkness when night falls and suck all the life from you, the same as the illness that darkens your lungs. You will wake in a cold sweat and a panic some night in a Dunquin lodging house, sure that you are being choked

27 23 February 1956.

to death, physically and metaphorically; the crowd you thought had left you alone have returned because they had never really gone away in the first place.

Crisis

Ní chuala go bhfios dom glór na ndaoine
Ag filleadh on rince sa doircheacht,
Ach do bhraitheas líonrith san aer im thimpeall –
Is bhí a fhios agam,
Gan iad a chlos,
Go rabhadar fillte bhí an t-aer im thimpeall chomh coillte acu.[28]

Crisis

I did not hear, as far as I know, the voice of the people
Returning from the dance in the dark,
But I felt an agitation in the air around me –
And I knew,
Without hearing them,
That they had returned, the air around me was so destroyed by them.[29]

The rabble that shouted out outside his window long ago were never half as menacing as this rabble. This new rabble is a knowledgeable and educated lot and they hold all the aces. The world is alive with claustrophobia and paranoia all over again, the hatred of fear and the fear of hatred – it has all come back …

The first of the diaries which mentions the various reviews of *Eireaball Spideoige* and Ó Ríordáin's reaction to them is the one spanning February 1953 to 8 April 1953. It's a very short copybook, just a dozen pages or so. And it's worth bearing in mind that there was a two-year gap in the diaries for the years previous to this and another eight months of silence

28 TÉB: p. 27.
29 Trans. M. Ó hAodha.

immediately afterwards. This means that these twelve pages is all that is left now from a period that spanned nearly three years of the poet's life and we don't know what was going on. Had Ó Ríordáin been keeping a diary during those three years at all and, if so, had he destroyed them or were they simply lost over time? Interestingly, the binding of the twelve-page copybook that we're left with is rough and torn, giving the impression that perhaps someone has gone through the copybook and pulled pages from it roughly or in a hurry. We'll never know.

The account begins in a relaxed-enough tone. Although the controversy and the debates are going on in the pages of *Inniu* and in *The Irish Times*, he has managed to push his worries and fears to the back of his mind; the implication is that this is just the regular deprecation of his work and it's what he would have expected, anyway:

> *I was given an 'injection' at the Bons [the Hospital] this afternoon – the last one. When I came out of the ward, I stood at the gate waiting for the 4.50 p.m. bus – A beautiful afternoon. Normally, I get restless and anxious, especially waiting for the bus. Either I'm in pain or I'm depressed thinking about the state of my health – or else, I'm thinking about poems I've written and finding fault with them – telling myself that I've never written a proper single line of poetry, that it was all just a dead form of composition. But suddenly, this afternoon, I forgot all my worries for once and looked around me at the afternoon and at the people. It was like a miracle. I was able to see properly again. The street and the sky were filled with wonder ...*[30]

The poet appears reasonably at peace with himself and with the world and on returning home from the city centre, he thanks God for all the good things in this life that he has given him. Over time, however, the swipes he's getting from the critics begin to hit home and have an effect on him.

By midnight on 8 March 1953, there is nothing that can come between him and the anxiety that accompanies the night, except for his diary writing. The March issue of the journal *Feasta* has just come out and he has read the latest review of his poetry in it:

30 D: 6 February 1953.

> *An unhappy day. I've got so much criticism from people like Mary McEntee that I'm afraid to write down a word of Irish. I'm reading* Parliament na mBan *and I'm very jealous of the author, his mastery of language.*
>
> *I don't have any confidence in myself any more at all. I'm going to write in English anyway now for the next while.*

Or the following, as noted on Good Friday, 3 April 1953. He doesn't bother mentioning what Corkery's verdict on *Eireaball Spideoige* might have been; he has a fair idea of what the Professor's likely 'take' was, anyway – Corkery held Máire Mhac an tSaoi and her emphasis on tradition in very high esteem and would surely have taken her side.[31] It looked to all intents and purposes as if the critics had won the day:

> *Lent has almost passed us by now and I haven't heard any church music. I'm lonely and cold and I don't get any pleasure in this language any more, not since the critics began trying to take it away from me. I visited Professor Corkery's house Saturday night last and I didn't sleep a wink that night with embarrassment.*

The criticisms and the controversy hurt Ó Ríordáin badly; his confidence in himself was shattered and it would never be the same again. The time when he could 'hang a verse on a sunbeam', so that it would never fall was gone forever now. His sense of doubt intensifies and he goes silent for a long time. Because, for all he knows, maybe the critics are the ones who have it right? Maybe Irish isn't the key to unlocking his sensibility after all? Maybe he'd got it wrong from the very beginning and only realised the truth now that he was chastised publicly?

Ó Ríordáin has lost the key to his poetry, but as he says bitterly in the privacy of his diary, it's not as if he was foolish enough to mislay it himself one 'windy night' but rather that it was unjustly taken away from him instead, as he confirms in the poem 'Tost' ('*Silence*').[32] And he won't forget or forgive those he suspects of responsibility for this theft

31 'Banfhilíocht agus Gaeilge', IT, 27 November 1975.

32 B: p. 28.

in a hurry either. Because it is they who are guilty of 'the unwritten mind', and all the years he'd entrusted to poetry, years for which he'd abandoned 'living'. The sanctuary or bolthole in which he'd felt secure prior to this has been taken away from him now and he's been locked out even from the room of the 'mind', the room of poetry that he's now been denied access to, he now associates entirely with his TB and his sufferings; they are one and the same as he makes clear in 'Tost', and when he leaves this place again, they will became separate and distinct aspects of his sensibility once more. This house and this room was where he'd always returned to his 'self' after every trip into the 'outside world' or the 'other', but now he envisions himself cast out and on the margins, a permanent 'outsider'. And it's little enough satisfaction to be able to say, as Ó Ríordáin regularly did – that at least you can't be hurled out to the margins if you're already there! The poet's necessity for 'listening' is gone now also, seeing as there is nothing left worth listening for. And maybe it's the best thing that ever happened to him: he no longer has to return home to a 'hearth without a fire' and the constant and anxious provocations of the mind that once awaited him.[33] He's free to hide out in the void from now on, secure in the emptiness that no longer requires his expression. From now on, perhaps he'll be less a watcher and more a man of engagement? But does he have the required ability or tools with which to engage or to return to the fray again? That's his greatest doubt at this juncture and the one that torments him the most. He falls back on the diary more and more often now that he cannot bring himself to respond through the medium of poetry:

> *There was a time, a few years ago, when I was writing regularly and when I felt that my thinking was developing from day to day, from poem to poem. My mind was something ongoing then. But now it's rare that I go to the house of my mind, whether day or night, and I wonder what she's up to. She used to weave a continuous pattern back then but now she just weaves random slivers, none of which are connected. Or I think so anyway. But sometimes I think the opposite of this, i.e. that she's still there spinning away underneath but that I don't pay her*

33 ES: p. 97.

any attention – but that I will again later and that then I'll reap the harvest. That's grand![34]

What's with this nervous and timid writing? Why am I not more brave? Isn't she my own language? Haven't I survived very serious bouts of illness? It isn't sickness that's getting to me now but language. There was a time when the language didn't worry me at all. I'd have hung a verse on a sunbeam. The scholars and critics knock us and put us down and they're just full of bitterness. Only a fool would pay any attention to them? But then there's a little voice inside that says maybe they're right. No sooner have I taken note of this voice but there's another little voice then that says the opposite.[35]

Mac Dathó is the name of the latest one to attack me: 'Mr. Ó Ríordáin is the author of one of the most ridiculously pretentious introductions to a volume of poetry that have been published for a long time.' Ha, ha! It makes no sense to leave the horns on a calf. Write for Department's leaflet No. 23 on dishorning cattle …

If I had any bit of good health I wouldn't be stretched out here surrounded by my enemies flinging darts at me.[36]

I must be a damned soul. I feel a hatred for humanity now in my heart, an unimaginable hate. This hatred is stronger than me. It's destroying me. One shouldn't be alone for too long. How come I don't go out of my mind? I'd just love to be able to disappear away beneath a cloak of madness. I'd have a sanctuary then. But out here exposed on the hill like this, I'm just an object of mockery. I can see them around me – petty little Irish speakers staring at me with hate and greed in their eyes. 'Be on the side of the strong' is their gospel. No wonder Joyce had to leave the country.[37]

I've written little poetry in the last few years. This thought just occurred to me a while ago. It sort of made me despair. So is this the end of me as a poet or a writer

34 D: 15 July 1955.
35 D: 12 February 1956.
36 D: 28 February 1956.
37 D: 6 March 1956.

of any kind? I believe that they think this in Dublin anyway. Maybe it was always a case of the shoe without a heel. Was I ever a poet or a literary man?[38]

Yes, when Máire McEntee farts, then Tomás de Bhaldraithe farts. Birds of a feather all farting as one … The night is getting colder. I'm getting older. I am bitter. Maybe it's not in me to do it any more. Let them off. I'm not finished yet, however. Oh Christ, but I've met many ugly people in the Irish language movement.[39]

I woke up tonight and I was feeling half-sick. Then I had a sudden vision of all the years that have passed by. I saw all those years in one go, in a way in that I'd never seen them before. A sudden insight/radiance and then darkness afterwards … But as regards the brief insight I got, the only thing I remember was all the barking insults that were thrown in my direction over the years. I saw them all grouped together as one. Sarcastic words, the words that are intended to destroy someone's confidence; I saw a cluster of them suddenly. They aren't worth much.[40]

When I woke a while ago I started thinking about the problems relating to literary matters and especially poetry – aspects of the writing that have tormented me for a long time. After years of consideration and wallowing, I've nearly reached that luminous point, that point of understanding in myself as a poet, if I am a poet. I reached it already before twenty years ago when I began writing poetry for the first time. But I must go off on my wanderings and lose my own light. I had to listen to Daniel Corkery and to heretics like him. Keep a grip on yourself, whoever you are. I'm not sure whether my understanding has returned, but I feel it has. And I think I've reached the place of faith also. This is in a very steep, high-up place and if you're unlucky enough to fall off that cliff, it is very difficult to get back up again.[41]

Europe in the morning! Is this Europe? There are people who'd prefer if it wasn't.

38 D: 22 October 1956.

39 D: 4 November 1956.

40 D: 4.55 a.m., 28 March 1958.

41 D: 30 March 1958.

'We need to protect our heritage from what is foreign.' Look at that cursed little heretic down in Crosshaven, Daniel Corkery from Anglo-Ireland, and he constantly banging on about a heritage that he never even had himself. But I wonder is it a question of heritage at all? It's a question of jealousy. Heritage isn't what Daniel Korkery [sic] is looking for; it's Daniel Korkery. That's the Hidden Ireland – namely Daniel Korkery himself.[42]

Awake. I'm not short of breath. I'm still anxious all the same. Suddenly, I thought of those verses that I put at the start of Eireaball Spideoige. *('Seo libh a chairde tríd an tír …') and I felt embarrassed. Ugly sentimentality! Why would anyone write that kind of shit?*

Gan ach comhairle eaglach ár gcroí
I lár na hoíche diamhaire

Tá baint agaibh le bualadh croí
Ar chuma an éin [sic] bheannaithe

Shit, shit, shit all of it! Bad as they are, all the same, it's enough to see these lines written on the page to awaken an insatiable desire for composition in man.[43]

Still on sick leave. I'm alone in the house. I'm not well. Rain drops falling. I don't know. Nyasaland. There's no redemption ahead for us. I'm sweating. I hear a raindrop smash itself against the windowsill outside. I feel lazy. The laziness of illness – languor *in Latin. Wherever you go in Spain, in France, in Munster, no matter how beautiful the spoken language, or how rich the tradition, the human being is tortured and tormented. How to bear this burden of living. As the poet said:*

Is deacair an t-ualach so d'iompar …
(It is difficult to bear this burden …)[44]

---

42 D: 8.12 a.m., 29 April 1958.

43 D: 5.15 a.m., 25 September 1958.

44 ES: p. 33; trans. M. Ó hAodha.

> *I used to write poetry in Irish until Daniel Corkery set his dead hand on her. My curse on that interferer.*[45]

> *Night. If I hadn't listened to their talk about metrics myself I'd be writing poetry today. But I listened to that little gobshite Corkery and others. That held me back.*[46]

As always, truth is more complex and tortuous than it first appears. Corkery and the critics had wounded him badly for a finish but they wouldn't have got away with it so if Ó Ríordáin hadn't given in to their theorising and shown them far too much deference over the years. That flaw was his; maybe it was his own fault, maybe the weakness was always his; maybe – and this is the most frightening thought of all – maybe Ó Ríordáin would have 'surrendered' to them and their like, even if they'd never existed at all.

A quick survey of the poet's diary entries in the decade following the publication of *Eireaball Spideoige* confirm that it wasn't solely the critics and their influence that led to the waning of Ó Ríordáin's poetic impulse, if it did indeed wane in later years. On a personal level, things are changing for Ó Ríordáin at this juncture also. The years are moving on. He's nearing forty years of age and has neither 'chick nor child'; he has neither wife nor children, nor anyone to call his own. When Ó Ríordáin occasionally mentions marriage it is solely in practical terms and there is little in the way of romance associated with it. He walks down Patrick Street in Cork and seeks out a friendly face or a face that might signify 'hearth and home', but more often than not, he receives the cold, proud and sometimes hostile stare of the young sophisticated city woman in return. They're not a world away from the beautiful and haughty women whom Marcus Aurelius saw long ago; the Roman emperor belonged to a different city and time but the city maintains its essence; such proud or 'superior' women encompass all that is the city and the youthful vigour that is his no more. And as for the women whom the poet knows, and whom he suspected might once have been in love with him, they have aged and

45 D: 17 October 1960.

46 D: 12.20 a.m., 13 February 1961.

grown less soft in his eyes. Every now and then he gets a momentary insight into the life he never experienced and the life he never lived. The image of a whore that flashes unexpectedly before his mind, as a group of priests or bishops pass him by procession, her earthy and lascivious image puncturing the pretence or solemnity of the moment. The sight of a pretty young woman's legs shimmering under the street lights at dusk as he drives home through the city in the pouring rain, back home to where the cats are his sole companions. The furtive glance at the girls and the boys wrapped around one another in pairs in the shady hedgerows as he passes them in the gloom, oblivious to the caveats and concerns of the Church; he knows who the powerful ones are in the world now, who it is that will prevail, and it's not the people whom one usually associates with spoils. The darkness of night rules the roost, after all, just as she overcomes the day. Open the door once you reach the house, the strip of light swallowing you up, then darkness again. Whatever authority or respect he'd garnered as a poet, he's accumulated the same again in terms of years that passed without issue, the years of delay and weariness that dragged him down. When Ó Ríordáin asks the pertinent questions in his poem 'In Absentia' – 'What is Recognition and Fame Worth?/Who'd Listen to You?' – he already knows the answer and, worse still, he strongly suspects that it's the crowd who never listen who have read things properly and who prevail in the end.[47] One day, he visits the site of the old dance hall again (the place where he'd once put on the plays) but he feels like an intruder, an old ghost who has returned to one of its forgotten haunts, a shadow on the joy of youth. This is a place for children now and he's an old man who has found himself in the wrong place, searching for a youth he can barely remember. He stands outside the door of the hall another night looking on and it suddenly comes to him that he has spent his entire life like this – on the 'outside looking in'.[48] There was a time in his life when he had somewhere to go and some company to keep but that's all gone now. He is on the outside now, in the absence of any physical or spiritual solace. He has been abandoned and shunned to the margin, to the dead limbo-

47 B: pp. 20–1.
48 D: 5 May 1957.

world, to the nowhere that is neither here nor there. And that constant fear at the back of his mind nags at him all the while, saying that maybe he never belonged 'anywhere' in the first place. Could it have been that he was in this state from the very beginning but that he'd never realised it? Had the truth been obscured from him all this time and he'd imagined the whole thing – that it was an illusion? – that his joy had just *seemed* more wonderful at the time, his despair more anguished? After all the years, maybe suffering has worn itself out, so that it is gone beyond suffering and become something else; maybe he has lost the ability to feel because he felt too much. The illness and torment of the years, both mental and physical, have worn him down to the bone, so that the only thing left now is the inevitable drift towards the end – towards death. The only sensation he's left with is a terrible exhaustion. The great storms are behind him now and he's the old man that he always was. He's become the physical manifestation of a 'cliché', the crusty and cranky old bachelor of tradition that he remembers from long ago, the sort of person whom children and young people instinctively avoided. In fact, the child inside the poet would have packed up and fled somewhere else if only he could – if only there was somewhere he could seek refuge.

Ó Ríordáin had thought about moving to Spain for a while, where the weather would have been far easier on his chest, but now this plan too has failed. When he applied for the scholarship that would have brought him there in 1955, he was rejected on the grounds that he was too old to be awarded it. Any future plans he has will have to be implemented closer to home, not that he puts anything in place in the end. He threatens to leave the chalet at the back of the house where he's been living for years but, needless to say, he doesn't do anything about it. He thinks of giving up his job in City Hall but doesn't – not for the moment, anyway; he'll put pen to paper and strike back at the critics who have attacked him, but he never does; he'll tell any 'do-gooders' who know him to 'take a hike', but he never does. He'll put an end finally to the recording of all his petty thoughts and concerns in the diary, and yet does he? The same rubbish repeated ad nauseam: 'What's the point in writing the likes of this hundreds and thousands of times: "Woken up! 3 a.m. A feeling of terror. Amn't I the real pity, Mary? Breathless. One has to put up with it

… etc., etc." Wasn't it easy to parody me and make a complete mockery of me.' (It was 4.55 a.m. on 23 March 1961 when he woke up and wrote this.) His name is laziness. Cowardice and his lack of manliness is proof of this. There's always been something in him that's held him back and prevented him from taking the initiative in life and it must be something in the genes – in the speckled Ó Ríordáins, he thinks, going way back, that means he's always so down on himself and others, and scribbling away in such negative fashion late into the night, rather than resolving his concerns effectively and with action. It's as if the same flaw reveals itself in each subsequent generation, the flaw of procrastination and the endless 'putting off' until tomorrow … and meanwhile nothing happens, nothing is achieved and none of his hopes and intentions on the personal or literary fronts ever come to fruition.

And when, if ever, will he be truly ready or adequately prepared to express his poetic vision? When will he finally be done with learning all the riches of Irish language and mastering it? The answer is never. He'll never be finished with it, he'll never have mastered the language to the standard that his critics proclaim. There'll never be an end to it and neither will there be a beginning to the poetic vision his sensibility cries out for. Ó Ríordáin admits as much, albeit half-jokingly, in the poem 'Údar' ('*Expert*'):

Is é a dúirt an t-údar so
Ná scríobhfadh focal go
mBeadh Gaeilge ar a thoil aige.

Do chaith sé a óige mhoch,
Is meán a aoise amach,
Is deireadh a laethanta,
Ag tóraíocht Gaelainne.

Ansan fuair bás de gheit,
Díreach is í aige.[49]

49 TÉB: p. 20.

An author once declared
he wouldn't write a word
until he had mastered Irish.

He threw his whole youth,
middle years and old age
into red hot pursuit
of the language.

Next thing, he died –
just as he qualified.[50]

Who knows? Perhaps the man he speaks of was already dead by then? And then there's another figure that's even more like the poet again: the crow from 'Preachán' ('*Crow*') who flew beyond the bounds of its ability and before the weather had permitted it to do so.[51] The trajectory of Ó Ríordáin's life is encompassed in those few lines about the youth that was never his, the poetry that was never granted, the relationships with women that were never experienced and were denied to him, even as a young man:

Tá mná na haoise seo
Níos féile féna gcuid
Ná bantracht óige an fhir:
Trua cás an fhireannaigh
A chaill a chumas fir
Sara mbog an bhaineannach.[52]

The women nowadays
Are more generous with their bodies
Than the women of the man's youth
Pity the man

50 Sewell, *Selected Poems*, p. 215. Trans. Frank Sewell.
51 TÉB: p. 19.
52 *Ibid.*

Who lost his virility
Before he'd a chance with the women.[53]

He might not be a total crow yet, but he's not far off it all the same. It's the withered old crow that's waiting for him at the end of the road he's traversed all these years. As Ó Ríordáin speaks in his piece 'Léaspairtí': 'he won't be at peace until he's assumed this old man's form.'[54] Or as he puts it in 'Alter Ego', you mightn't be quite at this stage but you're more like him than you are like yourself at this stage.[55] He's just a step ahead of you – one step forward, that is, or a few steps back – because it is backwards that both of you move ahead … his is your assigned form, he believes, the one that's destined for you. Meanwhile, until the extent of your own inadequacy manifests itself, grab hold of the next closest thing to you and illuminate what you can before the light goes out entirely. It might seem weak or insignificant but even the briefest of insights is better than nothing at all. Kerry poet Dónall Ó Gairbhia (Danny) had it right when he said: 'You leave nothing behind you [when you're gone] except for a handful of words.' Seize the moment and set your concerns regarding the continuity and consistency to one side, because there is no time; life is too short and such things don't really exist anyway. Visit the Gaeltacht in the summer and gather as much joy and expansiveness as will get you through some of the winter, at least. Our memories lose their power the more that the life that gives them meaning fades and the more years that go by, the harder the winters get. It will be endless winter before long, until everything fades to nothingness and silence … But let's live what's left of this life and taste its textures, even its most bitter aspects.

The last element in the Ó Ríordáin 'dispute' that we'll allude to here relates neither to metrics nor language but rather to the scheme that Comhdháil Náisiúnta na Gaeilge (the National Council for the Irish Language) regularly organised for Irish-language writers to spend time

53 Trans. M. Ó hAodha.
54 IT, 20 March 1971.
55 IT, 27 May 1972.

in the Gaeltacht improving their Irish. This is what Máire Mhac an tSaoi had said in relation to Ó Ríordáin's visits to the Gaeltacht in her essay published in *Studies*, Spring 1955:

> *Most of the time in the years since the book [ES] was published, he has spent in the Munster Gaeltacht. To this end, it is worth mentioning, he received financial help from Comhdháil Náisiúnta na Gaeilge. Certainly, this grant was very important and credit is due to both the granter and the recipient. One can see the positive results of this grant already in the most recent drafts of the poet's work.*

Such comments really upset Ó Ríordáin, especially what was said regarding taking money in the form of grants, and he made an official complaint in writing to *Studies*. They took no notice of him, however, as his complaint was never published and neither did he receive even a letter of acknowledgement from the journal's editor by all accounts. At least, this is what Ó Ríordáin always told people later; in fact, it was something that so annoyed him that he found it difficult to talk about it without getting angry. One imagines that his temper was up when he wrote this in his diary for 30 January 1957:

> *I got angry there just now thinking of that maverick Burke Savage, S.J., editor of* Studies. *I don't like this fierce anger that comes over me … It doesn't matter about the injustice that's done to you by others; it's the grievance that you hold yourself that really kills you.*

There's no trace of his written complaint (if indeed there ever was one), but his anger was understandable. Firstly, the way Ó Ríordáin saw it, he wasn't accepting money from anyone; if anything, he was losing money. The arrangement made was that the person proposed for the stint in the Gaeltacht was released from his official job for a certain, specified period of time and that the Comhdháil (National Conference) reimbursed their employer the absentee's wages. This was the system followed in Ó Ríordáin's case, the same as anyone else, as evidenced from the correspondence that passed between Donncha Ó Laoghaire, representing the Comhdháil, and Philip Monahan, City Manager, in September 1952, when the necessary arrangements were being put in place. The following, from Ó Laoghaire to the manager on 11 September 1952, for example:

Sir,

Special leave for Seán Ó Ríordáin

Thank you for your letter of 4 September. Based on the conversations I had with you since and with the Department of Local Government, I understand:

(a) that Seán Ó Ríordáin is due two months holidays from 15 September.
(b) that a new request needs to be made to the Department of Local Government for the next two months we mean (beginning 1 April 1953).
(c) that the Corporation will pay Ó Ríordáin's salary for as long as Ó Ríordáin is absent under this scheme and as based on an application from you that the Comhdháil will refund you a sum of money equal to that same salary.

The Comhdháil is very satisfied with these arrangements, and I thank you on their behalf for your co-operation and for helping arrange this.

From what I hear from Ó Ríordáin himself, I understand that he won't be able to go to the Gaeltacht from 18–22 September. Can one assume that he's entitled to the two months leave beginning the date of his departure?

As it turns out, Seán remained at work until Saturday 20 September and then went to Dunquin on 24 September, where he stayed with the Ó Conchubhar (O'Connor) family, on the northern side of the village for the next two months – until 23 November. £65 was his salary for two months in City Hall and this was the sum that the Comhdháil duly reimbursed City Hall. As regards Seán, however, he didn't receive any extra money or benefits, and by the time he'd paid for his accommodation he would have a good deal less money left over than would have been the case if he'd stayed at home by himself. Another thing was that Ó Ríordáin only had four months in Dunquin altogether under the auspices of the Comhdháil, so that Máire Mhac an tSaoi was incorrect when she gave the impression in early 1955 that he'd spent the guts of two years there in this particular instance. Any other period of time he'd spent in Dunquin in the meantime was during his own holidays, and he'd covered his own expenses.

The period between 15 May 1953 and 14 July 1953 was the second two-month period that the Comhdháil supported Ó Ríordáin's stint in the Gaeltacht at a cost of £73 13s. 4d. This was a total of £138 13s. 4d. for four months and if this improved his Irish and the quality of his poetry to the extent that some people claimed, then it was well worth it. But Ó Ríordáin clearly didn't see any major improvement in his use of the language (such a radical change in someone's level of Irish would have been virtually impossible to make within such a short period of time, anyway), and believed that it was the same Irish that he was always writing, a sort of refined personal language as based on ordinary people's Irish. By writing in the language of the 'inside' or the idiom as spoken by its last speakers, he was far more comfortable and in-tune with the values and cadences of the language, Ó Ríordáin would likely have argued.

Ó Ríordáin had dedicated his first major collection, *Eireaball Spideoige* 'to C', but it was to the people of Dunquin whom he dedicated his allegiance in *Brosna*. It was as good an example as any of how Ó Ríordáin's life had changed in the intervening years. If he'd entered a new period of life with his enhanced links westwards with the Kerry Gaeltacht, he'd severed some others that had arguably once been far more essential to him back east. Where poetry had once been his sole purpose – until the critics had ascribed a lack of care in this regard to him – he's aware now that the focus is on something else entirely and that they'll be watching him carefully from now on – in the same way as he'll be watching out also. As Ó Ríordáin said in his interview in *Scríobh 3* when Ó Mórdha asked him what he saw as the major difference between the two collections:

> *If there is a difference, it is this one more than any other – I got a lot of criticism when* Eireaball Spideoige *came out because of my Irish or my lack of Irish and this focused my attention on the language even more possibly – and maybe my attention is more focused on the language in* Brosna *than it was in* Eireaball Spideoige. *When I began writing initially, I wasn't thinking about the Irish at all, I was thinking about the poetry. It was after I'd come across Yeats and the others that I began using whatever Ballyvourney Irish that was left in my*

> *mind. In* Brosna *I suppose that I was adding to my Irish maybe. I read through* Eireaball Spideoige *and it has many errors in it, that's for sure. Now and again, I feel it going through it, I feel the thing called poetry somewhere in the air maybe. Other times again, I feel as if it is completely bland … as if there is nothing there at all …*
>
> *I'd say that maybe I had more inspiration somehow back then, maybe.*

'Maybe' is the operative word here and it's the word that appears more frequently from now on. The subjects beyond himself that he had written his poetry about to date – his childhood, the disease, the death of his mother, issues of love and philosophy, even the scruples themselves – the well he had sourced them in was nearly run dry and all that he had left now as the subject was the *self* – his own *self*, and that was a poorer and diminishing source, at best. He might finally have seen the light but he had paid dearly for it.

10

I Feel Life Falling

A sense of human emptiness and a hunger for belonging and the nausea that accompanies a life spent in the presence of your own sick body and the decay of others is a central theme of *Eireaball Spideoige*; it's as if many of the poems in the collection were a form of confession, a cleansing, an expiation. He would never get enough of the Gaeltacht to satisfy his needs, let alone to ever feel at home there; and he had an ambivalent attitude towards it at the best of times, anyway. Even if the Irish language was his literary métier and he loved it deeply, sometimes to the point of romanticising or idealising the community who spoke it, ultimately he didn't belong to that community. His attitude towards the Gaeltacht was complex and involved both attraction and rejection – as he explained in the following lecture given to students in University College Cork once. This brief excerpt is taken from the script of the lecture:

> *I eradicate people from my words. Then they become threadbare and I go to the Gaeltacht again to enrich them again, to enrich my speech. But then I begin to ascribe personal meanings to these rich words and I expel the people. It's dangerous to evaluate the words I use according to everyday human norms.*

He would continue to eradicate people from his words until, eventually, the living and the dead are one and the same in his 'gallery'; in the end, it makes no difference who is present or absent in this pantheon because they serve to constitute a type, a type that sustains a particular theory or philosophical view of his. His comments in the diary on 17 October 1960 are the *locus classicus.* No matter how often one is overcome on this aesthetic journey, this is the fundamental credo: protecting the 'me/self' against the 'they/other'. After all, they have the sanctuary of the 'institution', whether religious or lay, to fall back on – you (Ó Ríordáin) don't.

Even if just one individual elects not to acquiesce to the 'institutional' aesthetic, then it's a challenge to its authority and the institutional reacts accordingly to crush the individual revolt.

The law of the institution must prevail upon that individual and suspicion, mistrust and the culture of the 'surveillance' is the method. It is they (the 'others' out there) who are watching Ó Ríordáin out in the dark now, ready to cry out with derision. And there will be just one end to it if they get the better of him – a complete surrender or insanity. The poet has spent twenty years defying them at this stage:

> *I'm a ghost. I'm no longer a human being. I hate them. Who are this 'them'? The neighbours – the world outside – everyone other than myself. They are the 'them'. Where are they now? Conniving together out of hatred for me. What have they got against me? That I don't take the accepted approach in terms of interaction with others. That I don't accept the rules that pass for the societal or public ethic these days. They are simple people, is that it? Yes, in a way, but if you cross them in the wrong way, they are merciless, bloody, brutal. If you go on the drink, it's all right as long as you go on it the same way everyone else does. If you get angry it's fine as long as you get angry in the way that's considered normal. If you beat your wife, do it according to the rules, but if you do it either rightly or wrongly, it's then that you'd better watch out. Obviously, the maintenance of this public lie or front is essential to the survival of any community. I've noticed this myself when any small group of people come together, even a smaller group that has transgressed the public ethic of their own community – the first thing that happens is that a new or different public ethnic develops amongst the group and this smaller group adheres to this ethic just as a much bigger group would. Two groups who act to protect and bolster the public ethic are the priests and the police.*[1]

The question he has asked himself for a long time now is whether he abandoned one falsehood for another? Was it just a case that his initial falsehood was more diffused or expansive, given that he'd sourced it 'down amongst the people', and that it was healthier as a consequence? Was he, in

1 D: 17 October 1960; *Comhar,* May 1967.

reality, perpetuating the falsehood of his separateness and strangeness in his poetry, if indeed it was a form of perpetuation? Hadn't he perpetuated certain individuals or 'selves' in his poetry? And what difference did it make whether your work was an artificial fabrication or form of expression, or a transient one? Weren't they one and the same, anyway? The mad beauty of insanity that permeated his poetry, as Ó Ríordáin has put it in relation to Blake in 'Teangacha Príobháideacha' ('*Private Languages*'), and perhaps as relating also to Eliot's 'hallucinated vision', wasn't as far removed as one might think from the fear of insanity that worried Ó Ríordáin a great deal at times.[2] As a consequence, the poet is one of the first to demonstrate deep respect for the unruly and anarchic sensibility, wherever he comes across it. Regardless of whether it was Mad Sweeney who took the poet's place in 'In Absentia', or John Clare singing his way from the workhouse to the lunatic asylum in Northampton, or Patrick Galvin adopting the mentality of the insane woman in 'The Madwoman of Cork', or Ó Ríordáin's aunt herself tumbling into poetry when she'd gone insane, they are the creatures who speak in the purist and clearest way and without the taint of humdrum, everyday existence.[3] It's another thing again to be capable of expressing this realm of madness in art and in a language that appropriates to it. And this is the form of expression that Ó Ríordáin endeavours to access in 'Fiabhras': this 'geography of fever', as Seán Ó Tuama puts it; but it is more than this still, perhaps, it's a topography of the mind.[4] That which threatens to happen at the end of 'Saoirse' – the implosion of his imaginary world in the absence of a humane archetype to keep it steady – it has now occurred here. He includes the following short note with an early draft of the poem in one of his notebooks:

> *The picture frame jumping – melting, liquefying. Loyalty, some kind of love, keeps control over the frame. I thought of family . If I was unfaithful in my love for them, maybe they'd go to England.*

2 *Scríobh 4*, p. 15.
3 See 'Austin Clarke', IT, 18 May 1974.
4 Ó Tuama, *Filí faoi Sceimhle*, p. 19.

The fact that his brother was thinking of moving to England along with his wife and children was bothering Ó Ríordáin at the time. On 28 February 1955 he says as much in his diary:

> *Yesterday was the birthday of my brother's baby. 'An Canónach' (The Canon) is what I call him. We'd a great night in the 'Angelus' last night. My brother said that the city's full of carpenters, however, since the Lee Scheme came to an end and maybe he'll have to go back to England. I'm very familiar with this small family now and they with me, and I can tell you that these words of his went right through me. This life is empty enough as it is without them leaving as well. With the help of God, maybe they won't have to go away.*

His sister, Bríd, had been based in England for many years already. She'd emigrated there on 1 April 1949 and this is what Seán had noted the day prior to her departure:

> *I'm at home today. 'The Child' is going to England tomorrow. The poor girl. And the bishops and the doctors and the professors and the car dealers staying at home. 'A thousand thousand slimy things ...'*[5]

The last time she and her husband had said goodbye to Seán was on 28 August 1955, and he wrote a description of that sad afternoon, as published under the title 'Seal im aonar' ('*Alone for a while*'):

> *I said goodbye to some friends of mine who were going to England. When I was out of sight of them is when the loneliness really hit me and I felt sick. I knew that I wouldn't see them again for many long years and that we'd all be completely changed by then. I felt a certain sense of fate this afternoon. I'd just separated myself from them, maybe forever ...*[6]

(The poet foresaw this correctly – the next time she returned home was in February 1977 and this was for Seán's funeral.)

---

5 D: 31 March 1949.

6 *Comhar*, March 1955.

The old world beyond his window was changing irretrievably now and disappearing, as friend after friend and relative after relative passed away, and it wasn't as if the poet had ever had a large circle of friends or family. Turnbull died at Christmas 1954 and brought a lot with him to his grave. Fr Tadhg was still there all the while, 'my best friend in this world' as he described him in his diary entry for 30 January 1955. And yet, there was always a reticence or suspicion on Ó Ríordáin's part in relation to Seán Ó Tuama or Fr Tadhg or any of the others whom he considered his closest friends; they were surely either taking advantage of you or were hindering you in some way, he thought. In October of that same year, 1955, he writes about two of the circle who are still friends of his, despite himself:

> *I had supper in the Metropole last night with Fr. Tadhg* Ó *Murchú and Seán* Ó *Tuama. Fr Tadhg asked me to meet him yesterday afternoon. He never told me that* Ó *Tuama would be with him at all. The pair of them are friends of mine, supposedly. Yesterday afternoon and I stuck in between the two of them, I felt I think, as if I'd Bulganin on one side of me and Khruschev on the other. I felt hemmed in – as if I was being observed carefully. This man is a priest. He's a friend of mine. The other man's a friend of mine also, a man who defended my book and my views publicly. Isn't it really frightening that I don't trust either of them much! In my mind, I'm sure that they mean me danger.*[7]

People and life and the landscape altering form and becoming unrecognisable to him – and all right before his eyes. And all the while, he notes the same signs that are the passing of time repeatedly – the individual, the room, the view from his window, the darkness of night – all melting into one great confusion. Everything changing shape, position and perspective, each element melting one into the other, cancelling one another out, assuming a different form. Ó Ríordáin feels himself falling into this strange limbo-like existence where nothing seems to happen on the surface of things, an existence parallel with the 'real world' and yet entirely separate from it. He's transgressed the informal law of time he'd laid down for himself in 1949: 'No loitering'. The following excerpt from

7 D: 15 October 1955.

the diary (14 January 1954) is a good description of the place he's found himself in now. The term 'Tá' ('*It is*') is like the ticking of an interminable clock in background, counting down the evening:

> *I wasted the day today. There's a lamp hanging from the roof. It casts a red glow. It has made the room red. There's a bustling madness in the room by this light. I often spend an entire hour looking at this lamp. There's a picture of my grandmother on the wall. She was young then. I've no particular reason for thinking this but it seems to me that she must have had a normal and happy life when she was young. It's the fact that my own life is so dark and grim that makes me think this, I suppose. There's a bottle of wine (Sandeman Port) on the floor. A moment ago, I imagined that this bottle was a dog sitting on its haunches and staring me in the eyes. There is a candle on the chair next to the bed and the miserable remnant of another candle perched on the tip of the candle-holder beside it. Our race and our language is finished, if their standing depends on the likes of me.*

Who could forget the initial lines of the poem 'Claustrophobia'?

In aice an fhíona
Tá coinneal is sceon
Tá dealbh mo Thiarna
D'réir dealraimh gan chumacht ...

Next to the wine
is a candle. And fear.
The image of my Lord
is apparently without power ...[8]

One cannot get beyond Seán Ó Tuama's description of what he senses in these four lines: 'There's a desolation about the image here that is expiatory, as if we've come upon an altar where something's about to be sacrificed, the poet suspicious that he himself is the likely victim.'[9] 'Claustrophobia'

---

8 Trans. M. Ó hAodha.
9 Ó Tuama, *Filí faoi Sceimhle*, p. 22.

was awarded first prize in the Oireachtas poetry competition of 1954 and the poem was published in *Feasta* that same year, indicating that the diary excerpt and the poem itself were closely linked, both in terms of time and thinking. The atmosphere and sentiments are similar in both cases and the same applies to 'Fiabhras' (*'Fever'*), which was composed, we think, in early 1955. The atmosphere here differs only to the extent that the vertigo of 'Fiabhras' is the expansive confusion of day rather than the fearful constriction of night, as in other poems of his; the pointed flame of the candle radiates out upon the wider landscape he sees beyond his window and diffuses his anxiety and fear across a wider vista. The picture that begins to melt before his eyes as the fever kicks in is the picture of his grandmother that Ó Ríordáin mentioned in his diary entry for 14 January 1954. (Seán Ó Tuama is probably incorrect, therefore, when he says that 'maybe it's the picture of the "Lord" that's mentioned in "Claustrophobia"': the latter was a statue and not a picture as it happens.)[10] In fact, Ó Ríordáin mentions this picture frequently in his diary; the following excerpt encompasses both the picture's importance for him and the way he'd stare at it sometimes when he felt sick or at a low ebb:

> *I'm coming down sick again, I'm afraid. There's a picture on the wall beside me – my grandmother and her brother. I only ever look at it when I'm sick. I stare up at the roof of the house a lot when I'm sick too, up at the roof and at the bees up there. There's always a single bee perched here and there on the roof. They stay completely still there for a long time. I don't know what they do all the time. Each bee has its back to me so they're obviously standing all the time. Can a bee sit down at all or relax? Are they relaxing while they are always standing like that? There's water boiling in the kitchen. Someone's walking out on the road with heavy shoes. There's something stirring in the room – the breeze.*[11]

Closer still to the imagery and atmosphere of 'Fiabhras' is the diary entry (below) for March 1955. It is worth recalling that it was on 28 February that year that the poet spoke of his fear that his brother and his family

10 *Ibid.*, p. 22.
11 D: 26 April 1949.

might move to England, and even if this possibility wasn't a major element in the final (published) version of the poem, the idea that sentiments and feelings ('loyalty, love of some sort') are essential – i.e. that the family don't leave home and 'structures' don't break up or melt away – are vital to the poem's import nonetheless, as manifested 'physically' in the image of the picture frame liquefying and turning to nothing. In this case the exterior or physical world is expressive of the poet's deepest inner feelings and worries. Buttressed by the diary entries, we watch the fever take its course. The outside world recedes beyond his line of vision and his hearing grows increasingly indistinct as he loses touch with reality. The fever spreads and illness quickly fills his imagination and the entire room. Before long, the fever has taken control of the poet and it is through it that he sees and hears and comprehends and writes:

> *13/3/55 Sunday 12.30 p.m. Note that it's the 13th. You can feel it in the air. I'm wiped out here with a cold. I'm hot one minute and cold the next. I might as well be done with it and admit the truth to myself. The sun is shining in through the window. I'm shining out through the window. Outside there is summer, freedom and health. Inside here is fever, cold and fear. I am all three and each of the three at the same time – i.e. the latter three. Far away, at the back of the house, I can hear a radio. Now and again I hear someone's voice. I don't recognise the voice and I can't hear what they're saying either. Everything's unclear. That's the mystery of illness. Maybe it is death, my man. This sentence really alarmed me I can tell you. Yes, I have a slight fever. Wouldn't I be better off getting up?*
>
> *I checked my temperature there and I see that it's 99.4°F. I'm as well off staying in bed for the moment. There's a mist covering the hills so that I can't see them. There's a lorry going back the road.*
>
> *Have we had enough of this life? Am I worn out? I feel as if I can't go on any more.*
>
> *"Not with a bang but with a whimper."*
>
> *All the same, wouldn't it be lovely to be out in the sunshine today? There are many people out in the sun who have no peace. The Garda Síochána is a form of sickness. I never liked the Garda Síochána. How come I don't feel depressed now? Someone's going along the road whistling. There's not much music in that whistle. Dogs are barking in all directions, responding to one another. They're like the*

crowd in the Dáil. One dog gives a speech and another replies to it. A woman calls out and tells them to be quiet. A bird is whistling. I don't know what kind of a bird it is. The clock goes 'click-clack'. The shouts of children now. Morgan [Murphy] let a roar out of him. Silence. You'd think that some of the cars were aeroplanes. No one has any respect for the poor man. The poor man is alone in the world. G[eorge] B[ernard] S[haw] was a right idiot. He was a right braggart but then look at all the enjoyment he gave us all the same. Being sick makes you uneasy. I'm cranky in myself. I'm writing this just to pass the time. Eleanor Roosevelt. A real American. 'How come Americans are always laughing?' Seosamh Ó Dálaigh used always say. Roosevelt and Truman were always like that too but I think I've seen a frown on Eisenhower's face once or twice.

Tuesday 9.07 a.m. 15/3/55. In bed. I've been very sick since last Friday. A high temperature, shaking, coughing, a horrible feverish feeling. This morning I feel a crisis coming on.

Quamdiu, Domine, quamdiu? *[How long, O Lord, how long?] The schoolchildren are out on the road. Loud confident talk out of them. I think that I can hear them skipping. The bus has arrived. It steals away the children and all the noise.*

[A Sketch: a pole, electrical wires, two trees, the peaks of the hills and the sky.]

This is what I see when I look out the window. I feel cold and hot again. I'm shivering. There's nothing as ugly as shivering like this. Tomás Dhónaill – Crithineach.

Wednesday 16/3/55, 10.50 a.m. A fine day even if it's a bit foggy. I'm much improved today. The fever almost gone. I'm in a dark, cranky and nasty mood all the same. I'm arguing with the old women here. I'm arguing with the crowd in City Hall. They're all bastards as far as I'm concerned. Or could it be that I'm the one in the wrong? The way I see it, they're all crooked. Fr Tadhg Ó Murchú is being buried today. R.I.P.

I'll get up tomorrow at the break of day …

Was there ever anyone as full of hatred in the world as me? If I improved a bit and was able to sit out in the air for a while, maybe this would go away. It's unhealthy to be trapped in a confined space like this. To be outside where there is more space is far healthier. Throw any Christian into a hole, make him sick, give him fever, put terror into his heart, leave him in fear of death, leave him there with his enemies closing in, leave two ugly old wans looking after him, even if negligently so, but keep him alive when death would be a release for him. Then give him the same dose over and over again for the next eighteen years and see will he have malice in his heart. He'll have hatred and malice in his heart all right but he'll have an extraordinary light and joy in it also. 5.10 p.m. I've just spent a long day in hell. If I recover, I'll make sure that it'll be different the next time, I'm sick. I'll go into hospital or out in search of company, at home …

He's already recovering or coming to himself again when others make their appearance, those who had remained peripheral and on the margins of his perception until then. He'd been unable to incorporate these figures within his range of vision at the time or 'write them in', given the way the world outside had narrowed as the sickness expanded and encompassed his imagination and took over the room. Even if we can't say for certain that the writing of 'Fiabhras' and the diary excerpts above were contemporaneous with one another, they undoubtedly emerged from the same region of emotion and experience. The poem is a vast landscape: his knees pulled high in the bed are wrapped beneath the humid and feverish fog that is the illness, that which obscures the peaks of the 'mountains'; the remainder of his body up along is the 'plain'; the space between floor and window appears a great vista, a faraway journey that would be too gruelling to undertake now in his feverish condition. The window itself seems absolutely enormous. Time has changed and extended itself so that it rules the region that is the room, and so that yesterday or the day before belongs to 'long ago' and has a very different frame of reference. His temperature has gone sky-high too, dangerously high, and the landscape and the mountains beyond his window appear shrunken and tiny. His perception has altered completely and when he raises a thumb and forefinger, he senses that he could hold the 'tiny' church steeple between them; if he could only grab hold of the physical world outside in such a manner, he could gain control of the room again. Life has turned upside-down, inside-out. And isn't this in a sense similar to the first lines about the mountains in 'Saoirse', hills that were not God's creation but which emerged instead from the disregard which humanity had shown the world He created? The individual will have to pay for his sins in this living hell which he – the poet – has created. After all, it isn't just the heat and fever of the disease that causes the picture frame of perception to dissolve and disappear, but also the malaise that is his lack of faith in the entity that is the picture frame itself. The poem veers between one state of being and another so that it is beyond the poet's control:

Fiabhras

Tá sléibhte na leapa mós ard,
Tá breoiteacht 'na brothall 'na lár,
Is fada an t-aistear urlár,
Is na mílte is na mílte i gcéin
Tá suí agus seasamh sa saol.

Atáimid i gceantar bráillín,
Ar éigean más cuimhin linn cathaoir,
Ach bhí tráth sar ba mhachaire sinn,
In aimsir choisíochta fadó,
Go mbímis chomh hard le fuinneog.

Tá an pictiúir ar an bhfalla ag at,
Tá an fráma imithe ina lacht,
Cheal creidimh ní féidir é bhac,
Tá nithe ag druidim fén dhéin,
Is braithim ag titim an saol.

Tá ceantar ag taisteal on spéir,
Tá comharsanacht suite ar mo mhéar,
Dob fhuirist dom breith ar shéipéal,
Tá ba ar an mbóthar ó thuaidh,
Is níl ba na síoraíochta chomh ciúin.[12]

12 B: p. 26.

Fever

The bed-hills are ever so high,
fever the humidity in their midst,
the floor a long, long way off,
    and miles and miles away
    are sitting and standing in this world.

We are in sheet-country now
and can hardly remember a chair,
    but before we became a meadow,
    way back in our walking time,
    we stood as high as a window.

A picture on the wall is swelling,
the frame has melted into liquid,
with faith absent, this can't be stopped;
    things are closing in on me,
    and I can feel the world collapse.

A district is shooting from the sky,
a neighbourhood poised on my finger,
I could easily grasp a chapel;
    on the road north there are cows,
    and cows in eternity are not as still.[13]

Seán Ó Tuama recognised the shift that occurs in the last two lines of the poem:

> *And then, unexpectedly, we hear the first 'natural' sentence of the poem: 'On the north road there are cows'. This is the first sentence redolent of regular or everyday life, the first sentence that relates to a familiar landscape; and it's probably a sign of recovery.*

---

13 Sewell (ed.), *Selected Poems*, p. 147. Trans. Frank Sewell.

The conclusion to the poem saw a couple of changes when it was initially published. The first time it appeared in photostat form at the beginning of the anthology *Filí faoi Sceimhle*, the poem was titled '104°F' rather than 'Fever' and this is how the last verse went:

Dá gcreidfinn diongbhálta an chéad uair
Ní shobalófaí an pictiúir
Anois táim im eiriceach buan
Tá gach socair neamhshocair ó smacht
Tá gach fráma imithe ina lacht.

If I had believed firmly the first time
The picture would not have been reduced to froth
Now I am a permanent heretic
Everything steady is unsteady without rule
Every frame has been reduced to tears.[14]

The world returns to the quieter and more peaceful terrain that is the Sunday countryside, as the last traces of fever dissipate. Six months have passed since then and Ó Ríordáin is healthy again, and seems at peace in both body and mind:

> *18/9/55 Sunday 11.30 p.m. Spent a nice peaceful day today. Mass in the morning at the Church of the Sacred Heart. I went to confession yesterday. After Mass (10 a.m.) I went for a drive in the car out as far as Rylane. I sat down on the side of the road next to a bridge reading* The Sunday Times. *It was really relaxing just sitting there next to the lapping stream-water. (I've killed* Daddy Longlegs *now.) My mind lit up. I walked along the road for a bit. There were cows in a field. I stood next to the ditch and it wasn't long before a cow drifted over towards me; gradually, all the other cows came over. They were all very quiet, very heartbroken. This line came into my head.*
>
> *Will the cows of eternity be so quiet?*

14 Trans. M. Ó hAodha.

I thought I'd compose a poem. I began it like this:

Chonac ba ar an mbóthar ó thuaidh (I saw cows on the north road.)

Then it occurred to me to steal a line from Máire Bhuí Ní Laoghaire:

Maidin Domhnaigh Dé ('On Sunday morning of God')

Then I set it aside.

The cattle imbue the poem with some of the silence and eternity that is Sunday. Their arrival at the end of a another bout of fever was timely, even if the poet didn't manage to shake off this sickness. Not that he'd completed the fever that was the poem as of yet. There was at least one other occasion when he finished off a poem in this manner: by adding additional lines composed completely independently of the rest of the poem. In fact, it would be at an ungodly hour of night all of eleven years later that he would come up with those last few lines, by which time little had improved in terms of his own personal circumstances and illness:

Awake for three hours. Went through a couple of anxiety attacks. I got up and made two cups of Bovril and swallowed a tranquilliser. That did the job and I looked for a poem that I was working on a while back but which I didn't manage to finish. Although I didn't come up with any new line for it, I finally saw how I could finish it with a few lines that I'd previously composed. This gave me real peace of mind. The poem is 'Bean chaol suite ar chlaí'. *I hope the poem is good.*[15]

Whether it was or not, there were no further alterations made to the poem after this.

But let us return again for a moment to the juncture when he'd composed 'Fiabhras'. Thankfully for Ó Ríordáin, his brother's family and the children decided not to emigrate from Ireland in the end and the poet

15 D: 3.45 a.m., 5 December 1966. The poem can be found in LL: p. 23.

would incorporate many of their innocent and yet beautifully poetic and prophetic childish musings within the pages of his diary – their child-like brightness and lightness of their hearts, their imagination, their love. Unfortunately, however, these children, with their lightness of heart, were living quite a distance from Ó Ríordáin, on the other side of the city. He was sharing a house with very different people entirely – his aunts – one of whom would assume form in three of his poems: 'An Gealt' (*'The Crazy One'*), 'Bagairt na Marbh' (*'The Threat of the Dead'*) and 'Tá Pearsa Imithe as an Saol' (*'A Person has Gone Out of the World'*).[16] His aunts Mary and Gobnait are 'The Misses Linehan' referred to here and the people he refers to as 'witches' at one point in his diaries (16 March). He described the aunts in worse terms than this on a few occasions, so the one cited earlier isn't the harshest description he ever gave them. It was when they suffered from madness or after their death that he spoke of them in kinder terms and that he assigned them the respect and love that he was unable to show them in life. That said, it's not easy to forgive the cruel way the poet spoke of them at times, from the vantage point of today. And Ó Ríordáin himself felt guilty about this too and couldn't forgive himself, really, for his harshness towards them – he felt particularly guilty after they died – and when you read over the diary entries today it's easy to see why, particularly given the strange and somewhat strained relationship he had with them in the home that they shared.

Mary had retired from her last teaching post, in Cobh, by this time (1955) and had come to live in the house with them. Gobnait was the first of the sisters to come to live in the house and she was the last of them to leave it also, given that Seán's mother and Mary predeceased her. (The other sister, Kathleen, outlived all of them; she lived until 6 July 1966 – but she never lived with the others and she wouldn't have known Seán as well as the others as a consequence.) The following paragraph is as measured an account of their lives together as he wrote and it's not as if Seán comes out of it looking so well himself. It relates to Sunday 26 February 1956, the same day that he noted it in his journal:

16 B: p. 32; B: p. 33; LL: p. 20.

> *There's a party and a dinner in Sonny Callaghan's house tonight. I drove my aunt Gobnait there just now. That's how people get by – a little bout of company every now and then. My aunts don't have much in the way of company or pastimes, the creatures, and it's not like I'm much good to them on that score. There are two of them, Mary (a former teacher) and Gobnait whose [sic] still a practical person but is fairly miserable too. Gobnait still enjoys a bit of company but Mary is dour and resentful and prefers being by herself and a solitary existence from morning till night. I shudder when I think of the kind of life the three of us have in this house. There's nothing Christian about this life. The three of us are withdrawn in upon ourselves and how we survive this hermit-like existence, God knows. We've something lacking in us. We're estranged from the world, loveless. We're like a bunch of tormented ants. We're also damaged, and there's no balm for our wounds. It's complete loneliness here because none of us have any interaction whatsoever with one another; the three of us total loners, each in our own room.*

Mary was sent to the mental home for the first time on 17 November 1956. She'd been living with her sister Kathleen (Mrs Reynolds) for a short while prior to this. When Seán heard how she'd been ill and what they were doing to her in terms of treatment, he began to compose a new poem, only two lines of which materialised initially, lines that he noted in his journal for 11 November that year:

> *Do bhailigh léi i gan fhios dúinn*
> *Go dúthaigh daoine buile.*

> She left unknown to us
> For the realm of the mad.[17]

The second time she was admitted to the asylum was 17 February 1957, after she'd been at home for a week. She left the house in Inniscarra this second time and maybe the events of the previous day are those outlined in 'An Gealt'. As Ó Ríordáin wrote in his diary at 7 a.m. on the morning

17 Trans. M. Ó hAodha.

of 17 February, as they waited for her to be taken away, his aunt had been waiting for visitors from early the previous morning:

> *My aunt Mary is to go into the mental home in Dungarvan today. She spent yesterday waiting for important visitors to call in and say goodbye, the likes of the Pope, a bishop or two and some Fr Murphy or other. She had a meal prepared for them, and had it laid out on a special table since from seven in the morning. She couldn't understand why none of them made an appearance. 'I didn't see any sign of them yet,' she says, 'although I know they're definitely here.' That's a word that's often on the tip of her tongue. i.e. 'here.' There's something really mysterious about the word 'here' when you hear it from a lunatic's mouth.*

The mystery of insanity and the room merge in 'An Gealt'. If the poem 'Fiabhras' reflects a particular state of mind, it is also the tense mood that envelops the house on the morning of his aunt's departure, a tension that is almost at breaking point. 'Fuadar', 'géarú' and 'pléascadh' ('*rush*', '*intensity*' and '*frenzy*') define the atmosphere of 'An Gealt'. The lunatic has to leave the house so that the terrible tension of the room is 'released' and an appropriate response to the wild energy that is insanity can emerge (the poet implies). This madness never fully dissipates, however; it remains hidden there in the walls of his house; the same pent-up energy that is night in 'Claustrophobia' and the same dazed chaos (as manifested both physically and mentally) in 'Fiabhras' ('*Fever*') also defines 'An Gealt'. Ó Ríordáin might come to himself once the soft dawn light appears on the horizon but it was always a temporary respite in these years that were defined by fever and illness. And this is how it goes:

> *Tá ag géarú ar a fuadar ó iarnóin,*
> *Is go bpléascfaidh sí a haigne géaróidh,*
> *Tá an seomra ina timpeall ag géarú maille léi,*
> *Is na freagraí atá faighte aici, táid géaraithe dá réir,*
> *Ach cuirfear í go teach na ngealt le hamhscarnach an lae,*
> *Chun go maolófaí an seomra is na freagraí is í féin.*[18]

18 B: p. 32.

Her activity is intensifying since after noon,
And it will continue to intensify until she blows her mind,
The room around her is growing tense along with her,
and the replies that she has received: they have intensified accordingly,
She will be sent to the asylum at daybreak,
So that the room and the replies and she herself be unburdened.[19]

There was a strange confluence to the manifestation of his aunt's illness at this juncture of Ó Ríordáin's life, given that he was preparing his thoughts and ideas for the seminal essay 'Teangacha Príobháideacha' around this time. Where once there had been little enough of a relationship between himself and his aunt, Ó Ríordáin felt a new kinship with her, now that she'd reached that place which was a new conduit to the imagination and the power of words. She'd accessed the place where the purist of poetry and dreams inhabited, a place so pure and unsullied that nothing could ever corrupt it. Ó Ríordáin often sensed the same emotion in the atmosphere, something very similar to the mixed emotions he felt later when he waited for the doctor's considered opinion in relation to himself, which was preferable or of more value to the unique understanding or wisdom associated with madness or that which relates to 'good sense' and the entire control of one's faculties. The poet endures the cold tedium and loneliness of the 'outer life' now, rather than the region of the imagination that is interchangeable with the madness of dreaming, an 'elevated' place within the imagination that he'd come close to experiencing and giving expression to just a few times in his life. This place of dreams and poetry is accessible only to the very few and only on the rarest of occasions during the course of earthly existence, however. Blessed are those who never have to seek out its environs because they've already been granted admission:

I went to the mental home where my aunt is, after dinner. Anyone would think that she was sane the way she goes on. I spent a while inside in her own room with her. She spoke very sensibly and in a very dignified way and she listened to the news I had for her in a very understanding way. Eventually she said that

19 Trans. M. Ó hAodha.

we'd probably said everything that there was to say. We came out into the lobby, then suddenly she was a lunatic once more. 'Do you know what kind of a place this is?' she said.

'I do,' I said.

'But do you know who's here?' she said.

'I don't,' I said.

'Shaw's children,' she said. 'Isn't that shocking?'

'It sure is,' I said …

I think that what happened was that her words and thoughts fell into poetry. This is madness. A strange disease. The madness of tuberculosis is more interesting than tuberculosis because, I suppose, the mind is more interesting than the body. I wonder do I go a bit mad myself at times? Isn't it a heavy and complicated burden, this burden of living! Look at the diseases, the sins, the work, the hesitation, the heat, the cold, the fear, the joy! It is as if those poor patients who are lunatics in that mental home are trapped in a dream. They are trapped right inside the dream. I am very lonely again tonight. The night is shutting down and becoming as poison. I can feel it in my shoulders.[20]

The next day is the poet's birthday, but two days later again he notes in the diary for 4 December:

I was forty yesterday. I'm an old man now. A middle-aged bachelor walking through the streets and spotting teenage girls and girls in their early twenties …

Another dream, but one that he is fully cognisant of, rendering it powerless to Ó Ríordáin's mind.

He paid another visit to his aunt on Christmas Eve 1956, and puts pen to paper the following day, Christmas Day – thoughts which later see print in the essay 'Tráthnóna Liom Féin':

It's Christmas Eve. I felt a strong Christmasy atmosphere when I was leaving the mental home. The Christmas spirit fills the mental homes as well as everywhere else. I said goodbye to my female relative. 'Yes,' I said to her, 'a happy

20 D: 2 December 1956.

> *Christmas to you.' 'And also to you,' she responded cheerfully. I didn't pity her. Being free is no better than being hemmed in. Maybe it's better to be hemmed in. She's within her own realm of insanity. This is a tasty realm, even if it's a tormented one also. It is within such a realm when they have the madness of poetry in them. She's been transformed by this realm that she's found herself in. Look at how rich her speech is now. She is filled with inspiration. Look at the personal dignity that accompanies her. Ordinary people are always taken up with their own personal and petty concerns but it's the history of the world that bothers Toynbee, music was Beethoven's obsession, bringing the world under French dominion was Napoleon's dream. It's the same with my female relative. She won't eat Protestant food any longer in case this means Protestants take over the Gaeltacht. The Pope is angry with her because of some error she made. She is concerned with the major questions and has no time for petty issues. I met an educated man outside the mental home. He wished me a very happy and peaceful Christmas. His good wishes were a form of rhetoric really. That man isn't free either. He too is hemmed in, enclosed within the realm of rhetoric and has no time for petty issues.*[21]

Needless to say, such forms of 'elevated' language would find their appropriate place in Ó Ríordáin's 'Teangacha Príobháideacha':

> *Another type of people completely compose the most supreme of the private languages – the people who have been completely transformed, the likes of Saint Paul, John of the Cross, the great poets, the great writers of prose and crazy people. These are people whose native place has left its traces on their language, the same as everyone else, but who fell into the realm of holiness or poetry or madness so that their normal language was radically changed – or whatever language they use during their transformation.*[22]

The 'educated' or scholarly man would be assigned a different, yet appropriate, place in Ó Ríordáin's essay – this man for whom the magic of Christmas and the mystery of insanity were the same, and whose sole

21 *Comhar*, March 1961.

22 *Scríobh 4*, p. 15.

concern was the purity of expression. The source of the poet's fascination here is not so much with the thought that the crazy scholar communicates, but rather with the 'high' mode that is its expression, the same aspect that had clearly enthralled and inspired the 'educated' man in question. Ó Ríordáin became more and more familiar with such individuals in the years following the publication of *Eireaball Spideoige*. And it was the opposite of this man and his tribe of 'crazy scholars/poor fools' that Ó Ríordáin sought to defend himself against for the rest of his life – the 'other people' or those who spoke and wrote the language in such a clinical and rational way or 'with malice aforethought', as the poet himself put it in 'Teangacha Príobháideacha'. The people who have nothing with which to buttress their language and poetry but the icy logic and Irish idioms that are long-since dead and forgotten, the same as the people who once possessed them. There was no fear that the latter group (scholars and critics) would stray from this type of Irish of theirs or venture into the poetic realm of madness or irrationality, never mind make a grammatical error on the way.

This wasn't the first time that Ó Ríordáin had co-related the spheres of lunacy and poetry, needless to say. In truth, he'd made this link from the very first day he'd ever written poetry. 'Le solas na n-óinmhid/I gcreideamh an fhocail' ('*With the jester's light/In the faith of the word*').[23] In fact, he'd revisited this territory only very recently in his poem 'In Absentia', a poem we find first noted in his diary towards the end of the period spanning 4 December 1953 to 21 January 1956. The poet, the madman and the saint are all three aspects of the nature that is God as he understands Him because only they comprehend how the truth shall be revealed to them and pay no heed to the foolish voice that is this world. The end of his poem is based on St Matthew's Gospel; it is worth comparing Father Peadar's version (translation to Irish) with the concluding verses to Ó Ríordáin's 'In Absentia':

> *At that time if anyone says to you, 'Look, here is the Messiah!' or, 'There he is!' do not believe it. For false messiahs and false prophets will appear and perform great signs and wonders to deceive, if possible, even the elect. See, I have told you ahead*

23 ES: p. 87. Trans. M. Ó hAodha.

of time. So if anyone tells you, 'There he is, out in the wilderness,' do not go out; or, 'Here he is, in the inner rooms,' do not believe it. For as lightning that comes from the east is visible even in the west, so will be the coming of the Son of Man.[24]

Má deir aoinne leat
'Tá sé ar chúl an tí,'
Ná tabhair aon toradh air,
Bheadh fhios agat fé thrí,

Is fós má deirtear leat
'Tá sé sa raingiléis,'
Ná himighse amach
A chuardach feadh an lae;

Níl sé thall ná abhus,
Níl sé in aon áit,
Níl sé ach amuigh,
Is beidh sé amuigh gan fáil

Go dtí go dtiocfaidh fios
Mar dhuilliúr ar chrann ag fás,
Ansin sea a bheidh sé istigh,
Is beidh a fhios ag cách.[25]

If anyone tells you
'He's out the back of the house,'
Pay them no heed,
You'd know thrice if so,

Or if they tell you either
'He's out in the scrub,'

24 Matthew 24:23–27. 'The Destruction of the Temple and Signs of the End Times' *Holy Bible, New International Version,* 1973, 1978, 1984, 2011.

25 B: p. 20.

Don't go out
Looking for him all day;

He's neither here nor there
He's nowhere,
He's just outside,
And he won't be found

Until he sources wisdom
As a leaf on a tree,
Then indeed, he'll be in,
And everyone will know it.[26]

The coming of the Son of Man equals the arrival of the sage that the poet has been waiting so long for. It was in the Gaeltacht that he sourced the Irish word 'raingiléis', the word Ó Ríordáin used instead of Father Peadar's better-known word 'fásach' (desert), and a term the poet explained in one of his notebooks as follows: 'The place where the ground is sparse and rough.' ('Kruger blew the arse out of the primus' is the next sentence he writes in this notebook, indicating the mixture of earthiness and 'high idiom' that was the Irish of Dunquin – some of the terminology of which was about as far from the Bible as one could imagine!) Ó Ríordáin drew frequently on the Gospel of Matthew as part of his thinking and as evident in his diaries and notebooks. Later, in the same notebook where he includes the term 'raingiléis', for example, Ó Ríordáin includes a short translated excerpt from Matthew 11:10–17, at the place where Jesus calls Matthew out from the tax office. Ó Ríordáin's diary entry for 28 February 1956 also provides his own reading of Jesus' actions. Wherever else one sources wisdom it wasn't in the tax office, anyway:

I too sit in a tax office. Was I called to follow Him yet? If so, then it's a bad state of affairs. Will I be called? If I'm called, will I go?

26 Trans. M. Ó hAodha.

Whether he heard the call or not, he didn't heed it or follow it up – or not yet, at any rate. He'd wait for the call to come to him directly – the invitation to sanctity, to insanity, to irrationality and even inebriation – and he'd respond as necessary when the time came. Again and again, Ó Ríordáin addresses his response to that which is calling him, and yet his every response is the same. It's best to wait another while and see what else is left for him in the realm of poetry and language. If one waits long enough who knows what might happen? And yet if it wasn't for the endless delay, and the waiting, and the procrastination, he'd have moved on years ago and left the realm of madness and poetry far behind. Ó Ríordáin certainly viewed inebriation as another way to access something spiritual that was beyond the normal sphere of things – i.e. another way of speaking – or as he put it in 'Teangacha Príobháideacha', an essay he composed close to this time: 'It isn't the sober one who writes the private language but the drunken one.'[27]

In the case of 'Soiléireacht', it is the 'cleansed' or 'clean-scrubbed' that is located somewhere in the limen that is drunkenness and wisdom that is being investigated. This marginal, limbo-like region was Ó Ríordáin's normal 'stomping ground' after all – the place where madness and reason intertwine, darkness and light, the world of sleep and waking. The world as it once was for this particular artist flees just as he is about to expose it anew. The instrument is purified within the language, just as language is made pure within the instrument. Even the very essence of the word 'bottle' is not the same as it once was, given that it has now been perceived and understood with such clarity and purity of vision. This insight might not be as fine or as powerful when elucidated in prose (as compared with poetry) but the process of refinement has begun nonetheless. It was in the unlikeliest and most desolate of places that one might stumble upon that occasional diamond in the rough:

> *I'm in bed! Because I had the signs of a cold coming on yesterday, I left the office at 12.30 and went on the drink. I spent the whole day going from pub to pub drinking until it was night. No doubt, I made a fool of myself. Too much talk. How did I get home? That's something I don't know. It looks as if I stopped the car somewhere and*

27 *Scríobh 4*, p. 15.

> *fell asleep because I remember a woman's face against the window at one stage. I can't remember what she said. I think that it was Mrs Healy. God was definitely looking after me that I didn't cause a serious accident. I was blind drunk.*
>
> *Today again, I feel that freshness in the world that I always feel the night after a night's drinking. I've never seen paper as bright as the paper I'm writing on now, it seems to me. Everything about the world seems brand new and washed clean and clear.*[28]

It's with a line that he'd composed five months earlier in his diary (15 June 1957), but which he'd laid aside for the time being, that the poet begins his poem 'Soiléireacht' ('*Clarity*'):

> *Oíche dí ab ea an oíche aréir,*
> *Is le teacht na maidine chonac an domhan soiléir,*
> *Domhan chomh sciomartha ní cuimhin liom é*
> *Leis an domhan seo ar imeallaibh ár ndí aréir.*
>
> *Focal ann ní raibh doiléir,*
> *Ná baitheas cinn ná baic muinéil,*
> *Anseo is buidéalaí 'bhí fós buidéal,*
> *Bhí gach ní nite ina nádúr féin ...*[29]

> Last night was a drinking night
> And come next morning I saw the world clearly,
> A world so scoured that I cannot remember it
> In this world last night on the edge of drinking
>
> Every word was revealed in its fullness
> Every shape and form,
> The bottle was more bottled than ever
> All things washed pure in their essence ...[30]

---

28 D: 11.10 a.m., 8 November 1957.

29 B: p. 36.

30 Trans. M. Ó hAodha.

Moments such as this that moved him to write poetry were becoming rarer now, however. His aunt Mary died at five o'clock in the morning, on 6 October 1960, after suffering a heart attack. Ó Ríordáin had heard her complaining of pain in the middle of the night and he'd had to get out of bed himself and go in search of the doctor and the priest. There was nothing the doctor could do for her unfortunately and she'd passed away before the priest had reached the house. Seán mourned her later that same day, both in prose and poetry, after her remains had left the house:

> *The poor worn-out creature; she had it really hard in this life but she never let it get to her; she always had an elegant way about her. She spoke lovely cultured English too, the type of English that educated people in Ireland and that would nearly convince you that you didn't need to respond to her in Irish. I heard that noble-sounding English out of her late last night and as her soul was about to depart this world. She spent time in various asylums, bore her various mental illnesses with great dignity. She was laid out in the room today, the one that I'm in now. I hope she'll forgive me for whatever needs forgiveness.*[31]

In much the same way as he'd associated the crazy ramblings of madness with poetry previously, now the written poem is his relative's body, prone and stretched out in death in 'Tá Pearsa Imithe as an Saol' ('*A Person has Gone Out of the World*').[32] It is the poem that elucidates the nature of death by virtue of its idiom, its rhythm and the certainty and finality that permeates the black print on a page. The paraphernalia of death is duly laid out for the journey beyond this life, in much the same way as the definitive version of a poem finally sees print. Everything else is as nothing at this point, neither the alternative form of the poem, nor the lines that were never destined to see print. These are being sent away forever and it is solely the externals or the representations of them that shall speak on behalf of the original (form) that is no more:

31 D: 1 p.m., 6 October 1960.
32 LL: p. 20. Trans. M. Ó hAodha.

Do foilsíodh an cnuasach so is déanaí
De cheannaithe na mná so ar an mbord,
Do casadh a creatlach in aibíd,
Is bhí fuacht na heagarthóireacht' ar an ngnó.[33]

This latest collection of this woman's features
Was laid out on the table,
Her body was wrapped in a habit,
In an act as cold as an editor's.[34]

The identification between death and poetry is clear; as with the poem, death too necessitates an external and visible 'form' to filter it and to explain it; it needs its own poem, even if such an elegy or art form had never been the deceased's previously. Ó Ríordáin recalls the previous night when he'd had to go and call for the priest in much the same way as the poet might call upon or source the requisite words to express a particular emotion. The same thinking that underlies this poem – one must always seize the moment when poetry and life itself are in the air – also permeates 'Ná Fan' ('*Don't Wait*'), as evidenced earlier. The other trope common to Ó Ríordáin here is the identification between poetry and the act of confession; the cleansing of sin and the freedom that accompanies the purification of the soul:

Glaoch ola is ea an t-éamh a chloistear ón bhfilíocht,
Dá dheireanaí an uair caithfidh tú éirí:
Tá fuadar ag fáil bháis is é ina pheacaí –
Glan é chun go bhfuarfaidh sé sa chló is aingli.[35]

A call for anointment is poetry's entreaty,
No matter how late one must respond:

33 LL: p. 20.
34 Trans. M. Ó hAodha.
35 LL: p. 43.

The commotion of a dying sinner –
Cleanse it in cold most angelic print.[36]

This poem was written in time for the publication of the collection *Brosna* (1964) but he didn't include it. He held it back until *Línte Liombó* (1971), waiting until he came up with a better ending to the poem. Perhaps he thought that his aunt's place in that last verse had been subsumed within a comparison that wasn't really appropriate to her. His frustration with what he'd managed to come up with so far for the poem's conclusion (as cited above) is clear from his notes:

What place will she be assigned to up on-high? She looking for a seat amongst the souls. She blinded by the light, and the remnants of what affected her mind once. Life's words still worrying her.

One way or another, this is how he concluded the poem in the end; here is the penultimate version of the poem, as written sometime in the years between the collections *Brosna* and *Línte Liombó*:

Chím ag déanamh ar na flaithis í mar bheadh sí dulta amú,
I dallta ag an solas, an saol so fós ina súil,
Í in achrann i bhfocail atá anois ag dul ar gcúl,
An tsíoraíocht ina seilbh is í mall á sealbhú.[37]

I see her making for the heavens as if she's lost,
Blinded by the light, this life still visible in her eyes,
Tied up in words that are fading,
She comes to it late, eternity in her grasp.[38]

Her death left him with a lonely November and December that year (1960), the two months of the year that Ó Ríordáin associated most with

36 Trans. M. Ó hAodha.
37 LL: p. 43.
38 Trans. M. Ó hAodha.

the dead in his mind. In the meantime, another poem had come to him, one that was heavy with the dread of blackest night. This was 'Bagairt na Marbh' ('*The Threat of the Dead*'), as written at midnight on 21 October 1960, a fortnight after his aunt Mary died:

> *'Listen or the dead will awake.' Doesn't that statement sound strange in this house at midnight and the dead of this house barely just buried? I put a record on just now,* Úr-Chill Chreagáin *as sung by Aodh Ó Duibheannaigh, and the sound on the album was so high, too high that I was suddenly afraid that I might wake up the person who's just died. I believe that it's easy to wake the crowd like her who are newly dead – and who haven't fully left yet. A feeling of mystery and loneliness came over me for the first time last night and the same thing happened again tonight when I thought that maybe she could hear the record. Oh Christ, isn't it just as well that I don't believe myself completely, or I'd go mad here alone in this house.*

In fact, it's unlikely that Ó Ríordáin actually composed 'Bagairt na Marbh' ('*The Threat of the Dead*') a fortnight after Mary's death, given that he confided to his notes that she'd been 'buried three months' by the time he wrote it. In the poem, Ó Ríordáin envisages her returning to this world again and exacting her revenge on him, given that he hadn't let her rest either in this life or the next:

> *Tá an seomra teann le bagairt na marbh*
> *Ní féidir a bhfearg a shásamh*
> *Níl duine beo faram …*[39]

> The room tense with the threat of the dead
> One can't slake their anger
> No living person with me …[40]

If there weren't others in the vicinity, there were certainly plenty of spirits

---

39 B: p. 33.

40 Trans. M. Ó hAodha.

from the beyond always hanging around, his room flooded with the same eerie atmosphere that was 'An Gealt' (a poem which most appropriately appeared on the page opposite it on the publication of *Brosna.*) There is this one major difference between both poems, however: in this case now, the room is infused with his aunt's presence and it is she who is watching him, rather than the other way around; this time, he's the lunatic presence that provokes and incites her. This disconcerting and restless mood permeates not just the poet's sickroom but the entire house:

Níl torann dá ndeinim
Ná cuireann í ar tinneall,
I riochtaibh teacht dúisithe im láthair,
Bí ciúin, is ná cloiseadh an té atá nua-mharbh,
Nua-thitithe i néalaibh an bháis tú.[41]

There is no noise I make
That does not put her on edge,
As if she might awake in my presence,
Be quiet, and let not the one who is newly dead,
Let her not hear you.[42]

Ó Ríordáin was alone in the house half of the time at this juncture because Gobnait was often unwell and regularly went to stay with her married sister. So it comes as no surprise that the restless, nostalgic and lonesome atmosphere of long ago defines whatever he wrote then. The memory or presence of his recently deceased aunt was still palpable, both mentally and physically, and bolstered the anxiety that is the poetry and the night. The poet fights off his fears and immerses himself in it; isn't the ability to feel – even your worst fears – a richer experience than being rendered emotionless and inert, after all? The poet takes the temperature of darkness and abandonment, even as he hears others outside, wandering home raucous and drunk after a night on the beer. Let the others beyond

41 B: p. 33.
42 Trans. M. Ó hAodha.

his window remain blind and deaf. He alone gauges the night. Ó Ríordáin could have gone out on such a Halloween Night but he stays in and records his impressions of the inner and outer selves instead. He looks into the mirror and records his 'self', frightening as that may be:

> *Halloween Night 1960. 11 p.m. I'm alone in the house with the cat. Even if the atmosphere tonight isn't as strong tonight as it was on Christmas Eve, you can feel something in the air tonight. Tonight is the night of the dead, God bless them, and it's no night to be alone in a house where there was a wake recently. I feel a little bit lonely and fearful. The night is wet and uncomfortable. If only I could go out and have a drink! But I stayed and even if I didn't hear anything, I didn't feel comfortable. I had to try not to let my thoughts wander. I focused my attention again and again on the everyday things of this world, on the radio, etc. I was trying to force down the fear, trying not to remember the other life. If there was someone else with me in the house, I wouldn't think about the afterlife at all. If the other life exists, isn't it still there whether you're on your own or not? Yes, but you don't feel it until you're on your own, is it? You lose many things when you have company.*

He's made little enough progress, one senses, since the terrifying storm-filled nights of his childhood when he had to call on his mother to calm him down as the small window in his room was lashed by rain. It's at the stage now where he has to birth himself again every day, even if he is alone, and isn't it particularly appropriate then that he's got more than one persona in his writing, 'Céadna' included, so that he can re-invent himself again and again if needs be; unless there is no such thing, and he is actually one and the same with that depersonalised Fate which has steered every aspect of his life since the beginning of time – that same endless complaining of his, that same endless Irish language of his, the same errors.[43] There was a time when he'd chosen and embraced this fate, but now, with the years passing quickly, the time for voluntarily choosing such a life and literary commitment was long gone. And, just as Ó Ríordáin had reminisced on his childhood in Ballyvourney with some nostalgia, as

43 LL: pp. 27–9.

he moves into middle age his thoughts often shift to the Inniscarra of the late 1930s and early 1940s, the place that became his permanent home – the road at Bun an Chomair, the drama hall and the other places in the vicinity he'd once frequented. And still, beneath any slivers of nostalgia, we can sense the poet's unspoken regrets – the fact that he'd never gone down 'amongst the people' half enough and experienced that strange mixture of love and spite that was the Irish personality. Death is the one thing that calls him – the sole trope that never leaves his writing and his sensibility alone. It is always there in the background, stalking him every step of the way. Death is all-encompassing, a shadow on the periphery of his vision, and that haunted his work a long time before the death of his aunt, its dark presence growing stronger each day and mourning him in addition to all the others and the time that is lost now forever.

Ó Ríordáin looks at the trace of his foot in the mud one day and mourns those who are gone and those of his 'people' whose lives are nearing the end.[44] He mourns himself and bemoans the sparse tribe of words that he has left for his keening. We've become familiar with some of this tribe of 'words' over time, terms such as 'sceon' amongst them:

> *There is no word in the Irish language that I'm more familiar with than the word 'sceon' ('fear'). It's a cowardly state of affairs how often I feel anxious and fearful. As they say in Dunquin, 'sceon ar fad is ea mé' ('I'm all fear').*[45]

And he had another word that was close kin with 'sceon', the one he regularly hoped he wouldn't encounter – particularly after yet another anxious and restless night and with another day of pain and suffering and the ever-present torpor of disease awaiting him – and this was 'dúisithe' (awake), a term he once explained the contours of as follows:

> *9.15 a.m. Awake … It frightens me to write the word 'awake.' I've just emerged from the peaceful world of sleep to the anxious world of waking. I never wake up without feeling immediately afraid as, apparently, I associate being awake*

44 B: pp. 11–12.
45 D: 7 January 1955.

> *with trouble and pain. When I say (dúisithe) 'awake' what I'm really saying is 'Lord of Heaven, the time has come again that I must face the latest disaster that has inevitably befallen me, the latest health problems that have afflicted me, the latest spiritual torment I'm suffering.' (I never awake to joy but always to suffering.) 'And, oh Christ, I must confront and try and recover from all the disaster and illness and diseases of yesterday.'*[46]

And there was despair also as his constant companion, as exemplified in the following example, where the pair meet each other as if in prearranged appointment:

> *I woke at 5.30 a.m. and my relative was watching over me faithfully and patiently. Whoever else abandoned me, he didn't. Jealousy since I met [sic] is his name. He's been with me a long time.*[47]

And he'd be with him for a good while yet. On 3 August 1968 Ó Ríordáin's short essay 'Éadóchas maidine' appeared in *The Irish Times*. 'The world never looks too good at five or six o'clock in the morning' is its first sentence. Not that it looks much better at any other hour of the day either – particularly when, as in this poet's case, you have nowhere to go and nothing to do. This is a form of hell and you have got to suffer it. And perhaps its worst aspect of all is the repetitious or eternal monotony and sameness of it, and the mundane absence of thought and experience that defines it. Most terrifying of all, you can't remember how exactly you fell into this place or what brought you there in the first place. This is an existence that is interminable and because you cannot escape it and it goes on forever you might as well 'name' it or acknowledge it while you can. 'Tuirse' or (tiredness) is another, and perhaps the least distressing of terms. He locates this region on the map also and travels across it. There's no limit to how much you can know about this region of existence. It's a place that is exactly as it is described, just as it was in Don Quixote's case:

46 D: 21 October 1960.
47 D: 14 June 1967.

> *8.30 p.m. How can I study or do any writing? Between sickness and fatigue, I'm falling asleep from morning till night … When I wrote that word 'tuirse' ('fatigue') just now, you wouldn't believe the joy I got in that word – in the shape of the word, in the old memories associated with that word, in the meaning of the word, in the Irish-languageness of the word. I thought of Pound's phrase: 'Dá mbeadh mo thuirse-se ort, bheadh fhios agat.' ['If you had my fatigue – you'd know it.'] But you don't need to be sick to get the real flavour of that word. Maybe there are plenty of others who are healthy and who'd get ten times the flavour of that word 'fatigue'. But I have nothing. I didn't get anything.*[48]

Intervals of exhausted sleep as punctuated by the ceaseless partitioning of time. 'Isan bhFrainc im dhúscadh dhamh/In Éirinn Chuinn im chodladh.' ('*And France awake and alert/gentle Ireland still sleeping.*') Or at least, that's what he imagines, even if it isn't always like this. The poet returns to the diary and notes down whatever minor spoils he may have gathered while under the dream's influence, in the effort to augment his vision, even if sometimes he has found nothing there but another version of the world that he's been trying to escape. At least his documenting of the night means that he can temporarily delay the moment when he has to face a new day. After all, it's the individual who has nothing to document or nothing to say after his nocturnal wanderings who gets the worst abuse when the clock strikes 5 or 6 a.m. On 14 November 1962 he noted the following fractured impressions of the night before, as dawn approached and he felt the spectre of despair close in on him once more. Better his fractured impression than the full-blown nightmare:

> *I remember a few bits of dreams I had last night. I was abroad – somewhere very far away. There was someone with me – a man who was tied to me, his back to my back, the back of his head to the back of mine. He had some kind of a box or a helmet around his head. His job was to spit out my saliva – or something strange or disgusting like this. He had to lean back to do this. I think that the helmet was filled with water. It was hard work, he said, and he felt dizzy. We passed through London. I saw myself in the mirror of City Hall when I reached Cork city.*

48 D: 17 December 1957.

The sustenance this half-sleeping world of dreams provides him with is all he has, given that his ability to function and engage in the outside world is so limited. It's this inability to act or perform the deed that's left him in the subdued and forlorn state that he is in; this is the man whose health never recovered and whose illness never killed him, the man who never married, who neither truly became a clerk nor a poet, and a person who never truly accepted or interacted with others in the community and yet who never rejected them either; this is the man who never fully made the definitive decision on any matter, who remained in that liminal area, the limbo in-between. The recalcitrant individual who wouldn't listen to his inner self or to anyone else either, and even when he did, rarely acted upon such advice. Passing the days alone, passing time – with little notion of what might come tomorrow, or how time ought to be doled out or apportioned. Let tomorrow look after itself. It's not your problem; you're hard-pressed enough just getting through *this* one day – today.[49] Besides, tomorrow never did anything for you anyway, did it? This is enough is it not? – to look after this one person, this one body that's being torn apart by anxiety, regret and disease – never mind having to worry about others too. You are on your own in this one moment of time. You were always on your own.

The individual and the poem make the same journey, along a road and a range of experience that's ever-narrowing – until, in the end, they become as one. The artistic sensibility that was the poet's is running down the clock, sustained solely by fading nostalgia and memory – running to stand still. If the poet had sought solitariness and to end up on his own, he'd certainly got that – if anyone ever got it. There was one thing they'd kept from him all the same, curse them – and this was that stupid blubbering, childish and ignorant humanity of theirs. He'd always been too honest. There had been more poetry in the life than there had been life in the poems. As usual, he'd never been able to locate the failing within himself, to name it:

> *You can probably do worse than propose a new theory, i.e. a philosophical interpretation of one of the world's problems. You're caught within your own*

49 TÉB: p. 28.

> *net. These theories or philosophies harden within your mind and everything that will blow the winds of that theory and form it so that it's driven your way. It has to be distorted so that it can make its way through the gap that is theory.*[50]

In the old Gaelic tale 'Dearg mac Deirg', a story he'd learned years ago from Nell Mhattie, the king's son had put the witch under the injunction (taboo) that she only eat whatever food the wind blew to her through the eye of a needle. She wouldn't get fat on this any more than the poet would – certainly not as based on how much of this life might come to him through the eye of his own theory. More crucially still, what was the point in going on the same journey repeatedly to the inner world he'd already thoroughly ransacked, especially when there was nothing left to source any more? The cream that the poet had spoken of skimming in *Eireaball Spideoige* has hardened and entered the cow's horns.[51] This is the desolation that is a barren physical and emotional life, and about as far away as is possible from the fecundity and overflowing nature that one normally associates with poetry. It's no easy feat to compose poetry in such a bleak environment. Look around you; you've been confined to bed for the past two or three days, with the damp running down the walls. Half-read books scattered around the bed and on the floor. Little to no food in the house and not another soul in sight – not even someone who could hand you a cup of tea. A stack of empty cans next to the bed, ready to fling at the cat if he tries to get through the door again, seeing as he's already shushed him out plenty of times already. The smell of illness and infection – the smell of despair. They're all there, clear as day, with him in the room now and this man is under no illusions about who he is and what he's become – the life that's his. This thing that he does – this thing called writing – it is anything but writing in reality, isn't it? And even if it was writing, would he actually be grateful just for this fact? Hadn't he been to the well a thousand times previously when there had actually been something worth sourcing and what had he got for his troubles? And they'd been the charitable or giving Christian types too, hadn't they! No

50 D: 10 August 1967.
51 ES: p. 27.

doubt about it! Keep your distance or you'll get badly burned. Put a stop to all of this now. Do yourself a favour and burn this book in the morning while you're at it. Don't let them know how low you've fallen, whatever you do. That would just give them too much satisfaction, especially if they thought that they'd managed to drag you down to this level. The dream speaks to the poet and accuses him directly of being a coward. Why hadn't he stood his ground better instead of running away again?

This was additional dream-matter that didn't make it into prose, as usually happened come morning. It would have been forgotten completely if he hadn't formed a poem around it entitled 'Na Leamhain' ('*The Moths*'). This poem can be divided into three main elements: the setting, the dream and the message it expresses. The first verse and the last share the same setting and it's the atmosphere that is the dream which acts to separate them. It is an autumn night, the bedroom lights on late into the night; he's reading the book, turning the pages, the murmur of 'moth wings'. Then suddenly, and without warning, the abrupt assault, the injured wings, the 'fragile thing tormented'. The ghost of his humanity rears up within him and it suddenly occurs to the poet that he's the guilty one, the one who is responsible for all the pain that permeates the room. The real world and the world of dreams merge as one. The sudden assault in the silent darkness resurrects the memory of another night again when he'd felt those flimsy, helpless pages of the book between his fingers and understood the duty that fate had deemed his – 'to lay my hands on them', 'to save them' and bring them into the light again without blemish or harm. And then the sudden act of violence and devastation. His hand slips out on him and the 'holy dust' of the moth's wings is crushed like fine powder; the moment of beauty is destroyed:

Oíche eile i dtaibhreamh bhraitheas-sa
Peidhre leamhan-sciathán,
Mar sciatháin aingil iad le fairsingeacht
Is bhíodar leochaileach mar mhná.

Dob é mo chúram lámh a leagadh orthu
Is gan ligean leo chun fáin,

Ach iad a shealbhú gan sárú tearmainn
Is iad a thabhairt chun aoibhnis iomlán.

Ach dhoirteas-sa an púdar beannaithe
'Bhí spréite ar gach sciathán …[52]

Another night, in a dream, I felt
a moth's gentle wingspan.
Overarching, angelic, but infinitely
bruiseable, like woman.

I had to lay my hands on them
and not let them flutter away,
and deliver them to bliss,
and not violate their sanctuary.

But me, I spilled the magic powder
sprinkled on each wing …[53]

Now for the lesson of the poem, a lesson that's far from ethereal or dream-like in reality. Whereas before this the poet was half-reaching towards something that was almost unreachable or ineffable under the veil of sleep and dream, there's now a real awareness being conveyed here and it's this: the poet senses that he doesn't have it in him; he doesn't have the necessary 'marks (numbers) of manliness'. He's not man enough to be numbered/counted amongst them (i.e. the men), really. The dream serves to bolster cold reality in this instance. And if the sexual undertones were there earlier, they were only as an essential element of the whole – the fluttering wings that were 'womanly and sensitive', 'the taking possession without violation of the sanctuary', the 'holy dust' that spills – these are no longer reflections of something else but rather what the poet actually

---

52 B: p. 18.
53 Sewell, *Selected Poems*, p. 139. Trans. Francis O'Hare and Frank Sewell.

discovered in the emotions he's sourced.[54] The poet's sole role in this is to bring the sensations of the night to the poem and dress the words in the appropriate language, words that would do it justice. He was as oblivious as anyone else as to what the poem actually signified. And as the reality of morning draws in and he nears waking, the poet sees the poem in its true context and realises its insignificance in the greater scheme of things. He imagines the numbers (physically) walking out of the dream to him, as a form of conviction or authority. 'If you say that it is 150 miles between Cork and Dublin, you have a certain power over that road,' was how Ó Ríordáin explained this idea, when asked once. Because numbers and roads belong to other people, to the 'authority' that is the society outside his room – and not to him. The security and certainty that are these categories is paramount, as is the terminology of circularity that is logic and reason. God help the person who doesn't belong to any category at all, the individual whose life is that marginal or lacking in substance or meaning that their very existence appears futile. He won't be at that fair of voices or expression at all – whether as buyer or seller – the way things are looking. They can do fine without him, thank you very much. And when it comes to time totting up time, or counting, he doesn't figure in the calculations at all:

Is tuigeadh dom go rabhas gan uimhreacha.
Gan uimhreacha na fearúlachta go brách.

Is shiúil na deich n-uimhreacha as an mearbhall
Is ba mhó ná riamh a n-údarás,
Is ba chlos ciníocha ag plé le huimhreacha,
Is cách ba chlos ach mise amháin.[55]

and knew I'd always lack the numbers,
the numbers of the masculine.

54 Sewell, *Selected Poems*, p. 139. Trans. Francis O'Hare and Frank Sewell.
55 B: p. 18.

The ten numbers strode from the chaos,
greater than ever in authority,
and nations were heard engaging in numbers,
and all were heard but me.[56]

The crazy fool or the insect, it doesn't matter one way or the other; their dizzy, tortured flight is one and the same, as is their end – the complete annihilation that is the light, the obliteration that is the burning flame. The moths emerged from the darkness and caught Ó Ríordáin by surprise; and they've generated whatever crazy, panicked excitement that characterises this night. 'Níl cuil, níl leamhan, níl beach/Dár chruthaigh Dia, níl fear,/Nach dualgas dúinn a leas' ('*There's neither fly, nor moth, nor bee/As God created/That it's well-being isn't our duty*') he says in the poem 'Ní Ceadmhach Neamhshuim' ('*Indifference is not Permitted*') because 'they are part of us by rights.'[57] The same subject manifests itself in 'Na Leamhain' ('*The Moths*'), albeit in more mysterious form. And the moths aren't the only creatures and animals that the poet directs his artistic gaze at either, as we will see soon. The 'lack of manliness' that is the other side of this discourse is also a frequent aspect of Ó Ríordáin's thinking as we approach the mid 1950s and the end of that same decade, for example:

I'm not someone tonight who has control over himself. There isn't the slightest manliness in the anxious state I'm in. I'm letting fate do whatever it wants with me. I haven't got the manliness in me to take any part in the process.[58]

I think I'll probably be going down, i.e. to Hell. Not because of my bad deeds but because of my lack of courage, my lack of manliness. I'm living a life that I hate but I can't give it up ... There's another life there that I don't live and a life that it's my duty to live, an expansive life that would be ever-developing. But do I believe this, really? If I did, wouldn't I set myself free and undertake that life?[59]

56 Sewell, *Selected Poems*, p. 139. Trans. Francis O'Hare and Frank Sewell.
57 LL: p. 40; trans. M. Ó hAodha.
58 D: 7 February 1955.
59 D: 6 July 1955.

There's no reason to respond. Life still goes on, even if there's little enough of it to be found where the poet finds himself. He might be the old man in the court by now, all right – as Ó Ríordáin reminds himself on 27 May 1962 – but he has plenty of the ailments that bother women too, lying there every day on a half-frozen bed, tormented with thoughts and emotions … And no more than with his other thoughts and theories, it's not as if many of these have much of a reasonable basis to them in the real world (outside), 'Ní fear gníomha sinn' ('*We're not men of action*').

On Christmas Eve 1960 Ó Ríordáin heard the sad news that a cousin of his, Dónall Ó Drisceoil, had been sent to a mental home. Dónall's mother was Han, Seán's aunt (his father's sister), and seeing that he was a relative on his father's side, it set Seán to thinking about madness and the fear that such madness might have been passed on to him from that side of the family. You wouldn't mind, but wasn't such 'madness' already evident in the stubborn road he'd elected to follow in his own life as it was already? There was no question about that. And you wouldn't mind either but the madness or oddness would likely manifest itself anyway, wouldn't it? Particularly if it was his family inheritance, and irrespective of how much he tried to flee its influence. The mule was the son of the donkey and there was no two ways about it. This was a far from happy subject to be worrying about at Christmas-time:

> *They all have it, whatever it's called. My brother has it, my sister has it, that aunt has it, i.e. the mother of that Dónall who is in the mental home. My father and my uncle had it. I have it also. What's this? That we're Ó Ríordáins? Some kind of blindness afflicts you if you're an Ó Ríordáin, if you're one of the tribe. A blindness, an anger, a misery, a pride, a lack of charity, having a negative view of the neighbours, bitterness, malice for everyone, a cowardly sensitivity, the Ó Ríordáins have all of these in their blood.*[60]

'My grandfather had a hand in it.'[61] For the poet to seek out the source or root of his artistic sensibility was analogous with his soul seeking spiritual

60 D: 26 December 1960.
61 ES: p. 113.

calm and harmony. Ó Ríordáin utilised the scaffolding that was Catholic spiritual thought to engender the prayer within himself, and the prayer that was the racial inheritance (temple) of the Irish language. To be at one with the mind of God in poetry and 'to elevate himself like incense in God's presence by means of the appropriate act' – these two objectives were aspects of the same thinking in the poet's view.[62] The return to source and form within the tradition was itself a configuration of the eternal, an aspect of eternity itself. He listens to the voice – in the 'little-coat priest'[63] – because it has been ordained thus from the beginning, in the same way as he, the poet, seeks to strum on the 'harp that is the Master'. He's not long concluding, however, that the only 'Master' that's guiding things, really, is that of 'instinct' or 'inheritance', that which reveals itself in the boy's brown eyes which are but an ancient reflection of all the others who have come before – the lineage that is his in 'Súile donna' ('*Brown eyes*'). Or when he asks 'Ab shin a bhfuil de shíoraíocht ann, go maireann smut dár mblas' ('*Is that all eternity means, then, a small part of us living on*').[64] Or:

An mar seo tá an scéal mar sin –
Imeom ar nós an tsneachta anuraidh
Ach fanfaidh na clóanna fós ag filleadh …[65]

So, is this the way the story goes –
we all fade away like last year's snow
but the forms keep coming back on the scene …[66]

He's as certain of the likely response as he was years earlier: 'An bhfuil síoraíocht ann mar deir na naoimh?' ('*Does eternity exist as the saints claim?*') – from 'An Cheist' ('*The Question*').[67] It isn't really the same response, however, it turns out. Not for the poet, who still bears the same damned

62 ES: p. 13.
63 B: p. 24.
64 LL: pp. 10–13.
65 From 'Clóanna über Alles', TÉB: p. 29.
66 Sewell, *Selected Poems*, p. 225. Trans. Frank Sewell.
67 ES: p. 31; trans. M. Ó hAodha.

imprint and characteristics of the 'Speckled Riordans'. 'Níl ionam ach ball/De chorp san mo shinsir' ('*I am but a member of that ancestral body.*')[68] Now, he hears one of the younger generation talking down at the road (a girl), and he recognises the same thing in her as was in the generations before her, the same blindness or 'crankiness of the Ó Súilleabháins':

> *... just as the Ó Súilleabháins have heard it pronounced in the four generations that came before her. Death doesn't affect this cranky trait as long as Ó Súilleabháins continue to be born. The cantankerousness continues proclaiming itself and the Ó Súilleabháins are just the microphone for it. Great ... it is really important that there is something permanent in this life.*[69]

He's in writer mode again, and broadcasting the 'one message' that's been granted him. The inherited failings he sees in each generation is just another echo of what he'd said to Pádraig Murphy once in City Hall: 'everyone (in this life) is given just the one message', and the poet replicated it again in one of his most important essays years on:

> *I think that just the one message is given to each person. And constantly proclaiming this one message is what everyone does, no matter what it is that they actually say. Sustaining this message is what each person does continually ...*[70]

And if one consequence of Ó Ríordáin's literary project was to leave his 'self' behind after he was gone 'as further evidence of Humanity with respect to Humanity', another consequence was that he'd leave as his legacy examples of humanity's capability for pettiness and 'stupidity'.[71] It's a vicious circle that defines Ó Ríordáin's thinking – the constant exposition of this alleged 'inherited' tendency towards stasis or failure ('O'Riordanism') – that condition from which there is no release and which goes on frustrating him to the very end.

---

68 LL: p. 29. 'Toil' ('*Will*'), trans. M. Ó hAodha.
69 'Púcaí', IT, 10 June 1972.
70 'Teachtaireacht Amháin' ('*One Message*'), IT, 1 April 1970.
71 'Ná bac do bhac' ('*Don't impede your own impediment*'), IT, 17 June 1972.

And this thinking of his had other unintended consequences too – i.e. if it was indeed one's duty to source their native and appropriate form and the sensibility that expressed this artistically, rather than presenting a false or 'constructed' form of self, then you were surely damned for all eternity if one adopted such a native or 'inherited' form too enthusiastically or too completely.[72] In his case, the artist was in a 'no-win' situation, really, given that it had been written that the father's sins fell onto his sons and became their burden to carry on into the third or fourth generation. And what sort of a 'debt' would this poor poet inherit, given that he had no one of his own following after him to clear any part of it? There must have been some list of sins or failings due rendering back down the line for him, Ó Ríordáin thought, given how much he'd suffered in his life already. There is nothing amusing about this at all, noted as it is in the early hours of a cold winter's morning:

> *Awake still and frightened. My sins are the cause of this. The debt has to be paid. Who will pay it? Your family or your family's family. How do I know that I'm not paying for sins that were committed even before I was born! It's unlikely that anyone (i.e. a son or a daughter) will come after me to pay my dues. I've a big bill to pay so.*[73]

This was the concept of inherited 'debt' or psychic retribution/karma gone mad. And whatever had prompted such thinking on Ó Ríordáin's part, he was certain the debt had to be paid one way or another, and that it was a debt with a long history – 'Ó leag Ádhamh a shúil/Ár Éabha in tseanreacht' ('*From when Adam laid his eyes/Upon Eve under the old order.*')[74]

And what additional calamity had befallen him that he'd ended up in a place where they spoke bad English – never mind Irish – even as he sought to tap the source of his Gaelic inheritance as sustenance to his art? And what was the endless search for this 'inherited flaw', be it blindness or insanity, when one knew deep down that the flaw was there in you from

72 ES: pp. 18–20.

73 D: 5.50 a.m., 29 January 1961.

74 LL: p. 27; trans. M. Ó hAodha.

the very beginning and not in anyone else? Didn't he know this better than anyone and hadn't he any number of examples from his own life to confirm it?

As usual, it's when his anxiety and illness has rendered him powerless that he sees his predicament and understands the power and the healing that lies in the ritual of the everyday and the life he's forsaken for the sake of his art. The likes of this:

> *The day in bed. I feel sick. I didn't feel the slightest hint of joy today but only complete* tristitia *[sadness]. I realise today that there is no solace anywhere this side of the sunset. I'm going through a dark place – the valley in the shadow of death – and death is crawling on my skin. My aunt is keeping me company for a couple of hours here in the room tonight. Rare is wonderful! She's not bad company. She's pure honest. Slow. Her conversation like that of a priest. She's talking about the Carrigadrohid people, her home parish, where she was during the Christmas. Basic conversation. Describing people. Nothing exaggerated or made-up or theoretical. Keep the oars low in the water. She is part of a community. I've often noticed this in people, this understanding of the communal mindset and I've felt jealous of it. I always felt separate from it. There is a comfort and a warmth evident in my aunt's outlook. I never bother with these things except when I'm sick.*[75]

Gobnait died on the last day of November 1962. She'd spent thirty years living in that same house as him at Bun an Chomair. Or maybe it would be more correct to say that he'd spent thirty years sharing the house with her, given that Seán was the tenant all that time and not the other way around. Not only did Gobnait own the house in partnership with Mary, but the people and the place were hers also in a certain respect. She'd always prepared the dinner, lit the fire and ensured that the chalet at the back of the house was the poet's home. In fact, Gobnait was always the poet's strongest link with the outside world, if you excluded the clerical job that he'd been thinking of leaving since the very first day. Although he'd mentally left the job already by this juncture, he remained in it for

75 D: 7 January 1962.

another three years in actuality. And in many ways Ó Ríordáin had much the same attitude towards both his aunt and his job in those days: they were both areas of life that should be avoided, except when you had to deal with them, areas that you should push to the back of your mind or keep your distance from as much as you possibly could. But it's another story when you no longer encounter either or when they've disappeared from your life entirely. Did neither of them have that attribute known as humanity about them? And is their passing all the more poignant now given that they (or their potential humanity) have all but disappeared from his world? Isn't that enough in itself to warrant their mourning now that they're gone? And, in truth, the poet mourns more than this again; he also mourns himself – the pathetic and broken example of humanity that he once was. What a pity that he hadn't recognised years earlier how close he was to the person who's now gone, how alike they both were, really – how they'd been moulded from such similar clay:

> *I feel guilty in relation to this place I've been living in for the past thirty years now. It would be true to say that I've never shown any real interest in the place. i.e. in the activities of the people here for the past twenty years – over the past ten years, in particular. There was no point. The Gaeltacht and the city's intellectual life was the focus of my attention. There was nothing here, I thought, except poor and simple people who were of little interest given that they only spoke English – the broken English of Ireland. I'm afraid that we'd become too full of ourselves, too inhuman, us Irish speakers, the Gaelic revivalists. During all this time, my aunt (Gobnait) didn't neglect the local community, not a chance. She became one of them and signs on it – they respected her and were fond of her … Now I understand why it bothered my aunt so much when she'd to leave this place and go back to Carrigadrohid when she was sick. She left behind the place that she identified with and where she was understood. She'd been working on this place for years in much the same way that others work on a language.*[76]

It is far more difficult to bury the past or lament your kin than one imagines, however. She has passed away and yet she isn't gone; she lives

76 D: 6 December 1962.

on in the physical atmosphere of the house and in the communal memory. He'll love her and hate her in equal measure, irrespective of the different ways she manifests herself to him in the following years. There's no fear she'll be forgotten in death either because, unlike him, she's a link in the local communal chain and an important element in the community's ideation of itself. It's the other person, the one who's reliant on the life she created who's really left hurting at her passing. And what will be left after he (the poet) is gone – a handful of words, if that even? Who knows whether the language in which they were written will even survive, never mind the memory of the individual who wrote them. There'd been a time – a long time ago now – when he'd thought of bringing the community to him, of trying to Gaelicise them, but that was before he'd left them for this solitary existence in the place that neither community (whether English or Irish-language) could ever reach him. And, in so far as the poet has any possible remnants of an older community or way of life to share with others, it certainly isn't with the community closest to him – in Inniscarra – that he'll be sharing it. Detached from others and their humanity by the barrier that is language, a language that the poet has never been sure was ever really his, whether by inheritance or education. For all he knows, maybe these attempts of his to express himself in a language so marginal to the daily life of others and independently of every accepted social institution created for same – for all he knows, this is just an admission of his own oddness, the strain of madness he's always feared.

This is a question that's tormented Ó Ríordáin for years and one that he never actually solved to his satisfaction; the one thing that is very clear to him by now is this: he's the one who's lost out the most as a consequence of his entire life's project. It's never been a question of language – English or Irish – but rather of poetry and the role of 'people' within his realm of creativity.[77] And he's still tied up in knots and paradoxes, and there's no sign of release from any of them. If he hadn't isolated himself from that joy of community or public persona he gets an inkling of every now and then, he'd probably have given up on poetry and the search for his creative aesthetic years ago by now, wouldn't he? Therein lies the terrible irony of his life.

77 D: 1 July 1963.

It was just after the funeral of a local girl named Claire Kelleher, who died young and whom Ó Ríordáin knew, that he wrote the essay 'Coinsias Sochraide' (*'Funereal Conscience'*).[78] Her funeral was an occasion when Ó Ríordáin felt something small stirring within himself – a feeling that maybe he still had it in him to leave the solitariness of his room at the back of the house on occasion and renew himself in the 'social act' with others in a public setting. This thought has no sooner occurred to him, however, than he reverts to his distrustful or guarded self again, the self that we've come to recognise down through the years. The next moment, he senses that the public is conspiring against him and that the culture that is social norms and institutions has ostracised him because he's never abided by their protocols or rituals. Not only that but he feels as if he stands out almost amongst them like a 'sore thumb' because he's separated himself from the community all this time, so much so that he doesn't even know the rituals properly, he's lost the ability to act in accordance with the social norms that define everyday living:

> *In the graveyard during a funeral is when I get the strongest sense of community. Maybe this is because I have no relationship with them at all. When I visit the Gaeltacht my Irish improves. It's then that I see how poor and rundown it really is. A funeral is a renewal of a similar type. You find out (at a funeral) how poor and rundown your humanity has become, not to mention your social etiquette. I feel myself an oddball amongst the neighbours whenever I'm at a funeral. I feel myself starved with the hunger and dying with the thirst, in the absence of human contact. The air is alive with people and I'm soaking it all in. I feel that everyone else is acting out their lives in accordance with the public conventions except me. It's like as if they're all conspiring against me. I feel that they are contemptuous of me – that they know I'm not playing out my role within the community. I wonder do others have this funeral conscience too? Do they all feel as guilty I do? I feel awkward in my conversation and my manner. I suppose that your speech becomes impoverished and your manners get more coarse because you're separated from them for too long. Human beings make sense of the world through relationships. A person becomes abrupt or blunt when alone for too long.*

78 IT, 15 June 1974.

> *Interaction softens his words. Another thing that I noticed at the funeral was that the community have a firmer grip on the truth than I do. You have to be part of the community to be healthy, apparently. Your thinking gets weak and thin if you're alone. Individual logic gets a hold on you and you lose the flexibility of mind that is the community's.*[79]

Claire Kelleher was just twenty-five years old when she died on 1 June 1974. More likely than not, she'd been amongst that group of pretty young women who'd been with him that autumn afternoon in the orchard ten years earlier, women whose swift ageing had shocked him whenever he came across any of them years later:

> *I brought my brother over here this afternoon and he put a letter box in the door for me. I sent him home and spent the rest of the afternoon picking apples along with a number of pretty young girls until nightfall. Anything to do with apples reminds me of Robert Frost. But, again, there's no point in letting Robert Frost or anyone else come between you and the light, whether it's the afternoon light or the light of darkness. There was a group of girls there picking apples with me, girls aged between sixteen and eighteen years of age. As regards apples, housework or even good mentality, I feel that these girls are a lot more sensible and more knowledgeable than I am. Where do they get this good sense and understanding from? How come everyone was given such wisdom and understanding, despite how young they are, and I was left without it? 'Do you think that these apples are ripe?' I'd say to them, as if they were older than me. They know what people are thinking, what people are saying, what people would do on one occasion or another. They are part of a community and they think as part of a community – something that I was never able to do. I never rooted myself properly in any one place. A person without roots as torn between two languages – that's who I've always been.*[80]

The poet laments the trajectory of his own life and his stunted emotional development. Unlike the young women he describes, he never put down real

79 IT, 15 June 1974.

80 D: midnight, 8/9 September 1964.

roots anywhere, nor developed his sensibility in harmony with the rhythm of the seasons. And the truth is that his season or assigned portion of this life is drawing to a close from the mid 1950s onwards. It's not that he'd ever gathered too much to himself as part of his portion, anyway. There's no loneliness like the loneliness for the life that was never lived. 'Footfalls echo in the memory,/Down the passage which we did not take …'

The poet is more likely now to take a jaunt back to those happier and more expansive former times via his writing or his memories than any other way. Those sunny summer evenings when the bicycles passed by out on the forgotten road and the perfumed dusk drew in. There were more of those days that got away from the poet than stayed with him. The memory of that life may well have dimmed in the intervening years but it's all he has left and the only place he can source his former self. It certainly beats the dry and dull philosophy that underscores the emptiness of so much abstract thought. Two different July afternoons in two consecutive summers and the poet reflects on the extent of his life that became Inniscarra. However impoverished or abandoned he may feel (socially or culturally), it is his only home – and has been for most of his life, too:

> *Another day in the office. A lonely evening at home. In Inniscarra. I walked back the road as far as the graveyard and returned by the river bank. This place has descended into beauty. The river and the bridge so peaceful, and as lovely as a young girl … Loneliness is the human being's poem. I'd like to leave this place. I've been looking forward to leaving for a long time. I was never as lonely as I am now – seeing as they're all gone – my mother, my sister and my brother – but still and all, I always felt, and still feel the magic of the lazy summer afternoons here in Inniscarra. Cars and bicycles slipping past me and couples loving each other. Sentimentality! But Munster people were always like this. A rushed day and a lazy evening – this is as it was fated for us. But we are getting on in years and it's time to wake ourselves up.*[81]

> *A hot night. Thunder and rain threatening. I went up the Bun an Chomair road with Tom Bradley tonight, something I rarely do. I'm in the car too often*

81 D: 10.20 p.m., 9 July 1957.

> *... I really enjoyed the night and walking the road against the hill. It's a long time since I walked this road. I felt kind of lonely there when I thought back to my younger days when I was on this road more often than anywhere else. I've spent most of my life here in Inniscarra. I never did any travelling at all. And yet, a sentimental feeling came over me as I walked this road tonight as if I'd just returned home after being abroad for many long years. If I was abroad, this wouldn't happen to me at all I suppose. I always regret spending my life in such a boring and uninspiring place as this. But anyway, here is where I wrote whatever I've written, and a feeling stirred in me tonight that I can't feel anywhere else.*[82]

The return home is the theme of the next extract also, one of the very last we have from Ó Ríordáin, as relating to this theme of lost youth – but no less nostalgic or haunting for that. A neighbouring girl whom he'd courted twenty years earlier has returned to Inniscarra on a visit and the past when 'the joy of youth radiated on the evening roads' comes flooding back. Needless to say, such joyful, youthful days were as much a fiction and a form of nostalgia as anything else – and no one knows this better than the poet himself. The following excerpt is taken from the journal *Combar*, from March 1961, although he'd written it at 3.40 a.m. on 31 August 1960. It's easy for someone to see a summer evening long ago through rose-tinted spectacles, especially someone who yearns for the forgotten magic of the past:

> *There's a visitor in the village, here on her holidays. This woman lived here twenty years ago. She belonged to our youth. She's out of sync with the present time now. She acts now as if she was back twenty years ago again – all giddy. The giddiness of her teenage years doesn't suit this woman as she's nearly forty. Nevertheless, I don't find her way of behaving unnatural – because I understand it. She's on holidays. Not only did she move from one place to another, but she moved from one time to another. She returned to the time and place she was in twenty years ago. She took a break from where she was, in terms of space and time. Unfortunately, this area or space has moved from where it was long ago*

82 D: 11.10 p.m., 11 July 1958.

> *time-wise, so you could say that she's guilty of romanticising the past, but then she's also awakened some part of that old life in us too – so that you'd imagine sometimes that she's brought the area back twenty years in time also. I almost felt the lustre of youth on the roads this evening – the same lustre that was on those roads in the evenings as they were twenty years ago. But they didn't really have that lustre twenty years ago, as there never was any such glow on the roads back then. What is she really, this woman? She's our youth twenty years ago, not as we really were, but as how we imagine it was. We all got younger and so too did the area since she came amongst us – but it was a false getting younger.*

The following summer and the poet looks out at the seats at the front of the house and imagines all the relatives and friends who sat on them in the sweet summer evenings long ago. Then the return to the diary again, back to the source of his art; how many of these people are still evoked there or how many have left no trace at all? Aren't you lucky, really, to have anything to call your own by the time you come to the end, anyway? Even to have the imaginary itself – the life of the mind:

> *Tonight, when night fell, I looked at the old seats outside this house. I thought back to all the people that sat on them over the years (or some of them, I suppose). Some of them are amongst the hosts of the dead now, have mercy on them, e.g., my mother, my aunt Mary, John Hanlon. The rest of them are long gone. None of them left tonight. There were pretty young girls amongst the people that sat on these seats once. They were the days and the nights. Where are those girls tonight? Where is their prettiness gone? Many's the summer sin and winter sin that was committed around these seats. I am all alone now, I'm old.*[83]

83 D: 9 July 1961.

11

The Hardened Shell

Seán Ó Ríordáin was forty-three years of age in 1960. Who else would accompany him into old age? Other than the Gaeltacht people (Pound, An File, Charlie, Danny, Seosamh Ó Dálaigh, Bab Feiritéar, etc.), there were others such as Séamus Murphy (the sculptor who made a bronze head of Ó Ríordáin in July 1957) and his wife Máiréad, Seán Hendrick, Diarmaid Hurley, Bob Cotter and Kay MacCarthy – all English-speakers rather than Irish-language enthusiasts (i.e. they would all have spoken to Seán in English, as opposed to whatever small bit of Irish they might have had.)

Amongst this latter group was Isobel O'Shea, the woman whom Ó Ríordáin was closest to in his later years. Amongst the Irish-language contingent, Fr Tadhg was the poet's closest male friend, despite their often tense relationship. Ó Ríordáin had other friends in addition to Fr Tadhg who were also priests and whose status as clergymen didn't mean that he condemned them in any way: Aibhistín Valkenburg, Pádraig Ó Fiannachta, Seán Mac Cárthaigh and Cosslett Ó Cuinn. The Ó hÉigeartaighs, his publishers at Sáirséal agus Dill, were still loyal to Ó Ríordáin, as always, even as both poet and publisher were struggling. (When Seán Ó hÉigeartaigh died in June 1967, a copy of *Eireaball Spideoige* was placed in the coffin with him, along with a copy of Máirtín Ó Cadhain's *Cré na Cille* and *Dianmhuilte Dé* by Diarmaid Ó Súilleabháin.) Séamus Ó Coigligh was another close friend; he'd be Ó Ríordáin's soulmate for forty years (1937–77) and there had never been a bad word between them. Seán Ó Riada, Tomás Ó Muircheartaigh, Riobard Mac Góráin, Risteard Ó Glaisne and Diarmaid Ó Murchú, the editor of the journal *Agus*, were all friends, too. Aindreas Ó Gallchóir was a newer friend of Seán and was a man whom he regarded very highly, even for the English-language programmes such as 'The Ballad of Munster Towns' that he produced; in fact, Ó Gallchóir was one of the very few people whom he'd never dream of criticising in the diary. Seán Mac Réamoinn was another person he'd got to know in very recent times, even if Seán was unsure about his credentials in relation to poetry and literary matters (Mac Réamoinn had taken up a new role with Raidió Éireann in Cork, in September 1957). The way he saw it, Mac Réamoinn belonged to the hostile camp when it came to his (Ó Ríordáin's) poetry – ever since an essay of his on Máire Mhac an tSaoi's poetry that appeared in *Combar* in April 1957. (Such old grudges and suspicions would rear their ugly head every now and then in the following years – sometimes, in a way that wasn't entirely clear to either man – even after they got to know one another better.) There were younger scholars in the vicinity also, academics who combined both a sense of humanity and deep intellectualism – the likes of Breandán Ó Buachalla and Diarmaid Ó Mathúna. (Ó Ríordáin always held academics and researchers in very high regard; perhaps he'd shown them too much respect and deference, Ó Ríordáin would say near the end of his life, particularly given the torrid time they frequently gave him, especially around the time that *Eireaball Spideoige* was published.) Other scholars and Irish-language enthusiasts who came within Ó Ríordáin's radar at this time and whom he deemed as assets to intellectual and cultural life in the Irish language were Máirtín Ó Murchú, Gearóid Ó Crualaoich, Seán Ó Mórdha, Breandán Mac Aodha, Póilín Ní Chiaráin and Méabh Ní Chonbhuí, amongst others.

But how close was Ó Ríordáin to any of these people, really – if one were honest about it? No more than any other friend he'd have either before or after this. After all, they belonged to the 'elite' or the 'establishment', really, in a certain manner of speaking, no matter how different they were from the usual people Ó Ríordáin associated with. Was Seán Ó Tuama – a man he would end his friendship with quite soon after this – the most significant of them, given that he'd shared so much of his thinking on literature with the poet and helped establish him within the sphere of Irish-language literary criticism? Or was it all a front or a pretence in the end, really? (Something Ó Ríordáin increasingly wondered at this juncture.) All the talk and the friendship, and even the Irish language that they shared in common when they spoke? But then if it was a form of dishonesty to speak Irish in Ó Ríordáin's case, it would have been a much greater lie still if he'd gone with English-language culture and tradition. And yet, as against this again, the English language had thrived in Inniscarra and all around the poet for many decades now, and in ways that had never been the case perhaps as regards Irish. It is ironic, given this backdrop, that the few Irish-speakers whom Ó Ríordáin met up with from time to time in the city were almost like a group of gentlemen meeting at a club, their conversation oozing dignity, self-regard and the trappings of an elite within society; it was very different from Ó Ríordáin's normal everyday environment in Inniscarra. Every now and then, the honoured Gaelic guest would join them for a once-off event. On this particular day, it's the painter Seán O'Sullivan who joins the company. Which reality has most significance in the end?

> *In the office for the day. Dinner in the Oyster. Father Tadhg, Seán Ó Tuama, Aindreas Ó Gallchóir and Seán Ó Súilleabháin. They were discussing the Preparatory Colleges. They're being closed down. Irish is the language that's spoken in them. Ó Gallchóir says that it's the end of the Irish language in Ireland – the retreat has commenced. No one contradicted him on this. Suddenly I felt that we were a small isolated group, like the last followers of the Stuarts in England and Scotland. Like long ago when King James and Bonnie Prince Charlie were dead and gone, and the Windsors were firmly in control of power, and that small pathetic and unrealistic group – still loyal and pathetic – still taking on the world. We're a beaten people and I sensed that at least one of us was thinking right then that we should abandon this absurd revival publicly.*[1]

On another occasion, two years later, and it's just himself and Fr Tadhg who meet up:

> *I was at dinner with Fr Tadhg Ó Murchú on Thursday in the buffet. A young man was at the same table as us. He never said a word, never even acknowledged our existence. He looked unhappy. We were speaking Irish of course. It was as if hearing the Irish language really annoyed him. I told the priest how hostile this man looked. Fr Tadhg said that this didn't surprise him. Are we Irish speakers a crazy bunch, city Irish-speakers in a city where English is spoken? Is*

1 D: 16 March 1960.

it worse than this still? Are we dishonest – even to ourselves? Have we refused to face the truth? If we were native Irish speakers, just recently arrived in from the Gaeltacht, it would be another story, you might say. But we both spend most of our lives through English and then we come into this Buffet and speak Irish in public – faulty Irish at that. Not only this, but we've given to understand that it's a sin to speak English in Ireland – or, at least, that it's not polite. Do we believe ourselves fully? We're a strange tribe in a way. And what is it that we discuss when we meet, do you think? What else but the Irish language?[2]

They rarely met up without getting angry and having a row about something or other, sometime during the evening. Normally, the argument would kick off with the priest defending some aspect of the Church's authority and an irritated Ó Ríordáin challenging him on it; irrespective of whether it was the Pope's most recent Encyclical Circular or (local Cork) Bishop Lucey's interpretation of same, and Ó Ríordáin objecting to Fr Tadhg's consistent defence of the 'institution' or the institutional perspective. Or sometimes, it might be a completely unwitting remark from Fr Tadhg that would set things off between them. For example:

I was at dinner yesterday with Fr Tadhg. We've been going to dinner together regularly for many years now and whatever disease affects the two of us, we've hardly ever met up that I didn't annoy him or he didn't annoy me, and we've ended up arguing with one another. They say that you shouldn't have friendships with priests. As usual, he annoyed me yesterday. He told me that he and a number of other priests met up recently. He told them that there were two poets together in Dunquin this year, Thomas Kinsella and me. Fr Jerome Kiely immediately said that he'd put money on it that Kinsella was writing and not talking and that I was talking and not writing. It surprised me how angry Kiely's comment made me.[3]

Also, Ó Ríordáin had never liked the way Fr Tadhg was so fond of the 'gollywogs and public gollywoging' (i.e. the 'native' or 'colonised

2 D: 10 February 1962.

3 D: 3 July 1964.

peasant' who acts beyond his station and assumes the airs of a 'colonial' or 'gentleman').[4] Another thing that Ó Ríordáin never forgave his friend for was his class origins – the fact that the priest had 'farming roots, the rottenest roots in Ireland'.[5] Somehow Fr Tadhg had come to symbolise the vast emptiness and dullness of the Irish countryside in Ó Ríordáin's mind. Remember that Ó Ríordáin came from the landless class that made up the small villages, had lived most of his life on the outskirts of the city, and had tradespeople and artisans on his father's side of the family and business people on his mother's. Needless to say, as with every Irish family, Ó Ríordáin had roots in rural Ireland and farming too – and not very far back either – but it was with the astute and quick-witted mindset of the dealer that he related most. Here's how the poet explained the difference between the two mentalities – according to how he understood it – as he pays a visit to Roscrea Abbey in County Tipperary:

> *The vastness and emptiness of the countryside always depresses me. I always feel that country people are far busier and more effective than I am. Although I rarely see them, I sense that they are hostile to the likes of me. When I see two men chatting at a crossroads on a Sunday afternoon, I understand that there is nothing in the world as sombre as their slow conversation and lack of urgency. In that moment, I love city people and their urgency. I also think that country people don't understand literature and if they could, they wouldn't allow such a useless medium.*[6]

Far away hills are green and it's always somewhere else that the action is happening unknown to you – or that's what you think, anyway. But wherever the action is, it sure as hell isn't in the Oyster, anyway. What inspiration or stimulation worth talking about could emerge from these regular and dull dinners, if it wasn't for the usual 'dust-up' at the end when they all got on one another's nerves? Did anyone really believe in him? Did he believe in himself? Was this all just another element in the bigger

4 D: 18 August 1965.
5 D: 8 November 1965.
6 D: 31 May 1965.

charade that they'd been at for years? Ó Ríordáin is not so sure of himself any more. His confidence has taken a battering. He's not as certain of his vocation as he used to be and as he'll claim to be later – in public, anyway. The doubts circle around. Maybe the Irish language was his, but was she really his métier – or should she have been by rights? And wasn't it outside and beyond all of these places – the Oyster and the Buffet and the Tivoli and the Imperial – that the subject matter and the imaginary the poet sought was to be found? And if he managed to source it, had he any right to express whatever this sensibility was in a language other than the one he'd sourced it in? And how much of that sensibility had he managed to express in either language anyway? Was he a bit of a one-trick pony? The man who suffered and died in his doorway unknown to anyone – what did we really know of him, anyway, other than those short bursts of sadness and sentimentality? Deep down, you know whose territory this is and it's neither yours nor the stranger's nor is it the neighbour's himself. Concepts like humanity and empathy are all very well, but keep the small, grubby little everyman well away from it. That self is gone now; he's left us forever and disappeared into the eternal compassion that defines another place and another time. Let's be grateful that we still have a loving memory of him. He's dead and buried, the same as the others, and may he rest in peace, wherever he is. The funereal conscience once more:

> *That man was a great worker, very strong man, a poor and inoffensive man, a labourer who was low-sized and wide-shouldered. God love him, the poor fellow – he was sick for just a few months before he died. No one expected him to die. They were strangers to the area and they were shy and kept to themselves. They were also poor and uneducated, the poor creatures – God help them. He wasn't sent to hospital until a week before his death. They must have had many a black, empty and painful night, the pair of them, during winter, and everyone unaware, themselves included perhaps, that their situation was as bad as it actually was. When I looked at the house this evening, I thought of all the hardship that went on beneath its roof. Then I thought of all the places in the world where suffering has gone on, all the rooms people have died in, and all the beds people have felt the pleasures of the flesh on. But I feel guilty now when I see that empty house down at the gate below. I think that we've a duty*

> *to mix in amongst the poor and the abandoned. Our commitment should be to poverty and illness. Maybe this is because I was poor and sick myself during my life, but I don't think so. I believe that this is our inheritance – that it's in such places that God lives.*[7]

He'd meet Him still on the odd trip he took out of the house in later years, on those occasional visits to the mental home. A man who'd once had a name for poetry and a certain 'cachet' in the world of letters would call out to him from that abandoned place and ask him to keep him company every now and then. They're together once when the procession shuffles past them. The diary entry in relation to this includes a sketch of the 'corpse' being carried by two others:

> *'There's a corpse coming our way now,' said the poet. Sure enough, two patients arrived in carrying a stretcher with this Thing on it. The ridiculous creature lying on it in* sedes gestatoria *was a human being at one time.*[8] *A couple of other* sedes gestatoria *went past us, grotesque and crazy-looking creatures. Their clothes were tatty like you see on beggars, dirty old rags. There were some of these patients and not only had their hair greyed, but so too their faces and their entire personalities, their faces sunk and empty, like the eyes of an old dog. They were all part of that miserable and worn-out procession of the dead, however, and they moved in accordance with its rhythm. It gave them the liturgical dignity of the dead, not that they needed it, seeing as they were already distinct from every aspect of human destiny and had their own baleful fate mapped out. I noticed one sturdy, grey-coloured man who was barefoot and had nothing on but his shirt. Although his corpse was already that deep grey colour, he still appeared so calm and heroic that it gave you heart, even in that awful place. Dear heart, it is difficult to overcome the human spirit, even in the land of saints and scholars!*[9]

He paid the same man another visit some time later but he'd moved to

---

7 D: 17 April 1958.

8 The *sedia gestatoria* (gestatorial chair), lit: 'chair for carrying', was a ceremonial throne on which popes were carried on shoulders in times gone by.

9 'Lunatic asylum', IT, 10 April 1968.

England. On hearing this, Ó Ríordáin says: 'I felt lonely straight away. The poor man, however low he fell, he still had more go in him than I did. No wonder I feel lonely, I've no friends – only mad people'.[10] The poet had spent a good deal of his life hanging around with such 'marginal' people and yet he'd never engaged with them properly either. Ó Ríordáin had always admired the awareness of themselves and their place within the order of things that those deemed to be 'mad' had; as poet, he was but an interlocutor between their world and the world of others. 'I was never right. Still, I'm not a lunatic …'[11] Whether it was logic or madness that he required, the most important thing was that it was brought to its perfect or absolute level.

Another example of 'humanity's resilience' even in the face of authority or the system follows. And, as before, as with the madman or the old dog he associates with him in this instance, there's a certain status to both the person who rejects and he who is rejected. The status that is a form of bravery and dignity. In this case, it is the figure of the prostitute that Ó Ríordáin finds dignity in, even if it's only a half-hearted compliment, as he more regularly used this same term ('striapach' or prostitute) in a derisory way in his diaries:

> *I was driving in the city late at night, more than six weeks ago. It was after midnight. I saw two prostitutes standing against the wall on Brian Boru Street – waiting for customers. In a way, they must be commended for their courage. Theirs is an act of courage in a country where the authority of the Catholic Church is as strong as here – and there were probably never bishops as authoritative and as narrow and merciless as the lords we have here. The same goes for the clergy, and as for the public, they are as dour as their ecclesiastical masters. And yet, both women were brave enough to go out in public onto the streets and sell their fannies. It's really something! It's an example of human endurance.*[12]

Such sentiments aren't too far away from the sentiments of 'Do Striapach'.

10 D: 16 October 1967.
11 TÉB: p. 16.
12 D: 27 December 1964.

In this instance, the woman in question is nearly a saint in the poet's eyes; it's the 'desolation' and utter abandonment Ó Ríordáin associates with her that elevates and ennobles her in his mind:

from **'Do Striapach'**

Do chuais led cheird, is bail ó Dhia ort
Nár dhein fé cheilt do ghnó, a striapach,
Is taoi chomh lom anois id intinn,
Chomh mór gan maíomh gan éirí in airde,
Gur geall le naomh tú, a bhean gan náire.[13]

from **'To a Prostitute'**

You took up your trade, and God bless
you, prostitute, for not hiding your business,
and now your mind's so bare and blameless,
humble, without haughtiness,
shameless woman, you're near to saintliness.[14]

Another pair whom he comes across out on the street, wearing worn-out old rags are a man and a woman, both of whom have poverty written all over them. The poet recognises them as members of his same tribe. This life's victims always recognise one another. Here's Seán's perspective on their secret 'tribe':

It is clear that their poverty is grander and more noble than the grandeur of better-dressed people. One senses a dignity in their rags. You'd imagine that they chose these clothes of theirs deliberately because they are the only clothes that exude dignity in the world as they find it today. Another thing that one senses about them is that they live in a world of their own, in a world immune to the chaos around them. You'd imagine also by them, that anything else would be seen as

13 TÉB: p. 50.
14 Sewell, *Selected Poems*, p. 195. Trans. Mary O'Donoghue.

> *improper behaviour. I find they have complete faith in whatever spark has been granted them by the Holy Spirit.*
>
> *I met them again on Patrick Street the day before yesterday. What's seldom is wonderful. Himself looked at me for a minute. I think, and maybe it's arrogant of me even to think this – but, I think that herself noticed me and remembered me from that winter's day when I gave her a furtive glance, and that she roused him from his reverie and told him to look at me. He gave me a quick glance and then shifted his eyes away from me as quickly again as one of those educated eyes might do – the type who only need the one glance … And what his glance said to me was this – and again, it's somewhat arrogant of me to say it – but that he agreed with her that I was one of them too, that crowd who'd never had anything to do with the others.*[15]

It was the 'others' whom he met anytime he was in the Oyster, not that the people he's describing above had a whole lot in common with the likes of Fr Tadhg, however:

> *They speak a clipped, affected, polished English, a clongowesed, oxfordised, cambridgised Cork English. 'Cork* Idioma Castellano*' as Pearse Hutchinson once called it. You know by them that they are into money and rugby. Their trousers say 'yacht'. They'll be wearing different clothes tonight. The clothes they have on now in the middle of the day are informal in the most formal of senses. Their midday meal is only a snack compared to the dinner they'll have tonight. The name of the waitress who serves them is on the tip of their tongue, but they'd never know her surname – for the life of them. They speak loudly. It's obvious that they're used to giving orders. When I tell someone to leave, he leaves … Their conversation is golfy, clipped, fast, unintellectual, formal. The English spoken by the British aristocracy is the standard. None of them would put sugar in their coffee. Nothing would bother them except maybe sugar in their coffee. The coffee has to be black …*[16]

They might be the respectable and 'proper' sort, all right, but that doesn't mean Ó Ríordáin is equally magnanimous when it comes to describing

15 'Beirt chlúdaithe' ('*A Covered-Over Pair*'), IT, 20 June 1969.

16 'Proinnteach cáiliúil' ('*A famous Restaurant*'), IT, 11 April 1970.

them. He's the outsider, if there ever was one. You can almost see the smirks on the listeners' faces. That fake voice, hollow and high but which says nothing worthwhile. But then there's only ever been a thin border separating mockery and capitulation. He wouldn't find the God he was looking for in a place like this, anyway, no matter how hard he might look for Him there. And it wouldn't be in Daniel Corkery's authoritative statements on everything from turnips to art to nationalism, amongst a myriad of other subjects: *sequentia sancti Evangelii secundum Danielem* ('continuation of the holy gospel, according to Daniel'), as he puts it in a few places in the diary.[17] The old gospel was useless now, even the part of it concerning his right to write Irish, if it was indeed literature at all. It wasn't a gospel at all by rights but rather the same endless second-hand narrative that he had to keep proving to himself again and again:

> *I continue to pass the unavoidable afternoon in the presence of myself. I watch through the window and a wet asbestos roof. My mind is empty. It darts after interruptions. A car horn blew. My mind became horned. Which is worse, my Irish or my English – don't we understand sometimes that our English is more polished and fancier than our Irish? But read a piece of beautiful Irish and the English will feel empty to you.*[18]

> *When I die, it's down that I want to go. The people who refuse to accept, they're the ones who are all below. It's the humble ones who go up – that's if there is such a place as 'up'. There's little consolation in this world. Give humility a try, give the English language a try. Yes, humility in Heaven, arrogance and individualism in Hell. Would the infernal individualism compensate for the diabolic discomforts? Would the heavenly happiness compensate for the compulsory humility? Is the humility compulsory? Is it not a wise acceptance of reality? Is it possible to consider reality while angrily championing one's own ego? This English isn't worth anything. What is this Irish worth? I can't adapt my mentality to the English language. Is this a charade? Is it that I've nothing to say and that Irish is most appropriate when you haven't anything to say, but*

17 For example, 25 March 1960.
18 D: 3.45 p.m., 17 December 1957.

> *that English isn't? Maybe there's nothing to say in English. But others have something to say in English. I hope that it's like this: that* I have *something to say in Irish and that* I have *nothing to say in English. I've spent up to ten years deliberating as to what I should say but I've said nothing. Isn't it clear that I've nothing to say in either Irish or English.*[19]

Exactly three years from this, he'd read Beckett's *Malone Dies* and conclude that this was the greatest truth of all: that the individual has no story and nothing to say. 'Nothing is more real than nothing.' At the end of the day, the man lying prone on his sickbed is no wealthier in worldly or spiritual terms than anyone else. And what value has literary tradition and all that goes with it, in the incontrovertible presence that is the night, the truth and death? In the darkness, aren't you as well off fumbling for a pencil-stub or an insect – as anything else? This is your true wealth, after all – your private abandonment and desolation. But who's listening to you, anyway, especially in the case of a language as marginalised as Irish – other than those who are full of jealousy and spite? Or could it be that such an audience, albeit hostile, is better than no audience at all? Hadn't Frank O'Connor, Brendan Behan, James Joyce, Samuel Beckett and plenty of others simply left the country and it was only upon their 'return' (i.e. of these 'foreign' O'Connors, Behans, Joyces and Becketts) that they'd been shown a bit of respect. If Ó Ríordáin had been exotic or in 'exile' – would it have proved a different story? As with so many other postcolonial countries, this is a country where only that which is 'non-native' or 'exotic' is revered. And:

> *As for being traditional, it's unknown to oneself that one is traditional or, if you wish, it's completely despite oneself that one is truly traditional. Just be yourself and you'll be traditional. But as for being consciously traditional, as many of that loudmouthed class who frequent Irish-language circles are, this is the rule: Be consciously traditional and you aren't actually traditional at all, and you won't be either. Tradition is rooted in real life. It's not some kind of a posh uniform or little badge that you wear.*[20]

---

19 D: 3.45 p.m., 12 December 1960.

20 D: 22 September 1960.

It takes a strong man to continue dredging every aspect of the 'self' in such solitary fashion, and without the usual scaffolding of tradition, community or institution. And the time will come too when the theory and talk are no longer sufficient for the continued sustenance of the poet's inner life and when he'll falter. It is then that the constant disregard and hostility will catch up with him – when he views his life and his work as others see it. And seeing as he's got the best perspective of all on matters, the poet will condemn himself in more strident terms than any of the critics ever could. The truth always wins out in the end; there's no escaping it so it must be confronted head-on, no matter how grim or bitter it may be:

17/12/61 Sunday 3 p.m. Reading Feamainn Bhealtaine *by Máirtín Ó Direáin. Máirtín's focus is on the world out there, unlike me. His mind is swathed in a lovely Irish flag. His Irish is fluent and polished, and gradual, as characteristic of someone brought up speaking Irish on the Aran Islands. His childhood back west is what he recalls and records best.*

3.40 p.m. I'm tired of this dead speech! Even English itself would be better. Isn't my native language English? I've viewed and experienced all aspects of my life as intertwined through her. I spent today and yesterday and the day before that here in bed spitting out diseased saliva by myself. I'm dying. I've been taken for a ride – I took myself for a ride, I'm a public joke. I'm known as an Irish-language writer. I've spent my whole life and all of my energies with the Irish language and I'll never have Irish. I don't have anything and I never will except this dead thing that I pore over here. How did I deceive so many people? How did I deceive myself? Amn't I some bollox? Haven't I been promulgating something that I don't believe myself? Why all this b....xing around? To satisfy the snobbery in me, or the desire for publicity, or the desire for fame? The truth is a living thing. The truth is in Máirtín's Ó Direáin's Irish. It's alive. The truth isn't in my Irish or in me. No, and there's no life in it either. My Irish is corrupt and diseased, the same as myself. Is there anyone in Ireland as rotten as me, and as unproductive? If I recover from this illness I'll be out there spreading lies again! Oh, Oh, Oh – the pain of it. There's a certain suppleness, a certain cleverness, in this Irish of mine. All she's missing is truth and life.

It's difficult to say where the truth lies here exactly or what Ó Ríordáin's grasp of it was in this instance either. Time will tell. For the moment the truth is what he perceives it to be, no matter how unpalatable, and he has little shelter against it. If there's anything to shield him from its harshness, it is the word itself – the act of writing and everything that the word has ever illuminated. The fellow poet and his/her words are the only friendly aspects he has left to him against the hostility of the world that rejects the poet's song. The following was noted in his diary on the night of 11 August 1961 and appeared in print a full six years later in *Combar*, May 1967 as one of the 'Random quotes from a diary':

> *No matter who the poet is, no matter what age he is, the rest of the world is against him, it's hostile. His fate is mockery, suffering, disrespect. And he speaks the most directly of all. He speaks in the deepest and most enduring way. Because he's the tormented one, is it? When I read the words of the poets in any language that I can read them in, I sense ages, countries and languages melt away and I hear the human being himself speak, despite themselves. He is always the same humble and truthful person. Everyone, whether big or small, can access them. Every poet is your friend – especially when life is difficult for you. He doesn't try and trick you – no more than your own mind does. You are the poet.*

And if he was a poet, then it was the same humility and honesty that would guide him intact across the threshold of language and tradition. It's best not to reach beyond your fated station. Admit the weaknesses in your art and you have a new subject matter at hand. Disguise your weaknesses and you might as well be listening in vain forever, irrespective of how great and pretentious your aspirations might be.

> *A long day in the office. I'm alone here for the past two days … I'm not well, of course. This illness has made me tired.* Languor *is the Latin word for it. It's not a bad word for it. I'm reading Séathrún Céitinn and E.E. Cummings in between periods of exhausted sleep. Which of them are closest to me? I enjoyed them both – a lot. Cummings is closer to me time-wise and therefore in spirit, but the other man has something in him that's in me and that isn't in Cummings. The Irish language maybe. I'm getting a bit fed up of all this 'native culture/heritage' that*

> *the likes of Seán Ó Riada is always trying to source. I think that any true poet, like any good artist is someone who functions beyond such 'native culture' and nationalism.*[21]

You wouldn't mind but Ó Ríordáin had always been 'beyond' or on the 'outside', anyway, a marginalised status that neither art nor poetry would redeem him from. In a sense, it was irrelevant whether he was describing an old neighbour of his from back in the late 1930s or some members of the cultural circle that was the Palace in its declining years – you'll find the same message in both places, irrespective of context. He's the man standing in the middle of the doorway who's reluctant to enter, the same as the female figure of ancient folklore that doesn't conform to any category ever created. It's neither death nor life, sowing nor reaping – it's barely existing. The moments for renewal of his art are declining. There were only a few moments for such renewal in his life, none of which really stood out. He'll be living off these moments or experiences for the rest of his days and there's no change of course in sight now. There's a great nothingness ahead of him now, a state that is neither decline nor renewal. He's already felt whatever there is to be felt, and consequently fears that he's said whatever can be said. And it is all those unspoken things that kill you in the end. If there was one poet more than any other whose experience contrasted with his, it was the Poet of Dunquin, who proclaimed himself 'king of loneliness'. The Dunquin poet's 'loneliness' is of a different hue than Ó Ríordáin's, however; his loneliness is the warm and cosy solitude that defines the traditional 'community poet', who can call on the entire tradition (i.e. both the living and the dead) when required, whereas Ó Ríordáin's relationship with both constituencies is more turbulent, more complex and more insecure. The diary entry that follows here precedes the earlier one above by a couple of years and yet it undermines the 'categorisation' of time and subject so beloved of the academic or scholarly class. When everything in your life, whether for good or ill, is ascribed to the category that is 'long ago', it makes no difference how your life is portioned up. At 10.20 p.m. on 21 August 1961 is when he first begins writing this excerpt,

21 D: 19 March 1963.

but it's another three days before we catch up with him again – when he's finally managed to escape his own sensibility for a while:

> *Moon (3/4) very bright tonight and clouds scudding past. There's something mysterious in the night – because I'm alone, most likely. Didn't An File spend many a night at alone in Ballyvickery? But I'm a loner – in ways. Or am I? I was going to say that his mind is always accompanying the minds of others, when my mind is all alone and unaccompanied by any other mind. But it's hard to know whether this is true or not. After all, I interact with the sensibility of the Irish language and English, Latin, Spanish, French, which is something that An File doesn't have. I suppose that you could say I have had some contact with Russia and Greece and with other countries as well. But I think – and maybe I'm wrong about this – that I have contact with them in my own strange, churlish and unhealthy way – a way that leaves me as isolated as if I'd never had any contact with them at all. The clouds are still rushing past the moon and the moon overlooks them like a minister of state. What caused the depression that came over me tonight? Autumn is a lonely time of year. Maybe I finally understood that it's too late now – that I'll never do the business now – that I've lost my chance – that my life is just another pointless life that's passed by? Who knows? Loneliness is a bad thing. I'll probably be damned. I'm a tormented soul.*
>
> *11.35 p.m. I went over to the pub a quarter of an hour ago. I couldn't stand this abandoned place any longer. I only had one drink but it was a relief to have some company. [Y] was there and holding forth as usual; and his mistakes and misunderstandings were full of humanity and life. The company of others is a healing balm.*

As far as company was concerned, it was amongst his nieces and nephews (his brother's children) that he discovered the love denied him everywhere else, or which he himself had refused to accept. This childish, family love was the love given without question and without expectation of reward or advantage. It was they who kept the last of his life from crumbling to dust around him. He was particularly fond of Marian and Ó Ríordáin made frequent reference to the children in his diaries and prose essays, albeit that he never wrote a poem specifically for them. This might seem strange at first glance until we consider that he didn't feel it necessary for him to link whatever joy he felt with his anxieties or concerns – something which Ó Ríordáin rarely did in his poetry. The excerpt below was published in the essay 'An Taisceadán' in *Comhar*, May 1963; this essay appeared in the diary as two separate pieces – one on 16 October 1960 and another on 6 May 1961. Here's the *Comhar* version:

> *The children were like angels flying around me. They're no angels but rather little devils. Poetry is what they speak. Every time they open their mouths is an occasion of poetry. Their speech and their little thoughts relate to the world of the small ones, that life way back that we now refer to as the life of the child. They see things still, something that we no longer do. There is a little folklore and a little wonder in everything for them still. They speak prophetically therefore. What they say seems strange to us but it isn't to them. They aren't in search of strangeness, but the opposite. They like to be in fashion, to be as everyone else. Although they're a crowd who are full of wonder and even if their world is full of wonder, there's never any trace of surprise in their eyes, but the indifference of old-timers instead. Marian was talking, a rare thing for her. She's only four years old but she has something about her. She has some kind of a propensity for folklore in her. When she speaks, the conversation floods out of her similar to Lucky in Beckett's play. When this one starts twittering away, you know that you're in the presence of the spirit that is folklore. I can hear the fine and elevated speech of humanity through Marian.*

The second and the third excerpt (provided here) never saw publication. On 15 January 1961, this appears in the diary:

> *I'm alone in the house for over three months now. I no longer miss having company. I don't meet up with Fr Tadhg or Seán Ó Tuama any more. This doesn't bother me either. Is there anyone that I'm fond of left? Do I have love for anyone in me any more? There's at least one person that I'm fond of. That's Marian, my brother's daughter. She's three years old. I gave the children a spin in the car this afternoon – Peig, John, Eibhlín and Marian. There was a shrine on the side of the road and I stopped. The children were all 'holy' and 'holy God' and all the rest of it. And then Marian asked the question: 'Is it Mass?'*

Seán notes this third fragment in the diary on 30 January 1963:

> *I gave a trip up to my brother's house in Mayfield. I brought the children in the car down to St Lukes to bring a pair of shoes to the cobbler there. I drove them home again then. They were all with me except John. Here's who was with me: Peig (11), Eibhlín (7), Marian (5), Tadhg (3), Barra (1½). I watched them as they went in through the door of the yard that was open and disappeared out of sight. I suppose that they're probably the small community of people that I love most in the world. No one is as honest as they are, just people who are very old or very young. I felt a pain go through my heart. I'd be better off to try and put them out of my mind. I wonder does God feel this same unbearable love for all of us.*

It would be a long time before you would hear any of the crowd in the Oyster talk like that. It is the small things that break your heart and keep it from withering away. He would often take a trip over to his brother's house in Mayfield on a Sunday afternoon and then return home again to the solitariness of his own life and the long stretch of empty week ahead of him. Ironically, an empty week that was yet replete with the interminable questions. What value lay in that poem or diary that lay ahead of him on his return? Would he have been better off if he'd never had anything to do with poetry or if he'd never documented a single word of the inner soul that was his diary? But what else was there to bring him joy or peace in this life? You had to take it wherever you found it. And whenever it became too much for him, he might take another quick drive over to Mayfield again, where he'd pace up and down the floor of the house until he was finally able to relax again. He might have a small bite to eat – a bowl of soup in the kitchen with the family there, maybe – and go out to play with the children for another while – and then it was off home again. There was no point in offering him a bed for the night – even there in his brother's house – because he'd never stay with anyone and always preferred to go home to his own house come the evening. Still, it was this little family there who gave him the love and the tenderness that sustained him, even as the world around him became increasingly distant or unrecognisable to him. The more solitary he became, the more people outside his immediate family appeared more remote to him, and more recognisable in accordance with their class or their characteristics than anything else. It's as if the poet interprets the world outside and those who people it almost solely in terms of the past and what they once stood for. It's a long time now since they had an immediate, existent meaning for him; in a sense, he'd lost touch with them and their lives years ago. They're all one and the same now to the lone man in his room and whose home is solitude. The borders between past and present have dissolved and if there's any difference between them it may be that it is those people who have most recently crossed its threshold (the most recently deceased) that have brought some of the subject matter of his art with them. This is what Ó Ríordáin fears most in 'Gailearaí' ('*Gallery*'): that 'the shells of themselves' will solidify and set forever unless, on occasion, he can renew them again and make them live through the act of memory.[22] Could it be that the poem 'Gailearaí' was based on the reflection below? It is that picture of his grandmother again – it's the first that appears in his memory exhibition:

> *The chaste spring sun in through the window. A sun shadow from the window lighting the wall inside and the picture of grandmother when she was young. I knew her. Oh Lord, she's thirty years dead now! Isn't my mother seventeen years dead now! There's no one but myself in this room now but there's plenty of people in the space between the living and dead, in my memory. Maybe I'll call to them and they will make themselves present in my mind. It's the same presence for the living and the dead in this case. None of them are present physically. Is there any difference between the living and the dead when they present themselves in disembodied form before our minds? I don't see any difference. What happens is that we recreate subconsciously the mind and the body of the person who is absent, whether alive or dead. Maybe we can better recreate the living than the dead because we saw the living most recently. Sometimes, we can recreate the dead better, however. Therefore, as regards solitary reflection, they are one and the same …*[23]

22 B: p. 34.
23 D: 3 March 1962.

Gailearaí

Shiúlas i measc na bpearsantacht
'Bhi adhlactha i m'aigne,
Iad chomh slán i gcló is ba mhaith leat iad
Laistigh de phlaosc an dearmaid,
lad 'na ndaoine ansiúd i ngan fhios duit
Ag feitheamh leis an tagairt úd
'Dhúiseodh arís chun beatha iad:
Led mhachnamh féin is eagal liom
Gur deacair puinn den chuideachta
A thúirt ar ais chun aithne,
Ach ba mhaith leat iad a theasargan
Sula gcruadh an plaosc ar fad orthu,
Is ná beadh fanta id ghailearaí
Ach frámaí caoch' do-aitheanta.[24]

Gallery

I walked in among the personalities
Who were buried in my mind,
All as intact as you'd ever wish for
Within the skull of forgetfulness,
They are there unknown to you
Awaiting that mention
Which would awake them to life again:
It would be difficult with our own thoughts
to bring back many of the company to our acquaintance, I fear,
But you would like to rescue them
Lest the skull should harden on them completely,
And that there should only be left in your gallery
Vague, unidentifiable frames.[25]

---

24 B: p. 34.
25 Trans. M. Ó hAodha.

He'll visit Dunquin two summers later and discover another corpse to bury in his cemetery. A woman who was extremely feminine in manner and sensibility in the years when the poet first went there on his summer visits and for a good number of years later – she has since passed away. And so too has this aspect of his life, his Dunquin life – it's as dead as the joy-filled roads of Inniscarra in the early 1940s. But there is another death which the poet knows is greater than this again, a dual death, and this is his living lament for it – the death of all summer:

> *Dunquin is dead. She's still visible, that is to say that she's still there above ground, but it isn't really her that's there. She's not officially dead but that [X] that was once there years ago has disappeared completely. She's got little draw for anyone now. She hasn't got that thing any more. Something died completely in her. Her entire focus is on wealth now and she's eradicated the poetic aspect of her nature completely, and sacrificed it to that one aim. She's just a tomb now. She herself is buried in that tomb, or maybe it's just her passions that are buried there. Maybe the most interesting part of her still lives?*
>
> *As for myself, am I a tomb? If so, my poetry is at an end.*[26]

Bás Beo

Fuair sí bás ó anuraidh,
inléite ar a cló,
ní bean na bhfear í a thuilleadh
ach rud fuar gur ghéill sí dhó,
í féin an uaigh ina bhfuil sí curtha,
faraoir, beo.[27]

Living Death

She died last year,
As is obvious from her appearance,

26 D: 11 July 1964.
27 LL: p. 36.

She is no longer a woman among men,
But rather the cold thing to which she succumbed,
She herself is the grave in which she is buried,
Alas, alive.[28]

Maybe this was how his life had been fated from the beginning: people dying one after another, and the poet replicating what he could of them in the form of verse. It is always the abstract that triumphs – beauty or ugliness, age or youth, the tradition or the flaw – and not the artist who expresses it. One begins the journey with people but before long the people are merely symbols or abstract representatives of something else. And one becomes impatient or dismissive of them after a while, given that they've no real significance beyond their own abstract selves. They are powerless to Fate and can never develop beyond its strict confines. After a while, they are of more significance for the road that is their destiny than as individuals or people in themselves, given that their fate is pre-assigned almost from the beginning. They are accurate or inaccurate versions of an abstract thought or theory, but versions nonetheless. They may try to escape their restraints on occasion, but the master isn't long catching up with them again. And it's this 'master' or authority (the authoritative word) that is their conqueror in the poem 'An Feairín' ('*The Maneen*'), for instance. The individual is weighed up or assessed relative to the words or traits that encompass them – the cantankerousness or stubbornness that was the permanent stamp of the Ó Súilleabháins and the O'Ríordáins, for example. It's not always possible to embody an individual as neatly as was the case with Pound, whose personality his female neighbour captured so precisely within the space of a single word. Another character whose individuality was encompassed within the magic of just one word was Quixote. In fact, Ó Ríordáin's 'take' on Quixote might as well be a version of the poem 'An Feairín'. *In principio erat verbum* ('In the beginning was the word'): it was Daniel Corkery who said one night that 'Professor French had the appearance of Don Quixote and he'd never seen anyone else in

28 Trans. M. Ó hAodha.

his life whose face more perfectly resembled Don Quixote than him.'[29] Interestingly, Seán didn't know Professor French at the time, although he would get to know him some time after Corkery made that comment. And when he did finally meet French he recognised him immediately, as based on 'the master's' (Corkery's) word. On 9 January 1958 he jotted down his thoughts on this in his diary, thoughts which subsequently became the basis for an article in *Comhar* in March 1960:

> *I heard a man saying that a certain old person had the face of a Quixote and that he'd had that face since he was a boy. He said he'd also had that mindset and that whenever he died he still wouldn't be any more than eight years old. I hadn't seen this Quixote at the time but I finally saw it then. He was definitely a Quixote all right. He had the baby-faced look of a child about him. The sight of him frightened me a bit, this description was so realistic, although I hadn't understood until then what was meant by having a Quixote face. He fitted this description perfectly. That face was right there, waiting for me and you, and Quixote inscribed permanently on it. She'd been there for years as authorised by this other person's words. She'd never been able to escape the strictures of the word: Quixote. There was no fear that the man who'd given that word as a description of him would ever be contradicted. There was no fear this face would change over the years or become mean-looking. There's no nastiness in this Quixote face. It's always the same, from morning until night, humble and obedient to the station this man ascribed it, as someone assigned a punishment, or as ever-willing to bolster the definition or term. She is constantly adding to the term, morning and night, and when people are looking and when they aren't looking. This Quixote is isolated from people now in my mind as if it is no longer a person but an example. It's almost shameful for that face to be seen in public now constantly serving the other person's definition. It's as if its vulnerability has been paraded before the world so that everyone is aware of it. In the old days, people were struck by a magic wand and transformed into a goat or a hare. This face was struck by a magic wand and transformed into a word. You wouldn't listen to the man himself at all. It was his face that spoke. His face was his mind. A face that contains a whole life in the form of just one word as defined by someone else – the one who acts as the authority.*

29 D: 12 April 1957.

The female leprechaun and the beauty alluded to below are but different points on his theoretical compass, points that come and go, and irrespective of how they alternate or interact with one another they always remain affixed to the wheel, and the poet can never free them from it either. It's as if he spins them around the wheel for a spot of diversion in this instance. The following excerpt that saw publication is based on Ó Ríordáin's diary entry for 5 March 1956:

> *I saw a woman dwarf on Patrick Street last week. She'd a long nose. She wore glasses. A large head on small body like that fish that's known as the hard-nose (catfish). She was bow-legged. She had the look of a leprechaun about her. She was a fairly young woman, around thirty years of age, but her leprechaun appearance took away from her femininity. She looked very strange. Suddenly, I thought of another woman, a younger woman, a striking woman, a real beauty or very close to it. The woman dwarf reminded me of the stunner. There was a similarity of some kind between them. It was the strange woman's legs that put me in mind of the other woman initially. The beauty's legs weren't as short or as bent as the other woman's but if you shortened them a bit and bent them slightly, both women's legs would have been much the same. Then I looked at the shorter woman's face and she'd have been the same as the beauty if her nose had been made a bit longer and her face thinner. Clearly, the beauty's face is getting closer to that of the strange woman. They are both points on the same road. If there's a woman out there who's better-looking than the beauty, then she and the leprechaun are both moving in the opposite direction to her along the same road. If there's a woman more misshapen-looking than the leprechaun-woman out there, a woman who has similarities with her all the same, then the leprechaun and the other two women are becoming closer in form to her all the time.*[30]

Another girl he comes across one day has her surname written as clear as day on her face – the same as the Quixote that preceded her. The fact that her surname is Murphy is all the poet needs to assign her to her place within the pantheon of forms or 'types'. No matter how much they might disguise themselves, the 'Murphy characteristics' reveal themselves in this

30 *Comhar*, March 1960.

young woman. And to get to know her on a personal level or beyond the traits that her surname delineates is to interfere or disrupt her essence, her personality. Not only does the word define who the woman is in this case, but it also defines the poet himself:

> *I met … Murphy on Patrick Street today. A pretty girl, who's twenty-five years old. A city girl who works in the office. She looks well. She dresses well and speaks (English) well. She's polite. Familiarity breeds contempt, they say. I don't know this girl too well myself but I know her family very well. Suddenly, I saw through all her beauty and I saw those Murphy traits in her quite clearly. Suddenly she became a Murphy. She was more of a Murphy in that moment than she was a pretty girl. Whatever beauty she had, whatever dignified bearing, whatever sense of moderation, it wasn't enough. She had a particular surname permanently inscribed on her.*[31]

The others follow on in a line behind her now too, the 'personalities' and characteristics the poet has yet to create: Narcissus, the Nobody, the Prima Donna, The Human Cycle, the Son of Disaster – all of whom are 'types' more than they are real people. They are the poet's rightful heirs to the rabble that stood outside his window at one time, the only difference being that they've seen a more multifaceted evolution since those days. That said, they're only more interesting when each is considered in terms of their own individual nature rather than as part of the crowd. The corollary of this is that none can be expressed correctly as a type either, unless they are considered on the individual level first. You'd love to be able to see these people as they develop along the journey that is their amalgam of characteristics and personality. But, by now, life is become a fable for the poet, a fable that has little enough in the way of human life corroborating it. That said, the poet knows what his role is and where he stands in the story. He might be half-serious and joking at times (even if there's always something serious about them as well), but there's nothing particularly funny about this hierarchy of types when it comes knocking on your own door. You know what your fate is and you know that it is deadly serious.

31 D: 3 June 1961.

And sooner or later, it'll come calling on you, too, and when the memory of a half-lived youth and forgotten beauty is at stake, there's little scope for mockery or evasion. You understand where the significance of your life lies, now that you're forty-seven years of age. Although this didn't appear in print until 1971, it was originally noted in the diary on 12 June 1964. It is important to state that no woman who has been referred to in this volume at any stage prior to this is the subject of the next piece:

> *I saw a middle-aged, fat, ugly, woman the other night. She's married for years. Where has the snow that shone so brightly last year gone? I remember her when she was a beauty and when I realised that I was in love with her. She was all the beauty and joy in the world back then. And now, I don't care about her, one way or another. She's just a fat ugly old woman. It's other women, younger women, who have the sway now that she once had. It's the same old story of youth and beauty disappearing. But it's worse than this because they never go away but stay forever and we never stop desiring them. People are of no importance. They come and go. But youth and beauty stays forever and the older we get, the more we seek nothing but them. Young people between the ages of twenty and twenty-five were whom Marcus Aurelius always saw as he walked along the street known as the Via Appia. This is where the tragedy of the human condition lies, I think ...*[32]

Subsequent to this the poet will add few enough other pictures to this personal gallery of his and he'll be reliant on viewing the few that he has already on a repeated basis. The image of each individual becomes more indistinct as the years pass and his memories of those whom he once knew begin to fade. Even by this juncture, the edges are blurred and it's in the empty space between the lines that the poet is searching. He could be drawing sketches of them forever in an attempt to hold on to them and still the movement of time, but he can never retrieve their spirit, their soul. The only bright lights left in his life now are the innocent joy of his nephews and nieces, or the company of the cats or dogs. And there's the odd person too who'll never truly understand how little importance they really played in the life of this man they thought of as their friend ...

32 'Babhta suibiachtúil', IT, 23 January 1971.

The poem 'Súile Donna' relates to an interaction that took place on 9 September 1967 when he ran into a local boy whom he knew to see and whose lineage and family characteristics he was very familiar with, the same as the traits he ascribed to the Sullivans and the Murphys. People whom he once knew as a young man – their characteristics were made manifest and revealed themselves once again in the new generation. The poet recognises the next generation solely by reference to the past and the people whom he was once on familiar terms with; it is as the same reification of time almost, the same endless 'feminising' and 'masculising' right on into eternity. Fate had decided each individual's path and destiny long ago. Here's an example of destiny in action, and on the poet's own patch, too. How blind she is on this occasion, however!

Yesterday afternoon, I met a schoolboy, who was about six or seven years old. He introduced himself to me. Someone told me who his mother is. I know her. She was known as Lil Ní Shúilleabháin at one stage of her life. Then I noticed her eyes in this lad's head. Any man would have fallen in love with this woman, just for her eyes alone. I'd noticed her eyes from when she was a child. Beautiful brown eyes sparkling in her head. I associate her personality with those eyes. She was her eyes. And this lad had the exact same eyes. These aren't his eyes, however. They are hers. I found it strange yesterday to see them in someone else's body. No other personality could underlie such eyes except hers. How could a stranger take over her personality? But it couldn't be that these brown eyes began with Lil Ní Shúilleabháin either. There must have been others who came before her who had them also. They go back a long way and maybe they'll go on from generation to generation yet, on to who knows when. Can it be that we have no other form of eternity than this?[33]

Súile Donna

Is léi na súile donna so
A chím i bplaosc a mic,

33 D: 10 September 1967.

Ba theangmháil le háilleacht é,
A súile a thuirlingt ort;

Ba theangmháil phribhléideach é,
Lena meabhair is lena corp,
Is míle bliain ba ghearr leat é,
Is iad ag féachaint ort.

Na súile sin gurbh ise iad,
Is ait liom iad aige,
Is náir liom aghaidh a thabhairt uirthi
Ó tharla sí i bhfear …[34]

Brown Eyes

They're hers, the brown eyes
I see in her son's face.
It was a meeting with beauty itself
when they lighted on you.

It was a unique connection, too,
with her mind, with her body.
A thousand years disappeared
when they looked at you.

And because the eyes are hers,
it's strange to see them in him,
and I don't want to face her now
appearing in a man.[35]

One would have thought that the poet had finally stumbled on the answer to his own question as to which took precedent: the ego or the tradition,

34 LL: p. 10.
35 Sewell, *Selected Poems*, p. 169. Trans. Mary O'Donoghue.

the inner mind or the public expression? This isn't the case, however. His soul-searching is far from over. In fact, it would be for his later poems that Ó Ríordáin would really gain the true recognition and significance that was his. In the meantime, we find him delineating the two realms and laying down the borders of each – inner and outer, public and private – very strictly, for fear that one realm might slip across into another, something which was always very likely, given the fact that both realms were raiding one another already. The poet examines the marks of the nails in his hands and concludes that he has miraculously survived his own destruction and, indeed, the destruction of his very family. And who knows? Maybe there's still time for him to come to a resolution between the 'individual/the particular' and the 'communal/multi-faceted'. The excerpt below is part of a litany that he writes in the diary of 2 May 1970. 'Bíonn boladh Dé ón stail' ('*The stallion emits God's fragrance*') is the first line of the litany and where all the contradictions or dualities are brought together as one: male and female, chastity and lust, disease and health, pain and joy, youth and old age. The more perfectly the poet expresses these contradictions through his work, the closer he is to approaching God's handiwork in this world. Nothing really exists, not even God, unless they are unified in the artistic moment – in the act that is art itself:

Nuair is mó is mise mise is mise Dia
Nuair is mó is tusa tusa is tusa Dia
Níl Dia ann
Níl faic ann ach Dia.

The more I am myself I am God
The more you are yourself you are God
There is no God
There is nothing but God.[36]

36 Trans. M. Ó hAodha.

12

Slowly, the Night Fell

Seán Ó Ríordáin retired from his job in City Hall on 30 September 1965. He'd been threatening to retire for a long time, so much so that mention of him retiring had become a bit of an in-joke amongst his work colleagues there. He regularly gave notice of his intention to retire in his diary – every twenty pages or so. He notes it in his diary of 24 August 1965 – where he chides himself on not having it in him ever to take the plunge and hand in his resignation as he'd often intended. He'd never had a comfortable relationship with City Hall, anyway, and he'd had regular arguments with Philip Monahan, the manager there. From the early 1950s onwards, and until Monahan went out on pension in 1959, the relationship between the men worsened. There were many sources of contention between them, especially as relating to holiday pay and Ó Ríordáin's sick-pay entitlements. To have a member of staff who was absent as often as Ó Ríordáin was would have proven a major headache for any manager and Monahan was no exception: the fact that he was absent for such prolonged periods only made it more difficult from a manager's perspective as he had to train in someone to deputise for Seán each time and make sure the work was done. Then Monahan would have to find suitable work for the sick man whenever he returned to work again, never mind all the to-and-fro of correspondence that went between them in the intervening period – and all full in the knowledge that he could never rely completely or in the long-term on Seán, or on any likely improvement in his health. Ó Ríordáin could be out of work for months on end and then return to the office, but be gone again two or three days later. It's no wonder that Monahan's patience with him ran out after he'd been dealing with this on-off work situation for the best part of fifteen years. And as for Seán, one senses that he was only looking for an excuse to go on the attack. When he went to the Gaeltacht for the first time under the auspices of the Irish-language scheme, for instance, they didn't refund him in good time and he wrote a cranky letter to the manager on 14 October 1952 as follows: 'Contrary to the bargain made before I left Cork, I have received no salary since I came to Kerry.'

Ó Ríordáin received his money immediately upon receipt of this letter; a small misunderstanding and an office error had proven responsible for this, and Ó Ríordáin's situation actually had nothing to do with the manager and wasn't his responsibility at all. But on 19 February 1954 we find Ó Ríordáin complaining again; he hasn't been paid again and this time it's no misunderstanding, Ó Ríordáin insinuates, but something that's been done deliberately: 'I received no salary on the 15th inst. I should be glad if you would let me have an explanation.' Seán receives a response to his enquiry very quickly, albeit that the explanation he is given doesn't satisfy him one bit. Ó Ríordáin has used up all the leave that he is entitled to, the manager informs him, and from now on he'll be docked pay for every day he is absent. The manager's reply to Ó Ríordáin is dated 20 February 1954:

> *You received no salary in respect of the 15th instant because you did not present yourself for work on that day, and the amount of sick leave you have received recently has been very great.*

They spoke to one another about the situation and the manager said that he'd consider Seán's position – the outcome was the same, however, as indicated by Monahan's letter to Seán on 2 March 1954:

> *With reference to your application for payment when absent owing to illness recently, I do not think you are entitled to payment because the Local Government (Officers) Regulations, 1943, state that no salary should be paid to an officer when the sick leave granted to such officer during any continuous period of four years exceeds in the aggregate 365 days.*

Seán wasn't happy with this, however, and he wrote to the Minister of Local Government on 18 May, requesting that the City Manager's decision be overturned. His letter of request consisted of more than three pages of typewritten foolscap. The strongest argument Ó Ríordáin put forward was that both of his periods of illness and absence dating 5 May 1949 to 1 October 1950 and 14 October 1950 to October 1951 should have been excluded from the City Manager's calculations in terms of the leave that he'd now apparently used up. In support of this argument, Ó Ríordáin cited the following passage from the 'Circular Letter E. L. 7/52 (Local Government Officers)' as issued on 23 June 1952, instructing that in the case of tuberculosis 'that the period of special sick leave is to be disregarded in determining rate of pay under the regulations during subsequent absences, the periods immediately before and immediately after the special sick leave being treated as one continuous period'. The Local Government official who responded to Ó Ríordáin's claim agreed with his reading of the situation and suggested that the poet be paid for the periods he'd been absent; here's the end of the letter as sent by the department to the City Manager, dated 22 June 1954:

> *On the case presented it looks as though he is entitled to payment during the recent periods of sick leave. Perhaps you would look into the question and see if his grievance could not be remedied?*

This didn't resolve the situation either, however, as clear from the correspondence that followed. Seán's salary was cut again in the meantime, and the thing that really killed him about it was that it was the Sunday pay, a day that wasn't a work day at all, that was kept from him now the second time. He wrote again to the manager on 23 June as follows:

> *On the 31st of last month my salary was reduced by what I am told is one day's pay. As I had worked during the full preceding period, I thought that this was a mistake. I was informed in the Accountant's Department that, on the contrary, it was quite deliberate, and that the reduction was made owing to my absence from work on Sunday, May 16th. As far as I know, no other member of staff was penalised for being absent on that day, and I feel that I, like them, am entitled to full pay.*

The manager had had enough of Seán by now, however, especially given that he'd bypassed his authority by contacting Local Government about it;

this time he'd steal a march on him and play the game himself. One would think he was probably going slightly over-the-top when he referred to the 'offensive terms', 'extraordinary character' and 'extraordinary manner' of the letter from Seán he had to respond to, even if it was definitely a bit arrogant in tone. This is dated 25 June:

> *I have received your letter claiming one day's pay in respect of Sunday, May 16th.*
>
> *I think your claim is expressed in offensive terms. I am making an unfavourable record against you, and feel bound to caution you as to your future conduct. Your letter to me states that you worked during the full period preceding 31st May last, whereas, in fact, [you] were absent from work from 5th May until Monday, 17th May.*
>
> *Your claim, which is in respect of Sunday, May 16th, is of such an extraordinary character and expressed in such an extraordinary manner that I feel bound to take a serious view of your conduct, and I am accordingly sending a copy of your letter and of this letter to the Minister for Local Government.*

Ó Ríordáin had his own letter written for the Minister for 9 July, however: 'a perfectly truthful letter, seeking redress from the City Manager in a matter where, rightly or wrongly, I felt I was unfairly treated' is how he describes the complaint that had triggered their latest confrontation. This letter was two-and-half pages long and went into some detail on every point of contention. Because he was paid twice monthly, on the fifteenth day of each month and again on the last day of the month, he felt right to assert, he thought, bearing 31 May in mind as the completion date, that he hadn't missed any days within the period he'd outlined. But the fundamental issue was still: how to categorise the period 5 May 1949 to 1 October 1950 and 14 October 1950 to 8 October 1951?

Ó Ríordáin didn't want these periods counted as part of his natural sick leave entitlement but the City Manager had a different opinion on this and argued his case with the department just as Ó Ríordáin did. The arguments on both sides became more convoluted the longer the dispute dragged on. If Ó Ríordáin had been working in the civil service he wouldn't have been allowed back to work in October 1950 without being subject to a medical, the department official said on 29 October 1954, but seeing as the Corporation had neglected to do this, in his view, they would have to stick to the original decision they had made. The City Manager had a different view on this and he wanted a hearing on it. He rejected the advice of the department and wrote as follows on 4 November:

> *I have received your letter of the 29 ult. on the subject of Mr. O'Riordan's appeal disallowing him one day's sick leave.*
>
> *I understand you to argue that because the Corporation once gave Mr. O'Riordan more than the Minister permits it to give to him it should continue to do so indefinitely. It appears to me that the extent to which the Corporation should go beyond the Minister's Regulations is a matter entirely for its discretion.*
>
> *In those circumstances, I am not prepared to make an order allowing Mr. O'Riordan's claim.*

The next missive from the department wasn't in the form of advice or a request, however, because the manager received the following brusque instruction on 18 February 1955, and this was the end of the matter:

> *With reference to the appeal of Mr. Seán O'Riordáin under Section 10(2) of the Local Government Act 1941, I am directed by the Minister for Local Government to inform you that he has directed that Mr. O Riordáin's absence on sick leave between May 1949 and October 1951 be excluded in calculating his entitlement to normal sick pay. Mr. O'Riordáin should therefore receive full pay during his period of sick leave in January and February 1954.*

Ó Ríordáin was delighted at this victory of his, not because of the money – because he'd never had any interest in it – but because he'd finally got one over on 'authority' or the 'institutional mindset' for the first time in his life – and maybe the last.

He was finished now with his bouts of treatment in the sanatorium but he was far from finished with TB and the other infections associated with it. The signed sick certificates continue to arrive regularly from the doctor, stating that he'll be absent again for some time; usually, his illness is described as 'bronchitis', 'tracheitis and bronchitis', 'acute bronchitis', 'acute bronchial catarrh' or the like. To get an idea of how often he was ill, it is worth noting that according to the records of City Hall, for instance, Ó Ríordáin had fifty-three days leave in the twelve months that ended 22 December 1961; sixty-three days in the twelve months ending 15 December 1962, and seventy-four days in the twelve months ending 15 July 1964. His normal holiday allocation was eighteen days annually and, therefore, all the rest of the days he took as leave were sick leave, and there's no question that this was a big disruption to the activities of the office. Such prolonged periods of illness were a big hindrance to his writing also – or this is how Seán would certainly have seen it. And even if he had a more peaceful life under the new routine that followed Philip Monahan's retirement, it didn't mean that Ó Ríordáin was any fonder of the job, really. Ultimately, he was subservient to the 'system' or the 'institution' and an institutional mindset that he'd never accepted and that he'd had a tense relationship with for years. It was past time for them to finally see the back of one another. On 25 August 1965 Ó Ríordáin wrote to Patrick Clayton, Deputy City Manager, as follows:

> *I give herewith one month's notice of my intention to resign on grounds of ill-health.*
>
> *I enclose medical certificate.*

The medical certificate stated the following:

> *This is to certify that Mr. Sean O'Riordain [sic] is suffering from advanced bilateral fibrosis of the lungs as a result of previous bilateral Pulmonary Tuberculosis. His pulmonary function has been greatly diminished by the progressive fibrotic destruction of his lungs. He has now reached the stage when it is becoming increasingly injurious to his residual pulmonary function to try and carry on his work.*
>
> *He is a fit case for superannuation on medical grounds and I have been recommending this decision to him for several years past.*

The Deputy Manager requested of the doctor (26 August) that he add to the certificate that Ó Ríordáin was incapable of performing his official duties due to ill-health – in order 'to satisfy our legalistic minds here and to conform with the terms of the Superannuation Act.' The second certificate was received on 20 September:

> *I wish to state that in my opinion Mr. Seán Ó Ríordáin is permanently unfit and incapable of performing his official duties as a Clerical Officer of the staff of the Cork Corporation by reason of advanced chronic tuberculous fibrosis of both lungs.*

There was no going back now. A decision was made on what pension Ó Ríordáin would receive and an instruction from Walter MacEvilly, the new City Manager, was issued to this effect on 28 September:

> *To his service of 28 years 249 days there is to be added a period sufficient to bring his pensionable service to 34 years, and he is to be paid a lump sum of £1,338 15s. 0d. and allowance at the rate of £478 2s. 6d. per annum commencing 1st October 1965.*

By these calculations, Ó Ríordáin's official commencement date at work had been 25 January 1937. But now it's his last day there and it's time for him to say goodbye. Here is a brief extract from Ó Ríordáin's account in his diary of what he did on that last day in the office, 30 September 1965 (his description of that day is actually quite long – a full eight pages of handwriting in total). He returns to the office in City Hall after lunch:

> *The office staff were in before me. I was a little bit late, deliberately. I worked as hard as anyone for an hour. There was a crowd in the office because this is the busiest time. The office was closed to the public at three. During the afternoon I called into Patrick Clayton and presented him with two books i.e.* Brosna *and* Rí na nUile. *When it was nearly five Con Twomey brought a box into the office. It was a tape-recorder that the team in (City) Hall presented me with. £30 5s. 0d. is how much it cost. The neighbours gathered into the office, to see it and to say goodbye to me.*

It's only afterwards that he understands the real significance of that day. He wakes up at seven o'clock the very next morning with nowhere to go, except that it's permanent and forever now, the same as his battle with the solitary life. And he immediately puts pen to paper:

> *Just woke up a few minutes ago. A feeling of despair coursed through me. I know now that I've made the mistake of all mistakes in giving up my job – it was the only protection I had from myself – that I'll be eaten up now – that I'll eat myself up. I came out in a cold sweat at the thought of it. The books around me frightened me. Literature is okay in its place but it's not enough for your daily bread. It's a nice release from life's responsibilities on a half-day. We found sanctuary in it from life's duties. Where will we get relief from that now? Weren't we always looking forward to the break from routine on a Saturday but now every day is the same. It's not that I don't do any work, I hope that I will, but I don't have to work – I don't have to do it regularly, daily, at particular times, as most of my fellow creatures have to do. My brother's children will be more regular, more focused than me from now on. The absence of putting in the time and the lack of regularity will affect me. Another thing that I'll miss is urgency. I'll probably never feel that ever again. Who can live without urgency? He who hasn't an urgency about him has nothing between him and death, he has nothing to ease the grinding towards death. I was all urgency at one time.*

Another last link severed – perhaps the strongest one of all. There's no need for rush now. No one to hurry him any more, no one will miss him if he's not there. He has nowhere to be and nothing to do. It's no matter if he's early or late from now on either because they are terms that are irrelevant for him. In fact, the word 'time' itself barely has meaning any more. Day, evening, weekend – they're all the same now. Rather than increasing the time at his disposal, it is as if he has constricted time or eliminated the time that was his prior to this completely. And one can't accomplish anything if time itself has ceased. One cannot truly say that he has gained a new life now. It is more of a confirmation of his old life, really. This new state is what his life had been directed towards all along – it's almost as if he'd been moving towards this something for years – towards a sense of fruition, as if in a poem. The sole difference is that now his procrastination is worse than before, his cowardliness is more cowardly, his sense of alienation more extreme. This is the deferral of the moment and the fear of it, alienation and procrastination or its occasional corollary – a perfect sense of completion. Compounding this is the fact that his subject matter has got scarcer or more restricted. But then, hadn't this been the case from the very beginning? Another pattern is approaching its fulfilment, as if to say that he has been going in reverse all the time. The doubts return in abundance. He has set aside all his worldly responsibilities and cares for the sake of his writing but now he cannot write. Or was he ever able to write, really? Whoever suggested that? There's more time for Ó Ríordáin's doubts and insecurities now that he has no office to go to and no excuse to take his mind off the process of writing. It is now that one really understands the type who is more susceptible to doubt and despair:

> *But the man who has to be in the office at nine, at a press-conference for ten, at dinner for one, in Uppsala at six, his fate is portioned out and he's no danger to himself.*
>
> *But think of those poor pensioners whose official functions have been deprived them and who are no longer anything but ghosts* – laudatores temporis acti *['one who praises past times']! The former manager can no longer send an order out to the former doorman, even if the former underlings are always still a bit afraid of the former bosses. These creatures are no competition for the Uppsala man in the morning.*[1]

This poet had always been the underdog, but in the excerpt above one would be forgiven for thinking that he had almost given in or acceded to the societal establishment, now that he's in this new afterlife of his. What had he been preparing for all these years? Was this all that he'd set aside after his years of hardship and struggle? Is this it? Is this the 'self' that he'd sought after all these years? He knows now that he was never really separate from the search at all but rather an intimate aspect of the question – all the while. And if he should be destroyed as part of the artistic quest, as predicted, then it's a destruction born of inadequacy and timidity.[2]

1 'Éadóchas maidine' ('*Morning despair*'), IT, 3 August 1968.
2 ES: p. 80.

> *You can't separate from your own self in the end. We couldn't cope with it all other than that we're always hoping for change – a change in ourselves and a change that will never come. But even if this is what I've said and said honestly, I probably don't believe it fully either. I think that I'll probably escape from this strict bind and mould another personality for myself. I've changed over the course of my life, I must have, but, all the same, I think that it's the same pathetic, anxious person that's writing this today as would have written something similar twenty years ago.*[3]

God forbid that the 'self' that you searched for so assiduously and for so long was actually there with you all the time. Perhaps it's best to set the self aside for another while again, until the 'death bed' that is the very end, when it manifests itself again in all its perfection in the moment that all is revealed, that moment when the richness that is death erupts around us and we reap whatever it is we have set aside during this earthly existence.[4] As before, however, there is the other voice that whispers in the poet's ear, the doubting Ó Ríordáin that says this is nothing but the final trick and the cruellest of all. What if no one receives the portion they are expecting in the end; what if there is no levelling or balancing of the scales? And what's the point in waiting or hesitating any longer, anyway, when the probability is that he hasn't got that much time left and his doubts will soon be confirmed one way or the other? Hasn't he spent his life waiting already? And waiting for what? For health? For a boost or an impetus that never came? For that knock on the door? For Godot? He has a fair idea now of what he's been waiting for all this time, and it's not for some major revelation or resurgence in his art – but rather its opposite – the death of creativity, the demise of his art.

As regards that new flowering of his work that would happen, the play that would be written, the new style he'd develop – it wouldn't happen, there would be no new style or new play. He'd just continue adding random entries to the same old themes of the notebooks and observe the passing of the seasons instead: the death of summer, the birth of autumn, the crisp

3 D: 12 November 1965.
4 LL: p. 42; TÉB: p. 44.

freshness of the winter air burgeoning in late afternoon with the fading of the light. His life from now on would be spent 'absorbing eternity like a punctured shoe soaks up water'.[5] All divisions and protections gone as one feels oneself slowly slipping over the barrier as death gradually takes hold. One dies 'person by person, friend by friend, enemy by enemy'.[6] Death absorbs so much of you into itself that it is almost a release in the end. Ó Ríordáin's prose best expresses this gradual but relentless process, the sensibility that is gradually being numbed and put to sleep; the poet that is retreating from his métier, and coming to an end. While Ó Ríordáin traced this process in his public writings, he based his published articles and essays in this regard almost entirely on the diary entries, and it is in them that we get the clearest picture of his thinking at this juncture. The piece 'Treascairt an tsamhraidh' is based on his diary entries for 24 August 1965 and 20 July 1967 and when he mentions the storms of youth here, one cannot but recall the childhood storms that he attempted to tame within his poems.[7] Now that he's getting older, one senses calm and an approaching silence in the poet's writing, the last flurry that marks the end of days. The last days of summer are now but the brief flurry of a Sunday afternoon:

> *This afternoon for the first time in years I felt that the summer was dying and I could sense the winter returning. The night fell more quickly and there was a freshness in the air. But I'd already felt the overthrowing of summer even before I'd sensed the freshness in the air or before the night falling. Early in the evening, around seven, I noticed the sudden change of light and this light that was different from the summer light. It's a quieter light, this autumn light.*
>
> *The human being receives this blow every year, i.e. the disappearance of summer. Gradually, he gets used to it. Not only is there the heartbreak and unspeakable loneliness of this death of summer, but there is redemption also. There is too much freedom in the summer light. It is a scattering of humanity's hopes and longings. This yellowing of the light is a recreation, a renewal of the senses.*

5 'Éadóchas maidine', IT, 3 August 1968.
6 'Imeachtaí 1971', IT, 1 January 1972.
7 IT, 23 August 1968.

> *Even if it has its own light, it is nonetheless linked to the light that accompanies sorrow and when someone aligns their will to the will of God.*
>
> *Undoubtedly, this annual death of summer is linked to ageing and, in the end, with dying. The bustle of high summer is no longer threatening. Your strength lies now in secluding oneself beneath the blanket of winter, hiding within its privacy. The summer light is a bit public. It's a preparation for death all right. Our choices diminish with the arrival of death until it is logic, and a relief to go somewhere where there is no choice. Choice is a cause of storms, a lack of choice is calm. The storm relates to youth, however, and the calm to old age. A strange thing as relating to the death of summer, I think, is that we think this is the end of summer forever, because we'll never have such a season again and that this isn't just the death of this one summer but rather the death of summer itself. There is nothing but mercy in the autumn, a pause for reflection – a sentimental reflection the likes of this – so that the terror doesn't hit us too quickly. Then it comes – 'terror, terror, the first day of winter.'*
>
> *We are sentimental, a little soft in the head, this time of the year. We've a tendency for sentimentality in us. This loneliness that's the end of summer and the havoc and the coming darkness is the reason for this probably. We sense then that the summer was just a lie, a lie that we fell for. We seek out worldly things the most, things that are nothing but a lie – eternal youth, Damer's wealth, beautiful women, holidays in Andalucia, fame and fortune, complete knowledge of the copula. They are not at all and there is no loneliness like the loneliness for that which is not there. This joy that is summer in our minds, it isn't there, it was never there and it never will be there. This is the reason for our loneliness – that nothing exists except the void. You see a beautiful woman in the street. She is it. Every beauty that you've ever imagined is inscribed on her face. Get to know her and you'll soon find out that all the beauty of the world has gone into another woman that you see away from you on the street. You can't feel beauty or summer. Touch them and they fade away, because they don't exist.*

The same thing is true of 'Smaointe Geimhridh' ('*Winter Thoughts*'), published in *The Irish Times* on 2 October 1969, as taken from the diary entry for 1 September 1969. Another winter approaches, the same winter he thought he'd put behind him forever. Will he get away with denying its reality one more time? Another refusal to face up to the dying of the light, even if he's half-dead already? One senses more of a welcome for it than a denial in the excerpt below:

> *The summer has disappeared again. The days and years and we ourselves are disappearing into nothingness. Unamuno preferred the hell of nothingness.*[8] *This is why he had to believe in eternity. But there's a worse fate than death – if death represents nothingness. This is the fate of getting older. When you reach fifty years of age, a certain change comes over that's very scary. It is difficult to put into words. It's a living death. This is a preview of your real death. It's as if death is building away inside you. This change makes everyone equal in the same way as death. It hardens you, both inside and outside. But this ageing is a merciful form of change. Your emotions are being put to sleep.*

The piece 'Am Amú: Am Amú go Deo' ('*Wasted Time, Time Wasted Forever*') published in *The Irish Times* on 11 September 1971 is based on his diary notes for both 26 August 1971 and 4 September 1971. The day and its lazy passing hours have caught up with him again and he hasn't his piece prepared on time. So he heads back to the diary in search of material for his article and duly comes across a suitable piece of writing. This piece will be constructed on the negative attributions that are 'no', 'not', 'did not' – i.e. all the summers and parts of his life that he never really lived properly.

> *The summer is defeated again. The old wans are coming back from Salthill in the Morris Minor. They missed out on the weather again, unfortunately. But there are signs other than the old wans. I felt the freshness in the air that's the sign. A stab of pain went through me. Then the loneliness that's the end of summer began to spread, the loneliness that is no other spread all over the place. It's like a red sunset. Your heart fills with a rich colour. You think of all the things you'll never get to do, of all the summer trips you've never made, and that you'll probably never make now, of the relatives you never saw and are likely never to see, of the*

8 Miguel de Unamuno y Jugo (1864–1936) was a Basque novelist, poet, playwright and philosopher whose essays were very influential in early twentieth-century Spain. He was a Professor of Greek and Classics, and later the rector of the University of Salamanca. His major philosophical essay was *The Tragic Sense of Life* (1912).

graves the sun shone on in the summer and which you never visited. It wasn't right to let any valuable sliver of the summer pass without tasting it. But look at what you did! Think of all the summer people you never got to know. If another summer comes along, it won't be the same and neither will the summer people who'll be there either, and you won't get the same summer lamentations either – this year's summer lamentations are lost forever. But aren't the people you've never met, and the trips you've never made, and the unspoken voices you've never heard, and the lamentations that you've lost forever, aren't they the most precious things in this life and the greatest things you have in a way? You feel lonely now because another summer has got away from you without you experiencing any of it, as if it had never happened at all. And yet, that terrible aftertaste of summer is still in your heart because you couldn't hold on to it, because you've lost it forever. You are so confused that you sense it is that which you couldn't hold on to that is the greatest of all your possessions now. That is why, perhaps, there is a roof of happiness on this end-of-summer loneliness. We are end-of-summer creatures – creatures who are fated to lose everything forever. We are creatures of death. It is part of our magic that we should be losing every second, despite the fact that we are created with an unbelievable desire for the eternal and holding on to things. Late summer is the annual admission of that eternal hole in our pocket. Death becomes us. The end of summer becomes us. It becomes us to be losing things forever as such loss is a form of permanency. Everything we have lost has melted in the form of the loneliness that is in our hearts forever.

But it would be easy to find a more anxious mind, a more hurried mind. I hear them close to me, the small blows of the hammer. People are working away as always. They'll be all bustling also but they'll all fall into the light also. Wouldn't they fall into the light just the same, even if they remained idle? That's the question, isn't it? That's the difference, maybe, between going up on high and going down to hell. (You aren't telling me that you accept these things still?) I've spent the morning idle. Does this mean that I've put out the light of eternity? You wouldn't want to countenance it. Is wasted time the same as time that has gone astray forever? How wonderful is that word 'amú' ('astray')? Because of the long vowel at the end of it, it goes on forever, like an echo. 'Go deo' ('forever') is a similar kind of word, if two words can be termed as one. They both suit the meaning of the term. There is never any end to the word 'go deo' and as for 'amú', no one knows when we'll ever happen upon the person who has gone astray.

'Astray' is another sort of 'forever'. There is poetry in both these words, whatever poetry is.

The word 'fadó' ('*long ago*') is another similarly analogous word, a word beneath which lies the endless echo of eternity. By definition, Christmas resonates with the feeling or mood of long ago. The phrase 'long ago' explains 'Christmas'. Neither term would function correctly in the absence of the other. As evident here, Ó Ríordáin had always placed great emphasis on sourcing the correct 'word' or term to encompass the feeling he wished to engender. It was within such a term that he'd encompassed or 'tamed' the likes of Pound, after all. And not just Pound either; he'd captured many another feeling or night within the boundaries of the 'word' and calmed the emotion within him in the process. Over the years, Ó Ríordáin had also frequently sought out the 'texture of Christmas': he sought it in confession at the Dominican Church in Cork city; in the Midnight Mass, or in the hustle and bustle of the city centre in the days leading up to Christmas (e.g., the essays 'Rakryation' and 'Ainniseoirí'), or in the bottle of wine he brought home with him from the city and sipped alone in that small bit of a room that had no ivy or holly, nor even a fire; then up for the Christmas dinner to his brother's house.[9] And above anything else, it is in this correct application of the 'term' and the wholeness that is the 'word' that the poet found peace and spent so much of his life. The correct application of the 'word' and years pass by and meld seamlessly, one into the next, until they form a particular structure or harmony within his memory – until the memory and the word are as one within him.

It's Christmas, December 1972, and we find the terms that Ó Ríordáin loved interacting with one another in their own special manner:

I feel that the word 'fadó' ('long ago') is intimately linked to the Christmas. How long ago does something have to happen before it can be said that it happened long ago? I think that there's a certain sentimentality or loneliness associated with long ago. This 'long-ago' loneliness suits Christmas well. People's eyes fill with tears when they remember the Christmases of long ago. There is a power that is

9 'Rakryation', IT, 4 January 1971; 'Ainniseoirí', IT, 15 January 1972.

almost frightening in the term 'long ago'. It is a time full of dead people and dark nights and extinguished Christmases. It is from these extinguished Christmases that we sift through whatever aspects that we still think of as Christmas now, so that we can identify these aspects in every Christmas that comes our way. There's a heartbreak or sentimentality that's limitless in this thing because, I suppose, it reminds us of the impermanency of life and of our own mortality. When we were young, we associated long ago with elderly people and not with ourselves. There was no long ago in our lives then. Nothing had happened to us in our lives then that was ancient enough for us to associate it with long ago …[10]

The poem that comes closest to this winter atmosphere is 'Oíche Ghealaí' ('*Moonlit Night*'). The poet looks on as the battle between light and darkness rages in the night sky, much as he did years earlier in 'An Leigheas'. But unlike long ago, the battle never impinges on the poet in this instance, since he has gone beyond feeling or emotion by now. One senses here that Ó Ríordáin is saying his goodbye to conflicts or struggles of every type, and to the daunting joy of living, because this is no longer a suitable environment for it any more:

Tá mianach na tubaiste
In aoibhneas dufhulaingthe
Na loganna solais seo.
B'fhearr linn folaithe
An áilleacht obann so,
Níl slí i mbrollach di.
Níl cruth nach cumas di,
Múch i scamall í,
Is ragham don tigh.[11]

There is the possibility of disaster
In the unbearable delight
Of these places of light.

10 'Bhí fear ann fadó', IT, 30 December 1972.

11 LL: p. 32.

We'd prefer this sudden beauty
To remain hidden,
There is no room for it within one's breast.
There is no form that it cannot take,
Cover it in a cloud,
And let us go home.[12]

One feels there is more going on here than just the dousing of beauty and the light. Rest quietly in your room and let the night fall upon you slowly and steadily. This is different from the sudden extinguishing of the candle, and neither is it followed by a bout of dread or anger.[13] Don't broadcast a 'republic of light' in response to the night as you once did; the time for challenges and fighting is over.[14] He abandons colour and the manifestation of things as the darkness swallows him up. There's a certain hesitancy in the poet to let the life that's been engulfed resuscitate itself now again:

from **'Solas'**

Do thit an oíche diaidh ar ndiaidh
Go dtí gur mhúch an uile rud,
Do dhein comhdhubh de dhubh is geal,
Do chaill cathaoireacha a gcruth,
Do chuaigh an seomra ar ceal,
Do shloig an dubh an uile chruth:
I mbroinn na doircheachta tá domhan,
Is féidir liom é bhrath lem láimh,
Níl fanta ach a chuimhne agam,
Is leisc lem chuimhne é athchruthú ...[15]

12 Trans. M. Ó hAodha.
13 ES: pp. 42 and 68.
14 B: p. 13.
15 LL: p. 35.

from 'Light'

Night fell slowly, slowly
until everything was extinguished,
what had been black or bright one equal dark.
Chairs lost their form,
the room was annulled,
the dark swallowed every shape:
there's a world in the womb of darkness,
I can touch it with my hands.
All that remains to me is its memory,
my mind's reluctant to re-create it.[16]

When exactly Ó Ríordáin composed the poem isn't clear but the prose piece that accompanied it saw life at midnight on 11/12 March 1968 in his diary. The only obvious link between both pieces is the site of their composition and the first line of the poem. We can imagine him reading over the prose piece again, as if imbuing each sentence with the peculiar atmosphere that is the night, as if to hold on to the nostalgia of the moment for a little longer:

I spent the afternoon and the night listening to the radio. Gradually, the night fell and it became darker but I didn't light the room. It was a pleasant night of radio. Rare is beautiful. The standard of radio had fallen so low in recent years that you don't expect anything from it any more.

He had more than nostalgia for days past to worry about now, however. Whatever bit of money he had left was dead money now that it was 'tied up' and couldn't be touched for years.[17] He needed money from somewhere else and he needed it fairly urgently. The £1,338 15s. 0d. lump sum he'd received on leaving his job wouldn't last him long and certainly not until he was of an age to receive an annual pension of £478 2s. 6d. Well before

16 Sewell, *Selected Poems*, p. 179. Trans. Theo Dorgan.
17 TÉB: p. 44.

he'd resigned from his post (he seemed to have been thinking of giving up the job and mentioning it to his friends for donkey's years!), he'd written to Séamus Ó Coigligh (as he lay stretched out in bed sick at home) on 14 November 1950, and had added these few sentences to the tail end of the letter:

> *P.S. Do you know whether I'll ever again get another rouble? I thought that I'd a few weeks of half-pay due to me. Another P.S. I'm thinking of resigning from Local Govt. completely and making a living from writing. Between Raidió Éireann and the Irish-language newspapers and Scéala Éireann one could earn at least £10 a week, if you set your mind to it. But I don't care about that side of it. Something terrible needs to be said, and we all need to say some bit of it, but we have to approach it in pristine fashion, i.e. without any official religion, without patriotism, without any human bind whatsoever, without woman-love, without self-love, without mercy, without nobility. All one needs is hatred and a pen.*[18]

He was wrong because he needed more than this, and he wasn't long retired when he realised this either. He could have been the most successful writer in Ireland (never mind a lesser-known writer in a marginalised and minority language like Irish), and, realistically speaking, he still wouldn't have been able to carve out even a frugal living as a writer in Ireland. But trying to be a professional writer was very different from being a clerk, and in the eyes of most people in Ireland then, writing was not a real occupation but a form of recreational activity that someone might do at the weekends. Now that his clerical income was gone, Ó Ríordáin had to fend for himself; it was either that or starve. If it wasn't for the support of neighbours and family, he might as well have forgotten about the poetry.

Prior to his giving up his job, Ó Ríordáin had focused primarily on poetry; he'd written very little prose – just the short story 'Morrissey' as published in *Feasta* (January 1952), the Introduction to *Eireaball Spideoige*, the essays based on the subject matter from the diaries as published in *Comhar* ('Seal im aonar', March 1960; 'Tráthnóna Liom

18 Ó hAnluain, *An Duine is Dual*, p. 33.

Féin', March 1961; 'An Taisceadán', June 1963), and the *apologia* 'Teangacha Príobháideacha' ('*Private Languages*') as published in *Inniu* (August–September 1963). On the other hand, there were so many reflections and insights of his life's experiences and sufferings as stored away in his diary over a period of twenty-five years that he could now draw on, as appropriate, and make available for public consumption. But he'd also need to begin writing new prose material, perhaps as based on what he listened to on the radio or as based on his reading of newspapers or books. It mightn't be his ideal scenario but this is what he had to do to earn a living now. In fact, journalist and writer Breandán Ó hEithir had written to Ó Ríordáin a good few years earlier, on 5 February 1958, asking him whether he'd be interested in providing articles for the newspaper *Scéala Éireann*, but he hadn't taken up the offer. It would be a different story for the next while, however, and Ó Ríordáin would be seeking out opportunities rather than turning them down.

He received a letter in mid-November 1967 from Ciarán Ó Nualláin, editor of *Inniu*, asking him – if he was interested – to submit an article for the December issue of the newspaper. The article had to be in for 15 December but Ó Ríordáin only managed to post it that day so that the article was late arriving. This article, comprising extracts from his diary, appeared in print early in the New Year instead, on 5 January 1968. There was talk of his submitting further articles – Ó Nualláin was particularly interested in essays 'dealing with literary matters' and Ó Ríordáin began work on an article as relating to various Rabelaisian authors, an article he never managed to complete. Ó Ríordáin wrote to the editor to apologise as follows on 18 June 1968:

> *If you sought to write an article without seeking to write a brilliant article. I went to work as promised. The Rabelesian Voice as the subject – an interesting subject I think. (It's not enough just to be interesting, one has to write it also!) It proved too interesting. I had to read this and that, and then re-read it again. I filled a book with notes on Rabelais, Chaucer, Cervantes, Myles na gCopaleen, Joyce and Parliament Chloinne Tomáis. All the notes made me despair. Then I had a bout of illness in April. I had to continue with the articles for* The Irish Times *as I'd started them. Also, they were lighter.*

It was the same old story all over again. All the preparations with nothing to show at the end of it. But his work wasn't entirely in vain, as he was able to incorporate some of his research for this into various pieces that he had published in *The Irish Times* from time to time after this. He also drew on some of this same material when he gave a very blunt speech at the Aonach Urmhumhan in Nenagh when he responded to Máirtín Ó Cadhain at the 1969 Merriman Winter School.

In the meantime, Ó Ríordáin had made an arrangement with *The Irish Times* and the *RTÉ Guide* that he'd provide both with regular articles for publication. Two friends of his, Aindreas Ó Gallchóir and Seán Ó Mórdha, had acted as intermediaries on his behalf in relation to these opportunities. The *RTÉ Guide* was the first to get in touch with him to tell him that they'd welcome articles from him, on condition that such pieces related to radio or television. Ó Ríordáin had always been an avid radio listener but he'd only very rarely have had any interest in anything on television. The only thing on television that might have grabbed his interest would have been a special programme on the likes of Daniel Corkery or the sculptor Séamus Murphy, or a programme relating to the Irish language or nationalism. He never had a television set in his house and whenever he went on a visit to his brother's house, he'd deliberately turn his back to the television so as not to see what was being shown. Even in the case of the radio, however, the type of writing the *RTÉ Guide* were looking for would have run completely counter to his experience. Also, Leslie Faughnan, Assistant Editor at the *Guide*, had written to him with certain guidelines for the proposed articles, guidelines which Ó Ríordáin would have found difficult to comply with, given his writing experience and style as developed over many years. For instance, the editor had appended the following strictures with the initial invitation to publish, as issued on 29 June 1967:

> *The subject of an article would have to be connected, at least in a general way, with radio and television. If you are interested, it would probably be a good idea if you could let me have a rough outline of your subject and proposed treatment before you actually write the piece.*

This was Ó Ríordáin's response, as dated 19 July 1967:

> *Yes, I would be interested in writing articles for your paper. I do not think it would be possible for me to give a rough outline of the subject or proposed treatment beforehand. Subject and treatment come to me as a surprise – often unpleasant. My articles are based, I presume, on infused knowledge, direct, no doubt, from the Holy Ghost. In these circumstances you will, I am sure, appreciate that a rough outline would be pointless.*
>
> *I am prepared, however, to send you a specimen or specimens that you can accept or reject as you wish …*
>
> *P.S. I might be able to persuade the Holy Ghost to turn his August (or indeed September) attention to radio and television.*

Ó Ríordáin received another reminder on 10 August where he was asked to please adhere to the subject material that he'd been assigned to; he'd get five guineas for every 500–700 word essay. In the end, he had just one piece published in the *Guide*. It appeared on 8 December 1967 and comprised an account of the life and work of Father Peadar Ó Laoghaire, an account that tallied with the programme on the same subject that appeared as part of a school television programme broadcast just four days later; Ó Ríordáin himself had prepared the script for this TV programme.

At least, in this instance, all Ó Ríordáin had to write was what he sincerely believed in; the individual adheres to the literary model, as that is his own particular style. Some of this piece is on a theme analogous with that of 'Teangacha Príobháideacha': the mind and imagination of the individual writer being shaped and formed on the basis of the experiences and artistic expressions of the common man. The two aspects have the same heritage and they feed off one another and enrich one another in turn. As with Father Peadar and his *Séadna* characters, these are Ó Ríordáin's people too and he is as entitled to make literature of them as anyone else:

> *It seems to me that the style of Irish of Father Peadar is one of the purest and sweetest styles of Irish and that it was enough to make his name on a permanent basis. His Irish is Ballyvourney Irish but it's Irish that he'd been incubating for a long time, polishing it and licking it into shape … It's been*

> *said that* Séadna *isn't real literature. This is a ridiculous view, I think.* Séadna *is based on folklore, the same as* Peer Gynt. *When folklore is transformed in the individual's imagination, literature is produced. According to this understanding,* Séadna *is literature. One of the things that set the critics astray in this regard was the personality of Father Peadar himself. He was a rural man, a natural man, a simple man – a puritan, and a born priest. He was more of a strong man than a literary man really. I don't think he'd recognise good literature. I'm convinced that it was never his intention to compose this type of literature. All the same, Father Peadar was a talented and complex artist while he was writing* Séadna ... *He wrote as a rural man and not as an intellectual. He gave his characters their head. He let them speak for themselves. They were country people. He was inside them all the while. During the story, you sense a sensitive, sharp eye accompanying them all the while, the eye that is one of their own ...*

One can almost hear the measured rhythms of Father Peadar's Irish in the background. That was the beginning and the end of his writing for the *RTÉ Guide*, however. There was no further contact between Ó Ríordáin and the magazine after this, it seems. Both parties were happy to part ways and leave it at that.

In the meantime, Ó Ríordáin had started to provide articles for *The Irish Times*. He sent the first two of these to Donal Foley, the contact who'd been suggested to him, on 2 October 1967. The subject of his first article was Father Peadar, while Daniel Corkery was the subject of the second:

> *I'm sending you two articles, one on Daniel Corkery (author of* The Hidden Ireland*) and one about a funeral, to be published if they suit you. I think that I could send you articles on a regular basis from now on if you so wished. Seán Ó Mórdha (RTÉ) told me that you might be interested in some articles from me.*

Both these articles were based on material from his diary. He'd compiled the notes for the article entitled 'Dónall Ó Corcora' ('*Donal Corkery*') on hearing of Corkery's death on 31 December 1964, and it was while attending the funeral of a neighbouring woman on 3 May 1957 that he sourced the subject matter for the second essay, 'Tórramh'.[19] There was a certain delay between his sending the initial article and it appearing in print and he didn't receive any acknowledgement that they'd arrived from the newspaper at any stage in the meantime, something which upset him somewhat. When he didn't hear anything back, Ó Ríordáin assumed that the newspaper didn't find the articles of sufficient interest and that it was unlikely they'd accept any further material from him. He was due three pounds for the various articles he'd written over the first seven months of the year, by the time he wrote to Seán Ó Mórdha on 10 October 1967. He'd be lucky to pocket that much by the end of the year, he feared, the way things were shaping up. In the diary notes for 2 October 1967 he speaks of having 'to face the winter and old age and poverty'. It was probably past time for him to face the truth as well, the truth that had been lurking in the background for quite some time. He was finished as a writer, wasn't he – that's assuming he'd ever really been a writer the first day ever. At 2.40 a.m. on the Monday morning of 9 October 1967, the poet comes to the following conclusion:

> *I'm a while now dealing with despair, I'm a sad case, forty years of age by all account. Yesterday, I suppose, this despair changed and I felt free of it. It was the lie that got the better of me. Suddenly, I admitted to myself that I was finished as a writer, and not only was I finished but that I never had any talent for writing in the first place. I realised that I'd spent my life with a lie – engaged in a craft that I didn't have and a language that I didn't have either. If I have any talent, or if I ever had any talent, it was for drawing. I wasn't sure and I am not sure whether I have this talent or not but I'm always sketching, and it's against my will, once every ten years, that I compose a poem. I decided to give up writing and the lie associated with it. You wouldn't believe how much relief this gave me. It's a long since I felt this free. What ever possessed me to think that I was a bloody writer anyway? I feel so honest now that I think I could begin properly on writing – without any pretence … It's a strange thing but it was just after writing two new poems that I came to this view.*[20]

19 IT, 25 November 1967.

20 'Smaointe Fáin', IT, 24 June 1969.

The 'back-up' or 'grounded feeling' that went with that part of him that was the clerk was more necessary to Ó Ríordáin than ever, now that he was doubting himself as a writer again and having big misgivings about his life's literary project. A certain lack of reality is evident in some of his thinking at this point, in addition to a tendency to see nothing but hostility or enmity in others. It's as if he has pulled in on himself further, if that was possible. He writes of people conspiring against him from every quarter, the 'poisoning of the wells', 'slippery GAA methods' (as he wrote to Seán Ó Mórdha on 10 October 1967), or the 'bastard of a goalkeeper before him, blocking every gap and hole he finds', and his inability to trust anyone – himself above all.[21] Hard-nosed people who'd walk over anyone else to get what they want. And he's not tough enough for them because he's paralysed by animosity and self-doubt. It's the 'old story' of the critics all over again. Or as An File (The Poet) once proclaimed about the nuns in Dingle: 'Go bhfóire Dia ar an té a raghadh bocht ina measc' ('*God help those who'd go poor among them*'), or who hoped for some charity from them. Not a budge out of them at all. You wouldn't mind but the poet had lost so much respect for himself at this stage that he wouldn't have been able to bring himself to ask for mercy from them. They're all the same now as far as he's concerned – from your closest friend to your biggest enemy: they were how he'd always known them in his heart of hearts – the same as the powerful and those in authority had always been. It was might is right and screw the person who was down. As if to confirm this view, Ó Ríordáin received the following instruction from Cork County Council on 5 January that year – as addressed to a 'Seán O'Ríordán':

> *You are hereby requested to pay at my office, 7 Liberty Street Cork, WITHIN SIX DAYS from the date hereof, the amount of Rates due as already demanded, viz. £8 6s. 10d.*
>
> *And in case you refuse or neglect to do so I shall take proceedings for recovery thereof as the Law directs.*
>
> *J. Hogan*
> *Collector*

21 'Lucht spóirt', IT, 11 July 1968.

There you are! Like the landlords in the old days when the final warning had gone unheeded – 'Send out your wife to me!' – Ó Ríordáin duly complied. He had no choice. The month of February 1968 went by and although his first two essays had been published in *The Irish Times*, he hadn't received any word as to whether they were interested in more material from him. So he wrote again to Seán Ó Mórdha on 28 February 1968:

> *It's five months now since I sent any articles to* The Irish Times, *and a letter to them saying that I'd write for them regularly if they wanted. I didn't get any reply. It's two months since I wrote the second letter. Total silence. A rejection is fine. But if you want to destroy your enemy completely in body and soul, then put him on the long finger and leave him on the long finger. You'll break the heart inside the fucker. And he'll be left incapable of doing anything else because the constant living in hope and uncertainty won't let him. By now, I don't trust anyone. I can put up with anything except other people. When someone talks to me now, I can feel the man who's out to get me there in my chest. The worst thing of all is that I'm a human being myself …*
>
> *Don't think that I'm ungrateful to you. You did your best. But don't do anything. As far as I can see, every door is closed against it. I don't care so long as I know. There are other countries and languages and other prostitutes out there.*

There was more of the same in the letter: he hadn't received any payment yet for his article published in the *RTÉ Guide*; he'd given a lecture for the *Comhar na Meánmhúinteoirí* (Secondary School Teachers Partnership) in Cork [on 23 January 1968] but received no payment for that either; he hadn't even been asked permission for his poem 'Siollabadh' to be published in *The Irish Press* [10 February 1968] and worse again, it had been published accompanied by a 'really bad translation', a translation he hadn't been consulted about; Ó Ríordáin has also heard talk of Frank O'Brien's upcoming thesis on modern Irish poetry and knew that it wouldn't be favourable to him, anyway, given that Dáithí Ó hUaithne (David Greene) was 'O'Brien's supervisor at the time' and he'd been in the same critical camp as Máire Mhac an tSaoi and Seán Mac Réamoinn at the time that he was being 'venomously attacked'. It was just a year previously that An tOllamh (Professor) Breatnach had offered Ó Ríordáin a job in the

Department of Irish at University College Cork (on 18 February 1967, according to the diary) and although the poet had replied to him long ago (on 10 April 1967) saying that he was definitely interested in this, he'd heard nothing back since.

Ó Ríordáin had got it into his head by this time – as he says in another letter dated 10 October 1967 – that it was actually Seán Ó Tuama who was the person hindering his appointment to this post: 'it wouldn't do at all if Ó Tuama was speaking in one room on Ó Ríordáin and ÓR was in another room speaking on ÓR and the pair of them contradicting each other. If they were to contradict one another, then who'd be right?' In the case of the college lecturing position, the four who were angling in the background for the poet's appointment were Tadhg Ó Ciardha, Ó Ríordáin's old friend from his schooldays and then the Registrar at UCC; Risteard Breatnach, head of the department to which they sought to appoint him; the scholar and academic Seán Ó Tuama; and M.D. Mac Carthy, the then President of the University – all of whom were very keen to see Ó Ríordáin get the position. It was to the first two men especially that Ó Ríordáin should have been grateful, as they understood better than most how straitened his circumstances were and were doing their best to help him out. They came to an arrangement, finally, at the end of January of the following year, 1969: £400 was Ó Ríordáin's agreed annual salary and for this he was obliged to give about a half-a-dozen lectures a year on literary and cultural themes, in addition to making himself available to students for four or five hours a week. These responsibilities weren't huge but it has to be said that the salary wasn't huge either. As it happens, Ó Ríordáin's arrangement to supply newspaper articles to *The Irish Times* on a regular basis was put in place by 29 February 1968 and before all the details for the college job were in place. And yet, even then, Ó Ríordáin was suspicious about the intentions of some of the newspaper people and wouldn't have put it past them if they were celebrating getting a good 'deal' out of him on that one. As he wrote to the newspaper's art critic, Brian Fallon, on 15 August 1969:

> *I enclose article 'An Renaissance'. I sent an article 'Measúlacht' some weeks ago which you did not print. I met Donal Foley for a moment in Kerry and asked*

> *him if you had some objection to it. I think he said not but I am not sure. I would have sent an article sooner if I thought you would not print it.*

Needless to say, Ó Ríordáin always doubted the value or quality of his own pieces and whether what he wrote was worth publishing at all. His grim, self-deprecating humour was often a protective device, as he waited anxiously for the assurance he needed by the return of post. In the next piece, the humour is more a cover for his penury and the dire financial straits he is in – when he writes to the newspaper's assistant editor, Donal O'Donovan, on 11 June 1968 looking to see if he can be paid for the articles he's already sent on. He complains about how slowly he felt the articles were appearing in print and then:

> *I would be obliged if you would convey my correct address to your accounts department. They seem to be unable to get it right.*
>
> *I am very happy to be published by* The Irish Times. *Vile as my articles are, I am told they are read. Although my main objective is to increase the circulation of* The Irish Times, *I would not seriously object to a higher fee.*

He got the pay-rise he was looking for: from four guineas up to five guineas. Not that he'd ever be able to make enough from this occasional freelance work, or the books of poetry, to make a living from writing. At least, in the case of the poetry he'd someone in his corner that was fighting on his behalf: Bríghid Uí Éigeartaigh – who was always looking out for him in relation to RTÉ, the newspapers, various publishers and the editors of journals and magazines generally, and making sure that he got paid. As regards his role as a writer or public intellectual, Ó Ríordáin needed to argue his case in public, something he duly did in an essay in *The Irish Times* entitled 'Ní Íoctar Filí' ('*Poets Aren't Paid*') published on 20 July 1968, where he addressed the question of writing as a full-time profession and contended that the writer wasn't a charity case but rather someone who deserved to be paid for his work:

> *There are some innocent people in this country who think that poets and writers should be paid for their work in the same way as judges, bishops,*

priests, prostitutes, carpenters and TDs are paid. No one pays any attention to these crazy people. It's a completely opposite view in this country. They're currently giving pay-rises to Justices and the (government) ministers. If I understand the public's reasoning correctly, the reason for the pay-rises aren't the same in both cases. It seems that the judges will go to bad if they don't get very high salaries. It seems that the judges could be susceptible to bribery. The reason for raising the ministers' pay is so as to attract the best and the most able of ministers into politics. So these suit the wealthy classes, therefore. The integrity of one of these classes and the ability of the other class is dependent on money. Everyone knows the reasons for these and other similar-type increases off by heart. If you said to one of them, however, that they should pay an Irish-language writer for giving a lecture to secondary school teachers (say) or for reading poetry publicly, it would be the nearest thing to blasphemy in their eyes. They'd be shocked. To look for payment for writing in Irish or for anything at all in Irish! Where is our patriotism? Or maybe they might start laughing! You're a real optimist, aren't you! Isn't it a bad enough show already that they pay printers, proof-readers, typists, carpenters and stage-carpenters without paying writers as well! Writing isn't work. But if you don't earn anything, you don't get anything. Poverty suits writers because they haven't it in them to be corrupt …

It's the community who tell someone who he is, according to the sociologists. The bishop gets a certain degree of recognition, the professor another, the soldier another again, and each type behave themselves according to the type of recognition they are given. The writer in Ireland receives no such recognition. They criticise Irish-language writers because of their lack of productivity. Much of the blame for this lies with the community however. I can't see how you can practice a profession if you receive no encouragement, recognition or remuneration.[22]

One consequence of this was that the branch of *Comhar na Meánmhúinteoirí* (Secondary School Teachers Partnership) in Cork paid him immediately! Not that this solved all his problems – far from it! Truth be told, this wasn't how he'd planned to spend his time after he'd given up the clerical

22 'Gairmiúlacht' ('*Professionalism*'), IT, 20 November 1971.

job; he'd planned on pursuing the path of literature in peace, but rather than focusing on his poetry, he found all his time taken up with these various freelance jobs and deadlines – evenings, weekends, the long days and nights. Now that he'd given his artistic sensibility scope to develop for the first time with the benefit of additional time for writing, the direct opposite seemed to have happened and his time for the 'real writing' had narrowed instead. It was nearly worse to be sold to your own crowd than it was to the foreign master, given your own crowd had tighter control over you. His diaries had metamorphosed into something else again now – they were simply a preparation for the next article. Now, his best articles aren't the ones that were written spontaneously but rather the ones that were 'written' initially years ago in the diary. He's now the editor for the writer he was once – a writer he'd never duly respected anyway, and about whom he was still plagued with doubt. Where once the diaries were a form of preparation for the trade or proof-writing for the 'great work' that would come later – they'd now changed into something else. And the great work was going to these articles for *The Irish Times* and nothing else – much to his disappointment, the poet had only now come to realise this. His job now is to select the various excerpts and thoughts from the diaries and collate them together; it's as simple as that! Edit, cut, amend, disguise – but whatever you do, don't make any real progress as a writer!

And as with many article writers, there were times now when he found himself having to hold forth publicly on issues that he knew very little about. Sometimes, it was as basic as listening to the man in the pub preaching next to you and adapting his talk for the next article. Ó Ríordáin might have done this in conversation previously, but it was a first for him putting it into writing. Sometimes, now, he found himself taking on the role of the man with the cause to uphold or defend, a role that neither suited his 'elevated' aspirations as a serious writer, or as practised in the privacy of his own world; and neither did this new form of writing suit his personality, given that he was someone who spent his life with unresolved questions and difficulties and a disease that was incurable. He'd have to pay his dues now, however, whether he liked it or not. Or as Ó Ríordáin put it in his piece 'Teachtaireacht Amháin' – there was a heavy price to be paid for he/she who was misfortunate enough to hold forth or transmit that which wasn't your message.[23] He recognises immediately the false cloak that he's been obliged to adopt so as to produce this form of writing:

> *I bring the things that I have heard to the message that's been granted to me, if there is one. I think that everyone is given just one single message. It is this same message that the person gives expression to – no matter what they say. He brings his sustenance to this message ever afterwards. If he releases what he has accumulated without filtering it first, it isn't him who is speaking at all. And whatever he says isn't worth the ten of clubs. The voice that has no understanding is completely irrelevant. This is why he writes from himself. He waits until he's made blood and flesh and mind of what he stole.*[24]

It's easy to come out with the likes of this, of course, when he's got his wage-slip in his back pocket and consequently has the luxury of being a bit snooty about other hacks. This is just another trade to him in a way, even if he was never trained in it, as Ó Ríordáin explained to Brian Fallon in a letter dated 22 February 1975:

> *I think it is bad to keep on producing articles week after week without a pause – bad for me at least. The quality (such as it is) is bound to deteriorate. I am only a common whore, not a professional prostitute like a trained journalist – meaning no disrespect and speaking figuratively.*

The virginity of the diary is sullied forever in the poet's mind. He has one eye on the public palette and one eye on the truth. It's not a question of what he really has to say any more, but rather that which he's expected to say. One has to have a certain grandiosity and elegance now that you're on the same pages as 'Backbencher on the Saturday' or on the 'Arts and Studies' page on the Thursday. But how much of the real man or the real thinker are you getting? Just a small part, most likely. Every sliver of thought has to be a more remarkable reflection than the last; every phrase cleverer and more eloquent than that which came before. And even if it's blandness

23 IT, 1 April 1970.

24 'Iriseoireacht agus litríocht' (*'Journalism and literature'*), IT, 2 July 1968.

personified, at least it's a well-written form of blandness; it's fluent and silky dullness; this isn't the slow or hesitant tedium or dreariness you find sometimes in the diary, but rather a tedium that makes music of tedium. Even when one's admitting that one's vision has failed, one needs to say so in a way that sounds polished and eloquent. And the greatest sign of all that the vision has faded and failed is that he has to continually revisit all the 'nice bits' of writing and gather the most polished and ornamented material together. Here's an excerpt from the diary as written at 9.40 p.m. on 12 August 1968, when he's already been on the journalistic trail for about six months:

> *I write very little now, since I started writing for* The Irish Times. *I write articles now. Revealing my thoughts was what I did before. Which is better? I should be revealing my thinking in the articles. If I wasn't or if I am not, then what's the point? The worst thing of the lot is that my thinking isn't always enough for me. The article has to be good – a notable one. When my mind is dull, I think, I want to change it and replace it with a different mind, integrate nice pieces into it that have nothing to do with whatever bit of thinking I have at all. The likes of this is just a fraud and is padding. I should be satisfied with whatever mind and thinking I've been given. These nice asides that don't relate to the subject of the reflective piece I'm writing just make the articles uneven and confusing. Every bout of reflection, no matter how thin, has its own value. It's a while spent thinking. The other thing is just a covering over the cracks, a bit of decoration. And if I think that I'll get away with this trickery I'm wrong, because the only one I'm fooling is myself. It doesn't make things any better that the 'nice pieces' I put in are my own – that they were things I'd written before and that I thought were nice.*

Needless to say, Ó Ríordáin also had to draw on other material outside of the diaries to bolster the articles. The private reflections of his own inner world aren't enough; now that he's writing for a major broadsheet he's expected to reflect the mindset or conscience of the nation and the Irish public and yet, this is a man who never really knew some of his closest neighbours, a man whom (as far as I know) never even visited either Limerick or Galway, and was equally unfamiliar with Northern Ireland. If he was in Dublin ten times in his life, that's about it – and most of these were just day trips. The truth is that if it wasn't for his friends in RTÉ (the likes of Ó Mórdha and Ó Gallchóir) urging him to come to Dublin, and the fact that he needed the money so badly, Ó Ríordáin probably would never have visited Dublin at all subsequent to the 1948 Oireachtas. And it wasn't as if he socialised a lot, even on those few Dublin trips. Now, however, he's spouting off in public on both national and international affairs, or he's on stage in the Peacock theatre giving a powerful response to the arguments Thomas Kinsella made in *Éire-Ireland* (Summer 1967) with regard to the Irish writer and his/her relationship with their own country; now he's preparing scripts for television programmes and even taking part in them on occasion (e.g., *Iarphroinn*, *Féach*, *Writer in Profile*); now he's a 'big man' with the celebrity class up in Montrose, Dublin – with brandy and fine talk.

It was a hell of a change in Ó Ríordáin's life. And you wouldn't mind but for the man and the life that he'd come from and the fact that this new and sudden 'public' profile was partly an obfuscation of the truth, the reality that was the waning of his poetic powers.

He had another book of poetry in preparation at this time also. It is 13 March 1968 and we find Bríghid Bean Uí Éigeartaigh advising him to prepare an application for the Irish-American Cultural Institute literary prize. The page proofs needed to be ready by the end of June at the latest, she tells Ó Ríordáin and he posts his reply on the 14 March:

> *I've nothing done for the Oireachtas or for the American competition. I got worried about money-related issues and wasted time with* The Irish Times *and with* Inniu *etc., instead of doing proper work. Also, there is some sort of a cloud over me in this house, on my own. I see now that I can't work like this ...*

Two months later (11 May) and the collection still isn't finished. (In fact, the only poetry-related work he managed to undertake in the meantime was a translation of 'Cúl an Tí' that he did for the Aer Lingus magazine, *Cara*.) He thinks he might possibly have the collection completed within the fortnight:

> *I'm nearly gone mad. Instead of focusing on composing poetry, I'm completely taken up with minor issues. I've less than thirteen poems written. I'm not sure*

that I'll have a book done on time. I'd need until the end of the month at least and even then it would be a major achievement if I managed it. I won't send you anything yet in case I don't manage it. It wouldn't be of much use to give ten poems or so to the printers without being sure or even half-sure that I'd have enough done for a book. So, I'll really get down to work properly now and you'll hear from me again in a fortnight's time.

He receives another reminder again on 14 May that time has almost run out and that there would be no point in him looking for any additional time to finish the job either:

We'd need your manuscript by 14th of May at the very latest. The printer is waiting on it, but if he doesn't get it by then, we won't have the proofs in time for the competition.

By 14 June the deadline is well past and he knows that there's no chance whatsoever that he'll have the collection ready on time and that his chance of the prize has gone:

I'm ashamed to say that I failed to get the book of poems done in time. My health has improved over the last month and I've written five new poems. I'd only have 16 or 17 altogether and that would never be enough. I think that I've started on writing verse again and that I believe in it again. (I'd lost my faith in poetry for a long time.) Since I began again, if indeed I have begun, I feel that I could, if I forced myself, write many more poems. But there's nothing can be done now. I'm afraid that all the years that weren't made into poetry are lost now.

And so it goes on from day to day and from fortnight to fortnight until we reach December 1970 when he finally submitted the finished collection *Línte Liombó* – and even then, it practically had to be torn from him.[25] Twenty-two poems, none of them particularly long, formed this collection, just three or four additional poems to those he'd written a full year-and-a-half earlier.

25 See *Comhar*, May 1977, pp. 27–8.

His time has instead been taken up with petty issues and small bits of work. The literary review, radio programmes, pieces of poetry and prose as recorded for the Gael-Linn record, the occasional public lecture – even if he was often quicker to promise completion of same rather than actually delivery. The regular *Irish Times* articles were amongst the least important of his responsibilities and yet they were a long way short of the masterpieces of writing that he'd once thought he'd be capable of achieving if he'd only had the time and the opportunity. Remember the aspirations he'd once held before reality had come knocking: 'everlasting youth, incredible wealth, beautiful women, the holiday in Andalucía, fame and fortune, a full and complete knowledge of the structure of the copula.' It was the opposite nearly, that Ó Ríordáin had ended up with in all cases. He'd never had much in the way of youth or wealth or beautiful women and this wasn't going to change at this stage. He'd got the thin edge of the wedge, no doubt about it. As regards his newspaper articles, the quality of them varied. Some of them were better than others and went some way towards explaining who he was as a writer, while others found him attempting to explain something that he hadn't understood fully himself.

As stated in his diary entry for 11 January 1962, politics wasn't really Ó Ríordáin's thing. Likewise, when it came to campaigning on behalf of issues that were important to him, his attitude was more complex than at a first glance; even with respect to the Irish language, for instance, his private views and his public stances didn't always entirely tally. He lobbied very strongly as part of the campaign for the Irish-language school in Dunquin to be kept open, and yet there was a part of him that wasn't entirely in it either.[26] An excerpt from the diary tells us more – the inner self and the outer self interacting with one another:

Traces of blood still [in my saliva]. I'm in bed. I can't get warm. There was a knock on the door a while ago. A man from Dublin. The Dunquin School. Would I go to Dublin to help them again? I told him how I was – that I was sick. He left. To tell you the truth, I've had enough of them. My life has been spent in this

26 For example, 'Scoil Dhún Chaoin', IT, 23 September 1970.

> *bed. My childhood slipped away from me, unknown to me. This bed still has me in its grip. It's a black day for me today. One shouldn't succumb to a day the likes of this …*[27]

He'd remember the dark or black day when he'd forgotten the happier one, and the thoughts of the inner man when the public man was no longer significant. This isn't to say that he wasn't interested in politics from time to time, but its fascination for him lay in how he needed to adapt the rhythms of his own thinking to its machinations more than anything else. In the piece that follows, for example, the strange appeal that was war and the spilling of blood in times gone by is compared (in negative terms) with the bland nature of economics and the new European common market – a frequent theme in his essays. Ó Ríordáin would frequently refer to the 'rebirth' or renewal that the big event might bring, the 'spectacular' – no matter how horrific – that would shock him out of the dreary routine of life and shake him out of this deathly tedium. It's as if he seeks this, regardless of others; he needs something terrible to shake him up and it is precisely because he is unable to shake himself out of this deathly inertia that he needs it so badly:

> *The IRA issued a statement during the week saying that they intend giving up the bombing campaign on the border. The statement said that they weren't getting the support of the public any more because people's minds were focused on matters less important than partition. The governments, north and south, welcomed this statement. Although I was never in favour of this military campaign, I was left sort of lonely or nostalgic on hearing this statement. It's been part of the magic of Ireland for a long, long time, this fighting and spilling of blood for the sake of freedom. This is often how we let go of our bitterness. This economic Ireland that's being created by the likes of Lemass, we don't like it much. It's boring. It is no longer Ireland. You'd think by Lemass and Jack Lynch that we should be grateful to the countries of the common market just for letting us be in this world at all, we're that insignificant. I'm very dubious about Lemass. The country is full of foreigners … It's the foreigners who get*

27 D: 22 January 1973.

all the respect. The country is at a low ebb. There are minor, petty people in charge.[28]

The types he refers to would become even more petty and small-minded over time, in Ó Ríordáin's view, until the only archetype left was the Nobody; he saw the election of Lynch instead of Lemass as another sign of this trivialisation of Irish society (and particularly given that those two were preceded by the political and cultural colossus that was de Valera). Wasn't it the same pattern too in the US, Ó Ríordáin mused, with Johnson and Nixon taking the place of Kennedy – as stones replacing eggs – and Paul VI succeeding John XXIII as Pope – was the same thing happening everywhere now and not just in Ireland?

The terrible violence and blood-letting that was 1969 in Northern Ireland assumed even greater significance in Ó Ríordáin's eyes because not only did it deflect him – at least for a while – from the difficulties of his own life, but it was also a strange yet welcome distraction from the fact that Ireland itself was in a very bad way, economically and socially. It was as if the drama of life had renewed itself before the poet's very eyes and the old era of heroes and enemies and nations all hating one another was all part of a strange and vigorous form of rebirth. He begins noting these sentences in the dark and dreary dawn hours – at 4 a.m. on 18 August 1969 as the bleak rain falls on the roof outside and the atmosphere is heavy with a sense of powerlessness. Suddenly, he calls to mind the latest news and the events that are occurring in the world outside. This is *it* – the renewal that is required:

It's raining. A small moth is tormenting me. There's no doubt that we all like news. The more unusual the better. I heard a lot of things over the last few days that made me cry – not with grief but with pride. These are important days, it would be no harm keeping an account of them. We've never seen Ireland or England or the Orangemen or the human being clearly until now. Many things have been clarified by the bloody events of recent days.

28 D: 1 March 1962.

The poet felt he was seeing the death of consensus and compromise with the Nobody and all his progeny. It's the man and the woman willing to take a stand who matter now and who are significant. Individuals and countries drift apart so that the poet sees them more clearly and as if for the first time. This is the new societal paradigm – everyone with their own role in life and if you don't have a specific role or job, then you have no significance. Ireland is no longer a country for servant or messenger or the man who is an interlocutor. Every man must speak for himself or remain silent. Wasn't it like this that they'd once spoken to him so that he'd made poetry of them? – poetry that was pure and 'washed clean in its own nature'.[29] That which has the fresh tang of renewal in terms of speech and act and form – as the morning after a night of drunkeness. That which was asleep for a long time is awake and renewed once more. This is the joy that he thought was gone forever, now momentarily reborn. The poet describes this newborn world as it appears to him on midnight of 23/24 July 1969 – in the moment when it's clear to him that 'average' will no longer suffice, irrespective of one's status in this life.

> *Average was never a good leader, they say. And neither was* via media *ever a good leader either. That's how Lynch referred to himself when he was elected. Bernadette Devlin is no* via media. *One might say that Ian Paisley is no* via media *either. Pearse was no* via media *and neither was Connolly or Daniel Corkery. Captain O'Neill was a* via media. *What value was the evidence he gave? Where is he now? Paisley is always giving his evidence, no matter how miserable it is. Perhaps it needs to be given, so the truth comes to the fore. It's definitely part of the drama and it's bringing the arguments centre-stage. Anyway, it's Northern Ireland now. The protocols and handshakes are over now and the incursions into the north. We're all returning to ourselves. Ireland is returning to herself. It was never her destiny to be British or pro-British. For her to be Irish, she needs to be revolutionary. She was never destined to be a* via media. Via dolorosa *is her fate. Now, Lynch was responding well to Ireland when he referred to himself as a* via media. *Ireland was a* via media *at the time, i.e. she was teetering on being wiped out. She was rotting. But now –*

29 B: p. 36.

> *all is changed, changed utterly … The Ireland of Bord Fáilte Ireland is gone. It's irrelevant now. It is Pentecost. The Holy Spirit descended upon them … Derry has been derryified and Ireland has been irishified and Humanity has been humanised.*[30]

Ó Ríordáin creates a new internal monologue as based on his own history and the history of his people. And the persona he refers to becomes part of this new monologue also – they are simply terms of reference according to Ó Ríordáin's aesthetic and only significant with respect to the language they use. He'd always been fascinated by new terminology and the multi-voiced nature of them, but it's when people and events actually become the *via media* and when the multivoiced is reduced to the one common or collective 'discourse' that he loses all interest in them – and in history's monologue.

There was a good deal of 'posturing' in Ó Ríordáin's newspaper articles, needless to say, and behind all the 'brave talk' as appeared in the pages of *The Irish Times*, there's still a very anxious individual who's full of self-doubt, a man who always leaves the light switched on at night and keeps an imitation gun under the pillow, for fear of attack. The gap between the fictional 'self' he portrays in his newspaper pieces and the pretend gun he keeps beneath his pillow is not as wide as one might assume. Let's follow him for a while now out across the public arena, to the various gatherings and parties he attends – as often as not he's 'in attendance' on the imaginary level rather than being actually physically present at the event or occasion he's writing about in the newspaper article in question – but at least it's a release from the claustrophobia of his inner world. This is the same release or redemption of the sort that the poet felt in his piece 'Múscail do Mhisneach' ('*Awaken Your Courage*'), which was the beginning of his series on Haughey's island – Inishvickillane.[31] In our mind's eye, we see him take the road west back as far as Inch Strand in Kerry, where the Understanding Peasant is among the unexpected characters he meets along the way. And no sooner has he come across this character but he

30 'An Tuaisceart' ('*The North*'), IT, 10 September 1969.

31 B: p. 19.

provides him with a number of suitable sidekicks or companions. Here's how he develops the narrative in this first essay of his, the ending of which he hasn't worked out yet – though he has in mind a soft and sentimental or romanticised conclusion. The sky and the sea open in front of the poet as he travels west and form a single plane of newness and light. The more he moves forward, the quicker he receives admission to this new realm of experience:

> *On my way back west to Dunquin, I get my first view of the sea from Inch Road. My heart nearly stops. This water is a transformation of the inland world. It's a world of water from there westwards. Sea and sky come together in one big stretch of water. One is in the presence of eternity now. Water is eternity. Time is dry land. The claustrophobia of time is at an end – of the land. The* apertura *of eternity opens ahead of you. This sea means the desire of our hearts – The Land of Everlasting Youth. She means other summers. She means the dead back there whom we once knew …*
>
> *It means something within us that cannot be overcome. And it means the Understanding Peasant …*[32]

And even if, at times, the Gaeltacht was a subject which generated a dark and sardonic humour in him – the critical or satirical side of his imagination was exercised quite often by the figure of Conor Cruise O'Brien. Here's Ó Ríordáin letting fly regarding Cruise's very public criticism of the Irish-language movement at a filmed event in Waterford city:

> *But Cruise is the man who destroyed the Sacred Cow … He is the master. It is he who brought art to perfection. He knows that the cow with the most sacred tail is the ones that lows the loudest. His technique is based on this philosophy. This technique is similar to a drama – a four-part drama. Act I: He selects the Sacred Cow that is to be attacked. The destination day comes around or the destination night. Such a night was the night the ruckus happened in Waterford when he attacked the Sacred Cow that is the Irish language. It's not difficult to imagine*

32 'An Tuata Tuisceanach' ('*The Understanding Peasant*'), IT, 21 September 1974.

such an occasion. A public meeting. Journalists and television people all around the place like a great shoal of fish, all adding to the bluster and importance of the occasion. The air buzzing with the electricity of indiscretion.

Copies of Cruise's script being handed out to the crowd onstage. It doesn't take them long to locate the sentence they are looking for – that indiscreet and fateful sentence – the sentence that will get all the publicity – the attack on the Sacred Cow. They know well that this sentence will be there – that it'll be deliberately indiscreet, deliberately damaging from a political point of view, but a good scoop in the end. This lack of discretion, this brinkmanship, this safe form of danger, this cruise-manship, exhilarates and frightens them at the same time.

Then begins the second act of the play – the pleading that will fail. They start to urge him to omit the offending sentence. Corish sends a message to the chairman: 'For God's sake, ask him not to say that!'[33] *It's pointless. Corish knows that it's pointless. Cruise isn't for budging. They feel themselves threatened by a historical danger. Cruise loves the pleading with him. He knows that this sentence will grab all the headlines on television and in the newspapers. He knows that he'll be criticised – that the country will be on his case. People are scandalised by him. His heart swells in his chest with joy. His name will be a source of controversy, north and south. A row begins. The troublemakers get stuck in to one another. The purists get angry … The night is intoxicated. A new context has opened up. Everyone is high on the euphoria of it. Isn't he a really deep person! Isn't he really open-minded! An international figure dismissing the Sacred Cow the same as Patrick banished the snakes! A great thinker who's too educated, too sophisticated, for us peasants! …*

The third act in the drama. Cruise speaking and the air alive with brinkmanship and gombeen-gaeilgeoir-ism. The fourth act in the drama: A radio interview on the Sunday at 1 p.m. where he explains that he wasn't speaking on the government's behalf at all but entirely on his own bad-minded black-minded behalf and that only a heartless person wouldn't love him for it.[34]

33 Brendan Corish (1918–90) was an Irish Labour Party politician who served as minister for social welfare from 1954 to 1957 and from 1973 to 1977, leader of the Labour Party from 1960 to 1977 and tánaiste and minister for health from 1973 to 1977.

34 'Marbhghin Uí Chuanaigh', IT, 28 September 1974.

It wasn't as if one needed to be present on such occasions, and indeed it might be preferable if you weren't. After all, to see something with your own two eyes was a constraint on the imagination. 'I wasn't there. If I had been, I'd only have got a faulty perspective on it,' you would say. 'You need to be absent from these sorts of incidents in order to get a proper perspective on them. Soon, some of the crowd who were there on the night will be looking for information about it from me.'[35] This is how he spoke about a gathering at the Merriman School ('Scoil Mherriman') and even if it was a said as a joke, there was a certain core of truth to it all the same.

Ó Ríordáin agreed to take part in the Merriman School once, in early 1969, after the school's proceedings had already been published. His experience of the school underscored the piece below, even if he wasn't anywhere near the centre of the festivities himself. But, marriage today and pickles tomorrow, as they say. It's a rare moment of humour on his part and you certainly wouldn't begrudge him having a bit of a laugh at the expense of others:

> *Every scholarly belly was full of porter or of Scandinavian beer – how would I know? Expertise on drunkenness, the folklore of being twisted, the anthropology of drink, water sickness on linguistics. Swedes speaking Irish. There wasn't as mutual a spilling of seed as mutually learned since Vatican II ended. In view of this, it was necessary to drink.* Mens in alta rapitur *['the mind is driven high']. Our hearts stirring with prize-knowledge. Compared with this Remy Martini ruckus, the Renaissance would be the next closest thing to a Thomas Davis Lecture. Wouldn't it be just lovely for the baby, legitimate or illegitimate that would be conceived during these shenanigans! It would just pop right into the womb reeking of respectability. It couldn't be more dignified than if the child was conceived during the election of a pope, or if the gods themselves had erred. But, as they say, it's the Cumann Merriman today and pickles tomorrow. It is necessary to return to boring normality. And all the while, the North is like a festering boil in our shoe-leather.*[36]

35 'Scoil Mherriman (post mortem)', IT, 8 November 1968.

36 'Beoir Lochlannach', IT, 4 September 1971.

But even if Ó Ríordáin was 'on a roll' when he wrote the piece 'Scoil Mherriman (post mortem)', this hardly excuses him fracturing the rules of friendship and fairness, as he did later in this same article. The poet transgressed another basic rule also in the case of this article: he'd taken most of the material that he included in the piece straight from his diary (16 April 1966 and 23 June 1967) but hadn't edited it sufficiently or toned down his private opinions before making them public. The discussion that follows isn't to defend in any way what the poet did, but rather to try to explain the background and context to it. Basically, in the article Ó Ríordáin hurt Seán Mac Réamoinn with his insinuation that he hadn't an original thought in his head but simply adopted the views and perspectives of others and made them his own. This wasn't all that the poet said and neither was it the worst thing either. He'd always had a tempestuous relationship with Mac Réamoinn and had resented him for years.[37] Mac Réamoinn was like a weathercock, in Ó Ríordáin's opinion, someone who was always very aware of what way the wind was blowing and was ready to jump aboard the latest trendy themes and support whatever or whoever was in fashion. For a while it had been all the rage to say that Máire Mhac an tSaoi was the poet who encompassed everything in terms of the Irish language and tradition – as much as to say that no one else had what she had. Here's some of what Mac Réamoinn said in his article on Mhac an tSaoi's much-praised collection of the time, *Margadh na Saoire:*

> *But she didn't turn her back on education the way many others did: and while they were in thrall to foreign ideas and ways, and trying out new subjects and forms, she was exploring native heritage and tradition by all accounts – a while with her own personal cultural heritage, a while with the scholarly tradition of the ancients, a while with the heritage of the Gaeltacht ...*
>
> *They're [i.e. the original versions of the poems] free also, thank God, from the sort of monotonous neurosis that's fashionable with many pipers these days, and they convinced that they're playing the music of the universal ... It should be noted that the poet does not provide any prose introduction to the poems, and there isn't any glossary accompanying his statement that would better enable all*

37 For example, D: 17 April 1957; 16 October 1957; 7 December 1957.

> *of us to 'interpret' this collection and improve our understanding of it generally … Whatever it is she wishes to say in these poems, it is in these poems that it is expressed.*[38]

'Hey old fire-hook, guess who it is!' – Ó Ríordáin was sure that he recognised at least one person among those whom Mac Réamoinn was finding fault with in his article. Even if trends were always changing and nothing and no one (poets included) remained in vogue forever, the urge to be trendy and counted amongst the fashionable or 'in' crowd remained paramount, irrespective of whether one was discussing a school or a council:

> *I'm not criticising the School or Mac Réamoinn when I say that they're one and the same … He made a phone box out of the Second Vatican Council. Every patriarch and bishop and cardinal and theologian became a sort of a telephone when they came within his net. He spoke through them. Initially, he stole their mentality from them, directly and within the blink of an eye, because this is his talent. Then he questioned them using their own mentality. They were delighted to agree with him. Why wouldn't they? Weren't they actually agreeing with themselves? They wouldn't have recognised their own mentality being fed back to them through them, it was so electrified, enhanced and clarified …*
>
> *One thing that is forbidden him, by himself, the him having any idea of his own. Complete amateurism, the likes of that. He had no respect really. He's a manager of ideas. It's his job to absorb other people's ideas and fine-tune them, in a way that they could never do themselves.*[39]

A number of people complained about his article to Ó Ríordáin, amongst them his friend Aindreas Ó Gallchóir, who told him that the article was a 'bad day's work' and that it hadn't been 'done right'. Ó Gallchóir's letter really shook Ó Ríordáin and the same happened when he sought the advice of Séamus Ó Coigligh, who told him that he'd been out of order. Ó Ríordáin realised that he'd gone too far and that he had to rectify the situation. He wrote to *The Irish Times* on 14 November 1968:

---

38 *Comhar*, April 1957.

39 'Scoil Mherriman (post mortem)', IT, 8 November 1968.

> *I would consider it a great personal favour if you published this article, 'Seán Mac Réamoinn', as soon as possible. It would appear that some people considered my article on Scoil Mherriman a very severe criticism of him. This is not so at all. The present article refutes that idea. As Mac Réamoinn is an old friend of mine I would like to make it clear that I had no hostile intention.*

His 'revised' view was duly published, but if others were happy with his 'refutation', Ó Ríordáin wasn't one of them, that's for certain. 'Another article of mine about Seán Mac Réamoinn was published yesterday. I gave them the shit they were looking for this time around apparently,' he confided to his diary on 19 November.

In reality, Ó Ríordáin was convinced that he'd been right from the beginning; as he said in a letter he sent to Seán Ó Mórdha on 21 November, he couldn't have written the initial article if he hadn't got the inspiration for it from Mac Réamoinn in the first place. 'There's something about it. There's something there … People can be assessed according to this article. M. Ó Cadhain, B. Ó hEithir and Cian Ó hÉigeartaigh came best out of it, not because I praised them but because they just took it as a piece of writing and not as a personal attack on them.'

But if this particular 'dust-up' – if it could even be classified as a dust-up – had caught Ó Ríordáin by surprise, this wasn't so in relation to some of the other arguments that he deliberately brought on and which he found himself embroiled in before very long.

One of these was the controversy with Máire Mhac an tSaoi, a row that had history and an issue that had been festering inside him for nearly twenty years by this stage. They were never fond of one another anyway, but towards the end of 1969 he heard that Mhac an tSaoi had been recorded for a television programme as part of the series *Writer in Profile*, and that Seán Mac Réamoinn had been her interviewer. While the programme wasn't broadcast until some time later, and while Ó Ríordáin never actually watched the programme – as far as I'm aware – it was enough for Ó Ríordáin to hear about the programme to get wound up about it – even more so when he heard that it was Mac Réamoinn who'd interviewed Mhac an tSaoi. As he wrote to a friend of his on 16 December 1969:

> *It was revenge. They both have it in for me. He would not dare ... Mac Réamoinn ... wouldn't have it in him to attack me straight out. He chose this way instead. This civil war is as alive now as it was twenty years ago. Eliot says (in his essay on Milton) that a civil war never ends. I didn't respond to these attacks when they were first made on me, even if there were things that I could easily have contradicted. I don't know what I'll do this time. In the end, it doesn't matter about attacks. Nothing matters but the truth. And the other aspect of this is that poetry is something uncertain and mysterious. One never knows whether what they've written is poetry or not. What Mary means to do is to break my courage if she can. There's nothing that would anger her more than if she thought that I would publish superb poems. There's a basic enmity between us.*

One can forgive anything except that which you never had to seek forgiveness for: 'the years entrusted to poetry', 'the extra ideas and projects that were never written', the closed and empty void that was the sickroom he spent his life in. Certainly, if the attacks of the critics weren't entirely responsible for Ó Ríordáin's drive towards self-protection and self-doubt, they were a major factor nonetheless. And now, it was happening all over again, Ó Ríordáin suspected – whatever few years he had left to him, whatever writing remained to be done, whatever place he had reached in his development as a writer – they were attempting to cut it out from under him again, as he saw it. There's no doubt that Ó Ríordáin's suspicions of Mac Réamoinn and his motives were well-justified – this wasn't Mac Réamoinn's first time, after all; while assuming the role of interlocutor or peacemaker, he was also 'playing games', Ó Ríordáin suspected. As if to confirm the poet's suspicions, one of the first questions Mac Réamoinn asked Máire Mhac an tSaoi, when asking for her opinion of other writers in that segment of *Writer in Profile*, related to her views on 'my friend Seán Ó Ríordáin'. Her reply went as follows:

> Máire Mhac an tSaoi: *When it was originally published, I couldn't read Seán Ó Ríordáin's poetry, and I still can't read the first poems. I think that they are like something a computer would produce; now it isn't –*
>
> Seán Mac Réamoinn: *Oh, I don't agree with you at all about that.*

> Máire Mhac an tSaoi: *Maybe you don't, but you have to let me finish my thesis. Since he began to spend time in the Gaeltacht, his Irish has really improved and, in my opinion, there is a depth and a texture and a colour to his poetry so that he writes the kind of poetry that I write …*

Whatever else Ó Ríordáin picked up from others regarding Mhac an tSaoi's comments in that television programme, he certainly heard the cynical reference to 'the computer' because he referred to it later in his essay 'Rothair Dhaonna'.[40] As far as Ó Ríordáin was concerned, it wasn't important what Mhac an tSaoi or Mac Réamoinn said about him in such a programme; he'd already made his mind up about the pair of them years earlier and had judged them hostile to him; they were assigned to the 'enemies' camp forever after that – understandably so. It's at night when the same thoughts and doubts torment him and go around and around in his mind that he sees their hostility and dislike of him in all its clarity. It's going on for 1 a.m. in the morning and the world outside – past or present – is a hostile one replete with enemies:

> *I remember when it was Máire Mhac an tSaoi … and her followers who were attacking me in season and out of season. I didn't have Irish or poetry. My scruples were nothing but ordinary scruples. The entire scholarly Celtic world knows that a man can't be a poet unless his scruples are extraordinary ones. In one of my poor ditties, I said that 'gur líonadh an domhan le náire' (the world was filled with shame). This was bad Irish according to Máire Mhac an tSaoi even though you hear this said in every Gaeltacht in Ireland. My rhythms were too ordinary, the same as my scruples. I'm not a scholarly person and I wouldn't contradict her. I'm quite happy to let time takes its course. Time will tell if our work lasts … She had avant garde followers, like Seán Mac Réamoinn, Dáithí Ó hUaithne, Gearóid Ó Cléirigh. This Gearóid Ó Cléirigh is a very interesting example. He was in the Department of Foreign Affairs – no fear of him. He'd spend his summers duck-shooting in Wicklow with a pellet-gun – if memory serves me correctly. Although I was brought up in Ballyvourney and spent many a night in generous Nell Mhattie's house where she told us stories in sweet Irish*

40 IT, 22 February 1975.

> *– Dearg mac Deirg who went to the Eastern World Shrubs and 'Cac Money, a Chaipillín Bháin' and other stories when I was a child – Ó Cléirigh said that I was brought up too far away from the tradition to be capable of writing in Irish. He happens to be right, by God. But straight after that, he announced that he was going to translate Virgil's* Aeneid *into Irish – a man who was born and reared in Dublin amongst the English-speaking nobility. Into this camp was drafted Frank O'Brien, the American scholar who wrote the book* Filíocht Ghaeilge na Linne Seo.[41]

There was no point in telling Ó Ríordáin that he might have got it wrong and that maybe they weren't against him or meant well by him. Over the years he'd already sifted the evidence and judged otherwise. And he had more than enough proof to back up his view also. He wrote to Seán Ó Mórdha on 2 June 1970 and told him about something that happened while an interview with him (i.e. Ó Ríordáin) was actually being broadcast by Aindreas Ó Gallchóir:

> *I received the following message from Liam Ó Murchú:*
>
> *From T. F. Lyons. Summary of telephone calls received on Wed. May 20, 1970.*
>
> *Writer in Profile. Máire Mhac an tSaoi called during the programme to say that she'd never heard Irish spoken as well as she heard it spoken tonight by Seán Ó Ríordáin. She wanted to have this message passed on to S. Ó. R. through the producer.*
>
> *My own reaction? The shit stirred inside me with disgust.*

It would be exactly four years later before he plucked up the confidence to say anything against her in a public forum; he wasn't slow about gathering whatever ammunition he could in the meantime, however. It was an innocent enough 'dig' that he gave in the beginning but there's no doubt that he hit the mark straight away. It was at the end of the article

41 D: 12.40 a.m., 4 February 1970.

'Coinsias Sochraide' ('*Funereal Conscience*') that he got his dig in, one so subtle that few enough people would have noticed or understood what he was referring to. It's as if he has caught these two great Irish-language heroes out – and revealed by virtue of just the most minor incident that they're all 'fur coat and no knickers':

> *Congratulations to Dáithí Ó hUaithne and to Máire Mhac an tSaoi! It's virtually a miracle of deafness to be going to Dunquin for as long as people can remember without ever hearing the word 'leámharaic'.*[42]

Mhac an tSaoi responded to his jibe on the very same day his article was published:

> *Howth Head*
> *15.6.'74*
>
> *Dear Sir,*
> *I don't know where you got the impression that I'd never heard the word 'leáimhiric' [sic] before; I'm hearing that word since I first reached the age of reason, but always in the same context, as relating to an anecdote about Father Jones and the terrible flu. I'm of the opinion that the basis of this word is the English word 'maverick'. I'd be obliged if you published my letter.*
> *With kind regards,*
> *Máire Mhac an tSaoi*

Ó Ríordáin duly published Mhac an tSaoi's response to him in his article, 'An léamharaic'. He needed to go back and explain the context of the discussion in order that others could understand fully what they were disputing:

> *I said here 6 weeks ago that I was surprised Dáithí Ó hUaithne and Máire Mhac an tSaoi hadn't heard the word 'leámharaic'. I was referring to a radio programme entitled* The Words We Use *broadcast every Wednesday on Raidió*

42 IT, 15 June 1974.

> *Éireann. Diarmaid Ó Muirithe chairs it and David Greene, Alan Bliss and Dick Walsh are the experts on it. Dáithí Ó hUaithne said himself on this programme a while ago that he'd never heard the word 'leámharaic'. A few weeks later a letter from Máire Mhac an tSaoi was read out saying that she'd heard this word used herself in the context in which she described it in the letter, but solely in that context. Her understanding, if I understood her correctly, was that this word was only used with reference to Fr Jones and in that context only, and that the people themselves would never use it in normal speech. I've never heard any mention of a Fr Jones but I've heard the word 'léamharaic' in normal usage by the people of Dunquin for over twenty years. I knew from the radio that Máire Mhac an tSaoi had heard the word in a limited context but I was surprised that she'd never heard it used in ordinary speech. I should have said this initially, and I'm sorry if I upset her in this regard.*[43]

Ó Ríordáin wasn't beaten yet, however – not by a long shot. Now that he'd been assigned his own room in UCC, he had scholars and experts close by whose expertise and advice he could call on. Séamas Caomhánach, former Professor of Celtic Languages and (most appropriately) a fluent Irish-speaker who also happened to be from Dunquin, was the main person who provided Ó Ríordáin with advice in this instance. As it happens, Séamas Caomhánach had written to the producers of the programme at the time to provide them with his expert view on the use of the term 'leámharaic' in the dialect of Dunquin, and he'd passed on a copy of this letter to Seán, in case he wished to see it printed. Ó Ríordáin was keen on seeing Caomhánach's opinion in print and it was duly published. (The only changes to the text of the original letter relate to the spelling of a few words, none of which were relevant to the argument here.) It is clear whom the 'sages' Caomhánach refers to are; Dáithí Ó hUaithne (David Greene) is clearly the individual referred to here as 'author'.

> *The experts and the authors are wrong if they assume that the word 'leámharaic' emerged from Fr Jones; this is a common word in the Dunquin area for hundreds of years and it's still used in the speech there today. Another form of the word*

43 IT, 22 June 1974.

appears in Allagar na hInise [ed. 1928] – page 67 'leámhairic'. Also, the adjective 'leámharaiciúil' and the abstract term 'leámharaicíocht' are also common there. Doesn't it seem more likely that this term originated with the English word laverock, laverick, etc., than that it came from the word maverick?

Whatever else remained to be discussed about the etymology of the word 'leámharaic', that was the end of the argument concerning the term's usage, something Seán understood quite well when he boldly put an end to the argument by saying: '"leámharaic" is not a harsh word but it's probably a term best not used in the presence of female visitors, all the same'. Now who knew the place (i.e. Dunquin) better and was accepted more by the people there, after all? This was the end of that particular debate.

Ó Ríordáin had been preparing the ground for battle, however, and he wasn't about to retreat peacefully, particularly given that he'd just won this initial battle – in his opinion and in the opinion of others. He had a Gaeltacht man in his camp now, an expert adviser, a man who was a gifted writer in his own right, and someone who had extensive experience of literary criticism. This person found weaknesses and faults in Mhac an tSaoi's collection *Codladh an Gaiscígh* and forwarded them to Ó Ríordáin, and they subsequently discussed them in the university together. The initial point of attack on the criticism front was Mhac an tSaoi's use of the copula, and various examples were sourced on pages nine and eighteen of her book: 'Is mé tobar searbh ar shliabh' and 'Nuair gur coinneal an teaghlaigh ar choinnleoirín óir tú.' A third example of her poor usage of Irish was identified in Mhac an tSaoi's collection *Margadh na Saoire,* page seventeen, in case Ó Ríordáin needed further ammunition as back-up: 'Is ba cheol na fliúite le clos do ghlór ann', an example that wasn't needed as it turned out. Ó Ríordáin launched his counter-attack on her – with accompanying examples – in November 1975, but he didn't do so without first giving Mhac an tSaoi her dues as a poet, as was only right:

The first thing to say about the Máire Mhac an tSaoi, I think, is that she is a poet. Once this much is said, nothing else matters much. Dilige Deum et fac quod vis Dilige *or love God and do whatever you wish after that. Whatever*

> *makes someone a poet she has it in her – whatever strain of craziness or vulnerability.*[44]

He wasn't long getting to the point, however, and this was his strongest weapon of all: that Mhac an tSaoi's standing as a poet was based almost entirely on the richness of her language – and yet her Irish wasn't perfect or accurate at times, despite the claims of her admirers:

> *As a sculptor carves stone, she carves her poem in Irish. There's no doubt that the Irish language is her métier. With other writers of Irish, the language is just a medium of communication but, in the case of Mary Mhac an tSaoi, it's as if the Irish language becomes her work. This can only have one conclusion and this is that, sooner or later, she'll write poems that'll be just Irish alone – this is to say that they won't have any message in them but that they'll still be very readable and alert to emotions and art. The sole function of this Irish will be to be Irish that's* mac-an-tsaoithúil *– if one can envisage such a thing.*
>
> *While the work Máire Mhac an tSaoi has published the Irish is flawed at times, strange as it may seem. Maybe it's no longer a form of communication to her – but something which she moulds. Here's a line from her book,* Codladh an Ghaiscígh *– page 9:*
>
> Is mé tobar searbh ar shliabh
>
> *Maybe there's some explanation that I don't get, but as I understand it, this is bad Irish.*[45]

He got the explanation all right, but whether he accepted it or not is another story. This is how he interpreted the controversy publicly:

> *In the article I wrote on this woman poet a fortnight ago I said that this line was flawed:*
>
> Is mé tobar searbh ar shliabh
>
> *I received a letter from her since and she says:*
>
> *I suppose that this controversial sentence should probably have been printed*

---

44 'Máire Mhac an tSaoi', IT, 13 November 1975.

45 *Ibid.*

as follows: 'Is mé Tobar-searbh-ar shliabh'. It echoes nicknames and riddles in the folklore tradition, e.g. The Spirit beneath the Bridge, the Sphinx, Taliesin – as if to say 'Is mé Glór-i-gCoitín.'

This amendment to the sentence corrects the error in it. It's a tradition at this stage that any review of a work of Irish includes a criticism of the language employed in the piece, even if there isn't actually any fault in the text. Máire Mhac an tSaoi herself isn't without some skill in this business herself. Let's return to the issue at hand again. I consider this sentence to be flawed:

'Nuair gur coinneal an teaghlaigh ar choinnleoirín óir tú'

It's an awful shame to be finding fault with the Irish in this book given the beautiful poetry it contains ...[46]

Although another letter came to him the day that his article was published, a letter that referenced various aspects of his article, he didn't include any explanation or justification for the sentences he'd highlighted or any admission as to whether they were correct or not. And similar to the letters which preceded it, this one saw no personal reply to it from the poet either. In the sense that this 'civil war' continued on, it can be argued that perhaps Ó Ríordáin more than anyone else was the person who kept it alive. He wasn't going to let anyone away now, particularly anyone who'd hurt him in any way. He might have suffered an initial injustice, but Ó Ríordáin wasn't shy about adding fuel to the fire afterwards. He was going to fight back whether others liked it or not.

One alleged flaw which his critics regularly cited with reference to Ó Ríordáin's poetry was that there was too much philosophy or theory in it but, as Seán Ó Tuama put it – 'without the theory being woven correctly with the experience or sensibility of the poet'.[47] Ó Ríordáin refers to this supposed flaw in his work in 'Banfhilíocht agus Gaeilge' when he states: 'Ó Tuama considers even the smallest line of philosophy as a betrayal of poetry. I wouldn't like to limit poetry like this. I feel that Irish-language poetry is more a community poetry than it is a poetry of

46 'Banfhilíocht agus Gaeilge', IT, 27 November 1975.
47 *Studia Hibernica* 13 (1973), p. 152.

the individual.'[48] Seán Ó Tuama wasn't the first person to identify this aspect in Ó Ríordáin's poetry, however; another man, Fr Jerome Kiely, is the person referenced in the passage below from the piece 'Mearbhall', even if Ó Ríordáin neglected to mention his name after he transferred these sentiments from his diary (6 May 1969) to the published article. This wasn't the first time Ó Ríordáin had heard this view expressed in relation to his poems either. He'd noticed more than once that those who listened to poetry absorbed it as if it was theirs and acted as if they owned it afterwards:

> *I met a man on the street the other day and you could say that he was angry. He told me that the poetry of the intellect is useless, that reflective poetry isn't really poetry at all. But the poetry of emotion this is the real poetry, he said. He was fuming with anger. They all say that same thing – that intellectual poetry is no good. Why wouldn't they? That's what they've always been told. The best authors have told them this. They get into a right rage when they hear the word 'thought' as associated with poetry. Even though this is just a thought that they've stolen from others, they protect it more fiercely than if they'd come up with it themselves. It occurred to me that I'm not allowed to have any ideas in the poetry. I was reminded of that old saying – 'every saw to the head of the hake'. I suppose that there are many poets now who'd be too afraid to compose anything in case even a syllable of thought went into his poetry.*[49]

That said, we find the poet almost in agreement with his critics, judging by the conclusion to that same essay, particularly with regard to the sentiment that one cannot write 'poetry or prose writing in cold blood'. The same conclusion is evident from this next piece, as taken from his diary and published later. The intellect is permitted entry to the process provided it is conveying emotion at the same time; she should never lag behind (something that Ó Ríordáin, with great honesty, acknowledges in relation to certain poems of his, as we see later):

48 IT, 27 November 1975.
49 IT, 1 May 1971.

Dante was lucky that he fell in love with Beatrice. That's what made a poet of him – that he was so taken with her the first time he saw her. That's what awakened the poetry in him is a better way to put it maybe; as no one else would be as able to express his emotions as well as a poet would. This emotion is the heartbeat of poetry. Unless the poet rides on this wave of feeling, he isn't writing poetry at all. You need this emotion to be able to write at all. Even if it's an intellectual thing that he writes, it will still be poetry provided it surfs on this emotion. He is permitted good and evil if he rides the waves of such emotion.[50]

Ó Ríordáin's observations on poetry tend to be more accurate and correct when he isn't referencing his own poems. He is almost too strident or loud when making any public statement in relation to his own poetry or theories; it is the old chestnut of the public statement that is often underscored by self-doubt. In a way, this is why he was so sensitive to the criticisms of the reviewers – they frequently exacerbated his own doubts in relation to his poetry. Interestingly, while Ó Ríordáin was often engaged in the public defence of his literary views through the medium of his newspaper articles, he was simultaneously engaged in debating the same issues with his students in the university:

I think that 'Saoirse' is a healthier poem than any of the other 'philosophical' poems in Eireaball Spideoige, *because the philosophy or reflection in it was immediate, i.e. the reflection and the poem are contemporaneous. It was written suddenly and sparked in the impatience that goes with loneliness. It wasn't thought up far from the battlefield; it was an immediate form of reflection.*

From 'Saoirse' onwards, there is an end to philosophical musing at a distance. The poems relate more to what is immediately happening or what has just happened, rather than with any formulas, it's just letting the magic or granularity of the moment weave its spell in the shape of the words, the rhythms, the lines.

There's too much individual imagination (bad imagination) and too much remote philosophising in certain poems in ES, *e.g. strategic 'Oileán agus Oileán Eile', 'Na Blascaodaí'. I think the rhythm of 'Saoirse' is okay because the first few lines were expressed in impatience; that the natural rhythm of this impatience*

50 'Sleachta as dialann', IT, 13 January 1973.

> *underscores these lines. In 'Oileán agus Oileán Eile', I was searching for a magic place – a sanctuary within myself – everyone's island. I was inventing philosophy to come up with it. This is what left it lacking. 'Saoirse' is completely different from this. 'Saoirse' consists of what happened. There's philosophy in 'Saoirse' but it's a philosophy that happened. She emerged from an instant impatience. It's a philosophy that says your imagination and your secret island is worth nothing – it's better to be a member of a community – to be low. 'Saoirse' is healthier than 'Oileán agus Oileán Eile', I think, not because it's a better philosophy but because it happened and it wasn't worked out. Cf. 'Teitheadh' and 'Adhlacadh mo Mháthar'. A six-month sorrow and slightly romanticised ['Adhlacadh mo Mháthar'] v. immediate sorrow. The mechanics of sorrow is evident in 'Teitheadh'.*

These latest salvoes were just a pale imitation of the attacks that he'd been subjected to himself years earlier. But then, how was he to know whether the most recent poems he'd composed weren't also but a pale imitation of the verse he'd been capable of once – years earlier, when 'the sea had announced herself' with that great swell of inspiration – if such a moment had ever occurred?[51] Because it was a common cry of Ó Ríordáin's from the very beginning of his literary odyssey that his poetic powers were waning or in the past. As early as 5 January 1943, he speaks of the time when the poems came easily to him and it's the period 1940–41 that he particularly associates with the flourishing of his poetic imagination. On the evening of May Day (1943), he speaks of the slow tide that has followed on from the swell there once was:

> *I know that I haven't got it in me to write anything except something dull tonight. I don't feel the warmth or the madness in me any more. Last year, writing one page and I'd be delight [sic]. And it was the joy of that memory that prompted me to start writing again just now …*

Ó Ríordáin had been confiding similar sentiments to his diary for years and yet this doesn't mean that he hasn't hit upon the blunt truth in this

---

51 B: p. 28.

instance. Some of the critics and supposed 'experts' had been claiming for years that his poetic impetus was gone and had produced the requisite negative reviews to support their assertions. The negative review by 'Flann Mhac an tSaoir' of Ó Ríordáin's collection *Brosna* was just a reiteration of a theme. The initial sentences of the review and the negative attributions as associated with the poet, his book and even the class he belonged to were enough to give the game away:

> *Ireland's a very small world. The Irish-language world is even smaller again. Something that means the critic's path isn't an easy one. It's not easy to sleep on a friend's hurt. Is it better to say nothing? Is there enough literature being written in Irish to be able to judge it properly or to assess its value? Is it better to let well enough alone and not to discourage people who are stretched to the farthest point of their ability and to be upsetting very nice people whom you've got great respect for and all for nothing? Because I don't believe that literary criticism has any affect [sic] on the writer. It's the same all over the world. The novelist, the playwright, the poet, their attitude towards the critic is the same as the man who's afraid of the dog when passing a strange house in the wilderness of the night. On edge, waiting for the attack.*
>
> *Not that I'm going to go barking at Seán Ó Ríordáin, poet, and* Brosna, *the latest collection of poetry from him. He'll get enough bark and bite just for the title of the collection. Random pieces, the odd stroke here and there. The delivery doesn't always match the build-up. A shot here and there and here again. The odd one that hits the target, the occasional piece that escaped the net and got away – and left us gob-smacked, sometimes.*

Another piece by the same man appeared in *Comhar,* in May 1967, entitled 'Smaointe faoi Nuafhilíocht na Gaeilge' ('*Thoughts on Modern Irish-Language Poetry*'). In this case, the critic chose a poem from *Eireaball Spideoige* – 'Na Blascaodaí' – as an exemplar of Ó Ríordáin's work and compared it with 'The Given Note' by Seamus Heaney. While he claims that Ó Ríordáin's poem is a better one in the end, he criticises it so heavily in the first part of his review that his later praiseworthy comments are rendered meaningless:

> *The poem is in no way as well-formed as the English poem. There isn't the same certainty or mastery of expression in it. The form isn't as assured and its construction less artistic. The poet isn't as sure of himself or of the things he wants to say, and he hasn't the same facility of language to express it. The metre is too loose, too easy; it's clear that it was formed under stress, as if the poet had to force the meaning out despite the barrier of language. It's a very good example of the difficulty the Irish-language poet has nowadays, someone who's using a medium of expression they had to learn. In one word, his facility with the language doesn't match his poetic ability.*
>
> *But, that said, Ó Ríordáin's poem says far more than does the English poem ...*[52]

Not unnaturally, Ó Ríordáin was very upset by this: '"Flann Mac an tSaoir" has made a vicious attack on me in this issue – an attack of the type that Máire Mhac an tSaoi made on me years ago,' he says in the diary entry for 28 May 1967, having just read the article. What drove Ó Ríordáin really crazy was the statement in another section of the review that of the seven poets who brought out a book in 1964 there wasn't a 'native Irish speaker among them, even if it's claimed that Seán Ó Ríordáin is a half-native speaker.' Ó Ríordáin began writing a letter of response to this but didn't pursue it any further, a response which went something like this: 'The critic didn't say that all of the reviewers are learners of Irish. I don't recall that anyone who was a native speaker found fault with my Irish. "It is claimed that Seán Ó Ríordáin is a half-native speaker" – supposedly – as much as to say that this is an empty claim.'[53] Deep down, Ó Ríordáin knew that it wouldn't be with a reply which refuted such criticism that he'd achieve anything, but rather through the public composition of his art and the poetry itself. He was finding it very difficult to compose new poetry at this juncture, however. The critic wasn't going to be any help to him on this score and anyway, as he'd said to Tomás Ó Floinn later, wasn't it the critic's job to 'tell the truth and tear apart the work if

52 *Combar,* May 1967.

53 As taken from the end of Ó Ríordáin's diary for 22 April 1967 to 26 June 1967.

necessary?'[54] It wasn't a question of challenging people or attacking them but rather that there were people whose job it was to critique the work of others and that was the beginning and the end of it. In his latter years, Ó Ríordáin suspected that whatever poetry he still had in him was just the 'leavings' of the sack; there were times too, near the end of his life, when he wondered whether it was better to forget about it altogether rather than to attempt to compose new literature if his heart wasn't fully in it.

A few weak attempts to source the well of inspiration and youth follow once more. His exhaustion is palpable, however, as measured out in words and phrases. The last weak breaths drifting through the embers as a reminder of another time and place, a place that no one can ever return to:

> *29/5/68. 6.45 p.m. How come nothing ever happens? How come I can't compose poetry any more like it was the beginning of the world?*

> *11 p.m. Night has fallen on a long summer day. I spent part of the night pruning shrubs and chatting with Dr Long. Without any writing done. I often write poems about things that happened a long time ago but which are written down in the form of prose notes. I realised tonight that it's better to write poetry in the present moment – if such a moment happens. How else can one capture time in the form of poetry?*

> *13/10/69. 10.15 p.m. It's the 13th all right. Nothing disastrous happened but neither did anything worthwhile either. I haven't reviewed A. O'Rathaille's poetry yet. I'm all over the place. How is it that I can't compose any poem? The poems were once about ordinary life, about ordinary thoughts, about ordinary feelings. Is there anything else left below? Or is it the case that I'm too lazy to raid the place below any more? Or is it that I am no longer willing to risk searching below in case I find out for sure that there's nothing left there. There are still surely fish there if one has the will to go fishing. There are too many books and stuff in my way. I'll probably have to force away this dumbness. Force is necessary to take virginity. Is it laziness? Is the laziness hardening in me? I*

---

54 'Gaeilgeoirí goilliúnacha' ('*Sensitive Irish-language enthusiasts*'), IT, 21 August 1971.

> *was reading Desiderius, Céitinn and Sgéal Mo Bheatha (Domhnall Bán Ó Céileachair) tonight, and they are all nice forms of prose in their own way. I don't know whether I get as much pleasure from poetry or the jargon of poetry any more? It's probably a lack of ability – like the person who is spent.*

As in the piece just cited, he'd no shortage of excuses: the word 'gnáth' (usual/normal) slipping through the net from him – but the excuses, like his 'talk', were hiding the truth of the matter now. The truth was that he'd lost trust in himself and in the 'word', just at the very time when he needed to keep faith the most. He was the tradesman who blames the fact that he has too many tools; he was too busy to write poems; he'd ruined things with all those articles for *The Irish Times.*[55] Those articles and the College-related matters were 'sucking the life' out of him and dictating his work and allocation of time for him.[56]

Although he begins his piece with the excuse that he's been 'castrated by the prose' in 'Drochfhilíocht agus Deascoláireacht' ('*Bad Poetry and Good Scholarship*'), he isn't long getting to the nub of the issue, as he understands it. He's referring here to the poems that he had published initially in *Scríobh 1* and then in the collection *Tar Éis mo Bháis:*

> *Those poems had plenty of faults but there was one thing that isn't possible to improve upon and which I shouldn't be forgiven for and that is that they weren't imbued with any life. What do I mean by this? It's difficult to say, but I think I know what it is. You have an inner sanctuary within you – a sort of a factory. Fragments of life fall into this and crystallise. They become shadow stones. What happened to you is in these shadow stones and is continuously happening – or you've made your own of that outer life in there, if you understand me. If you can get into this sanctuary and manage to carry away some of these shadow stones with you on your pens, your words will be imbued with life – whether these words are in the form of prose or poetry. Your own seal will be on these words, and yet it will surprise you how rich, how exotic they will be …*
>
> *Whatever's written outside this sanctuary is nothing but invention – this is to*

55 D: 20 September 1968.
56 D: 4 April 1969.

> *say that they're merely words and nothing else – words that aren't imbued with life. Nothing more needs to be said. There's no need for critics. We all know what the story is here. I was unlucky enough to let* Scríobh 1 *publish my compositions instead of dipping the words into the light …*
>
> *You can't invent a dream.*[57] *It's rather that you become a dream. If you don't become a dream, then don't pretend you did, but just stay silent.*[58]

In his review of *Tar Éis mo Bháis* (*After my Death*), Seán Ó Tuama argued that Ó Ríordáin was more of a versifier rather than a great poet subsequent to the publication of his collection *Brosna.* ('Seán Ó Ríordáin ceased to be a major creative force after the publication of his second book of verse, *Brosna* in 1964.')[59] It was Ó Tuama who had announced Ó Ríordáin's arrival as a great poet, and now he was announcing his departure. Even if Ó Tuama waited fifteen years after Ó Ríordáin's demise as a poet, and two years after his death as a versifier, for fear he'd spark the dogs in the street and until the poet's soul had safely crossed to the other side, and even if his pronouncements of his poetic birth and death were slightly premature perhaps, the chances are that Ó Ríordáin would have agreed with him to some degree. The poet wasn't in the business of giving responses to critics in his latter years, however. And even if Ó Ríordáin had either the energy or the inclination to respond to them, the words were drying up; increasingly, he'd begun to wilt beneath their burden. This was a new country he'd found himself in now, one that would never be inscribed on any map:

> *Cold damp weather. I went through such despair yesterday that words lost their meaning. All standards and values were blown sky-high. I drifted into an area that's never been named. Therefore, if real, there are probably no words in any language for these things …*[60]

57 cf. 'Taibhrithe', IT, 16 December 1968.

58 IT, 18 January 1975.

59 *Scéala Éireann*, 15 March 1979.

60 D: 3.30 a.m., 10 April 1972; 'Éadóchas' ('*Despair*'), IT, 15 April 1972.

No wonder he had trouble responding, given the circumstances and the terrain he was attempting to source such words in – some of which we'll explore in the next chapter. What was there left that he could do? *Colligite Fragmenta* ('Collect the Pieces').

> *I got a letter from Con Prior in London this morning. He'd found, he said, a little poem in English ('your little poem is very amusing') which I wrote long ago about Artie Mannix (R.I.P.) amongst his papers. I don't know why, but I immediately felt that whatever I had to do was done – that I'm finished. I also received in the post a copy of some prose pieces that appeared in* Comhar *years ago. I felt again that my life's work is over – that my life is over. The stuff that was just drafts, as I thought at the time, they were my life's work.*[61]

61 D: 18 March 1976.

13

Riordanisation and Cat-Scape

One familiar trope in Ó Ríordáin's poems was his animal imagery. In *Eireaball Spideoige*, images of animals are used primarily in a comparative context: the image of the respectful little donkey who stands for 'the devout old woman/performing the Stations of the Cross', or the flow of the poet's thoughts in tandem with the woman praying in the church, thoughts and feelings whispering as the pony's tail that 'swishes in the air'.[1] He'd always been very fond of animals and not just in the poetic sense or as utilised for comparative purposes in poems such as 'An Lacha' ('The Duck'). A masterful portrayal of a duck's ungainly waddling movement, the words of this poem express the absurdity that is the poet's image better than any picture or portrait ever could. Interestingly, he claimed to have written 'An Lacha' prior to the publication of *Eireaball Spideoige*, although this isn't what one would assume from the diaries.[2] In the diary that marks the end of the period 16 February 1958 to 4 November 1958 we find reference to this poem. Perhaps the version that eventually appeared in print was the final rendering of a poem he'd written nine years earlier:

> *Ducks have a very common (ordinary) voice. I can't imagine that they ever frequented the Oyster Tavern in Cork. Ducks have the speech of the ordinary people. The thrush and the blackbird have the dialect of the upper classes. The poor ducks are slow and dirty, but the blackbird has the pure extent of the sky behind it. The duck is a right miserable specimen. He cannot even walk properly. It falls*

1 ES: pp. 70 and 50.
2 *Scríobh 3*, p. 174.

> *sideways from one foot to the other – over and back, over and back. A real clumsy way of walking. But look at the movement of the blackbird or the thrush. It is straight and true as a fishing rod that's wrestling with a heavy fish – there's nothing hesitant or unsure there.*[3]

The poem remains at the level of imagery, however. He notes the signs and records them for posterity, whether in prose or in poetry. He doesn't go any further or develop a particular moral or message as based on it; not that this is always the case, however. One could read a great deal more into a line such as 'The little cat/Stretched lewdly out on the hearth', and there is a naturalness and grace to the image of the ram's horns in 'Ifreann', an image within whose contours Ó Ríordáin sought to reflect some of his own nature.[4] In the poem 'Malairt' and also in the introduction to *Eireaball Spideoige*, Ó Ríordáin had already begun to experiment with the exchange of imaginative qualities that was the child's mind and that of the horse. Such transformations or exchanges symbolise the changed state that comes over the poet when composing poetry. In this regard, his poems containing 'animal imagery' bear similarities with the poems that explore the 'tradework' (e.g., shoe-making). If there is a consistent theme running through nearly all of Ó Ríordáin's poems, it is the question of poetry and composition itself. (This is a subject that both fascinated him and tormented him all his life.)

It isn't the process of exchange or transformation that engages us in 'An Cat' ('*The Cat*'), however, but rather the image of the lone cat-person battling the falling darkness of night and the terror that accompanies it. We watch as the blindness falls and envelops this lonely half-human/half-animal like a great screen. The cat's eyes are the poet's; the candle is the room's sole illumination. Both are lit up with the fear that burns through the dark world around them:

> *An cat d'fhágáil amuigh*
> *Sa chaochoíche leis féin,*

3 D: 26 April 1949.

4 ES: pp. 48 and 105.

Is an spéir ró-ard mar thigh,
Ní dhéanfainn a leithéid.

Dhá shúil mar dhá thoitín
I dtóin na hoíche i gcéin,
Is sceon i gcroí chaitín,
Ní dhéanfainn a leithéid.

Féasóga cíortha ag crith
Is ionga troda réidh,
Iontaoibh phiscín a lot,
Ní dhéanfainn a leithéid.[5]

Leave the cat outdoors
alone in the eyeless night,
under the sky's pitched height—
I would never do that.

Two eyes cigarette-bright
faraway in the deep dark,
its little cat-heart afright—
I could never do that.

Combed whiskers twitching,
and claws drawn for a fight.
Kittenish trust turned to spite—
I would never do that.[6]

One senses that he didn't really need to go further or provide us with this explanation:

5 ES: pp. 54–5.
6 Sewell, *Selected Poems*, p. 43. Trans. Mary O'Donoghue.

Mar d'ólas smaointe an chait,
Is d'fhair an cat go géar
Na smaointe im shúil ag teacht,
Is d'fhásamar araon.

Do deineadh díom leathchat,
Ba dhuine an cat dá réir,
An caidreamh a scoilt,
Ní dhéanfainn a leithéid.[7]

For I took in the cat's mind,
and the cat watched tight
my mind sliding into sight,
and we both gained together.

I turned half-cat alright;
so too the cat turned man.
Break up a kinship that tight?
I could never do that.[8]

The poet made the same mistake in 'Malairt' when he felt obliged to explain the relationship that defined both:

from 'Malairt'

Agus b'fhollas gur thuig sé chomh maith sin an brón
I súilibh an chapaill,
Is gur mhachnaigh chomh cruaidh air gur tomadh é fá dheoidh
In aigne an chapaill.[9]

7 ES: pp. 54–5.
8 Sewell, *Selected Poems*, p. 43. Trans. Mary O'Donoghue.
9 ES: p. 63.

from 'Switch'

And it was plain to me, that he'd realised the sorrow
in the horse's eyes so well,
So deeply had he contemplated it, that he was steeped
in the horse's mind.[10]

This is the rationality of the mind overwhelming the imaginative sense and it wasn't the last time he'd have this problem in his poetry – the impulse towards absolute logic or clarity, and it proves a weakness now when we read the poem years later. It proves difficult for us to get underneath the poem and source the experience that went into it as it was actually being written. This difficulty should not preclude us from digging below the surface of the words and attempting to understand the circumstances and the atmosphere that gave rise to the poem, however. It was Ó Ríordáin's close friend Séamus Ó Coigligh who provided us with the background to the poem 'An Cat', as Ó Ríordáin didn't go into it in the diary:

> *A back-window in the house was broken once and Seán told his brother Tadhg. Tadhg came out from the city and measured the window, and he was just about to replace the pane of glass, when Seán screamed: 'What are you doing there? How can the cats come in at night if the window is closed like that?' And that was that:*
>
> *To leave the cat outside …*[11]

Other poems that bear similarities with 'An Cat' are 'Catchollú' ('*Incatation*'), 'Aistriú' ('*Transfer*'), 'Piscín' ('*Kitten*') and 'Eireablú' ('*Tailing*'). Add to this the poem entitled 'Tar Éis Dom é a Chur go dtí Tigh na nGadhar' ('*After Sending him to the Doghouse*') and this comprises a significant portion of Ó Ríordáin's work. It's a body of work that relates to the smaller and apparently less important creatures of this world, the type that Ó Ríordáin had always had a particular empathy for. It's as if he's holding

10 Sewell, *Selected Poems*, p. 61. Trans. Ciaran Carson.
11 *Combar*, May 1977.

on to this world just about, even if he's not always sure of how he himself shapes up to the animal or what his relation to it may be. It's as if all that remains of this life for him is what can interact with this small animal or its nature. As the poet put it in the aforementioned poem 'Do deineadh díom leathchat/Ba dhuine an cat dá réir' ('I became the half-cat, the cat became human').[12] This search for alternative forms of his poetic self is more prominent in his work from the 1960s onwards. He searches and scours until he finds that thing, the form that is his reborn self. Sleep or reflection. Putting in the day. The cat's place amongst its fellow creatures appears more stable or secure than is the poet's among the people – because the cat is simply acting as a cat and in accordance with its own nature:

> *Mild weather. Winter is over. My heart making honey, as is rare for me. I'm getting older, however. What's ahead of us? I never read the works of Juvenal. I think I will not hang myself today.*
>
> *Is there anything as lonely as a living cat? There's a kitten lying in the darkness outside in the kitchen. Even if he had the light itself, he couldn't read a book or do any practice for himself. They say a cat has no capacity for thought. I wonder. When I go into the kitchen and when I switch on the light, the cat gets up and I can see in his eyes that he's working out what I'm going to do. If he thinks that I'm about to try and grab him, he jumps up from the chair suddenly and hides under the table. It seems to me that he's already been thinking a little bit. He comes out to the car to me every evening when I arrive home. Isn't that thinking? How does he spend the night and the day? He can't always be asleep. How does he pass the time? No wonder he has that lonely look about him. One can't attend to him.*[13]

> *I saw one of my two cats cleaning herself with her paws the other morning. There's no doubt that there's something about a cat washing herself. She looks as if she understands that she has permanency in this place and that she'll have this forever – that she'll never get old, nor anyone else in the house, and that*

12 LL: p. 30. Trans. M. Ó hAodha.

13 D: 29 January 1962.

this house will be here till the end of time – that she has complete faith in her ownership of this house and in the status quo – that this is a permanent world that time will never destroy.

I often see people too, who have this settled or fixed look about them. As for me, I can't find joy in anything but feel as if the world is melting away before my eyes. It often happened that it was the others who left and that I stayed, and yet I never felt the permanency that they felt.[14]

The poem 'Catchollú' ('Incatation') emerges from the poet's envy of the ancestral permanence that is the cat. This new term 'catchollú', as invented by the poet, is apparently another form of the word 'ionchollú' (incarnation). (Even if the poet intends no deliberate disrespect to the Christian concept that is the word 'incarnation', it is worth mentioning that some of the poems as relating to the question of nature, form-shifting and the natural world come close to denying that there is an afterlife or supernatural world at all; not that this particular poem 'Ionchollú' is the best example of this, however.) The cat promulgates its cat-nature and its cat-ness when it stretches itself out – in this case, she is a female cat as befits her latent reproductive and life-generating qualities. This is when she appears and acts most truthfully in accordance with her nature as a cat, when there is nothing that is more natural to her. The line 'í féin atá sí ag rá' ('it is herself she speaks') echoes Hopkins' line 'myself it speaks and spells'. Another time and the cat is teetering on the edge of personhood in the form of prose: 'A cat loves to be a cat. They love to clean themselves with their paws as if making the Sign of the Cross.'[15] Even if the sense of peace the poet seeks emerges in 'Catchollú' with the actual transformative moment or the 'embodiment' that is this new 'cat-creature', it is in the more general dissolving of boundaries that we feel the poem's particular power. The boundary is porous and one can traverse it either way. The poem 'Catchollú' bears similarities to a slow-motion film which records each movement and turn of the cat as she expresses her cat-like nature. Slow the film down initially and then let it roll forward in a single continuous

14 D: 26 May 1966.
15 D: 11 January 1968.

movement and you have every cat ever conceived and those that have yet to be born. The cat that you observe nearly comes to represent a new race, she speaks with such precision concerning her tribal inheritance:

Is breá leis an gcat a corp,
Is aoibhinn léi é a shearradh
Nuair a shearr sí í féin anocht,
Do tharla cait 'na gceathaibh

Téann sí ó chat go cat
Á ndúiseacht as a ballaibh,
Fé mar nár chat í ach roth
De chait ag teacht is ag imeacht.

Í féin atá sí ag rá,
Is doirteann sí slua arh ea í
Nuair a shearrann an t-iomlán,
Á comhaireamh féin le gaisce.

Tá na fichidí catchollú
Feicthe agamsa anocht,
Ach ní fichidí ach milliúin
Tá le searradh fós as a corp.[16]

The cat worships her body,
just loves to unravel
when she shook herself tonight,
it rained cats by the catful

She turns from cat to cat
at the stir of a paw,
more like a wheel than a cat
shifting to and fro.

16 B: p. 37.

> She expresses herself,
> sheds a catalogue of skins
> at full-stretch, she counts
> herself and preens.
>
> Tonight I've seen scores
> of incatations,
> and still to come,
> not scores but millions.[17]

As regards the poet, his human manner seems to recede until his behaviour is almost cat-like and it is difficult to separate the human and the cat forms from one another. He has spent so much time in the company of the cat, the poet explains, that his patterns have come to resemble it. Even if there is something slightly comical about the meshing of these different natures and forms, this isn't really the truth of it. This exchange of forms is really just another example of the waning and death of the poet's artistic powers. It's as if he disappears into the authority and seal of nature that is the cat forever, now that he's lost all human agency:

> *Tomás Ó Canáinn gave a lecture last night at the University, a superb lecture. I really enjoyed it. I forgot about myself for as long as the lecture was on. But sometimes my attention slipped and suddenly I understood that I was visible – that people were looking at me. Then I'd focus on presenting myself properly – assuming the proper image, so to speak. It occurred to me today that I conduct myself as a cat does when I'm amongst other people because it's always cats that I live in the house with. I'm always noting what cats do. Cat behaviour is my standard behaviour by now. Whatever a cat does is what I do now unknown to me. I was there as a cat last night. When I stretch myself, it is the same stretch that my cats do.*[18]

17 Sewell, *Selected Poems*, p. 161. Trans. Frank Sewell.
18 D: 12 November 1971.

Compare this with:

Dá n-iompóinn féin im chat,
Dar liom go mothóinn ait,
Go mba dheacair dom an scrabhadh
An t-eireaball is an mí-amha
Do lánshamhlú lem shamhail.[19]

Hard to imagine that,
but if I were to turn cat,
I think I'd find it odd,
the scratching awkward,
the tail, miaow-miaows,
not to mention the claws.[20]

He is 'en-tailed' nonetheless, however. He awakens from slumber and the transformation has happened. Here she comes, the maiden, as day battles night, between waking and sleeping. We've walked this territory with him too often by now:

I woke up a while ago and these lines come to me:

Aistrigh a cló cait
Id aigne go bean,
Agus chífidh tú
Go mba bhreá an bhean í
Dá mbeifeá id chat fireann.[21]

Change form o cat
In the mind, change form to woman
And you'll see

19 From 'Eireablú' ('*Tailing*'), TÉB: p. 25.
20 Sewell, *Selected Poems*, p. 219. Trans. Frank Sewell.
21 D: 8.15 a.m., 5 December 1969; LL: p. 24.

That she'd be a fine-looking woman
The male cat you'd be.[22]

When he received the proofs of *Línte Liombó* from the publishers, Sáirséal agus Dill, he wrote back to Bríghid Bean Uí Éigeartaigh on 18 January 1971:

> *I read the booklet immediately. Unfortunately, it didn't take me long. It was like a flash of lightning. I got an insight that I hadn't got previously when I read all the verses together, in book form. I saw the life I live – empty, completely empty.*[23]

Despite such talk, he was enacting a scene that he'd experienced and understood and explained many times before. Here is how Ó Ríordáin saw things on New Year's Day 1969 at 1.40 a.m., and as revisited again, in his article 'Caidreamh le Dia agus le Daoine' ('*The Relationship with God and with People*') four weeks later:

> *One of the difficult questions in this life is the relationship with our fellow human beings. Thinking back now on the poems I published last year, it occurred to me that it's obvious from them that I need to spend more time in the company of other people (God help these other people!) and that whatever impetus I had from the solitary life, if there was any, is gone. The voice in those poems appears barren and lacking in humanity and civilisation. Interaction with other people enriches the language, the mind, poetry. Contact with others is a form of civilising. You have a certain interaction with other people as filtered through books but it's a form of interaction that's lacking, even if it's a quicker one. It's normally a congress with the dead. But* ga dtam ris*! We've discussed this many times before. I hope that no one needs to discuss this after us.*[24]

This was the one mistake he made – assuming that further discussion

22 Trans. M. Ó hAodha.
23 *Comhar*, May 1977, p. 28.
24 IT, 29 January 1969.

would prove unnecessary. It *was* necessary, given that his story was the lack of a story and the biggest thing in his life was the void or absence at its heart. The empty gap that he constantly sought to fill, but which he only rarely succeeded in doing so. The vain attempt to hold on to something familiar or close by – so that he might root himself, even within the void. In the end, any fibre of being, any living creature, no matter how static it appears, will suffice for the poet. 'A kitten sitting still beneath the stool' who is yet to be 'fully-kittened' because it is yet to have the rhythmic movement that is the cat, as the poet explains to his fellow westerners in 'Piscín'. As regards the difference the poet sees between East and West (i.e. that which he feels necessary to explain to his audience – something which he has yet to do by the end of the poem), it is worth referring to the diary entry for 3 June 1969: 'I think that Western poetry is only prose compared to Eastern poetry.' And it's in prose that he defines the meaning of his poem. The kitten stands for Christ while the poet is Paul who presents it/Him to the people. We see the same empathy at play here as was in 'An Cat' ('*The Cat*') and also in 'Tar Éis Dom é a Chur go dtí Tigh na nGadhar' ('*After Sending Him to the Doghouse*'): the empathy and compassion that is pain, suffering and all that unnecessary fear. All three are present – 'The trembling body' that is the kitten, the Passion of Christ and the long-suffering individual whom we are all familiar with by now – all meshed together. The frightening joy that suffuses terror 'framed' momentarily:

Chonac piscín fé stól anocht
Frámaithe díreach,
É teite ón bhfothram le corp
Eagla an créatúir.

Piscín mothallach ag tuar gach oilc,
An radharc ab aoibhne ...[25]

I saw a kitten under a stool tonight
Framed exactly

25 'Piscín' ('*Kitten*'), TÉB: p. 15.

Having fled the noise
Out of sheer fear, the creature.

A shaggy kitten predicting every evil,
The most delightful sight …[26]

He loses sight of his vision momentarily and then tries to explain further what it is he seeks to express. It makes no difference whether it's the people of the West or the East that you're addressing in the absence of sufficient guidance to show the way. On an initial glance, it may seem unjust to take this one poem of Ó Ríordáin's in isolation, but then again, this was essentially the long poem of his life, a life that was now grinding slowly towards the end. The poem 'Piscín' ('*Kitten*') therefore needs to be read within the wider context of Ó Ríordáin's life and work and his interactions with the 'world outside'. The passion that he'd once had as a younger poet is now exhausted and yet it is still a painful memory in his mind. It is no coincidence that Ó Ríordáin noted Yeats' words below in the very first diary he ever kept. He understood better than most what his fellow Irish poet Yeats meant when he said in 'The Nineteenth Century and After':

Though the great song return no more
There's keen delight in what we have:
The rattle of pebbles on the shore
Under the receding wave.

There's nothing in his later diaries that surpasses the poet's agony relating to his pets – the dogs and the cats – in terms of the heart-rending and moving nature of his descriptions. Privately, Ó Ríordáin laments the well-known figures of his day as the years pass – those whom he'd got to know publicly or through their writings: Pope John XXIII, President Kennedy and his brother Robert, Daniel Corkery, Seán Ó hÉigeartaigh, Máirtín Ó Cadhain, Seán Ó Riada, Fr Tadhg, de Valera, Mícheál Ó Gaoithín, Pound,

26 Trans. M. Ó hAodha.

Kruger, Séamus Murphy and others; the death of each in turn left another gap in the poet's life. In a sense, they were the heroes in the artistic sense whose talent, generosity and imagination had kept him going over the years and distracted him from his own difficulties. And yet, in spite of this, their passing affected him less than did the violent deaths of these small animals that he himself was responsible for. Whereas the well-known people had the whole world outside to lament them with all the necessary ceremonial and recognition, the only person who could bear the grief of his pets passing was the poet himself.

Each of the animals belonged to Ó Ríordáin and to his life alone. Their company was his company, no matter that it was short-lived. In fact, the smaller or less significant their lives might seem, the more devoted and committed he is to their celebration and remembrance. And yet this makes him the Judas who betrayed 'his own' and handed them over to their deaths. He was Judas now, when a short time earlier he'd been Saint Paul explicating Christ's nature through the transformation that was the cat in the artistic act of the imagination. As evidenced in the diary entries that follow Ó Ríordáin felt very guilty about handing over some of his pets to their deaths. It preyed heavily on his mind. Again, as evidenced in 'Fiabhras', we need to faithfully trace the coordinates of the poet's emotions and thinking, no matter how sentimental or pathetic we might deem them on an initial or cursory glance. It's a sad state of affairs and yet one still has *something* if one has an experience that is outside oneself at this stage of your life, something else to channel one's suffering and compassion towards.

It might be outside him and yet it still takes something from him at the same time. Where can your imagination flee to or find refuge in now that she torments herself? Ó Ríordáin was so affected by the fate of his pets that he committed long pieces to his diary on four occasions – and he'd written a poem subsequent to his third entry also. But he's really the man who's ageing and in decline now when he's given up the last bit of regular company he has left. His heart is torn inside him; he's inconsolable:

> *18 October 1960, 10.20 p.m … I did something this afternoon and I'm afraid that it wasn't much to my credit. I put Atom, the house-dog here, into the Animals' Home in Cork, i.e. to be put down. Atom was poor, dirty, old, but*

she was weak, defenceless and without a word in court. I grabbed hold of the creature this afternoon as she stared up trustingly at me and threw her into the car. She urinated right there and then. If you saw the ruthless hangman who took possession of her in the Animal Home! A former sergeant in the Garda Síochána – whom I knew. Your man placed a knotted noose that still had a few bloodstains on it around her neck and Atom was nabbed, the poor creature. If I'd been man enough to bring her home even then. I'm an ugly individual. She's probably died a horrible death by now. The only consolation I had coming home was the blessed stink of her urine in the car. What an ugly bourgeois act! This afternoon, I took away the soul of one of the creatures God created for my own comfort's sake. How come I didn't think this earlier on today? There's no doubt about it but the human being is an ugly creature.

19 October 1960, 1.30 a.m. Woken up. I'm not as bad as I was last night, the drink, God bless it.

I spent the evening chatting with Bob Donoghue and I have nothing for my trouble. There's nothing to report even after this long night of talk. Down beneath our talk, and through our talk was the image of that poor dog 'I'd sent to death.' I was there at the counter acting the part of the literary gage ['prince'] knocking back drinks, and the poor dog was in another part of the same city receiving the drink of death. When I think of her there at the hangman's mercy, I associate her with Christ somehow. Judas was a gentleman compared with me. Mine was a safe and treacherous deed … The case of the dog was far worse than that of Christ. The fact that the dog was brought low in the presence of death and in the presence of his killers is what makes it really pitiable altogether.

18 May 1963, 7.40 p.m. I'm frightened of the cat. She's going crazy through the house crying. She gave birth to three kittens this morning and I gave them to a girl to drown them in the river an hour ago. Those small animals emerged from the womb just last night or this morning. No wonder they were so dear to her. Every cry she gives goes straight through you. I wish I could find an adjective shocking and lonely and desolate enough to describe that terrible 'liach' sound she is making. I don't know any adjective that can do justice to the sound. Midnight. I've been into the city and made a bad confession in the meantime. I felt as if the Latin in the absolution was damning me. I had two drinks back in Heelan's. I paid a short visit to the Choral Festival while I was in the city. I felt the city and the world hostile to me.

The cat is crying all over the place. It would tear the heart out of you. Those little kittens and the mother that she could give her love to them are dead or dying. That cat would kill a bird without the slightest pity or mercy, and yet look at the depth of her nature as regards her own brood. I feel that cats and people are hostile to me tonight. I feel God Himself as hostile to me. What sort of a person am I? I'm a bad person, I'm afraid. Even the crowd who don't spend any time thinking are better than me.

19 May 1963, 6.30 a.m. The cat is beneath the bed crying. For as long as I was awake last night, she never stopped and she was still mewing pathetically outside the window this morning when I woke up an hour ago. She's under the bed now moaning ceaselessly. There's a loneliness, and an anger, and a searching in her voice. She knows that I'm the cause of it. I wonder does she think that I have them? 5 p.m. … The cat still crying at home. Wherever I go in the house she follows me. She's my conscience following me around.

14 August 1968, 5.35 p.m. A fine day again but a day of despair. Yesterday was bad but today was even worse. I'm in the pit of hell. Rover was a stray dog. I say 'was' because he may no longer be alive now. I had him here originally. He came to me in the winter [note: 'winter 1966–7'] and stayed. Then I moved him up to Mayfield to my brother's house. He's there ever since. He always had a great welcome for me whenever I called there. The woman of the house was getting tired of him because he was snapping at strangers. I put the creature into the Dogs' Home today. Three of the children went with me. He knew that something was up when he reached the door of the Dog's Home. But the dog-man put a tie on him and he had to go. I've wiped a lot of welcome from my life thus far and it's not as if the welcome for you gets bigger as the years pass. No wonder my heart aches. I'm a sort of Judas.

If despair tightens its grip any more deeply in me, I'll go out of my mind. There's some kind of charity lacking in me and it causes the vacuum in my heart.

Poor Rover was a poor, friendly goodhearted dog. It was this goodhearted nature, maybe, that caused him to end up in the dog parlour with his destroyers. If he's still alive, awaiting death and denied of his liberty. It was a beautiful summer's day. I watched a show with the children around 2 p.m. I welcomed myself along. I sat down in the small grassy yard behind the house. He lay down next to me, his head on my knee, fully trusting of me. He was probably made homeless and became a wild dog because he had the manners of a house dog about him.

We come upon the poem in a different place now, a poem that had initially appeared lighter in theme and far more formal than the emotions that engendered it. The poem's metrical pattern only adds to its atmosphere of formality:

Tar Éis Dom é a Chur go dtí Tigh na nGadhar

Ná bí am buaireamh a ghadhair,
Fáilte tú chuireas den saol,
Ba tú an fháilte a bhíodh fial romham,
Cé mé chuir deireadh led ré.

Taoi id aonar anois a ghadhair,
Más gadhar fós tú is nach scáil,
I measc do namhad gan trua duit,
Ag fanacht le goin do bháis.

Bhí do chroí gadhair fial, mór,
Ní raibh de mhaoin agat ach grá,
An dream a ghráis d'íheall ort,
Is gan ionat, monuar, ach gadhar fáin.

Bhí béasa gadhair tí agat,
Is támáilteacht gadhair fháin,
Níl ded ghrá rothaig sa mbith anocht
Ach a bhfuil im chroí ded chrá.[27]

27 LL: p. 30.

After Sending Him to the Doghouse

Don't be at me like this, dog.
I had to do it.
You were my warmest welcoming friend,
though it was me that had to end your days.

You're on your own now, hound,
if you're still a dog and not a shade,
surrounded by enemies without mercy
as you wait for the death wound.

Your big dog heart was always loyal,
love was all you had in the world,
but the ones you loved betrayed you,
and you only a poor old stray.

You had the ways of a house dog
with the deference of a stray
Now all that's left of your bounding love
is here in my sore heart tonight.[28]

On the fourth occasion, not only did Ó Ríordáin write an entry in his diary about how he felt (1 a.m., 11 October 1968) but he also published some of what he'd written as part of one of his *Irish Times* articles under the title of 'An Turas Deireanach' ('*The Last Journey*').[29] If we read the diary entry, the article and the poem in unison, it is possible for us to get a better picture of the circumstances that were the composition of this poem. We can see that the classes of people and creatures that Ó Ríordáin had carefully collated and arranged in his own mind were all melting into one another in his imagination now. In the end, they're all the same, an amorphous mass of individuals, a series of heads or faces;

28 Sewell, *Selected Poems*, p. 175. Trans. Mary O'Malley and Frank Sewell.
29 IT, 13 February 1969.

nothing has a centre any more – they're just a plethora of 'non-persons' moving from one body to the next. Ó Ríordáin had seen the signs well before this, no doubt, that this is how it would unfold: the leprechaun-woman and the beautiful maiden, the eyes of one woman transposing and becoming one with those of her son. The aforementioned transferral of images and visages was clearer then, however, than it is in this case. By now, the people's visages are becoming blurred and it is just two giant torsos he imagines rather than a series of faces or heads. The 'Seán Ó Baoill' he references is the same man who'd used the word 'fódúil' ('deep-sodded, earth-like') when speaking to Ó Ríordáin years earlier, a word the poet had associated with a particular magic or mystical quality ever since.[30]

Ó Baoill was mentioned in the privacy of the diary (3 March 1975) but when Ó Ríordáin came to discuss images for his sketching in an *Irish Times* article, he referred to him in anonymous fashion:

> *I've nailed X's head now. I realised some time ago that X has a certain similarity to Ernest Blythe who died recently. Every time I think of X now, it is Blythe's head that I have. I can't wait until I meet X again so that I see his real face again and see whether this will get rid of Blythe's head. Blythe's head swallows up X's head always. One day, I managed for a moment to imagine X's face as it really is, but it disappeared immediately as quickly again and it's Blythe's head forever now.*
>
> *Blythe had bad Irish that was very good. X has the same. They're both realists. There's always a certain awkwardness about realists. This awkwardness is honest. These two forms of awkwardness are at odds with one another in my mind. There's a sort of a polish about priests, government ministers, school inspectors, bank managers, and Blythe had this polish about him also. X has a similar polish about him. No wonder the two became entwined in my mind. This polish applies to the Sunday, to summer collars, to being freshly shaved, to umbrellas.*[31]

30 'F. Ó Dúill', IT, 29 March 1968.

31 'Stair agus Béaloideas', IT, 10 July 1975.

These ideas partly saw poetic form in the poem 'An Blaosc Mícheart' ('*The Wrong Skull*').[32] He'd still have to return to his various visages and 'categories' again later and revise them or validate them as necessary.

Shortly before Christmas 1976, I visited him in hospital, in Sarsfield Court. Given the similarity of some of its ideas with the way Ó Ríordáin developed his thought over the years, I brought along a copy of an essay that had just appeared in *Time* magazine, 13 December 1976, which described the new science known as 'sociobiology'; 'Genes über Alles' was the title of this piece and it was from this that Ó Ríordáin took the title of his poem entitled 'Clóanna über Alles'. Not that Ó Ríordáin had to go far to source the subject for this poem. Hadn't he had it right next to him for years? That said, he'd never been more in need of it than at this moment. Eternity was threatening … if there was such a thing as eternity, that is. Each point of reference has gone astray. The 'self' that was his subject matter since the beginning was on the point of annihilation and disappearance: one tiny part of it left behind him in a handful of words that no one would read, and that weren't worth reading anyway – or so the poet felt. A life spent as death's godparent. And the next day that might never come – the day that was never meant to come and yet it had done so. Who could tell? One day, Ó Ríordáin looked at a sketch he'd drawn on the cover of *Measgra Dánta* thirty years earlier, and then turned to look at the cover of another book, *The Bog People* by P. V. Glob (a copy of which Seán Ó Mórdha had given him) where he saw a picture of a man's head, a man who'd been in the bog for 2000 years and yet whose features were so well-preserved that it looked as if he'd only been buried there yesterday. The confluence that is permanence and impermanence as captured together. 'Cló na con, cló an duine' ('*The imprint of the dog, the imprint of humanity*') still recognisable despite the centuries of bad penmanship and the erosion of time. As for the dog who was once sketched or the man whose skull survived, only fate still holds or preserves anything of their essence now. The pen and the bog are the gods of this world and there is no other god here. There is no escaping the message of time, even if its message is actually framed as a question.

32 TÉB: pp. 30–1.

from **'Clóanna über Alles'**

An mar seo tá an scéal mar sin –
Imeom ar nós an tsneachta anuiridh,
Ach fanfaidh na clónna fós ag filleadh,
Leis an bpointeáltacht chéanna cruinnis,
Ag iompar con is duine
Ár macasamhail ní sinne?[33]

So, is this the way the story goes –
we all fade away like last year's snow
but the forms keep coming back on the scene
with the same pinpoint accuracy,
delivering up a hound or a human
like us but not the same man or woman?[34]

Unsurprisingly, as he neared the end of his days, Ó Ríordáin returned to the very source of life – the skeleton that is the framework for the human being and the essence it engenders; it's as if by their existence, he is reassuring himself as to his own reality, that he's still living and breathing despite all the difficulties and devastation of his life. The poet is now counting the hours and the days down, drawing time out to its very end.

from **'Mise'**

Sin é,
Sin inspioráid,
Sin mise.
Níl d'inspioráid ar an saol domhsa
Ach mise,
Ná duitse
Ach tusa,

33 TÉB: p. 29.
34 Sewell, *Selected Poems*, p. 225. Trans. Frank Sewell.

Ach cá bhfaighead é,
Sé sin mise? ...[35]

from 'Me'

That is it,
that is inspiration:
me.
There's no inspiration in the world for me
but me.
Nor for you
but you.
But where can I find him,
me, that is?[36]

It is most appropriate to finish this poem on a question. If the answer to this question was to be revealed on his deathbed, then the poet didn't have too long to wait. One line in his poem, 'Mar bímse ar aimsir ag an saol', is an alternative version of another line he'd written a long time ago in 'Cnoc Mellerí': 'Aige tá na manaigh ar aimsir.' (*'The monks are in his service.'*)[37] This was a reference to death also. One could even go back as far as the day that Ó Ríordáin first read a copy of the compilation of Irish love poetry entitled *Dánta Grádha,* when he made a similar comment: 'Tá sí ar aimsir ag an ngrádh' (*'She's in love's service'*).[38] This wasn't an issue that concerned him in his personal life for the majority of his life and yet it highlights a theme and a form of language that ran through his poetry for many years. Even if his physical and writing life was drawing to a close, it was important for Ó Ríordáin to pursue every last strand of his poetic impulse to its ultimate conclusion.

---

35 LL: p. 42.
36 Sewell, *Selected Poems*, p. 185. Trans. Frank Sewell.
37 ES: p. 65. Trans. M. Ó hAodha.
38 O'Rahilly, T. F. (ed.), *Dánta Grádha: an anthology of Irish love poetry of the sixteenth and seventeenth centuries* (Browne and Nolan, London, 1916), p. 125.

14

'No Help I'll Call'

Seán Ó Ríordáin passed away in Sarsfield Court (St Stephen's Hospital) in Cork at 11.20 p.m. on Monday 21 February 1977. He had been unconscious for the previous twenty-four hours. It was more than a year since he'd suffered a very bad turn health-wise – in January 1976. He'd had many bouts of serious illness down the years but this bad turn proved the most definitive of all, even if he did survive for another year after this. Then, suddenly, the end came. And the poem that is the night fell for the last time. He was in the same place he'd spent most of his life when the beginning of the end came – in that small room at the back of the house that overlooked the river and the road – it was 5 January 1976.

He tried to set out for the doctor in Sarsfield Court alone, something he'd managed often before. One of his neighbours, John P. O'Connor, suspected that Seán mightn't make it to Sarsfield Court and so he followed him in his car. Seán had only gone two miles when he collapsed. They called for help and a doctor arrived on the scene immediately. They were on standby at the Mercy Hospital when they arrived, as the doctor had telephoned ahead. John P. O'Connor brought him there in his car and the medical staff came out to meet them the minute they arrived. Ó Ríordáin didn't want to go in with them but they brought him upstairs despite his protestations. His condition worsened and one of the senior doctors was called. He examined Ó Ríordáin and was immediately quite concerned about his condition:

> *'You don't like the look of me,' I said to the Doctor [X]. 'And you don't like the look of me either,' said he. 'I don't like the look of you, you can take it from me,' I said.*[1]

---

1 D: 17 January 1976.

In fact, the poet confided an account of what happened earlier that evening prior to his collapse, and even if he noted it in his journal four days later, it's a piece of writing that's imbued with a strong feeling of death. There's no doubt that death means business this time. He might not have had it in him to record the trajectory of death's approach when it was actually happening but he still had a good memory of it. What is it – this thing called death? It is the unity of all feeling? Is it the final or completed version of something? Or is it just the ultimate silence and tranquillity? Whatever it was, he'd always thought he'd be able to record a glimpse of it when it came. He feels a duty to leave an account of it that can be accessed after he is gone. Because, before too long, everything will be assigned to the category that is afterwards:

> *This struggle with death lasted from ten at night until ten the following morning – without a break. The battle didn't engender any solidarity between myself and the senior doctor, however. I suspected that I wouldn't live until morning. It was a strange thing – very strange? – but this didn't bother me too much. It wasn't up to me any more. I'd left the responsibility for this on someone else's shoulders. They could save me or not, it was up to themselves. My mind was about to go. It wasn't just me that would suffer. Maybe I'd be the least person who'd suffer – when I wouldn't be there any more. But that's something that was bothering me – a little? – a lot? that I wouldn't be there any longer? I knew it was touch and go, that I'd gone past what I could cope with. I was really suffering a lot with it. I hope that my death when it comes isn't as hard as this. Amongst those who comforted me the most was a beautiful young nun. She was the most humane of them all. I didn't know at the time that she was a nun – Dorothea from Castletownbere. She caressed my forehead and told me that she'd had to learn my poetry at school. For the first time ever, I thought that there was some importance to my mind – what she had amassed – that I had some importance – that I had come closer to perfection in some way – not closer to perfection but to unity maybe – than I'd previously imagined. I was getting an insight into myself – from outside myself almost. I was about to separate from myself – or that's how I understood it anyway.*[2]

---

2 D: 9 January 1976.

The news wasn't long going around: he was at death's door, they said. A new twist on the old story. People were enquiring after him, something that had never sat well with Ó Ríordáin at the best of times. He could tell what was happening – the vultures circling the near-corpse. Who'll be first to swoop on the carrion?

> *Seán Ó Mórdha (7 Days) was on the phone from Dublin. Mac Réamoinn was enquiring about. They've got the scent of death. They'd prefer nothing better than if they had the news of my death before anyone else. They're the media them.*[3]

They'd have to be patient another while yet. His heart was very weak but he'd hang on for another while yet. But where was the ultimate relief that he'd always expected? *Quamdiu, Domine?* ('How long, Lord?') The terrible tiredness that seeks its final outlet. Another while listening to the footsteps in the hospital corridor and watching the door to see who might come in. Needless to say, no one comes. No one ever came. He'd been watching out for them all these years, watching out and listening but had anyone ever been listening to him? The same terms that have defined his poetic journey manifest themselves again even at this, the most critical juncture of his life. There's that word 'dúisithe' ('*woken*') again. And there's more of them from the same stable – 'dream' and 'act' in particular. And there's also 'self' and 'them'. Each to its assigned station, except for he who was always outside, anyway – the perennial failure:

> *Just woken up. I fall into a very heavy sleep here. The nurse will come around (I hope) and give me a sleeping pill. I've spent the day stretched out on the bed reading or sleeping. I only had one visitor – Isobel Ní Shé – and she only stayed 15 minutes. I'm wiped out and exhausted. I'm afraid now that the nurse won't come around at all; maybe she came around already and found me asleep. She won't come. Blast her anyway. I could call her but I've no excuse to really. I've no shortness of breath and nor am I anxious but I'd still love to sleep for a while. Aren't they tight with the tea too, the hoors, or just tight full stop! One has to be cautious. I'm in a world full of very able simpletons. Herself and thousands like*

3 D: 17 January 1976.

> *her can perform a miracle, the likes of which would never be in my gift, but they're not capable of any reflection. They're capable of deeds but they're not capable of the thinking that accompanies those deeds – or that's what I think anyway. This is what makes them dangerous. They're almost like people who are acting in their sleep. One can't communicate with them. I was woken from the dream apparently, but left without any facility for action, and very early on also. (The TB did this, maybe, or maybe I was always awake.) Anyway, I feel that I lost the rhythm of the dream – that I'm not wrapped up within the dream. It's a scary thing to live in a world where people are asleep, and yet have every power, and you're the only one who's awake, and, worst of all, you're the one who's been gelded and they're the ones who are capable. Because you can't do anything except through the dream. The bishop, the architect, the carpenter, the pilot, the lawyer, the farmer, the radio-man, the housewife, the nurse, fast asleep and yet they are still running the world. The idle ones are the only ones who are awake. They see what's going on but they can't do anything, because they're just spectators. They're sent to the asylum or left on the side of the road. They're only headed for the dung-heap. The people who woke up are people who failed. You can't function unless you participate in the dream.*[4]

It was in Sarsfield Court that Cearbhall Ó Dálaigh, President of Ireland, visited him on 2 February:

> *He's a tidy, sallow-skinned man. He looks younger than his picture. Something about his clothes that makes him fancier-looking than fancy. No one could have been nicer, more easygoing, friendlier or more concerned about me. Fr Tadhg would really have loved the day – it would be like a sliver of God's Kingdom to him – but there's some kind of lack in me that means I can't partake fully in anything. I'm always standing to the side. I was like that even the night I was dying. When I'm called one way, I head the other.*[5]

Tokens of mutual respect and friendship were duly exchanged. The President had brought a bouquet of flowers and a book of Spanish poetry, while Seán presented him with two of his own books – the only two of his four

4 D: 11.55 p.m., 19 January 1976.
5 D: 14 February 1976.

books of poetry then available in Cork city. (He managed to make sure that the President got all four books of his the following day after copies of his other two books arrived in the post to him from the publishers.) The President stayed that night in the Arbutus Lodge Hotel and at 12.40 a.m., 3 February, wrote the following note to Seán on a piece of paper and included a nice financial contribution to the envelope:

> *As regards the thing we referred to before, perhaps if you didn't mind, you might be good enough to take on that job that Sweet-tongued Seán Ó Riada requested: to compose a few words of poetry in relation to Éamon de Valera (if appropriate, so that, maybe we could get someone to put music to them – now that Seán isn't with us any more.) But you're the best judge of what can be done or not ... Whatever's produced, it's not my call or anyone else's either as regards publishing it and all that – it's entirely up to you.*

Ó Ríordáin struggled to write the necessary material just as Ó Riada struggled to compose the necessary music, but what bothered the poet most was knowing that this talk of him writing this specially commissioned poem was just an excuse for giving him this money and that his donors weren't really bothered if he never actually delivered it. Other people were insisting to him that he should accept the money without question. The President actually had to try and convince him to take the money. Another letter arrived from the presidential residence, the Áras, on 10 February, thanking Seán for the additional books. He certainly wasn't 'buying' the suggested poem from him and nor was he pressurising the poet in any way whatsoever:

> *As I explained in the note I wrote from 'Arbutus', that little donation is just a small acknowledgement on the part of the Irish people of what you've done to date. As regards that thing that Seán Ó Riada mentioned – it's your own decision completely: Pegasus is no wild horse.*

Less than two months later, on 1 April, Ó Ríordáin was transferred from Sarsfield Court to the Shankill Hospital. He was nearly forty years now going in and out of hospital on a constant basis and this was his third different hospital in a row. He'd remain here in Shankill until he was strong enough to go home again. The President paid him another visit on 20 April, while Seán was still a hospital patient. Ó Ríordáin noted a brief description of this visit as follows: 'There isn't much to tell. He presented me with a scholarly book, a book his wife published last year.'[6] The book was *Cath Maige Mucrama*, as arranged by Máirín O'Daly, and published by the Irish Texts Society. Ó Ríordáin enjoyed this visit, the same as he did the first one but … (There always had to be a 'but' so that the poet could never really relax or be himself. And what 'but' was it this time?) Thinking back on it afterwards, Ó Ríordáin said:

> *There were two Cearbhalls there every time he came to see me, as in Cearbhall, the President, and Cearbhall, the human being. It's both surprising and honourable (whatever that is) that the President came, it doesn't matter who he is. But it's a heavy load to carry and it's a huge thing to have the President of the State to face it. Cearbhall, the human being did his best, therefore, to bear the burden and to ease the curse that I have to carry – because he has to bear them himself, the same as me …*[7]

Wasn't this it again? The individual has drifted closer to the theory before he/she can be fully represented or expressed. What remains is all that was there from the very beginning – the taste of the ashes in one's mouth. One has no option but to return to one's life – to one's writing. The empty return to the void from whence one emerged. It has always been thus. Here now again was the gentleman brought low, the man who was an exemplar of what the Irish nation stood for in Ó Ríordáin's view, a man he'd been delighted to see become President and who emphasised destiny and tradition and who 'holds himself as if there'd never been any break in the tradition'.[8] What else could one say for a finish other than that it was nice of him to call on the poet and enquire after him. Ó Ríordáin wasn't ungrateful in any way and yet he wouldn't have set any great store by the

6 D: 20 April 1976.
7 D: 29 December 1976.
8 'Neamhurchóid', IT, 11 January 1975.

President's visit either. It was a nice gesture on the President's part and one he'd respected and that was the first and the last of it.

In a similar vein, Ó Ríordáin had said that he wouldn't publicly accept the D.Litt. *honoris causa* that the National University of Ireland offered him, and yet he also didn't want people to think that he was ungrateful. He didn't attend the conferring ceremony – ill health ensured that he couldn't have been there anyway – and the President of University College Cork, Professor Tadhg Ó Ciardha, accepted the doctorate in his absence. Ó Ríordáin saw the clip from the conferring ceremony on television that night in hospital and Raidió na Gaeltachta also ran a programme the same night called *An Bíogadh* ('The Pulse'). Various people sent the poet their congratulations on his award. 'I received a telegram from Seán Mac Réamoinn in Latin: "Euge doctor et vates." This should have been a joyful day for me but it wasn't.'[9] The television programme *Féach* also featured Ó Ríordáin on 12 April, a programme which included older footage of the poet in one of his earliest interviews. God rest the faithful souls of the dead. The programme also featured Seán Ó Tuama discussing Ó Ríordáin's writing with Proinsias Mac Aonghusa. 'Maybe you'll be disappointed to know that his prose isn't as good as his poetry. The character and theme of his poetry is doubt – doubt about the nature of life. There is too much certainty in his prose,' Ó Tuama opined at one point. This was a new literary sin, it seemed – i.e. certainty.[10] Let them off.

From the very first time he'd published his writing, Ó Ríordáin had always been defined by others and he'd had to abide quietly by their theories and judgements, silently watching and listening from the sidelines. To be honest, he'd have been embarrassed if someone had referred to him as 'doctor' – he was a right joke now.[11] It wasn't that he didn't respect the academic title but rather that it didn't suit him. He knew what academic scholarship entailed and it wasn't really his thing. For instance, Séamus Ó Coigligh mentioned that Ó Ríordáin insisted on getting a loan of Celtic scholar Thurneysen's Irish grammar book when he was working on *Rí na*

---

9 D: 8 April 1976.

10 D: 12 April 1976.

11 *Combar*, May 1977, p. 35.

nUile in conjunction with Seán S. Ó Conghaile C.SS.R., and he looked for the original Latin versions of Saint Augustine's *Confessions* when he wrote a review for *Comhar* (September 1967) of *Mise Agaistín* by Father Pádraig Ó Fiannachta.[12] Privately, Ó Ríordáin would say that such projects were just tip-toeing around the edges, really, and served to highlight his lack of scholarship. But even if he didn't ever study at university himself, Ó Ríordáin never shied away from questioning the academics in print or in person, whenever he got the opportunity. He owned every volume of the Irish Academy's Irish-language dictionary, for example, and he also had a regular subscription to scholarly journal *Éigse*. In the case of older Gaelic literature, he wasn't happy unless he consulted the original source in order to get a better flavour of the work in question. There was many a hospital waiting room in which Ó Ríordáin had the first volume of O'Grady's *Silva Gaedelica* with him. If he was admitted to hospital in a hurry, it sometimes happened that he'd send his nephew Seán home to get his copy of it. Amongst the books that people noticed him reading in hospital shortly before his death were *Bethada Náem nÉrenn* (Plummer), the oldest version of O'Rahilly's *Táin Bó Cuailgne* – he liked this version of the book far better than Kinsella's – and *Aislinge Meic Conglinne* (Meyer). The poet's writings mention him reading many other similar books – for example, his article 'Mis agus Ruis Dubh'; the story explored in this article was based on his joint reading of *Celtica* and Aonghus Ó Dálaigh.[13]

Ó Ríordáin found the cold and detached nature of academic life with its BAs and MAs difficult, however. He just wasn't suited to the academic life, he felt, and it came as no surprise to him that the students rarely called to his room to him: they sensed they would only be wasting their time.[14] It wasn't worth the university's while employing him, really, given that he wasn't able to fulfil some of the responsibilities they wanted him to fulfil. And even if he had been capable of doing his job to their satisfaction, his poor health just didn't allow him. He had no option but to resign until he was either better-prepared for the work in hand or until

12 Ó hAnluain, *An Duine is Dual*, p. 50.

13 IT, 17 March 1973.

14 D: 6 May 1969; D: 27 October 1969.

his health improved. Could they freeze his salary but still keep him on the teaching staff? (It wasn't a huge annual salary, anyway – it never went above £675 pounds a year at any stage.) Ó Ríordáin made enquiries and the authorities explained to him that the arrangement wasn't set in stone and that he could leave or stay at any stage, if this best suited him. Here's how Professor R. A. Breatnach's sympathetic letter ended as sent on 27 February 1976, a letter that put him at his ease:

> *There's only one solution to this situation really and that's to resign from the job or die, and I'm hopeful that it won't be either of them. This leaves you with a dilemma, I realise, but I know that this is a great place for poetry.*

The university continued to pay him up until 30 September 1976 when he finally decided to give up on the arrangement. Ó Ríordáin never cashed any of the payments that he felt he didn't deserve. These uncashed cheques were found scattered around the house subsequent to his death. You wouldn't mind, but his financial circumstances were never particularly good, although he did see a certain improvement in the summer of 1976 when the Arts Council awarded him a literary bursary of £2,500 pounds. This was the only substantial sum he ever made from his literary endeavours aside from the £500 that he received on winning the O'Shaughnessy Prize 'for twenty years of talented writing and new ideas in relation to literature and life in general' as the programme said on the occasion of the award, the night of 31 October 1971 (he was also in the frame for the Ossian-Preis but he didn't live long enough to receive this award).

He left Shankill Hospital on 22 April 1976 and went home. He'd managed very little writing while in hospital, even for the diary. He made some notes on Breandán Ó hEithir's *Lig Sinn i gCathú* as if he was possibly preparing a review of this book. Did Ó hEithir belong to that highest class of writer, the Rabelaisian writers? 'Rabelaisian to my mind means that "your sins are forgiven".'[15] This is something that a Rabelaisian writer would never do, i.e. forgive you your sins or release you from your difficulty. He takes advantage of everyone, which Ó hEithir doesn't do.

---

15 D: 6 April 1976. 'Rabelaisian' means to display earthy humour; bawdy.

This flaw in his work means that Ó hEithir can't be counted amongst the really top writers. But then, isn't a person's flaw frequently also the same as their talent?

> *Ó hEithir has a sweet healthy style. There's something about it. You feel him in the presence of human tragedy and trying his best to save whatever he can – or in the middle of the confusion and trying his hardest to make as much sense of it as possible …*[16]

Another writer had appeared now to take Ó Cadhain's place, even if there was no way that he was on the same level as him. Ó hEithir could be added to the cultural fabric that was Gaelic Ireland in the same way as writers such as Peig and Father Peadar, Ó Ríordáin felt. There's a sense of history there with all three writers and a clear understanding of the people they've come from, their behaviour and their way of thinking; their words pure and unfiltered. Ó hEithir's work was the type of writing that you could praise or criticise without causing harm to it. It had a sense of permanence or stability about it in that sense … a sense of permanence that Ó Ríordáin needed now that his health was declining badly and death loomed closer still.

He was readmitted to hospital in Sarsfield Court towards the end of May 1976, a period of illness that one gets a better sense of from both the diaries and his article in *Scríobh 3* (pp. 29–31). He was in hospital when he heard that his cousin Dónall Ó Drisceoil had died from cancer; Dónall was only forty-five years of age and had suffered from schizophrenia for the previous twenty years. The poet's family had suffered a great deal with various illnesses throughout the years, no doubt about it. Ó Ríordáin had a phone installed in his house on 23 June, something he should have had done years earlier, and which his hospital surgeon, Maurice Hickey, had encouraged him to do on many occasions. Until he was too weak to do so any more, however, he'd refused to let the telephone technicians into the house. In fact, Ó Ríordáin left the hospital without permission on the day that the men came to install the phone – so that he could be there to

16 D: 2.45 a.m., 26 April 1976.

let them into the house himself – in itself an indication of how ill he was at this stage. No sooner had the men finished their work but Ó Ríordáin phoned Sarsfield Court Hospital himself mischievously claiming to be a doctor – even giving the name of the doctor he claimed to be – and claiming that Seán Ó Ríordáin had been killed in a car accident and that it was outrageous that they'd allowed a patient in no fit condition to drive home and to leave hospital. (Even when in the full of his health, Ó Ríordáin was a very bad driver.) The poet returned to the hospital that afternoon.

We find him back home again on 18 July, writing the prose piece that would become the basis for his poem 'Clóanna über Alles'. In the prose piece that he wrote at home, Ó Ríordáin included a note that never appeared in the poem, however: 'A Chríost, tá uaigneas orm agus is fada uaim m'óige.' ('*O Christ, I am lonely and I miss my youth long ago.*') From then on he was between home and the hospital every couple of weeks as his health declined further. He was readmitted to hospital again in Sarsfield Court on 9 September and discharged again eleven days later. On 23 October he had an accident while driving, when his car overturned on the main road into Cork city. He was lucky to escape with minor injuries on that occasion, but spent another week in hospital. He goes silent for the whole of November and well into December.

You'd telephone him sometimes and he'd pick up the receiver immediately and in surprise – almost as if he'd been expecting a call from someone. Normally, then, you'd be waiting a long time before his drowsy voice began to respond – in sluggish and apologetic fashion. It was clear that you'd disturbed him with your call but he'd never dream of telling you that he'd have preferred if you hadn't called. He'd keep chatting then for as long as he was able to keep up any meaningful conversation – given the heavy medication he was on – and our conversations often lasted up to an hour. After he'd said goodbye, you'd often wonder whether you'd done more harm than good by waking him from his heavily medicated midday slumber. And, no doubt, you'd have wondered even more about this if you'd fully understood what the poet meant by the word 'dúisithe' ('*awakened*'). We find him noting a few sentences again on 10 December when he begins writing in the last account book (diary) he'll ever use. He's back in hospital again and he won't ever be coming out:

Block 8, Floor 2, Sarsfield Court is my address. Today was one of the worst days of life and that's saying something. I've been exhausted beyond belief since morning. I couldn't even shave myself …

He did improve slightly, however. He makes it to the end of another year; though the signs are ominous:

Yes, I've spent Christmas in Sarsfield Court – 'quietly', as they all say. Healthwise and as far as my breathing is concerned, I haven't felt this well for many years. This is the first year in twenty-six years probably, that I failed to go to Dunquin, and it's the first year for twenty years that I didn't publish anything. Maybe that's no harm – not to publish a word.

The usual murmuring sound that is the hospital. One group of people leaving and another arriving in. He feels disconnected from everyone now, however. January 1977 draws to a close; he's almost paid his dues – his life's dues.

There's no one here amongst the patients or on the staff to talk to. I don't know if there's anyone anywhere that I could talk to. The likes of me and my contemporaries are all in the earth by now. That's where I should be myself too. When an old bachelor ages there's no one to look after him. I lived on for too long even when death was threatening me or issuing me its invitation since I was a boy. I never took up the invitation, and I'm paying for it now. It's a disaster to be cautious. It's best to give in. I'm not sure if I ever saw until tonight just how badly I went astray in this life. Maybe this whole thing with the Irish language was a mistake too. Maybe my problem is a lack of charity. Words were always more important to me than people and now I'm left with nothing. They don't need me. Anything that used to interest me on Raidió Éireann is over now. Life is gone in another direction. This hospital floor is full – there are nearly forty people here – but I wouldn't dare strike up a conversation with any of them. We wouldn't have anything to say to one another, as far as I know.

Cabhair ní ghoirfead go gcuirfear mé i gcruinnchomhrainn,
Dar an leabhar dá ngoirfinn níor ghoiride an ní domhsa
[Gaelic Poet, Aogán Ó Rathaille (1670–1726)]

The poem which this couplet was taken from can be found in full at the end of the first ever diary he kept – the one that ended April 1940: he was following the pattern to its end. The solitary existence, the Irish language and the book that he recorded it in.

Ó Ríordáin took a sudden turn for the worse at 3 a.m. on the morning of 13 February. An Indian doctor gave him an injection in an attempt to stabilise him but it had no effect. ('The British were right to wipe out the f….rs!' he scribbled in his diary.) At 2.15 on 14 February, he somehow managed these few tormented sentences:

> *Is Jesus Christ there? Where is he? How come he doesn't help me? Help me. There's no one else. I'm in a bad way. I've no living friend. I've a pain in my chest. Shortness of breath.*

The priest was called. He was an elderly Franciscan, a man who had a lot of experience in caring for the dying. He told Ó Ríordáin straight out that he was dying and that he had very little time left. Initially reluctant, Ó Ríordáin received Holy Communion and the sacrament of Extremunction from him. The institution or unscrupulous authority had triumphed in the end. It hadn't completely, however. On 15 February, even as his handwriting becomes more illegible, he writes: 'I was anointed for the first time tonight.' Then, in large letters across the same page: 'This isn't to say that I'm a Catholic.' Who's to say that he was or wasn't when he couldn't say so himself?

At 2 a.m. on 16 February he put down the very last sentences he ever wrote. His writing is so weak that one can barely make it out. There's one sentence in the middle that's illegible but the rest says as follows:

> *What a night. I had a special nurse, Mrs Holly. I was anointed. A lecture from the doctor [X] on religious issues. He doesn't believe in eternity. That said, he doesn't mind not blessing himself. I was happy to hear of my impending death, not the opposite.*

That was Wednesday morning. His condition had improved little by the Friday when I went to see him. He was very afraid of the thought of death. He wanted the truth and yet he couldn't face it. Whether truth or lie, it was too late now to make any difference.

'Do I look terrible?' he asked.

'To be honest with you, I've often seen you looking a thousand times worse.'

'You can stick your honesty up your arse.'

They were the last words I remember him saying to me. They weren't the worst *valedictio*. His voice had gone weak by the Sunday, what was left of it. A nurse was making him swallow a few drops of whiskey with a spoon. He had the pallor of death. A woman appeared at the door, who'd recently returned from a trip to Lourdes or Fatima; she could provide him with a healing balm, if they let her in to see him. She didn't know Seán very well at all, but her son had told her that he was very sick. They stayed with Ó Ríordáin till the end, and for a good while afterwards also. They were very decent people.

I left Séamus Ó Coigligh there with him after me. This was only right. Séamus described the rest of that evening in an article he wrote for *Combar*, May 1977. Seán died the following night. The death certificate noted: 'Cardio-respiratory failure. Congestive cardiac failure. Pulmonary fibrosis.'

Whatever the reason, this is the piece of his writing that has remained imprinted on my mind, even after all these years (from his diary for 1 September 1957):

> *The Poet of Vicarstown says he's the king of loneliness. Loneliness is my king tonight. I have the loneliness of childhood in me. I was always cut off from childhood and yet I always felt very close to it. There are some people and they're never right until they're wrapped up in their old age. They're not themselves until then. Childhood suited me, I think. That was the mindset I always had – the childish mindset of youth.*

Ó Ríordáin had already left instructions that he be brought back west to Ballyvourney for burial and it was there, in Reilig Ghobnatan on 24 February 1977, that he was laid to rest alongside his other relatives. He'd left them behind a full forty-five years earlier as he set out on the road to adversity. He'd left it *all* behind then – his youth, his health and the individual who had a place within the community, in addition to the word 'dúchas' ('*native place/mindset*') and what this meant. Their loneliness had followed him east and it was as if this was his final attempt to return home. Despite his great love for her, this place contained more of *him* than his mother's place of Inniscarra had ever done. He was buried in the same family plot as his father, Seán, his grandfather, Seán Breac, and his grandfather's spouse, Bríd Ní Fhionnagáin. A plaque was erected later with the following inscription, as taken from the poem 'Toil' ('*Will*') engraved on it:

Níl ionam ach ball
De chorp san mo shinsir.[17]

I am but a member
Of that ancestral body.[18]

In this place, he'd have a sense of constancy and of the eternal that he'd never had in life. The stone inscription on the wall in front of the house in Inniscarra was another sliver of poetry:

Ní dual do neach a thigh ná a threabh a thréigean.[19]
(It's not natural for someone to abandon their home or tribe.)

This wasn't the house he'd had in mind when he'd written that poem, but it was the house that had become an indelible part of him nonetheless over many decades. And it was a house that may well have proved more important in the long run than the one that he'd immortalised in the poem. In the end, it was just another of the questions, another of the mysteries that Ó Ríordáin had wrestled with throughout his writing life. I can still see him in my mind's eye today – he's still there, traversing that same road of atonement between Inniscarra and Ballyvourney, still seeking out our redemption.

---

17 LL: pp. 27–9.
18 Trans. M. Ó hAodha.
19 B: p. 41.

Bibliography

Books

Blaisdell, Bob (ed.), *Selected Poems of Gerard Manley Hopkins* (Dover Thrift Editions, Dover, 2011)

Corkery, Daniel, *Synge and Anglo-Irish Literature: A Study* (Cork University Press, Cork, 1931)

Crotty, Patrick, *Modern Irish Poetry: An Anthology* (Blackstaff Press, Belfast Press, 1996)

Davis, Wes (ed.), *An Anthology of Modern Irish Poetry* (Harvard University Press, Harvard, 2013)

Ibsen, Henrik, *Peer Gynt* (Signet Classics, New York, 1964)

Ibsen, Henrik, *The Collected Works of Henrik Ibsen* (Palala Press, Warsaw, 2015)

MacDonagh, Thomas, *Literature in Ireland: Studies Irish and Anglo-Irish* (The Talbot Press, Dublin, 1916)

McFarlane, James (ed.), *The Cambridge Companion to Ibsen* (Cambridge University Press, Cambridge, 1994)

Nic Ghearailt, Eibhlín, *Seán Ó Ríordáin agus An Striapach Allúrach* (An Clóchomhar, Dublin, 1988)

Ó Brien, Frank, *Filiocht Ghaeilge na linne seo* (An Clóchomhar, Dublin, 1968)

Ó Cadhla, Stiofán, *Cá bhfuil Éire?: Guth an Ghaisce i bPrós Sheáin Uí Ríordáin* (An Clóchomhar, Dublin, 1998)

Ó Cadlaigh, Cormac, *Guaire an Oinigh* (Oifig an tSoláthair, Dublin, 1939)

Ó Ceocháin, Donall (ed.), *Saothar-Dámh Sgoile Mhúscraighe ar n-a sholáthar a croinicibh na dámh-sgoile* (Oifig Díolas Foillseacháin Rialtais, Dublin, 1933)

Ó Coileáin, Seán, *Seán Ó Ríordáin; Beatha agus Saothar* (second edition, An Clóchomhar, Dublin, 1982)

Ó Coileáin, Seán (ed.), *Seán Ó Ríordáin: Na Dánta* (Cló Iar-Chonnacht, Galway, 2011)

Ó hAnluain, Eoghan (ed.), *An Duine is Dual* (An Clóchomhar, Dublin, 1980)

O'Rahilly, T. F. (ed.), *Dánta Grádha: an anthology of Irish Love Poetry of the Sixteenth and Seventeenth Centuries* (Browne and Nolan, London, 1916)

O'Rahilly, T. F. (ed.), *Measgra Dánta I: Miscellaneous Irish Poems* (Cork University Press, Cork, 1927)

O'Rahilly, T. F. (ed.), *Measgra Dánta II: Miscellaneous Irish Poems* (Cork University Press, Cork, 1972)

Ó Ríordáin, Seán, *Eireaball Spideoige* (Sáirséal agus Dill, Dublin, 1952)

Ó Ríordáin, Seán, *Brosna* (Sáirséal agus Dill, Dublin, 1964)

Ó Ríordáin, Seán, *Tar Éis mo Bháis agus Dánta Eile* (Sáirséal agus Dill, Dublin, 1964)

Ó Ríordáin, Seán, *Línte Liombó* (Sáirséal agus Dill, Dublin, 1974)

Ó Ríordáin, Seán, *Scathán Vearsaí* (Sáirséal agus Dill, Dublin, 1980)

Ó Tuama, Seán, *Nuabhéaraíocht, 1939–1949* (Sáirséal agus Dill, Dublin, 1950)

Ó Tuama, Seán, *Seán Ó Ríordáin: Saothar an Fhile* (Mercier Press, Cork, 1975)

Ó Tuama, Seán, *Filí faoi sceimhle: Seán Ó Ríordáin agus Aogán Ó Rathaille* (Oifig an tSoláthair, Dublin, 1978)

Sewell, Frank, *Modern Irish Poetry: A New Alhambra* (Oxford University Press, Oxford, 2001)

Sewell, Frank (ed.), *Selected Poems: Seán Ó Ríordáin, 1916–1977* (Yale University Press, New Haven, 2014)

Tindall, William, *A Reader's Guide to James Joyce* (Syracuse University Press, New York, 1995)

Washington, Peter (ed.), *Keats: Poems* (Everyman's Library, London, 1994)

Yeats, W. B., *The Poems* (Everyman's Library, London, 1992)

Archive

Seán Ó Ríordáin Papers/Aircív Sheáin Uí Ríordáin (1940–1977): 20 boxes, Special Collections, UCD, Dublin (Reference code IE/ÓR)

Index

Symbols

A

B

G

H

I

J

K

L

M

N

P

R

S

T

U

V

W

Y